Roman Emperor Zeno

'We have two ears and one mouth, so we should listen more than we say.'

Zeno of Citium (Diogenes Laërtius,
Lives and Opinions of Eminent Philosophers, VII.23)

'[I]n particular, I studied History, which adds flavour to moral instruction by imparting pleasurable knowledge of past events, spurring the reader by the accumulation of examples to follow the good and shun the bad.'

William of Malmesbury, *Gesta Regnum Angolorum* II prol. I

Roman Emperor Zeno

The Perils of Power Politics in Fifth-century Constantinople

Peter Crawford

Pen & Sword
MILITARY

AN IMPRINT OF PEN & SWORD BOOKS LTD.
YORKSHIRE - PHILADELPHIA

First published in Great Britain in 2019 by
Pen & Sword Military
An imprint of
Pen & Sword Books Ltd
Yorkshire – Philadelphia

ISBN 978 1 47385 924 1

A CIP catalogue record for this book is
available from the British Library.

Printed and bound in the UK by TJ International Ltd, Padstow, Cornwall.

Pen & Sword Books Limited incorporates the imprints of Atlas, Archaeology, Aviation,
Discovery, Family History, Fiction, History, Maritime, Military, Military Classics,
Politics, Select, Transport, True Crime, Air World, Frontline Publishing, Leo Cooper,
Remember When, Seaforth Publishing, The Praetorian Press, Wharncliffe Local
History, Wharncliffe Transport, Wharncliffe True Crime and White Owl.

For a complete list of Pen & Sword titles please contact

PEN & SWORD BOOKS LIMITED
47 Church Street, Barnsley, South Yorkshire, S70 2AS, England
E-mail: enquiries@pen-and-sword.co.uk
Website: www.pen-and-sword.co.uk

Or
PEN AND SWORD BOOKS
1950 Lawrence Rd, Havertown, PA 19083, USA
E-mail: Uspen-and-sword@casematepublishers.com
Website: www.penandswordbooks.com

Contents

Acknowledgements

I would like to give thanks to those who have contributed in some way to the production and publication of this work, many of whom are becoming part of an established team.

To Phil Sidnell and Pen & Sword for once again giving me the opportunity to write about Ancient History. My sincere apologies for the delays to this manuscript.

To Noble Numismatics for again granting me access to their excellent archive; to my sister, Faye Beedle, for making sense of my vague instructions and outlines to present such excellent maps and diagrams and to the artists and photographers whose images have been consulted and detailed within.

To Matt Jones and his team who turned that collection of photographs, diagrams and maps into this colourful tome.

To the online library of University College London and the staff of the History department for providing help and resources through 2016/2017.

To Dr John Curran for not only providing me with the encouragement to continue along this 'career' path but also acting as a sounding board to bounce ideas off and a conduit for some weird and wonderful academic articles when other avenues were not so fruitful.

To all the staff, past and present, at Queen's University, Belfast, and Dalriada School, Ballymoney, for all the time and effort you have put in to get me this far.

To all my predecessors and peers whose works have been consulted, digested and cited within. I hope to have done you all justice.

To all my friends, I promise that some of that home-brewed ale will be on the way soon … I cannot promise it will be drinkable though!

To my grandparents for all their enquiries and questions about how my book is going. It is getting somewhere at last …

And to Mum … we finally got that bookcase installed, so the ceiling should not be caving in any time soon … hopefully!

gratias vobis ago

'Among those seeking power there is no middle ground except either triumph or complete failure.'

Tacitus, *Histories* II.74

'When you play the game of thrones, you win or you die. There is no middle ground.'

Cersei Lannister in G.R.R. Martin,
A Song of Ice and Fire: A Game of Thrones, Ch.45

Introduction

A Roman Game of Thrones

Much like my previous literary outing on Constantius II, the seed of this work was planted during my PhD research on 'Late Roman Recruiting Practices'. The section of my thesis which involved Zeno involved the military domination of Aspar, the increasing use and growing threat of the *foederati* and the Machiavellian paradigm of Roman recruiting in playing opponents off against one another. The prolonged preoccupation of Leo I and then Zeno with the Goths and Isaurians may have seen these 'barbarian' groups become too much of a crutch for the eastern military of the late fifth century, perhaps displayed by the necessity of significant military reform under Anastasius after the migration of the Goths in 488 and the revolt of the Isaurians in 491. The very fact that Zeno, a supposedly 'semi-barbarian' Isaurian, was able to become *Augustus* in the first place would also seem to present proof of the continued ability of the Roman Empire to integrate and Romanize foreigners despite the trials and tribulations it had faced through the fourth and fifth centuries.

Despite the intricate politicking surrounding Zeno, his seventeen-year reign is frequently reduced to the briefest of mentions as the emperor who was on the throne in Constantinople when the Western Roman Empire was consigned to the dustbin of history in 476. Indeed, the fifth-century eastern empire in general gets something of a limited press in favour of the collapse of the West, the domination of Attila the Hun and the Justinianic *revanche* of the 530s. This largely reflected the paucity of the sources and in particular the lack of a surviving secular historian between Ammianus Marcellinus and Procopius of Caesarea; however, as will be seen, there is plenty of information about the fifth century and Zeno. The accelerating growth of Late Antiquity as a subject all its own beyond Constantine, Theodosius and Justinian has seen areas such as the fifth century receive increasing attention. Some modern historians have found the reigns of Leo and Zeno to be particularly fruitful in terms of articles due to the lack of in-depth research on various aspects of the period, and there has been work focusing largely on aspects of Zeno's reign. To my knowledge though, there has yet to be an extended look at Zeno's entire life and reign in English, so a significant part of the inspiration for this book stems from wanting to help fill that gap.

There were other reasons for focusing on Zeno. Not only is there a personal interest in the emperor on the throne when the West fell, but Zeno was also one of the few Roman emperors to be forcibly removed from the throne only to regain it. His very (adopted) name, while recognisably Greek, has a strange, almost other-worldly feel to it in the English-speaking world (*Zen'ō* does literally mean 'King of All' in Japanese). Perhaps it is the unfamiliar 'Z' in the name of a Roman emperor that seems a little more exotic? While it was not in the forefront of my mind when I proposed Zeno as the subject of a book, it became impossible to ignore that at least on a subconscious level I had been drawn to this era through my interest in G.R.R. Martin's *A Song of Ice and Fire* and the immense popularity of its TV adaptation, *A Game of Thrones*. The similarities between the affairs of the empires ruled from Constantinople and King's Landing can be striking: multiple parties vying for control of the throne, political manipulation, military manoeuvrings, family in-fighting, regional conflict, usurpation and monarchs in exile, religious strife, repeated betrayals and broken alliances, all on a background of the barbarian 'other' lingering at the fringes.

It is this intriguing Constantinopolitan game of thrones which has been frequently bypassed by many of the more general histories of the period. During the earliest days of Zeno's reign, there were anywhere up to eight factions vying for power and influence: Zeno, Verina, Basiliscus, Illus, Armatus, the Senate, imperial courtiers and the Roman army. And this does not take into account other factions within factions and other parties with vested interests, competing for imperial attention or looking to take advantage of infighting: Theoderic Strabo, Theoderic the Amal, Odoacer, what was left of the western government, individual provinces, governors, local commanders, the Persians, Armenians and Caucasians in the East, Samaritan rebels, various barbarian tribes along the Danube, barbarian kingdoms like the Vandals, various religious groups and individuals, and the odd usurper thrown in for good measure. This book will be the story of how Zeno attained a position amongst such players, came to sit on the imperial throne (twice) and then largely overcame most of these problems.

Unfortunately, despite the fifth century seeing persistent warfare across the Mediterranean world and beyond, the lack of depth in the sources leaves extremely slim pickings when it comes to the intricate description of battlefield manoeuvres and none from the reign of Zeno. Perhaps the only battle to involve Roman forces in the fifth century where it is capable of reconstructing a battle map of any detail is the checking of Attila by Aetius' coalition in the Catalaunian Fields in 451, which does not feature in the pages that follow. The only battle able to appear in battle map format took place in the same year as Attila's check and did not involve Roman forces – the Battle of Avarayr between the Persians and the Armenians.

Sticking to a military-political approach to Zeno would miss out a significant part of the story and overlook the main reason for his terrible reputation in much of the surviving source material - his religious policies. In just over a century and a half since the Roman Empire had become ruled by Christians, several emperors – Constantius II, Valens and even the great Constantine – had fallen foul of religious figures due to their supposed heterodox beliefs and policies. Zeno was far less confrontational than some of his predecessors, hoping to achieve compromise at times of political turmoil, but it would all be for nought as his reputation became tied up with the reception of that compromise, which was to turn sour after his death.

Many of these political, military and religious aspects of Zeno's reign intertwine, so while the layout of this work will largely follow a chronological progression, there will also be significant thematic and geographical elements – there is an extended chapter on Zeno's religious policies, while his interactions with the western empire and the eastern frontier are congregated in two separate chapters despite involving extended periods of time. This in itself requires some occasional overlapping and retreading of information, but hopefully it will not become unnecessarily repetitive. Given word limit constraints and the need to keep this piece accessible to most readers, some areas have been set aside for another day. An inspection of those recorded serving under Zeno at court, in political office and in the military could have shone some light on his ability to put the right men in the right place. A look at the limited entries attributed to Zeno in the *Codex Iustinianus* could have provided more on the social, economic, military and religious problems the empire faced between 474 and 491.

Hopefully, I have struck the right 'academically researched for popular consumption' balance with the narrative and analysis providing a good look at the Roman 'Game of Thrones' which took place around *Flavius Zeno Augustus* in the second half of the fifth century.

Sources

For the life and reign of Zeno, the student of history is confronted with the lack of a complete secular historian. Modern compilations such as the *Prosopography of the Late Roman Empire* do show that there is plenty of information out there for late antiquity, but it requires manoeuvring through a quagmire of fragmentary works, unreliable narratives, religious pieces and later historians of varied standard importance, usefulness and bias. It would take a full book alone to catalogue and describe all of the primary material consulted herein, but some of the more prominent sources require elucidation.

It would be hyperbole to say that there are as many fragmentary historians as there are fragments, but there are certainly considerable numbers of both. Despite their state, some provide extremely useful information about the mid/late fifth century. Perhaps the most famous is Priscus of Panium, whose eight-volume classicizing history likely covered the period between the accessions of Attila the Hun and Zeno (*c*.433-474). A well-used source by other writers, Priscus' fragments prove invaluable on Attila, his court and its relations with the empire. The '*Byzantiaka*' of Malchus of Philadelphia, a sophist in Constantinople, seems to have covered the reign of Constantine I to that of Anastasius; however, its fragments only cover 474-480. He was praised for his concise style and composition, although he was 'patently hostile to Zeno and the Isaurians'.[1]

A native of Isauria, Candidus was likely a secretary to a leading Isaurian, perhaps a *comites Isauriae*, Illus or a rebel against Anastasius.[2] His history encompassed the reigns of Leo I and Zeno, but only survives heavily epitomized in the *Bibliotheca* of Photius, who considered Candidus' style unpleasant. It is probable that Candidus was 'writing in the distinctly anti-Isaurian climate after Zeno's death in 491 … [and that] the whole thrust of his history was a riposte to … Malchus'.[3] Candidus was not the only Isaurian writer; several other histories - by Capito, Christodorus and Pamprenius - were written 'to champion their importance and prestige'.[4] The anonymous *Life of Conon* in particular aims to portray Isauria's barbarian, bandit and pagan past being tamed and civilized by members of Isaurian society, setting itself up as a reply to the negative portrayal of the *Miracles of Paul and Thecla*.[5]

More well-known as the historian of the reign of Justinian, Procopius of Caesarea provides relevant background information for the mid–sixth century wars with Persia, Vandals and Goths, and 'views Zeno's reign with objectivity and perspective'.[6] His panegyric *On Buildings* recounts the history of the building of the Church of Mount Gerizim by Zeno, which provides information on the Samaritan revolt.[7] Another useful sixth-century historian is Jordanes, a *notarius* in Constantinople of Gothic origin, who composed two histories, *Romana* and *Getica*. These were heavily influenced by the Gothic and Roman worlds their author inhabited, and highlighted the interactions between the Goths and Romans, something which was particularly useful for Zeno's reign given his involvement with two Gothic groups. The disputed relationship between Jordanes' *Getica* and that of Cassiodorus demonstrates potential bias in favour of Theoderic the Amal over Zeno.[8] Another Constantinopolitan official to write a history was the Illyrian Marcellinus Comes. His *Annales* covered 379-534, with an anonymous continuator adding further information down to 566. Although his work is in Latin and used western sources like Orosius and Gennadius, he was primarily interested in events at Constantinople, with his position giving him access to public records.[9]

The *Chronicle* of John Malalas, an Antiochene bureaucrat serving in Constantinople, not only provides useful (and problematic) information about Zeno's reign, it may also present an example of the potential alteration in tone and opinion that can come with the change in an author's personal thoughts, their surrounding and their sources. When writing about the mid/late fifth century, Malalas appears anti-Chalcedonian, but by the end of his work in 565, he is showing support for Chalcedon.[10] 'Named for the methods it presents for calculating the date of Easter',[11] the anonymous *Chronicon Paschale* of the 630s writes about the fifth century as well, although its use of Malalas as a source decreases its value.[12] The same can be said for the seventh-century *Historia Chronike* of John of Antioch, which imitates much of Malalas, as well as the likes of Eusebius and Ammianus Marcellinus.

Malalas was also the original source for a significant part of the Syriac tradition. Born in Amida and studying at the Zuqnin monastery, John of Ephesus undertook missionary work amongst the remaining pagans in Asia Minor, before becoming the non-Chalcedonian bishop of Ephesus. The second book of his *Ecclesiastical History* incorporated the reign of Zeno, but it only survives in fragments within the *Zuqnin Chronicle*.[13] This was a Syriac compilation of four separate works which follows Eusebius, Socrates and John of Ephesus before the final section provided a more personal account of the Middle East after the Muslim conquests. The third part provides some information on Zeno, although its exact authorship is unclear. It was originally identified as the work of Dionysius of Tel Mahre, a late eighth-century Syrian, but this was rejected in favour of an anonymous monk from Zuqnin or a certain Joshua the Stylite. This section of Pseudo-Joshua the Stylite focused on the Anastasian War of 502-506, but included a synopsis of Romano-Persian relations from the death of Julian in 363 and accounts of the Persian kings Peroz I, Balash and Kavadh I.[14]

Written around the same time as the Pseudo-Joshua, Theodore Lector's *Church History* was divided into three parts, the third section of four books with Book III looking at the reign of Zeno. His work does not survive in full but it was used by various later historians, who preserved some useful fragments. Lector was a firm Chalcedonian, willing to 'glorify in his work the ardent defenders of the Council'[15] and criticise its opponents. Theodore also ridiculed those who attempted to maintain the unity of the Church through negotiation, including Acacius and Zeno, although he did not paint them as heretics as others did. Instead, he 'reproached them for their willingness to make dogmatic concessions and inclination to negotiate with the heretics'.[16]

The *Ecclesiastical History* of Zacharias Rhetor was written in the 490s during the reign of Anastasius. While his anti-Chalcedonianism is clear and he was not above distorting material for his own ends,[17] Zacharias did not allow his approach to blind him completely. He demonstrated some support for Zeno and the *Henotikon* as an attempt to maintain Church unity. Zacharias' history is only extant as volumes III-VI of the mid-sixth century work of a Pseudo-Zacharias. This anonymous writer was a monk in Amida and used the library of the anti-Chalcedonian bishop, Mara.[18] The extent to which the anonymous monk preserved the work of Zacharias is not known. Maybe he translated Rhetor's Greek to Syriac or merely compiled already translated works; however, other Greek passages from Zacharias' history preserved elsewhere suggest that the Pseudo-Zacharias did not translate/copy Rhetor's work verbatim.[19]

In an ironic twist, the only reason some original Greek of Zacharias survives is because the Chalcedonian historian, Evagrius Scholasticus, used his history as a source for Zeno's reign. A survivor of the Justinianic Plague, Evagrius was a sixth-century lawyer and government official from Antioch. Like Zacharias, he was no radical and looked favourably on Zeno's attempts at unity through the *Henotikon*, although he focuses more blame for disruption on John Talaia and Peter Mongus than Acacius. While Evagrius wrote several theological works, only his six-volume

Ecclesiastical History from the first Council of Ephesus in 431 to his own time in 593 survives. While he focused heavily on his home city and religious affairs, Evagrius does also address secular events.[20]

Zacharias' works were not just limited to ecclesiastical history. While pursuing a legal career in Constantinople, he wrote hagiographies of the anti-Chalcedonian Peter the Iberian, Isaiah and Severus of Antioch. These works provide an 'apologetic representation'[21] of their subjects and appear to have been written to defend them from supposed connections to paganism and Illus during his revolt against Zeno, a perspective put forward by the *Philosophical History* of Damascius.[22] Even with troubles over authorship and compilation, these hagiographies provide useful information about the continued struggles between Christians and pagans, and Christological doctrines during the reign of Zeno and the impact they could have on the political situation regarding the revolt of Illus.[23]

Another hagiography of Peter the Iberian was written by John Rufus, an Arabian monk ordained by Peter the Fuller during the reign of Basiliscus, who also compiled the *Plerophoriae*, a collection of traditions and anecdotes about prominent anti-Chalcedonians. A radical opponent of Chalcedon, Rufus intentionally ignored virtually all attempts at compromise, including the *Henotikon*.[24] An alternative view of the religious tensions in Palestine under Zeno is provided by the hagiographies of Cyril of Scythopolis on John the Hesychast, Euthymius and Saba.[25]

The most prominent hagiography of the late fifth century is the anonymous *Life of Daniel the Stylite*, who stood atop a pillar just north of Constantinople for thirty-three years and provided advice to Leo I and Zeno. The life was written by a disciple of the saint between 494 and 496, and due to 'his excellent knowledge of court rumours and intrigues'[26] he may have had some connection to the imperial court. Unlike many of the other religious sources, Daniel's views on Christology are not completely clear. His criticism of Basiliscus might suggest a dislike of anti-Chalcedonianism and several pro-Chalcedonians, Zeno included, do receive a positive reception, although his approval may reflect the author's and possibly Daniel's positive view of their efforts to unite the church rather than their Christologies.[27]

These eastern sources do not provide the only viewpoints on the Christological controversies. The Church of Rome had its own position to ponder with regards to Chalcedon, the Acacian Schism and Zeno's attempts to unite the Church. The *Gesta de nomine Acacii*, which is attributed to Pope Gelasius (492-496), although it may instead belong to the pontificate of Felix III (483-492), summarises the Roman view of the controversies surrounding the deposition of Acacius in 485.[28] There is also a cadre of African writers who provide some insight into the reign of Zeno, religious politics and relations between Constantinople and the Vandals. Victor of Vita is something of a mystery, aside from being from Vita and serving as a clergyman in Carthage during the reign of Huneric (477-484). Given that his aim was to drum up support for the Catholic Church in Africa, Victor's work includes dramatic flair and exaggeration of Arian Vandal persecution.[29]

Another western pro-Chalcedonian, Liberatus, archdeacon of Carthage, wrote a chronicle in the mid-sixth century. Due to his exile as part of the 'Three Chapters' controversy, he was able to make use of the *Gesta*, Roman synodal documents and a variety of other Latin and Greek sources. Virtually no eastern individual receives a positive treatment from Liberatus aside from Leo I due to his consultations with the episcopate.[30] Another African caught up in the 'Three Chapters' controversy was Victor of Tunnuna. Despite being a Latin-speaking African bishop, Victor 'spent a good deal of his later life in Constantinople'.[31] This proved something of a double-edged sword. As an historian, it gave Victor access to information and sources he would not have had otherwise; however, personally, it proved a problem due to his beliefs, leading to various periods of internment and exile. His *Chronicle* of 444-567 was largely focused on the occupants of the major metropolitan sees, but does provide plenty on ecclesiastic politics within Constantinople.[32]

Even as the centuries progressed, due to the *Henotikon*, Zeno remained an attraction for historians. Aside from his name and his being the bishop of the Egyptian city of Nikiu in the late seventh century, little is known about John of Nikiu. It is not even certain what language he wrote in, Greek or Coptic, as his chronicle only survived through an Ethiopian translation of an Arabic translation. John was generally positive about Zeno, although given the hijacking of the *Henotikon* by Anastasius, this does not demonstrate whether Nikiu was pro- or anti-Chalcedonian.[33]

The Macedonian dynasty of the ninth/tenth century proved particularly important for the preservation of information on the reign of Zeno. Theophanes the Confessor, an eighth/ninth-century Constantinopolitan aristocrat-turned-monk, wrote a *Chronographia* of the period 285-813. His information is occasionally suspect and his sources are disputed, but he did use Theodore Lector for much of Zeno's reign, incorporating 'multiple additions which make the original Theodore's account more "sharp", giving more negative evaluations of both Akakius and Zeno'.[34] Another to use Theodore, along with Cyril of Scythopolis, was the ninth/tenth-century anonymous *Synodicon Vetus*, which focused on synods.[35]

Twice patriarch of Constantinople (858-867, 877-886), Photius was a prolific writer; his most important work being the *Bibliotheca*. This was a collection of extracts and abridgements of 280 classical works, many of which would otherwise be lost, including Candidus and Malchus. Another compilation to preserve otherwise lost material was the tenth-century encyclopaedic Greek lexicon of 30,000 entries called the *Suda*.[36] The tenth-century emperor Constantine VII Porphyrogenitus saw to the creation of the *Excerpta Historica*, a collection of extracts from ancient historians, including sections of John of Antioch, and the *De Caermoniis*, which provides official records of the coronations of fifth-century emperors.

The tenth-century Melkite Church provides two authors who wrote in Arabic: Eutychius, Patriarch of Alexandria, and Agapius, bishop of Syrian Hierapolis.

A celebrated doctor, Eutychius wrote a world history to his own time. It has not come down to modern times in its complete form, with details from Zeno's reign lost or removed by a later revisionist. What can be discerned is that Eutychius was a fervent Chalcedonian and he allowed that to colour his opinion of Zeno, calling the emperor a 'Miaphysite' in another instance of an ill-defined, negative and incorrect use of such a term.[37] The *Kitab al-Unwan* of Agapius used Greek and Syriac sources that do not survive in full, meaning that while his own history has many missing pieces, it remains a useful historical source for the late Roman Empire.[38] Another Arabic history, the *Kitab al-Tarikh* of Abu l-Fath, preserves a Samaritan perspective of the fifth century, although it is of 'questionable historical value and often incompatible with sources of late Antiquity'.[39]

Michael the Syrian, twelfth-century Patriarch of the Jacobite Church, was a prolific writer of various genres - canonical, theological, liturgical, historical. His twenty-one book history used at least 150 different sources, with John of Ephesus, Zacharias Rhetor and Jacob of Edessa primarily used for Zeno.[40] A century later, another prominent Jacobite bishop, Gregory Bar Hebraeus, was another prolific Syriac writer. He produced a combined world and church history, which focused on the Near East, giving information about a part of the empire that was largely ignored by the sources for the reign of Zeno.[41] The later 'Byzantine' period also provided useful compendiums of early sources. The eleventh-century John Zonaras probably relied heavily on John of Antioch for Zeno's reign; the late eleventh/early twelfth-century *Compendium Historiarum* of Kedrenus used Pseudo-Symeon, Theophanes, George the Monk and the *Chronicon Paschale*; and the fourteenth-century Nikephoros Kallistos, whose *Church History* drew upon Theodore Lector, Evagrius and Theophanes and portrayed Zeno in a poor light.[42]

Contemporary material is also preserved in the letters of many prominent church individuals – popes, patriarchs and bishops – between themselves, and with the emperor and other clergy and monks. Popes Simplicius and Felix III corresponded with Acacius, Basiliscus and Zeno.[43] Severus of Antioch wrote nearly 4,000 letters, of which about 300 have survived, while the letters of Philoxenos of Mabbug provide useful information about the Antiochene patriarchate during the 470s and 480s.[44] Care over the provenance of such letters must be taken, as certain groups were not above perpetuating forgeries. The majority of Acacius' letters to Peter Mongus may be later creations to portray the former as an ardent anti-Chalcedonian to bolster Mongus' reputation, as Acacius had remained in communion with him.[45] The monks of the *Akoimetoi* monastery near Constantinople created a collection of ten letters to Peter the Fuller supposedly from Felix, Acacius and other bishops regarding the *Trisagion* hymn of the Divine Liturgy.[46]

The legal sources are not particularly bountiful for the late fifth century, languishing in the gap between the *Codex Theodosianus* of 438 and the *Codex Iustinianus* in 534. The latter incorporates about fifty to sixty laws of Leo, Zeno and Anastasius, 'a very small proportion of the legislation of these emperors'.[47] Most of these laws are heavily truncated, with their introductory information removed, limiting the understanding of their circumstances. It is also difficult to ascertain how widespread the implementation of these laws was meant to be. Laws promulgated in Constantinople might not have had much bearing on the rest of the empire and may never have meant to.[48]

Numismatics can also provide useful information about the state of the empire at a particular time and place. The circulation of coins can imply how well the Roman economy was operating, while a large amount of coins in a particular area is a good indication of a strong imperial presence at a particular time. Most importantly for a time of political disruption and usurpation, coins can demonstrate who held power at certain times, as well as the outward appearance presented by the imperial court. In the instance of Zeno, coins show his inferior position to his son, Leo II, his deposition by Basiliscus and his brief acceptance of Leo Basiliscus as *Caesar*. The *Roman Imperial Coinage* remains the most useful collection for Roman numismatics, with Volume X by J.P.C. Kent (1994) focusing on *The Divided Empire, 395-491*.[49] Archaeology can also provide information about various events and their settings, whether it be the layout of Constantinople, the fortifications of Isauria or the damage done to various Balkan cities by Gothic and Hunnic forces. It can also highlight Zeno's building programme in various regions and cities; however, unless there are accompanying literary sources, it is difficult to ascertain when certain edifices were constructed, who was behind their establishment and what their context was.[50]

The extensive footnotes and bibliography demonstrate the sheer number of historians and works which have been consulted in the preparation of this work, but it would be remiss of me to not mention three which I have found particularly useful. The various articles of Brian Croke have been particularly useful in unravelling many of the embedded assumptions about Zeno, the imperial family and court in the second half of the fifth century. There are the eminently readable works of Peter Heather on the late empire, barbarians, Goths and Theoderic the Amal. Finally, Rafal Kosinski's 2010 monograph, *The Emperor Zeno: Religion and Politics*, proved invaluable for Zeno's religious policies. It provided a tremendous amount of information not just from Dr Kosinski himself but also a vast array of secondary material which may otherwise have eluded me. While purchased new, the fact that my copy is no longer in the best shape is testament to the amount of use I have gotten out of it.

From this wide range of sources, the image they provide of Zeno is largely negative. This would not be entirely surprising, as plenty of Roman emperors have deserved a poor reputation through their actions and intentions; however, it appears that 'quite often the sources ... do less than justice to Zeno'.[51] Of particular consequence is that many of the writers appear to have used the same material. Therefore, what might seem like a ubiquitous depiction, backed up by multiple sources of diverse origin, period, viewpoint and genre, can be traced to perhaps a single individual who had an interest in depicting Zeno harshly either through intentional deception or mistaken interpretation. It will be part of the brief of this work to dig through any such injustice done to the emperor Zeno in his depiction by the primary sources.

Spelling Conventions

Given the various languages that sources for the fifth century were written in – Latin, Greek, Armenian, Syriac and Arabic – it becomes important for the sake of clarity to establish spelling conventions. As I freely admit to having only the most fleeting knowledge of some of these languages, I have endeavoured to maintain consistency, rather than apply any sort of linguistic principle. Hopefully, this does not create any difficulty in the identification of an individual or place.

More prominent Anglicized versions of personal names will be used over Latin or Greek, so we will be in the realms of Zeno, Leo and Theoderic rather than Zenon, Leon and Theodericus. The eastern neighbours of Rome present a slightly trickier problem as the same name can have many different spellings. The limited political and military interaction with the Persians, Armenians and other Caucasians during the reign of Zeno condenses much of the interface with such names to a single chapter. That said, there can be some considerable differences in spelling of the same name in the Graeco-Latin-Germanic (with Hunnic thrown in for good measure) world of Europe as well. The most extreme example from this work's *dramatis personae* is that of the man who deposed the last western Roman emperor and ruled as *rex Italiae*. In the sources, there are at least eight different versions of his name recorded: Odoacer, Odoacar, Odovacar, Odovacris, Odovacrius, Adovacris, Οδοαχος and Οδοακρος. It is unsurprising then that there is no firm conclusion on where his name originates from. As will be seen, I have used 'Odoacer'.

As for cities and regions, the Anglicized ancient name of an existing town, city or region prevails in the text, such as Constantinople over Istanbul, Antioch over Antakya or Gaul over France. Roman era provincial names will also be used over modern equivalents, although on many occasions a lesser-known place name will be accompanied by its more modern equivalent or a more famous nearby location to aid in its identification. As for the empire as a whole, while some trace the beginning of the 'Byzantine Empire' to the refounding of Constantinople by Constantine in 330, I am of the opinion that the empire based on that new imperial capital and the eastern provinces remained recognizably the Roman Empire for at least another three centuries after that time, if not all the way to 1453.

List of Emperors and Kings

Roman Emperors 395-518

		Theodosius I	379-395	
West			*East*	
Honorius	395-423		Arcadius	395-408
Constantius III	421		Theodosius II	408-450
Ioannes (usurper)	423-425			
Valentinian III	425-455		Marcian	450-457
Petronius Maximus	455			
Avitus	455-456			
Majorian	457-461		Leo I	457-474
Libius Severus	461-465			
Anthemius	467-472			
Olybrius	472			
Glycerius	473			
Julius Nepos	473-480		Leo II	474
Romulus	475-476		Zeno	474-475
			Basiliscus	475-476
			Zeno (restored)	476-491
			Anastasius	491-518

Sassanid King of Kings 399-531

Yazdgerd I	399-420
Shapur IV	420
Khusro	420
Bahram V	420-438
Yazdgerd II	438-457
Hormizd III	457-459
Peroz I	457-484
Balash	484-488
Kavadh I	488-496
Djamasp	496-498
Kavadh I (restored)	498-531

List of Maps

All maps and diagrams were drawn by Faye Beedle - www.fayecreative.designbinder.com

List of Illustrations

Coins – all coins courtesy of Noble Numismatics – www.noble.com.au

THEODOSIUS II gold solidus, issued between 408–420 from Constantinople mint.

VALENTINIAN III gold solidus from Rome mint.

MARCIAN gold solidus from Constantinople mint.

AELIA VERINA gold tremissis, issued between 462–466 from Constantinople mint.

LEO I gold solidus, issued between 468–473 from Constantinople mint.

LEO I gold solidus from Constantinople mint.

BASILISCUS gold tremissis from Constantinople mint.

ANASTASIUS I gold solidus, issued between 491–498 from Constantinople mint.

ZENO gold solidus from Constantinople mint.

ZENO gold solidus from Constantinople mint.

ZENO gold solidus from Constantinople mint.

ZENO gold tremissis from Constantinople mint.

THEODERIC I/ANASTASIUS I gold tremissis issued by Theoderic I in the name of Anastasius I from Rome mint.

PEROZ I silver drachm from Susa (?) mint.

BALASH silver drachm from Susa (?) mint.

KAVADH I silver drachm issued in 521 from Dywan/Dinawar (?) mint.

Walls of Constantinople – Restored section of the walls near the Pege Gate. (© *Bigdaddy1204*)

Pege Gate. (*Courtesy of CrniBombarder!!!*)

Missorium of Aspar – Aspar and his eldest son Ardaburius (c.434). (© *Sailko 2008, Museo Archeologico Nazionale in Florence*)

Leo I – Louvre. (© *Marie-Lan Nguyen 2009*)

Weight of Theoderic – Silver inlaid bronze weight, featuring the name of Theoderic, issued by prefect Catulinus in Rome, 493–526. (*British Museum; courtesy of PHGCOM*)

Ariadne Augusta. (*Kunsthistorisches Museum, Vienna; courtesy of Andreas Praefcke, 2009*)

Chapter 1

Under Pressure: The Roman Empire of the Fifth Century

'[Cato] makes speeches in the Senate as if he were living in Plato's Republic, instead of this sewer of Romulus.'

Cicero, *Letters to Atticus* II.1.8

Appearances Can be Deceiving: Decline, Division and Disunity

Look at a map of the Roman Empire in 420 and you might be forgiven for thinking that talk of a decline was a little overblown. In terms of outline, the empire does not look all that different from its fourth-century predecessor. Even a generation later at the outset of the 450s, while some regions had fallen out of imperial control – Britain, western Gaul, western Spain and the province of Africa – the overall integrity of the empire appears to be sound. But appearances can be deceiving. On such maps, the eye is immediately drawn to the presence of barbarian tribes establishing their own proto-kingdoms on formerly imperial territory: Franks, Burgundians and Goths in Gaul, Suebi in Spain, Vandals in Africa and the opening gambits of German tribes in Britain. Surely their establishment had been at the point of a sword, bringing all kinds of death, destruction and decline to the Roman Empire?

The great movement of Germanic peoples – the *Völkerwanderung* – had seen numerous tribes cross into Roman territory either as displaced refugees, desperate migrants or opportunistic invaders; however, it is too simplistic to say that this influx caused the imperial infrastructure to crumble. The Roman state had proven capable of resisting such intrusions along the Rhine-Danube frontier in the past, and at least two barbarian tribes operating on Roman territory by the turn of the fifth century – the Goths and the Franks – were there by the invitation of the Roman government. Something had to have changed within the Roman Empire for its policies to fail so spectacularly in the late fourth century. The lack of clarity about what that something might have been was summed up by Alexander Demandt in his 1984 work, *Der Fall Roms*, where he tabulated a list of 210 reasons for the decline of the Roman Empire.[1]

While some Roman decline seems assured, looking at the same map would seem to present a more definitive confirmation of the division of the Roman Empire into eastern and western halves; however, again, the reality was not so straightforward. The division of 395 was hardly the first time there had been more

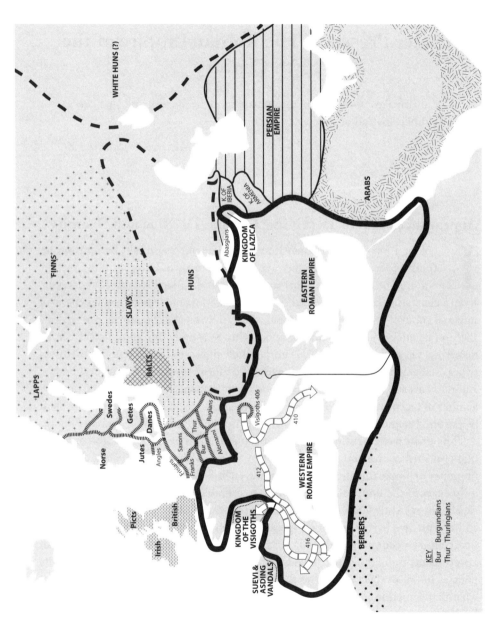

Roman Empire in 420

than one emperor ruling different parts of the empire at the same time. The fourth century had begun under the 'rule of four' that had been the Tetrarchy; the death of Constantine I in 337 had seen the empire divided between his three surviving sons; while there had been at least two reigning emperors since Valentinian I elevated his brother Valens in March 364. None of these was ever taken to be a proposed permanent division of the empire into separate states, so there is no reason to suggest that the succession of Arcadius and Honorius as eastern and western *Augustus* respectively on the death of their father, Theodosius I, in 395 was meant to represent one either.

Dynastically, there was no divide at all. Aside from a brief western interlude with the usurpation of Ioannes in 423-425, the Theodosian dynasty ruled both halves of the empire until the mid-450s. Eastern emperors frequently acted on what they saw as their duty to maintain the dynastic stability and territorial integrity of at least some parts of the west. Eastern forces campaigned in the west and several western *Augusti* owed their selection to an emperor of Constantinople. In terms of laws, most generated by Constantinople or Ravenna would feature the name of both emperors, so long as he was recognized by the respective imperial courts. Right up until the expiration of the western empire, and indeed beyond that, this division into Eastern and Western Roman Empires was technically non-existent.

In reality, there was a growing division between East and West as the fifth century progressed. Many aspects of what would make for a permanent split were in place before the death of Theodosius I. The growth of Constantinople had made it so that the empire had two imperial capitals, each with its own court, Senate, armies, clearly defined spheres of influence and all attendant bureaucracies. These alone had not been a problem during the periods of east/west division of the fourth century; the major differences post-395 came in the type of governments which controlled each half. In the last months of his reign, Theodosius had left his eldest son Arcadius to rule at Constantinople while he travelled west to deal with the usurpation of Eugenius; however, Arcadius was still only 17 and needed help, with the choice falling on the praetorian prefect Rufinus. As Arcadius proved uninterested in ruling, this gave the Constantinopolitan government a civilian feel. This contrasted with the more military government set up under Stilicho in the West after Theodosius' victory over Eugenius at Frigidus. The subsequent demise of Theodosius left these civilian and military-led governments in place, with Stilicho and Rufinus appointed as guardians of their respective young emperors. This contrast was exacerbated by Stilicho's claim that he had been named guardian of both Theodosian sons. This led to political confrontation between East and West, which distracted Stilicho and undermined the imperial response to the likes of Alaric.

The longevity of several Theodosian emperors also proved a significant issue. It was not only Arcadius who proved unsuited to imperial rule – Honorius,

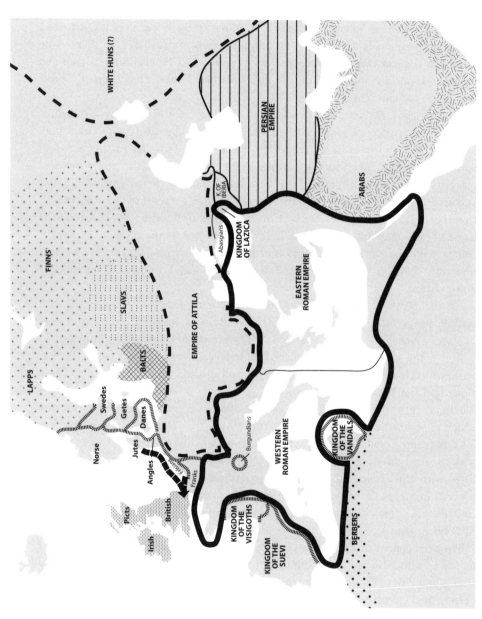

Roman Empire in 450

Theodosius II and Valentinian III were all long-reigned but largely ineffective. These emperors also acceded to power at young ages: Honorius was 10, Theodosius II was 7 and Valentinian III was just 6. This allowed other individuals to lead the imperial government. Theodosian women like Galla Placidia, Pulcheria, Eudocia and Eudoxia wielded increasing influence over the future of the dynasty, providing a legacy for Verina and Ariadne of the House of Leo. The failure of Theodosian emperors to take the field at the head of the army after 395 saw increasing power fall to generals such as Stilicho, Flavius Constantius and Aetius. The effect was slightly delayed in the East by a limited demilitarization, but as will be seen, Aspar was a well-established power behind the throne by the mid-450s. Along with the Suevo-Goth Ricimer in the West, the Alan Aspar also demonstrates the rise of Romanized barbarians within the military hierarchies.

The rise of non-Theodosian or non-imperial powers behind the throne led to divergent and even opposing policies. This was exacerbated by Ravenna and Constantinople facing different problems caused by their differing geography. Barbarians crossing the Rhine or Danube into western territory were immediately into the heart of the western empire, and while Illyricum and Thrace were similarly vulnerable, the eastern empire ruled a wide arc of rich territory from the walls of Constantinople through the Middle East to Egypt, which was largely free from invasion. In the West, not even those provinces separated from the European continent by the sea – Africa and Britain – proved safe from barbarian conquest. Therefore, while it was not a planned and definitive political split in 395, dynastic politics, personal ambitions, geography and military decline made it one with the fullness of time.

It was not just politically that the Roman Empire was no longer quite so united. The fourth century had seen the triumph of Christianity in the Roman Empire, going from a persecuted minority to the faith of the imperial family and ultimately the empire itself within a century. One of the biggest reasons why Christianity had been so successful was its strong organization, taking many of its cues from the Roman Empire itself. However, without a persecuting pagan empire to provide a lightning rod for all the energies of the Church, Christianity become more introspective. Local autonomy, regional cultures and philosophical debate sparked disagreements over various aspects of doctrine.

This meant that while the Roman state was united under Christianity, Roman Christianity was far from united. The focus of this doctrinal dispute was the divinity of Jesus of Nazareth – as the Son of God, had He been created by God and was therefore in some way inferior? Succeeding Ecumenical Councils – Nicaea in 325, Constantinople in 381, Ephesus in 431 and Chalcedon in 451 – had attempted to settle this issue, but the introduction of various terms only served to further muddy the waters and provide more areas of disagreement. The decline of the western empire and the growth of Constantinople as an imperial capital also prompted disunity within the Church hierarchy. The pope came under pressure from the patriarch of Constantinople in terms of influence, while other eastern

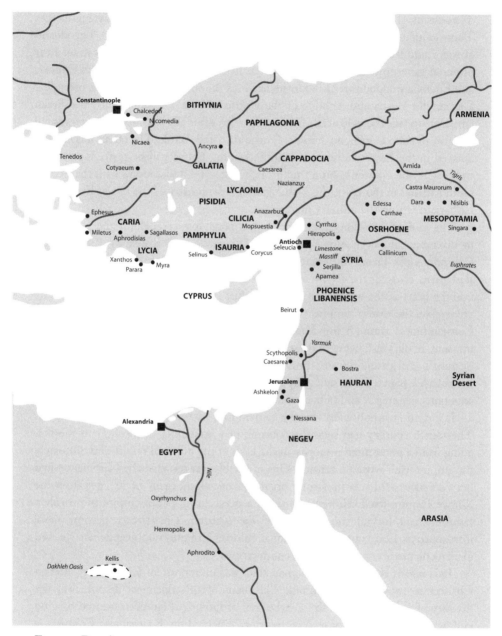

Eastern Provinces

patriarchates – Antioch, Alexandria and Jerusalem – rankled under the doctrinal and hierarchal primacy of Constantinople. This was to cause significant trouble not just for the Roman church but also imperial authorities, with Zeno spending a lot of his reign attempting to find solutions to these problems.

Christianity may have won out in the fourth century, but that did not mean that other faiths disappeared overnight. Various forms of paganism remained prevalent throughout the fifth century, although those issues may be as much Christians portraying pagans as more of a political and religious nuisance than they really were. Jews were portrayed in a similar light, with past revolts used as justification for viewing them as 'fifth columnists'; however, the only involvement Zeno would have with Jews was when Christian groups partook in their own anti-Semitism. It was the other ethno-religious group in Palestine who were to cause Zeno political, religious and military trouble: the Samaritans.

The Spectre of Attila

The Samaritans were not the only internal military problem faced by Constantinople in its eastern provinces. As will be seen, Zeno's own Isaurian countrymen continued to be a source of considerable political and military disturbance. The eastern Roman provinces also bordered a series of non-Roman kingdoms. Where there had once been the Achaemenid Persian Empire crushed by Alexander the Great, and then the Parthian kingdom, which had resisted the triumvirs Crassus and Antony, there was now the Sassanid Persian Empire. Since the 230s, Romano-Persian relations had seen repeated conflict; however, while the territorial and religious squabbles of the other kingdoms of the Middle East – Armenia, Iberia, Lazica and Caucasian Albania – might occasionally drag in the two great powers, Rome and Persia had their own internal and external distractions. This meant that the 'apparently never-ending cycle of armed confrontations'[2] took a prolonged rest during the fifth century.

The quiet which overtook the fifth century eastern frontier could not have come at a better time for Constantinople as its other major frontier, the Danube, was coming under increasing pressure. Legionary bases all along the river put vast amounts of wealth in the pockets of soldiers, leading to a significant number of towns of increasing size such as Naissus and Singidunum growing in the Danubian hinterland. This combination of military and agricultural infrastructure on top of the rugged terrain saw Danubian manpower become much sought after, leading to men of such origins becoming candidates for imperial power throughout the third and fourth centuries. This imperial backing saw those towns not only grow further but become adorned with temples, churches, palaces, theatres, aqueducts, roads, statues and villas.

However, these decades of growth came to a shuddering halt in the late fourth century. The crushing of the Limigantes by Constantius II in the late 350s upset the tribal balance beyond the Danube, with the Goths establishing themselves as a dominant force. They proved a very tough nut for Valens to crack in 367-369,[3] although he was successful enough to leave the Goths desperate to seek his permission to settle in the empire. The subsequent disaster at Adrianople in 378 was only the beginning of decades of damage to this once formidable defensive line. Various barbarians crossed into imperial territory increasingly unmolested, ravaging farmland, sacking cities, reducing Roman resources and depleting imperial control of the region.[4]

The baton of harriers of the Danube was taken up by the Asiatic terror whose arrival in eastern Europe had played a significant role in sparking this earliest Gothic step in the *Völkerwanderung* – the Huns. While the exact history and origin of this nomadic confederation is disputed, they had arrived north of the Caspian Sea from Central Asia by the 360s, where they came into contact with the Alans and Goths. The eastward expansion of the latter provoked an explosive reaction in the early 370s, and in a mere handful of years the Huns had destroyed a century of Gothic growth and subjugated all the tribes from the Caucasus to the Hungarian Plains.

The first generation of Hunnic dominance along the Lower Danube was remarkably quiet. There were raids west and south, and Huns appeared in the Roman army as mercenaries, but these interactions were on a small scale. It was not until 395 that Hunnic raids increased in size, perhaps encouraged by the absence of eastern forces in the West. The Huns not only crossed the Danube and raided as far south as Thrace, they also streamed through the Caucasian passes and attacked Armenia, Cappadocia, Syria, Mesopotamia and possibly even Palestine and the outskirts of the Sassanid capital at Ctesiphon. Hunnic raids west in the first decade of the fifth century may also have sparked waves of barbarian crossings into the western empire, including the Italian invasion by Radagaisus and the collapse of the Rhine frontier in the face of Vandals, Alans and Suebi in 405.

The first decade of the fifth century also demonstrated how quickly the allegiance of the Huns could shift. In 400, the men of the Hunnic leader Uldin living in the area which now encompasses Bucharest in Romania intercepted and killed the rebel *magister* Gainas, sending his head to Constantinople. In 406, Uldin was an ally of Stilicho against Radagaisus and may even have facilitated the capture and execution of that Gothic menace after the battle of Faesulae. Uldin looked every bit the useful Roman ally; however, in the interim between his killing of Gothic enemies of the Roman state, he had proven a threat to the Romans. In 404/405, Uldin's Huns raided Thrace, crossing the Danube again in 408, capturing Castra Martis – modern Kula in north-western Bulgaria – and then proceeding to raid Thrace once more.[5]

The career of Uldin demonstrates some evidence of a growth of Hunnic royal power, but they were still nothing like a centralized group. Indeed, the episode at Castra Martis may reveal that Uldin's power was on the wane. In conversation with a Roman commander, Uldin proclaimed that he could conquer every people enlightened by the sun and demanded a suitably astronomical tribute; however, his underlings were more impressed by the Roman offer and defected in large numbers. This diplomatic failure seems to have struck hard at Uldin's base, with his Hunnic following dwindling, large numbers of Scirian allies killed or captured by the Romans and the Alans seemingly able to strike out on their own. The collapse

of any centrality achieved under Uldin or its general lack is also demonstrated by
there being several bands of Huns serving in various parts of Europe: Alaric and
Athaulf had Hun mercenaries in their employ, who were attacked by two separate
Hunnic groups in Roman service in 409.[6]

The next generation of Hunnic activity is poorly recorded, but there is enough
to highlight that the various groups were a continued problem for the empire.
Charaton, another 'regal' Hun, had to be placated with presents from Honorius,
while in the East the praetorian prefect Anthemius went to great lengths to build
up eastern defences with the expansion of fortifications along the Danube, its fleet
and most famously the land walls of Constantinople in 413. Not before time, for
in 422 major Hunnic raids penetrated right to the outskirts of the imperial capital,
and were only bought off by an annual subsidy of 350 pounds of gold. On top
of that, Pannonia became a battleground between Roman and Hunnic forces in
the 420s, while the *magister militum* Aetius obtained significant Hunnic support in
establishing himself as the power behind the western throne.[7]

While the Huns were clearly a threat and 'their inroads carried them at times
deep into the Balkan provinces … they were always either driven out or bought
off'.[8] However, that was all to change upon the death of the Hunnic leader Ruga in
around 434. He was succeeded by his two nephews, Bleda and Attila. The brothers
were quick to capitalize on the foundations laid by their predecessors, forcing
Constantinople to pay 700 pounds of gold *per annum* and open Roman markets
to Hunnic trade.[9] Bleda and Attila then used the financial and territorial security
provided by this treaty to tighten their grip along the Danube. They brought many
of the disparate Hun groups under their sway through a combination of bribery,
coercion and promises of military success. This more united Hunnic force was then
able to exert more direct control over the various tribes which had fallen under its
sway in the 370s – Goths, Gepids, Rugians and Sarmatians – with greater central
organization allowing for a larger Hunnic 'imperial' army. This in turn allowed the
Huns to extend their suzerainty to the Germanic tribes of the Upper Danube and
even parts of the Rhine.

By the time the Romans revisited the treaty in 440, they found a tribal empire
beyond anything they had ever faced. Claiming that the Romans had broken the
treaty by not paying their annual subsidy, Attila and Bleda flexed their muscles in
Pannonia and Moesia, capturing all the major cities of the hinterland during 441
and 442 and delivering a string of defeats to the leading eastern general, Aspar. The
Huns then drove into Thrace, only to turn back due to bribery, disease or an uprising
near their heartland.[10] In 443/444, Theodosius II again refused to pay the subsidy
and was initially met with no Hunnic response, perhaps due to the combination of
any disease or uprising, western distraction and the death of Bleda in *c*.444. Attila
retaliated in 447 with his greatest raid on the eastern empire. Hun armies burst
across the Danube and drove deeply into Thrace, sacking Serdica, Arcadiopolis
and Philippopolis. The Theodosian walls likely saved Constantinople from assault,

but this did not stop the Huns from driving further into Roman territory, with Attila's men reaching Thermopylae and winning a large victory in the Thracian Chersonese, modern Gallipoli. This brought Theodosius II to the negotiating table and Attila was quick to point out that he was owed tribute arrears, demanding 6,000 pounds of gold. He also insisted on an increase of the annual subsidy to an eye-watering 2,100 pounds of gold and that the empire recognize his control of a five-days' march wide belt of land along the southern bank of the Danube.[11]

Attila may have continued to drain the eastern empire had it not been for him being dragged into western affairs. In 450, Aetius, Valentinian III and Geiseric encouraged Attila to attack the troublesome Gothic kingdom of Toulouse. This fitted in with the Roman policy of using barbarian armies against one another, but with Attila making preparations to cross the Rhine, it would not take much to see him diverted to grander imperial ambitions. That spark came in mid-450 with the arrival of a eunuch messenger at the court of Attila, carrying a ring, promises of riches and a plea for help. The originator of this message was the sister of Valentinian III, Justa Grata Honoria, who was being forced into a marriage she did not want. Attila chose to view this plea as a marriage proposal and demanded that Honoria be released to him, with half the western empire as her dowry.[12] Inevitably, these demands were rejected and Attila invaded Gaul in early 451.

The western Roman army was in no shape to stand up to Attila alone; thankfully, Aetius was a master of diplomacy, demonstrating to the barbarian nations of Gaul that it was in their best interests to stop the Hunnic rampage. On 20 June 451, in the Catalaunian Fields,[13] Aetius brought a force of Romans, Goths, Burgundians, Franks and Alans to bear against Attila the Hun. The Roman-led allies stood firm, unwilling to break their defensive line, perhaps happy to play for time in draining Attila of his resources. It has long been difficult to gauge the actual results of the battle, either in terms of the result or its effects on Attila's aims. It has even been suggested that much of the battle narrative is a classicizing invention, playing on the Battle of Marathon.[14]

The likelihood is that while Attila was checked enough for him to retreat from Gaul, his army had not suffered any debilitating casualties because the following year, the Huns invaded Italy. Major cities like Aquileia, Verona and Milan all succumbed, while only superstition over the fate of Alaric, famine and a papal-led embassy discouraged Attila from attacking Rome itself. A Roman invasion of the Hunnic heartlands may also have encouraged Attila's retreat, while also emboldening the emperor Marcian to withhold the annual subsidy for 452. This drew Attila's attention back east; however, before he launched his latest grand campaign, he married a young Germanic beauty called Ildico, only to die on his wedding night.[15] The death of Attila ostensibly led to the collapse of his empire. The squabble between his numerous sons over who would succeed their father presented an opportunity to the subjugated tribes to break free from Hunnic control. This culminated in the Gepid-led victory at the Battle of the Nedao River in 454, ending Hunnic suzerainty over the tribes along the Danube.

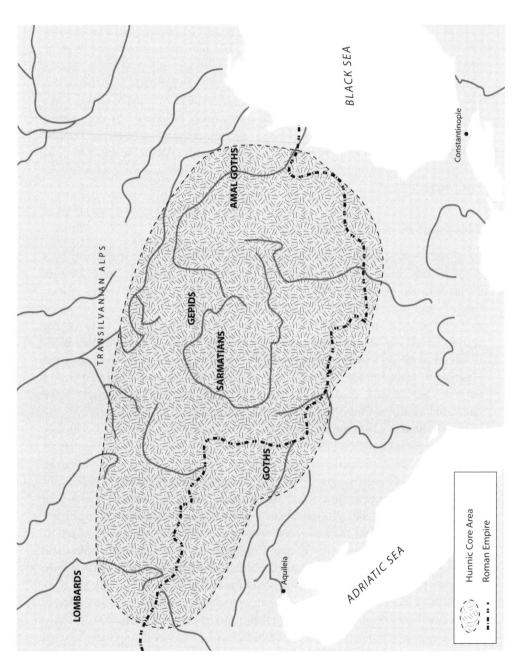

The Hunnic Empire of Attila c.450

The collapse of such a large empire would seem a positive for the Romans, but Attila's death and the defeat of his sons at Nedao multiplied Roman problems. Freed from Hunnic control, a vast number of tribal groups of varying size were scatter-gunned across much of the Rhine-Danube. Therefore, even though the reign of Attila is outside the period of Zeno's prominence (although it is not impossible that a young Zeno served in some of those Roman armies swept aside by Attila in the 440s), the fallout of events in 453/454 casts a large shadow over much of this work. Many of those who interacted with Zeno were greatly influenced by the Hunnic yolk: the Goths of the Theoderics, Odoacer, the numerous tribes along the Danube and the still significant Hunnic remnant under the sons of Attila. He might be dead and his empire dissolved, but the spectre of Attila still haunted the peoples of the Mediterranean.

The Jewel in the Eastern Crown

For all the growing pressure and damage done on the Danube frontier and provinces of the Balkans, there was one bastion the eastern empire could rely upon. Despite its prominence in Mediterranean politics, Constantinople was a young upstart city in comparison to virtually all of its neighbours. It had only been refounded by Constantine I in 330, admittedly on the already Romanized layout of the ancient Greek city of Byzantion, originally founded in the seventh century BCE. It was situated 'on a peninsula strategically placed to control the crossing of the Hellespont, from Europe to Asia, and equipped with abundant sheltered waters for large fleets to lie at anchor, both in the Bosphorus itself and particularly in the Golden Horn that snakes up its eastern shoreline'.[16]

By the time of Constantine's death in 337, it was barely half-finished, still only sparsely populated, with no rich landowners and lacking a secure water supply. It was left to his son Constantius II to make Constantinople the *Nova Roma* his father had envisaged. He greatly expanded the Constantinopolitan Senate, with significant financial inducements to convince those rich landowners to move to the city. The accompanying expansion of its bureaucracy saw to it that through the fourth century Constantinople became the centre of eastern political administration. Much as Rome had come to embody the Roman Empire in the past, Constantinople came to signify the imperial grandeur and hierarchy in the East. Such was its stature and importance to the imperial regime that fifth-century emperors rarely left their capital, and for any rebels against the throne or barbarian invaders it became a target which could not be ignored. The perpetual imperial presence within the city also made it a labyrinth of political intrigue, which would eventually sprout the term 'byzantine'.[17]

Constantius II also oversaw the building and completion of some of Constantinople's most famous landmarks, but none were more important than the truly monumental defences – 'rarely has any city been so well guarded'.[18]

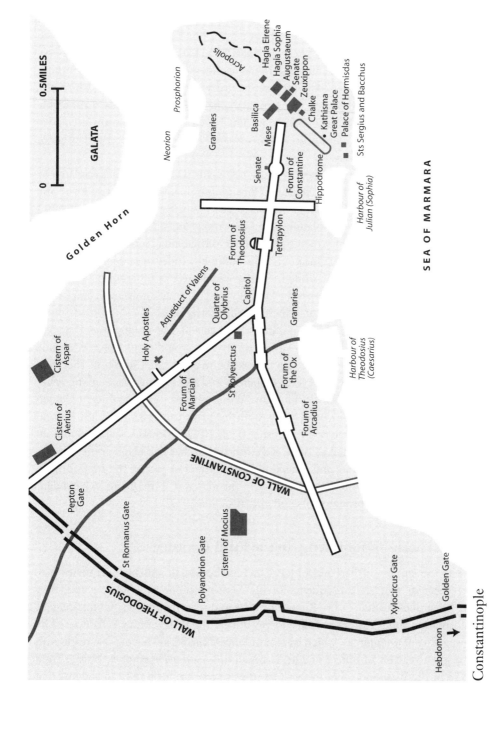

Constantinople

Constantius completed Constantine's expansion of the city walls, but by the end of the fourth century, the city had already outgrown this Constantinian Wall, leading to the already seen expansion under Theodosius II.[19] By the time these Theodosian Walls were finished, the size of the city had been doubled and an enemy would have had to overcome a 20m wide, 10m deep moat and a 20m flat killing zone before even reaching the outer walls. These were 2m thick, 8.5m high and studded with ninety-six defensive towers at 55m intervals. If the enemy managed to get through those obstacles, there was another 20m of terrace before reaching the main wall, which was 5m thick, 12m high and dotted with another ninety-six towers. These formidable fortifications would not be successfully breached until over a millennium later, after the invention of the cannon. Large sections of the Theodosian Walls and their gates still stand in Istanbul today.

While all of the land enclosed by these new walls was not heavily populated or even built up, by the mid-fifth century, Constantinople was 'the largest city of the Mediterranean, with a population estimated at over half a million'.[20] Such rapid expansion and extensive population posed enormous logistical challenges, but the Romans had long experience of supplying huge settlements. Several vast, open-air reservoirs, dozens of subterranean cisterns and many miles of aqueducts brought and stored water for the city, while the coast was dotted with harbours of varying size bringing in goods from across the known world, although none more important than the grain fleets from Egypt, which fed the metropolis.

However, Constantinople was not just a spectacle of size and logistics. The city was bedecked in imperial and holy architecture that would inspire awe in anyone lucky enough to walk its streets. There was the magnificent Church of the Holy Apostles, the burial place of several emperors and the resting place of the relics of St Andrew, St Luke and St Timothy. While not yet the magnificent domed structure still visible today, which was built by Justinian in 532-537, the second Hagia Sophia inaugurated by Theodosius II on 10 October 415 was no doubt an impressive building. Added to those were other churches like Hagia Irene, forums such as those of Arcadius and Theodosius, the imperial palace, the hippodrome, triumphal arches and the Senate House – 'the city was in its pomp, resplendent with marble facades, bronze roofs and gilded statues'.[21]

The Eastern Roman Army in the Fifth Century

While the success of barbarian incursions in the fourth and fifth centuries may have been as much a consequence of the Roman decline as it was a cause, they mark a serious decline in the Roman Empire and its armed forces. Unfortunately, information about eastern military forces during the fifth century is hampered by the paucity of the sources, which leaves students of the period having to wrestle with that great registry of offices and army units, the *Notitia Dignitatum*. Dating from *c.*420 in the West and *c.*395 in the East, the *Notitia* has been used to suggest that the empire was capable of fielding up to 600,000 regular soldiers.[22] However, the *Notitia* presents several problems.[23] Not only is the eastern half of the registry two generations removed from the 450s, it provides a snapshot of no particular time. That snapshot is also inaccurate as it records offices and units that 'should' be in certain places, rather than those that actually were. As it also made little attempt to quantify men on the ground, any figures derived from the *Notitia* can only represent a paper strength, almost certainly nowhere near fighting strength. Furthermore, the *Notitia* did not record non-Roman units serving alongside the regular army. Could Stilicho really have had access to 113,000-strong field armies and 135,000 *limitanei* when he had to strip Britain and the Rhine of men just to provide an army to defend Italy? And while the eastern military had not faced the same influx of barbarians as the West, the damage done to the Balkan frontiers and armies will have meant that the 104,000 field forces and 248,000 *limitanei* suggested by the eastern *Notitia* likely represents very wishful thinking, not only for the 450s but 395 as well.

The Eastern Field Armies of 395

Field Army	*Notitia*
Praesental I	21,000
Praesental II	21,000
East	20,000
Thrace	24,500
Illyricum	17,500
TOTAL	104,000[24]

The impression given by other sources is that 'the organisation of the eastern army scarcely changed throughout the fifth century';[25] the field armies made up of the successors of the classical legions and the *auxilia* in particular seem to have remained at similar dispositions until at least the mid-sixth century. Despite their considerable numbers in the *Notitia* and repeated use in armies and garrisons, the *limitanei* gained a poor reputation as soldiers. The assumption is that their lesser status and privileges must have meant that they became little more than a regional police force or peasant-soldiery. Justinian reputedly even removed their pay and status as soldiers.[26] However, this was almost certainly overblown: '[I]f the *limitanei* were so useless then at least one emperor between Constantine and Justinian would have noticed.'[27] The highest status part of the 'regular' army was the *scholae* and *protectores*, who made up the imperial guard; however, as Leo I found it necessary to establish the *excubitores*, it may be that these guards had already begun their descent into ceremonial units.[28]

That the *Notitia* and other sources frequently only list regular units can give the impression that the army only recruited Roman citizens, but that had virtually never been the case. From the moment the Romans came to rule peoples not enrolled in their citizen body, non-Romans had become a vital part of the Roman army, first serving beside the legions as allies and mercenaries, and later taking their place in the legions themselves. By the late empire, non-Romans were a prevalent part of the regular army, although not necessarily a majority.[29] Non-Romans also made up the *foederati*. Originally these were groups serving under treaty obligations that implied submission, but as the centuries wore on, this idea waned. By the sixth century, the *foederati* were described as those non-Romans who served not because they had 'been conquered by the Romans but on the basis of complete equality'.[30] This progression will be seen during the reign of Zeno with the Goths of the Theoderici, while the treatment of the Isaurians could present some blurring of the lines regarding *foederati*. Non-Romans also continued to serve alongside the Roman army for a single campaign as mercenaries, varying in type according to the needs of the army and what was available. This willingness to employ non-Romans meant that a list of peoples serving in the fifth-century Roman army includes every people that the Romans were in contact with: Huns, Gepids, Bulgars, Franks, Burgundians, Goths, Vandals, Suebi, Berbers, Arabs, Armenians, Caucasians and Persians.[31]

A growing use of non-Romans might suggest that there was some trouble recruiting Romans. Even with the growth in demographic studies of the Roman world, it is difficult to prove any drastic reduction in population.[32] Perhaps military service in the fifth century was unattractive to Roman citizens due to poor pay, poor conditions or a poor general attitude to military life. This might be highlighted by how the pay reforms of Anastasius I provided a strong Roman army in the early sixth century, starting a trend that was to last well into the seventh century that when the Roman government had the funds, they could find sufficient recruits to build good armies.

Recruitment of increasing numbers of barbarians may also reflect a growing tactical shift in ancient warfare, particularly the perceived decline in effectiveness of infantry as the manoeuvrable horse-archers of the steppe became more prevalent.[33] However, while the Romans did hire and train their own horse-archers, this decline in infantry and increase in cavalry has been overplayed in the past. While the proportion of cavalry and other specialists may have increased to provide greater variety, speed and power, when it came to pitched battle, sieges, garrisons, rugged terrain and warfare in general, infantry remained the dominant soldier type. And as the purveyor of the best infantry, the Roman army remained a force to be reckoned with in both size and ability.

As well as remaining capable of military reprisals against unruly barbarians, the Roman Empire was willing to buy them off, with survival and cash proving powerful incentives for negotiation. However, as with the Huns, the concentration of wealth in the hands of specific barbarian tribes and families during the fourth and fifth centuries encouraged increasing centralization amongst tribal groups.

It is no surprise then that those groups who could attract followers, attain cash and establish themselves on Roman territory – Vandals, Goths and Franks – were the groups who developed strong central kingships. It must also be noted that each of these groups were fortunate to be led by some of the more capable individuals of Late Antiquity: Geiseric, Theoderic, Alaric and Clovis respectively.[34]

In spite of territorial losses, political and religious fracturing, financial and administrative decay and military contraction, the Roman Empire of the mid-fifth century remained the leading state of the Mediterranean, with a population and army of various cultures, faiths and skills capable of defeating any of its foes. However, the arrival, conquests and collapse of the Hunnic Empire presented the Roman army with more than just a single foe. Even at a time when the eastern frontier was quiet, the glut of tribes and proto-kingdoms operating on formerly imperial territory would have overtaxed the Roman army presented by the *Notitia*, never mind the increasingly undermanned or mercenary armies being fielded in the names of Rome and Constantinople. Roman use of such barbarians in their army also increased the number of men of barbaric origin at the higher levels of imperial politics, introducing further elements into an already crowded contest for political power, particularly within the monumental walls of Constantinople.

Chapter 2

The Romanized 'Barbarians':
Isauria and the Origins of Zeno

'one person's "barbarian" is another person's "just doing what everybody else is doing".'

Susan Sontag, *Regarding the Pain of Others* (2003)

Internal Barbarians

The man who was to become the emperor Zeno was born in a region of the Eastern Roman Empire called Isauria, in what is now the mountainous south of Turkey. It had been well inside the Roman frontiers for up to five centuries by Zeno's birth in *c.*425; however, it had a long-standing reputation as being semi-civilized and as a source of perpetual trouble to neighbouring provinces due to a proclivity towards raiding and banditry. This apparent semi-barbarous existence proved both a strength and weakness – their living conditions produced hardy men who made useful military recruits, which provided a route to increasing political influence. This supposed lack of civilization provided a persistent barrier to full integration into the Roman body politic, with the upper classes of Constantinople unwilling to fully accept Zeno and his compatriots. But how had Isauria and its inhabitants acquired and seemingly retained such a reputation over the course of five centuries of Roman control?

The region called 'Isauria' jutted out from the belly of Anatolia, between the plains of Adana and Pamphylia, and was made up of the Taurus Mountains and their rugged foothills north of the Cilician coast. From the time of the Hittite conquest of the region in the mid-second millennium BC, the inhabitants had spoken Luwian, an offshoot of Hittite. As use of Luwian continued perhaps down to the sixth century CE, it is not much of a stretch to suggest that concomitant culture, art and architecture survived as well. This shared language, culture and geography encouraged their neighbours and overlords to lump the inhabitants together under the name 'Isaurians' even before the arrival of the Romans in the first century BCE.[1]

However, this masks that the Isauri, who inhabited the mountains south-east of Lake Trogitus and were concentrated around the town of Isaura Vetus, were just one of the tribes in the region. There were also the Homonades, Lalasses, Kennatae and probably more, who likely shared a bloody history with the Isauri, only to be terminologically subjugated to them. This may make the Isaurians more a regional than an ethnic group, although the Isaurians referred to themselves by the collective name of *Cetae/Cietae*. This also appears on Graeco-Roman coins, inscriptions and literary sources, suggesting some level of cultural unity was sensed by Greeks, Romans and the Isaurians themselves.[2] But even the identification of this group of Luwian tribes as the 'Isaurians' is not the end of the problems. Under the Roman provincial system, the descriptor 'Isauria' took on more than one administrative meaning on top of pre-existing regional, ethnic and tribal meanings. This urges caution when dealing with anything labelled as 'Isaurian'.[3]

The entire region of southern Anatolia had a reputation for raiding long before the legions entered the area and it has been argued that no ancient imperial power ever gained complete control of the Isaurian hinterland.[4] The source of this difficulty was the terrain. The Taurus highlands can reach up to 3,000m above sea level, leaving timber as the only natural resource and limiting agriculture to small pockets of transhumant pastoralism. This, along with their inter-tribal feuding, caused most Isaurians to follow 'a lifestyle which does not lend itself to control by central states'.[5] Many highland Isaurians likely lived close to the line of subsistence, so any meteorological or outside harm to their already meagre yield will have left them little recourse but to resort to brigandage.

This mountainous terrain also helped shield the Isaurians from the civilizing effects of Hellenism and Romanization, much like other parts of the empire that were either mountainous or transhumant – Basques, Berbers, Illyrians. This opened them up to the vitriol of Roman writers, who 'generalise and vilify their "barbaric" opponents'[6] as greedy rapacious marauders. By the second century CE, Isaurians were classed as 'internal barbarians',[7] a prejudice which could see them deprived of citizenship rights. They are even seen being treated similarly to Germanic tribesmen – thrown to wild beasts in Iconium or tortured for certain crimes.[8] However, it is difficult to make any definitive conclusions about the nature of the Isaurians from these stereotypes. Also on the second-century list of 'internal barbarians' were Egyptians and Jews, neither of whom would be considered uncivilized. By the second century CE, pastoralism may have been replaced as the predominant Isaurian lifestyle by settlement dwelling, husbandry and the trading of olives, grapes, flax, grain, wool and timber with Cilician ports.[9] Consistent with this transition to a more sedentary lifestyle, the Isaurians may have ceased to be a threat to the surrounding provinces, becoming 'a fairly typical, if not particularly prosperous province for three centuries in the Principate'.[10]

Care must also be taken in dealing with the terminology used to delineate what kind of trouble the Isaurians posed to imperial authorities. The sources use the same words – *latrocinium* and λεστεια – for brigandage as they do for robbery, rustling, racketeering, barbarian invasion, rebellion and usurpation.[11] And as the Isaurians were recorded partaking in all of the above, some distinction is necessary, whether it was the extent of the territory involved or the Roman response. When small

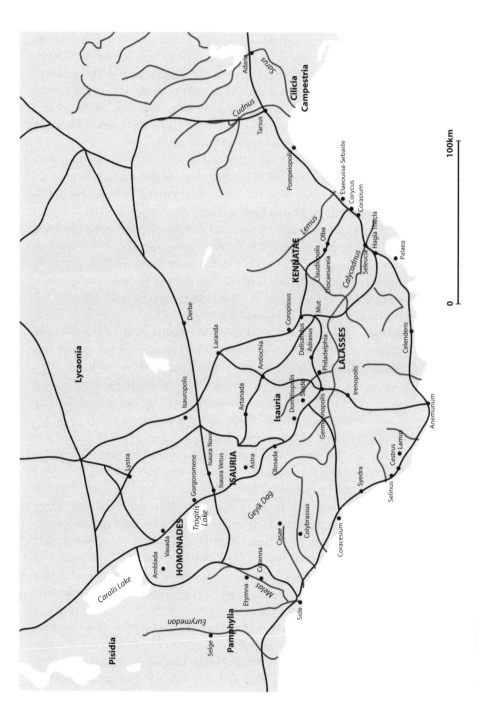

Isauria and Cilicia

detachments in or near Isauria were adequate in the first and second centuries, providing little more than a local police force, Isaurian *latrocinium*/λεστεια might be best translated as localized robbery or rustling. However, by the mid-fourth century, when there was need of a permanent legionary garrison and Ammianus gives the impression of the region crawling with troops, forts and castles, a translation of rebellion or revolt might be more apt.[12]

A History of Imperial Disgruntling

Given the terrain and the influence it had over their lifestyle and behaviour, it could well be imagined that the Isaurian tribes had been causing trouble for all their various imperial overlords – Hittites, Assyrians, Babylonians and Persians. Large punitive expeditions were launched against Isauria at various points in the pre-Roman era, although more out of retribution for raiding rather than attempts to bring the region under tight control. Their murder of Balacras, a satrap of Alexander the Great, shows how little respect for even the most famous of rulers the Isaurians had. Perhaps in response to this outrage, Perdiccas launched a bloody punitive strike into Isauria in 322 BCE, but the Isaurians remained 'largely free from outside interference for the next 250 years'.[13]

The Romans first penetrated the Isaurian hinterland in 78-74 BCE. Publius Servilius Vatia captured Isaura Vetus by diverting the Carsamba River, but despite his celebrating a triumph and receiving the *agnomen* 'Isauricus', there was no firm Roman control of the area. The territory nominally changed hands between Rome, Mithridates of Pontus and Deiotaurus of Galatia, before the pirate havens of Lycia, Pamphylia and Cilicia drew the attention of Pompeius Magnus during his anti-piracy campaign of 67-66 BCE. It could be that such first impressions, even if piracy was more by the Cilicians than the Isaurians,[14] likely impacted negatively on the Roman stereotyping of the Isaurians as a single group of bandits. But while he was successful in subduing the pirates, Pompey did not extend direct control over the Isaurians to any great degree. Cicero soon had to march into Isauria from his Cilician province to punish a chieftain called Moeragenes, while Marcus Antonius transferred the region to Polemo and then Cleopatra. Seemingly the Romans began to think that 'it was better for the region to be ruled by kings rather than subject to Roman governors'.[15]

Octavian continued this policy of indirect rule, entrusting the region to Amyntas of Galatia, who founded Isaura Nova (modern Zengibar Kalesi) in an attempt to impose order on the Homonades. The succession of client kings went down through Archelaus I and II of Cappadocia and then to Antiochus IV of Commagene by 38.[16] But this should not suggest that the Isaurians were under any more control than they had been in the past. Amyntas was killed fighting the Homonades, and was only avenged by direct Roman intervention over twenty years later. The Cappadocians also required direct Roman aid in 6 CE and 36; the governor of Lycia Pamphylia struck into Isauria sometime in the 40s, while an uprising under Troxoborus needed the *praefectus equitum* Curtius Severus to intervene in 51.[17] There seems to have been little attempt by the Romans and their client kings to exert full military control over Isauria; any solid hegemony enforced at the point of a sword was not respected for any extended period by its inhabitants.

It may not have been until the reign of Vespasian that Isauria was fully incorporated as part of a Roman province, and even then it was not achieved in any way conducive to long-term security. The Isaurian hinterland was joined to the plain of Cilicia Campestris to form the province of Cilicia, but the fertility, wealth, trade and urbanization provided by the Cyndus, Sarus and Pyramus rivers (the modern-day Tarsus Cayi, Seyhan and Ceyhan rivers respectively) was in stark contrast to the Isaurian mountains, foothills and valleys. Such contrasting topography saw the two halves of the province develop at different rates and in different directions.

After the intervention of Curtius Severus in 51, the sources fall silent over Isauria for virtually 200 years. There is always danger in drawing conclusions from historical silence, but with the likes of Tacitus, Suetonius and Cassius Dio writing in that period, that silence may be telling. Perhaps creeping Romanization, urbanization, financial growth in the plains and investment, road-building, colonization and occasional direct intervention in the hinterlands had produced more success in pacifying Isauria than usually thought.[18] The epigraphic record may demonstrate the increasing Hellenism of Isauria and a general acceptance of Roman rule,[19] which in itself may have brought greater regional prosperity and therefore a reduced need to resort to brigandage. The expanding definition of 'Isauria' is demonstrated during this period of 'peace' by Hadrian in 138, when he established the province of Tres Eparchiae of Cilicia-Lykaonia-Isauria. In this name, 'Isauria' signified a wider area than that surrounding Isaura Vetus and Isaura Nova.[20]

That 200-year absence of Isaurian raiding may be connected to the long periods of political stability which encapsulated the High Roman Empire. That Isaurian raiding seemingly returned in the mid-third century with Rome on the precipice of military and political collapse may also be of little real surprise. And even after two centuries, the Isaurians had not forgotten their roots – 'the terrain was simply too well suited for hiding bandits',[21] with the second-century poet Lucian demonstrating that the stereotype of the 'Cilician brigand'[22] had also not faded away. The raiding returned to such an extent that the Isaurian highlands were considered a *quasi limes*, an internal frontier between civilization and barbarism.[23] The source for the renewed outbreak of Isaurian raiding, the *Historia Augusta*, is of dubious worth. It claims that Severus Alexander won victories over the Isaurians and that the highlanders attempted to raise their own usurper called Trebellianus against Gallienus. It then has Probus settling veterans in the region in an attempt to suppress brigandage, claiming that 'it is easier to keep brigands out of these places than to expel them'.[24] All of these stories of renewed Isaurian aggression could be retrospective additions, reflecting the trouble of the fourth century rather than the reality of the third.[25]

However, there is other evidence of potential Isaurian trouble in the third century. Walls may have been built at Lamus in the 260s, adding some credence to the idea of an uprising under Gallienus,[26] while Zosimus records a brigand leader striking into Lycia and Pamphylia during the reign of Probus. This is further backed by the discovery of the siege site of this brigand at Cremna and an inscription dedicated to Probus from 278/279 by the governor of Lycia and Pamphylia.[27] Shapur I capturing some Isaurian cities could have seen the Isaurians looking to their own tribal leaders, like Trebellianus, with a similar episode taking place under Probus following the Gothic invasion of 276.[28] Perhaps the Roman response to regional self-help was so heavy-handed or non-existent that it saw the Isaurians turn on the imperial government due to anger or opportunism.[29]

After two centuries of seeming pacification, Roman control over the Isauria highlands was slipping. Diocletian's separation of Isauria from Cilicia was likely not only part of his policy of provincial subdivision, but also a reflection of defensive necessity. He was also the first emperor to install a permanent garrison at Seleucia made up of the legions *I*, *II* and *III Isaura*, which were still present there in 353, with the latter two still there by *c*.395.[30] An inscription from Colybrassus in Pamphylia also records the presence of *I Pontica* in the region in *c*.288,[31] which was 'an unlikely destination in the absence of major problems'.[32] Clearly, the Isaurians were turning into a 'profound security threat',[33] necessitating the transformation of southern Anatolia 'into a militarized zone that regularly diverted imperial troops and attention'.[34] And yet trouble continued, with a *vicarius* of Asia intervening in Pisidia against brigands – who were probably Isaurians – in 343.[35] Such reckless aggression may reflect that the Isaurians were 'distressed by severe hunger'.[36] Whatever harvests or herds they maintained may well have failed during this period, leading to attacks on major cities and depots regardless of the Roman military presence. Diocletianic Isauria bore little relation to the land of the original Isaurians, covering the south-east coast of Asia Minor, a coastal strip of Cilicia Tracheia, the remote reaches of the Taurus Mountains and the Isaurian Decapolis.[37]

'The astounding frequency of [the] eruptions'[38] reported in Ammianus may represent a far more accurate picture of Isaurian brigandage than the record of the previous century.[39] In 353-354, Isaurians raided across the Taurus Mountains, attacking Seleucia and its three-legion garrison, with only the intervention of eastern field units driving them back.[40] Within five years, the Isaurians forced Constantius II to empower Bassidius Lauricius as a *comes* in order to restore order. The new *comes* captured a fort taken over by brigands, garrisoning it as Antiochia, while a certain Aur. Ioustus fortified the highland town of Irenopolis. Both of these sites were situated along main routes through the Isaurian highlands, suggesting that the Romans were in danger of losing control of the province without major intervention.[41] In 367, with Valens distracted by the Goths, the Isaurians attacked and overran Cilicia and Pamphylia, defeating the Asian *vicarius* in short order. It took the imperial army to drive the Isaurians back to their hinterland, with further fortifying of important positions.[42] But this did little to prevent Lycia and Pamphylia being targeted once more in 375, with the communications between Caesarea and Constantinople threatened as well. This forced Valens to send field army units to regain control and then rebuild the damaged roads.[43]

The limited material for the late fourth/early fifth century suggests that Isaurian trouble continued. The *Notitia Dignitatum* depicts Isauria as so 'bristling with fortlets [that] it had come to be cordoned off as an enclave of active resistance'.[44] The *comes Isauriae* in 382 constructed the sea walls at Anemurium with the aid of *I Armeniaca*, which may be linked to attacks on Cilician cities by a certain Balbinus under Theodosius I, with some Isaurian rebels drafted into the army.[45] There was a large-scale revolt in 404, perhaps in reaction to the rebellion of Tribigild and Gainas. For four years, the Isaurians cut a swathe across Asia Minor, into Syria, Armenia and Pontus, across the sea to Cyprus and even into Palestine.[46]

After the defeat of the 404-408 revolt by imperial troops, it was another thirty-three years before the Isaurian tribes are recorded on the warpath. This could be due to the extent of the imperial intervention in 408, or perhaps more likely it is the poor state of the sources. In this 'new' outbreak, their strikes into Syria were again only ended by intervention from imperial forces.[47] And as will be seen, this 441 revolt and subsequent revolts up to 491 came at a time when there were Isaurians holding significant positions at court, demonstrating that even after over 500 years as part of the Roman Empire, the Isaurians were not a united people. Isaurians raided Rhodes in 466 in a dispute over their pay, while Zeno himself had to deal with the raiding of Indacus Cottunes in 479.[48]

Despite the strategic importance of Isauria on the communication and trade routes between east and west, Rome had significant trouble in imposing her authority and having it respected over the Isaurian tribes after the 'usurpation' of Trebellianus. Periods of unrest seem linked to the availability of imperial manpower and resources. When able to bring its forces to bear on the Isaurian tribes, the Roman army was capable of keeping the bandits in check. However, when distracted by Persians, Goths, Huns or rebels, the army presence diminished to the extent that Isaurian bandits troubled large parts of the Roman east.[49]

Counter-intuitively, the partial Romanization of Isauria contributed to the increased threat it posed. Those highlanders who became sedentary under Roman rule evolved into an elite, who combined local control with regional participation in Roman government. Such individuals amassed self-perpetuating power and wealth, which garnered support from the highlanders and made them militarily useful to the empire. But when the highlanders broke off from the empire, such a client/patron relationship saw the sedentary elites provide rebel leadership, which made them a much more dangerous and difficult prospect. The combination provided the Isaurians with several generations of high-level political power, and even when he became emperor, Zeno would still face real difficulties from amongst his countrymen – to them, he 'was only the most prominent of several Isaurian leaders, each of whom led their own men and were potentially their own bosses'.[50] It would require the systematic destruction and uprooting of this elite in the 490s to bring the region under firm imperial control.[51]

Christianity Amongst the Isaurians

The cultural dichotomy between the urban Cilicians and the rural Isaurians was also reflected in their religious proclivities; the former were much more likely to be Christians than the latter. That is not to say that the highlanders were all pagan. The process of Christianization may have been slowed in a similar manner to how the terrain had sheltered the Isaurians from Romanization, but by the fifth century many Isaurians were to prove themselves sufficiently Christianized to be at the forefront of Roman politics. The emperor Zeno himself would prove his Romano-Christian 'credentials as a traditional imperial patron in his greater "homeland" of Isauria-Cilicia'.[52]

However, prominent careers and the emperor's building of churches in Isauria was not enough to rehabilitate the Isaurians, particularly in a world of elevated polemic post-Zeno. Therefore, in order to fit into Roman political and religious life, Isaurian elites had to adopt Roman architectural techniques and Greek language. One of the best ways to achieve the latter was through the patronising of a cadre of educated, pro-Isaurian writers, who could portray the Isaurians as a single homogenous group with its own Christian history, complete with the prestige and cultural maturity necessary to legitimize their position within the empire. The non-extant writings of Capito, Christodorus and Pamprenius praised the religiosity of their countrymen, while Candidus tried to place the Isaurians in a biblical context, claiming that they were descended from Esau.[53] This was a peculiar choice of ancestor given the negative connotations surrounding Esau, and there must have been more to it than the similarity of 'Esau' to 'Isauria'. The relationship between Jacob and Esau had become prominent in arguments over natural slavery in the ancient world, stemming from the works of Aristotle and renewed by Philo of Alexandria and Basil of Caesarea.[54] It is likely that Roman writers preyed upon or even invented this connection to present the Isaurians in a brutish, subservient and inferior light. Perhaps Candidus was attempting to appropriate this alleged descent from Esau for a more positive usage proving the ancient and Biblical origins of the Isaurians.[55]

Such a process continued after the decisive victory of Anastasius in the Isaurian War, with Isauria increasingly brought into the Roman world 'through church institutions, employment in the army and the church'.[56] This imperially imposed completion of the processes of Romanization and Christianization is reflected in the recreation of Isaurian history in the *Vita Cononis* and the few fragments of

Capito.[57] This was a more nuanced approach to Isauria's barbarian past: they had been pagan bandits, participants in the poor treatment of Thecla, but by accepting Christianity and Roman civilization, they were just like any other part of the Roman Empire.[58] Their cultural and religious maturity was further displayed by the fact that they had been tamed and cultivated by Conon, who was himself an Isaurian. This not only integrated the Isaurians into Christian Roman society but also promoted the propagandistically useful 'blurring of Romanitas and Christianity as supra-ethnic identities'.[59] As Roman citizens and orthodox Christians, unlike many of the barbarians in the imperial hierarchy, it was perhaps inevitable that one of them would eventually rise to the position of *Augustus*.

Paving the Way: Isaurian Recruits and the Career of Zeno the Patrician

However, at the outset of the fifth century, Isaurians were still regarded as partially Romanized, which not only increased their threat but also their potential usefulness. Their mountain pastoralism made them formidable fighters, 'well disposed to army life and action'[60] and therefore valuable recruits for the Roman army. This was because the Romans had long surmised that military service could be an effective means of social and political control. It could well be then that each of the periodic outbreaks of Isaurian brigandage or revolt from the mid-third century through to the late fifth century culminated in the incorporation of Isaurians into the Roman army. Of course, as with previous barbarians such as Tacfarinas, Arminius and Alaric, the familiarizing of the Isaurians and their leaders with Roman military techniques almost certainly further increased the threat these 'internal barbarians' could cause to the Roman state should they rebel again.

Could it be that the Isaurians remained 'barbaric' and uncontained because the Romans did not want to get rid of a valuable recruiting resource? The imperial government had held back from totally destroying barbarian groups in the past and would do so again so as to maintain access to militarized barbarian manpower. And Constantinople would prove capable of the kind of overwhelming destruction of much of the Isaurian population and lifestyle by the end of the fifth century. But then this might be accepting a pro-Roman gloss, suggesting that they were purposefully not defeating these internal barbarians rather than being unable to do so.

Recruiting of Isaurians may have accelerated during the fifth century due to the extent of the Roman intervention in 408 and the growing threat from the Huns. Such major recruiting drives saw Isaurians 'disproportionately represented in the ranks of the Roman army and in its leadership wherever the army was stationed'.[61] Also demonstrating their continued dual status as internal barbarians and Roman citizens, Isaurian recruits were found serving in regular units, ethnic *foederati* units and perhaps even as mercenaries. An Isaurian unit under Longinus took part in the policing of the Council of Ephesus in 431; St Saba's father, Ioannes Conon, was sent to Alexandria to serve in an Isaurian unit stationed there in around 444; while a large Isaurian contingent under Marsus took part in the Vandal expedition of 468.[62] Isaurians were also frequently found amongst the increasingly popular *bucellarii* of large landowners and other non-imperial individuals.[63] Leo I legislated against such private forces, but this did little to assuage this trend demonstrating the loss of the imperial monopoly on military force, which saw the emperor 'increasingly reduced to being the biggest spender in a world of private armies'.[64]

The dissemination of power in non-imperial hands increased the potential for military instability, which erupted after the death of the Leos – civil war between Zeno and Basiliscus, Zeno and Illus and then Anastasius and Longinus, each of which were focused almost completely on the ownership of Constantinople and Isauria. The Isaurian origins of many of the major players saw considerable Isaurian manpower deployed on the part of Isaurian generals; however, their history as bandits meant that there was 'the use of massive personal wealth by political opponents to buy support in Isauria'.[65] As will be seen with Ardaburius, the idea of a non-Isaurian trying to buy the support of Isaurians against other Isaurians shows a lack of ethnic solidarity amongst the Isaurian tribes. Such mercenary attitudes must have played into the Isaurian reputation 'for coveting wealth … [with] the constant need for warlords to buy the loyalty of their followers'.[66] And viewing the Isaurian leadership in such a way, the emperor Zeno may only be 'the most successful *bucellarius* of them all'.[67]

These examples demonstrate that Isaurians were not only serving in their own 'national' units and as mercenary *bucellarii*, but also under their own commanders. This enabled Isaurian officers to ascend the military hierarchy, and by the 440s they were in the highest military and civil positions, such as the *comes* Longinus, Neon, governor of Euphratensis, and in particular the *magister utriusque militiae per Orientem*, Flavius Zeno the Patrician.[68] While there is little known about Flavius Zeno before 447, the chances are that he took on a Greek name so as not to appear 'barbaric' and that he must have had a distinguished Roman military career to have been appointed eastern *magister*.[69] While it could be evidence of just how stretched the empire's resources had become, with the Illyrian, Thracian and praesental *magistri* deployed to deal with the incursions of Attila, Flavius Zeno was deemed competent enough to be called to the capital with a significant force of Isaurians to take up the defence of Constantinople in 447.[70] Theodosius II and his court must have felt that he had done a job worthy of reward, for Flavius Zeno served as consul in 448.[71]

This honour saw Flavius Zeno dragged into the politics of the imperial court in opposition to the eunuch Chrysaphius, who enjoyed power and influence beyond his official position of *comes sacrarum largitionum*.[72] The specific bone of contention was Zeno's resistance to Chyrsaphius' appeasement of the Huns, with the Isaurian's influence having grown 'so great that he was able to forestall a diplomatic arrangement with Attila in 449'.[73] After a failed attempt to bribe Edeco, one of Attila's chief bodyguards and possibly the father of Odoacer, the future king of Italy, the Hun demanded Chrysaphius' head. The imperial court responded by buying Attila off with a promise of 700lb of gold per year. Supposedly, this deal was intentionally kept from Zeno as it was feared that he would revolt against the idea of buying freedom from Attila instead of handing over Chrysaphius.[74] He may even have been plotting to kill Theodosius II at the time of the emperor's death in 450, although it would be peculiar for a treasonous plotter to then be rewarded with the position of patrician in 451.[75]

Zeno the Patrician disappears from the historical record after 451, possibly deposed by Marcian before dying sometime before 457.[76] Regardless of his fate, that he was able to mix it with Chrysaphius, plot against the emperor, be entrusted with the defence of Constantinople and be given several high-ranking titles meant that Isaurians were well-established in the corridors of power. It also highlights how, despite this prominent position, the Isaurians were 'only conditionally subject to Rome',[77] willing to turn against the central government if they felt it suited them. This was not much different to other periods of Romano-Isaurian history but now in the mid-fifth century, instead of posing a threat to the provinces of southern Anatolia and Syria, the Isaurians were a threat to the position of the emperor himself.

Tarasis, son of Kodisa, from Rousoumblada

Early biographical material on the man who would become the emperor Zeno is scant. His date of birth is not specifically recorded, although some idea can be calculated from the recording of Zeno's age upon his death on 9 April 491. Unfortunately, the sources do not agree about the length of Zeno's life. Malalas says he was 60 years and 9 months old, Slavic sources suggest 65 years and 9 months, while the *Chronicon Paschale* says 65 years and 9 days, although as its author used Malalas as a source, the discrepancy is likely an error by the former. That said, Malalas was not beyond errors in recording the age of emperors, claiming Theodosius II died at 51 when he was 49 and that Anastasius died at 90 rather than the more likely 88. Despite these chronological issues, Zeno was likely born some time between 425 and 430.[78]

Zeno's actual name is also a source of dispute. On the surface, this seems a little strange. His regnal name was *Flavius Zeno Augustus*, highlighted on his coins and papyri.[79] However, this was not his birth name, with him seemingly changing it to Flavius Zeno upon his advent as a major player and supporter of the Leonid dynasty in *c*.466. Plenty of sources record the emperor Zeno's original name, and in the process of unwinding the mysteries tied up in that name, other biographical details emerge in the name of his father and seemingly the original name of his hometown; however, that unwinding process involves a parade of distortions.

The full name of Ταρασικοδίσσα 'Ρουσουμβλαδεώτου – Tarasikodissa Rousoumbladeotou – is provided by Candidus, and is largely followed by Agathias.[80] The likes of Malalas and the *Chronicon Paschale* provide recognizable, although stunted versions, which could provide some help in deciphering the meaning of the name.[81] However, from there the versions become increasingly distorted. The *Exerpta de insidiis* records Στρακωδίσσεος; Evagrius has Ἀρικμήσις; John of Nikiu has 'Trascalissaeus', which seems to have influenced later sources like Theophanes' Τρασκαλισσαῖος or the Slavic Траскоʌнсειа.[82] Given this morass of transliteration and distortion, it might seem as though Zeno's original name is lost, but it would seem a little illogical to put more faith in someone like Malalas or John of Nikiu over the Isaurian Candidus.

But even deciding that Candidus' version should be preferred does not solve the mystery of Zeno's birth name completely. Some have translated this as 'Tarasikodissa, son of Rousoumbladeotes',[83] giving the name of Zeno and his father. However, the prevailing wisdom is now that instead of being a patronymic, Rousoumbladeotou refers to a city called Rousoumblada as Zeno's original birth place.[84] Rousoumblada may be the original name of Zenonpolis, one of the Isaurian Decapolis, meaning that Zeno came from the hinterland but was potentially part of the urbanized elite.[85] The meaning of Tarasikodissa is also disputed. It may be an amalgamation of two separate names, Tarasis and Kodissa/Kodisas, with the suggestion that Tarasis was Zeno's original name and Kodissa was the name of his father. The 'distortions' of John Malalas – Κοδισσαῖος – and the *Chronicon Paschale* – Ζήνων ὁ Κοδισσεὺς – could support this,[86] but Tarasis and Tarasikodissa were known names in Asia Minor. So while Tarasis, son of Kodisa is the prevailing interpretation, support remains for Zeno having been born Tarasikodissa.[87]

But why did Tarasis/Tarasikodissa change his name? The usual reason given is that his birth name was too obviously Isaurian, with all the 'barbaric' notions which came with it. If he was to provide something of a counterweight to Aspar, he would have to appear less open to accusations of barbarism than the thoroughly Romanized Alan *magister*. He would be better able to achieve that as Zeno than as Tarasikodissa. Perhaps it was Leo I who chose the name Zeno to make the man chosen to marry his marry his daughter, Ariadne, more acceptable, although there is little support for this.[88] Why then did Tarasis or Leo settle on Zeno as a new name? Not only was it a thoroughly Hellenic and therefore 'civilized' name, it also harkened back to the career and successes of Zeno the Patrician.[89] It has even been suggested that Zeno the Patrician was the father of Tarasis,[90] with the latter not only naming his first-born son after the boy's grandfather but also then taking on the name Zeno when it came to needing a 'civilized' name. This familial connection is very unlikely, for surely it would have been mentioned in the source material.

That is not to completely rule out any connection between Tarasis and Zeno the Patrician beyond their shared Isaurian origins. Being of age for military service by the time Zeno the Patrician was called to defend Constantinople in 447, perhaps Tarasis was amongst the Isaurians who went to the capital with the *magister militum per Orientem*. Zeno the Patrician could therefore have been something of a patron for Tarasis, a bond he felt honour-bound to reflect in his choice of Romanized appellation. In so doing, Tarasis could also have been making a play for the loyalty of any remaining supporters of the Patrician, something which Leo will have been keen on if the whole point was for Tarasis to be an ally against Aspar.[91]

While evidence regarding Zeno's father is laced with issues, there is some more concrete information about the rest of his family. His mother was called Lallis, who outlived her son, dying sometime in the 490s, probably in her 80s.[92] Zeno was not the only child of 'Kodissa' and Lallis. They are known to have had a younger son called Longinus, who would play a prominent role during and after Zeno's reign. Such a Romanized Greek name may suggest that Longinus also changed his name; however, Longinus was a popular enough name amongst Isaurians for it to have been his name from birth. The younger brother is accused of being a bad influence on Zeno due to his immorality, stupidity, arrogance and licentiousness, although this likely reflects the reaction to his Isaurian origins and his threat to Anastasius in the 490s rather than any real personality faults.[93] There is also some mention of a third brother called Konon, although the only two sources that mention him are much later and may be misidentifying Longinus.[94]

Zeno had had a wife before marrying Ariadne, which would not be surprising given that he was in his late 30s or early 40s by 466. He is referred to as a widower, and a certain Arcadia is listed as a wife of Zeno. However, Arcadia is named as Zeno's second wife, which is either an error and should read Ariadne, or there is a third, otherwise unknown wife of Zeno from before both Ariadne and Arcadia.[95] A headstone of an Arcadia that stood for centuries at the foot of the steps to the Topoi, near the Baths of Arcadius in Constantinople, could be Zeno's former wife.[96] The *Suda*, perhaps using Malchus, also records Zeno having a son before he married Ariadne, presumably with Arcadia, who was also called Zeno. He seemingly died at a young age of dysentery or extravagance. No other source confirms this and the connection between Malchus and the *Suda* has been doubted, although there is some record of Zeno having other children beyond Leo II. Some traditions record Zeno having two daughters, Hilaria and Theopiste, and an illegitimate son, whose daughter married Aspar's youngest son, Ermanaric.[97]

The potential identity of members of Zeno's family can provide some idea of the position Zeno enjoyed before his alliance with Leo. It could be that his father, whatever his name, held a prominent position amongst the Isaurians for his son to inherit, although this is assuming that power among the Isaurians could be passed on through generations. Many barbarian tribes were ruled by a kratocracy ('rule by the strong'), so Tarasis would have had to prove himself worthy of such a leadership role with his actions, something he appears to have been capable of doing given his promotion by Leo I. Exactly who Arcadia was could also impact on the view of Zeno as less an 'internal barbarian chieftain' and more a rather typical Roman officer. Arcadia's name might suggest a Constantinopolitan family, as does that of Valeria, Longinus' wife. Both names also had potentially imperial connotations – Arcadia to the Theodosians and Valeria to the Leonids. And if the headstone near the Baths of Arcadius was of Zeno's wife, Arcadia, it would seem that at least some of Zeno's family were already well-established.

For Zeno to have married a potentially prominent Constantinopolitan lady could further suggest that he was 'part of a civilised provincial Isaurian elite, which had emerged by the 5th century'.[98] Such connections within the imperial capital might also explain why Leo chose Tarasis as an ally and son-in-law – he already knew and indeed trusted him. The incident which marked Zeno's arrival on the imperial stage, the disgracing of Aspar's son, Ardaburius, with the revelation that he had been in contact with the Persians, could also present hints at Zeno's position within Isauria and indeed the imperial hierarchy. It centres on how Zeno was able to gain access to the letters of the *magister militum per Orientem*. Could Isaurian raiders have intercepted this correspondence at the behest of Zeno? It has been somewhat *de rigueur* to portray Tarasis as a tribal chieftain, called down from his mountain stronghold to serve his emperor. But even if this is playing too much into the barbarian stereotype, either through anti-Isaurian propaganda post-491 or a more modern misconception, perhaps Tarasis was a regional power, commanding 'his own detachment of Isaurian *bucellarii*, maintaining his influence in the mountain areas of Isauria'.[99] Some sources go as far as to suggest that Zeno held the title of *dux* amongst his Isaurian brethren.[100]

But this still might be applying too 'barbaric' a portrayal of the Isaurians. While Zeno was an Isaurian, this does not mean that he must be a tribal chieftain. He will have had his own tribal roots, but being from the Isaurian Decapolis likely saw him more integrated into Roman political and military hierarchies. There may even be little reason to claim that he followed a different path to leading Roman soldiers in general. He would hardly have been given command of the *protectores domestici*, joined other generals in the field against tribal forces in 467 and then been given a promotion to *magister militum* by 469 if he was a totally barbaric tribal chief coming down from his mountainous redoubts at the head of a column of barely Romanized raiders in 466.[101] And even if Zeno was an Isaurian tribal leader, he 'was only the most prominent of several Isaurian leaders, each of whom led their own men and were potentially their own bosses. Zeno could not simply or naturally command the allegiance of other Isaurian generals such as Illus, but had to win it.'[102] This would not have changed even when he became *Augustus*.

Rather than as a local Isaurian leader, Zeno could have held a prominent position within the Roman military hierarchy before 466. To have intercepted Ardaburius' Persian correspondence, perhaps Zeno was serving on the eastern magisterial staff at Antioch, where Ardaburius could even have tried to involve Zeno in whatever he was plotting. Or maybe Zeno was a prominent figure at the imperial court, possibly a *protectores domestici* of Leo. As a *protectores*, Zeno may have been sent east on assignment by Leo, who was acting on some suspicions or merely carrying out a routine inspection.[103] However, these ideas of Zeno's position pre-466 are 'purely hypothetical and based on very tenuous clues'.[104] Even if the name and position of Tarasis, son of Kodisa, are somewhat problematic, he must have been in some position of power either in Isauria, Constantinople or both for Leo to view him as a man worth promoting and then marrying into the imperial family.

Chapter 3

Enemies in the State:
The Gothic 'Nations' of the Theoderici

'Remember … the ABC I taught you when dealing with the Romans.

'A: accept nothing

'B: believe nobody

'C: check everything'

Laidlaw (2008)

Barbarian Opportunity Knocks

By the mid-fifth century, the weakness of the Roman frontiers had made sure that the Isaurians were not the only 'internal barbarians'. To try to compile a list of the peoples, tribes and clans that had seeped into Roman territory would be somewhat futile. Even the Danube frontier by *c*.460 presents considerable issues of identification following the break-up of the Attilan empire. However, for the reign of Zeno the two most important groups were the Goths of Thrace and the Goths of Pannonia. Geographical descriptors are required, for not only did these two groups have their own political ambitions, but they both used to be labelled as 'Ostrogoths' and were simultaneously led by a Theoderic (which rather aptly means 'king of the people' in Gothic). Such descriptors are also required as these two Gothic 'nations' were far from the only Gothic groups recorded in the sources. Another remained under Hunnic domination until at least 467, while there were two others still settled in the Crimea and around the Sea of Azov. There were also the Goths of Radagaisus and Bigelis, neither of which seem to have had anything to do with the Thracian and Pannonian groups. There were also several Gothic groups already settled elsewhere on Roman territory as federates, like that of Sidimundus near Dyrrachium, descendants of those who supported Tribigild and Gainas, or the 'Visigoths' who migrated west and eventually set up their own kingdom at Toulouse.[1]

These Gothic 'nations' were not only a military problem for the Roman Empire; such barbarian leaders were growing increasingly powerful and forthright within Roman political circles, with some even capable of threatening the Roman emperor himself. This was the result of non-Romans having assumed positions of leadership in the Roman hierarchies throughout the previous 150 years; whether it was Bonitus the Frank serving as a leading general of Constantine I, Bonitus' son Silvanus being well-enough placed to supposedly make a dash for imperial power, or the struggle for power between the half-Vandal son-in-law of Theodosius I, Stilicho, and the Gothic leader Alaric. By the 460s, both imperial courts were led by decidedly non-Roman powers behind the throne: in the West it was the Suevo-Goth, Ricimer, while the East was held in the vice-like grip of the Alan, Aspar.

Non-Romans serving alongside and then in the legions was a long-established policy, but since the late fourth century, beginning with the Gothic treaty of 382 signed by Theodosius I, large non-Roman contingents were being settled on Roman territory without being disarmed or dispersed, and under the command of their own leaders rather than local Roman government. In return, they provided military manpower to the Roman army. These tribes having such 'a considerable degree of legal and political … autonomy'[2] weakened the powers of cultural integration the Roman state and its army had long deployed in managing such barbarian settlers. While this *foederati* system did not sprout fully formed in Theodosius' Gothic dealings in the aftermath of Adrianople, it continually evolved from a one-off, slapdash arrangement into more formal treaties by the mid-fifth century.

The likes of the Thracian and Pannonian Goths would marry these two ideas of Romanized leaders achieving prominent political positions and attaining a prosperous *foederati* position for their 'nation'. However, there would be an extra dimension to their operations. The domination of the Huns had altered the outlook of many tribal leaders. The Roman Empire was no longer something to just aspire to join or trade with; it was something to exploit. By taking onboard this Hunnic lesson but without discarding the benefits of imperial service, the Thracian and Pannonian Goths could strike a balance between being an imperial army provided with pay and supplies, and a raiding and extorting barbarian nation, similar to that which made Alaric and his Goths such a threat to the western government in the late fourth/early fifth centuries. For the Roman emperors, it meant that even as they served as an 'imperial' army, these Goths could never be fully trusted for the moment they felt that the empire was shirking its obligations or simply wanted to increase their stipend, they would revert to their raiding ways.

The Thracian Goths

Upon the advent of Zeno to a position of influence in Constantinople, it was the Thracian Goths who enjoyed the privileged position in eastern politics, primarily through their geographic position in Thrace and a marriage alliance with the most senior eastern general, Aspar.[3] This exalted position is demonstrated further by their presence in the garrison of Constantinople and Theoderic Strabo's ability to demand to become *magister militum praesentalis*.[4] How and when these Thracian Goths came to be established so close to the imperial capital is open to question. It appears that they were a conglomeration of clans and tribes who had escaped the Hunnic yolk, but not necessarily all at the same time. Their 'foundation' may have come as early as the 420s, when Roman forces drove the Huns out of Pannonia, liberating their Gothic subjects and settling them in Thrace as *foederati*.[5] A case could be made that the first fully developed *foederati* treaty involved these Thracian Goths. The empire gained manpower and depleted their enemies, while the Goths replaced the oppressive, hand-to-mouth overlordship of the Huns with a privileged position within the Roman army, political influence in Constantinople and 'recognised land rights which supplemented their yearly pay'.[6]

Throughout the mid-400s, the Thracian Goths may have been bolstered by other arrivals, making them 'the product of several separate bouts of immigration into the Roman Balkans'.[7] Either that or they were a band of Goths who broke off from their brethren in the immediate aftermath of the Hunnic defeat at Nedao and sought service with the empire.[8] The latter may fit just as well as the former, although for the Thracian Goths to have such a prominent position near and within Constantinople by the 460s could support a longer relationship with the East than the mid-450s.

The first leader recorded for the Thracian Goths was a certain Triarius,[9] whose Latin military name may reflect extended Roman service in his family. He may have had some blood ties to the Amal family, which would add another dimension to the confrontations between the Thracian and Pannonian Goths, although Amal propaganda denied any connection.[10] Triarius was not to see these Gothic altercations as he died sometime in the mid/late 450s, but it was a reflection of his dominance of the Thracian Goths and his position within the Roman hierarchy that his son Theoderic succeeded him as both leader of their tribal 'nation' and as their representative in Constantinople. In order to differentiate this Theoderic from the leader of the Amal Goths, the sources refer to him as *Theodericus Triarii filius*,[11] although he became much better known by the nickname 'Strabo', meaning 'squinter' and likely reflecting him being somewhat cross-eyed.[12]

The record is largely silent about these Goths and their role in imperial politics, likely because they made up part of the military support for Aspar, who was such an over-riding presence that little discussion was made in the sources about who his supporters were. It was really only with the removal of Aspar in 471 that the position of Theoderic Strabo as an independent actor comes into focus, particularly as he rebelled against Leo as a result of the emperor's Ardaburii butchery. It might be asked why Strabo would risk his privileged position in Thrace over the murder of Aspar. It may have been something of a pre-emptive strike due to the expectation that Leo would try to remove any vestiges of Aspar's faction. Unfortunately for the Thracian Goths, not long after they had shown themselves an opponent of the ruling *Augustus*, another Gothic 'nation' arrived in the eastern Balkans, keen to assume a similar position of privilege that the Thracian Goths had enjoyed for several decades.

The Amal Goths of Pannonia

The story of the Amal Goths is much better fleshed out than that of the Thracians, due to their eventual success in setting up their own kingdom in Italy. However, there is also the constant threat of being taken in by courtly propagandists. This is best on show when it comes to the almost complete manufacture of a long history of Amal control over significant sections of the Goths. According to Jordanes, the Amals ruled all of the Goths on the basis of descent from mythical, semi-divine heroes in the middle of the third century until the Hunnic conquests. They maintained their dynastic succession through the years of Hunnic dominance to re-emerge as rulers of half of the Goths in the 450s. Upon Theoderic's death in 526, 'legitimate' power was passed on to the seventeenth generation in the form of Athalaric.[13] Virtually all of this is complete fantasy, the concoction of Theoderic's court in Italy to provide legitimacy for his dynasty.[14]

The Gothic people were far too divided and disseminated by the 450s for anyone to rule over half of them. The same can be said for before the Hunnic conquests. Amongst various demigods and mythological heroes, the only member of this Amal genealogy of any credence is Ermanaric, a Greuthungian king known to Ammianus Marcellinus.[15] Rather than being an Amal ancestor, the Ammian depiction of Ermanaric has been appropriated by pro-Amal sources to create a connection that just was not there. The same appears true for the 'Amal' leaders after Ermanaric, where even defeated enemies of Valamir, Theoderic the Amal's uncle, have been incorporated into the Amal genealogy. Valamir did fight and defeat Vinitharius and then married his granddaughter, Vadamerca, which would suggest that Vinitharius was either not an Amal or that there had been an Amal civil war. There are also considerable chronological issues in this genealogy, with Vinitharius appearing in both c.375 and c.450.[16] It is also worth noting that when these Amal Goths were faced with military defeat at the hands of Belisarius in the 530s, they had 'few qualms in deposing the last representative of what the *Getica* supposes to have been a family of demigods who had ruled them since time immemorial'.[17]

The history of the Amal dynasty was far less spectacular, but no less colourful. Rather than from the mid-third century or even the late fourth century, Amal control of what became the Pannonian Goths likely originated late in Attila's reign or in the aftermath of Nedao. The latter is more likely as it is doubtful that Attila would have allowed the concentration of so much power in the hands of a non-Hun subordinate.[18] As the Hunnic empire collapsed, any vestiges of authority were up for grabs amongst the low-level tribal sub-commanders and a series of contests between them likely took place. Therefore, rather than the latest in a 200-year line of kings, Valamir should be viewed as a ruthless warband leader who forced his way to prominence, killing a certain Vinitharius, marrying Vadamerca for legitimacy and then seeing to the elimination of various Gothic families. These defeats of fellow Goths may explain why Jordanes seems to mistake Valamir for a Hunnic conqueror of the Goths called Valamver/Balamber. This hints at Valamir emerging from the post-Attilan maelstrom along the Middle Danube at the head of a strong Gothic 'nation' but with a lot of Gothic blood on his hands.[19]

While this more realistic approach to the origins of Amal control over the Pannonian Goths completely undermines Theoderic's claims to legitimacy, it increases the Amal achievement in attaining and maintaining control of such a dangerous, disparate and heavily militarized group. Rather than relying on a long-standing tradition of family rule, the lack of primogeniture meant that the Amals had to prove themselves as dynamic and ruthless leaders. They also displayed enough strength, bravery, charisma, intelligence and ability to provide for their men and their families that the Pannonian Goths were willing to follow successive Amal leaders across various parts of the Mediterranean world: Pannonia, Epirus, Macedonia, Greece, Thrace, Asia Minor and Italy. The same would have to be said for Triarius and Theoderic Strabo with regard to the Thracian Goths. Had they proven unable to provide for their followers, they would soon have lost their position.

It is not clear as to how Valamir threw off the Hunnic yolk. Goths fought at Nedao,[20] but specifics about the role of the Goths of Valamir are lacking. It has been suggested that they either did not fight at all or even that they fought for the Huns.[21] Whatever his initial stance, Valamir exerted his independence after the Gepid-led Germanic victory at Nedao, leading to conflict with the sons of Attila in 453/454, where the latter failed to rein Valamir in.[22] But then how did these Goths end up living in Pannonia, a province of the Roman Empire? The traditional approach, following Jordanes, is that they received it as federates from the emperor Marcian sometime between 453 and 457;[23] however, by the reign of Marcian, Pannonia was not the Roman emperor's to give away. Through the 440s, it had been the scene of heavy fighting between Roman and Hunnic forces, which ended with Theodosius II and Valentinian III ceding large parts of Pannonia to Attila.[24] It could well be then that it was Attila who was responsible for the plantation of Valamir's Goths in Pannonia; Marcian's involvement may only have been a recognition of a *fait accompli* after the Attila collapse. At best, Marcian achieved some suzerainty over Valamir and therefore could claim to have recovered Pannonia. Jordanes suggests that Marcian agreed to pay a subsidy to Valamir, although this is not mentioned in any other source.[25] Ultimately, Roman control of Pannonia slipped away in the 440s never to return fully, with combinations of Huns, Goths, Gepids, Sarmatians, Lombards and Avars controlling it for the next 150 years.

While the Amal Goths were now established ostensibly as a free people in Pannonia, Valamir's success did not come with unrivalled power within the Pannonian Goth 'nation'. His two brothers, Theodemir and Videmir, retained control of their own groups of the Pannonian Goths settled around what is now Lake Balaton in modern Hungary. The two younger brothers may have ceded some pre-eminence to Valamir, but they still maintained their own distinct positions and

policies. Their groups settled separately from one another, and frequently acted and
were treated independently: Valamir was targeted by Huns and Scirians without
the involvement of his brothers, Theodemir attacked some Suebi by himself
and Videmir would not follow Theodemir east in 473. This lack of complete
centralization of power reflects the disparate origins of the constituents of the
Pannonian Goths and that their unification was a relatively new development.[26]

Not All Theoderici 'Goths' were Gothic

It is too far to represent either Gothic 'nation' as anything approaching 'mini,
ancestral, culturally homogenous proto-nations'.[27] Indeed, they were not made up
solely of Goths; the ruling elite may have been Gothic, but even they had no trouble
intermarrying with non-Goths. It would hardly make sense for Strabo and the
Amals to limit their manpower solely to Goths, particularly for the latter who were
more clearly mired in the post-Attila bloody quagmire that was the Middle Danube.
Neither group would have turned away any Scirii, Gepids, Sarmatians, Huns,
Suebi, Rugians or even Roman provincials looking to join them, so long as these
new recruits were willing to submit to their leadership. Whether such barbarian
tribal 'nations' had a group identity or not remains a contentious issue, with either
answer having important consequences. No separate identity or any deeper ties
than kratokratic instincts and the ability of their leaders to project power might
mean that these groups 'were never more than loose and shifting agglomerations of
disparate warriors'.[28]

Another continuing debate is over exactly what the makeup of these 'nations'
was – purely military or a more societal group that farmed and traded, only turning
to military action when it was necessary? The answer to this question impacts
upon their potential threat to Constantinople and perhaps also their resilience
as a 'community', and even their abilities to amalgamate with existing populations
to form a kingdom. Their subsequent negotiations with imperial representatives
and the numbers attributed to them might suggest that the Pannonian Goths were
established farmers to some degree. The armed forces of 10,000 listed for
Theodemir's group 'can only exist in a relatively developed economic context, when
enough surplus wealth is being produced by non-fighting farming populations to
feed, clothe and arm them'.[29] Their establishment in Pannonia may have helped
such a trend towards farming, but then they were only there for no more than
twenty-five years, which does not seem long enough for a substantial increase in
population through farming techniques. The suggestion must then be that some
of these Goths were already farmers before their settlement in Pannonia. However,
Theodemir's 10,000 requires clarification – was this really his number of warriors,
or was it the tribal total? It seems large in comparison to many other fifth-century
tribal groups, but then the Goths had been a sizeable group before their Hunnic
oppression and the Amal Goths represent a conglomeration of various tribes rather

than a single family-led tribe. It would also help explain why the Roman army seemed to have so much trouble with them, or at least a great deal of reticence in risking battle against them.

Just because individuals and entire groups could move into and out of such tribal confederations does not mean that there was no real identity or solidarity in these groups. The idea that there might have been as many as 10,000 warriors, which could suggest up to 50,000 people, working together for a prolonged period may suggest that some of these conglomerations had their own hierarchies in place – rulers, high-grade, low-grade and slaves. Given that thousands would not join up or stay if they were permanently slaves, there was likely some idea of progression within the confederation. And to control such numbers, it is likely that the leadership had a political system of sorts, particularly some kind of commissariat of logistics to distribute food and funds. With such a hierarchy, the likelihood is that 'the strength of individual affiliation to the group's identity fell off dramatically'[30] further down the scale.[31]

Closer Amal Ties with Constantinople

As already seen, there was some contact between the Pannonian Goths and Marcian, but despite Jordanes' claims, it is unlikely that there was an imperial subsidy. It was the lack of subsidy rather than an imperial failure to pay, along with starvation, which led Valamir and his brothers to strike into Roman Illyricum between 459 and 462. This eventually brought the new emperor, Leo I, to the negotiating table and earned the Goths 300 pounds of gold *per annum*. This will have been enough to stave off any economic distress behind these raids, allow the Amals to further secure their position amongst the Pannonian Goths and likely bring others under their banner, although this could be a double-edged sword as any further growth in numbers would have exacerbated any lack of resources in Pannonia.[32]

The prolonged Romano-Hunnic conflict of the 440s had likely left the surrounding area in poor shape. The succeeding three decades provided little respite for recovery, culminating in a large-scale war between the Pannonian Goths and a coalition of Suebi, Scirians, Sarmatians, Gepids and Rugians, with a climactic battle on the Bolia River in the late 460s.[33] However, it would be dangerous to overplay this idea of Middle Danube destruction causing the Pannonian Goths to move. Other tribes such as the Gepids were happy to remain there for another century. Jordanes' claim that the area had been exhausted of spoils may hint that the Amals were not yet keen to settle down completely into an agricultural life.[34] It could also be that the Pannonian Gothic victory at Bolia was far from the complete success that Jordanes would have it be believed: 'Increasing competition between the Huns' former subjects may have made the region progressively less attractive as a homeland.'[35]

In return for his annual subsidy, Valamir promised good behaviour amongst his followers and had sent Theodemir's son, Theoderic, as a hostage to the imperial capital.[36] This could suggest that there was some dynastic manoeuvring taking place, with Valamir removing Theoderic from any position within the hierarchy of the Pannonian Goths where he could build a reputation and bonds of trust. Theoderic being only an 8-year-old boy in 463 and Valamir having no male heir might undermine such a suggestion, but they do not preclude it. However, looking for a dynastic squabble may be reading too much into this arrangement: 'All this was routine. Since time immemorial, Rome had demanded high-status hostages to ensure that treaties would be compiled with.'[37] By taking hostages, the Romans not only hoped to keep their friends and relatives in check, they also hoped to Romanize the barbarian, who would then return to his tribe and 'influence the foreign policy of his group in directions that served Rome's interests'.[38] This was not without its risks. Sometimes those hostages receiving a Roman education or the tribesmen serving in the Roman army would use that education and training against the Roman state. Following the likes of Arminius, Tacfarinas and Alaric, Theoderic the Amal would prove to be another 'ungrateful' product of the Roman hostage system.[39]

Clearly, 'internal barbarians', whether literal non-Romans like the Goths or figurative barbarians like the Isaurians, were a real issue for the imperial court at Constantinople in the mid-fifth century. Even trying to incorporate them into the body politic of the Roman Empire came with its drawbacks. Sectarian dislike within the capital was enflamed by the promotion of the likes of Zeno and the Theoderics to the highest offices, while it increased the military threat posed by the tribes as the likes of Theoderic the Amal used his Roman education and Roman tribute against the Roman state.

Chapter 4

Puppet on a String? The Reign of Leo I

'There is something behind the throne greater than the king himself.'

Sir William Pitt (House of Lords, 1770)

Aspar and the Imperial Successions

The seeds of the personal feud that helped propel Tarasis, son of Kodisa, to the imperial throne in 474 were planted seventeen years earlier on the death of the emperor Marcian on 27 January 457.[1] His demise from disease, perhaps of gangrene of the feet brought on by a long religious procession, was followed by an eleven-day interregnum. Some latitude should be given as Marcian's death, despite him being 65, may have been somewhat sudden, but such an 'unusually lengthy interlude suggests a power struggle'[2] going on behind the scenes out of the view of the people, the army and perhaps even much of the Senate.

It might be considered that there was no obvious imperial candidate, although this was not strictly correct. Marcian did have a daughter called Marcia Euphemia who had married a certain Anthemius, who was of good Constantinopolitan stock and strong lineage.[3] After having studied under the neo-Platonic philosopher Proclus in Alexandria, Anthemius led a distinguished career, although it was one seemingly thrust upon him in rapid succession after his marriage to Euphemia in 453. He was sent as *comes* by Marcian to serve along the Danube in around 453/454, and while he was probably more involved in rebuilding defences than actual campaigning, his imperial father-in-law rewarded Anthemius with a raft of honours and promotions. He was given the title of *patricius*, the position of *magister militum praesentalis* and the consulship in 455, with Valentinian III as his colleague.[4] Such a meteoric rise could easily suggest that the emperor was grooming his son-in-law for the highest office. Indeed, it would appear that many expected Anthemius to succeed to the purple as Marcian had done – through marriage to the daughter of an emperor.

Anthemius was not the only candidate of good breeding and connections. Even with the demise of the male side of the Theodosian family tree by 455, there were still some Theodosian women. They had shown themselves to be the real driving force behind the dynasty since 395 and in the 450s they could continue to bestow legitimacy on an imperial candidate as Pulcheria and Licinia Eudoxia had done for Marcian and Petronius Maximus respectively. In the process, any man married to a Theodosian woman could claim more of a right to the throne than Anthemius, as Marcia was not a Theodosian. This was the route that Ancius Olybrius attempted to follow in bettering his claim. Unfortunately, the Vandal sack of Rome in 455 meant that the only two available Theodosian women, Eudocia and Placidia, both daughters of Valentinian III and granddaughters of Theodosius II, were in captivity in Carthage. Olybrius travelled to the Vandal capital to secure a marriage with Placidia, perhaps fulfilling a betrothal; it may even be that Olybrius and Placidia were married before 455.[5]

However, neither of these men ascended the imperial throne in 457, and nor was it anyone with a Theodosian connection. At the vital moment, Anthemius supposedly showed some reluctance, lacking '*cupido imperii*',[6] leading to his being set aside, although it is far more likely that he faced opposition from the other power players. While Marcian had raised him to one of the two *magister militum praesentalis*, Anthemius was by far the junior of these two most powerful military officials. And unfortunately for Anthemius, his senior colleague had no interest in seeing him on the throne. That colleague was Flavius Ardaburius Aspar, and this was neither the first nor the last time he was involved in the imperial succession.

It is clear from his name that Aspar's family did not originate from amongst the 'civilized' peoples of the Mediterranean. He is usually regarded as being of Alanic descent, a semi-nomadic Iranian people situated north of the Caucasus but frequently swept up in the westward migrations, such as that of the Sarmatians, Vandals and Huns. Some sources regard him as a Goth, which is not out of the question as much of his military support and perhaps two of his wives were Gothic. His father, Ardabur, may also have married a Goth, making Aspar himself a Gotho-Alan.[7]

Regardless of his specific origins, they were clearly barbarian, so how did Aspar find himself able to influence the imperial succession? Barbarians had been becoming more prevalent in the Roman army throughout the fourth and into the fifth century, but the East had seen a process of limited debarbarization. The reason for this was the revolt of Tribigild in 399. This Goth used his Roman rank of *comes militaris* and poor treatment by the government to encourage his Gothic unit to rebel. He then subverted the loyalty of the barbarian element of the imperial forces sent against him and incorporated other discontented elements such as slaves, deserters and possibly Roman provincials.[8] He resisted two armies sent against him, and when Tribigild himself was killed in skirmishes, leadership of the revolt fell to one of the *magistri* he had resisted, his fellow Goth, Gainas. With the combination of his army and the rebels of Tribigild, Gainas took control of Constantinople for a few months in 399.

His own incompetence and the opposition of the city populace soon put paid to Gainas,[9] but he and Tribigild had succeeded in escalating mistrust in foreigners. While the departure from using barbarian manpower was not total for practical purposes, there was a deliberate effort to keep Germans from powerful positions in the army, with the number of eastern generals with Greek or Latin names increasing from around 66 per cent to about 80 per cent.[10] While Constantinople might have felt that they had found good balance between limiting barbarian influence in the upper echelons of power without overly compromising military manpower, the policies enforced seem to have limited integration. Non-Roman officers did not necessarily become citizens and a prohibition of intermarriage between *gentiles* and Romans was enforced. Even a successful and loyal general such as Fravitta had to ask for imperial dispensation to marry a Roman. This led to prominent barbarians in Roman service binding themselves together through marriage, which in turn consolidated a lot of their power and influence into a single house, allowing them to pass authority on to the next generation.[11]

This was best seen in the marriage between the daughter of Plintha the Goth and the son of Ardabur the Alan, who just happened to be Aspar. By itself, this would not have changed much had the policies of limited demilitarization and debarbarianization continued; however, within two decades, eastern armies were on the move and they needed barbarian manpower and leadership once more. This saw Plintha serve as *magister militum praesentalis* for twenty years and attain the consulship in 419, while Ardabur took command of imperial forces during the short-lived Persian War of 421-22 and received a consulship in 427.[12] The Gotho-Alan family of Aspar was not just the most predominant barbarian family in imperial service; it was amongst the most predominant in Constantinople full stop, well-connected and highly Romanized. Its connection with the Thracian Goths was not some opportunistic congregation contracted on a whim to impose greater control over Theodosius II, Marcian or Leo, or even 'a self-styled faction or cabal with its own overriding ethnic agenda'.[13] It was a long-standing and expanding alliance between those already ensconced in the corridors of Constantinople and those well-established as Gothic *foederati* in Thrace.

Aspar wasted little time in extending the web of alliances surrounding his Ardaburii family. He married three times – the aforementioned daughter of Plintha, an unknown woman and then a relative of the Gothic leader, Triarius. By these wives, Aspar had three sons – Ardaburius, Patricius and Ermanaric – and two daughters. No doubt Aspar will have looked to achieve favourable matches for his daughters, although there is no indication of their names.[14] Ardaburius married a woman called Anthusa, although she is also of uncertain identity. She was linked to a cloud-seer of Cilician descent, but this would be a strange match for the son of a general of such dynastic ambitions.[15] Instead, Anthusa may have been a daughter of the Isaurian general, Illus, although this also raises issues. Any marriage link between the competing families of Aspar and Illus would be flagged up more in the sources; however, it would not be surprising had Aspar looked to neutralize potential rivals by tying them to him. One other proposition on the nuptials of Ardaburius is that there are two Anthusas – the Cilician seer who was the wife of a general sent to fight in the West, possibly Damonicus, and the daughter of Illus, who was perhaps Ardaburius' second wife.[16] Whoever his wife was, she bore Ardaburius a daughter called Godisthea, who in turn married the prominent general Dagalaiphus and gave birth to Ariobindus, eastern *magister* and consul under Anastasius.[17] The proposed marriage of Aspar's second son, Julius Patricius, would become a bone of particular imperial contention.

Aspar did not rise to prominence solely on his familial connections. His father's position did enable him to participate in high-level campaigns, such as the Persian War of 421-22. He earned enough of a military reputation in Mesopotamia to be selected as a general alongside Ardabur during the eastern expedition to overthrow the western usurper Ioannes and install Valentinian III in 424/425. While still a junior partner, it was Aspar who emerged as the real military victor over Ioannes after his father was captured at sea; the highlight being his conquest of the previously impregnable Ravenna, complete with the rescue of his father and the imprisonment of the usurper.[18] Shortly thereafter, Aspar also defeated a Hunnic contingent led by future western generalissimo, Aetius. This double success saw Aspar not only rewarded with a western consulship for 434 but also dispatched to Africa to help Boniface deal with the Vandals from 431, attaining the rank of *magister militum* which he would hold for forty years. This expedition proved a blot on Aspar's military record as he failed to prevent Geiseric's takeover of this important province. This was followed up in the 440s by defeats by Attila, which led to the suggestion that Aspar's influence was on the wane.[19]

However, Aspar remained a favourite of Theodosius II and was seemingly present to witness his passing on 28 July 450. The extent to which Aspar's political power had grown is demonstrated in the suggestion that he was in a position to intervene in the subsequent imperial succession. He may even have been key in the choice of Marcian, a former underling of his, supposedly overhearing his nomination by Theodosius II on his deathbed. Even the putting forward of Pulcheria as the main mover in the accession of Marcian, given that she would provide him with Theodosian legitimacy through marriage, does not nullify any role of Aspar. Perhaps the Theodosian princess and the Alan general forged a *détente* to see Marcian elevated to the throne.[20]

Whatever role he played in the succession in 450, it is clear that Aspar was able to enhance his position throughout the reign of Marcian. So much so that in 457, he was perhaps little less than a shadow emperor, able to choose who would sit on the throne of Constantinople.[21] It is difficult to fully comprehend his aims during the succession crisis of 457, but it could be that he felt that Anthemius was too well connected and independent.[22] It could even be that Aspar had designs on the throne for himself or his sons, with Anthemius presenting too much of a dynastic continuation. Theoderic the Amal later claimed at a church synod in 501 that Aspar was offered the imperial throne by the Senate in 457, but turned it down stating, 'I fear I would launch an imperial tradition.'[23] During his time as a hostage, Theoderic could have heard Aspar grumbling over that lost opportunity when it became clear that his chosen puppet was not the pushover that he had hoped.[24]

It is not known what Aspar meant by any such 'enigmatic observation'.[25] Perhaps he was content to remain behind the throne and held 'some genuine respect for legitimacy of emperors'.[26] He could also be hinting at the issues of his Arianism, his Alano-Gothic heritage or even reopening the imperial throne to the strongest general. The former is favoured by the sources and would rear its head again with the proposed accession of Aspar's son, Patricius.[27] It should also be noted that Theoderic had the ulterior motive of presenting the Constantinopolitan Senate as willing to hand the imperial title to an Arian barbarian as it could provide a precedent for the Roman Senate to follow to his benefit in the early sixth century.

Flavius Valerius Leo *Augustus*

Rather than take the imperial title for himself or his sons in 457, Aspar chose one Leo Marcellus, enthroned as *Flavius Valerius Leo Augustus*. It appears a strange choice – Leo had no prior imperial connection, was of obscure origins, underwhelming military position as *comes et tribunus* and was probably in his mid-50s.[28] Aspar must have known Leo personally as he would not have chosen an unknown quantity to serve as his mouthpiece on the imperial throne. Leo's unit, the *Matiarii*, was stationed close to Constantinople at Selymbria and was likely one of the six *legiones palatinae* under the command of Aspar in his role as *magister militum praesentalis*. Leo may even have been the *curator* of Aspar's estates. The raising of a member of his household would not be unexpected given Marcian's former position as an Ardaburii *domesticus* before his elevation in 450.[29]

Such a combination of poor lineage, obscurity, age and close connections to Aspar makes it seem that Leo was meant as a place-holder, elevated to allow Aspar to pave the way for the accession of his own family. This has also encouraged the assumption that Leo was but a humble Balkan soldier, dragged from anonymity to serve as Aspar's emperor.[30] However, even with Aspar's power, considerable opposition from the Senate, military and people might be expected had the Alan general chosen a complete nobody to don the purple. Therefore, Leo's obscurity is exaggerated for propagandist effect. He is more commonly described as being of Bessian stock, although he is also listed as an Illyrian Dacian, with the change from the latter to the former perhaps an attempt to portray Leo as a barely Romanized barbarian, something which would be repeated with Zeno.[31] It is much more likely that Leo's position as *comes et tribunus Mattiariorum* at Selymbria saw him as 'a relatively senior and experienced military figure',[32] and given their similar age Leo and Aspar may have served together for years.

Even being of less obscure origins and having a more prominent career behind him, Leo had become *Augustus* on the influence of Aspar, 'and would naturally be expected to comply with Aspar's preferences and plans'.[33] The sources clearly thought so, with the likes of Priscus, Malchus, Candidus, Procopius and Jordanes all hinting at Leo being under Aspar's control, while in the letters of Pope Leo I,

Aspar appears as an illustrious patrician and almost a co-ruler.[34] For so many sources to agree, little attempt must have been made to hide his role. Indeed, it could be that if 'Aspar's ultimate power was his capacity to manage the imperial succession',[35] rather than just his network of alliances, he had to be seen wielding that power.

This could be seen in the prevalent role Aspar played during Leo's coronation in early February 457. Having been acclaimed by the army at Hebdomon, Leo enjoyed a long procession through Constantinople to the Helenianae Palace, being well-received by the public more for the occasion than any personal popularity. Aspar joined the emperor in the imperial carriage, kissing Leo's hand as he boarded. And when Leo alighted in the Forum of Constantine to greet the Senate and the Prefect of the City, he was offered the *modiolus* gold crown by the *princeps senatus*, who just happened to be Aspar as well. For the remainder of the ceremony, Aspar cannot have been too far from his emperor; his power there for all to see.[36]

Being so thoroughly overshadowed by Aspar is perhaps reflected in the reception of Leo in modern sources. In an era of great importance to the history of the Roman Empire, Constantinopolitan politics receives unsatisfactory focus. Leo receives even less press than the likes of Anastasius and Zeno.[37] A major part of that lack of focus is the paucity of sources, but certain historiographical trends and ideas have undermined the depiction and depth of investigation on Leo. His depiction as a 'puppet' emperor, whether accurate or not, and the focus on imperial women of the fifth century, Christological debates and the careers of Attila, Aetius, Aspar and others may have seen Leo overlooked.[38] This was not just a modern tendency. More contemporary historians were frequently non-committal when it came to Leo's reign. The collapse of the West was hardly an era that Roman historians would want to recount, while the likes of Malchus highlight that later emperors like Anastasius may have made a conscious effort to disassociate with Leo due to his Chalcedonianism and connections with Zeno. Malalas is more nuanced, willing to portray the positives and negatives of Leo, while Procopius and the *Suda* provide a more positive military hard-man presentation. And it is not as if Leo's reign was devoid of interesting and important events. Not only were there his relationships with Aspar and Zeno, there was also his involvement in the growing importance of the Church in imperial politics, the disastrous Vandal expedition and his dealings with the crumbling imperial grip on the western provinces. And while it is not the aim of this work to completely right the lack of attention on Leo, his reign and the circumstances surrounding his deteriorating relationship with Aspar are crucial to the career of Zeno.

While Leo would prove to be not as pliable as Aspar would have hoped by the mid/late 460s, there are some suggestions that some of Leo's early moves were partly inspired by a wish to attain some freedom from Aspar – his Christological stances and closeness to Daniel the Stylite, his creation of the *excubitores* as an elite palace guard in 460/461 and the promotion of his brother-in-law, Basiliscus, to *magister militum per Thracias* in 464.[39] When listing such actions and proposing a 'whispering campaign'[40] against non-Romans, it is tempting to see an ever-progressing plan by Leo and his allies to strengthen his imperial position in opposition to Aspar. However, caution must be maintained. It is more likely that there was little real overall planning or connection between these moves, and Leo would need to have been an extremely patient man to have waited so long before moving to strike against Aspar.

Aspar will also have found that Leo came with a collection of ambitious and conniving personages in the form of the new imperial family. The only known natal family of Leo was his sister Euphemia, who played no role in politics, although Leo did not forget her and visited her every week in Constantinople, while she dedicated a statue to her brother.[41] The threat came from the other side of the new imperial family. Leo's wife, Aelia Verina, would prove a more than capable player in the game of thrones. She also had at least three siblings: an unnamed sister was married to Zuzus, another unnamed sibling was the mother/father of Armatus, and her brother Basiliscus. These men would prove as ambitious and problematic as Verina.[42]

In keeping with the reports of Leo's barely Roman, Bessian origins, the very Romanity of Verina's family has been called into question. The source of this supposition is John of Antioch's recording of Armatus' assassination in 477 by Onoulphus, brother of the *rex Italiae*, Odoacer. The passage can be interpreted to suggest that Odoacer was brother to just Onoulphus or to both men. In the latter case, this would make the king of Italy a nephew of Verina and Basiliscus, and more importantly could suggest that the empress and her imperial brother were of barbaric descent. Surely such a relationship would have been commented upon by even the poor sources that survive? John of Antioch is likely two centuries removed from Leo's reign and there are several historians much closer to the period who might be expected to have mentioned such a connection but are silent. At the very least, Odoacer might have made it known that he shared some link to the eastern *Augustus* to shore up his legitimacy in Italy in the late 470s.[43]

One prominent familial reason why Aspar may have chosen Leo over Anthemius or many other mid-level military men is that like Theodosius II and Marcian, Leo and Verina had no sons and, being of middle age, were perhaps not expected to have any more children. Even more useful to Aspar was the fact that Leo and Verina had a daughter, Ariadne, who could provide imperial legitimacy to whomever she married. That said, the fact that Leo and Verina did have another daughter not long after Leo's accession demonstrates that both he and Verina were still of child-producing age. Aspar surely breathed a huge sigh of relief when the child born soon into Leo's reign was a Leontia rather than a Leo.[44] Without a male heir to perpetuate the Leonid line, Aspar could look to influence the marriages of Ariadne and Leontia, and seems to have extracted a pledge from the emperor that Ariadne would marry Patricius. Aspar's second son certainly appeared to be on the up early in Leo's reign, serving as consul in 459, and may also have been present in the imperial carriage during Leo's coronation.

But this pledge was not enough for Aspar. He wanted Patricius married to Ariadne as soon as protocol would allow and for his son to be named *Caesar*, essentially marking him out as heir apparent.[45] 'Yet, as Ariadne grew up, Leo procrastinated in the hope of keeping the throne within his own family',[46] recognizing the bind he was in should he become too dependent on Aspar. But if Leo was already wrangling under the Aspar yolk, there was as yet to be no real move to curb the Alan's influence. Both Aspar and Ardaburius remained *magistri*, while Ardaburii allies Vivianus and Dagalaiphus became Praetorian Prefect in the East and consul respectively. When Vivianus ascended the consulship in 463, Aspar's power seemed stronger than ever.[47]

However, in April 463, Aspar's dynastic plans for Patricius and Ariadne were thrown into disarray. With the birth of Leontia showing that they were still capable, Leo and Verina were desperate for a male heir. In the summer of 462, Leo sought divine intervention through Daniel the Stylite, stood atop his column at Anaplous along the Bosphorus from Constantinople. The emperor asked Sergius, a disciple of St Simeon the Stylite, now amongst the followers at Anaplous, to forward his plea to Daniel. Soon after, Verina conceived once more and after what must have been an anxious wait, she gave birth to a boy on 25 April 463. Elated, Leo had foundations laid for a third column for Daniel.[48] It could well be imagined that Aspar was far less happy with the securing of the Leonid line, particularly if the newborn was almost immediately created *Caesar*, marking out his position as imperial heir.[49] While he could still hope to influence Leo and his new son, Aspar's plans for Patricius were seemingly in ruins and he also faced the growing influence of Verina. As the mother of the imperial heir, Verina saw her prestige sky-rocket, enough to warrant the title of *Augusta* and her own coinage.[50]

This dynastic bliss and the securing of the imperial succession did not last long. The omens had not been good, with a horoscope cast about the birth of the new imperial heir providing grim reading. And so it was to prove. Just five months later, the infant son of Leo and Verina was dead.[51] Despite the air of confrontation that was to ferment between the imperial family and Aspar and the open designs of the latter for the imperial throne, there was no hint of foul play in the sources over the death of the young boy. And while that does not rule out any involvement of the Ardaburii, this was just another case of infant mortality in the ancient world, with Leo and Verina's son dying at a young enough age to have no name recorded.

Growing Confrontation

The succession was now up in the air again, with the marriages of Ariadne and Leontia once more fundamental to the future of the imperial dynasty. For Aspar, the long-standing betrothal of Ariadne to Patricius was paramount, and he must have been growing impatient, especially as Leo and Verina continued to prevaricate while simultaneously promoting the example of Pulcheria, the Theodosian empress, who in choosing her consort was also choosing the emperor.[52] The surviving Theodosian women and their husbands had grown as a threat, for while Aelia Eudocia had died in Jerusalem on 20 October 460, Licinia Eudoxia and her daughter, Placidia, wife of Olybrius, had returned to Constantinople in 462. Anthemius had been retained as *magister militum praesentalis* and allowed to take the field, where he defeated the Goths of Valamir at some point between 459 and 462,[53] while Olybrius holding a consulship in 464 might be 'both a statement of recognition by Leo and a concession to his influence'.[54]

During Olybrius' consulship, a disaster overtook Constantinople that was to provide many of the major players with an opportunity to shine. On 2 September, a large fire broke out near the arsenal at Neorion, supposedly due to the carelessness of an old woman with a candle; it spread east as far as the old temple of Apollo, south towards the Forum of Constantine and north to the Forum Tauri, burning out of control for three days.[55] If there was a chance to show himself a proud, capable *Augustus* who could take the bull by the horns and be the saviour of at least part of the city, Leo failed to take it. Instead of meeting the problem head on, he did exactly the opposite, fleeing Constantinople up the Bosphoran coast to the shrine of St Mamas, where the imperial court would be established for the next six months.[56] With the emperor shying away from the job, Aspar seized the opportunity. If the *magister*'s prestige could have risen any higher than it already was, then saving the lives and property of those in the imperial capital would surely do it.[57] Brooding in his temporary palace, the activity of Aspar likely further encouraged Leo to take steps to challenge the domination of his leading general. The appointment of Verina's brother, Basiliscus,[58] as *magister militum per Thracias* and then consul of 465 may have been the first steps in promoting those loyal to the family of Leo rather than that of Aspar.

Given that Aspar's youngest son, Ermanaric, was Basiliscus' consular colleague, this was not yet a full-on attempt to emerge from his *magister*'s shadow. However, the events at a meeting of the Senate, not long after Leo's return from St Mamas in March 465, might suggest otherwise. A seemingly hitherto unknown Isaurian, Tarasis, son of Kodisa, arrived in the capital, likely from an assignment with the staff of Ardaburius, the *magister militum per Orientem*. The soon-to-be rechristened Zeno produced a series of Ardaburius' letters to the *conventus*. They detailed correspondence between the eastern *magister* and the Persian king, which included the former attempting to induce the latter to invade Roman territory.[59]

The letters were read out to shock and horror; and why not? This was a Roman general, son of the foremost imperial subject, attempting to betray the empire. Leo was outraged, or acted so, as he surely already knew the content of the letters, having previously seen them or perhaps even because he was their co-author in a ploy to discredit Aspar's son. As *caput senatus* and presiding consul respectively, Aspar and Ermanaric were both present at this reading. The former reacted with great surprise at this treasonous revelation, although it must be considered that if Ardaburius was in contact with the Persian king, there was a fair chance that Aspar was involved. He quickly disassociated himself with his eldest son's actions and backed Leo in whatever punishment the emperor chose to inflict, reputedly saying:

> 'You are the master and have full authority; after hearing this letter I realise that I can no longer control my son; for I often sent to him counselling and warning him not to ruin his life; and now I see he is acting contrary to my advice. Therefore do whatever occurs to your Piety; dismiss him from his command and order him to come here and he shall make his defence.'[60]

This raises the matter of what either side could hope to gain from such plotting. By potentially creating this scandal, Leo would have been looking to embarrass Aspar by discrediting Ardaburius, forcing him either to share partly in his son's disgrace or to virtually disown him. Ardaburius' motives are more unclear. Just why would he attempt to induce the Persian king to invade the empire? Never mind the treasonous nature of such a move, it would have put Ardaburius in the firing line as *magister militum per Orientem*. But then perhaps that was the whole point. As a Roman commander, Ardaburius will have had the utmost faith and confidence in his eastern field army and any reinforcements to defeat a Persian invasion. Such a victory would have greatly increased the already immense prestige of the Ardaburii, and the crisis of a Persian invasion may have seen Leo turn over more authority to Aspar. It is possible that rather than conspiring with the Persian king, Ardaburius was carrying out part of his mission as eastern *magister*, conferring with the Persians over the behaviour of the Armenians, Laz, Iberians and Albanians, as well as providing promised funding for the defence of the Caucasian passes from Hunnic raids. Perhaps this proposed Persian invasion was actually of one of the recalcitrant Caucasian kingdoms, with the Romans in the guise of Ardaburius agreeing not to get involved.

It is difficult to come to any firm conclusions regarding the veracity of these accusations. The shock and horror of both Leo and Aspar could easily be put on for appearance's sake. The latter's composed response in disassociating himself from his eldest son's actions could be the actions of a man loyal to the empire or a shrewd operator capable of calculating risk and reward on the hop. Of course, such a composed response could easily be interpreted as something more orchestrated. Would a surprised father not leap to his son's defence if he knew nothing of these accusations? The lack of an outburst might be taken as Aspar having at least some knowledge of Ardaburius' actions or of the imperial plot against his son.

Leo stripped Ardaburius of his position as *magister* and his title of *patrician*.[61] He was recalled to the capital in disgrace and any defence or denial he offered failed to see him reinstated or absolved of guilt. What is surprising is that if Ardaburius was considered guilty of such an egregious act of treason, why was he not faced with execution? Either he was able to mitigate some of the outrage of Leo, feigned or real, with his explanations or Aspar remained too influential for the emperor to execute his eldest son regardless of the crimes involved.

This incident had a negative effect on Ardaburii plans and influence as 'the balance of power within the court of Leo began to tilt away from Aspar'.[62] Leo was quick to take advantage. Ardaburius was replaced in the East by Flavius Jordanes, son of another prominent general. This appears like a continuation of the *status quo*, as Jordanes was another protégé of Aspar; however, an encounter with Daniel the Stylite had seen Jordanes step way from the Arianism of his family and much of the Ardaburii alliance. Leo seized this opportunity, taking Jordanes to Daniel for his blessing, which established the general as an orthodox Christian and a supporter of the emperor.[63]

The disgrace of Ardaburius, together with the vacancy in Thrace, had allowed Leo to place his own appointees in high office – Basiliscus in Thrace, Jordanes in the East and Zeno in the capital. The emperor seemed keen to continue to build on that momentum. In 465, Leo announced that he would serve his third consulship in 466 alongside Flavius Tatianus, who Marcian had appointed *patrician* and Prefect of the City. Tatianus had retained imperial favour under Leo, serving as an envoy to the Vandals in 464, albeit unsuccessfully.[64] Recognizing the gradual eroding of his previously dominant position, Aspar was indignant at this consular choice.[65] He had been angling for Vivianus to hold the consulship of 466, which would have been his second in three years. Leo might even have given his tacit approval of this appointment, only to then take advantage of the disgrace of Ardaburius and appoint Tatianus instead. It could also be that the 'unlikely but reliable'[66] Tatianus was chosen first, only for Aspar to object, putting forward Vivianus as a better candidate. The sources are not clear on the events surrounding the nomination of Leo's co-consul for 466. The summary of Candidus compounds the promotions of Zeno, Vivianus and Tatianus, which took place over the course of several years, into one exchange between Leo and Aspar,[67] while many sources record that Leo was consul *sine collega* in 466. Some western sources list Tatianus as his colleague. This could suggest that Tatianus was a western consul,[68] but it is more likely that his appointment was originally announced, only to be withdrawn and this information not reaching the West.

Any removal of Tatianus from the consulship begs the question of what took place. Perhaps the opposition of Aspar encouraged Leo to reconsider his choice, but if it did, it was not enough to see Vivianus appointed in Tatianus' place. The rather abrupt disappearance of Tatianus might instead suggest that he died before or not long after assuming the consulship, a victim of Aspar or 'Father Time'. The latter seems more likely, as Tatianus was already an old man by

466, having moved to Constantinople in 388 to finish his education,[69] while the elimination of a consul by Aspar would have been a scandal.

The position of City Prefect of Constantinople also caused friction between *magister* and emperor. Aspar wished for 'someone of like mind and Arian belief',[70] but Leo could not allow an Arian city prefect and made his own choice without consulting his general. The limited sources do not allow for a certain identification of Leo's choice, but it was either his daughters' tutor, Dioscorus, or a certain Diapharentius.[71] Furious at being ignored, Aspar confronted Leo. Tugging at the emperor's cloak, he proclaimed, 'Emperor, it ill befits the wearer of this garment to lie.' Unsurprisingly irate at this direct affront to his imperial glory, Leo replied sharply, 'And it's not fitting that he should be constrained and driven like a slave either.'[72] Zonaras suggests that this confrontation took place over the proposed elevation of Patricius to *Caesar*, an argument that had simmered since 457.[73] There was also seemingly persistent disagreement over various religious policies, due to the emperor's orthodoxy and the general's Arianism, even if Pope Leo considered both defenders of Chalcedon.[74] Leo and Aspar had disagreed on the repudiation of Chalcedon by Amphilochius, bishop of Side, in early 458. The emperor had wanted to deal harshly with the bishop, but Aspar persuaded Leo to leave Amphilocius alone.[75] Now, eight years later, Aspar tried unsuccessfully to prevent Leo's deposing of Timothy Aeleurus, who had usurped the see of Alexandria and orchestrated the murder of the Chalcedonian patriarch, Proterius. Leo 'was not turning out to be the compliant emperor Aspar had expected'.[76]

The Rise of Zeno

In this state of heightened tensions between Aspar and Leo, the man responsible for precipitating Ardaburius' disgrace, Zeno, was promoted to the position of *comes domesticorum*. While he may not have been appointed immediately after revealing the treasonous letters, 'he was probably made *comes* in late 465/early 466'.[77] This hints that Zeno was already a prominent member of the *protectores domesticii*, perhaps even one of the *decemprimi*, the ten most senior *protectores*, and well-known to the imperial family. However, the emergence of this Isaurian commander as a power within the imperial palace and progenitor of the Leonid dynasty is not straightforward.

This promotion is usually seen as a reward for his facilitating the dismissal of Ardaburius, with the underlying assumption that this 'tribal chief' was elevated beyond his station by an emperor looking for allies. However, 'to be entrusted with this position, Leo must have felt that Zeno was qualified and trustworthy',[78] and in terms of status, if Zeno was already a *protector*, he held the rank of *clarissimus* and the promotion to *comes domesticorum* made him an *illustris*.[79] Rather than a bolt from the blue then, his ascension to a prominent position within in the imperial household was the latest step on a logical career progression.[80] By inviting Zeno and his family, probably still Arcadia and their son, Zeno, to live in the imperial household, Leo was perhaps also offering Zeno protection 'from any vengeful actions on the part of Ardaburius and his father'.[81]

The potential for Zeno's promotion to be part of a usual military career may also undermine the notion that Leo was using Zeno to escape Aspar. While this notion was long-professed by modern scholars;[82] it has also been rejected as being 'pure fiction'.[83] The sources only state with confidence that Zeno gained imperial favour by providing the evidence that saw Ardaburius dismissed; for example, the *Vita Danielis Stylitae* merely says that 'a certain Zeno ... came to the emperor'.[84] If Leo had been intriguing in such a way to see Zeno promoted directly against Aspar, why does it seem that the whole episode of Ardaburius' disgrace was needed as a catalyst? As emperor, he could have just elevated Zeno without such an overt display of good service. At best, the revelation of Ardaburius' treasonous correspondence was a welcome addition to any intrigue and an embarrassment for Aspar, but hardly overly important to the rise of Zeno. And yet, the meagre sources have it that 'it is the very revelation of Ardaburius' correspondence with the Persian king which provides the context in which Zeno first emerges into public light'.[85] Providing the kind of service which a secretary could have performed in delivering letters to the *conventus* is hardly the act of a man who would be considered as an opponent for the strongest general in the empire. It is more likely that Zeno was merely doing his job and was promoted to *comes domesticorum* due to a record of consistent good service rather than as a direct threat to Aspar.

Another part of the idea that Leo sought to use Zeno against Aspar is the suggestion that Zeno arrived in Constantinople at the head of an Isaurian army, who could protect the emperor from Aspar's Goths.[86] This assumes that Zeno derived his power from being the head of an Isaurian faction and that there was 'an overly simplified model of Gotho-Isaurian rivalry'.[87] There is little evidence that Zeno was accompanied to the capital by a large contingent of Isaurians intended to stand up to the Ardaburii and their allies. Nor is there much reason to see him as a tribal leader of *comes foederatorum* instead of a Roman officer on a regular career progression, with at worst a small cabal of *bucellarii* around him.

Candidus does not suggest that the Isaurians suddenly flooded the capital in great numbers; only that this was their initial appearance as a power at court.[88] Both Procopius and Agathias are misused in suggesting that they support the idea that Zeno brought a large cadre of Isaurians. Neither focuses on the period of Zeno's rise to prominence in Constantinople. Procopius only mentions Zeno recruiting 'cowards and wholly unwarlike men'[89] to the palace guard, which does not reflect the 'barbaric' reputation of Isaurians or even mention Isaurians at all. Agathias does say that Isaurians were recruited, but he is referring to the period after Zeno's restoration in 476, not 466.[90] Similarly, Procopius is speaking about 'since the time Zeno succeeded to the throne',[91] which would mean sometime in 474. Neither then is focusing on Zeno's 'arrival' in Constantinople in 465 and cannot therefore be used to highlight him arriving at the head of an Isaurian army.

Zeno certainly relied on Isaurian support in 476, with them becoming a large part of the imperial army after that, which contributed 'to the notion of undue dependence on Isaurians'.[92] A group of Isaurians also arrived in the capital in the late 460s after a failed raid on Rhodes due to not receiving their pay.[93] Their welcoming by Zeno partly explains his depiction at the head of an ethnic army, but the date is uncertain and it may be anachronistic to apply it to Zeno's rise in 465. This seeming lack of any Isaurian force arriving at Constantinople with Zeno or already established in the capital to unite behind him against Aspar spoils any notion that Zeno's rise was a reaction to the growing power of the Isaurians within the Roman military, substituting one under-Romanized military strongman for another.

Another development linked to Zeno's reputed flooding of Constantinople with Isaurians is Leo's founding of the *excubitores* as a palace guard corps. Suggestions that such Isaurian recruits were joined by Thracians and Illyrians have not prevented it becoming something of an 'unqualified certainty'[94] that the *excubitores* were made up of Isaurians and linked to the rise of Zeno. There are significant issues with this assumption. Leo did not found the *excubitores*; they had been part of the imperial guard for four-and-a-half centuries since their founding by Tiberius.[95] Instead, he gave the *excubitores* a more specific command structure and role in the palace guard, with the *comes excubitorum* becoming of senior rank and later capable of acceding to the imperial throne like Justin I and Tiberius II.[96]

John Lydus is the only ancient source for Leo's reforming of the *excubitores*: 'Leo, who was the first to establish the so-called *excubitores* as guards of the side-exits of the *palatium*, put into service only three hundred to accord with ancient custom.'[97] He makes no mention of it being an Isaurian unit and there is no suggestion that these 'new' *excubitores* were under the command of Zeno. There is also no indication that the changes to the *excubitores* took place upon Zeno's advent to prominence in the mid-460s. They could easily have taken place any time in Leo's reign up until that point.

Aside from these inferences, there is nothing else known about Leo's reshaped *excubitores*; nothing about its specific make-up besides being of 300 elite troops or how it would be recruited or from where, so the idea that the original Leonid *excubitores* were all Isaurians is not backed by any ancient source. As a unit of the best soldiers, there will have been Isaurians in the *excubitores*, but it does not definitely follow that they came to Constantinople with Zeno. They could have been part of any following that Zeno the Patrician had established in the city; they could be linked to any number of other Isaurian commanders or may have earned their promotion by being amongst the best soldiers in the Roman army.

While each had some of their countrymen as their supporters, neither Zeno nor Aspar had a true ethnic faction behind them, precluding any real notion that Constantinople was the battleground of barbarians. However, that does not rule out the presence of an Ardaburii faction and an opposing alliance between the imperial family, Zeno and others. By 466, these two factions were squaring up to each other with increasing frequency. The actions of Ardaburius, the appointment of consuls and *magistri* and religious policy had provided flashpoints between Aspar and Leo, but now with the promotion of Zeno, a well-trodden battleground was about to be revisited – the marriages of Leo's daughters and ultimately the imperial succession – and in that battle, Leo was about to make a decisive move.

Wedding Bells and Tiny Feet

Sometime in 466, Zeno married Ariadne. The union was certainly dynastic in nature, thrusting Zeno into the role of progenitor of the imperial family, but it was not a scandalous match between a semi-barbarian and an imperial daughter 'to secure the support of a large band of Isaurians to counteract the influence of the "Gothic faction" led by Aspar'.[98] Zeno was a distinguished career soldier already high up in the imperial hierarchy, and 'as *comes domesticorum* and *illustris* Zeno was perfectly eligible'.[99] If his first wife was of good Constantinopolitan pedigree, Zeno's Isaurian roots had already been established as no obstacle to marrying into good stock. He was certainly no less eligible than Patricius in terms of rank or ethnicity.

The marriage is sometimes connected to Zeno's promotion to *comes domesticorum*, but there were perhaps several months between these two developments. It is also possible that in 465 Zeno was still married to Arcadia and as 'there is no hint of enforced divorce',[100] she may have died not long before or after Zeno's promotion. It would be strange for Leo to have planned for Zeno to marry Ariadne while Arcadia still lived, particularly if she was part of a prominent Constantinopolitan family. Ariadne's age may also undermine the idea that Leo planned her marriage to Zeno, at least in terms of immediacy. By 465, Ariadne may not have been of marriageable age. She would need to have been born in 454 to meet the youngest acceptable age for marriage in 466, and given the proposed closeness of age between Ariadne and Leontia, who was born after 457, Ariadne may have still been a teenager upon her marriage to the near 40-year old Zeno.[101]

The marriage of Zeno and Ariadne therefore seems more of an opportunistic response to Aspar becoming more forceful in his demands. Through the incidents with Ardaburius, Jordanes, Tatianus and Zeno, Aspar may have felt that his grip on supreme power was slipping and therefore decided to try to coerce Leo to acquiesce to the marriage of Ariadne to Patricius. Zeno's recent elevation to *illustris* and the death of Arcadia made him a suitable candidate to marry Ariadne rather than give over the future of the imperial succession to the Ardaburii. In turning to Zeno, Leo was taking a decisive step in the alienation of Aspar. The general's plans of placing his family on the imperial throne now seemed dashed.

One can imagine Aspar's anger at this turns of events. The emperor who he had placed on the throne possibly on the promise of marrying his daughter to Patricius had not only given her to someone else, he had chosen the man who had been instrumental in the disgracing of Aspar's eldest son. Indeed, the situation got worse for Aspar. Within a year, the union of Zeno and Ariadne fulfilled its dynastic duty with the birth of a child in late summer 467. More importantly, that child was a boy.[102] While the demise of Leo and Verina's son provided warnings over being hasty, the newest member of the imperial family was quickly confirmed. Named after his delighted grandfather, Leo II almost immediately took his place as the imperial heir of Leo I. This is perhaps best shown in the description of a mosaic in the *parekklesion* chapel called *Hagia Soros* beside the Blachernae. While the tenth-century writer mistakes Leo II for the son of Leo and 'Veronica', this chapel was built by Leo and Verina to house the robe of the Virgin Mary, depicting them with their new grandson.[103]

The translation of the robe of the Virgin Mary to this chapel may also further show how Leo used religion to isolate Aspar and his Arian allies. Part of the tradition surrounding the robe saw two otherwise unknown brothers and generals, Galbinus and Candidus, once close associates of Aspar and Ardaburius, renounce their Arian beliefs and set off on a pilgrimage to the Holy Land. There they found the Virgin's robe in the possession of a Jewish woman, whom they tricked out of it and presented it to Leo,[104] who was quick to associate his reign and his new grandson with this 'source of power and patronage not open to Aspar'.[105] Such recognition of the weakness of Aspar's Arianism may also be seen in Leo's increasing connection to Daniel the Stylite. Over time, Leo went from being too busy to meet the bearer of St Simeon's tunic and petitioning Daniel through intermediaries, to travelling to him personally and even bringing men like Jordanes for baptism and foreign dignitaries such as Gobazes, king of the Laz, to Daniel on his column.

However, 'monopoly of the power deriving from his association with relics, especially the Virgin's robe, and with holy men such as Daniel, would not protect Leo from the more worldy machinations of Aspar'.[106] Even if by 467 Leo was seriously plotting a decisive move against Aspar, the support of his new son-in-law and the securing of the succession through Leo II still did not make him feel secure enough to strike. Despite Ardaburius' disgrace and the snubbing of Patricius as Ariadne's spouse, Aspar retained a lofty position at court through his positions as *magister militum praesentalis*, *caput senatus* and at the centre of a system of alliances that spread through the civilian and military hierarchies. The Alan general's position remained safe, but the pressure was growing. Something was going to have to give.

Chapter 5

The Pressure Grows: Huns, Vandals and Assassins

'New Rome will be destroyed

'By the attacks of new vandals.

'God always remains silent.'

Stojanovic, *Circling* (1978-87)

The Attilan Aftermath in the Balkans

While Zeno had assumed the role of progenitor of the Leonid dynasty, he was not present in Constantinople for the birth of his son. Keen for him to win some military renown, Leo had appointed Zeno as either *magister militum per Thracias*, in succession to Basiliscus, or as *comes rei militaris*. Therefore, Zeno was likely in the field when Leo II was born. However, there is a lack of certainty over details of Zeno's first Thracian deployment, namely when it took place and who he was fighting. This mess led to the rather wonderful academic sidestep of Otto Maenchen-Helfen that 'fortunately it is not our task to straighten out the confused chronology of those years'.[1] Here, we have to give it a go.

While Leo II was seemingly born in late summer 467, which is by no means a certainty, Zeno's campaign in Thrace is recorded as being after he became consul, which was not until 469.[2] This is likely an error by the biographer of Daniel the Stylite, conflating Zeno's two separate Balkan campaigns into one – the first of 467, when he served along with Basiliscus, Anagastes, Ostrys and Chelchal, and the second in 469, which was cut short by the machinations of Aspar. The confusion over who Zeno was fighting in Thrace may have some consequences for the growing conflict between Leo and Aspar. He seems to have been fighting Goths, which could indicate Theoderic Strabo. This would not be surprising, although it would be a daring move by Leo to fight useful Roman *foederati* and high-profile Ardaburii allies situated close to Constantinople.[3] This would be an early indication that Zeno and Aspar were on a collision course, but the likelihood is that Zeno was fighting a mixed force of Goths and Huns.[4]

The presence of Huns and the limited clarity over the identity of these Goths highlight the turbulent nature of the Danube frontier following the collapse of Attila's empire. Large numbers of tribes were coming into conflict with each other and Roman forces as they attempted to forge their own independent path. Despite the presence of Thracian and Illyrian field armies backed up by regional garrisons and frontier forces, in the winter of 465/466, a group of Huns under Hormidac crossed the Danube, pillaged Dacia and struck as far as Serdica, modern Sofia in Bulgaria. Serdica itself had been through the wars already in the mid-fifth century. It had suffered a heavy sack by Attila in the late 440s, and while it had recovered enough to have a metropolitan present early in the reign of Leo,[5] its defences and garrison likely remained in disrepair by 466 as Hormidac captured Serdica with little recorded fuss. Anthemius led out his praesental forces from Constantinople and blockaded Hormidac within Serdica. Only when the Huns were close to starvation did they accept Anthemius' offer of pitched battle, and while the Roman effort was briefly undermined by the defection of their cavalry commander, himself a Hun, Anthemius led his infantry to victory.[6]

In the midst of this Hunnic attack on Dacia, envoys reached Constantinople from the Pannonian Goths and the Sciri. These groups had been embroiled in tit for tat raids throughout the mid-460s, with one Scirian attack leading to the death of Valamir. Now under the senior command of Theodemir, the Goths appealed to the Romans for aid, as did the Sciri, who may have had Edeco, father of Odoacer and former high-ranking lieutenant of Attila, in a prominent position at this time, along with his other son, Onoulphus.[7] Being confronted with pleas for aid from both sides provided Leo and Aspar with an opportunity to present a united front; instead, they ended up with contrary views. Leo wished to help the Sciri, perhaps in the hope of punishing the Goths for their attacks on Illyricum in c.459/462 and even overturning Marcian's recognition of their settlement in Pannonia. Aspar argued that they should ally with neither and just allow them to continue fighting each other. Both could claim that they had the best intentions for the empire in mind by weakening barbarian enemies, but when the decision came as to what the empire was going to do, Leo's increased confidence shone through. He wrote to his general in Illyricum ordering him to give aid to the Sciri. With the distorted chronology of these events, it is possible that it was this subsequent Romano-Sciri action against the Goths that saw the death of Valamir, rather than a previous Sciri raid.[8]

Leo again showed his growing confidence in the face of another embassy that arrived at Constantinople in mid/late 466. The envoys were from the Huns of the Attilan family. After Nedao, the surviving sons of Attila, Dengizich and Ernach,[9] had become the focus of the vain attempts to hold together their father's empire. Forced away from the Hungarian grasslands, Dengizich looked to the Hunnic clans of the Lower Danube and the Ukrainian steppe – a varied list of Kutigurs, Onogurs, Utigurs, Saragurs, Ourogs, Sabirs, Akateri and more.[10] The interchangeability of many of these tribes in the ancient sources has seen them lumped together as Huns, Avars and Bulgars. Such umbrella terms are not necessarily incorrect, but they can mask how frequently these tribes were enemies of one another and the general chaos of the region.

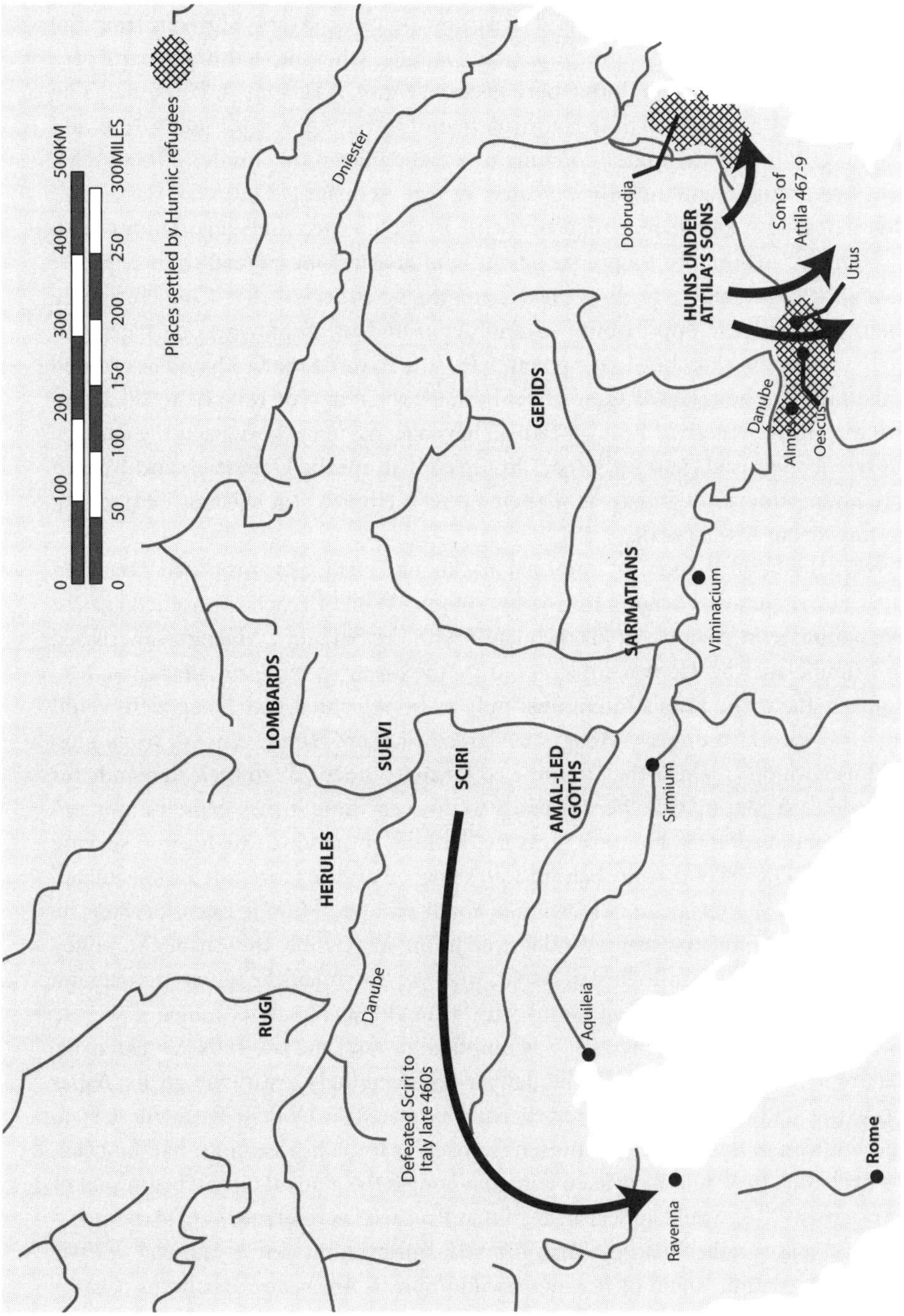
0 100 200 300 400 500KM
0 50 100 150 200 250 300MILES
Places settled by Hunnic refugees
Dniester
Dobrudja
HUNS UNDER ATTILA'S SONS
Sons of Attila 467-9
Utus
GEPIDS
Danube
Oescus
SARMATIANS
Viminacium
LOMBARDS
SUEVI
SCIRI
AMAL-LED GOTHS
Sirmium
HERULES
RUGI
Danube
Aquileia
Defeated Sciri to Italy late 460s
Ravenna
Rome

Collapse of the Hunnic Empire

Whilst demonstrating the energy of his father, any thoughts Dengizich might have had of restoring an empire of Attilan dimensions were thwarted by the violent reluctance of the Sabirs and what may be proto-Avars.[11] Driven from the steppe, Dengizich returned to the Lower Danube, where he led his tribal forces in an attack on a group of Goths, perhaps even those of Valamir in Pannonia. The attack seemed judiciously timed, for the main Gothic force was absent on a raid of its own, but whether taking too long or weighed down by plunder, Dengizich's men were caught and heavily defeated by the returning Goths at Bassiana.[12] This defeat saw Dengizich, together with Ernach, enter into negotiations with the Romans, looking 'to secure sufficient land and income to feed their nation'[13] through a treaty and a trading post. It might be expected that Constantinople would welcome the opportunity of another round of employing one barbarian group against another, but Leo's recent hard line towards the Goths was extended to the Huns as he rejected their offer. Perhaps the emperor refused to do a deal with the Huns because of his own Balkan heritage, having experienced the damage and terror their raids had inflicted. On top of that, maybe Dengizich and Ernach were attempting to negotiate as if their father's empire still existed, demanding ransoms on an Attilan scale.

Irked by such a show of imperial backbone, Dengizich proposed attacking imperial territory and driving to Constantinople. While Ernach counselled against such action, citing trouble in his own lands with the Saragurs,[14] Dengizich crossed the Danube anyway. He was intercepted by the *comes rei militaris* Anagastes, who enquired about the Hun's intentions, only to be informed that Dengizich would only deal with Leo directly. Anagastes agreed to allow Hunnic envoys to pass on to Constantinople, where they found Leo far more amenable to their demands for land and cash, stating that 'he was ready to do everything if they came to him and offered him obedience. He took pleasure, he said, in nations which came seeking alliances.'[15] The exact reasons behind Leo's change of heart can only be speculated upon: perhaps he was genuinely worried about renewed Hunnic raids; perhaps he was focusing on his upcoming Vandal expedition; or possibly this change in policy reflects the continued influence of Aspar, who was 'fearful of the Huns encroaching on the domain of the Thracian Goths with whom he was so closely allied'.[16]

While the threat of Dengizich was nullified for now, the late 460s saw extensive military action in the Balkans. The danger was seemingly great enough for Aspar to take the field in person; however, this may be a mistake by Priscus, as 'there is no other indication that Aspar was present himself at these proceedings, had he been, it is likely that he would have been named amongst the generals at the beginning of the fragment'.[17] It would appear instead that Priscus was referring to οἱ Ἄσπαρος – men of Aspar – rather than the man himself. But even the senior *magister militum praesentalis* sending some of his men in addition to Anagastes, Basiliscus, Ostrys and probably Zeno suggests that there was significant trouble. The recently disgraced Ardaburius is also recorded in the field sometime in 467/468, killing the

Gothic leader Bigelis.[18] While the record of this action is limited to Jordanes, there appears to be little reason to think that he has made a similar error as Priscus. That Ardaburius was deployed at the head of Roman forces so soon after the exposure of his treason surely reflects the continued power of the Ardaburii. He may even have been *magister militum per Illyricum*, although it is more likely that he was serving in the field on behalf of his father or along with the likes of Ostrys.[19]

It is possible that Zeno spent some time with the οἱ Ἄσπαρος serving in this campaign. Indeed, while Anagastes was already on the scene and Basiliscus had his own Thracian field army, Zeno may have been in command of praesental forces. Of the commanders from the capital to take the field in support of Anagastes and Basiliscus, Zeno was likely the ranking officer. Even if he was only a *comes rei militaris* rather than a *magister*, Zeno's positions as imperial son-in-law, father to the heir apparent and *comes domesticorum* surely placed him above Ostrys and Ardaburius. This might suggest that there was as yet no major trouble between Zeno and Aspar, and that the Alan *magister* was willing to cooperate with Leo and his son-in-law for the good of the empire, although it might well be imagined that Zeno did not serve against Bigelis, which would have put him in the immediate vicinity of Ardaburius.

The deploying of up to five generals – Anagastes, Ardaburius, Basiliscus, Ostyrs and Zeno – reaped success for Leo, for there were soon more Huns asking for a settlement on account of starvation. The commanders on the ground again forwarded Hunnic envoys to Constantinople, and in the meantime agreed to feed the Huns as long as the barbarian column broke up into smaller groups. One of these groups contained a large proportion of Goths and was guarded by the aforementioned οἱ Ἄσπαρος, who were under the command of Chelchal, an officer of Hunnic origin. He summoned the Gothic leaders from amongst those under his care and explained that Leo would not treat with them separately, and that the Huns were under no obligation to provide them with anything. Angered by these 'revelations', these Goths turned on their Hunnic allies and perpetrated a massacre. By their intriguing, Chelchal and these 'men of Aspar' had succeeded in removing a significant part of the threat posed by these Huns.[20]

Whether this was a plot by Aspar or an action signed off on by Leo is unknown. The fact that the Hunnic massacre began with a group guarded by οἱ Ἄσπαρος highlights that there were plenty of allies of Aspar involved in the campaign – Ostrys, Ardaburius and Chelchal – but Anagastes, Basiliscus and seemingly Zeno also participated. Leo could easily have been privy to such machinations and even been their architect, deploying all the forces at his disposal to bring order to the Balkans in preparation for his Vandal expedition the following year. This campaign of 467 also suggests that despite some dissension between them, Leo and Aspar were still able to work together.

That does not mean that there were no plots in the workings. While he had rendered a good service to the empire in his defeat of Bigelis, Ardaburius continued to scheme on behalf of his family. Before 469, when both he and Zeno were in the capital, he attempted 'to attach the Isaurians to him'.[21] There is no explanation as to whom these Isaurians might have been, and the attempt was betrayed to Zeno by Martinus, an οικειος of Ardaburius. It may also have been around this time that Ardaburius married Anthusa, a daughter of Illus. That Ardaburius thought he could bring Isaurians to his side undermines the idea of 'ethnic factions' at court, rather than supports it. He was probably not even targeting Zeno. Indeed, Candidus suggests that he had bigger fish to fry as he hoped to use these Isaurians – 'κατὰ βασιλέως' – against Leo himself. The decline in relations between the emperor and the Ardaburii seemed set to shift into a higher gear.[22]

Leo I, the Western Empire and the Vandals

Aspar was perhaps not the only rival Leo felt the need to deal with. His successes against the Amal Goths and the Huns of Hormidac propelled Anthemius back into the spotlight. Having such a well-connected and high-profile man now winning military victories increased the threat he could pose to the throne, particularly as in early 467, Leo II had not yet been born. The Ardaburii might look to use Anthemius to undermine the emperor, although Aspar too could have seen him as a threat. Therefore, Leo had to both placate and remove Anthemius. He found his chance by looking west. Playing it up as a reward for his service and recognition of his pedigree, Leo put Anthemius forward as his candidate for western *Augustus*.[23]

The western throne had been vacant for eighteen months since the death of Libius Severus in August/September 465.[24] This interregnum was seemingly caused by negotiations between Ricimer and Leo, which may have commenced as early as 461 after the execution of Majorian and stalled initially over Ricimer's elevation of Severus in November 461. The crux of the negotiations seems to have been that if Ricimer wanted aid against the Vandals, he would have to accept Leo's candidate for the western throne, and the *magister militum* eventually agreed in late spring 467.

Being a successful general, consul and patrician with a link to the Theodosian dynasty saw Anthemius accepted as emperor outside Rome on 12 April 467.[25] The promise of a large-scale expedition against the Vandals and marriage to Alypia, daughter of Anthemius, won over Ricimer.[26] However, it could be that Ricimer was not all that pleased with the choice of the well-heeled, well-connected and apparently capable Anthemius, particularly if he seemed able to win the backing of the Italian aristocracy. Having been the supreme power in the West for a decade, Ricimer will not have taken kindly to Anthemius exerting his own agenda. Leo's ability to impose a settlement and an emperor on the West at the very least demonstrates that in East/West relations, he was not to be viewed as a puppet of Aspar. If anything, his enthroning of Anthemius, threatening of Geiseric and gaining of the support of the quasi-independent Dalmatian general Marcellinus shows that Leo was growing in stature.[27]

It may be that 'Leo was engaged in detailed strategic planning for his mission against the Vandals as early as March/April 467',[28] or perhaps much earlier with his refusal to send aid against the Vandals in 461.[29] Could it be then that Leo embarked on the enthronement of Anthemius purely because he wanted someone he could trust on the western throne when his forces were deployed against the Vandals? This could also highlight his growing independence, particularly as Aspar was opposed to the expedition. But what exactly was the reason for this aggressive policy towards the Vandals, beyond any call for aid from Ricimer? Aside from their continued occupation of the province of Africa providing three decades of embarrassment, the Vandals had used whatever ships they could find to not only raid the coasts of the western Mediterranean but also lift its islands from the faltering grasp of the Roman government. Sicily, Sardinia, Corsica, Malta and the Balearics would all eventually be incorporated into the Vandal kingdom. Italy was also the target for raiding, including one that culminated in the fourteen-day sack of Rome in 455, which saw the removal of vast amounts of treasure and captives such as Licinia Eudoxia, Placidia and Eudocia.[30]

Given the extent of the damage that the Vandals had done to the integrity of the Roman state, Leo's expedition of 468 was not the first imperial attempt to retake Africa. Theodosius II had sent an expedition in 441, but it only got as far as Sicily before war with the Persians and Huns forced a recall. Ricimer and Majorian had gathered a significant force at Cartagena in mid-461 with the aim of crossing to Africa. Through treachery, either of locals or even Ricimer himself, Geiseric's fleet caught that of Majorian unawares near Cartagena on 13 May 461 and destroyed it. This Vandal victory brought both the imperial courts to the negotiating table and resulted in an agreement between Leo and Geiseric in 461/462. This treaty was far more politically involved than any previous arrangement with the Vandals, although it stopped short of recognizing the Vandal kingdom. Geiseric agreed to release Placidia and Licinia Eudoxia to Constantinople and to rein in his raiders. In return, Leo recognized the marriage between Eudocia and Huneric. 'The treaty of 461/2 marked Geiseric's entry into the labyrinthine world of high imperial politics',[31] and he quickly proved a more than capable player. With Eudocia now his daughter-in-law, the Vandal king launched an appeal on her and Huneric's behalf to a share of the estate of Valentinian III. This was an incendiary claim, for Valentinian's estate could be construed as the western empire itself. Unsurprisingly, this claim would never be accepted by the Romans and would be renounced by Huneric during his reign as Vandal king.

This Theodosian link provided another avenue for Geiseric to interfere in imperial politics – Placidia's husband Olybrius and his own imperial candidacy. The Vandal king pressed for Olybrius to succeed to the western throne, perhaps even in succession of the murdered Majorian. There may even have been some tacit agreement from Leo to support Olybrius' candidacy as part of the settlement in 462.[32] These Vandal connections to the House of Theodosius will have irked

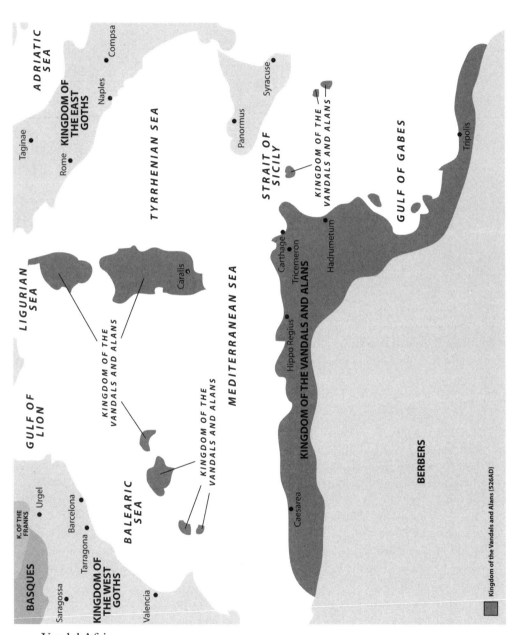

Vandal Africa

Ricimer, and any acquiescence to Geiseric's backing of Olybrius on behalf of Leo may well have been a catalyst for the cooling of East/West relations after the death of Majorian in 461. However, the failure of Leo to see to the elevation of Olybrius and Geiseric's refusal to come to terms with Ricimer meant that any improvement in relations between Constantinople and Carthage was short-lived. The embassy of Tatianus in 464 was not even granted an audience by Geiseric.[33] This may have been one of very few errors on the part of the great Vandal king. The appointment of Olybrius as consul for 464 and sudden disappearance of Libius Severus the following year could suggest that Tatianus was going to propose a way to see Olybrius crowned the next western *Augustus*. Instead, Geiseric's dismissal of the embassy unseen may have seen Leo rescind his backing.

With the end of Libius Severus' reign, Geiseric will have expected Olybrius to ascend to the western throne, and while the eighteen-month interregnum must have raised suspicions, the pronouncements of the embassy of Phylarchus in 467 will still have come as a shock. Anthemius, not Olybrius, was to be western *Augustus*, and if the Vandals did not refrain from raiding Italy and Sicily there would be war. He left with accusations of Rome's breaking of the treaty of 462 ringing in his ears.[34] Furthermore, Leo may already have been making plans for an African expedition, which may not have escaped the notice of Geiseric. And even if there had been no official clause in the treaty that Leo would support Olybrius, Geiseric could point to Roman military action against the Vandals, with Marcellinus capturing Sardinia in 466/467. However, Leo could argue that this was only a response to Vandal raids not only continuing in the West but also extending into the eastern Mediterranean, with the Peloponnese, Egyptian coast and even Alexandria not beyond the audacity of Geiseric's raiders.[35]

Given this deterioration of relations between the Vandals and the empire, with all sides reneging on various clauses, the elevation of Anthemius could be seen as a Roman declaration of war. It marked a definitive nullification of the agreement of 462 on the behalf of Leo and Ricimer, with the latter deciding that it was worth an eastern appointee as western *Augustus* to gain aid against the Vandals. This too suggests that Geiseric had overplayed his hand. His political interference, obstinacy and continued raiding had seen Ravenna and Constantinople agree that diplomacy was to be abandoned.

'The Fourth Punic War' – The Disastrous Vandal Expedition of 468

The failures of Theodosius II and Majorian, as well as that of Aspar in the 430s, suggested that even with a sizeable navy and army, a Roman reconquest of Africa was not a simple affair. Despite this, Leo committed fully to this 'Fourth Punic War',[36] raising an enormous force. According to Priscus, 100,000 ships were assembled, but this is either hyperbole or an error mistaking ships for men. John Lydus' 10,000 ships appears equally hyperbolic. Modern scholars emend this to 1,100, which is closer to Cedrenus' figure of 1,113 vessels.[37] These ships will have been of various sizes, from major warships to small cargo and trading vessels, so it is difficult to ascertain how many men they were capable of carrying to Africa. Procopius records 100,000 men for the expedition of 468, although some doubt has been cast on this number as 'both high and suspiciously round'.[38]

However, there is room to assuage that doubt. While it is true that Procopius records that it took 500 ships to ferry the $c.18,000$ in 532[39] and a similar ratio would place about 35,000 soldiers in Leo's expedition, Procopius also lists that those 500 ships included up to 30,000 sailors. A similar ratio, removing some of the 1,100 ships as warships rather than troop-carriers, would see perhaps 50,000 sailors in the fleet of 468, some of which will also have been fighters. That still comes up short of the 100,000, but the extra $c.15,000$ could be made up from the forces of Marcellinus and Ricimer. So while there may not have been 100,000 soldiers in the Roman expedition to Africa in 468, the combination of soldiers and sailors of Leo, Marcellinus and Ricimer could have reached the 100,000 recorded by Procopius.[40] Even if the size was exaggerated by sixth-century sources 'keen to highlight the contrast with Belisarius' more modest [and successful] expedition in the 530s',[41] the likelihood is that Leo's force was of significant size.[42]

While 100,000 men may have been within the numerical capacity of the empire, was it within its financial capabilities? The frugal Marcian is recorded as having collected 7.2 million *nomismata* during his reign, and with one *nomisma* or *solidus* the equivalent to 1/72 of a Roman pound, it might be that Leo had access to about 100,000 pounds of gold. The figures for the money spent on this expedition range from the 1,300 *centaria* (130,000 Roman pounds) of gold reported by Priscus and Procopius, to the 64,000 pounds of gold and 700,000 pounds of silver by John Lydus and to 65,000 of gold and 700,000 of silver by Candidus.[43] A limited amount of the total expenditure may have been endured by the western empire, but the lion's share will have been borne by the treasury of Constantinople. Seemingly, Leo could afford it. But only just, and this demonstrates the great risk he was taking and the potential rewards he was expecting to gain from conquering Africa.

So if the empire could just about afford such a force, where did it come from? As to be expected with an empire that still stretched from the Danube to the Sahara and from Italy to the Euphrates, the expeditionary force was suitably polyglot. The Thracian, Illyrian, Dalmatian, Egyptian and praesental armies will have provided contingents, and they were populated with Roman citizens from their regions, supported by any number of barbarian groups – Goths, Gepids, Huns, Arabs – with many pressed into service through the Roman victories of 467. Any forces offered by Ricimer and Anthemius will also have included Roman citizens and Germanic tribesmen from the western provinces and kingdoms. Leo's reaching out to Titus and his *bucellarii* in Gaul may also be linked to the emperor looking for soldiers for his expedition, even if Titus soon resigned his commission in favour of exploring his faith with Daniel the Stylite.[44] The Gothic allies of Aspar may also have provided a contingent, likewise the Isaurians. Indeed, there seems to be more than one contingent of Isaurians in the expedition. The force of Heracleius of Edessa and the Isaurian Marsus seems to have had a considerable Isaurian contingent. The Isaurians who had just arrived in Constantinople after their raid on Rhodes may have been enlisted in the expedition.[45]

While 'the massive logistical efforts behind the ambitious attack offer evidence of the continuing military capabilities of the twin regimes when acting in unison',[46] wielding such a large three-pronged attack was not only a vast logistical undertaking but also a tremendous leadership task. Leo did have a series of military commanders at his disposal: Aspar, Ardaburius, Ostyrs, Anagastes, Zeno and Basiliscus, several of whom had won success during the Balkan campaigns of 467. There were also western candidates in Anthemius, Ricimer and Marcellinus, who had also recently won renown on the battlefield. Leo did choose from this list, placing command of the expedition in the hands of his brother-in-law, Basiliscus, complete with a promotion to the position of *magister militum praesentalis* vacated by Anthemius.[47] Aspar likely opposed this appointment of a Leonid to such a prominent command, and that is before his personal thoughts about Basiliscus both as an imperial rival and military commander are taken into account. Could Aspar have expected to be offered the Vandal command given his previous experience in Africa and the West, even if he did not want the command? 'One can presume that Aspar could have had the command if he wanted it',[48] but the idea 'that Aspar declined to lead the expedition because of his reservations about its likely outcome is ... disputable'.[49] While Aspar remained the senior *magister militum praesentalis*, the appointment of Basiliscus as his praesental colleague and as commander of the Vandal expedition, and his replacement as Thracian *magister* by either Zeno or Anagastes, demonstrated further independence on the part of Leo, although Ardaburius did join the expedition so Aspar's 'faction' was not being completely ignored.[50]

While Basiliscus and perhaps Ardaburius provided the main command of the eastern contingent, there were various sub-commanders. The Egyptian contingent, which was sent to attack Tripolitana, was under the command of *comes rei militaris* Heracleius of Edessa and the Isaurian Marsus. Another commander perhaps linked with Egypt was Damonicus, who had served as *comes sacri consistorii et rei militaris Thebaici limitis* in the past, while the *dux* Ioannes was also involved. Marcellinus was given command of the western Roman contingent of the expedition, which along with his own federates, could have been between 10,000 and 20,000 men.[51]

Such a 'colossal imperial military force should have overwhelmed the Vandals'.[52] That it did not would seem to be largely due to the weather and ambition. The Roman plan was more involved than simply striking at Carthage to cut off the head of the Vandal snake. Marcellinus had already been driving Vandals out of Sardinia and Sicily, while Heracleius and Marsus would land in Tripolitana and march towards Carthage, capturing Vandal cities as they went. These prongs could have had several aims. They removed avenues of retreat and resupply from the Vandals, as well as removing forces from Geiseric through death and imprisonment. The conquest of Vandal outliers also concentrated remaining resistance in Africa, where Basiliscus could then use overwhelming force to destroy the kingdom outright. This was no Roman raid or even subjugation of the Vandal kingdom. The expedition was aimed at completely removing the Vandals as an independent people, incorporating them as subjects of the empire and conscripting their men into the army.

The first half of this ambitious plan worked rather well. Heracleius and Marsus landed in Tripolitana and captured Tripolis, before continuing their march west along the North African coast to the old province of Byzacena. Marcellinus followed up his capture of Sardinia by completing the recapture of Sicily in time to provide a harbour for Basiliscus' fleet. With these pieces in place, the next stage was for Basiliscus to cross to Africa, defeat the Vandal fleet and then meet up with Heracleius for a march on Carthage, defeating whatever armies Geiseric could muster against them. This stage also seems to have begun rather well. Heracleius' successes seem to have continued, while Basiliscus made the crossing to the African coast, perhaps defeating some Vandal ships which tried to intercept him.[53] He anchored off the town of Mercurium, about 40 miles from Carthage, named for the temple of Mercury on the promontory, which is now Cape Bon in Tunisia. The loss of Sicily and Tripolis, together with the arrival of the vast imperial fleet, sparked panic in Carthage. Geiseric himself was gravely worried, surprised that his brinkmanship had seemingly brought about the ruin of his kingdom.

This was as good as it got for the Romans. Even before Basiliscus had departed Sicily for Mercurium, there had been signs that not everything was going to plan. Western power politics had interfered in the make-up of the expedition, for when Basiliscus left Sicily, Marcellinus and his men were not with him. Ricimer seems to have manufactured the Dalmatian general's missing of the boat. Perhaps the western *magister* felt that he could not spare the manpower, but it is more likely that he resented and even feared the growing stature of Marcellinus, who had the support of both Leo and Anthemius. Further victories in Africa may have put Marcellinus in a position to threaten Ricimer's position as the power behind the throne.

Further suspicion falls on Ricimer when in August 468, Marcellinus was murdered 'treacherously by one of his fellow-officers'.[54] The killing likely took place after the departure of Basiliscus for Africa, but as the dates of the movements of the expedition are not recorded, it could be that Marcellinus was killed before the expedition left Sicily, providing a definitive reason for his absence at Mercurium. However, had Marcellinus been killed while Basiliscus was on Sicily, the supreme commander of the expedition may have seen to the appointment of a successor to the command of Marcellinus' men, although this likely advocates too much power to Basiliscus. Could he really have interfered directly in western affairs in opposition to Ricimer? Regardless of the reason, Marcellinus was not present at Mercurium and while it is difficult to say if he would have made any difference to events, the presence of a confident general could have swayed the actions of Basiliscus. Geiseric was surprised and pleased when he heard of the assassination of Marcellinus, repeating the phrase spoken of Valentinian III on the murder of Aetius: 'the Romans had cut off their right hand with their left.'[55]

And so it was to prove. Heracleius and Marsus continued their approach from Tripolis, brushing aside any Vandal resistance, but as they approached Byzacena, they found no trace of Basiliscus' army. The supreme commander had failed to make any kind of landing at Mercurium. This was very peculiar, for such was the confusion and panic at Carthage at the arrival of the expedition that if Basiliscus 'had undertaken to go straight for Carthage, he would have captured it at the first onset, and he would have reduced the Vandals to subjection without their even thinking of resistance'.[56] So what was the reason for this inactivity? It was at least partly due to the reactions of Geiseric. The old Vandal king may have been surprised at the sheer presence of the vast Roman armada, but he had quickly overcome his awe. He armed as many of his subjects as he could and sent whatever fleet he had on hand to shadow the Romans at Mercurium. However, the most important thing he did was to send envoys to Basiliscus. They succeeded in acquiring a five-day truce, reputedly by claiming that Geiseric would submit to whatever terms of surrender Leo chose to impose, although it is more likely that they bribed Basiliscus to withhold action for those five days. As will be seen, there may have been other reasons for the Roman commander to agree to a cessation of war.

Given the overwhelming Roman forces arrayed against him, it is difficult to see what Geiseric might achieve with a five-day truce. It was hardly enough to form an army capable of standing up to the expedition on land or to prepare Carthage for a siege. The answer comes in the Vandal king's knowledge of his kingdom and use of local intelligence. Unbeknownst to Basiliscus, he had anchored his fleet in a position vulnerable to onshore winds. Geiseric's seeking of a truce was almost solely to allow him to prepare his own ships for an attack when the wind changed. And these were no usual preparations. Demonstrating the extent to which even the Vandal fleet was outmatched by that of the Romans, Geiseric took a risky course. He had his fleet tow a number of empty ships with them to Mercurium. When the onshore winds came, these empty ships were set alight, hinting that there were some combustible materials on board, and directed into the huddled mass that was the Roman fleet, which was anchored close together and now pinned to the coast by the wind:

> And as the fire advanced in this way the Roman fleet was filled with tumult, as was natural, and with a great din that rivalled the noise caused by the wind and the roaring of the flames, as the soldiers together with the sailors shouted orders to one another and pushed off with their poles the fire-boats and their own ships as well, which were being destroyed by one another in complete disorder.[57]

Many of those which survived the fire found that the Vandal fleet was waiting to ram them. This saw significant numbers of ships either sunk or fixed in place for Vandal boarding parties to swarm all over them, taking the ships and their crews as booty.

While Basiliscus and Ardaburius managed to escape, both Damonicus and Ioannes are recorded as having chosen to drown rather than surrender. The latter is recorded by Procopius as having killed 'very great numbers of the enemy … [and] threw himself into the sea, [rather than] come under the hands of dogs'[58] when faced with capture by Genson, a son of Geiseric. There may be some issue with two different sources recording the same death for two different men, but it would appear that at least one high-ranking commander chose death over humiliation; even if the story is entirely made up, it may demonstrate just how calamitous the battle off the *Promontorium Mercurii* had become. Up to half of the combined Roman fleet – perhaps over 500 ships – was either burned, sunk or captured. The expedition was over: 'The instant loss of such a large part of the expedition emasculated the imperial project.'[59] Some attempt was made to suggest that Leo had to recall Basiliscus, Heracleius and Marsus to the capital to face down a plot by Aspar,[60] rather than admit the extent of the calamity at Mercurium; however, this conflates the retreat of Basiliscus in 468 and the later retreat of Heracleius and Marsus from Tripolis in 470, which they had held since the defeat of the expedition at Mercurium.

There is no escaping the conclusion that, despite the promising start, the Vandal expedition of 468 was a complete disaster. The Vandals not only still controlled Africa, but their position had been improved, not only due to the prestige gained for seeing off such an enormous Roman attack but also to the significant amount of ships, men and equipment they managed to capture. Buoyed by their success, the Vandals looked to strike against the territory of Constantinople, reputedly attempting to invade the Peloponnese, hoping to use the Mani Peninsula in Laconia as a base for future raiding. When Geiseric's men attacked the Maniot city of Kenipolis/ Taenarum, the inhabitants repulsed them with heavy losses. In retaliation, Geiseric attacked Zacynthos, killing many inhabitants and taking 500 captives, whom he had hacked to pieces and thrown overboard on the journey back to Carthage.[61] There is no record of Geiseric attempting to remove Heracleius and Marsus from Tripolis after Mercurium, but it is likely that the Vandal king at least investigated the possibility. Perhaps the Roman force was considered too strong to oust. Despite his attacks on Greece, it is possible that Geiseric was still happy to negotiate a cessation of hostilities with the empire. This was aided by growing pressure on the Balkans and the intrigue surrounding Leo and Aspar, and Anthemius and Ricimer, coming to a head. Heracleius and Marsus were recalled to the capital, allowing the Vandals to retake Tripolis, perhaps under some kind of peace treaty in 470.

While 'the western imperial court was fading as a theatre for political ambition',[62] there still remained a connection for Geiseric to exploit. The expedition of 468 had revealed the split between Ricimer and Anthemius, which was to grow over the next four years into a fully fledged civil war, with the latter besieged in Rome by the former. Leo attempted to quell this fight by sending Olybrius to mediate, ridding himself of that threat in the process. It is even claimed that Leo sent a letter to Anthemius urging him to kill Olybrius, only for this letter to fall into the hands of Ricimer, who used it to gain the support of Olybrius. This appears more a ruse by Ricimer, but whatever it was it worked to his advantage and Rome was soon taken, with Anthemius executed on 11 July 472. He was succeeded as western *Augustus* by none other than Olybrius, suggesting that Ricimer and Geiseric had come to an arrangement by early 472.[63]

The Vandal king had gotten what he wanted, and for a brief moment in August 472 might have felt that he could have gained further influence over the western court with the death of Ricimer. This was not to be, as Ricimer's nephew, Gundobad, became *magister militum*. Geiseric was probably not that disappointed at this, nor when the demise of Olybrius before the year was out removed Vandal interest in the imperial succession. Control of the western court was more a poisoned chalice than a holy grail by this stage, and the ensuing chaos in Italy allowed the Vandals to regain Sardinia and Sicily with little fuss.[64]

Burnt by the expedition of 468 and inwardly distracted, Constantinople cared little about these Vandal reconquests, and Geiseric signed a 'perpetual' peace treaty with Zeno in 476.[65] This highlighted not only Zeno's lack of interest in the West but also how the Vandal kingdom had grown in stature and how religious considerations had grown in importance. Geiseric agreed to halt raids on Roman territory, release any remaining hostages, open some Catholic churches in Carthage and allow the homecoming of some religious exiles. In return, Vandal authority in North Africa and the western islands was officially recognized. The Vandal kingdom itself was dealt with as a state rather than the tribe of Geiseric, with the treaty expected to last beyond the death of the signatories. This seems to have been the case, for 'relations remained relatively good between the eastern empire and the Vandal kingdom until the campaign of Belisarius nearly 60 years later'.[66]

Apportioning Blame

For all the prestige Geiseric would gain through his resistance in 468, the expedition was a disaster for Leo. His financial gamble had failed spectacularly and the imperial treasury seemed to lie empty. The failure of the expedition also provided another major flashpoint between Leo and Aspar. The specific focus was Basiliscus. The leader of the expedition had returned to Constantinople with about half of the fleet. For his disgrace, Basiliscus was soon in fear for his life, having to seek sanctuary in Hagia Sophia, and was only rescued through the intervention of Verina. But even the support of his sister and something of a pardon from Leo could not overcome the embarrassment Basiliscus had brought to the imperial family. He had to be removed from public view, so Leo had his brother-in-law packed off to Heraclea in Thrace, where he would still be in 471.[67]

However, the flashpoint between Leo and Aspar came over why Basiliscus had let disaster overtake the expedition. Rather than excellent use of the terrain and conditions by the Vandals and poor knowledge and strategy from Basiliscus, the surviving sources focused on more insidious reasons for the defeat. Basiliscus is accused of various forms of treason;[68] Priscus and Procopius in particular did not hold back in the criticism of Basiliscus' motives, accusing him of cowardice, greed, negligence and treachery.[69] However, there being several different motives suggests that 'there was obviously uncertainty at the time about what had led to the destruction of most of Basiliscus' fleet'.[70] Worse than cowardice, greed and incompetence is the accusation that there was an overriding political motive behind all of Basiliscus' conduct; that he 'played the coward'[71] rather than actually being one. This would mean that the emperor's own brother-in-law had been intentionally complicit in the loss of thousands of men and hundreds of ships.

Worse still, Basiliscus' treason was reputedly 'a favour to Aspar in accordance with what he had promised'.[72] The lack of clarity in the sources makes it difficult to explore any relationship between the *magistri*. Candidus, who as an Isaurian might look to paint both in as poor a light as possible, does not mention Aspar in connection with the failure of the Vandal expedition; however, other sources do. As well as Priscus and Procopius, the Spanish chronicler Hydatius records a Suevi embassy reporting back home 'that Aspar had been cashiered and his son executed after they had been discovered plotting with the Vandals against the Roman Empire'.[73] Even if this report contains false information – Leo did not cashier Aspar or kill Ardaburius in 468 – the envoys have picked up on suspicions that Aspar was somehow involved with the failure of the expedition. Later sources such as Theophanes and Zonaras largely drew on Priscus and had little option but to repeat this mix of incompetence and Aspar-inspired treachery.[74]

But why was Aspar opposed to the Vandal expedition? The sources claim that Aspar orchestrated the disaster because he feared that 'if the Vandals were defeated, Leo should establish his power most securely'.[75] Certainly the returning of Africa to the empire would have been a huge boost to Leo's credibility, not to mention the tax revenues and corn supplies to bolster Roman finances. Perhaps Aspar 'repeatedly urged upon Basiliscus that he should spare the Vandals'[76] because he viewed Geiseric as a potential ally like Theoderic Strabo. He could even be advocating the usual Roman barbarian policy of not destroying enemies because they could be next year's allies, particularly when such an action put Roman soldiers at risk. Aspar certainly knew the risks of African campaigning. Maybe the legacy of his defeat in the 430s and the failures of the 440 and 461 expeditions were a large part of Aspar's opposition in 468: he knew the financial and manpower implications of failure. Jealousy could also play a part, for if the emperor's expedition prevailed, he would have achieved something that Aspar could not. Leo could even say that he had fixed Aspar's mess.[77]

However, it is a significant leap to go from opposition to sabotage. That the sources thought that Aspar made that leap may be using hindsight, given the benefits the fallout of the expedition's failure seemed to bring Aspar. In such a ruthless portrayal, targeting Basiliscus for destruction provided an opportunity to kill two political birds with one stone. Through his promotion to *magister milium praesentalis*, appointment to the Vandal command and his familial connections, Basiliscus had become a substantial obstacle to Ardaburii plans. By undermining Basiliscus, Aspar will have been undermining Leo too and demonstrating that his own power was still potent. Personal revenge could also be a factor – the disgracing of Basiliscus was direct retribution for the disgracing of Ardaburius. The contest between Leo and Aspar may well have been entering a new and potentially deadly stage. But would Aspar really have threatened the existence of the expedition for his own ends? Would he have let his eldest son go on an expedition he knew was doomed to failure? It would be more likely that Ardaburius' presence was encouraged by Aspar so he could regain some prestige and trust.

And even if Aspar was acting against the expedition, why would Basiliscus agree to work with him to sabotage it? It has been suggested that 'perhaps Basiliscus had promised Aspar he would be a more accommodating emperor than his brother-in-law'.[78] Procopius thought that Basiliscus was 'extraordinarily desirous of the royal power [which] he hoped would come to him without a struggle if he won the friendship of Aspar',[79] but this is also almost certainly tainted with hindsight. If he was acting on imperial ambition, Basiliscus could well have had the same reservations about the Vandal campaign as Aspar – success made Leo harder to influence. Ardaburii support would certainly help in those imperial pretensions, with complicity in the failure of the expedition the Alan general's price for that support. However, Basiliscus allowing his own imperial pretensions to influence his dealings with Aspar and Geiseric still leaves some questions unanswered. Did Basiliscus really think that the backing of Aspar was worth the disgrace of a life-threatening military disaster? Was Ardaburii aid really worth more than arriving back in Constantinople the conquering hero with Geiseric's head on a pike? If the answer to both of these was 'yes' then perhaps this is why Malchus considered that Basiliscus was slow in understanding and easily deceived.[80]

But for him to be a willing participant in the cutting of his own political throat on the promise of an alliance which would do him little good, either with his reputation ruined or his life ended at Mercurium, is surely beyond credulity. Two experienced and prominent generals would not be so blasé about orchestrating an imperial military debacle. The disaster was instead caused by Vandal abilities, limited Roman local knowledge, Basiliscus' poor admiralship and the ongoing disputes within the western establishment.[81] Aspar's effect on the failure of the expedition may instead be limited to his lack of involvement.

It is worth noting that for all the blame apportioned to Basiliscus, Aspar, Ricimer and Geiseric, none is attributed to Leo himself. This shows one of the major benefits of the emperor not leading the army in person. While he could claim all the *kudos* from a successful campaign, he could also be isolated from the calamity of defeat. But despite blame being apportioned elsewhere, the disaster must have stalled Leo's political momentum.[82] Another man sheltered from the fallout of the Vandal expedition was Zeno. Despite holding military rank in Thrace, his position as *comes domesticorum* kept Zeno within the vicinity of the capital. Indeed, the disgrace of Basiliscus improved Zeno's position further, with him being appointed consul for 469.[83] However, before his consulship was at an end, Zeno had followed Basiliscus into semi-exile. The reason behind this requires focus to switch back to the Huns and the Roman generals dealing with them.

The 'Protest' Revolt of Anagastes

Despite his manpower having been seriously depleted by the defections and massacres perpetrated on the urging of Chelchal, hunger for revenge or just hunger full stop saw Dengizich continue to raid Roman territory. Unfortunately for him, while the Vandal expedition had drained away a proportion of Roman field forces in the area, not all of them had returned to their garrisons after the success of 467. Anagastes and his army had remained in the area and there were to be no negotiations this time. In a crushing Hunnic defeat, Dengizich was killed and his head taken to Constantinople to be paraded through the streets.[84] This is usually dated to 469, following Marcellinus Comes; however, as the *Chronicon Paschale* places the death of Dengizich during the consulship of Anthemius in 468, it may be that Marcellinus has confused his dating systems. His mistake may be to have assumed that an event recorded as taking place during the indiction of 1 September 468 to 31 August 469 took place in the calendar year 469, rather than 468.[85]

It could well be then that Dengizich was dispatched by Anagastes in late 468. The Gothic general is also recorded defeating and killing Ullibos, a Gothic chieftain in Roman service who had rebelled.[86] Despite these victories, Anagastes was put out by his lack of reward, which was exacerbated by being passed over for the consulship of 470, which Leo put down to refusing to appoint an epileptic such as Anagastes to the post. This slight was further compounded for Anagastes by the subsequent selection of Jordanes, *magister militum per Orientem*, for the consulship instead. While Jordanes was a suitable candidate, there was a long-standing enmity with Anagastes. The latter's father, Arnegisclus, had caused the treacherous death of Jordanes' father, John the Vandal, three decades earlier in 441. This succession of snubs led Anagastes to embark on some kind of rebellion.[87] Given the sidelining of Basiliscus and the growing mistrust of Aspar, it was left to Zeno as the most high-profile commander in the vicinity to deal with this revolt.

The details surrounding the revolt and the imperial response are plagued by dating issues, the targets of campaigns and positions held by certain individuals. While the early 470s have been put forward,[88] the likelihood is that being placed after the Vandal expedition of 468 and the death of Dengizich in 468/469 establishes Anagastes' revolt in mid/late 469. This date is backed up by the likely announcing of Jordanes' consulship of 470 at the same time, particularly if it was a major factor in sparking Anagastes' revolt. However, the sources are far from clear as to who Zeno was sent to campaign against. Some do not mention a specific enemy, although it is usually supposed that this enemy was barbarian in nature. The Pannonian Goths have been suggested, although they were supposedly fighting Suebi along the Danube at this time; other Gothic or Hunnic raids in the wake of those of Dengizich, or even Dengizich or Ullibos, have also been suggested as well as Anagastes.[89]

Zeno was sent to Thrace not long after becoming consul in 469 to deal with a 'barbarian disturbance',[90] which suggests Goths or Huns. However, the Greek used by the anonymous biographer of Daniel the Stylite – ταραχῆς βαρβαρικῆς γενομένης – is far less clear than simply 'barbarian disturbance'; ταραχή was more normally applied to domestic trouble in the fifth century, while βαρβαρική could infer barbarian involvement or hint at the identity of the antagonist. Even though they were opponents at the time, John of Antioch links Anagastes and Ullibos, calling them 'Scyths with a tendency to rebellion',[91] and if one source could refer to Anagastes as a non-Roman, Daniel's biographer could see a rebellion by a Romanized Goth as a 'barbarian disturbance'.[92] It has also been pointed out that if the defeat and death of Dengizich is consigned to 468, then there is no recorded barbarian threat to Thrace in 469.[93] This may then limit Zeno's target to a Roman rebel. Given that Anagastes killed Ullibos before he himself rebelled, the chances are then that Zeno was sent into Thrace to deal with Anagastes.

The picture is also clouded over the positions of these men. Anagastes and seemingly Zeno were serving as *comes rei militaris* in 467, with Basiliscus as Thracian *magister*. However, there is no direct evidence as to who succeeded Basiliscus in Thrace upon his promotion. Both Anagastes and Zeno are recorded as Thracian *magister*,[94] but the sequence is uncertain. It has been assumed that Zeno briefly became *magister* in 467/468 before being succeeded by Anagastes.[95] Such an assumption faces problems if the death of Dengizich is moved from 469 to 468, particularly if Anagastes was *magister* when he defeated the Hun. With that, it would appear more likely that it was Anagastes who succeeded Basiliscus in Thrace.

Before the discovery of the *Vita S. Danielis Stylitae*, and even by ignoring it, historians felt the need to look beyond Thrace for Zeno's magisterial position. Despite nomenclature not being his strongest suit, some have followed Theophanes in considering that Zeno was eastern *magister* from around 467, which overlooks Jordanes, while Bury proposed that Zeno was acting as *magister militum praesentalis*, positions held by Aspar and seemingly still Basiliscus.[96] The idea of Zeno holding another magisterial position when being sent into Thrace in 469 could tally with Anagastes being his target. The only reason for Zeno to be deployed to deal with a threat would be that the Thracian *magister* was otherwise engaged, and given that there was no barbarian activity in 469, it might be surmised that that threat was the Thracian *magister* himself. As Zeno was appointed Thracian *magister* in the same year that Anagastes rebelled, it would seem then that the two events are linked. The likelihood is then that Anagastes succeeded Basiliscus and when he rebelled in 469, he was stripped of that position and succeeded by Zeno, the man sent to deal with him.[97]

This would seem to clash with the recording of Zeno as having taken up the position of *magister militum per Orientem* during his consulship of 469.[98] Zeno's holding of two separate magisterial positions in 469 need not be a problem. The source of this rectification is the revolt of Anagastes being short-lived. On the surface, it was a very dangerous threat to the security of the empire given the importance of the Thracian field army in defending the approaches to Constantinople and the Danube. However, Anagastes appears to have been happy to make his point with the threat of rebellion rather than actual rebellion. With the lack of fighting and its short-lived nature, the 'revolt' of Anagastes looks more like an armed protest. He was quick to submit to Leo diplomatically, with the emperor equally quick to welcome Anagastes back into the imperial fold, restoring him to the position of *magister militum per Thracias*. Therefore, Zeno was probably Thracian *magister* only for a very brief time, allowing him to become *magister militum per Orientem* before the end of 469. But why had Zeno gone from staying in the capital to protect Leo to becoming general in the east? The answer comes in the latest escalation of the feud between Leo and Aspar.

The Attempted Murder of Zeno and His Escape

That Leo would send his most high profile supporter out into Thrace away from the capital at a time when Aspar was still present and Basiliscus was in semi-exile suggests that either the revolt of Anagastes was viewed as overtly dangerous or that Leo thought there was little personal threat from the Ardaburii. The latter notion is tempered somewhat by the emperor turning to Daniel the Stylite to ask his opinion of this proposed campaign; the holy man prophesized that Zeno would be the target of a conspiracy but would escape unharmed.[99] In response to this warning, Leo beefed up his son-in-law's security with a contingent of his own personal forces.[100] Unsurprisingly given the involvement of a saint's predictions, Leo's precautionary actions ensured the fulfilment of the prophecy. Despite being of the imperial household, the men sent to protect Zeno from a conspiracy turned out to be the conspirators themselves. Aspar and Ardaburius persuaded them to kidnap and murder the emperor's son-in-law. Before the trap could be sprung, Zeno was tipped off and managed to escape to the relative safety of Serdica.[101]

For Ardaburius and Aspar to carry out such an overt attack on Zeno with Leo's own men meant that the gradual erosion of their power and influence was starting to affect them. The choice of Zeno as Thracian *magister* may have been the final straw for Aspar, who had had to watch the man who had disgraced his son receive a raft of promotions: *comes domesticorum*, consul, perhaps *patricius*, husband of Ariadne and progenitor of the Leonid imperial line,[102] on top of a series of other pro-Leonids receiving high-office. When Anagastes ended his 'protest', he not only offered the emperor his allegiance, he provided evidence of Ardaburius' connivance against Leo. Could the 'protest' and the attempt on the life of Zeno have been orchestrated by Ardaburius and Aspar?

As with the Persian and Basiliscus intrigues, it is difficult to ascertain just what Ardaburius or his father would hope to gain from the rebellion of the Thracian *magister*. It might have been an attempt to get Zeno out of Constantinople in order to kill him so 'Aspar and Ardaburius could more easily expect to re-assert their position at court'.[103] While orchestrating a revolt of a disgruntled general seems a contrived way of removing Zeno from the capital, it is less extravagant than their proposed involvement in sabotaging the Vandal expedition. Even though this plan did not fully succeed, with Zeno escaping to Serdica and Anagastes returning to imperial loyalty, the Ardaburii had got what they wanted. This was because despite his survival, Zeno was 'best advised to keep well clear of the capital until events turned more favourably in his direction'.[104]

From Serdica, Zeno moved on to the Long Wall and then Pylai,[105] although the exact identity of this 'Long Wall' is not certain. Was it the Anastasian Long Wall, 55km west of the capital, or was it the fortification across the neck of the Thracian Chersonese?[106] If the Anastasian Wall was built from scratch by Anastasius, then it was not there to be visited by Zeno in 469. However, what would become the Anastasian Wall was perhaps built in the 440s. A definitive archaeological answer has yet to be reached.[107]

It has been suggested that Zeno had no reason to detour to the Thracian Chersonese,[108] but he did have cause to be wary of the capital and the main routes to it. There had just been an attempt on his life, carried out by men supposedly loyal to his father-in-law but instead working for the Ardaburii. The idea that any Isaurians in the capital could have protected Zeno from such overt violent intent is overplayed.[109] The roads from Serdica to the capital were also rendered dangerous by the continued presence of the plotters and any barbarian groups roaming the area, especially Theoderic Strabo and his Goths.

It is likely that Zeno did hope to return to Constantinople after his flight from Serdica. However, he refrained from the direct route. As he moved south to the Thracian Long Wall, no doubt Zeno was looking for information regarding the safety of the route and the capital. That he had not received a definitive answer might be speculated from him not taking ship for Lampsacus or even Cyzicus, but instead he sailed the length of the Sea of Marmara for Pylai, 'the beginning of the highway across Anatolia into Isauria and Cilicia, and seems to have been mainly used by emperors and high officials'.[110] While Pylai lay at the beginning of these routes, if he was already planning to head to Antioch, joining the land routes at Lampsacus or Cyzicus would have been a quicker and safer option. At the very least this suggests that he was keeping his options open. That Zeno then turned back north to Chalcedon again suggests that he hoped to return to the capital and could indicate that he had yet to be appointed eastern *magister*. It is unlikely that he would risk crossing to Constantinople having taken the long way around just to be appointed *magister*. Instead, word of his appointment to the east likely reached him at Chalcedon.[111]

Another potential alteration to be made to Zeno's escape route is his destination being not Antioch but Isauria. Malalas calls Illus' escort of Zeno to Constantinople in 476 'his second return from Isauria',[112] with the first likely coming at the climax of the Leo-Aspar confrontation in 471. This could mean that Zeno departed Chalcedon for Isauria in 469, or at least ended up there at some stage, only for him to hear later that he had been appointed eastern *magister* and move on to Antioch. While something of a conundrum, in the context of Zeno's escape into 'semi-exile', his appointment as *magister militum per Orientem* appears slapdash. Zeno not returning to the capital will have seemed strange and even embarrassing, so Leo attempted to make the appointment appear as part of his plans. In reality, transferring Zeno from Thrace to Antioch was a largely transparent recognition of the fact he had essentially been driven from the imperial capital and the emperor had been unable to stop it. Aspar ruled supreme once more, the emperor Leo being 'powerless and isolated in the imperial capital'.[113]

Chapter 6

The Puppet Becomes the Butcher:
The End of Aspar

'every once in a while, the lion has to show the jackals who he is.'

Uncle Mike, *Poolhall Junkies* (2002)

Zeno's Eastern 'Exile'

While it may have been a last minute appointment dictated by circumstance, Leo and Zeno likely assumed that the latter's time as *magister militum per Orientem* would be brief. Instead, it would be nearly two years before Zeno could return to the capital, and the area commanded by the eastern *magister* meant that he did not have a quiet time. Antioch saw Zeno become involved in religious politics through his relationship with Peter the Fuller. More importantly for the security of the provinces, Zeno was also faced with some military threats during his tenure as eastern *magister*.

The first came from his own kinsmen, as a rebel called Indacus Cottunes had established himself in the *castellum Papirii* – the Fort of Papirius in Isauria, built and named for Indacus' father, himself an Isaurian brigand.[1] Isaurian raiders could have played a part in Leo's decision, encouraged by Aspar, to send Zeno east; however, the exact timing of these events is not certain and this could be a convenient occurrence for Leo to use it as a propaganda smokescreen. An incipient Isaurian revolt may also undermine any suggestion that Leo had sent Zeno east to be closer to his Isaurian powerbase,[2] although subduing threats to the imperial peace and showing himself to be foremost amongst the Isaurians cannot have harmed Zeno's standing. Faced with an old-style Isaurian raider, Zeno responded by sending troops to expel Indacus from the Papirian fort before the end of 469, although it is unclear if these men were successful. Indacus did survive this imperial response and may even have remained in command of the fortress as he was present there in 484. Zeno's men may have just moved to quell Indacus' brigandage rather than expel him from the stronghold.[3]

Zeno was also faced with a pro-Persian secessionist movement that had arisen in Tzania, a region within the Roman-allied kingdom of Lazica. Zeno sent some Roman soldiers to the Lazican leader, Gobazes, although this Romano-Laz force was unable to subdue the Tzani. Persian attempts to aid this secessionist movement through proxies saw an Iberian invasion of Lazica and Tzani raids spilling into Roman Armenia by late 470. This seems a poor result for the Roman Empire,

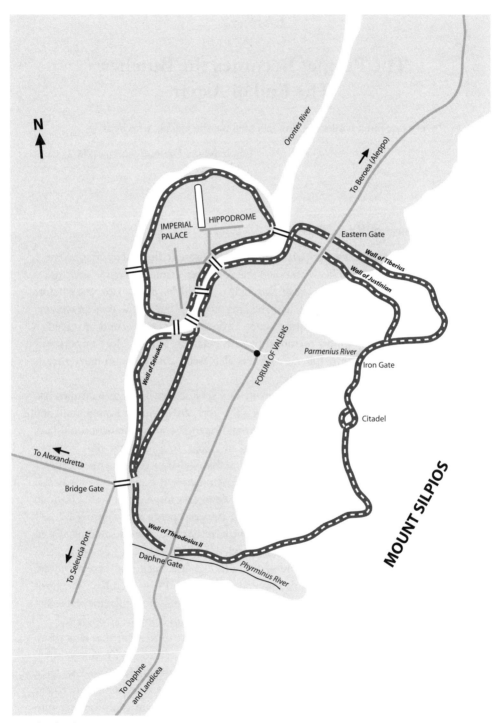

Antioch

but as will be seen later, being able to pull back from the internal turmoil of these Caucasian kingdoms may have saved the empire from the greater headache of proxy conflict turning into a full-scale Romano-Persian war.[4]

Zeno had no direct involvement in either of these military excursuses, which would be a recurring theme throughout his career with him employing others to lead the fighting. While some might call this cowardice, it could be a pragmatic decision from Zeno, recognizing his own personal lack of military flair and leadership, much as how previous emperors such as *Augustus* and Diocletian had done. However, it is unlikely that he could have established himself in a prominent position amongst the Isaurians without some sort of martial ability. Instead, his lack of field leadership could be due to the growing eastern trend which saw no emperor lead the army in person between 395 and the early seventh century.

Aspar Gets What He Wants: The Elevation of Patricius

While distracted in the east, Zeno will have kept in touch with Leo over the growing tensions in Constantinople, and it had certainly not been quiet in the capital. 'Either by careful planning on his part or accidents of circumstance which he shrewdly exploited',[5] the neutralizing of Basiliscus and Zeno allowed Aspar to reassert complete dominance over Leo. He was not going to waste any time in solidifying that dominance for future generations. Therefore, the emperor quickly found himself under increasing pressure to make good on the promises he had reputedly made early in his reign – the elevation of Patricius to *Caesar* and betrothing him to one of his daughters. Leo had long prevaricated over this and had even married Ariadne to Zeno to prevent capitulating, but now the Alan general imposed his will. In 470, he was able to bask in the glory of seeing Patricius named as *Caesar* and betrothed to Leontia as Leo acquiesced, either 'to gain the goodwill of Aspar'[6] or accepting 'the reality of Aspar's authority'.[7]

The dating of Patricius' elevation and his marriage to Leontia to 470 is not universally agreed. Some suggest that Patricius was elevated as early as the late 450s;[8] however, not only would both Ariadne and Leontia have been too young to countenance a marriage (although not a betrothal), had Patricius been elevated to *Caesar* in the late 450s, far more coins depicting him as such would have been issued.[9] It has not been infrequent for historians to suggest that the marriage and elevation took place in separate years, although placing either as early as 468, which Theophanes may have, overlooks the ebbs and flows of imperial politics at that time. It is unlikely that Leo would have countenanced Patricius' elevation and marriage to Leontia before the 'exile' of Zeno in late 469.[10]

The elevation of Patricius as *Caesar* also raised significant questions surrounding his Arianism. An Arian Patricius *Caesar* would have been in stark contrast to the rest of Leo's reign, which had been profoundly anti-Arian. Their churches and any congregation of Arians had been banned.[11] Any opposition to the conversion of Patricius to Catholic orthodoxy would not have been the first time that Aspar had stood up to the doctrinal policies of Leo and Gennadius. He had argued with the emperor over the banishment of Timothy Aeleurus, meaning 'the Cat' or 'the Weasel', in 459/460 and is thought to have been behind the law of 457 that granted heretics the right to a decent burial.[12] He also argued with the emperor in favour of the appointment of Arians to important positions. As already seen, Leo had used the Arianism of Aspar as part of his plan to emerge from his shadow by fostering closer ties with orthodoxy.

Leo's success in promoting orthodoxy was demonstrated in the reaction to the very notion that the new heir might be an Arian. Great tumult amongst the Senate, people and clergy of Constantinople led to a protest march headed by patriarch Gennadius and the monk Marcellus from Hagia Sophia to the Hippodrome. They voiced their opposition to an Arian *Caesar* and fear of a repeat of the 'atrocities' committed under previous 'Arian' emperors. Eventually, Leo had to assure the crowd that Patricius had forsaken his Arianism for orthodoxy. Opposition was so great that 'if Aspar still wished his son to be *Caesar* then the son would have no option but to declare himself orthodox'.[13] It is unlikely that any such declaration quelled opposition, especially when Patricius was the son of Aspar and part of a largely Arian alliance, but that there was the slightest hint of Patricius becoming *Caesar* without forsaking his Arianism is a testament to the power of Aspar in 469-71.

Patricius' profession of orthodoxy would also have removed the obstacle to his marriage to a daughter of Leo. Strangely, no source actually names Leontia as the daughter-in-law of Aspar, betrothed or actual. As Ariadne was already married to Zeno and seemingly in Antioch with him, Leontia was left as the only other candidate; however, this is not universally accepted. Given that she was born during the reign of Leo, it is possible that by 470, Leontia was not yet old enough to be married. If that was the case, for Patricius to marry a daughter of Leo there would either have to be a breaking of accepted marital practice or Ariadne would have to have been divorced from Zeno. While the former might be possible, the latter would require Ariadne to remarry Zeno after the ousting of Aspar as they were husband and wife up until his death in 491.[14] As the sources mention no underage marriage, divorce and remarriage, it would seem like an unnecessary complication to portray Ariadne as Patricius' wife. It was an early teenage Leontia who was to be the imperial link for Aspar's burgeoning dynasty.

This must have been particularly galling for Leo as he was essentially announcing the son of his enemy as his designated heir and allowing him to marry his daughter. He had avoided such a move for over a decade and may have thought that it was behind him following the birth of Leo II. Several sources record not only the growing despair of Leo but also the unsurpassed power of Aspar and Ardaburius. The *Vita Marcelli* recalls a certain John incurring the wrath of Ardaburius, with Leo proving powerless to protect him. Even the sanctity of Marcellus' monastery was no obstacle to Ardaburius, who had his retainers besiege the holy place and threatened any who opposed him.[15] The *Vita Marcelli*, along with the *Vita Simeon Stylitae*, also records the power of the Ardaburii making them essentially emperors in their own right. At the translation of Simeon's remains to Constantinople in 470/471, Aspar and Ardaburius were 'honoured like kings in the areas of their authority'.[16] John Lydus reports that due to the seeming end of his independence, Leo 'not merely quitted the court – with phantoms haunting him as though he were an Orestes wanting in manhood – and dwelt elsewhere, but even came seriously to consider quitting the city itself'.[17]

Leo's disappointment and reticence in broadcasting the elevation of his new Caesarian son-in-law is demonstrated in his coinage. There are no issues depicting Leo and Patricius, and while there has been some suggestion that certain coins hosting a seemingly redundant 'C' on the reverse signify Patricius' time as *Caesar*,[18] this has been explained as a mistake in the reuse of a die from Constantinople in Thessalonica.[19] It might also have been expected that Patricius would be nominated for the consulship of 471 alongside the emperor Leo, as that was a common occurrence for a new heir to the throne. That this did not happen might hint at not only the emperor's reticence but also that he had plans in the making to remove the Ardaburii. However, Patricius' elevation may have come late enough in 470 for the consuls of 471 – Leo and Caelius Aconius Probianus – to have already been nominated. Probianus was also a western nominee by Anthemius, so Leo is unlikely to have run roughshod over the western *Augustus* and his appointment. Patricius and Aspar may have expected a consulship in 472 to celebrate the former's elevation, but circumstances would prove that impossible.

The sources pass over Patricius' period as heir apparent in relative silence. He visited Alexandria, where he was met with all the pomp and ceremony due a *Caesar*, although the purpose of this visit is not explained. It may have been a patronage mission, showing the Alexandrians that all was fine despite the Vandal debacle. Perhaps Aspar was keen to have his son seen by the public in his new imperial guise, while Leo may have been happy to get one of the Ardaburii out of the capital, particularly if he was planning some drastic action.[20]

To undertake and then survive any such drastic action, Leo would need all of his allies. However, at this time, he was faced with religious-based opposition from a far more unexpected source – Zeno himself. Upon his 'exile' to Antioch in 469, Zeno was accompanied by the anti-Chalcedonian monk, Peter the Fuller. Peter began to rally anti-Chalcedonians against the Antiochene patriarch Martyrius, inviting monks into the city to promote his views, particularly his addition of 'who was crucified for us' into the *Trisagion*, 'suggesting that God and not just Christ had suffered in the flesh'.[21] The following of Peter and the indifference of Zeno saw Martyrius appeal to Leo in person. While the Antiochene patriarch was gaining the support of Leo and Gennadius in the capital, Peter made his move. He had himself established as patriarch of Antioch, with the returning Martyrius forced to resign due to civil unrest, violence and Zeno's failure to intervene.[22] Leo was furious. He exiled Peter, who fled upon hearing the news, and addressed a law to Zeno, dated 1 June 471, forbidding monks to leave their monasteries, to discuss doctrinal matters with the people or to incite rebellion amongst the 'simple minds of the populace'.[23] While this law suggests that Zeno was still eastern *magister* on that date, was Zeno still in Antioch at this time? Could he perhaps have been heading west already?

And what of Basiliscus? Had his time in Heraclea removed him completely from imperial politics? A curious episode in the sources could suggest that Basiliscus was still militarily active in 470. While the failure of the Vandal expedition in 468 had removed him from the capital, Basiliscus seems to have remained *magister militum praesentalis* and it may be that he was now given the opportunity to repair his reputation in 470 by leading another African campaign.[24] He may have reached Sicily with the aim of linking up with an overland expedition marching from Tripolis, having taken ship from Egypt under the command of Heracleius and Marsus. Defeating Vandal forces and capturing cities as they moved west, these forces came within striking distance of Carthage only for a peace settlement to be hammered out with Geiseric. The abruptness of the end of this campaign, especially with a potential victory in sight, suggests that Leo had more important fish to fry with Basiliscus and the men under his command: the time to deal with the threat of Aspar was fast approaching.[25]

However, this 'Fifth Punic War' seems extremely familiar, even repetitive. That is because the sources used for this proposed second expedition of Basiliscus are by no means clear in the dates of the events they address. Procopius ties in the advance of Heracleius and Marsus from Egypt through Tripolis with Basiliscus' defeat at Mercurium and therefore the 468 campaign, with no mention of a second attempt in 470-71. It is perhaps only his immediate jumping to the destruction of Aspar and Ardaburius 'not long afterwards'[26] that narrows the gap between these exploits in the West and Leo's butchery enough to suppose another expedition. Paul the Deacon conflates the events of the Vandal expedition of 468 with Anthemius' tenure as western *Augustus*, the elevation of Patricius in 470 and Leo's move against Aspar in 471, making it difficult to say that he supports the notion of a second expedition.[27]

It is Theophanes who provides the most ammunition for the suggestion that Basiliscus returned west. Not only does he devote a section to the expedition of 468,[28] he also records the advance of Heracleius and Marsus as taking place in 470, with the additional note that the two generals 'had harassed Geiseric more than the fleet of Basiliscus had done'.[29] This would place Basiliscus once more at the head of a naval squadron aimed at Africa. Theophanes also then links the subsequent peace treaty with Leo's desire to have Basiliscus, Heracleius, Marsus and their forces back east for the plot against Aspar. However, Theophanes has misplaced the overland expedition of Heracleius and Marsus to 470, attaching Basiliscus and his fleet, when in reality it was all part of the 468 expedition, with Heracleius and Marsus retreating from Tripolis in 470. This would suggest that there was no direct military connection between any treaty with Geiseric and Leo's removal of Aspar in 471. An inscribed statue of Basiliscus at Philippopolis in commemoration of his achievements could be dated to 471/472 and therefore perhaps in recognition for his forcing of a peace treaty on Geiseric.[30] However, this statue could easily have been a reward for other achievements.

The whole idea of a 'Fifth Punic War' in 470 is a phantom born of poorly worded, conflated and misdated source material. All the events ascribed to this campaign, aside from the peace treaty and Leo's need to bring his men home for support against Aspar, should be attributed to the 468 expedition, with the defeat of Basiliscus' navy at Mercurium forcing Heracleius and Marsus to retreat to Tripolis until signing it away to Geiseric in 470. With the existence of his second African chance rendered unlikely, Basiliscus was almost certainly still in exile at Heraclea throughout the period 468-471, even if he did nominally retain the position of *magister militum praesentalis*.

With Zeno and Basiliscus removed from the capital and Patricius now installed as heir-designate, Aspar could celebrate what seemed his ultimate subjugation of Leo. As the emperor was of advanced age and possibly even somewhat infirm,[31] the Alan general may even have been counting the days until the enthroning of his son as sole *Augustus* and the beginning of an Ardaburii imperial dynasty. But if he was, Aspar was to be in for the rudest of awakenings. The old and infirm Leo was by no means a spent force, and he had been sufficiently backed into the proverbial corner to be left with little option but to earn his sobriquet of the 'Butcher'.

Leo Gets What He Wants: The Destruction of the Ardaburii

While the 'Fifth Punic War' might have been a phantom, the reasoning behind its proposed sudden calling-off proved to be very real. The confrontation between the imperial family and the Ardaburii, fourteen years in the making, was about to come to its bloody crescendo. The sources do not provide any real depth on the events that led up to Leo's desperate strike against Aspar, Ardaburius and Patricius, requiring some speculation.[32] On top of tiring of his authority being overshadowed by Aspar and being plotted against by Ardaburius,[33] Leo's motive for moving against the Ardaburii may have been sparked by his own sense of self-preservation. Leo may well have feared that the Ardaburii intended to have him killed so Patricius could accede to the throne before circumstances changed.[34] Leo's response to this perceived threat to the Leonid grip on the imperial throne from the Ardaburii was simple – 'he killed them'.[35]

While that was a straightforward solution, it was not a straightforward task. Aspar was the senior military official, leading senator, centre of a network of alliances, father of the heir to the throne and had such a stranglehold over Constantinople that Leo will have had to move with caution as he attempted to bring together a plot. While removed from Constantinople, both Basiliscus and Zeno were likely still in contact with the emperor. Basiliscus was not overly far removed from Constantinople at Heraclea, and as already seen, Zeno was receiving laws and perhaps even rebukes in Antioch. Those communiqués may even have seen Zeno encourage Leo to resort to butchery, and included a summons back to the capital, possibly before the law of 1 June 471, for Zeno to have arrived at Chalcedon by the time of the strike.[36] Given that he would provide assistance in the aftermath, the emperor likely contacted Verina's nephew, Armatus, now serving as *magister militum per Thracias*. The recall of Heracleius and Marsus from Tripolis in 470 also seems part of Leo concentrating his allies, although this might have appeared suspicious. Leo will have wanted to keep knowledge of any plot to as few persons as possible for fear of it reaching Aspar and his allies.

This all infers that the plot against Aspar had been well-planned. Not only had allies been placed in strategic positions,[37] Aspar's youngest son, Ermanaric, had been deliberately lured to Chalcedon, delivering him into the hands of the arriving Zeno.[38] However, it could instead be that the Leonid plot to oust Aspar was far more spur of the moment. His perception of a threat against his life may have seen Leo jump into desperate action with little backup in place – Basiliscus and Armatus seemingly moved no closer to the capital, while the evacuation of Heracleius and Marsus may only be connected by the sources through incorrect hindsight and Zeno may not have arrived at Chalcedon in time.

There are certainly issues with the inference that Basiliscus and Zeno were placed to provide military support for Leo against the inevitable backlash. It is difficult to see how much protection they provided in the immediate aftermath. Theophanes claims that Basiliscus, Heracleius and Marsus provided aid,[39] but in reality it appears that the *excubitores* and perhaps any loyal praesental forces provided the only tangible help to the emperor within the city. Zeno was seemingly still in Chalcedon, of little use to Leo, and would remain there until Theoderic Strabo became a problem.[40] Indeed, none of Leo's allies appear to have been close enough to Constantinople to provide physical aid. Perhaps this was in hope of not tipping off Aspar, but it exposed Leo to the threat of Ardaburii reprisals.

Whatever the level of planning, the actual attack contained some choreographed elements. The Ardaburii were called to the imperial palace for a *conventus*, which would not have aroused any suspicion as Aspar, Ardaburius and Patricius were senior officials. What will have come as a great surprise to the Ardaburii, their allies and likely many supporters of Leo was when the eunuch *cubicularii* drew their weapons, pounced on Aspar and Ardaburius and cut them down in cold blood, their bodies thrown from the palace in sacks.[41] The fate of Patricius is somewhat clouded. He was present at the bloody *conventus* and was at the very least seriously injured before perhaps managing to escape to safety, never to be heard of again. In a letter to Ricimer in 472, Leo reports that he had Aspar and Ardaburius put to death, without any mention of Patricius, which could be taken as evidence that he escaped and may even have been still alive as of that date.[42] His marriage must have been annulled or ended, as Leontia was soon to marry Marcianus, although this gives no indication of his fate. While the sources are too patchy to provide a concrete outline of his fate, Patricius was almost certainly a casualty of the same massacre that claimed the lives of his father and elder brother, dying at the time or later of his wounds.[43] This was not the final end of the Ardaburii family. Ermanaric, having fallen into the hands of Zeno at Chalcedon, was sent to Isauria, where he reputedly married a daughter of an illegitimate son of Zeno. He would be allowed to return to Constantinople after the death of Leo, becoming an ally of Zeno. He revealed a plot by Severianus and led a force of Rugian troops against Illus in 484.[44]

Word of the massacre quickly spread, and it is here that the lack of clear planning by Leo may be revealed. While the Constantinopolitan populace seem to have been happy with the outcome, shouting 'the dead man had no friend – except Ostrys',[45] the emperor had little help against the 'large band of Goths and *comites* and other followers, and a large number of supporters, whom he called *foederati*',[46] who rioted. Ostrys rallied another group of Goths and attempted to break into the palace. Only the presence of the *excubitores* and other imperial guards saved Leo. Prevented from getting to the emperor, Ostrys and his allies fled the capital with Aspar's Gothic concubine. Given that the streets of Constantinople were awash with rioting, to save time and avoid danger, Ostrys may have headed to one of the much closer harbours and taken ship for Thrace rather than tried to make his way from the imperial palace to the city gates, a distance of at least 4 miles.[47]

In Thrace, Ostrys raided various estates, probably the large imperial lands near the capital and was joined by other Ardaburii allies, including the Gothic *foederati* of Theoderic Strabo.[48] These vengeful Goths were dealt with by Armatus in his role as Thracian *magister*, who showed a particularly ruthless and bloody streak in ordering many of the Goths he captured to have their hands cut off. Theoderic Strabo would later cut off the hands of his own prisoners, seemingly in response to Armatus' mutilations.[49]

Despite these threats from Ostrys and the Goths, Leo was not in any great danger in the aftermath of his dispatching of the Ardaburii. Any unrest in the capital was short-lived following the expulsion of Ostrys, with the imperial guard and city garrisons able to bring order to the streets. Indeed, this lack of any real backlash could be evidence that the idea of Aspar being at the centre of a vast web of close-knit political alliances and at the head of a militarily dominant Alano-Gothic faction within Constantinople and the wider empire should be played down;[50] or that perhaps at this crucial time, Aspar's allies proved to be of little use. Many may have decided that Leo had so comprehensively outwitted them that there were better prospects in retaining their positions within the imperial hierarchy than risking revolt, especially with virtually the entire Ardaburii family annihilated. This lack of revenge missions may also be reflected in the refrain heard in Constantinople of 'the dead man had no friend – except Ostrys'.[51] It seems that Leo was happy to accept this state of affairs, for there does not seem to have been any real purge of those thought to be allies of Aspar.

There were only a couple more minor issues raised in the aftermath. One was the potential unpopularity of Zeno in the imperial capital. Any hatred for the Isaurian might have been 'so intense and widespread in Constantinople that he did not re-enter the city until after his son Leo was made co-emperor in 473',[52] a prolonged absence that would encompass Leo II's appointment as *Caesar* in 472.[53] However, this seems speculative as the sources do record him returning to the city from Chalcedon shortly after the demise of Aspar.[54] Another lingering issue was Theoderic Strabo. Despite Armatus having dealt with him, there were still some problems that needed to be ironed out. Instead of looking to avenge Aspar, the Gothic leader claimed the right to inherit the dead general's position through their family ties and Strabo's own military record. Leo responded by dispatching Pelagius, a *silentarius*, to meet with Theoderic regarding this claim: 'The barbarians gladly received him and in turn sent envoys to the Emperor, wishing to be friends of the Romans.'[55] Despite this respectful tone, trouble was to emerge from these negotiations. When Leo rejected Theoderic's initial demands, the Goth launched attacks on the nearby cities of Arcadiopolis and Philippi. These attacks lacked intensity, but they did drag on through what remained of 471, through 472 and on into 473. By this time, the lack of supplies saw the Gothic need for food bring them back to the negotiating table, where Leo appointed Theoderic as *magister militum praesentalis* in succession to Aspar.

Given that this position had remained vacant since Aspar's demise, Leo was likely prepared to appoint Theoderic as *magister* in 471. Rather than any imperial reluctance to promote Strabo, the delay in the appointment originated with Leo's rejection of the other demands of Theoderic, namely more land and ownership of Aspar's entire inheritance. By appointing a family relation of Aspar to one of the most high-profile military positions in the empire, Leo demonstrated that he had no problem with replacing one powerful individual with another so long as the new individual was loyal to the Leonid dynasty. That said, neither Strabo nor Zeno were as powerful as Aspar had been, so while the removal of the Alan *magister* may have been good for Leo in terms of his imperial authority, the lack of a powerful military figure, coupled with the emperor not leading the army in person, may have led to increasing unrest among the soldiery, contributing to the sedition and mutinies under Zeno and beyond.[56]

There is an interesting contrast between Leo's removal of Aspar and the similar removal of Aetius by Valentinian III. In promoting Zeno, keeping Basiliscus close, attaining the loyalty of the *excubitores* and being willing to negotiate with Strabo, Leo was laying the foundation not just of his removal of the Ardaburii but also of his own survival in the aftermath. This was what Valentinian III neglected to do when having Aetius executed. He had no general or bodyguard to protect him when Aetius' allies sought revenge. Aetius had also been the Roman to 'defeat' Attila, so Valentinian had a far harder time of attacking his military record, while Leo could portray Aspar as a traitorous barbarian with at best a mixed military record.[57]

While the removal of the Ardaburii had gone far more smoothly than Leo could possibly have hoped for, 'views were mixed on the justice of this move'.[58] Leo clearly thought he was justified and had done well in ridding himself of Aspar, going as far as to recommend to Anthemius that he get rid of Ricimer.[59] The contrasting of Leo/Aspar with Anthemius/Ricimer could see Leo's butchery painted in a positive light as saving the eastern empire, while Anthemius failed by not doing away with his German *magister*. Praise for Leo was ramped up in the sixth century, where Procopius likely reflected anti-barbarian rhetoric prominent during and after Justinian's reconquests.[60] However, Leo's new nickname of 'Butcher' was meant as an insult to show the distaste of some sources for the action.[61]

Leo's Butchery, Ethnicity and Factionalism in Constantinople

The mixed reaction to the murder of the Ardaburii also reflects the ambiguous depiction of men like Aspar – a contradictory combination of a blurring of the lines between Romanity and barbarity and the continued potency of that barbaric trope. Any 'strict polarisation between the "barbarian" Aspar and the "Roman" Leo is largely a creation of our sources'.[62] The sources can also provide contrasting approaches depending on their origin. For example, western propaganda sought to paint the Germanic Ricimer as a noble Roman protector against the Galatian Greekling, Anthemius.[63] By the 460s, eastern imperial interference in western government was far less welcome than the control of a Romanized barbarian strongman.

Despite having spent 'five decades as a member of the upper echelons of Roman society',[64] Aspar's barbarian heritage was still a target for attack. While it may only take two generations for a barbarian family to be viewed as Roman, that stigma did not dissipate so easily.[65] This was also demonstrated in the depictions of Leo himself, and then Zeno. Their respective Bessian and Isaurian origins were 'barbaric' enough to be a detriment, especially in the political cauldron of Constantinople. It was only natural then for Leo to try to undermine Aspar by attacking his Alan origins and, perhaps even more usefully, his 'Arianism'.[66] Of course, given the questionable 'Romanity' of virtually all of the major players in the 460s and 470s, the hypocritically tinged accusations of barbarity from supporters of these men are largely of political convenience or reflect the feelings and/or influences of commentators.

Even with a long career as a Roman general and senator, and being the son of a Romanized general and consul, Aspar was in no position to assume the imperial throne, otherwise he surely would have attempted to do so either in 450 or 457. Despite Theoderic's loaded claim in 501,[67] Aspar's barbarian origins and Arian beliefs disqualified him, much as it had done for Ricimer.[68] That said, Aspar's attempts to place his son Patricius on the imperial throne demonstrate that at least he thought that it was possible for his family line to rule. Both he and Ricimer felt that any barbaric faults could be bred and educated out of their bloodlines through marriage alliances. Aspar went further in purposefully giving his second son, Patricius, a good fifth-century Roman name.[69]

But while learning the language, behaviour and culture of the Roman world could gradually integrate local elites and barbarian tribesmen,[70] 'heresiology was increasingly used alongside long-standing stereotypes about barbarians to demarcate the Roman, orthodox world'.[71] Refusing to accept orthodoxy was refusing to accept Romanization. This could raise the cynical question that if Aspar, Ricimer and Theoderic really wanted to be accepted as 'Roman', why did none of them simply convert to orthodox Christianity? Patricius had little problem with professing orthodoxy in order to be elevated to *Caesar*; however, it is difficult to measure the levels of faith within an individual and it cannot be ruled out that Aspar refused to convert due to his faith in Arianism.

Men like Aspar may also have clung to their Arianism and barbarity to differentiate themselves from orthodox Romans. Playing these dual identities opened up opportunities for alliance on both sides of the Roman-barbarian divide. Being within the imperial government and appearing Roman provided status, wealth and power, but links to barbarian tribes gave access to power that his Roman competitors could not reach. Aspar by no means played on this dual identity to the extremes of Romanized general/barbarian raider/Germanic proto-king. In that regard, it would be Odoacer and Theoderic the Amal who would follow in the footsteps of Alaric. On the other hand, Zeno largely shunned or at least did not play up his Isaurian roots, probably because they were too unpopular in Constantinople. The plotting of Illus could suggest that Zeno was right to not promote Isaurians further as a consequence of their traditional confrontations with imperial government and each other.

Even if Aspar and Ricimer felt that they could have made the leap to the imperial throne through embracing orthodoxy, they may have felt that it was not worth the risk. Roman elites in Italy and Constantinople might have provided them with support, but they may not have taken to a barbarian *Augustus*. At the same time, accepting Catholic orthodoxy could have cost them support amongst their Arian brethren, so by assuming the imperial mantle someone like Aspar or Ricimer may become less powerful. The allure of imperial office had also declined throughout the fifth century, with Constantius III complaining about the loss of freedom that came with being emperor.[72] Aspar may therefore have chosen to remain the power behind the throne, maintaining his influence but also his freedom rather than risk decreasing influence over the army.[73]

The removal of the Ardaburii family has long been 'cast as the replacement of the German/Gothic faction with the Isaurian faction'.[74] There is a litany of quotations to be lifted from modern historians to this effect.[75] However grandiose these proclamations are, do they really represent an accurate picture of politics in the imperial court at the time, or is this an 'overly simplified model of Gotho-Isaurian rivalry'?[76] Was there even a Gothic faction at court? There were plenty of Germans serving in the imperial government and the army, although not all were allies of Aspar. Some, like Anagastes, were staunch opponents of the Ardaburii, which at the very least shows that any existent Gothic Ardaburii faction had not united all Goths. The aftermath of Aspar's murder demonstrates that there were significant numbers of Goths in the imperial capital. The Γοτθικην χειρα – military contingent of Goths – recorded in Malalas as belonging to Aspar could be a private army or warband, but it is far more likely that this was merely a unit of the Roman army attached to Aspar in his role as *magister militum praesentalis*.

While it is unlikely that there was a Gothic faction at court, that does not preclude 'the deliberate creation of a new ethnic power-bloc to balance that of Aspar'[77] based on the Isaurians. However, there is very little evidence of an Isaurian contingent helping Zeno rise to prominence at all. As already suggested, Zeno was promoted to high rank as part of natural progression of his military career and aiding of Leo against Ardaburius and Aspar, rather than due to his Isaurian origins.[78] There are very few high-ranking Isaurians known from the reign of Leo beyond Zeno, Marsus and Illus;[79] that number would grow after Zeno's restoration by Illus in 476, after which the presence of an Isaurian faction is more likely. Claiming that this faction of Illus was formed in the mid-460s as a counterbalance to Aspar is to go beyond the sources.[80] It may even be that most known Isaurians came from the same three families,[81] which means any Isaurian faction was created along familial rather than ethnic lines.

The very depiction of the Isaurians as an ethnic group is itself somewhat problematic. Not only were they Roman provincials, as seen earlier, but being 'Isaurian' was far more a geographical descriptor than an ethnic or linguistic one. It was perhaps not until the Isaurians became the imperial challengers to Anastasius that they became caricatured as semi-barbarians.[82] Instead, the Isaurians should be viewed in the same light as the Illyrians and Pannonians of the second and third century: hardy fighters honed in the rugged terrain of their homeland; perfect recruits for the Roman army. That would make them more a regional than an ethnic faction.

Even if there was some existence of factions in the capital, there were plenty of occasions that shared ethnic origin meant nothing to solidarity. Aspar and Ostrys fought Goths in 467, Chelchal the Hun encouraged Goths to kill Huns and Zeno campaigned against Isaurians, while Ardaburius felt he could bring Isaurians to his side. On such occasions 'ethnicity or provincial origin was plainly subsidiary to imperial service and policy'.[83] Many of the sources also refuse to identify the participants by ethnic labels. Candidus might call Zeno an Isaurian, perhaps out of some regional pride, but in the fragments of Priscus, Zeno is only identified as the son-in-law of Leo. The anonymous biographer of Daniel refers once to Zeno as being Isaurian by birth, the *Chronicon Paschale* only introduces him as Isaurian, while Theodore Lector and Cedrenus do not mention Zeno being an Isaurian at all.

Leo did slowly build his own power-base, distinct from that of Aspar, but it was certainly not an ethnic one exclusively dependent on 'hardy Isaurian mountaineers'. Not only did Leo have Isaurians as his allies, he also brought together Goths, Vandals, Gauls, Verina's family and almost certainly some Bessian/Thracian allies. As emperor, he will also have been able to command significant sections of the army and the palace guards.[84] With this multi-ethnic group, which is only labelled as 'Isaurian' because Zeno would be its ultimate benefactor, Leo broke the domination of Aspar and the Ardaburii rather than any hold of the Germans over the imperial government.

The unravelling of the long-supposed ethnic factionalism leaves the destruction of the Ardaburii to be explained in other terms. One interpretation is that Ardaburius was as much the primary target as his father. He had been the source of various controversies and problems, but getting rid of just him would incur the wrath of Aspar and Patricius. Family annihilation was safer for Leo than a surgical strike. It is also possible that the doctrinal difference between the orthodox empire and the Arian Ardaburii was a particular stumbling block for Leo.[85] It does seem that Leo confiscated Aspar's estates and gave them over for the building of orthodox churches, following his own law whilst perhaps simultaneously keeping them out of the inheritance of Theoderic.[86] However, there are two much more prominent reasons for the liquidation of the Ardaburii – personal enmity and the succession. Leo wanted his grandson, Leo II, to succeed him, with Zeno and Ariadne to act as regents, but Aspar's forcing of the elevation of Patricius to *Caesar* threatened the future of the Leonid dynasty. This attack on his family's future saw Leo take 'drastic pre-emptive action'.[87] This marks the bloody *conventus* as the culmination of 'a conventional dynastic rivalry amongst aristocratic families'.[88]

The murder of Aspar and his sons in 471 is usually explained as 'marking a decisive turning point in the fortunes of Roman imperial power in the fifth century'.[89] The lack of a Gotho-Isaurian rivalry not only alters the perception of the reign of Leo and the domination of Aspar, but also the understanding of the reign of Zeno, which becomes less a contest between sections of that Isaurian faction and more a series of 'divisions between two families and their political allies'.[90] While it seemed to secure the stability and future of the throne, the plot to remove Aspar saw the family of Verina elevated to a higher profile, with Basiliscus returning to court and Armatus achieving further prominence. This paved the way for another round of imperial musical chairs after Leo's death.[91]

The Migration of the Pannonian Goths

By the time Leo had brought Strabo back into the fold through negotiation in 473, the political scene in and around Constantinople was in the process of welcoming another new player – the Pannonian Goths. They were last heard from in the context of their war with the Scirii whilst they were still in Pannonia, but now they were looking to move closer to the centre of imperial power. The catalyst for that move may have been the return of the 18-year-old hostage, Theoderic the Amal. The timing of his return also may have been linked to the death of Valamir at the hands of the Scirii. This had seen Theodemir inherit Valamir's followers and his unofficial position as leader of the Pannonian Goths.[92] Theodemir's seemingly immediate promotion of Theoderic to some level of leadership represents the start of 'more deliberate moves to concentrate authority'.[93]

However, the death of Valamir may have occurred in the mid-460s, which would significantly reduce a dynastic element as a factor in Theoderic's departure from Constantinople. He may have been released from the capital as part of the political developments in 471 surrounding the demise of Aspar. Staying in the capital could have seen Theoderic caught in the anti-Aspar/Gothic crossfire, so Leo released him in the hope of keeping the Pannonian Goths on peaceful terms at a time when imperial forces were preoccupied with Strabo's rebellion. Conversely, Leo could have sent Theoderic home with a proposal to have the Pannonian Goths replace the Thracian Goths as the empire's go-to *foederati*.

Whatever the reasons behind his release, 'Theoderic's most immediate need was to establish some legitimacy as the son of his father and potential leader of the group'.[94] He therefore led a successful plundering raid against Sarmatians located near Singidunum, with or without his father's knowledge.[95] This strike towards Singidunum may reveal some grander Gothic ambitions. His time in Constantinople showed Theoderic 'the limitations of the Goths' current situation in Pannonia'.[96] Risking life and limb for the increasingly meagre scraps of the Attilan ascendancy did not appeal, certainly not compared to the vast tribute that the Thracian Goths received, which was seven times more than the 300lb of gold *per annum* that Valamir had obtained from Leo. The aftermath of the destruction of the Ardaburii provided the Amals with an opportunity to usurp Strabo's position. Pointedly, the Amals failed to return Singidunum to the Romans after they took it from the Sarmatians, and this may seem like the opening move in the risky gambit that Theoderic now proposed. Singidunum controlled the major routes into the eastern Balkans from Pannonia, and Theoderic may now have encouraged Theodemir to travel these routes in order to offer his Goths to Leo as *foederati*.

Probably in early 472, Theodemir took the momentous decision to move the entire Pannonian Goth 'nation' east. But persuading his father was only one of the obstacles facing Theoderic. While there had been some strides made in the centralization of the Amal monarchy, if the warrior class did not join the Amals in great numbers, the Pannonian Goths would be easy targets. Theoderic and Theodemir likely appealed to the martial pride of the warriors: they should follow in the footsteps of their forefathers who had migrated and won great victories. However, the downside was equally clear. While they might try to portray themselves as willing helpers for the empire, imperial authorities could easily view them as yet another barbarian invader looking to extort land and wealth – after all, that is exactly what they were – and the eastern army was still a formidable enough force. The likelihood of being welcomed with clenched fists rather than open arms unsurprisingly saw some dissent within the ranks. Pannonia, where they were their own masters, might be a harsh environment, but surely that was to be preferred to the death or oppression offered by facing the Roman army? For some, it was a risk not worth taking. This was a real test of the Amal leadership.

Here, the propaganda of Theoderic's later Italian court intervenes again. Through Cassiodorus, Jordanes records that the Gothic departure from Pannonia was caused by Theodemir being begged by his men to lead them somewhere, with the casting of lots sending Videmir west to Italy and Theodemir east towards Constantinople.[97] This was not only an attempt to hide the 'deeply predatory intent'[98] of the move from Pannonia, but also that it had led to a serious disagreement within the Gothic leadership. Videmir had no interest in moving, and his withholding of up to a third of the total Amal strength likely occasioned a definitive power struggle within the Pannonian Goths. Fighting cannot be ruled out, but Theodemir's seniority, Theoderic's recent victories at Singidunum, their combined strength surpassing that of Videmir and the opportunities offered by Constantinople swayed many of Videmir's followers to throw their lot in with the father/son duo. As will be seen later, Videmir did not retain enough men to pose any kind of threat to the mess that was Roman Italy in the mid-470s. Theodemir was now the undisputed leader of the Amal family, with Theoderic as his heir.[99] Their success can also be seen in the need for 2,000 wagons to contain all of their number and belongings. Theodemir and Theoderic did not just mobilize the warrior elite of their 'tribe' – they were taking virtually their entire group with them.[100]

Setting off through Singidunum in late summer 472, the Amal target was Thessalonica, the primary city of the prefecture of Illyricum. However, that was over 700 miles from Lake Balaton, a distance made harder by mountainous terrain, various settlements and enemies en route. The Sarmatians around Singidunum offered no resistance due to the threat of attack by the entire Amal force, and the Goths headed on towards the first real obstacle, the Roman-held city of Naissus. Despite being the birthplace of three emperors – Constantine I in c.272, Constantius III some time in the mid/late fourth century and the future Justin I in 450 – Naissus was not the thriving metropolis it had once been. Its very prosperity had made it a target for the barbarian raids of the fourth and fifth centuries. Its nadir had come in 443 when Attila wrought his particular brand of devastation on the city and the surrounding area. This is evident from the records of Priscus for 448:

> When we arrived at Naissus we found the city deserted, as though it had been sacked; only a few sick persons lay in the churches. We halted at a short distance from the river, in an open space, for all the ground adjacent to the bank was full of the bones of men slain in war.[101]

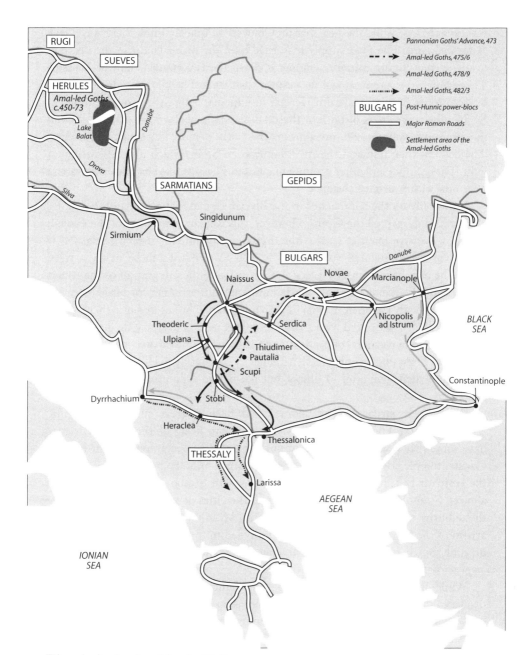

Theoderic the Amal in the Balkans

That Justin I was born in or near Naissus just two years after Priscus' grim assessment might suggest that Priscus was employing poetic licence, yet the city was likely still in a sorry state by the time the Amals approached in late 472. That they had little trouble occupying whatever remained of Naissus suggests that there was no garrison, while the fact that they moved on quickly hints there was a lack of farmed land. The food supply may have been the major factor in the decision to divide the Gothic column, sending it down the two routes south of Naissus. Theodemir led a column down the eastern pass, while Theoderic headed down the western route through Castrum Herculi to Ulpiana, before the group reunited at Scupi. The narrowness of both of these hill passes may also have played a part in the decision to split the column, allowing the Goths to move more quickly to Scupi. The column then followed the main highway to Stobi, which also fell without a fight. Thessalonica and other prominent cities in Thessaly like Heraclea and Larissa were now within striking distance.

It was only on the approaches to the Illyrian capital that a Roman force under Hilarianus intercepted the Goths. However, this Roman army was not big enough to deal a decisive blow, at least without risking unaffordably heavy casualties. If Hilarianus was appointed specifically by Leo to deal with these newly arrived Goths, he may have been given leeway to investigate the integration of the Amals as *foederati*. Hilarianus certainly needed imperial authorization for his subsequent negotiations with Theodemir, even though it is claimed he entered into them 'of his own accord'.[102] Confronted with a large force threatening to attack the praefectural capital, the Roman general offered gifts and land in the immediate vicinity in return for leaving Thessalonica unharmed. After gladly consenting to Hilarianus' proposal, Theodemir died soon after of illness, but not before appointing Theoderic as his successor.

While their strike at Thessalonica had been a great success in gaining Theodemir and Theoderic territory closer to the heart of the empire, it may have somewhat worked against them in their hopes of becoming a major force at Constantinople. By presenting Leo with another military problem, they forced the emperor to transfer troops from dealing with Strabo to Thessalonica. This allowed Strabo's men to raid freely 'among the cities of the Via Egnatia, burning the suburbs of Philippi and laying siege to Arcadiopolis'.[103] Inadvertently, the arrival of the Pannonian Goths had partially led to the restoration of the 2,000lb of gold annual payment to the Thracian Goths and a promotion of Strabo to *magister militum praesentalis*.[104]

While the Amal Goths had a good settlement in Thessaly, they had not displaced the Thracian Goths. On the surface then, Theodemir and Theoderic had only exchanged one tract of potential farming land for another. Thessaly was far less war-torn than Pannonia and had better trade links, but the Amals had made themselves a target. Leo may soon be directing Strabo to evict the new interlopers. However, appearances may be deceiving. By denying the Amals an annual subsidy, Leo may have been intentionally sowing discord between the two sets of Goths. As the empire could only pay one group, for Theoderic the Amal to achieve that annual payment would have to see the demotion of Strabo, setting the two barbarian groups on a political and military collision course.

His treaty with Leo demonstrates that Strabo was wary of the new arrivals, with stipulations such as he 'should be "sole ruler" of the Goths, and that the emperor should not give admission to anyone who wished to cross into his territory'.[105] Strabo had every reason to be alarmed given the nature of 'service' and membership of such tribal conglomerations. While there will have been family retainers of intense loyalty to the Amals and Strabo, the major part of such groups owed their loyalty to the man who could provide for them. The appearance of a second Gothic group gave many of these men further employment options beyond Strabo or the Roman army. Should Strabo show any weakness, he might soon find a steady trickle of his manpower heading for Thessalonica or Constantinople. Of course, the same can be said for Theoderic the Amal, and given his lack of an annual subsidy it was a problem that he was more likely to face. The result of such pressure would certainly encourage the Amal into a desperate act in 475, so it is very possible that in 473, Strabo was attempting to secure his position before the seemingly inevitable Amal strike. It is doubtful that this agreement of 473 will have held for long with Leo looking for an opportunity to have the two Gothic factions square off against one another to the benefit of the empire. However, fate intervened with the death of the emperor at the beginning of 474.

Chapter 7

A Father Succeeding his Son: The Making of *Flavius Zeno Augustus*

'After three years had passed, the Lord took the infant, the pious emperor Leo, into His eternal kingdom; and he went to the land of his fathers, and left the empire to his father.'

Vita Danielis Stylitae 67

Leo Iunior Augustus

With the Ardaburii dispatched and their Gothic allies largely contained, Leo could focus on ordering the imperial succession how he wanted. Fortunately for the emperor, despite the machinations of the Ardaburii, they had failed to terminate any of those in Leo's succession plans. The entire branch of the Leonid dynasty meant to take on imperial responsibilities upon Leo's death all escaped east in 469.[1] And it was now time to restore them to Constantinople. Given how little military help Zeno provided during and after the massacre of the Ardaburii, it could be that his recall from Antioch was more about who he was escorting back to the capital – Ariadne and Leo II. The removal of Patricius had left the empire without an obviously designated heir, so getting Leo II back to the capital as safely as possible to secure the dynasty will have been a priority. Zeno's subsequent tardiness in crossing over to Constantinople may therefore be less to do with his personal lack of popularity in the capital than a refusal to bring Leo II back to Constantinople until his safety was guaranteed.

The record of Leo II's short life is littered with chronological problems. Essentially, for the most basic outline of young Leo's life, we require three pieces of information – date of birth, age on death and date of death – and the sources only provide a reasonably secure date for the latter. This is only made worse by the lack of clarity on other events such as the date of his parents' marriage and Zeno's whereabouts, vocation and task when Leo II was born. It is left then to work backwards from what is the only reasonably secure date recorded for Leo II – that of his death in November 474. It is usually accepted that Leo was 7 years old when he died, meaning that he was born between December 466 and November 467 and conceived between March 466 and February 467. This is all based on Malalas being correct on Leo's age when he died;[2] however, there is an alternative reading. Malalas' phrase ὧν ἐνιαυτῶν ξ, could mean 'seventh year' rather than '7 years old'.[3] This would potentially place Leo's birth in 468. It is not completely clear if Malalas is listing complete years or the current year at the time of death, although when listing Anastasius' death at 90 years and 5 months, Malalas is speaking of years completed.[4] If it is the same with Leo II, then the young emperor was already 7 years old at his death.

This would place Zeno and Ariadne's wedding between January 466 and February 467, with it suggested that early in that period might be less likely due to the emergence of Zeno as a prominent player in Constantinople only in 465. His undermining of Ardaburius may not have been enough for Leo to immediately hand over his eldest child to Zeno. There may also have been the additional issue of Zeno's first wife, Arcadia, still being in the picture.[5] But this lack of time in the limelight should not necessarily dull the idea that Zeno and Ariadne tied the knot rather quickly. Given that Leo was keen to secure the succession and find allies against Aspar, there is a good chance that having settled on Zeno, the emperor heaped positions upon him all at once. Such a position brought not only power and prestige, but also pressure. Ariadne and Zeno needed to provide an heir as soon as possible, and given the age of Leo II on his premature demise, 'they appear to have obliged'.[6]

However, the entire idea of Leo II being 7 years old can be doubted. A more literal reading of the *Vita Danielis Stylitae* could suggest instead that Leo II was born in 471 and was therefore only 3 on his demise.[7] This is based on the suggestion that Daniel's biographer records the length of Leo II's life at three years rather than his reign, positing a marriage between Ariadne and Patricius in 468, a subsequent divorce before the demise of Aspar, the marriage of Ariadne and Zeno in 470, the birth of Leo II in 470/471 and then his death in 474 aged just 3.[8] This does not fit in with other chronological understandings, especially as it would have been strange for Zeno to have been 'still absent at the war' during the winter of 470. The only conflicts he was in any way involved in around this time – the 'protest' of Anagastes, the raiding of Indacus and the Tzani secession – were either over by 469 or did not involve Zeno leaving Antioch.[9] Any date in 469 for Zeno being 'still absent at the war' would make Leo II 4 or 5 upon his death in 474. However, this 'impossible interpretation appears to be based on a misguided quest to prove the literal chronological accuracy of every statement in Daniel's *vita* at any cost and in spite of any other testimony'.[10] Even more impossible is the claim by Procopius, which is surely an error, that Leo II was only a few days old when he succeeded his grandfather in 474 and therefore less than a year old when he died.[11] Despite attempts to promote alternatives, the prevailing interpretation is that after the marriage of Ariadne and Zeno in *c*.466, Leo II was born either in 466 or 467 and then died in November 474 at the age of 7.[12]

Regardless of his age, Leo I made it clear that he intended for his grandson to be his successor. However, it is not entirely clear when he enshrined this intention with a promotion to *Caesar*. Leo's advancing years and failing health,[13] as well as the shock at the continued power of Aspar, must have encouraged the emperor to solidify his succession plan; 'having struggled so long to secure his own succession, creating a *Caesar* from within his own family was a guarantee of imperial continuity, not to mention religious orthodoxy'.[14] Leo II's official elevation cannot have occurred before the deaths of Aspar and Ardaburius in 471. With the need for a clearly defined succession after the removal of Patricius, the elevation likely took place sometime in 472 after Zeno and his family crossed to Constantinople from Chalcedon. Leo may have initially planned to elevate Zeno to *Caesar*, so he could act as something of an imperial placeholder for his son. However, the populace were quick to make their dislike of that idea known. They did not believe in Zeno's Christological orthodoxy and did not like the idea of an Isaurian assuming the throne. There was even a massacre of Isaurians in the capital in around September/ October of 472, although the reason for this is not clear.[15] Leo had faced similar opposition over the elevation of Patricius, but the emperor could now make his own decisions and in this he listened to the public. With Zeno removed from contention, there was only one choice – the sole elevation of Leo II.[16]

The more usual attribution was to place Leo II's elevation in October 473, backed by the tradition of a newly elevated *Caesar* holding the consulship the following year and Leo II was consul in 474. However, much like with Patricius, if Leo was elevated late enough in 472, the consuls for 473 would already have been decided.[17] It 'would make better political sense'[18] for the elevation to take place earlier than October 473, with the combined testimony of Theodore Lector and Cedrenus, with some backing from Victor of Tunnuna, suggesting that Leo II was *Caesar* before November 472. An anecdote recalling Leo *Caesar* presiding over games in the Hippodrome when ash from a recent eruption of Vesuvius began to fall may also see the elevation moved to sometime in 472.[19]

However, the dating of this Vesuvian eruption has been disputed. Marcellinus Comes has it in 472, the *Chronicon Paschale* dates it to 469 while Theophanes puts it in 474.[20] Marcellinus is to be preferred over two such later chroniclers, but his date is not solid given the inconsistency of his dating system. If Marcellinus used the indiction system for the year of the Vesuvian eruption – 1 September 471 to 31 August 472 – over the consular year of Marcianus and Festus – 1 January to 31 December 472 – then the eruption may have been in the second half of 471. This encompasses a period which would be too early for the ash to fall on Constantinople in November 472, but provides the latitude for the eruption and therefore the games presided over by Leo *Caesar* before the end of 472.

Another issue with the source material is the lack of numismatic evidence. Given that there was no personal reason for Leo I not to have Leo II on coins as there was with Patricius, the lack of issues of Leo *Augustus* and Leo *Caesar* was perhaps because the younger Leo was only *Caesar* for a relatively short period of time.[21] The reason for this is depicted on coins – his elevation to *Augustus*. On those surviving issues, 'two emperors are enthroned and both are crowned, signifying that both are *Augusti*.[22] This is backed by Leo II's consular nomenclature as *Leo Iunior Augustus*, suggesting that he needed to be differentiated from the still alive Leo I. This intimates that Leo II was *Augustus* before the beginning of 474, going against the more usual idea that Leo II only became *Augustus* on the death of his grandfather in January 474.

There is another source of information about the elevation of Leo II which had long been overlooked – the *De caerimoniis* of Constantine VII Porphyrogenitus. It provides a template for the ceremony involved in the elevation of a *Caesar* to *Augustus*, including potentially that of Leo II. It was largely discarded due to its perceived inaccuracy on the position of Eusebius, *magister officiorum*, a position he may not have held until 474, and in its dating of the coronation to November in the consulship of Leo the Younger.[23] The problem with Eusebius being *magister officiorum* is that there is another well-attested man in this position at this time, Hilarianus. He was definitely *magister officiorum* on 27 March 470,[24] but a series of undated laws from the months when Leo II and Zeno were joint *Augusti* – 29 January to November 474 – list both Eusebius and Hilarianus as *magister officiorum*. The usual fix was to view Hilarianus as being in position from before March 470 through to the joint reign of Leo II and Zeno, and then being succeeded by Eusebius, removing any chance that Eusebius was in a position to oversee the elevation of Leo II to *Augustus* in late 473.

However, Hilarianus is also attested as *magister officiorum* under Zeno after November 474,[25] opening the door for him to have held that position twice, either side of Eusebius. It could be that Hilarianus' skills were needed elsewhere, such as leading an army in Illyricum against the Pannonian Goths.[26] Given that Basiliscus had Theoctistus as his *magister officiorum*, it would seem that Hilarianus held the position until the removal of Zeno in January 475. If Hilarianus held the office on two occasions, punctuated by a military command in Illyricum, then there was a gap for Eusebius to have served in that role from late 473 to sometime in 474, meaning that he could have overseen Leo II's elevation.

This possible explanation of one of the issues with this source provides some impetus then to investigate the more glaring error – the listing of the ceremony to elevate Leo II to *Augustus* in 474 during his sole consulship. This seems irreconcilable; however, the shared name of grandfather and grandson could have caused some textual problems. Perhaps μιχροῦ has been accidentally used in the *De caerimoniis* instead of μεγάλου. The former 'makes no sense ... [while the latter] makes perfect sense'[27] by placing the ceremony of 17 November in 'the consulship of Leo the Elder' in 473. It seems then that while fixing the errors in the *De caerimoniis* is not definitive, there is enough doubt to prevent its complete rejection.[28]

The potential restitution of *De caerimoniis* can therefore provide a detailed account of Leo II's elevation to *Augustus* on 17 November 473, while again hinting at Leo I's increasing age and infirmity. Under the guidance of Eusebius, who as *magister officiorum* oversaw the ceremony, officials, soldiers, ambassadors and the general population gathered in the Hippodrome. Cheered on by the populace and soldiery, Leo I appeared along with the Senate. Recognizing the difficulty the emperor was having with standing, the soldiers and people chanted 'sit down, we beg you', allowing the emperor to perform the ceremony while seated. Leo then dispatched Eusebius and some patricians to bring Leo II into the Hippodrome from the *triclinium*, where he had been waiting with patriarch Acacius. The imperial chamberlain, Urbicius, then presented Leo I with a crown to place on the head of the new *Augustus*, wishing him luck in his new role. Leo II was then acclaimed by the people and the soldiery, with the latter promised an accession donative of five *nummi* and a pound of silver.[29]

Leo II was now *Augustus*, although Leo I retained his seniority. The examples of child emperors in the fifth century – Arcadius, Honorius, Theodosius II and Valentinian III – had not been positive. All four had not been renowned for their leadership abilities, relying on their generals, officials and female relatives, allowing for the domination of men like Aetius, Ricimer and Aspar. Perhaps fortunately for the empire, Leo II had considerable support from within his own family: his father was an established general; his mother, Ariadne, was the eldest child of Leo I; his grandmother, Verina, was a formidable political operator in her own right; his aunt, Leontia, was married to the prominent politician Marcianus; his great uncle, Basiliscus, was senior *magister militum praesentalis*; and his first cousin once removed, Armatus, was *magister militum per Thracias*. On the surface then, it appears that the regime of Leo II was a closely knit family unit with natural allies in many prominent positions. However, this is to overlook the personal ambitions of all of those family members: Verina, Basiliscus, Armatus and Marcianus were to prove problematic for the main protector of the new regime – Leo II's father, Zeno.

Following his return to Constantinople, there is a lull in the record of Zeno's movements and role in the imperial hierarchy. It is possible that he did not hold any official position, aside from *patricius*, until he became *magister militum praesentalis* in 473/474. He is unlikely to have stayed as *comes domesticorum* after being forced to Antioch in 469, and he likely relinquished his position as eastern *magister* upon returning west in 471.[30] Even without an official position, it can be imagined that Zeno helped Leo re-establish his position in the aftermath of the butchery of the Ardaburii. Perhaps he was given a role in evaluating the loyalty of those within the imperial hierarchy, particularly when Leo meant for Zeno to have a prominent role within the regime of Leo II. However, the combination of racism, elitism, religious and pro-Aspar feeling meant Zeno remained unpopular in the capital, leaving him without an imperial position beyond father of the new *Augustus*.

The Death of the Butcher and the Accession of the Isaurian

If public dislike of Zeno had led to the shelving of a proposed promotion to *Caesar* in 472/473, it was to be put to the test again in early 474. Speculation surrounding the health of the emperor playing a role in the promoting of Leo II to *Augustus* was correct – *Flavius Valerius Leo Augustus* was dying. Leo I was not a young man; indeed, he seems to have been born in the first years of the fifth century, suggesting that he was perhaps 70 by 471. Therefore, while it might seem convenient to continually associate any decisive move of Leo with a personal fear of his impending end, it is a perfectly acceptable supposition. In the case of Leo II's elevation to *Augustus*, it could be entirely accurate. A little more than two months after the ceremony of 17 November 473, Leo the Butcher died of dysentery, aged 73.[31]

There is some dispute in the sources over the exact date of Leo I's death. Early 474 is agreed upon, but various dates in January and February are recorded: *Auctarii Hauniensis, Continuatio Hauniensis Prosperi ordo posterior* has 18 January; Theophanes reports January; the *Necrologium* suggests 30/31 January; and Cyril of Scythopolis notes that Leo died 'at the end of the first year after the death of the great Euthymius', whom he records as having died on 20 January 473. Malalas' date of 3 February may have been preferred in the past but may reflect the day that news of Leo's death reached Antioch, rather than the date it happened. This has seen the 18 January of the *Auctarii Hauniensis* become more prevalent as the date of Leo's death.[32]

Leo's reign had been a peculiar one. At over sixteen years, it provided the kind of stability that the contemporary western empire lacked, but for periods it also provided the same kind of disastrous hands-off approach of the Theodosian minors and Ricimer's puppets. Indeed, Leo is often portrayed as being solely the acquiescent puppet of Aspar right up until Zeno encouraged him to kill his master. Even if this picture of him is overplayed, it cannot be overlooked that Leo did owe his elevation entirely to Aspar. While his wife and in-laws would prove capable players of the game of thrones, they and Leo cannot have engineered his rise from one of several palatine commanders to *Augustus* in the face of Anthemius and Olybrius. There is no escaping that Leo became emperor because Aspar chose him.

However, Leo did prove that escaping Aspar's control was possible. Some of his actions represent not only his own growing freedom of action but also that he and/or those around him understood how social, cultural, religious and imperial politics could be used to differentiate his own position from that of the 'barbarian' Arian, Aspar. It is also not necessary to choose between the removal of the Ardaburii being the culmination of a decade-long plot or spur-of-the-moment attack brought on by desperation. The reality was likely a combination of both: Leo and his allies having worked to establish enough freedom of action to have Leo II recognized as the heir to the throne, only to be pushed into a final showdown after the Alan general orchestrated the quasi-exile of Basiliscus and Zeno and forced the elevation of Patricius to *Caesar*.

While his relations with Aspar have come to characterize the reign of Leo, there are at least three other aspects which were just as important – his pro-Chalcedonian religious policies, the Vandal expedition and that for all his supposed ruminating over the succession, his death left a 6-year-old as sole emperor. Zeno's reign would be plagued by the religious distractions, military weakness and political vulnerability caused by these actions. His error over the succession, specifically the position of Zeno, was immediately addressed upon his death. While Leo might have made known his wish for Zeno and Ariadne to act as regents for Leo II, his caving in to supposed Constantinopolitan opinion on Zeno meant that there was a lack of legitimacy to this regency. This gap was soon filled.

As little as a fortnight into the sole reign of Leo II, the young *Augustus* had his father Zeno crowned; and not as *Caesar* but as *Augustus*. It is not all that surprising that Zeno would be elevated to the same position as his son. If it was felt that Zeno required a boost in popularity, loyalty and legitimacy, how better to achieve that than to make him *Augustus*? If this promotion was linked to Zeno's ability to command respect as the imperial regent of Leo II, could Ariadne perhaps have been promoted to Augusta at this time in 474? There may be some AEL ARIA-DNE AVG *solidi* dateable to this period, although they may belong much later in Zeno's reign or even to that of Anastasius.[33] If both Zeno and Ariadne were meant to be regents and being seen to make decisions for Leo II, then their lower rank than an enthroned *Augustus* may have appeared as a breach of protocol. Zeno's elevation may also demonstrate an acceptance of the realities of infant mortality. The imperial family had already been faced with the tragedy of the death of Leo and Verina's infant son, and Leo II was by no means out of the reach of a young death. Given how the year 474 would play out, perhaps it was perceived that Leo II was a frail little boy.[34]

In keeping with the negative spin surrounding Zeno, it was claimed that the crowning of the Isaurian came through the manipulation of Leo II, who placed the crown on his father's head by accident, trickery or 'against custom'.[35] However, an existing emperor placing the crown on his chosen imperial colleague was hardly against practice, and Zeno had little reason to manipulate his son when he had almost complete control over him. If there had been any public voicing of dislike of Zeno, he will have wanted his elevation to be as legitimate as possible. 'The more likely version is that it was a properly planned public ceremonial',[36] with Leo II crowning his father in the Hippodrome with the agreement of the Senate, patriarch Acacius and the *magister officiorum*, Eusebius, before Zeno then promised the usual accession donative to the military.

Even with the suggestion of an official, public ceremony, the entire notion of Zeno becoming co-*Augustus* could still have been his own idea. However, there were several prominent groups and individuals who felt that not only should Leo II have a regent but that Zeno was 'the most appropriate man to handle this task'.[37] The only other potential candidates would have been from amongst the imperial family, and with Basiliscus still somewhat sidelined and Armatus deployed in Thrace that left Ariadne and Verina. The Theodosian dynasty had shown that strong women could be promoted to positions of regency but as they were still women, not to be trusted above men. This left Zeno as the straightforward choice.

His elevation could also have been on the initiative of the imperial family, specifically Ariadne, and the Constantinopolitan Senate. Senators are also recorded voicing worry over the age of Leo II, who was young enough to be ineligible to sign the documents needed of an emperor, determining 'that his father Zeno should hold the sceptre of the empire'.[38] The sheer idea that Zeno had a public coronation also demonstrates the support of his family and the Senate, as Ariadne, Verina and senators all took part.[39]

It was long held that Zeno's accession took place on 9 February following Malalas,[40] but as with Leo's death, it has been questioned whether Malalas was recording the date of the elevation or the date that news of it arrived in Antioch. An alternative date comes from the continuation of *Auctarium Haunensis Prosperi*: the fourth day of the Kalends of February – 29 January.[41] Depending on the dates used, the period of Leo II's sole rule was between six and twenty-two days, and even from such a short period, there were two identifiable coin issues. One set shows the boy emperor holding a globe and standing on a low platform; a second, seemingly later set removes the platform.[42] From the elevation of Zeno, both father and son are displayed as *Augusti* but it is the son who is presented as senior emperor, which is unsurprising considering that it is through his maternal bloodline that his right to rule came. Despite being Leo's father and Ariadne's husband, Zeno had no real right to rule at all. A similar portrayal of this superiority of the Leonid line is displayed in their joint laws – '*Impp. Leo (Iunior) et Zeno AA*' – Leo II always appearing first.[43]

The Death of Leo II

Son and father ruled jointly for much of the rest of 474, likely with Zeno taking charge behind the scenes, while the young Leo provided the numismatic, legislative and public face of the regime. It can also be imagined that Zeno, Ariadne and other members of the imperial family and hierarchy were taking the initial steps in Leo's education, preparing him politically, militarily and ceremonially for what could have been a reign of half a century or more. But any such preparation would not bear dynastic fruit, for before 474 was out, Constantinople was in imperial mourning again.

The joint reign of son and father lasted just ten months, with Leo II perhaps barely making it through a full year as *Augustus*. He was still alive on 10 October 474 when a law was issued in his name,[44] but 'in the eleventh month of his consulship … in the month of November of the thirteenth indiction, in the year 523 according to the era of Antioch',[45] *Leo Iunior Augustus* fell ill and died. Unlike previous occasions, there is much less reason to take issue with Malalas here as he is very clear, citing not just the Julian, indiction and Antiochene dates, but also his source in the lost chronicle of Nestorianus, who ended his history with the death of Leo II. Both

Theodore Lector and Theophanes back up this dating of November 474 by stating that Leo ruled with his father for ten months – January to November.[46]

The circumstances of Leo's demise seem similarly clear – some form of illness, a not uncommon occurrence at any stage of human history.[47] That said, the young Leo was in a vulnerable position, surrounded by ambitious individuals and those who would like to see his father wield significantly less power at court. The actions of Verina and Basiliscus in the wake of Leo's demise could be used to fuel rumours of their involvement in dispatching the boy emperor either to weaken Zeno or to improve their own imperial ambitions. There were also rumours that his own parents, Zeno and Ariadne, had something to do with Leo II's disappearance from public view to secure Zeno's grip on power. Victor of Tunnuna records that Ariadne, fearing for the life of her son, with Zeno identified as the threat, spirited Leo II away to a local church, replacing him with a doppelgänger, whom Zeno later had murdered. So successful was Ariadne in hiding her son that he survived until the reign of Justinian (527–565).[48] For such a curious story to appear in an otherwise trustworthy *Chronicle* suggests that Victor had at least some basis for it.[49] Perhaps there was a former boy-emperor serving in the church by the time of Justinian's reign: there was such a candidate in the form of Basiliscus, son of Armatus. He was elevated to *Caesar* as part of the deal which saw Armatus abandon his allegiance to Basiliscus in favour of Zeno in 476. When Zeno then removed Armatus, he was left with a young co-emperor. Rather than have the young boy killed, Zeno had him enrolled as a reader in the Blachernae Church on the Golden Horn, perhaps on the intervention of Ariadne on behalf of her young relative.[50]

Sending deposed emperors to churches was something of a trend in the mid/late fifth century – the western *Augusti*, Avitus and Glycerius, were made bishops of Placentia in 456 and Salona in 474 respectively. Basiliscus *Caesar* was later recorded as a highly capable bishop of Cyzicus. Exactly how long Basiliscus had remained at Blachernae or when he became bishop of Cyzicus is unknown. But given how it was expected that a bishop could not be elected until his 30th birthday, and how Basiliscus *Caesar* was likely not much more than 6 years old in 476, he would not have become bishop until the very last years of the fifth century. To then make it to the reign of Justinian, he would have to have lived until his mid-50s, which was hardly a big stretch, even in the ancient world.[51]

This might suggest that Basiliscus *Caesar* could have been the origin of this rumoured fate of Leo II, but it still seems like a big misidentification for Victor of Tunnuna to make. Or does it? During the joint reign of Leo II and Zeno, their coinage bore the legend DN LEO ET ZENO AVG. All of a sudden though, coins appear with DN ZENO ET LEO NOV CAES, leading to all kinds of questions about the nature of Leo II's reign.[52] The solution to this problem was to highlight that this LEO NOV CAES was not Leo II but someone else. One suggestion was that DN ZENO ET LEO NOV CAES were otherwise unrecorded sons of Basiliscus *Augustus*,[53] who ruled alongside his eldest son Marcus. Basiliscus is recorded as having had other offspring, and 'Zeno' and 'Leo' would be appropriate 'names for sons of the husband of Zenonis and brother of Leo I's widow'.[54] However, the sources do not mention any other *Caesares* of Basiliscus.[55]

These DN ZENO ET LEO NOV CAES coins are also not clear on what they depict in terms of the imperial title of each individual – was DN and CAES to be applied to both? The latter appears singular, with CAESS more likely when applied to *Caesares*, which seems to make the coin apply to a *Caesar* called Leo and a *dominus noster* called Zeno. This cannot apply to Leo II and Zeno but to the only other time when Zeno shared imperial power, and that was with the son of Armatus, who is also known as Leo Basiliscus. The similarity of name, age and sharing of imperial power with Zeno must have seen the stories of both boy-emperors converge, with the less well-known Leo Basiliscus' life subsumed by that of Leo II, 'to explain the continuing presence of an erstwhile boy-emperor named Leo'.[56]

Regardless of these rumours, had Zeno, Basiliscus or someone else done away with Leo II, much more would be expected from the sources about the murder of an emperor. It is very unlikely that Zeno would be involved in the removal of his son, as Leo II represented his best link to imperial legitimacy. Getting rid of him would have seriously undermined his position. The likelihood then was that Leo II died quite suddenly of an illness in November 474. His place of burial is not recorded, but has been suggested as being alongside his imperial predecessors in the Church of the Holy Apostles and perhaps even in the green Thessalian marble tomb of Leo I. He had been emperor in various guises – *Caesar* under Leo I from no later than October 472; co-*Augustus* with Leo I from 17 November 473; sole *Augustus* from 18 January 474; and then co-*Augustus* with Zeno from 29 January 474 until his demise in November 474, leading to the recording of him dying in his third regnal year.[57]

This raised some questions over what was entailed in these 'three regnal years'. The solution came from the moving of Leo's initial elevation from 473 to 472 and counting his stint as *Caesar* as part of his reign. Leo II's third year as an emperor may only have been a couple of weeks old by November 474; he may even have been ill over the anniversary of his elevation, but in Roman inclusive counting, his reign was three years old.[58] Malalas also provides some problems over the length of Leo II's reign by stating that 'after the reign of Leo the Elder, Leo the Younger ruled for one year and twenty-three days'.[59] Leo II only ruled as *Augustus* for around ten months after Leo I's death in early 474, and it was likely just over two years between his first assumption of imperial power as *Caesar* in around November 472 and his death in November 474. It seems that Malalas has counted Leo II's time as *Augustus* from November 473 until his death as being 'one year and twenty-three days', which is possible given the lack of exact dates. In suggesting that the reign of Leo I ended at the beginning of that of Leo II, Malalas is either making a mistake or he means to suggest that Leo I's sole reign ended on the elevation of Leo II in November 473.[60]

The death of Leo II left sole power in the hands of Zeno, one of the few times in history where a father has succeeded his son. While a peculiar scenario, this was the natural order of succession and it should have boosted the security and strength of the imperial throne as a frail minor had been replaced by an experienced general. However, the removal of Aspar had left a power vacuum that the aging, unwell Leo, the underage Leo II and the unpopular, barely legitimate Zeno were unable to fill completely. Had Zeno been the last survivor of the Leonid faction, his succession would have been better received, but there were not only several allies of Leo and enemies of Zeno still in prominent positions, there were also several members of the imperial family – Verina, Basiliscus and Armatus – who were ambitious enough to take advantage of Zeno's lack of popularity and legitimacy.

As the usurpation against Zeno, dated to 9 January 475,[61] happened less than two months after his assumption of sole power, this might suggest that it was more a spontaneous outburst than a well-planned move. However, it could be the exact opposite.[62] The final illness of Leo II might have triggered the move, but if Leo II was known to be a sickly child, Verina's family may have been planning Zeno's removal long in advance of his assumption of power. It could even be that they would have sought his removal even if Leo II had not died young. Clearly, the imperial family did not like the idea of power resting in the hands of Zeno as father of the emperor. They liked the idea of supreme power passing to him even less.

Chapter 8

A Brief Imperial Interlude:
The Usurpation of Basiliscus

'My family is my strength and my weakness.'

Aishwarya Rai Bachchan

The Meddling Mother-in-Law and her Ambitious Brother

The death of Leo II in November 474 left his father vulnerable. Zeno was still married to Ariadne, but without his son he had been shorn of a significant part of his legitimacy. It was not long before his enemies sprung into action, initiating whatever plots they had planned to remove the Isaurian. Due to the speed with which Zeno's position collapsed in early 475, there must still have been ill-feeling towards him from various political, military, social and religious hierarchies within Constantinople. There were not only members of the imperial family – Basiliscus, Verina, Armatus and their in-laws like Zuzus and Leontia's husband, Marcianus – but also Theoderic Strabo, Illus and his brother, Trocundes.[1]

The leader of the Thracian Goths was more than eager to join a plot to remove Zeno. Not only did he suspect Zeno of connivance in the murder of Aspar, but also following the death of Leo I, Zeno had taken control of many of the political and financial affairs at Constantinople. This perhaps saw him fiddle with the fiscal agreements made between Leo I and Strabo. That said, Zeno will also have recognized that his position was far from secure, so he is unlikely to have risked provoking Strabo. Indeed, hostilities between Strabo and Zeno did not erupt immediately upon the latter's accession. There was time for Strabo to capture the *magister militum per Thracias*, Heracleius, and an exchange of letters to arrange Heracleius' ransom and release. Conflict broke out upon the subsequent murder of Heracleius at Arcadiopolis.[2] With Theoderic the Amal somewhat content around Thessalonica, the Roman field forces under the command of Illus concentrated on Strabo and prevented a repeat of the damage done in 471-73. It can be no surprise then that Theoderic Strabo threw in with the plotters looking to remove Zeno from power. While Illus' position at Constantinople demonstrates the extent to which some Isaurians had become entrenched in the capital, his willingness to side against Zeno undermines the idea of a united Isaurian bloc, as well as any anti-Isaurian motive. The support of Marcianus has also been suggested as indicating some senatorial and even non-Isaurian, non-Gothic military support for the revolt.[3]

Zeno surely recognized the weakening of his position entailed in the death of his son, but the palace coup in the earliest days of 475 took him largely by surprise as he was forced to slip out of Constantinople, effectively giving up the imperial title without a fight. That the coup seems to have originated in Heraclea gave Zeno sufficient time to escape, with his ability to again evade danger perhaps leading to the suggestion that a deformity made Zeno a runner 'beyond human measure'.[4] Within days of Zeno's flight from the capital, Basiliscus was proclaimed emperor, his son, Marcus, was made *Caesar* and his wife, Zenonis, Augusta on 9 January 475 at Hebdomon Palace by palace officials, the Senate and representatives of the army. Recognition from the provinces and the West soon followed.[5]

However, while this seems like a straightforward redistribution of power within the imperial family, it was quickly proven to have been anything but. There is lack of agreement over who the leader of this plot was and who the preferred candidate to replace the absconding Zeno was. The likelihood is that Verina and Basiliscus plotted together, and it was always the plan for Basiliscus to assume the imperial mantle.[6] The rapidity of his coronation and the smoothness of the transition highlight that there was only one plot taking place in the first week of 475. The seeming origins of the coup in Heraclea,[7] where Basiliscus had spent much of the previous six years, may hint at his centrality. His military experience may have helped bring in Illus and Trocundes, and the support of the rest of the imperial family may well have come as power shifted to Zeno with the death of Leo II. Verina may even have crowned Basiliscus herself.[8] This would not be the only time that Verina would crown a challenger to Zeno.

There is an alternative narrative which focuses less on Basiliscus and more on Verina as the focal point of anti-Zenoid sentiment.[9] This story sees Verina, unsatisfied with being an imperial widow, mother-in-law or sister, hoping to use the connections she had made over years by the side of Leo I to broker power and place her new lover, Patricius, on the throne.[10] He had been a trusted ally of Leo I, having served as his *magister officiorum* and been the man to read out the treasonous letters of Ardaburius to the consistory.[11] If Verina had planned to elevate Patricius, she failed spectacularly. The ambitious Basiliscus either thoroughly outmanoeuvred his sister or took advantage of any hesitation or reticence in the implementing of Patricius' elevation.

However, this story seems less likely than Verina and Basiliscus working together to ensure his appointment. It hinges on a widowed empress not only thinking herself influential enough to unseat a ruling *Augustus* but to then bestow the imperial title on a non-imperial individual like Patricius. There are also issues with the portrayal of Verina. Her relationship with Zeno is far from clear in the sources. She backed him during the brief reign of her grandson, Leo II, reputedly warned Zeno of the incipient palace coup which deposed him and then provided financial aid in his attempts to regain the throne;[12] hardly the type of relationship which would see her leading a plot to unseat Zeno. While this pro-Zeno Verina may be an attempt by some sources to restore her reputation, the negative power-hunger of Verina may itself be more a reflection of the hostility of Candidus and John of Antioch rather than an accurate depiction of her actions in late 474 or early 475.

Even with the downplaying of Patricius as the intended imperial candidate of Verina, he does appear as an important figure in the souring of relations between Verina and the three main players in early 475. There is a reported falling out between Verina and Zeno, caused by the emperor refusing a request made by the widowed empress, which could explain a sudden shift in her support from him to another candidate. The nature of that request is not recorded, but it could be that Verina asked permission to wed Patricius. It could be that her anger over this snub was taken advantage of by Illus, who promised to bring about the elevation of Patricius in return for Verina's support for the removal of Zeno.[13] The Isaurian general went back on whatever promise he made by backing the coronation of Basiliscus, which was to have grave consequences for Patricius, who was executed by the new *Augustus*.[14] This earned Illus the deep-seated enmity of Verina. The execution of Patricius would also provide a reason for any falling out between Verina and Basiliscus beyond him potentially usurping her own attempted usurpation.

Even if Basiliscus was always the intended recipient of the throne, there may be other reasons too for the siblings falling out. Perhaps Basiliscus had failed to live up to promises he had made to Verina, such as recognition of any relationship with Patricius or a prominent position at court, repaying her with Patricius' execution and Zenonis *Augusta* perhaps overshadowing her sister-in-law. Verina may have disliked Basiliscus' anti-Chalcedonian policies. This is predicated on Verina holding the same strong Chalcedonian views as Leo.[15] Even if she did not hold strong religious views, Verina could have used the unpopularity of Basiliscus' policies as a convenient excuse to abandon her allegiance to him.[16] Outmanoeuvred, tricked, betrayed or opportunistic, Verina may have begun to plot the return of Zeno almost immediately, and when this was revealed, she was forced to take refuge in a Blachernae church and was saved only by the intervention of Armatus.[17]

Despite the smooth transition of power to Basiliscus, there remained a problem for the plotters to face – Zeno was still at large. He had managed not only to escape Constantinople with a small cadre of followers, but cross to Chalcedon and set out across Anatolia, with Ariadne seemingly joining him via a perilous sea voyage.[18] If Zeno had hoped that the eastern field army would back him, allowing him to make Antioch his base, he was let down and had to retreat to one of the mountain redoubts in Isauria. This was a peculiar situation, one with little precedent in the five centuries of Roman autocracy. Men had laid down the imperial title before, but this was an emperor shorn of his power but able to escape execution to fight on for his crown.

The new regime immediately sent Illus and Trocundes to Isauria to flush out the deposed *Augustus*. The location of Zeno's redoubt is not certain, although Theophanes records it as Sbide, possibly a small town north of Germanicopolis, about 10km from Zenonopolis.[19] Regardless of where it was, archaeological surveys of Cilicia and the Taurus Mountains[20] provide a basic outline of what Illus and Trocundes faced – 'high walls on top of a bare mountainous crag … well supplied by cisterns with water, and with lots of hidden ways of getting food inside at odd moments, these fastnesses were essentially impregnable'.[21] But for all that Illus and Trocundes could not get in, Zeno could not get out. Without a colossal change of luck, he would die in that redoubt. Fortunately for Zeno, a colossal change in luck is exactly what he got.

On the surface though, what happened next in Isauria seems like Zeno's luck had only become worse. A year into their attempted blockade, in the spring of 476, Illus and Trocundes captured Longinus, Zeno's brother.[22] It might be expected that the Isaurian generals would have executed Longinus or threatened to in order to induce Zeno to surrender. However, demonstrating the fluidity of loyalty in the face of opportunity, they decided that Longinus was far more useful to them as leverage. The rule of Basiliscus and his unfulfilled promises might also have encouraged the Isaurians to switch sides – they may already have been in talks with Zeno[23] – but the capture of Longinus made them take the plunge, calling Zeno down from his fortress and marching back to Constantinople to put him back on the throne.

'How to Make Enemies of Friends and Alienate People' – The Reign of Basiliscus

There were still substantial obstacles in the way of the Isaurian trio, particularly as the reign of Basiliscus had gotten off to a strong start. He had support from several different factions, institutions and individuals – the Senate, palace officials, Strabo, Illus, Armatus and Verina. The defection of the Isaurian generals does not seem to represent a massive shift in power away from Basiliscus *Augustus*. However, the usurper's honeymoon period had come to a rather abrupt end as unfulfilled promises and his own actions alienated virtually all of his supporters.

As already seen, Verina may have turned against him, either through his stealing of the throne, his execution of Patricius, his policies or broken promises. It is also suggested that Zeno had been able to take a significant portion of the imperial treasury with him. Given the financial promises Basiliscus made to various parties, finding funds severely depleted was an enormous, perhaps fatal, setback to his nascent regime. Basiliscus also found that several of his promises were incompatible. Essentially, he had four military backers – Strabo, Armatus, Illus and Trocundes – and only two positions to offer as *magister militum praesentalis*. In choosing to give these top positions to Strabo and Armatus, he may have begun the alienation of the Isaurian brothers at a time when he expected them to deal with Zeno, a snub possibly exacerbated by his sharing of the consulship of 476 with Armatus.[24]

Despite having been in revolt, Theoderic Strabo was brought back into the imperial fold on the accession of Basiliscus. Along with his restoration as *magister*, Basiliscus

also gave Strabo various unnamed honours, wealth and property in the capital.[25]
Presumably any suspension or alteration of the annual subsidy to his Thracian Goths
made by Zeno was reversed, restoring these Goths as imperial *foederati*. Despite that,
Strabo was still not happy, for unlike with Leo in 473, Basiliscus refused to promote
him to senior praesental commander. That position went instead to Armatus, who
Strabo personally despised. Rumours abounded that Zenonis, the wife of Basiliscus,
coaxed her husband to pick Armatus as consul and senior *magister militum* because
she and Armatus were lovers.[26] Regardless of such rumours, it made sense that
the imperial family would promote one of its own as head of the army given the
expectation of loyalty from Armatus. But such an expectation would soon be proven
ill-judged, while Strabo was none too happy about having been 'surpassed in honour
by a young man who thought only of his hair and attending to his body'.[27]

Despite this snub, Strabo may have increased his court influence by having
various Goths placed within the Roman military hierarchy, the palace guards, the
scholae and the Constantinopolitan garrison. Such aspersions must be treated with
caution as they come from a speech made by Zeno after his restoration and in the
run-up to a proposed war against Strabo. Indeed, he went as far as to claim that the
Thracian Goth 'persuaded Basiliscus to disband the army on the grounds that they
were sufficient by themselves'.[28] While such a claim is clearly an exaggeration, there
was likely some basis for Zeno to make such a propagandist leap.[29]

Perhaps, given his wish to succeed Aspar and his icy reception of Armatus'
seniority, Strabo was laying the groundwork for the assumption of an Ardaburii-like
position of influence at Constantinople based on his Gothic troops being in prominent
positions. It would be common, perhaps even expected, that a power player such as a
magister militum would have placed his men in influential, strategic positions. Aspar
had done it; Zeno would do it; why would Strabo not have tried to do so?[30] Any such
reinfiltration of Goths into the corridors of power may not have been all that well-
received by some and could have reflected badly on Basiliscus himself. The people
may also have been unimpressed by a growing Gothic presence in the city, while the
increasing number of Arian Goths will have irked the Church.

Basiliscus and the *Encyclical*

In the midst of this alienation of various parts of his own support, Basiliscus and
Zenonis stepped into the arena that had been the graveyard of many an imperial
reputation – religion. The mid-fifth-century dispute was largely, although certainly
not solely, focused on the findings of the Council of Chalcedon, convoked by
Marcian in 451, which in Christological terms found that Jesus had both human
and divine natures. Opponents of this formula believed that the human and divine
characters of Christ were inseparably combined in a single nature, and were
sometimes called Miaphysites from the Greek μία, meaning 'one' or 'single'. and
φύσις, meaning 'nature'.

But this less than straightforward division does not tell the whole story. There were Nestorians, who believed that the divine and human natures in Christ were so distinct as to be almost two separate people inhabiting the same body, a belief condemned at Ephesus in 431. There was also Eutychianism, which stressed that Christ's divine nature overcame his human one, but in so doing created a new blended nature, a belief condemned at Chalcedon in 451. There was also Monophysitism, itself rejected at Ephesus and Chalcedon, a perhaps more over-arching term from μόνος, meaning 'only' or 'one', and φύσις, that saw Jesus as having a single nature, either divine or a combination of divine and human. Chalcedonians were quick to lump followers of a 'single nature' doctrine together with Eutychianism under the name 'monophysite', which became a disparaging moniker regardless of its aptness as a descriptor of their Christology. Similarly, these 'monophysites' lumped Chalcedonians and Nestorians together under the term 'dyophysite' or simply called them all Nestorians.

While Chalcedonian orthodoxy was the official Christology, anti-Chalcedonianism had significant support in the East, particularly amongst the people of Egypt and Syria as opposed to the ruling elites. So forcefully held were such beliefs that they frequently led to significant unrest in the provinces between the different adherents, especially when the imperial government attempted to intervene and impose whichever doctrine it was supporting at the time. Clearly, it was a religious and political quagmire, one that, as emperor, Basiliscus (and later Zeno) would have to face up to at some point, although he would probably have looked to steer clear so early in his reign as it could only invite trouble.

Unfortunately for Basiliscus, the dispute landed right on his doorstep in the spring of 475 courtesy of his newly appointed *magister officiorum*, Theoctistus. An Alexandrian native, Theoctistus supported the anti-Chalcedonian wish to have the banished Timothy Aeleurus restored as patriarch, and provided a group of Alexandrian monks, including his own brother Theopompus, with an imperial audience.[31] It has been suggested that the monks would not have travelled without some assurance of an audience, which could lend credence to the idea that they set off upon word of Basiliscus' accession. The idea of contact between the regime of Basiliscus and the supporters of Timothy leading to this delegation could be bolstered by the presence of Theopompus. The fact that he was the brother of the newly appointed *magister officiorum* could be too much of a 'simple coincidence'.[32]

However, coincidences do happen, and as the death of Leo II, the accession of Zeno and the usurpation of Basiliscus had all happened in the winter months when the sea lanes were closed, any journeys to and from Alexandria will have taken at the longer end of nine to twenty days.[33] Therefore, so early in Basiliscus' reign did these monks arrive that they probably intended to petition Zeno, hoping that the seeming end of the Leonid dynasty meant an end of imperial support for Chalcedon, only to arrive after the coup of early 475.[34] It was only through serendipity that Theoctistus became *magister officiorum* and played a prominent role in the religious policies of

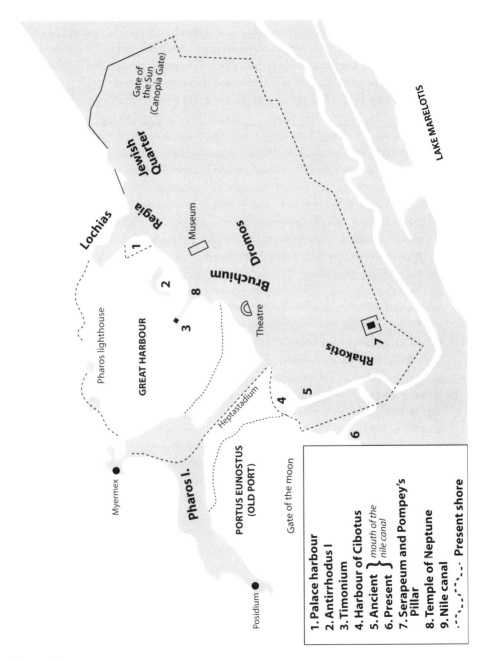

Alexandria

the new regime, allowing his brother and fellow monks to gain an audience with Basiliscus.[35] There was another individual recorded as having a strong influence on Basiliscus' religious policies – his wife, Zenonis. She had connections to the Eutychian monks who remained in or near Constantinople.[36] However, as with any women appearing in a position of power and influence, caution must be taken as Roman sources are not above painting Zenonis in a negative light in order to explain away the unpopular actions of the men she had influence over.

In focusing on Theoctistus, the Alexandrian monks or Zenonis as influencing religious policy, it can be easy to overlook the most important opinion of them all – that of Basiliscus himself. So far, the major events of his career have been accompanied with a reason to explain why Basiliscus was not in control of his own destiny: being Leo's brother-in-law saw him appointed *magister*; the machinations of Aspar saw to the debacle of the Vandal expedition; Verina led the plot to oust Zeno; and now it was his wife and *magister officiorum* who were formulating his religious policies. All of this overlooks the potential cunning of the new emperor. If he had no role in orchestrating these events, then he is perhaps one of the most fortunate men to ever find himself on the imperial throne. His machinations might not have always worked out, but he had brought together many disparate factions to clothe himself in imperial purple. It would therefore be unwise to overlook his own beliefs and calculations over the formulation of his policies.

So was Basiliscus a staunch anti-Chalcedonian? It is difficult to ascertain his beliefs from his actions. Negotiating and working with the supporters of Timothy does not make Basiliscus himself one of those doctrinal supporters. He may have just seen Timothy, Theopompus and the Alexandrian monks as a way to bring stability to Egypt, with its tax base and grain. Such a determination to win over Egypt may have been why Basiliscus quickly sent word to Alexandria about his accession, leading to the fast arrival of the delegation of Theopompus.[37] Whatever the circumstances of their arrival in the capital, the Alexandrian monks were not to be disappointed. Against the objections of patriarch Acacius,[38] Basiliscus had Timothy Aeleurus restored to the Alexandrian see after sixteen years of exile, while Peter the Fuller was reinstated to Antioch.[39] These recalls did not go down well in orthodox Constantinople, but would not be all that troublesome if Basiliscus had just left it at that.

Instead, he continued to listen to the anti-Chalcedonians around him, marking a sea change in the religious direction of the imperial government. Throughout March 475, Basiliscus' advisers and new Christological allies, led by Paul the Sophist and the recently returned Timothy,[40] produced a document which was to demonstrate the true extent of that *volte face* and go a significant way in restricting the length of Basiliscus' reign. On 9 April 475, Basiliscus issued a circular letter, known as an *Encyclical*, which confirmed the decisions of the Council of Constantinople in 381 and First Ephesus in 431, but focused on the creed promulgated by the Council of Nicaea in 325 as 'the only *Credo* free of errors'.[41] Chalcedon and the *Tome* of

Pope Leo were condemned, any copies were to be burned and the decisions of the Second Council of Ephesus of 449 were to be restored. Despite not setting out a Christological definition of its own, the *Encyclical* was clearly putting forward the traditions of Alexandria.[42]

Three separate versions of this important document have survived – a summary by Ps-Zacharias and the full texts of Evagrius and the *Vaticanus Graecus*. However, it is not clear which is the closest to the original as there are differences between them.[43] Is the text of Evagrius slightly watered down? Is the *Vaticanus Graecus* version the result of the slightly later Synod of Ephesus? Does Ps-Zacharias report the gist of the original *Encyclical*, complete with reference to the Second Council of Ephesus, which was later removed following negotiations with Acacius?[44]

The *Encyclical* is important not just for its transforming of imperial religious policy and the damage it did to Basiliscus' reign, but also for the relations between the Roman state and the Christian Church. This was an imperial edict directly interfering with the articles of faith agreed at a Council; worse still, the *Encyclical* was not enshrining the decisions of a synod or council in law, but those of an imperial appointee, and contained considerable legal penalties for those who refused to accept it. Bishops and priests were faced with deposition, 'while monks and laymen would be threatened with banishment, property confiscations, or even [the] death penalty'.[45] The *Encyclical* seemed like it could be establishing something akin to caesaropapism (with the head of state also the head of the church) in eastern religious politics.

The incumbent anti-Chalcedonian regimes in Syria and Egypt welcomed the *Encyclical*, while the imperial capital was in uproar.[46] The utter horror of Constantinople did not stop some sources from trying to distort that reception. Not for the first time or the last, the doctrines of Acacius and his reaction to the *Encyclical* were misrepresented, with claims that the patriarch initially supported the anti-Chalcedonianism of the new regime, supposedly offering lodgings in Hagia Irene to Timothy Aeleurus. The subsequent falling out was not due to any dogmatic differences but because Acacius feared being replaced as patriarch by Theopompus. There is some hint of doctrinal disagreement, with Paul the Sophist being unsuccessful in persuading Acacius to sign up to the *Encyclical*.[47] Furthermore, Acacius was not far wrong in any concerns he had over being deposed. Rumours circulated of an official council being called in Jerusalem for late 475 for the purpose of deposing Acacius and replacing him with Theopompus.[48]

The likelihood is that not only was Acacius not a supporter of the *Encyclical*, he was actively against it and the policies of Basiliscus from the very start. Any depiction otherwise is almost certainly part of the attempts to show Acacius' differences with Timothy Aeleurus and Peter the Fuller in terms of anything other than their beliefs. As Basiliscus and his doctrinal allies were proven to be far less popular than was originally assumed, Acacius became more overt in his opposition, ordering the closure of all Constantinopolitan churches to Timothy. The remaining supporters of Eutyches in the capital also made Aeleurus feel unwelcome. So while Basiliscus had offered Timothy the hospitality of Constantinople, many of its denizens were less than impressed by the reinstated Alexandrian patriarch and made his stay as unpleasant as possible.[49]

Timothy soon felt the need to depart; he did have a patriarchate to reclaim in Egypt. However, he was not going to let the journey there go to waste. Recognizing the problem with the *Encyclical* being an imperial order, Timothy called a synod at Ephesus for some time between July and October 475.[50] Despite the opposition of the Constantinopolitan see, Antioch, Jerusalem, Ephesus and Alexandria were under the control of the anti-Chalcedonian camp. The *Encyclical* was signed up to by perhaps 200 bishops, and while there is doubt over Ps-Zacharias inflating such a number to more than that which ascribed to Chalcedon in 451, there does appear to be a significant support for the *Encyclical*.[51] Only Acacius and Pope Simplicius remained implacable opponents, so it is unsurprising that Timothy would look to have Chalcedon condemned by a synod. The rapturous reception Timothy Aelerus received as he re-entered Alexandria can only have bolstered his convictions. Once the Chalcedonian patriarch of Alexandria, Timothy Salophakialos, had been shipped off to a monastery at Canopus, Aeleurus was reinstalled as patriarch. He called a synod of Egyptian bishops, which condemned Chalcedon and had the name of Dioscorus, deposed by Chalcedon, restored to the diptychs, his remains brought to the city and buried in the tomb of Alexandrian bishops.[52]

While the Alexandrian see and prominent churchmen may have supported the *Encyclical*, this is not necessarily cast-iron evidence of the doctrinal feeling across those regions and the empire as a whole. The sources do paint a picture of general acceptance. Egypt was clearly happy to have its anti-Chalcedonian Cat-weasel back and most of Palestine followed the lead of Anastasius. Antioch is more uncertain. There is no clear evidence of Peter the Fuller acting decisively in an anti-Chalcedonian manner, aside from perhaps his consecration of vehement anti-Chalcedonian John Rufus. Bloody riots are recorded in Antioch at this time, which may demonstrate hostility towards Peter, although Theodore Lector claims that these disturbances were due to Peter's additions to the *Trishagion* rather than his position on Chalcedon.[53]

It All Comes Crumbling Down: Chalcedonian Revolt and the *Anti-Encyclical*

From what seemed like a strong political and religious position, the regime of Basiliscus collapsed remarkably quickly. While the actions of Verina, Illus and Zeno played a significant part in bringing down the usurper, the role of Acacius and the supporters of Chalcedon in Constantinople should not be overlooked. Following his initial silence, born of self-preservation and hope of negotiation, the restoration of Timothy, the *Encyclical* and the synod of Ephesus saw Acacius come out fighting at the head of the Chalcedonian faction. His determination to stand up to the doctrine of the usurper's regime was further strengthened by the zeal of the various monasteries in and around Constantinople.

The exact origin of overt opposition to the *Encyclical* and Basiliscus is not clear. Writers like Ps-Zacharias place Acacius at the centre of unrest from the start, inciting the church, monks and people of Constantinople to revolt. Theodore Lector has Acacius being forced out of fear for his safety to side with the people and the monks in defence of Chalcedon, although a later fragment of Theodore depicts Acacius at the centre of opposition to Basiliscus' policies. The *Vita Danielis Stylitae* suggests that Acacius only proceeded with open opposition 'after certain circumstances', perhaps when Basiliscus tried to remove him as patriarch, while Malchus has the monks successfully defending Acacius from the threat of banishment, possibly from the Ephesian synod.[54]

There is a brief silence from Acacius which causes many of these issues – was he silent because he was not opposed to the *Encyclical* or because he needed to keep his head down in order to keep it intact? Without a direct answer from Acacius himself, it is easy to see him as an individual swept up in the opposition of the monks and people, elevated to leadership of the revolt due to his position as patriarch. But it is equally possible to see him as publicly quiet but very active behind the scenes, inciting monastic and popular leaders to revolt while perhaps providing himself with plausible deniability. The lack of consensus from the sources might be a testament to how successful Acacius was in diverting attention from any leadership role he had in the earliest days of the Chalcedonian revolt against Basiliscus.

When Acacius took up open opposition to Basiliscus, he did so whole-heartedly, ordering Constantinopolitan churches to adorn themselves with black cloth as if they were in mourning. He also turned to the only eastern Chalcedonian who matched him in prominence – Daniel the Stylite.[55] Basiliscus had tried to gain his support for the *Encyclical*,[56] but Daniel had already shown that he was pro-Chalcedon and was not about to change his mind. So invested was he in protecting Chalcedon and demonstrating how dangerous he felt the *Encyclical* was that Daniel did something he had not done in over fifteen years – he came down from his pillar and made his way to Constantinople.

The effect was electrifying and decisive. The alliance of this great holy man, the patriarch, the monasteries and the population proved irresistible to Basiliscus. The emperor removed himself to Hebdomon, forbidding the Senate from dealing with Acacius, suggesting that he feared they might negotiate away some of his anti-Chalcedonianism or side with the other anti-Basiliscan forces massing in Asia Minor.[57] This move to Hebdomon was not quite an abdication, but given the developments in Isauria, Basiliscus had shown himself unwilling or unable to stand up to the opposition of civil and religious leaders. Many of his erstwhile allies, some of whom may already have been disgruntled over lack of reward, must have been asking themselves whether or not he would meet the coming military challenge with the same kind of vacillation. When the time came against Zeno and Illus, most would decide that the answer was 'yes' and that Basiliscus was unworthy of their support.

If things were not bad enough for the reputation of Basiliscus' regime, a fire broke out in the Chalkoprateia district of Constantinople and quickly spread to consume homes, churches, the palace of Lausus and an imperial library containing 120,000 volumes.[58] This marked Basiliscus as ill-omened, especially in the eyes of the enraged Chalcedonian majority in the city. It could be that in heading to Hebdomon, the emperor was fleeing the fire, as that palace had served as a refuge from fire for emperors in the past. However, Hebdomon was also an important army camp, where Basiliscus himself had been acclaimed emperor, so perhaps he was preparing for military action against his growing list of opponents.

Whether he was fleeing the raging fires of the Chalcedonian uprising or actual flames wreaking havoc in the streets of the capital, Basiliscus was not yet a dead duck emperor. However, his subsequent actions and capitulations ensured that he was. So desperate was he to placate Constantinople that he entered into feverish negotiations with the representatives of the uprising. Through senators and then in person, Basiliscus agreed to reconcile with Acacius, 'publicly retracting his support for anti-Chalcedonianism'.[59] In humbling himself before the patriarch, the usurper spent whatever political capital he had left.

The extent of his capitulation was shown in the new document which Acacius and the Stylite managed to extract from Basiliscus – the so-called *Anti-Encyclical*.[60] On the surface, this document gave the people of Constantinople what they wanted: Nicaea was reaffirmed as the symbol of orthodoxy, Nestorius and Eutyches were condemned and a new general council was prohibited. However, omissions from the text show that this *Anti-Encyclical* was far from a full reversal of the anti-Chalcedonian stance of Basiliscus' regime. The Council of Chalcedon was not mentioned and there was no call for the removal of anti-Chalcedonian bishops, although Basiliscus may have written to Timothy, ordering him to allow Chalcedonian Alexandrians to follow the decisions of Chalcedon.[61] It could be that Basiliscus did not mean for the *Anti-Encyclical* to be enforced throughout the entire Church, but as more of a short-term placatory measure in the capital. It was almost completely ignored throughout the rest of the empire.[62]

A timeline of the collapse of Basiliscus' regime can be somewhat brought together. Letters of Simplicius from January 476 do not mention any uprising, possibly suggesting that Basiliscus was not forced to Hebdomon until February or March, although travel time could place the revolt several weeks earlier with the letter of Simplicius not mentioning it because it had not yet happened when Basiliscus wrote to the pope in late 475. However, a revolt in late 475 would see Acacius in nominal control of Constantinople for up to six months, which seems unlikely. Also, dating Basiliscus' return from Hebdomon to late July because Zeno returned to Constantinople 'not long after'[63] Basiliscus humbled himself before

Daniel and Acacius is probably too late.[64] So it would therefore seem that Acacius and Daniel raised the Chalcedonian revolt against Basiliscus in the last days of winter or the first days of spring in 476.

While the *Anti-Encyclical* was not formally accepted anywhere outside the capital, the circumstances of its composition went a long way to destroying the regime of Basiliscus. News of the Chalcedonian revolt in Constantinople may have influenced Illus and Trocundes to defect to Zeno, with perhaps even a senatorial commission arriving in their camp ordering them to make contact with Zeno. While this idea comes from a later source, it is not out of the question given the outbreak of revolt and Basiliscus already being seen as not trusting the Senate.[65] If that was not enough poor publicity, scarcity of funds forced Basiliscus to not only renege on some of the financial promises he had made but also to raise taxes, sell offices and extort money from the Church, all undertaken under the avaricious eye of the eastern praetorian prefect, Epinicus. A favourite of Verina, Epinicus became so unpopular through his money-maker schemes that Basiliscus had to dismiss him.[66]

However, the support of Strabo, Armatus and the praesental armies meant that Basiliscus still had the upper hand over Zeno and Illus. But this was soon to change. The latest undermining of Basiliscus' position came near Thessalonica. The death of Theodemir some time in 475[67] had seen Theoderic the Amal became the leader of the Pannonian Goths. Keen to establish himself and improve the lot of his people, Theoderic decided to enter the political game surrounding the imperial throne. The Amal made contact with Zeno and promised to support his attempts at restoration by moving into Thrace to distract Strabo in return for all of the benefits accorded to the Thracian Goths by Leo in 473 – the position of *magister militum praesentalis*, lands in Thrace and the large annual subsidy. Zeno jumped at the chance to have his own 'Gothic nation' fighting for him. Strabo made a similar offer to Zeno, but personal animosity, coupled with the chance to do damage to both Gothic groups, saw Zeno side with the upstart Amal.

The exact timing of Theoderic the Amal's contacting of Zeno is not clear. It might be expected that he had some kind of assurance of imperial support upon his move towards Thrace.[68] However, there is no direct record of the movements of the Amal Goths between the accession of Theoderic and their appearance some 250 miles north at Novae in Moesia Inferior in 476.[69] Given that this was another occasion where the entire Amal Goth 'nation' packed up and headed north, an inference made by the recording of their return journey in 478/479 as involving women, animal herds and large baggage train,[70] it would be most likely that they followed the quickest route. This would have been back through Stobi and on to Serdica and Oescus before reaching Novae. It might be expected that these cities suffered attacks, but that may well depend on whether Theoderic was already in contact with Zeno. If the Goths were acting as imperial allies rather than opportunistic raiders, Stobi, Serdica and Oescus may have been spared.[71]

The choice of Novae could suggest that Theoderic moved before contact had been made with Zeno, as it was along the routes to Thrace rather than strictly in Thrace. The Amal himself later stated: 'I chose to live completely outside Thrace, far away towards Scythia … [where] I should trouble no one, yet from there I should be ready to obey whatever the emperor commanded.'[72] This could also suggest that Theoderic made the move with the intention of grabbing the attention of Zeno, or even Basiliscus. Novae was a good strategic choice as it was heavily fortified and controlled an easy Danube crossing, offering a defensive position to fall back upon and an avenue to gain more barbarian support should things go poorly.[73] Even with the added security of Novae, it would be a colossal roll of the dice for the Amal to up sticks and move to a position to challenge a main ally of the emperor without having some assurances from Zeno. But then, the move from Pannonia had been a similarly colossal gamble.[74]

The sources do not record the involvement of the Amal Goths in the restoration of Zeno, but the move to Novae, contact with him in Isauria and their promotion to the former position of Strabo's Goths after the removal of Basiliscus suggests that they were true to their promises.[75] At a time when Zeno and Illus were approaching from the east, the Pannonian Goth incursion drew Strabo away from Constantinople, draining the usurper's remaining manpower. It also 'incidentally intensified Gothic rivalries',[76] and in the summer of 476 it looked like the Pannonian and Thracian branches were about to square off over 'the prospect of a prosperous future in the eastern empire'.[77]

With Strabo distracted by the Amal, this left Basiliscus having to rely solely on Armatus to head off the Isaurians. While a decisive confrontation might have been hoped for and Armatus duly led an army possibly comprised of Thracian and praesental forces out of Constantinople, Basiliscus might have been better served keeping his last army in the capital, if only to keep a closer eye on his general. It would be reasonable to think that Basiliscus could trust his nephew, but Armatus proved to be as ambitious and opportunistic as his uncle. Near Nicaea, Armatus came into contact with Zeno and Illus – Trocundes had gone to take command of Syria.[78] Zeno offered all the usual courtly privileges, which amounted to confirming the positions and titles Armatus already held, but to sweeten the deal he pointed out that while Basiliscus had an heir in Marcus *Caesar*, Zeno did not and would need one quickly to secure his restoration. He therefore offered to elevate Armatus' son, Leo Basiliscus,[79] to *Caesar* and heir to the imperial throne.[80] With Armatus fresh from the capital, where he would have seen the troubles of the Basiliscan regime, this dynastic promise sealed the deal. Basiliscus' last army defected, intentionally taking the route to Isauria which would fail to intercept Zeno. By August 476, the route to the capital and restoration was clear.

With his support gone, Basiliscus must have seen the writing on the wall. A cavalcade of personal missteps and the general ruthlessness and opportunism of his enemies, allies and family had rendered him militarily and politically impotent.

So as the city gates were opened to admit Zeno and his forces, Basiliscus and his family sought sanctuary in Hagia Sophia or the Blachernae.[81] They only agreed to surrender if their blood was not shed. Zeno agreed, exiling Basiliscus, Zenonis, Marcus and other children to a fortress in Cappadocia, recorded as Limnae, Cucusus or Saemis. However, there was a twist in the tale. The emperor ordered the usurper and his family to be cast into a dry cistern where 'they should be destitute of food and clothes and every kind care',[82] so they would die of starvation or exposure in the winter cold, keeping his promise to not shed their blood.[83] The sources are not united in the details of Basiliscus' fate and this whole episode has been questioned. Perhaps Basiliscus was beheaded rather than condemned to any elaborate, symbolic demise in a cistern.[84] True or not, the outrageous execution of Basiliscus and his family would come back to haunt Zeno when it came to the reporting of his own death in 491.

Even though it had not seen much in the way of military campaigning, Basiliscus' twenty-month reign on the imperial throne had several long-term effects on the Roman Empire. His religious policies were to have a vast influence on its religious politics. For the first time, an emperor had overturned the decisions of a church council by imperial decree, with harsh penalties for those who did not change their position. The empowering of the anti-Chalcedonian movement was to provide a real headache for Zeno. The circumstances of Basiliscus' deposition would also prove problematic for the re-enthroned emperor. Much like with Basiliscus' usurpation, Zeno's restoration involved a lot of promises to ambitious men – Illus, Armatus and Theoderic the Amal. There were still other problems to solve amongst the supporters of Basiliscus, such as Theoderic Strabo and members of the imperial family like Verina. Would Zeno prove any better than the deposed usurper in actually delivering those promises and dealing with his family and enemies?

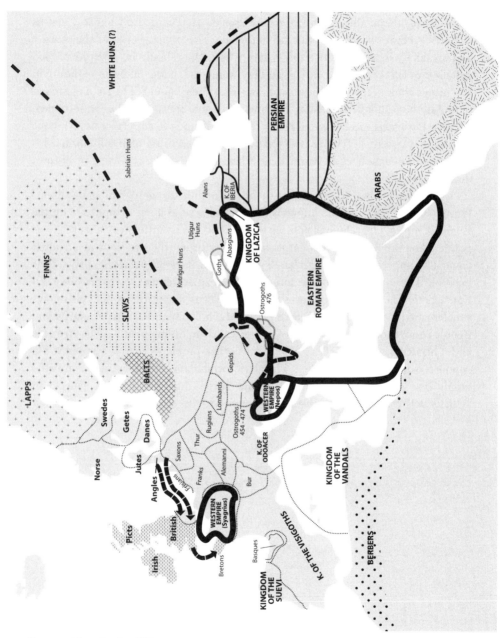

Roman Empire in 476

Chapter 9

Beholden to All: The Price of Zeno's Restoration

'Barzini's dead. So is Phillip Tattaglia, Moe Greene, Strachi, Cuneo.
Today I settle all Family business.'

Michael Corleone to Carlo Rizzi, *The Godfather* (1972)

Removing Rivals

With Basiliscus and his family dealt with, it might seem that Zeno was secure on the imperial throne. In reality, he was far from it. In order to be able to come down from his Isaurian hideaway, march to Constantinople, oust Basiliscus and reoccupy that throne, he had made many deals with many devils. In the military sphere alone, he had made promises to Illus, Trocundes, Armatus and Theoderic the Amal; all of whom had supported Basiliscus in Zeno's ousting in early 475 only to change sides when it appeared that they had more to gain out of disloyalty. Such mercenary tendencies could not be relied upon. Therefore, it was not long before Zeno decided to act to reduce his number of debtors and in the process reveal himself as a ruthless schemer and breaker of promises in the mould of Machiavelli's Prince, Mario Puzo's Michael Corleone or G.R.R. Martin's Tywin Lannister.

Who would be the first devil to feel Zeno's sharp knife between his shoulder blades? The answer was rather straightforward. The two Theoderics were keeping each other occupied in the Balkans with a prolonged staring contest; Trocundes was absent in Syria; and Illus still had Longinus as a hostage. That left Armatus, 'an arrogant dandy who liked to dress up as Achilles and parade in the Hippodrome'.[1] Such behaviour cannot have endeared him to many in Constantinople or his army – it was part of the reason why Strabo hated him so much, especially when he was supposed to be the foremost general of the empire given his position as senior *magister militum praesentalis*. His already poor reputation took a further nosedive with the sheer naked ambition of his betrayal of his uncle Basiliscus, the man who had promoted Armatus to his lofty position in the first place. Despite that general unpopularity, Armatus represented the most dangerous of Zeno's new 'allies'. This was due to the terms of his defection in August 476. Not only was he *magister militum praesentalis* for life, but his son, Leo Basiliscus, was the heir apparent. Should anything 'unfortunate' happen to Zeno, Armatus would suddenly be senior commander of the army, father of the ruling *Augustus* and regent, as Leo Basiliscus seems to have been still a boy in 476.[2] The sources felt that this would be a lure that

Armatus would be unable to ignore for long. He had betrayed Basiliscus, so why would he not betray Zeno when the empire might fall into his lap?[3]

While on the surface, Zeno was fulfilling his promises to Armatus, behind the scenes, the emperor was searching for an accomplice to make sure that the 'for life' part of Armatus' magisterial title was short. He found his assassin in a certain Onoulphus, half brother of the new king of Italy, Odoacer,[4] and, as seen earlier, perhaps even a relative of Armatus. Showing the quite literal as well as figurative cut-throat nature of Constantinopolitan politics, Onoulphus owed his promotions to *comes* and then *magister militum per Illyricum* to the backing of Armatus. But whatever loyalty, personal or familial, Onoulphus might have felt for Armatus, it was quickly overcome by the promises of Zeno as he had little issue sticking the knife in when the emperor came calling, cutting down Armatus while he was on his way to the Hippodrome in late 476 or early 477, with some other former members of Basiliscus' regime possibly following him.[5] There was little uproar at the emperor's instigation of the murder of his most senior general, a man who had helped him regain the throne and was a cousin of Ariadne. Any complaints were either muted by the sources or were muted in general. Could Armatus have made himself so unpopular that his murder was met with little more than a shrug of the collective shoulders? There was certainly no rebellion similar to the aftermath of the murder of Aspar. Zeno made sure to mitigate any potential negative reaction by treating Leo Basiliscus with leniency. As already seen, he was stripped of his position as *Caesar* and compelled to enter the Church, eventually becoming Bishop of Cyzicus.[6]

One down, three to go. But that was to be the end of the easy removals. The others were more popular with their men and now had the forewarning that Zeno had no problem with the extrajudicial killing of those responsible for his restoration. While Onoulphus will have been well rewarded and Zeno had removed a potent threat to his rule, perhaps the man to gain the most from the assassination of Armatus was Illus. The *magister officiorum* was now unquestionably the most powerful man at court. He may also have encouraged Zeno to do away with Armatus,[7] although it is also claimed that Illus was shocked by the murder and may have briefly taken refuge in Isauria, fearing that he might be next.[8] If the account of John of Antioch is to be believed, Illus did have something to be scared about. Buoyed by the successful removal of Armatus, Zeno attempted to have his Isaurian benefactor assassinated in the summer of 477. The effort failed and the slave employed to commit the crime, Paul, was handed over to Illus. To placate the livid Isaurian general, Zeno appointed him sole consul for 478 and was forced to rely so heavily upon him that Illus is referred to in similar language to Aspar – almost all-powerful.[9]

The failure by Paul was not the only attempt on Illus' life in the months following Zeno's restoration. In 478, an otherwise unknown Alan soldier was tasked with murdering the Isaurian consul *sine collega*, but once again the perpetrator failed to kill his target.[10] But what would killing Illus really have accomplished? Trocundes would have inherited his brother's position at the head of their Isaurian army and would probably have been able to force Zeno to recognize him as Illus' successor in Constantinople. Then there is the position of Longinus, whom Zeno almost certainly viewed as his successor – killing Illus would not have seen him released. Either Zeno did not particularly care what happened to his brother or perhaps Zeno was not behind the assassination attempt on Illus. But if it was not the emperor, then who was it?

While Paul the slave had been handed over to Illus, on this second occasion it was the man who employed the unknown Alan who was carted off to the custody of Illus in Isauria: the former praetorian prefect of Basiliscus, Epinicus. When visiting Antioch for the funeral of his brother, Aspalius, Illus confronted his captive and through interrogation discovered that it was Verina who had ultimately been behind this latest assassination attempt, perhaps in revenge for Illus' role in the execution of Patricius. But then even if Verina was not involved, the actions of Paul the slave, the unnamed Alan and Epinicus proved that someone – or someones – were out to get Illus, as well as other leading commanders.[11] Either Zeno was attempting a Michael Corleone-style removal of his two biggest problems in Constantinople at around the same time or the imperial matriarch was playing out her own personal vendetta against an Isaurian general while Zeno removed an unpopular dandified *magister*.

Whatever the circumstances behind these attempts on Illus' life, their failure had significant repercussions. Seeing literal knives out for him, Illus packed up and left for Isauria, leading to enough unrest amongst a portion of the field army that Zeno had to send them back to winter quarters. This in itself was not necessarily a disaster, but the timing of it proved problematic as the Balkan part of Zeno's grand *Godfather*-like neutralizing of his enemies had fallen through rather spectacularly. While the relationship between the imperial family and the Isaurian general deteriorated, they still shared the mutual objective of retaining Zeno on the imperial throne, and events in Thrace saw to it that there was something of a 'temporary reconciliation'.[12]

Imperial Double-cross

Zeno's problem in the Balkans was that the Theoderici confrontation triggered by the Pannonian Goth move to Novae had largely failed to materialize. The Amal presence had drawn Strabo away from Constantinople, allowing the overthrow of Basiliscus, but the two 'Gothic' forces seem to have been too evenly matched. Strabo received rations and pay for up to 13,000 men, not all of whom will have joined him in moving towards Novae, while it may be possible to extrapolate a number in the region of 10,000 for the Amal.[13] This deterred either Theoderic from pressing for a decisive battle. Only the involvement of imperial forces would tip the balance, something that Theoderic the Amal was keen to point out to Zeno. Together they could crush Strabo once and for all.

However, that was not necessarily what the emperor wanted. Destroying Strabo could essentially entail replacing one dangerous Gothic general with another whilst risking valuable imperial manpower in the battlefield. Zeno may also have received word that he might have backed the wrong horse. While not yet a haemorrhage, the proximity of the 'Gothic' forces was leading to a steady trickle of men from the Amal camp to that of Strabo. This seems a little strange given the imperial backing of the Amal, but he 'was not yet the all-victorious ruler of Italy, but a young leader who had risked his men in a major gamble'.[14] Theoderic Strabo was well-established in Constantinopolitan politics and was viewed by some as the heir of Aspar. That could easily sway ordinary tribesman to change sides.

Yet the loss of imperial favour must have undermined the appeal of service with Strabo. In 477, representatives of Strabo approached Zeno for employment, but were turned down as the emperor claimed not to be able to pay both groups at once. This not only shows that Strabo's men may have become reliant on imperial funding, but that the Pannonian Goths were receiving imperial subsidy. Theoderic the Amal had not only been confirmed as *magister militum praesentalis*, he was also given the title of patrician, along with vast personal wealth, likely in a similar vein to that provided to Strabo in 473, while Jordanes suggests that Zeno adopted the Amal in the Gothic fashion.[15] While this looks like out and out war against Strabo and that the emperor had stuck with the young Amal pretender who had aided him in reclaiming the throne, circumstances would prove that this was to be only Zeno's first steps in playing the two Goths off against one another.[16]

The winter of 477–478 saw the emperor and the Amal come to an agreement over how to deal with Strabo. Amal forces would march from Marcianople through the Haemus Mountains, where the anonymous *magister militum per Thracias* would join him with 10,000 infantry and 2,000 cavalry on the march towards Adrianople, where they were to be met by a further 20,000 infantry and 6,000 cavalry.[17] The size of these forces looks like what was supposed to include not just the Thracian field army but perhaps one of the praesental forces, likely that supposedly under the Amal's command, and even the Illyrian field army, under the command of Onoulphus c.477–479. Together with the significant garrison forces of Thrace, this looks like a plan to annihilate the Thracian Goths, as Strabo's 13,000 would be no match for the 48,000 of this proposed Romano-Amal alliance.

But even before looking at the outcome of this agreement, suspicions should have been raised. Was the eastern empire capable of putting such numbers into the field in 478? On paper, absolutely. If the Thracian, Illyrian and twin praesental field armies were anywhere near the strength recorded for them in the *Notitia Dignitatum*, not to mention what was left of the frontier and garrison forces of the Balkans and Danube, they could supposedly bring together up to 131,000 men.[18] However, even without going into the deficiencies of the *Notitia*, Zeno was operating in 478, not 395. A lot had changed in those eight decades. That Strabo and the Amal were so close to the capital, in the pay of the state and able to interfere in politics suggests that mustering 40,000 men to fight in the Balkans was not as straightforward as Zeno's promises to Theoderic the Amal. However, Zeno did put significant forces into the field for the campaigning season of 478; just not for the reason promised.

Having already moved to Marcianople, away from the defences of Novae and into striking distance of Strabo's men, the Amal Goths found themselves left high and dry. The Thracian *magister* and his 12,000 men failed to appear at the Haemus, and then near Adrianople, the 26,000-strong army also failed to arrive. On top of that, and perhaps more importantly, the paymaster Claudius and the promised pay did not materialize. Theoderic would complain bitterly about this to the Roman diplomat, Adamantius, outside Dyrrhachium eighteen months later in 479.[19] Worse still, the imperial guides who did join the Pannonian Goths led them along a steep rugged path through the mountains. This was slow, hard going given that the 'Gothic' force included cavalry, wagons and baggage. But worst of all was that after not being reinforced or paid and led up the mountainous path, the Amal Goths emerged from the hills straight into the teeth of the Thracian Goths.

This would not be the first or the last time that two armies accidentally blundered into one another, but this was not one of those occasions. This had been planned from the beginning; orchestrated by an emperor determined to remove all of his rivals in one fell swoop. While Amal support had helped his restoration in 476, Zeno was disappointed by the lack of a set-piece battle between the two Theoderics to whittle down their ranks. So now in 477–478, he decided to bring about one by manipulating the Amal and perhaps holding some talks with Strabo to discover his position. It all seemed to have worked perfectly as the two 'Gothic' forces came face to face. But it was then that the problems of Zeno's *Godfather*-like extermination started to rear their heads. In Thrace, the two Theoderics refused to fight. Zeno's manipulation had been too obvious. Strabo is recorded explaining the betrayal to the Amal, pointing out what Zeno had hoped to accomplish.[20] This is almost certainly a rhetorical device deployed by Malchus; the Amal surely did not need Strabo to point out what had happened.[21]

There is some hint that Theoderic the Amal was still willing to commit to battle against Strabo. Not only is there this reported conversation where Strabo goes to great lengths to point out the obvious imperial manipulation, there is also the suggestion that the Pannonian Goths refused to countenance fighting Strabo under the availing circumstances. If some of his own men threatened to desert or join Strabo, some must have felt that Theoderic the Amal was still willing to fight even without imperial assistance. Faced with a reluctant army, an inevitably bloody confrontation and an opponent willing to do a deal, the Amal reined in any destructive tendencies. Instead, it would be his betrayer and his empire that would be the target for his rage.

Zeno will have realized that there was a possibility that his plan for a mutual Goth on Goth slaughter would fail. There were just too many warning signs for neither Theoderic to figure out what was going on – two sets of reinforcements not arriving, pay going undelivered and guides leading the Gothic armies into each other. The outcome must have been a disappointment, but not a disaster. He almost certainly had planned for this as part of his mobilization of up to 30,000 infantry and 8,000 cavalry. Instead of these two imperial forces arriving to mop up the remnants of the two Gothic forces, now it would have to deal with both of them. More empty promises and their pre-existing enmity may well have made it so that the two Gothic forces could be picked off one at a time, and even if the two Goths could fight together, Zeno still had the larger army in the field.

Or at least he should have. This is where the failed assassination attempts on Illus did their most damage. His retirement to Isauria caused the benching of a significant portion of the imperial field army, meaning that Zeno now lacked the strike power to deal with the two angry Goths. The Amal in particular was spoiling for a fight, not just because of the anger he felt at the betrayal of Zeno but also because of the dripping away of his forces to Strabo. He needed a military success to keep them happy and to fill his own coffers and ration stores. Agreeing something of a non-aggression pact with Strabo, the Amal led his forces along the coastal route towards Constantinople, hoping to force an accommodation out of Zeno, while raiding the countryside to sustain his army and punish the Romans for their subterfuge.

With two angry Goths on the loose and having a limited army to confront them, Zeno had to negotiate. With the Amal on a vengeance-fuelled rampage, getting an agreement out of him would have been difficult; although that did not prevent the emperor from trying. Zeno reputedly offered 1,000lb of gold, 40,000lb of silver, annual payments of 10,000 *solidi* and the hand of a leading Roman aristocratic lady, perhaps the daughter of Olybrius.[22] When the irate Amal rejected this, the emperor had to deal with Theoderic Strabo. Given their history, it is surprising that they would even contemplate an agreement. But both men were pragmatic, willing to temporarily set aside past differences to get what they needed at that exact moment – Zeno needed to reduce the forces openly hostile to the empire, and Strabo needed gold and rations to pay and feed his followers. Much like with the Amal Goths, past glories would only keep Strabo's following together for so long, and if he had been attracting men from the Amal's ranks then his need of resources will have increased. So when presented with the chance to re-enter imperial service, Strabo bit Zeno's hand off at the offer of soldier's pay for 3,000 men, reappointment as *magister militum praesentalis*, command of two *scholae* units, the restoration of property and rehabilitation of his relatives.[23]

With Strabo restored to imperial favour, Theoderic the Amal must have known that their non-aggression pact was no longer worth the paper it was not written on. At any moment Zeno could succeed in buying Strabo's breaking of that gentlemen's agreement and put the Roman army into the field. Theoderic the Amal's days looked numbered. But that would be against Roman barbarian policy – removing the Pannonian Goths by risking Roman forces would leave the Thracian Goths without a counterweight and probably much stronger having absorbed the defeated Amal remnants. Instead, Zeno left Theoderic the Amal to his own devices, which entailed raiding the Thracian countryside and threatening cities as he moved west along the 700 miles of the Via Egnatia from Constantinople to the Epirote city of Dyrrhachium.

While he had removed a threat from the immediate vicinity of the capital, the circumstances cannot have made Zeno popular with those provincials in the path of the Pannonian Goths. Several towns and cities of the Balkans interior, still not recovered from Hunnic and Gothic raids, were subjected to the anger, frustration and hunger of the Amal. The archaeology of Philippi and Stobi bears the scars of a sack around this time and may be linked to the Amal travelling on the Via Egnatia.[24] Worse for the Romans was the failure of local forces to prevent the Amal making a dash for Dyrrhachium and capturing the city in the summer of 479 through the subterfuge of a certain Sidimundus, Gothic nephew of Aedoingus, *comes domesticorum*. Taking such a 'highly defensible and strategic port'[25] greatly increased the Amal's bargaining power, while the material and reputation benefits allowed him to sit and wait to see what developed between Zeno, Illus and Strabo.[26]

What did develop was the arrival of an imperial envoy, Adamantius, to whom Theoderic the Amal vented his spleen over Zeno's egregious betrayal the previous summer.[27] Yet Theoderic remained willing to serve at the behest of his imperial betrayer. If his non-combatants were allowed to settle in a Roman city of Zeno's choosing, the Amal promised the emperor 6,000 of his best men. He then went on to suggest what these men could be used for – the first was a rehashing of the plan for 478, with the Amal Goths joining together with imperial field forces to crush Strabo, allowing the Amal to reclaim the position of *magister militum praesentalis* and to live in Constantinople. His second suggestion was dynamic and risky but also strangely prophetic: Theoderic offered to use his forces to re-establish Julius Nepos on the western throne through an invasion of Italy. It is unlikely that Theoderic was truly interested in moving to Italy in the summer of 479, particularly if it might include leaving his non-combatants behind. Perhaps he was attempting to provide a less favourable option to make his own preferred choice of a renewed alliance against Strabo look more acceptable.

This is putting faith in Malchus recording a truthful conversation between the Amal and Adamantius and not using hindsight over Theoderic's eventual travelling to Italy almost a decade later. Developments in Dalmatia within months could suggest some connection to this proposed conversation. Before 480 was out, Nepos was dead, murdered by his own men, and the *rex Italiae* Odoacer had struck into Dalamtia, defeated Nepos' murderers and annexed the entire territory. While likely sparked by the murder of Nepos, could Odoacer's Dalmatian attack also have been somewhat encouraged by rumours of Theoderic's offer in 479? This stretches credulity, but if nothing else it might suggest how well-connected both Theoderic and Odoacer were when it came to events in territories outside their control.

Having to capitulate to Strabo must have really stuck in the emperor's craw, so the offer of aid to undo that capitulation will have appealed, especially if it included neutralizing the strategic damage done by the Pannonian Goth capture of Dyrrhachium. However, perhaps even before Adamantius could forward the Amal's proposals to Zeno, a significant blow was struck by imperial forces against the Pannonian Goths, which altered imperial strategic thinking. In his dash to Dyrrhachium, Theoderic had left many of his non-combatants and baggage train to catch up. They failed to arrive. Between Heraclea and Dyrrhachium, an ambush by Sabinianus, Onoulphus' successor as *magister milium per Illyricum* and opponent of negotiations with the Goths, saw 2,000 Gothic wagons, their collected booty and 5,000 prisoners taken by the Romans. This altered the negotiations, but the sources do not focus on the aftermath of the destruction of the Amal's baggage train. There was a proposal where the Goths would spend the winter of 479/480 in Epirus and then be settled in Dardania, but buoyed by victory and listening to Sabinianus, Zeno saw an opportunity to defeat the Pannonian Goths once and for all and ignored any agreements reached between Adamantius and the Amal.[28] This left Theoderic the Amal with very few options. While Amal forces may still have outnumbered those of Sabinianus, was Theoderic really prepared to risk the very survival of his people as an independent 'nation'? Instead, he chose to wait, holding back any bloodlust of his men over the loss of their families and demonstrating the growing stature of Theoderic as a leader. He was soon to be rewarded. Inevitably, the agreement between Zeno and Strabo had not lasted long.

The Two Revolts of Marcianus

The collapse of this agreement between Strabo and Zeno in 479 was another plot against the emperor. The prolonged conflict with the Goths had an adverse affect on Zeno's already low approval rating, in particular after the attempts on the life of Illus, who appears to have been popular with the Constantinopolitan populace. The emperor may even have felt that there was enough popular dissent, political conspiracy and military mutiny to leave the capital, crossing the Bosphorus for Chalcedon, from where he summoned Illus to help deal with these problems in late 478. The Isaurian general duly arrived at Chalcedon but then refused to re-enter Constantinople, citing the confession of Epinicus and the continued threats to his safety. In order to bring about a 'temporary reconciliation',[29] Illus fell back on a staple of ancient negotiations – he demanded more hostages.[30] Custody of Longinus, Paul the slave and Epinicus was clearly not enough, as Illus demanded perhaps the most high-profile imperial hostage possible who was not Zeno; he wanted Verina. It might be expected that the emperor would have laughed off the idea of giving up his mother-in-law as a hostage, but such was his need of Illus' support that Zeno felt he had no option but to acquiesce. In late 478, Verina was packed off into an Isaurian exile from which she would never return. While Ariadne cannot have been too happy at seeing her mother shipped off to the semi-barbarian backwater, Zeno was probably not all that displeased with giving up his conniving mother-in-law. Perhaps it was Zeno himself who was behind the Isaurian exile of Verina, although this seems unlikely and he will not have appreciated being blackmailed by Illus.[31]

While it might have cost him prestige and support within his family, getting Illus back onside could not have come at a better time for Zeno. Not only were there rampaging Goths in the Balkans, there was also another revolt on the horizon. The emperor had taken action against suspected enemies within the capital, with a special court composed of Illus and three senators sentencing many allies of Strabo to flagellation and exile.[32] But the latest rebellion did not come from an Ardaburii remnant or friends of Strabo. As with the usurpation of Basiliscus, it came from a scion of the imperial family; however, it was not technically the Leonid imperial family who were trying to pry the purple from Zeno.[33]

The candidate was Flavius Marcianus, and first and foremost he was a son of the western emperor Anthemius. On top of that paternal link, Marcianus was an incredibly well-connected man: through his father he was descended from the fourth-century usurper Procopius, who was a relative of Julian; through his mother, Marcia Euphemia, he was a grandson of the eastern emperor Marcian; and his sister, Alypia, was married to Ricimer. Such a prominent position had seen Marcianus married into the Leonid imperial family as the husband of Leo and Verina's second daughter, Leontia. He had supported the usurpation of Basiliscus in 475, but while there is no record of his reaction to Zeno's restoration, it is likely that much like so many others, Marcianus tacitly accepted the toppling of Basiliscus.[34]

Perhaps spurred on by the exile of Verina, who may even have encouraged sedition from her house arrest in Isauria, Marcianus rebelled against Zeno in late 479. He was supported by his brothers, Procopius Anthemius and Romulus, and the otherwise unknown figures of Busalbus and Nicetas,[35] but Marcianus was going to need more support than that to overthrow the emperor. He and his family spread promises of wealth and promotion amongst the military and political classes, deriding Zeno for his failure to deal with the Goths, his reputed uncouth behaviour and Isaurian origins, but he needed more of a focal point. He looked to galvanize what remained of the Leonid family by reproaching Zeno's exile of Verina. Any lasting admiration for Leo could have been mobilized by the perceived poor treatment of his widow. However, it was the status of his own wife, Leontia, that Marcianus made the central part of his claim.

On the surface, Marcianus had no better claim to the throne than Zeno. Both were married to imperial daughters, and given that Ariadne was older than Leontia and Zeno had fathered Leo II, stirring up arguments over who had the superior claim looked unlikely to get Marcianus anywhere: a cut and dry case of primogeniture in favour of Ariadne and her husband, Zeno. However, Marcianus based his 'superior' claim on what would become a legitimate succession determinative within Constantinople – *porphyrogenitus* ('born in the purple'). This right of succession favoured those born to their fathers after he had become emperor, so as Leontia was born after Leo became emperor and Ariadne before, Marcianus could claim that Leontia was the preferred candidate of God and so he had a superior claim to Zeno. Whether there was any support for *porphyrogenitus* or this was just the link to legitimacy for Marcianus, the revolt gathered traction.[36]

Marcianus and his allies quickly gathered a mixed force at the House of Caesarius and succeeded in commandeering many of the ships sailing the Bosphorus, potentially cutting communication between Zeno and his allies. They then attacked the imperial palace and the house of Illus. Their reconciliation over Verina had enabled Zeno and Illus to return to the capital, but now in the midst of Marcianus' revolt, they found that rebel control of the streets and the Bosphorus prevented imperial and Isaurian reinforcements entering the city. This forced the emperor and his general to rely on whatever loyal men they had in Constantinople for the first night of the revolt. Illus' men and likely parts of the imperial guard managed to defend the palace, but Zeno required a bit of luck to evade capture and to retain his throne.

That bit of luck came when, almost inexplicably, with final victory in sight, Marcianus delayed his final attack until the next day. When he launched what he thought would be his decisive strike, he found his opponents dug in and supported by regular army units. Unbeknownst to Marcianus, Zeno and Illus had used their night's respite well, not only regrouping the forces they already had in Constantinople but also getting reinforcements across the Bosphorus from Chalcedon. While the advice of a certain Pamprepius is mentioned as helping Illus, perhaps Zeno had got word to a navy squadron stationed near Constantinople and sent it to ferry across Illus' army. For those men to enter the city without a fight and not come to the attention of Marcianus would suggest that either the rebels were lax in enforcing their perceived control of Bosphoran shipping or it was never really in their control and nor was much of the city. Against an army of well-trained, well-positioned and well-led professionals, the cobbled-together and seemingly unsuspecting forces of Marcianus stood little chance and were quickly beaten.[37]

Defeated and captured, Marcianus was sent to Cappadocian Caesarea, where he went through the increasingly prominent ordination as a priest to remove him as a candidate for the throne. His wife, Leontia, was confined to the *Akoimetoi* monastery at Constantinople, a reflection of not only her support for the rebellion but perhaps also the threat of her status as *porphyrogenita*.[38] Zeno would have been well within his rights to have had Marcianus executed for attempting to usurp the imperial throne, but it is likely that his familial connections saved Marcianus from death. But then imperial family links had not saved Basiliscus. Perhaps his inability to execute Marcianus reflects the continued weakness of Zeno's position.

It is possible that Marcianus saw the failure to execute him as a further sign of how weak and ill-suited Zeno was for imperial rule. Despite his forced ordination, Marcianus soon fled Caesarea, determined to continue his fight for the throne.

Again trading on his name, limited resources, opposition to Zeno and no doubt myriad promises, he managed to cobble together another small army. The one source that mentions this second 'revolt', John of Antioch, regards this force as made up of farmers and peasants, which reads like a literary trope used to disparage a rebel.[39] While Marcianus' force must have contained such undesirables, it is possible that he recruited some local militias and perhaps even some more regular forces passing through the region. Perhaps the clearest evidence that Marcianus' force was not completely made up of the dregs of Anatolia was that he attempted to use it to capture the major city of Ancyra, although it could be argued that such a move demonstrates Marcianus' weakness and desperation rather than any level of strength.

Regardless of the makeup of his new army, Marcianus was again thwarted by the forces of an Isaurian general working for Zeno; this time it was Trocundes. That the *magister militum per Orientem* took the field in Galatia suggests that this second attempt by Marcianus took place over a longer period of time than his attempted seizure of Constantinople, as it would have taken the eastern *magister* time to reach Ancyra from his eastern base. Captured again and then reunited with his wife, who must have been dispatched from *Akoimetoi*, Marcianus was sent to what was fast becoming the prison for opponents of the imperial regime – the fortresses of Isauria, this time the Papirian fort, where he was placed under the guard of men of Illus.[40]

It was fortunate for Marcianus that he fell into the hands of Trocundes rather than Zeno, as a second rebellion could easily have seen the emperor overcome whatever discouraged him from executing Marcianus in the first place. While his final fate is not known for certain, Marcianus, Leontia and their daughters[41] were valuable prisoners for Illus. It is suggested that the Isaurian general tried to use their imperial connections to his advantage in 484 when he sent Marcianus as an envoy to Odoacer. In travelling to Italy, Marcianus may have been able to reunite with his brothers, Procopius Anthemius and Romulus, who had also managed to escape there. Other supporters of Marcianus were punished by Zeno through imprisonment and property confiscations, but the most important backer of the revolt required more authoritative and even controversial action. That supporter was Theoderic Strabo.

Ouch! The Unfortunate End of Theoderic Strabo

Upon hearing of Marcianus' revolt against Zeno, Strabo immediately marched towards Constantinople. By the time he arrived in the outskirts of the capital, the revolt had been put down and Zeno's envoys were demanding answers. Strabo's answer was a bald-faced lie – he had been racing to Constantinople to aid Zeno against the rebels in his capacity as *magister militum praesentalis*. When nobody believed him, Strabo dropped all pretence and welcomed refugees from the failed revolt, including Procopius Anthemius and Busalbus. Zeno demanded that Strabo hand over these rebels, only for the Goth to refuse.[42] This led Zeno to replace Strabo as *magister militum praesentalis* with Trocundes, which might explain his presence near Ancyra to detain Marcianus. The emperor went a step further and declared Strabo an enemy of the state. But while this may have deprived him of Roman resources, Strabo's demotion and outlawing did little to change the strategic situation. Zeno still lacked the military resources in the Balkans to deal with both Theoderics at the same time, and his Illyrian/Thracian forces were already shadowing the Pannonian Goths at Dyrrhachium. This may explain why Zeno had to look east to the Isaurian brothers to provide manpower against Marcianus. With Illus' troops needed to protect Constantinople, there were few if any available Roman forces to protect the Thracian countryside from Strabo.

In an attempt to at least distract Strabo, the emperor fell back on the tried and trusted tactic of playing barbarian foes off against one another. He found his instrument of distraction amongst the Asiatic tribes beyond the Lower Danube, listed as 'Bulgars', but potentially either Kutrigur Huns or proto-Avars; however, in 480, they were more probably remnants of the Hunnic tribes of Dengizich defeated a decade previously. While the identity of these Bulgar-Huns was not all that important for Zeno and his employment of them was well within the bounds of accepted practice, how he was proposing to use them raises a few eyebrows. Given that Strabo had just marched towards Constantinople, he was deep in Roman territory far removed from the Danube.

Zeno was paying a barbarian tribe to invade Roman territory. As such tribal raiders could not be expected to concentrate their attacks solely on Strabo, Zeno was exposing the citizens of Moesia and Thrace to further depredations. While it was somewhat explainable from political and military points of view, it cannot have helped Zeno's popularity with the provincials. Of course, they will not have known that this latest barbarian raid was imperially sanctioned, but they will have noticed the lack of an imperial response to both Strabo and the Bulgar-Huns. This dubious action does seem to have worked, distracting Strabo for the campaigning season of 480, but by the following year, Strabo was on the prowl once more. Did Zeno not have the funds or the will to pay the Bulgar-Huns again? Or had Strabo dealt with them to such an extent that they could not be used again?[43]

In 481, Strabo mobilized his entire force and marched directly against Constantinople. The first Gothic assault fell upon the main gates of the city, only to be beaten back by Illus' men. It seems likely that Strabo had no real expectation of taking Constantinople by assault. Perhaps he was gauging the strength and preparedness of the garrison forces, or was making a demonstration against the city in an attempt to spark a revolt against Zeno within the palace.[44] Having been a prominent member of the Ardaburii faction, Strabo probably still had some connections within Constantinople, even after Zeno and Illus' attempts to exile them. He was also currently giving shelter to Procopius Anthemius, so perhaps he planned to elevate him in place of Zeno.

After his initial attack failed, Strabo moved his men around the Golden Horn to Scyde to probe the seaward defences. When this provided no evidence of an opportunity to storm the city and no movement within to oust Zeno, Strabo was forced to move again. This time he went to the small harbour towns of Hestiae and Sosthenium, in an attempt to cross to Bithynia, only to be frustrated by the Roman navy. As assailing Constantinople from Asia Minor was even more difficult than from the landward side or across the Golden Horn, Strabo's proposed crossing to Asia Minor must have been in an attempt to raise it in revolt against Zeno and cut off Illus' communication with Isauria. Isolating the Isaurian general might have encouraged him to act against Zeno, while any sign of weakness in Illus could have encouraged the ever-opportunistic Zeno to make another attempt to remove Illus permanently.[45]

Strabo's gambit failed in all its aims: the Theodosian Walls stood firm, there was no coup in Constantinople and the Goths did not get across the Bosphorus. This left Strabo in a quandary as to what to do next. He had overestimated his connections in the capital and the extent of opposition to Zeno, particularly in the light of Illus' continued interest in maintaining his fellow Isaurian on the throne. Having burnt all of his imperial bridges, Strabo could expect to be the target of a full military reprisal from the empire. His only hope now was to find allies, and the only one of any substance in the area was holed up in Dyrrhachium. Whether meeting up with the Amal Goths was his objective or he was merely fleeing from Constantinople along the quickest road, Strabo moved west along the Via Egnatia. Attributing such aims to Strabo at this time is speculative, but if he was wary of Zeno and Illus combining their available forces against him, moving towards the Amal might make at least some sense. Perhaps together the Theoderics could defeat the force of Sabinianus keeping an eye on Dyrrhachium before it could link up with other imperial forces.

Whatever his plans along the Via Egnatia, they would not come to fruition. While encamping at Stabulum Diomedis, near Philippi, Theoderic Strabo suffered one of history's more unfortunate demises. Attempting to break an unruly horse, Strabo was thrown from the animal. This was hardly a rare occurrence, but the real misfortune came with where and how Strabo landed; instead of getting the wind knocked out of him, Strabo landed 'on an upright spear standing at the side of his tent'.[46] Impaled on his own spear was an ignominious end for a Gothic leader who had matched wits with Roman generals and emperors for two decades, and given how history would pan out, he gets unfairly sidelined in favour of his Amal namesake. More experienced in leadership and in dealing with the Romans, Strabo had maintained a prominent position in Roman politics despite the opposition of the ruling *Augustus*. However, it was this personal enmity with Zeno and his misjudging of Constantinople almost a decade after the death of Aspar that eventually led to the ruin of Strabo.

Even at the time of his death, Strabo was still in a better position militarily than the Amal, as he likely still commanded a superior 'nation', one that stayed together under his son, Recitach. The question was now to be whether or not Recitach could follow in his father's footsteps, building on the reputation of Strabo. However, while Theodemir had paved the way amongst the Pannonian Goths for his son to take sole command, the suddenness of Strabo's death meant that the succession within the Thracian Goths was far less linear, and as a result far bloodier. Recitach shared the leadership with his otherwise unknown uncles,[47] and while he quickly did away with them, this led to insecurity regarding Recitach's position, not helped by rumours that he had murdered his father in revenge for a beating. Their proximity, the sudden change in leadership and the legacy of his father's attacks on Constantinople saw Zeno target the Thracian Goths for destruction.

Making a decisive move against the Thracian Goths meant a change of tack towards Theoderic the Amal to free up the forces in western Greece. This was not entirely straightforward. The death of Sabinianus sometime around 481 had removed an obstacle to peace between Zeno and the Amal,[48] but the rejection of the Amal's offer of delayed departure for Dardania in the winter of 479/480 had left Theoderic soured by the bad faith of the imperial court. Perhaps in contact with Strabo, the Amal may have already launched some further raids on Greece. In 482, unshackled by the demise of Sabinianus and bolstered by the death of Strabo, the Pannonian Goths expanded those raids on parts of Macedonia and Thessaly, sacking Larissa even in the face of the Roman forces of John the Scythian and Moschianus.[49]

Therefore, when imperial representatives arrived in the Amal camp to offer a peace, Theoderic was going to make the emperor pay for his repeated deceptions. The result was a new arrangement in 482–483, which saw the Amal Goths settled in Dacia Ripensis and Lower Moesia and their leader appointed senior *magister militum praesentalis*: 'After a decade of intermittent movement and fighting, the great gamble had paid off.'[50] The extent to which Theoderic's fortunes were turned around by the actions of Strabo and then his death was shown by the Amal achieving a position that Strabo had never managed – the consulship of 484:

> No individual who owed his political prominence to the fact that he was in command of a non-Roman military force had ever received such an honour before. Clearly Zeno had been forced to find something entirely beyond the norm to pay off Theoderic for the double-dealing off 478.[51]

Such a promotion into the elite circles of Constantinople may also have brought Theoderic into whatever plans and plots Zeno had for Recitach. In late 483 or early 484, after leaving a bathing house on his way to a banquet in Bonophatianae, a district in Constantinople, Recitach was murdered on the instigation of Theoderic.[52] Zeno was almost certainly involved, as surely Theoderic would not have risked ordering a murder in the imperial capital without some sanction. The fact that Recitach was in Constantinople at all would suggest that the Thracian

Goth leader had been invited to the capital for discussions with the emperor. Perhaps Illus had reached out to the new leader of the Thracian Goths and Zeno was keen to prevent any such alliance.[53]

Together with his removal of his uncles, Recitach's murder triggered the disintegration of the Thracian Goths. The sources do not provide any real information about what really happened; however, if forces acting on behalf of Zeno had inflicted a decisive defeat on the Thracian Goths, even the scant sources that survive would record it. Perhaps those lesser chiefs left in command by the loss of Strabo and Recitach could not decide which of them should lead the group going forward and they gradually went their separate ways. Some seem to have enrolled in the Roman army, as Gothic names are represented in its ranks for the next generation;[54] perhaps others merely faded away to be absorbed by Balkan populations or returned across the Danube to 'barbaricum'. Jordanes records Thracian or Moesian Goths still living in Moesia by the mid-sixth century:

> They are a numerous people, but poor and unwarlike, rich in nothing save flocks of various kinds and pasture-lands for cattle and forests for wood. Their country is not fruitful in wheat and other sorts of grain. Certain of them do not know that vineyards exist elsewhere, and they buy their wine from neighboring countries. But most of them drink milk.[55]

However, a significant proportion of Strabo's men transferred their allegiance to the strongest independent general in the vicinity: Theoderic the Amal.[56] This might hint at some other involvement in the murder of Recitach; perhaps the Amal was in contact with some of those sub-commanders of the Thracian Goths. This was also not something that Zeno would have wanted. He may only have one Gothic force to deal with but it was now a stronger, more numerous force; if he had to confront it militarily, it would involve risking imperial forces or relying on Illus, neither of which the emperor was keen to do.

Upon his restoration to the throne in mid-476, Zeno had been beholden to a series of individuals and groups who could be enemies or allies from one season to the next depending on which way the political wind was blowing. Perhaps demonstrating how influenced he had been by either his Isaurian origins or the success of Leo's massacre of the Ardaburii, Zeno's initial aim was a Corleone-style annihilation of his numerous opponents. This had only been partly successful, but over the following years, through a mixture of good timing, good fortune and good, old-fashioned ruthlessness, Zeno achieved a more piecemeal reduction of his opponents. By 484, Zeno had neutralized, dispatched or outlasted Basiliscus, Zenonis, Marcus, Armatus, Leo Basiliscus, Verina, Marcianus, Procopius Anthemius, Romulus, Theoderic Strabo, Recitach and his uncles and the Thracian Goths. However, this did not bring security to Zeno's reign. If anything, it may have increased the peril it was in, for in decreasing the number of his opponents, Zeno had concentrated more power and influence on those who remained, specifically Theoderic the Amal and Illus. To be free to govern the empire as he saw fit, Zeno had to find a way of getting rid of these two immensely powerful generals at a time when he was lacking overwhelming military force and had other political and religious problems to deal with.

Chapter 10

All Quiet on the Eastern Front?

'Rumours of war from distant frontiers ... Victories were still being won, but against increasingly fearsome opponents. The waves crashing against bulwarks of Persian power appeared to be growing more violent with every passing year. Whole tribes of people, whole nations, were on the move.'

Holland (2012), p.69

A Brief History of Romano-Persian Interactions

Ever since the legions had moved into the eastern Mediterranean in the first century BC, Rome's main adversary had been the occupant of the Iranian Plateau. From the 220s, that had been the Sassanid Persians, when they emerged from the province of Persis, Fars province in modern Iran, under Ardashir I to overthrow the Parthian kingdom. To consolidate his new position as King of Kings, Ardashir turned his attention to the Roman provinces of Asia, claiming that 'he would win back everything that the ancient Persians had once held, as far as the Grecian Sea, claiming that all this was his rightful inheritance from his forefathers'.[1] While it would be four centuries before the Sassanids ever came close to achieving such a lofty aim, these initial strikes demonstrated that the nascent Sassanid state was not a pushover. Large cities like Dura-Europus and Antioch were captured, huge victories at Barbalissus and Edessa were won and a Roman emperor was taken prisoner in 260. The Roman response to this new Iranian threat had begun poorly, but after a strong rearguard action in the Taurus Mountains, pro-Roman forces led by the Palmyrene ruler Odenathus not only restored the frontier but also marched on the Persian capital at Ctesiphon. Internal instability then saw much of the last decades of the third century remain largely peaceful.[2]

When war broke out again in 296, Armenia was the focal point. Its king, Tiridates III, had tried to take advantage of a Persian civil war, but once Narses had emerged as undisputed Sassanid king he launched a series of reprisals. As Armenia was a Roman ally, Narses knew this meant war with Rome, in this case Diocletian and his fellow Tetrarchs. The initial contest at Carrhae in 296/297 saw the defeat of Galerius *Caesar*, although he was quick to avenge that humiliation with a decisive victory over Narses near Satala in 298. The subsequent Peace of Nisibis in 299 established Roman dominance over Armenia, Iberia and northern

Mesopotamia for almost forty years. That this peace lasted so long is surprising – the Persians were undoubtedly unhappy about their lost territory and it would be expected that at least one Roman emperor would try to build upon their dominant position in the East. However, as both the Roman and Persian worlds collapsed into several bouts of internal fighting and short-lived reigns, the status of Mesopotamia, Armenia and Iberia was less important than who would rule in the East and West. By the time Rome and Persia came to blows again in the mid-330s, the merry-go-round of imperial succession had left Constantine I as Roman emperor and Shapur II as Sassanid king. It was the latter who launched a series of attacks on Rome's provinces and allies, although he did so due to the former's warmongering. On the premise of defending Persia's Christians, Constantine had been gathering his forces for an eastern expedition; his son, Constantius II, had already been dispatched east to oversee preparations. Shapur was merely getting his retaliation in first.

Over the next twenty-five years, Shapur II 'retaliated' on numerous occasions, repeatedly driving into Roman territory. However, while there were some Persian successes at Singara, Bezabde and most famously at the siege and sack of Amida, the defensive strategies of Constantius II prevented Shapur from making significant territorial gains. It was only when the Romans went on the offensive that results changed. The Persian expedition of Julian in 363 was a complete disaster. Unable to capture Ctesiphon and constantly harassed by Shapur's forces, the emperor was killed in a skirmish. To extricate the remainder of the army, Julian's successor, Jovian, had to sign away Armenia, Nisibis and Singara and all territory beyond the Tigris, undoing 150 years of Roman expansion. Shapur's triumph was somewhat short-lived as the Romans re-established parity in the eastern theatre with the limited victories and diplomatic manoeuvring of Valens. This had seen the status of Armenia again become a contentious issue, but a solution was at hand. Under Theodosius I and Shapur III in around 386, Armenia was partitioned: the Romans absorbed their half as a province on the death of Arsaces III in 387 and the Persians established their own Arsacid sub-kingdom of Persarmenia.[3]

This agreement between the two empires held and even fostered a mutual respect. This saw Arcadius appoint the Persian king Yazdgerd I as guardian of his son and heir, Theodosius II, in his will,[4] a tradition which would continue on and off for the next 200 years. By the fifth century then, it appears that the two great empires saw each other as equals, leading to longer periods of peace and shorter, less sanguinary wars, although this reduction may be more to do with internal opposition or other foreign foes[5] – the Romans with the Huns and Goths, the Persians with the tribes of the Central Asian steppe. That is not to say that peace reigned completely throughout the fifth century. These were still two heavily militarized empires. Any *Augustus* or *shahanshah* could quickly overturn a prolonged period of peace in the search for military glory, a distraction from internal problems, financial gain or imperial legitimacy.

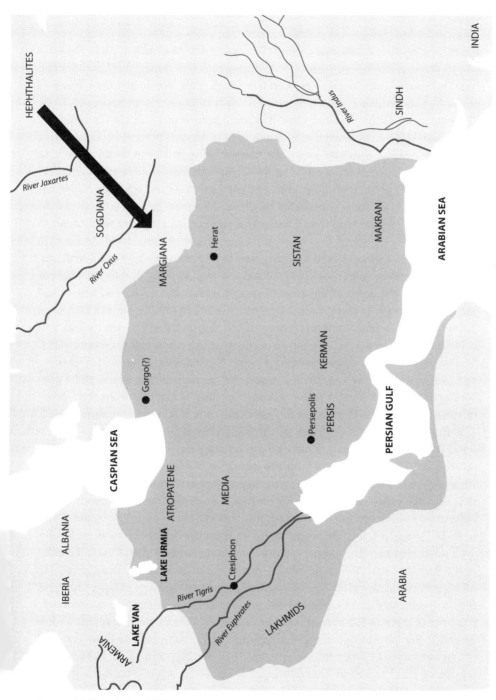

Sassanid Persia in 476

The 'Proto-Crusade' of 421/422 and the War of 440

The removal of Armenia as a geographical flashpoint had not quelled one of its underlying issues – Christianity. Since the conversion of Constantine in the early fourth century, Roman emperors (with the exception of Julian the Apostate) had seen themselves as the protectors of all Christians. This in turn saw the Christians of the Persian Empire viewed as a potential 'fifth column' and an opponent of the Zoroastrianism of the Sassanid state. Any move against intransigent Christians by the Persian king could be used as a *casus belli* by a Roman emperor, as Constantine I did with Shapur II in the 330s. The Sassanid king therefore found himself in something of a no-win situation. If he was strong and long-lived he could interject in the religious politics of his empire and even suppress the religious minorities when they were perceived as causing problems. However, he risked the ire of the Roman emperor if he targeted Christians. If the Persian king was too lenient on those minorities he could find himself facing the opposition of the Zoroastrian priestly class, as Yazdgerd I did for being seen to be embracing Jews and Christians. His depiction as a 'sinner' by Sassanid sources was not only due to his religious policies. Since the death of the great Shapur II in 379, the nobles and priests had grown increasingly brazen, with the former being responsible for the demise of Yazdgerd I's two immediate predecessors. He responded by having priests and nobles executed – a perceived political necessity which blackened his reputation.

For most of his reign though, Yazdgerd's lenience towards Christianity and distractions of the two parties meant that peace between Rome and Persia continued. That prolonged peace was to reach half a century from the victory of Valens' generals at Bagavan in 371 until the time war broke out again in 421. The reason behind this outbreak was that a group of Persian Christians took it upon themselves to destroy some Zoroastrian temples, leading to some Sassanid repression.[6] Theodosius II took up the mantle of 'Christian protector', waging a war in 421–422 which almost took on the appearance of a 'proto-Crusade'.[7] Perhaps reflecting the expected extent of this conflict, Theodosius removed men from the Balkans to bolster the forces sent east and replaced them by letting some Goths settle in Thrace, possibly the precursor to the Thracian Goths of Theoderic Strabo.

To fight this war, Theodosius appointed Ardabur, father of Aspar, as commander of the Roman eastern forces. Ardabur dispatched a column under Anatolius to join rebels in Persarmenia while the Alan general himself crossed into Persian Arzanene. He was intercepted by and defeated the main Persian force under Narses, seemingly a brother of Bahram V. The Sassanid force retreated, only to then strike into under-defended Roman Mesopotamia. Recognizing the Persian plan, Ardabur marched to Mesopotamia as well, forestalling any such attempt and then, bolstered by reinforcements,[8] moved to besiege Nisibis. Despite this positive start, the Romans found their enemies multiplying. Not only was a large Persian force marching to the relief of Nisibis, Bahram V had gained support from the Lakhmid Arabs. Worse still, Huns had attacked the Balkans, brushing aside whatever defence the Goths provided, and were threatening the outskirts of Constantinople.

Ardabur's forces defeated the Lakhmids under the walls of Nisibis, with many thousands reputedly drowning in the Mygdonius, but Theodosius II and his advisors felt that they could not afford war on two fronts and ordered Ardabur and Anatolius to retreat. This may have allowed the Persians to besiege Theodosiopolis; however, exactly which Theodosiopolis this was or when it took place is not clear. If it is Armenian Theodosiopolis, modern Erzurum, the siege belongs in 421, while if it is Osrhoene Theodosiopolis, modern Ras al-Ayn, it could be after Ardabur's retreat from Nisibis. The siege is presented as being of significant size, lasting up to thirty days and involving thousands of soldiers backed up with siege engines. However, the story that the Persians were only convinced to abandon the siege when one of their sub-kings was killed by a stone-thrower who supposedly looked like Thomas the Apostle, who was encouraged by the city's bishop, Eunomius, somewhat limits the usefulness of the source. After the Roman evacuation of Persian Mesopotamia and Persarmenia, the war of 421–422 fizzled out. The *magister officiorum*, Helio, was charged with negotiating terms of cessation and in 422 obtained a return to the *status quo ante bellum*, an agreement not to interfere in the Arab relations of the other power and mutual religious tolerance. As Theodosius had largely got what had seemingly been his reason for going to war – the toleration of Christianity – the war of 421–422 was trumpeted poetically as a great success.[9]

This cessation of war in 422 and the distractions of the respective empires brought another generation of peace to the Mesopotamian frontier. It should always be noted that just because there was official 'peace' between Constantinople and Ctesiphon does not mean that the frontier was altogether peaceful. Keen for any upper-hand on or distraction of their opponent, both the Romans and Persians were surely engaged in constant information-gathering and espionage. This could have escalated with foreign agents using religion and culture to cause trouble in Armenia, Iberia and other regions, and even to wage proxy wars through the likes of the Arabs. However, even if there was an ongoing campaign of mutual misinformation and destabilization, there was a public display of diplomatic cooperation centred on the Caucasus Mountains and a mutual enemy of the Romans and Persians. That enemy was the Huns and the cooperation came in the form of Roman financial contributions to the Persian defence of the passes through the Caucasus. The Romans were willing to countenance providing such assistance because while the Caspian Gate was in Persian hands, any Hunnic force to get through the Caucasus was as much a threat to Roman Armenia, Anatolia and Syria as it was to Persian Media or Iran.[10]

John Lydus posits a mutual agreement coming about through the treaty of Jovian leaving the Persians to defend more territory than they could manage.[11] The great Hunnic raid of Asia in 395 proved that this threat was by no means a mirage dreamt up by Persians and locals.[12] But even with such proof, the exact nature and regularity of these payments are contentious. The description from Lydus has been used to suggest a formal treaty between Constantinople and Ctesiphon; however, while there was communication over Rome's contribution to the Caucasus defences, any payments may have been far less regular and structured than any treaty might entail.[13] Perhaps the arrangement was something of an *ad hoc* affair with the Persians asking for payment when they felt they needed or wanted it, and the Romans paying up when they could or wanted to. Indeed, the modern disagreement over the nature of these payments may reflect their contemporary depiction. They were 'viewed as diplomatic subsidies by the Romans, [but] for the Sasanians these payments were unambiguously tributary evidence of Roman subordination'.[14] Non-payment was grounds for military action.[15] It might not have been seized upon every time the Persian king's entreaties were rebuffed by the Roman emperor, but such refusals could be depicted as a gross insult should the *shahanshah* be in a position to embark on a war.

This appears to be the case when Yazdgerd II, son and successor of Bahram V, came to the Persian throne in 438. Keen for a successful military campaign, Yazdgerd chose to take the refusal of Theodosius II to pay the subsidy in 439/440 as a *raison de guerre*. His decision can only have been helped by Theodosius II refusing to pay the subsidy because Hunnic raids and an African campaign meant he could not afford it. These military engagements may well have seen the Romans remove some men from their eastern frontier, further emboldening the Persian king to invade Roman territory in 440. The subsequent war was even shorter than its 421/422 predecessor. The area around Nisibis is hinted at as being the centre of Yazdgerd's raiding, with perhaps the city itself a target, which would require it to have changed hands since the war of 421–422. The only other aspect of this conflict recorded by the sources is that poor weather hindered the Persian advance, allowing the Romans to get their forces into the field. To Theodoret, the thunder and hail was evidence of God's support of the Romans.[16]

This delay did little to bolster Roman participation in the war and before the year was out, Theodosius had sent Anatolius to treat with Yazdgerd in the Persian camp. Demonstrating his other distractions, the emperor gave the Sassanids the Caucasian payment he 'owed' and agreed to not build any new fortifications in Mesopotamia. But why did Yazdgerd accept such a basic peace deal? He too agreed not to build fortifications in his part of Mesopotamia and the payment does not seem to have been of enormous proportions. It may be that the Persian king was content with having made his point to the Romans and to his own nobles that he was willing to fight. He also had his own distractions. Soon after the peace signed with the Romans, Yazdgerd and his generals were striking into Persarmenia, defeating rebels, capturing many Armenian nobles, priests and troops, and sending them to the eastern provinces. He then moved on into Iberia and the Caucasus to secure the passes.[17]

In terms of direct military action, the cessation of the war of 440 was to be the end of Romano-Persian conflict in the fifth century. However, there were to be several flashpoints throughout the next six decades which could have brought the two powers to war should either be in a position to wage it. The distractions of the Persians were equally drastic to those faced by Leo and Zeno, and for a brief period in the mid-480s may have threatened Sassanid control of the Iranian plateau.

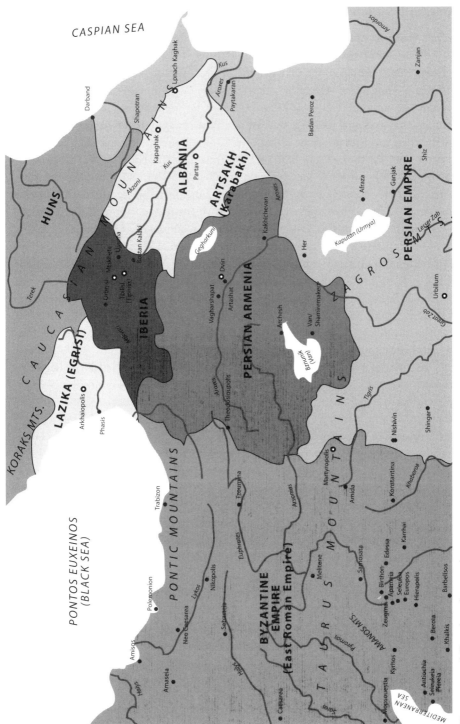

Roman and Persian Armenia

Persian Problems I: Armenia and the Battle of Avarayr 451

Before looking further east to new enemies, the Persians still had to deal with a persistent problem – Armenia. Bahram V turned his attention to the Persarmenian subkingdom at the end of the war of 421–422. It had been without a king since 418/420 when Shapur IV had made his play for the Persian throne. The lack of a king had seen the Armenians eject many of the Persian garrisons and live in a state of anarchic independence for several years. Rather than install a member of his own family, Bahram reinstated the Arsacid dynasty one last time. The choice fell on Artaxias/Ardashir IV, but he proved unpopular with some of the Armenia population, seemingly because he was fostering close relations with the Romans. Constantinople retained an interest in expanding its influence in Persarmenia with the foundation and fortification of Theodosiopolis on the Armenian border in around 420–421, which in itself could be seen as part of the outbreak of the war of 421–422. So wary were they of the Romano-Arsacid association that a band of Armenian nobles appealed to Bahram to annex Persarmenia as a Sassanid province. This was opposed by the Christian population, as they would rather have a poor Christian ruler in Ardashir than any kind of non-Christian. Despite this opposition, Bahram deposed the Arsacid dynast and made Persarmenia the newest satrapy of the Sassanid state under a Persian *marzban* governor in 428.[18]

This annexation was met with opposition, which only grew as Yazdgerd II began to get more involved in the religious politics of his empire. Religious minorities came in for some harsh treatment as Yazdgerd attempted to spread Zoroastrianism. Jews were prohibited from observing the Sabbath, the Jewish community in Isfahan attacked local Zoroastrian priests after the execution of some of their leaders, while 153,000 Assyrian Christians were reputedly massacred in Kirkuk. It was in Persarmenia that Yazdgerd's religious oppression sparked the greatest reaction. The Persian king issued an edict imposing Zoroastrianism as the 'official' religion of Sassanid Armenia, leading to the demolishing of churches, building of fire-temples and establishing of Zoroastrian priests by force.[19] Yazdgerd would not have introduced such a potentially divisive measure if he did not have some Zoroastrian support within Persarmenia. However, there were a significant number of Armenian Christians willing to fight for their faith and they found leadership from Vardan Mamikonian.

The subsequent revolt came to a head at what sources record as the truly monstrous Battle of Avarayr on 26 May 451. Armenian sources present the Sassanid force on a scale barely matched until the Industrial Age – 200,000-300,000 men.[20] The Persian king was capable of recruiting forces in the several tens of thousands from within his own realm, and still had allies amongst the Zoroastrian Caucasians including what was recorded as 40,000–60,000 Armenians, but he was in no position to field an army of 300,000. It must also be noted that this Persian force at Avarayr was more likely a regional force rather than the grand army of the King of Kings.

However, the Sassanid force did include two corps of elephants and their fearsome elite cavalry, the Immortals.

Vardan appealed to Constantinople for aid, but the empire was embroiled not only with the Huns but also with the death of Theodosius II on 28 July 450 and the subsequent accession of Marcian a month later.[21] Mamikonian also looked to his Caucasian neighbours for help, sending forces to claim the Derbend Pass for the Caucasian Albanians, who responded along with the Iberians by sending men. Vardan may even have succeeded in attaining some Huns from north of the Caucasus.[22] The religious element of the revolt may have encouraged far more Christian peasants to join up, swelling the numbers if not the quality of the Caucasian-Hun force of Vardan, but it is unlikely to have reached the recorded 66,000. That said, even with many inexperienced or raw peasant troops, the noble core contained many veterans and the well-respected and coveted Armenian heavy cavalry.

Despite the wide array of regions, petty kingdoms and peoples represented at Avarayr, such overall numbers – perhaps over 400,000 men – are impossible to accept. That there was no direct involvement from either the Persian king or the Roman emperor significantly reduces the possibility of the armies even reaching 30,000-40,000. The forces involved were more likely closer to a tenth of the numbers recorded; perhaps 20,000-30,000 Persians versus 6,000-8,000 Caucasians. The Persians likely had a significant numerical superiority, a superiority only increased by the defection of a group of Christian Armenians under Vasak Siuni as the two armies squared up to one another across the Avarayr Plain, separated by the Tghmout tributary of the River Arax.

Vardan divided his force of cavalry, archers, spearmen and swordsman into four corps. On his right, he placed a mixed forced of infantry and cavalry under Koren; his centre was made up of infantry under Nershapuh Ardzruni; and he took personal command of the mixed infantry and cavalry corps on the Armenian left. The fourth corps was held in reserve under his brother, Hamazaspian. The Persians, under the command of Mushkin Miusalavurd, were divided into five corps – mixed cavalry and infantry on their left, an infantry centre supported by elephants, a massed corps of various cavalry units on their right, another elephant-supported infantry corps in the centre second line and a reserve guard in the rear. Before battle was joined, Vardan addressed his men, invoking the deeds of the Maccabees, who in winning their freedom from the Seleucid Greeks over 600 years previously had overcome massive odds in fighting for their faith.[23] Catechumens were then baptized and communion was taken. Mushkin will likely have told his men that they need only resist the initial Armenian charge and then make their numerical superiority tell.

The Battle of Avarayr began with a mutual advance towards the waters of the Tghmout. The religiously inspired Christian Armenians had the better of the fighting, holding the Persians back from gaining a foothold on their bank of the river. The inevitable charge of the heavy Armenian cavalry drove segments of the Persian wings back. However, it seems that the Armenian left was over-zealous in

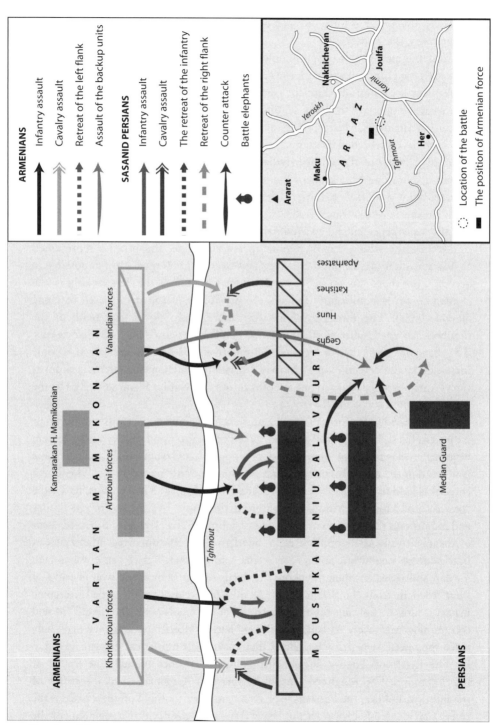

Battle of Avarayr

its charge, throwing itself into as much confusion as it did to the Persian right flank. Vardan responded by gathering the rest of the left wing, along with his reserve, to try to retrieve the situation, with some success. Hamazaspian aided the Armenian centre against the elephants, while Vardan's reconstituted left wing drove the Persian cavalry away from the river and towards the rear of the battlefield.

Vardan's decisive action appeared to have put the Sassanids on the back foot, with their massed cavalry right wing dispersed and the Persian commander now within striking distance of Vardan's cavalry. However, the Armenian left and reserve had over-committed and were now detached from the support of the rest of their army. They were soon assailed on all sides by various Sassanid forces – the elephant corps from the second line, the reserve guard and a reconstituted cavalry corps. As the Persian cavalry included Huns and had a tradition of employing steppe tactics, it could be that the collapse of the Persian right was something of a feigned flight, meant to draw the Armenians into over-extending. More likely, it was something of a welcome bonus for Mushkin that the temporary collapse of his cavalry wing had led to the destruction of the Armenian left.

Isolated and overwhelmed, Vardan Mamikonian went down fighting, dying a martyr's death, along with several hundred other Armenian nobles. Without their leader, not to mention their left wing and reserve, the Armenians and their Caucasian allies fought valiantly, but by the end of the day their resistance had been broken and the survivors dispersed into the highlands. While Mushkin was of a mind to use the knowledge garnered from Vasak and other defectors to track down the survivors, Yazdgerd II was happy to have made his point on the battlefield of Avarayr. He called Mushkin off and informed the Armenians that if they ended their insurrection, they would be allowed to build their churches and maintain their faith under a tolerant *marzban*.[24] Despite this lenience, some Armenians continued their rebellion from hideouts in the western and northern highlands, even encouraging the Huns to attack and destroy the re-established Persian garrison at Derbend and raid Persian territory.[25] However, while it would become 'a symbol of resistance and remembrance against their Zoroastrian neighbours',[26] Avarayr had been a decisive defeat for the Mamikonians and their Christian allies, and for the time being shut down the biggest threat to the Persian peace on their western frontier.[27]

Persian Problems II: The Tribes of the Steppe and the Battle of Herat 484

It was just in time too, for in the east another persistent Persian problem had refused to go away. During the 421–422 war with Rome, the Sassanid north-eastern frontier collapsed under an attack from the steppe, with the rich city of Marv falling to the invaders. This was by no means the first time that the Persian east had come under pressure from steppe nomads. Even the great Shapur II had great difficulty in the mid-fourth century dealing with an influx of such steppe barbarians, called

Chionitae and possibly Kidarite in origin. But who were these enemies at the eastern gates of the Persian Empire in the early 420s? There appears to be two successive groups – Kidarites and Hephthalites. Frequently, these groups are classed as merely some of the easternmost parts of an immense Hunnic 'nation', stretching from the Central Asian steppe into central Europe. The Kidarites, also referred to as Chionitae, Hunas or 'Red Huns', may have been a Hunnic clan, which replaced the Kushans in the early fourth century. However, the physical depiction of the Hephthalites has raised doubts over their Hunnic identification. They come across as far less 'ugly' in the sources than the Huns, lacking the Asiatic complexion, but they do demonstrate aspects of the Hunnic lifestyle, particularly their elongating of skulls and horsemanship. Perhaps these 'White Huns' were Aryans like the Persians and Parthians but had adopted Hunnic customs on the steppe.[28]

In the 420s, the conquerors of Marv were Kidarites, and having procured peace with the Romans, Bahram V moved east in search of revenge. He was successful in killing the Kidarite leader, Varhran II, in *c*.425, regaining many of the lost riches and restoring the Oxus River as the boundary between his empire and the steppe tribes. However, Bahram's setting up of his brother, Narses, at Balkh as governor of the eastern provinces and Yazdgerd II moving his court to Nishapur in 453 for a large-scale Kidarite campaign shows that the Kidarites remained a threat. They may even have forced the Sassanids to pay them tribute.[29] Before he could make any definitive steppe intervention, Yazdgerd II died in 457 and the Persian succession fell into another round of dispute amongst his sons, Hormizd and Peroz. As the eldest son and seemingly closer to the capital, Hormizd III had himself crowned, forcing his brother to flee east. Within two years though, Peroz had returned at the head of an army – but it was not a Persian army; instead, it was a force of Hephthalites. While he had turned to enemies of the Sassanid state for military aid, Peroz did have internal support from the influential Mihran family, so this was not a barbarian takeover. But it was a takeover: in 459, Hormizd III was defeated and replaced on the Sassanid throne by Peroz I.[30]

Peroz's reign had not started in the most auspicious terms. Not only had he used Hephthalites to take the throne and been faced with opposition in Albania and Armenia, but large parts of the Sassanid kingdom were racked by drought and famine. Despite his reputation as an ostentatious dandy,[31] Peroz tackled these problems head on, reducing taxes, spending state funds on the poor and forcing his nobles to subsidize famine relief. This programme was reputedly so successful that it was still spoken about in positive tones centuries later.[32] Having alleviated some of these internal problems, Peroz turned to his main external problem – the steppe tribes. In doing so he would earn a reputation as 'a daring and warlike man',[33] although it would cost him his life.

On the death of Yazdgerd II, the Kidarites had again begun raiding Persian territory in the early 460s. Peroz lacked the manpower to face down these raids, with appeals to the Albanians, Armenians and even the Romans not providing enough men to contemplate a large-scale invasion of Kidarite territory. The Persian king therefore resorted to negotiation, compromise and treachery. He agreed to send technical aid and even his sister to the Kidarite leader, Kunkhas, although rather than his sister, he sent an imposter. When he realized this deception, Kunkhas sent back many of Peroz's 300 military experts maimed or disfigured and the raids continued. Peroz finally found the needed manpower in 467 by taking a page out of the Roman barbarian playbook – he would pit Hephthalite against Kidarite. This Sassanid-instigated Hephthalite-Kidarite War of 467 ended in the elimination of the Kidarites.[34]

However, the Hephthalite victory expanded the threat they posed to the Sassanids. Peroz may have cultivated a personal relationship with the Hephthalite leader, Khushnavaz, but it did not prevent these 'White Huns' from turning on their erstwhile Persian allies in 469, perhaps because Peroz had reneged on any promises made in 459 or 467. Peroz had built on the infrastructural foundations of his father, Yazdgerd II, with the continued strengthening of border capitals with fortified garrisons and supply depots, but this did not stop the Hephthalites from seizing Balkh and much of Bactria. More concerning was Peroz seeing the need to build a 150-mile wall across the Gurgan Plain.[35] Steppe conflict had expanded beyond Transoxiana and the eastern Persian provinces. The Iranian heartland of the Sassanid state was now under threat as the Hephthalites founded a capital at Gorgo on the Gurgan Plain, just to the south-east of the Caspian Sea.[36]

Peroz may have fought a series of battles against the Hephthalites on the Gurgan Plains in *c*.469, only to suffer the ignominy of defeat and capture,[37] although these battles may be a misplacing of a later conflict, which would result in Peroz's capture and ransom. That conflict in the early 470s was provoked by an insult from Khushnavaz. Peroz and his Albanian allies invaded Hephthalite territory with such ferocity that Khusunavaz was sent into headlong retreat. Or so it seemed. The likelihood is that the Hephthalite retreat was feigned. Thinking that supreme victory was at hand, Peroz forged on after his foe. However, in leading his men into the hills and valleys, the Sassanid king's forces entered unsuitable terrain. When the forces of Khushnavaz turned on Peroz, the Persian king met with heavy defeat sometime between 471 and 474 and was taken hostage. The ransom imposed to buy his freedom was unsurprisingly harsh. Persian strongholds and land were surrendered, heavy tribute was imposed and to make sure it was paid, Peroz's chief priest, daughter and son, Kavadh, were all sent to Khushnavaz as hostages.[38] The most humiliating spectacle, though, was Peroz being forced to prostrate himself before the Hephthalite king. The Persians made great hay out of the idea that the Roman emperor paid them tribute, and it was a great diplomatic and political shame to be paying actual tribute to barbaric horsemen. When trying to throw off the steppe yolk, Yazdgerd II had made a show of stopping that payment and Peroz himself had reneged on similar payments, contributing to Hephthalite raids. It can come as no surprise then that as soon as

Kavadh had returned from three years as a hostage in *c*.477, Peroz was planning another attempt to defeat the Hephthalites.[39]

But Khushnavaz and his horsemen clearly presented a tough prospect. Small wonder then that Peroz reached out to Zeno for financial aid against their shared 'Hunnic' enemy.[40] Whatever money the Roman emperor provided, any observer of the Sassanid force gathering in the eastern foothills of the Elburz Mountains will have felt that Peroz had spent that money well – anything from 50,000-100,000 men comprised of spear, sword and archer infantry, light, archer, heavy and Immortal cavalry and probably a corps of elephants. Marching out through 'Alexander's Wall', Peroz drove at the nearest Hephthalite settlement, possibly Gorgo itself,[41] finding it deserted. This initial move may not be part of the decisive campaign of 484, as Gorgo is considerably distant from the eventual focus of fighting 1,000km to the east around Herat. Whether marching across Hephthalite territory or returning home to then strike east later in the year, Peroz led his vast host to Bactria, recapturing Balkh. While there, the Persian king was approached by Hephthalite emissaries but he rejected any talk of a negotiated peace. Had he not just driven the Hephthalite army 1,000km from their base at Gorgo? But given succeeding events, Khushnavaz was not aiming at a negotiated settlement either; he was merely buying time.

Recognizing that Peroz was heading in the direction of Herat, the Hephthalite king sent small contingents to irritate the advancing Sassanid column. By the time the Persians reached Herat, they were thoroughly frustrated and Peroz was keen to seize on any opportunity to attack. Suddenly, that opportunity presented itself. Opposite the Persian position outside Herat, the Hephthalites had made a mess of whatever manoeuvres they were attempting. Small groups had become detached and the main army itself was in disarray. The Sassanid cavalry hurtled across the desert, the scent of impending triumph only intensifying in the nostrils of the Persians and their steeds as the Hephthalites broke and fled through the centre of the battlefield. Such an orderly rout should have raised suspicion, but the Persian force only saw a fleeing foe to be run down. So blinded were they that the Persians missed that the battlefield had been excavated extensively. Too late, the Persians found the ground opening up beneath them and thousands of horses and riders were plunging into a huge trench filled with stakes and other maiming devices. The Hephthalites peppered the entrenched Persians with arrows and finished off any men attempting to climb out. The rest of the Hephthalite force surrounded the chaotic Persian lines. In a storm of arrows, missiles and cavalry charges, the immense host of Peroz ceased to exist; the King of Kings himself was dead, along with seven of his sons.[42]

Such a calamity could have done irretrievable damage to the Persian state; indeed, if loyalty to the Sassanid dynasty, its ideology and structures had not been so strong, and if the Hephthalite state had not been so young, the Iranian plateau may have fallen to these 'Huns'.[43] That is not to say that Iran was free from degradation in the aftermath of the disaster at Herat. For two years, the Hephthalites raided the Sassanid east with impunity. It took the intervention of Sukhra of the Karen to prevent these raids becoming a more permanent change in the balance of power. Sukhra then saw to the elevation of Balash, another son of Yazdgerd II and brother of Hormizd III and Peroz, to the Sassanid throne. Despite this Karen-led military recovery, Balash still felt the need to sign a peace treaty with Khushnavaz, agreeing to pay a huge tribute.

The Caucasian Kingdoms: Future (and Present) Flashpoints

As already seen, the upkeep of the passes through the Caucasian Mountains had become a bone of contention between Rome and Persia in the late fourth century and on into the fifth. As the two great empires proved either unwilling or unable to take direct control of the Caucasian passes, some responsibility fell upon various local peoples – Laz, Iberi and Albani. The Colchian kingdom of Lazica had been a Roman ally for most of the previous 500 years. The kingdom of Iberia in the centre of the Caucasus had a similarly long Roman clientship, which had only ended with Julian's disastrous Persian expedition. Albania was a subkingdom of the Parthian and then the Persian state, although it had not been out of Rome's reach with the likes of Pompey and Antoninus Pius exerting influence over the region. The Peace of Nisibis had seen Albania become a Roman protectorate, only for that to be overturned by the treaty with Jovian.

Tensions began to rise between these local peoples and their imperial overlords at the height of the Hunnic threat in the mid-fifth century. In around 456, the Lazican king, Gobazes, was accused of negotiating with the Sassanids to throw off Roman hegemony. In response, Marcian dispatched a military expedition, which required the acquiescence of the Persian king as it involved marching very close to the border with Persarmenia. Through military force and the envoy, Dionysius, the message was delivered to Gobazes that either he or his son must abdicate. By 466, Gobazes had accepted this judgement and stepped down before visiting Constantinople, where he was treated favourably by Leo, including a visit to Daniel the Stylite. However, the visit also involved a reprimand as Gobazes' dealings with the Sassanid king had destabilized the Caucasus.[44] This was highlighted by the invasion of Lazica by King Vakhtang I of Iberia, which would only have happened with the approval of his overlord, the Sassanid king.

This abortive Iberian venture was not the end of the fallout. In 468, the Lazican kingdom was faced with a pro-Persian secessionist movement in its mountainous north by the Tzani. Gobazes, seemingly still in a position of power, led an army into Tzania, reinforced by resources and even men provided by Zeno in his role as eastern *magister*, but failed to reincorporate the breakaway state. Another Sassanid-sponsored Iberian invasion of Lazica may have hindered Gobazes' efforts.[45] The outcome was that while Roman influence remained in Lazica, the Persians now had a foothold in Tzania. However, this merely upped the military and financial burden of the Persian king, for he was now responsible not only for the Derbend Pass but also the Dariel Pass. This in turn escalated Persian calls for the Romans to contribute to the Caucasian defences.[46] This division of hegemony over Lazica would see the Romans become more heavy-handed over maintaining their last outpost in the Caucasus, to the detriment of relations with the Laz, who would eventually turn to the Persians for aid in the 540s, leading to the twenty-year Lazican War of 541–562.

After a failed assertion of independence in *c*.406–409 saw it spend the first half of the fifth century under tight Sassanid control, the second half was something of a golden age for the kingdom of Iberia. The upturn in its fortunes coincides with the long reign of Vakhtang I, seemingly from 447-502, if not 522. Unsurprisingly for a proposed reign of fifty-five to seventy-five years, Vakhtang was only about 7 when he acceded to the throne, so the upturn of his kingdom's fortunes cannot have been all his own work. Such a proposed long reign and some trouble with the names Vakhtang went by raises problems over the semi-legendary nature of his position in Georgian history.[47]

He was still in his minority when Iberians joined Vardan Mamikonian at Avarayr, although by the mid-450s he came of age in time to save his country from a Hunnic raid, reputedly killing a giant in single combat. He also led the first Iberian invasion of Lazica, an action which may have seen him rewarded with marriage to a daughter of Hormizd III. His reputation as a useful client of the Persian king can only have risen with his providing military aid to Peroz against the Hephthalites and his second intervention in Lazica in *c*.468. The resultant division of the Lazican kingdom benefited Iberia, with Vakhtang receiving some suzerainty over the Tzani, as well as other areas of the Caucasus.[48]

This increase in his power saw Vakhtang rankle under the Persian yoke, an irritation only enflamed by the presence of a pro-Persian viceroy and the promotion of Zoroastrianism amongst the Christian Iberians. As with any other client wanting to escape his overlord, Vakhtang sought a rapprochement with Zeno. Demonstrating the religious nature of the Iberian irritation with Persia, the negotiations involved Vakhtang asking for the elevation of the Iberian Bishop of Mtskheta to *catholicos*, a symbolic independence of not just the Iberian Church but also all of Iberia. Vakhtang also attempted to gain assurances of Roman military aid against the inevitable Persian retaliation. He is even recorded marrying a Roman imperial daughter, although who this Helena was is not clear. She may have been an illegitimate daughter of Zeno, merely a relative of the emperor, or she was a third daughter of Leo and Verina.[49]

Through these Roman promises, Vakhtang stepped up his bid for independence by expelling pro-Sassanid nobles and Zoroastrian priests in the Caucasus. This brought an armed response from Peroz in the late 470s. Roman aid arrived but only in time to negotiate a truce between Vakhtang and the Persian king, which saw the Iberian monarch reaffirm his client status, providing troops and tribute to Persia. Peroz made the token gesture of agreeing to stop the propagation of Zoroastrianism in Iberia.[50] This humbling did little to assuage Vakhtang's desire for independence and he did not have to wait long for another opportunity. By adhering to his treaty obligations to provide soldiers to Persia, Vakhtang discovered just how badly the war with the Hephthalites was going. Surmising that Persian retaliation would be slow, the Iberian king went after the most high-profile of his pro-Persian underlings, Varsken, the current viceroy of Gurgak.

In putting Varsken to death in 482, Vakhtang was not only declaring his challenge to Persian suzerainty once more, but may also have been purposefully aiming to secure aid from the Armenians. This is because Varsken had been married to Shushanik, daughter of the martyred Vardan Mamikonian, but had reputedly tortured her to death for refusing to convert to Zoroastrianism with him in 475. Even with that, Vardan's successor, Vahan, was reticent about providing help and a recent Persian invasion had left Albania unable to offer support. Nevertheless, the coalition of Iberian, Armenian and Hunnic forces under Vakhtang drove the Persian garrisons out of Iberia. The Armenians followed this up by defeating the Persian governor of Armenia at Akori and then again at Nersehapat.[51] However, the Persian army returned in 483 to ravage Iberia, forcing Vakhtang to flee and again seek the aid of Vahan.[52] The Mamikonian leader obliged, marching his forces to the Kura River to join Vakhtang; however, Roman and Hun reinforcements failed to materialize. Worse still, the Armenian nobles whose loyalty Vahan had suspected expressed their willingness to desert. The subsequent Battle of Akesga was a crushing defeat for the Iberians and Armenians, with Vahan having to flee into the highlands and Vakhtang to Lazica.[53]

Fortunately for the Armenians and Iberians, the Hephthalites intervened. The Persian army ravaging Iberia was withdrawn to join Peroz's fateful campaign of 484, allowing Vakhtang and Vahan to re-establish themselves in their kingdoms. Balash was in such a weakened position that he not only acquiesced to negotiation with Vahan but was in no position to force Vakhtang from his pro-Roman stance, despite Iberia seemingly remaining a Sassanid client. As the Romans and Persians remained at peace and Zoroastrianism was not imposed, an uneasy truce won out between client and master in the last decades of the fifth century.[54]

The last years of Vakhtang's life are somewhat confused chronologically. He seems to have died during Kavadh I's invasion of Iberia, but when this invasion took place is not clear. He may have died in c.502, which would put this Persian invasion during the Anastasian War, possibly after Vakhtang refused to help Kavadh. In this scenario, the Iberian king is recorded dying a heroic death, storming the Persian camp and killing a son of Kavadh before later succumbing to his wounds. However, it is here where the disagreement over the length of his reign comes in. Procopius' rendering of Vakhtang's sobriquet *Gorgasal* – from the shape of the helmet he wore – as Gurgenes could see the Iberian king survive until 522. The incorporation of the events of the reign of 'Gurgenes' with that of Vakhtang sees him faced with Iberia being forcibly brought under Persian suzerainty and a viceroy established at Tblisi in 518. Another Persian invasion in 522 saw the old king die in a Lazican exile.[55] Much like with Lazica, the division of loyalties within Iberia would see it become a focus of a Romano-Persian war from 526–532, when Kavadh I tried to impose Zoroastrianism. This conflict ended with the kingdom of Iberian falling under even tighter Persian control.

The easternmost of the Caucasian kingdoms, Albania, bordered Persian territory and in the fifth century had less direct contact with the Romans. The ruling Arsacid dynasty not only had Parthian origins but also close ties with the Sassanid dynasty through marriage. However, Christianity had spread to the petty kingdom in the early fourth century. This reflected Albania's Armenian links, with the actual name 'Albania' perhaps being of Armenian origin.[56] Such connections to Armenia and its own Christianity meant that Albania had similar reactions to the attempted imposition of Zoroastrianism by several Sassanid kings in the fifth century. This saw Albanians join Vardan at Avarayr in 451, after he helped them gain control of the Derbend Pass.

In 459, as the civil war between Hormizd and Peroz was playing out, the Albanian king, Vach'e II, a cousin of the warring Sassanid brothers, made his play for independence. He no doubt reached out in the usual directions for aid – Constantinople, Armenia and Iberia – yet he also looked north to the Huns and Alans beyond the Caucasus. Vach'e's control of the Derbend Pass allowed his new Transcaucasian 'allies' to pass through the mountains and ravage Persian territory. The newly enthroned Peroz was quick to retaliate in kind. Having already used Hephthalites to overthrow Hormizd, Peroz had little problem allowing another set of Huns through the Dariel Pass to ravage Albanian territory.[57]

This rebellion continued until either the abdication or death of Vach'e II in 463. Peroz refused to allow the accession of a new Albanian king, and for the next twenty-four years Albania was subject to Persian rule, probably through a viceroy established at the new Albanian capital of Perozabad.[58] It was not until 487 that the Albanian monarchy was restored by Balash, as part of his attempts to bring stability to Persian affairs post-Herat. It might be imagined that there was some unrest in Albania, as there had been in Armenia and Iberia, for Balash to allow the formal accession of Vach'e's brother as Vachagan III. The new king sponsored the continued growth of the Albanian Christian Church to the extent that he became known as 'the Pious'. However, despite seemingly having a son, the death of Vachagan III in c.510 saw the end of the Albanian Arsacid dynasty. It would be replaced by a dynasty of Parthian Mihranids, who ruled under Persian, Roman, Khazar and Arab suzerainty until the early ninth century.

A Non-Event: Zeno, the Persians and the Treaty of Nvarsk

Despite the defeat at Avarayr and some relaxing of Yazdgerd's enforced Zoroastrianization, Persarmenian Christian resistance continued, with the focus falling on Vahan Mamikonian, nephew of the fallen Vardan. The Armenians might have looked to take advantage of the civil war between Hormizd and Peroz, but the victorious Peroz was quick to make his presence felt in Caucasia, keeping both the Armenians and Albanians in line.[59] The machinations of Gobazes did bring a Roman force into Lazica in the mid-450s and Tzania in the mid-460s, and probably contributed to Vahan asking for aid but receiving unfulfilled promises from Leo.[60] Peroz may have also shown some inkling of forcing Zoroastrianism on Caucasia during the 460s, although no direct confrontation emerged as Peroz became increasingly drawn east to deal with the steppe tribes.

It was the actions of Vakhtang I of Iberia which brought Vahan Mamikonian and his Armenian Christians into conflict with the Persians once more. Further attempted Zoroastrianization and perceived Persian weakness saw the Armenians join the Iberians in revolt in the early 480s. This did not go well, the Caucasian coalition suffering such a heavy defeat that it should have been the end of the matter, much as Avarayr had been. Instead, the monumental defeat of Peroz at Herat in 484 turned what was a lost cause into an extremely strong bargaining position for Vahan.

With the Sassanid state in disarray, Balash needed to shut down the Caucasian revolt as quickly and bloodlessly as possible. He may also have been wary of an increasing Roman presence in the East as Zeno freed himself from various Gothic and Isaurian distractions, although the emperor will have been looking for any reason not to take up the mantle of 'Christian protector'. Pre-484, the reason had been the presence of Peroz's forces in the Caucasus and the Persian king pointing to the continued issue of the Huns. Rather than intervene in Armenia, Zeno sent funds to help Peroz's Hephthalite campaigns, although these dried up when the war went badly. The emperor may even have offered some financial aid to the Hephthalites upon hearing of reputed Persian support for Illus, an accusation that Zeno may have been willing to hear given his 'revealing' of Ardaburius' connivance with Persia. Post-Herat, with his forces occupied in Isauria, Zeno will have encouraged any non-violent end to hostilities in Caucasia. With Balash similarly inclined, this led to negotiations opening between the Armenians and Persians.

The result was the Treaty of Nvarsk of 484. The focus is usually on how this agreement provided religious freedom to Persarmenia, with Armenian Christians free to worship; however, it went much further than that. In allowing the destruction of all fire-altars in Persarmenia, banning any new constructions and denying land to Zoroastrian converts, the Treaty of Nvarsk seemingly authorized discrimination against Armenian Zoroastrians. The treaty did not formally recognize Armenia as independent from Persia, but the recognition of Vahan as supreme commander of Armenian forces and as *marzban* governor gave the Armenians a great deal of control over their own destiny.[61]

While a sensible move post-Herat, these negotiations did not make Balash popular at home. Roman intervention against the Tzani in the form of Zeno's brother, Longinus, can also not have helped the Persian king's position.[62] Within a year of his accession, Balash was faced with a rebellion from within the Sassanid dynasty. Zarir is a little-known figure, either another son of Yazdgerd II or a son of Peroz. Reputedly

Balash needed military aid from his newly appointed Persarmenian governor, Vahan Mamikonian, to put down the revolt, although the chronology is muddled. It is uncertain if the revolt of Zarir belongs in 484 or 485, making it potentially either a catalyst or a consequence of the Treaty of Nvarsk. This was not the last family trouble Balash faced. Upon the choice of Balash as king, Peroz's son, Kavadh, fled to the Hephthalite court where he had spent three years as a hostage. There, he married a daughter of Khushnavaz and persuaded his new father-in-law to repeat the trick performed with Peroz nearly thirty years earlier – providing a Hephthalite force to place Kavadh on the Persian throne in 488. Such an action must have been helped by Balash's lack of popularity in some Sassanid circles, including Sukhra of Karen, who retained a great deal of power under the new regime.

Kavadh I's reign would last well beyond that of Zeno, but it was not to be a settled one. His attempts to intervene in Armenia were rebuffed by Vahan, who had used the conditions of Nvarsk to help Christianity flourish and build a unity that not only faced down the Sassanid king but also, in concert with Vachagan III of Albania, repelled a Hunnic invasion in 489. Vahan died sometime before 510, succeeded as *marzban* by his brother, Vard. By 514, Kavadh had succeeded in deporting Vard to Persia, although he made no real attempt to reverse the religious freedom granted to Armenia for fear of another rebellion.[63]

Kavadh also faced rebellion from the Albanians and opposition from various factions of nobles, all on the backdrop of continued tributary status to the Hephthalites. Indeed, the proposed way of dealing with his nobles was to promote Mazdakism, which demanded that the nobility share their wealth with the poor. This led to inevitable trouble as the nobles joined with the Zoroastrian clergy to depose Kavadh in 496, replacing him with his brother, Djamasp. However, in 498, Kavadh returned to the throne at the head of another Hephthalite army. Desperate to pay the tribute owed to the Hephthalites and to distract from the social problems caused by Mazdakism, Kavadh used the refusal of Anastasius to continue paying subsidies to the Persian state as a *raison de guerre*, sparking the Anastasian War in 502, ending over a century of peace between the Roman and Persian empires, barring a campaigning season or two in 421/422 and 440.

Romano-Persian relations in the fifth century come across as something of a non-event. Bloody battles, epic sieges and wide-ranging campaigns were replaced with two brief confrontations, hands-off proxy wars and cooperation against mutual enemies. The Persian kings of the fifth century were reasonably capable for the most part, but the situations faced by their empire – war, famine, drought – frequently placed them in weak positions. Yet while the Sassanid state had not had its best century, it remained a powerful player in the Middle East, capable of defeating the Caucasian kingdoms on various occasions and standing up to the Roman field armies. The Persian king also remained a focus of Roman dissidents, with Ardaburius, Illus, Gobazes and the Tzani all seeking some kind of involvement of the Persians in Roman-controlled territory. Of course, the Romans too remained a focus of anti-Sassanid activity amongst the Caucasian states, with the Armenians, Iberians and Albanians all recorded seeking aid from Constantinople. While the Roman help did not always appear, Roman forces were still active on the eastern frontier. However, any Roman territorial ambitions in Mesopotamia were frequently frustrated by poor timing. When the call came from Armenians, Iberians, Albanians and Laz, the empire was instead busy dealing with Huns and Goths, reeling from the Vandal expedition, facing down internal dissension, convalescing over a dead *Augustus* or a combination of some or all of the above.

It was perhaps during the reign of Zeno that the biggest opportunity was missed. As an emperor with internal, financial and legitimacy problems, it would not be surprising had Zeno looked to reopen old wounds in the East. The opportunities were clearly there with the Hephthalite invasions and Caucasian rebellions; late 484 in particular looks like a perfect opportunity, with the Persian state laying prone after the disaster at Herat. A Roman invasion of Mesopotamia, supported by an alliance of Vahan Mamikonian, Vakhtang, the Albanian Arsacids and the pro-Roman Huns north of the Caucasus, would surely have made considerable inroads against the Sassanid state of Balash. However, Zeno was restrained by the circumstances prevailing in his empire, particularly the revolt of Illus.[64]

It must also be noted that while the Caucasians represented useful allies for the Romans at the outset of any proposed campaign, they would quickly become a band of potential troublemakers should that campaign be successful. Many of the cultural, military and religious problems faced by the Persians in Caucasia would merely pass to the Romans. Sharing a religion was not enough, particularly as many Caucasian Christians held different Christological opinions to the empire. While these kingdoms were willing to play one empire off against the other in search of their independence, such situations only resulted in an exchange of masters, leaving the cycle to repeat itself.

Perhaps Zeno, the imperial court and Roman military hierarchy had come to agree with Cassius Dio's summation of conflict over Mesopotamia: '[I]t yields very little and uses up vast sums.'[65] But before any suggestion that this 'cycle of armed confrontations'[66] between the two superpowers of the ancient world was not quite so never-ending, it must be borne in mind that the fifth century was an aberration in Romano-Persian relations; one which did little to change how they viewed one another. When war did break out again in 502, it was because Kavadh felt the need for the credibility and financial boost that a victorious campaign against Rome could bring. The resultant Anastasian War greatly resembled past contests, with the initial inroads of the Persians at Amida and Edessa soon rebuffed by the Roman army, leaving the frontier back where it had started. The accidental prolonged peace of the fifth century had very few consequences.

Chapter 11

Zeno, the Christological Crisis and Imperial Religious Policy

'It's the ones who believe in gods who make the trouble.'

Tyrion Lannister, in *A Song of Ice and Fire:*
A Dance with Dragons, Ch. 27, by G.R.R. Martin

'What has the emperor to do with the church?'

Optatus, *Against the Donatists* III.3

The Council of Chalcedon 451

Given the protracted squabbling over the imperial throne, usurpations, plots, revolts and events in Italy which punctuated Zeno's reign, it is not surprising that his political and military career is very much the focus of the works written about this purple-clad Isaurian.[1] However, it is his religious dealings which gained Zeno his rather poor reputation with a large section of the sources. As will be seen, much of this stems from misrepresentation, either intentional or genuine errors born of the difficulty in delineating an individual's beliefs. The focus of many of Zeno's religious policies was the reaction to the Council of Chalcedon in 451, which sparked doctrinal divisions which still exist to this day. Not that Chalcedon was the origin of these problems. Even before the emperor Constantine began the conversion of the imperial hierarchy, Christianity was having trouble maintaining doctrinal unity, not least the relationship between the divine and human natures within Jesus of Nazareth. Previous councils at Nicaea (325) and Constantinople (381) were thought to have achieved unity but ultimately failed, leading to a third ecumenical council at Ephesus in 431 and then a fourth at Chalcedon in 451.

Showing how deep-seated and long-lasting many of these Christological disputes could be, the two major issues faced by Chalcedon in 451, Eutychianism and Nestorianism, ostensibly had their origins in the Christology of Apollinarius, acting Bishop of Laodicea in the 360s. What became known as Apollinarianism was based on the idea that Jesus had a human body, a lower soul but a divine mind. This opened a Christological can of worms. The most vehement opposition came from Theodore of Mopsuestia, who stressed that Jesus must have had human free will and because of that his divine and human nature existed whole within the oneness of Christ.[2] This dispute came to a wider audience through the rise of one of Theodore's followers, Nestorius, to the Constantinopolitan patriarchate in 428. Suddenly, this doctrinal dispute was at the heart of the empire. What became known as Nestorianism required Jesus to have lived a fully human life for redemption to have taken place and for his divine nature to have not suffered. This opened Nestorius to attack, forcing him into various rounds of linguistic gymnastics to get across his point that 'Christ was to be a single entity, with one will and intelligence, inseparable and indivisible, remaining dual in nature'.[3]

Cyril of Alexandria took up the mantle of opposition to Nestorius, although in expressing his own ideas of moral, physical and ontological union within Christ, he too had to partake in similar linguistic gymnastics, with the added problem of regional differences in the meaning of specific words such as φυσις – 'nature'.[4] Nestorius was deposed by the Council of Ephesus in 431, but it was not until 435 that some agreement between Antioch and Alexandria was reached through careful rewordings of Cyril.[5] This compromise pleased few. Into that maelstrom came Eutyches, a Constantinopolitan monk, who professed that Christ had two natures but only up until the Incarnation, after which he had one indivisible nature that had completely engulfed the human side. This was a further muddying of the Christological waters, a quagmire now occupied by Nestorians, Eutychians, Antiochenes, Alexandrians, the new Constantinopolitan patriarch Flavian and Pope Leo I.[6]

Such a mess required a council, with Theodosius II calling another for Ephesus on 8 August 449. However, this Second Council of Ephesus only made things worse. It was essentially hijacked by the Alexandrian patriarch, Dioscorus, Eutyches and their allies, leading to the deposition of Flavian and many Antiochene bishops without much debate. This led to this second Ephesian council being poorly received by a large proportion of the Church and quickly relegated from the status of ecumenical council. It became known instead as the *Latrocinium Ephesinum* – the 'Robber Council of Ephesus'.[7]

The Flavian opposition to Second Ephesus received a shot in the arm with the accession of Marcian, as both he and Pulcheria supported Flavian, Pope Leo and the Antiochenes.[8] The emperor and his empress therefore called another ecumenical council for 451. Marcian was keen to prevent a repeat of the debacle at Ephesus, so the host city was moved from Nicaea to Chalcedon. Imperial control was maintained through the presence of eighteen imperial officials, including Anatolius, *magister militum praesentalis*, Palladius, praetorian prefect, and Tatianus, prefect of Constantinople.[9] This hands-on approach to Chalcedon could be seen as interference and the promotion of Pulcheria's preferred Christology; however, a less cynical view would be that the emperor was trying to restore unity to the Church through debate. Some common ground was reached between the 'orthodoxies' of Pope Leo and Cyril of Alexandria,[10] but finding a definitive definition of the faith proved problematic. At the urging of Marcian, a compromise was found which professed 'the mystery of the Incarnation by making use of four negative statements:

without confusion, without change, indivisible, inseparable'.[11] By depicting this as a definition rather than a creed and a negation of the views of Nestorius and Eutyches, on 25 October 451, 454 bishops signed up to the decisions of Chalcedon.[12]

In overturning many of the decisions of Second Ephesus, Chalcedon opened itself to scrutiny. Some viewed its decisions as having a Nestorian tinge, particularly due to its deposition of Dioscorus, even if he was more targeted for his canonical abuse than his Christology. Given that a significant proportion of the Church refused to negate their support for Nestorius, it seemed that the Christological definition agreed at Chalcedon was not worth the paper it was written on.[13] The Council of Chalcedon also saw the increasing prominence of Constantinople as an ecclesiastical centre, much to the chagrin of the papal legates. However, rather than at the expense of Rome, Marcian sought to improve the position of the Constantinopolitan patriarch in order to reduce the prominence of Alexandria and perhaps Antioch too, whilst elevating Constantinople to a position worthy of the imperial capital. While the papacy would support the doctrinal findings of Chalcedon, the popes disliked the position accorded to Constantinople, even though it clearly put Rome first. The very act of assigning the Eternal City a place in the hierarchy was seen as questioning Rome's 'unchallenged' primacy within the Christian world.[14]

This meant that as soon as it concluded, the Council of Chalcedon began to unravel. Very few individuals seemed keen to defend its decisions and stances; not even the bishops themselves. Many were claiming that they had been coerced into signing up to the Council's decisions,[15] with Marcian's involvement making him an easy target for anti-Chalcedonians. The most vicious reaction to Chalcedon came in Palestine, where a group of monks, led by Theodosius, gained widespread support by depicting the council as the restoration of Nestorianism.[16] They demanded that their bishop, Juvenalius, retract his support for Chalcedon, and when he refused, he was driven out and Theodosius the monk was elected as the new Bishop of Jerusalem. The resultant confrontations led to bloodshed, including the murder of Severianus, Bishop of Scythopolis.[17] It took an armed imperial response to restore Juvenalius to Jerusalem by mid-453, but this did little to quell the anti-Chalcedonian hostility in Palestine.[18]

Anti-Chalcedonian fervour was also ready to boil over in Alexandria. While Proterius, the successor of Dioscorus, had his Chalcedonian orthodoxy questioned by the pope, for having signed up to Chalcedon, he was rejected by the followers of Dioscorus. Violence broke out in Alexandria and was only quelled by military intervention. Proterius attempted to stabilize the situation by banishing two of his most important opponents, Timothy Aeleurus, and the deacon, Peter, but this only exacerbated the trouble.[19] Three deaths saw matters in Alexandria come to a head. The first was that of Dioscorus in exile on 4 September 454, which saw his followers declare the Alexandrian see vacant; a clear rejection of Proterius. They could not make any real move while the emperor was willing to use armed force against them, but when Marcian died on 27 January 457, Dioscorus' supporters elected Timothy Aelerus as patriarch. The *comes Aegypti* Dionysius responded by banishing Timothy to Mareotis,[20] but this only enflamed matters and led to the third and most shocking death to affect Alexandrian church politics. On 28 March 457, whilst celebrating the Eucharist, Proterius was murdered, his body dragged through the streets and then burned in the Hippodrome, possibly on the connivance of Dionysius.[21] The see of Alexandria thus fell into the hands of Timothy, who solidified his position by consecrating numerous anti-Chalcedonian bishops throughout Egypt.[22]

The accession of Leo I initially brought a relaxation of the enforcement of Chalcedon due to the prominence of Aspar, who had supported Timothy Aelerus, and the influence of the moderate Constantinopolitan patriarch, Anatolius.[23] However, as has been seen, Aspar's Arianism provided Leo with an avenue towards independence by supporting Chalcedon. This may be demonstrated by the election of the more hard-line Chalcedonian, Gennadius, as patriarch of Constantinople on the death of Anatolius on 3 July 458.[24] Less willing to resort to force, Leo proposed a debate between the pope and Timothy, followed by a new council. Pope Leo refused, stating that the Council of Chalcedon could not be superseded, while Timothy denigrated the pope as a 'Nestorian'.[25] Faced with such intransigence, the emperor conducted a survey of various bishops and monks across the empire on the legitimacy of Timothy Aelerus and the Council of Chalcedon, encouraging the holding of local synods to gain a more wide-ranging picture of the opinion. The response was not unexpected – Timothy's usurpation of the Alexandrian patriarchate was condemned and Chalcedon was upheld, if unenthusiastically.[26]

The near unanimous voice of his survey empowered Leo to demand the resignation of Timothy. The 'Cat-weasel' refused and his followers caused frequent rioting in Alexandria throughout the late 450s and early 460s. This left Leo with no option but to have Timothy arrested and exiled to Gangra in Paphlagonia.[27] The emperor's representatives continued to try to persuade Timothy to accept Chalcedon. Four years later, it was clear that these pleadings had failed and Leo decided that Timothy needed to be further removed from Christological debate, leading to Aelerus being sent to Cherson in the Crimea.[28] He was eventually replaced as Alexandrian patriarch in summer 460 by another Timothy, a Pachomian monk from the Canopus monastery, known as Salophakialos, which meant either 'white cap' or 'wobble cap'. He proved a good choice, for while he was pro-Chalcedon, he was willing to extend the olive branch to his anti-Chalcedonian opponents, bringing some calm, at least for now.[29]

Aside from Egypt and Palestine, opposition to Chalcedon during the 450s and 460s had largely been muted. Leo's survey had revealed begrudging acceptance, although there is a lack of evidence about what various regions really thought beyond the opinions of certain individuals, providing perhaps a deceptive picture of acceptance.[30] The silence from many regions could be more an ignoring of the

Chalcedonian definitions. Certainly the doctrinal developments in 475 would prove that there was a vocal opposition to Chalcedon.

Influencing Zeno: Peter the Fuller and Acacius

It is difficult to ascertain the doctrinal beliefs of Zeno before or after he acceded to the throne. Isauria was largely pro-Chalcedon but the influence of Antioch, which became increasingly Miaphysite as the fifth century progressed, might reflect Zeno's beliefs and policies. That assumes that Zeno was closely linked with the religious persuasion of his native Isauria. One later source, Michael Psellus, regarded Zeno's father as being a Catholic, but then this source regards Leo I as Zeno's natural father. It has also been suggested that Zeno had to be baptized due to being a pagan when he arrived in Constantinople, although anti-Zenoid sources would have made more of this.[31] Being considered a potential ally of Leo I, Zeno likely held orthodox beliefs. He certainly cannot have been an Arian or a clearly defined heretic in the mid-460s.

Development of Zeno's doctrinal beliefs may be detected in his relationship with Peter the Fuller. A monk of Constantinople, Peter left the capital for Antioch around the same time that Zeno was appointed *magister militum per Orientem* in 469. The sources disagree about the exact nature of their relationship. Some see Peter befriending Zeno, joining his retinue and accompanying him to Antioch.[32] Others do not record any real acquaintance before their arrival in Antioch, suggesting that the Fuller fled east because his Christological beliefs were becoming increasingly incompatible with the Chalcedonian capital.[33] In Antioch, Peter fell in with the local anti-Chalcedonians,[34] although there is very little evidence of a strictly anti-Chalcedonian stance held by him at this time. He appears more hostile to Nestorianism, while leading anti-Chalcedonians treated him with a lot of mistrust.[35]

. As seen earlier, Peter and his allies orchestrated the flight of the Antiochene patriarch Martyrius and saw Peter consecrated as his successor, much to the chagrin of Leo, who had Peter deposed in 471. The sources accuse Zeno of varying levels of complicity. Opponents saw him as the Fuller's protector, aiding in the removal of Martyrius and pressuring the Antiochenes to accept Peter as patriarch at the Synod of Seleucia.[36] The Roman tradition of Liberatus and the *Gesta de nomine Acacii* give no mention of Zeno playing a part in the removal of Martyrius or the elevation of Peter, but it is difficult to make any argument from that silence. On top of that, the Roman tradition may rely on the account of Acacius, who is unlikely to highlight how the emperor supported a heretic.[37] However, this does not confirm Zeno's complicity. Perhaps he was left with little choice, with Peter and his allies threatening an escalation in violence. The accusations of Nestorianism made against Martyrius and the Synod of Seleucia provided a cover for Zeno's actions having been somewhat forced upon him. This would in turn mean that little can be derived of Zeno's personal beliefs from his association with the Fuller.[38]

Regardless of what role he had played in Peter's elevation, the judgement of Leo in early 471 meant that Zeno was to restore Martyrius and depose the Fuller and exile him to Upper Egypt. Peter was removed but escaped to Constantinople, seeking refuge in the *Akoimetoi* monastery. He remained there, perhaps having had his sentence commuted to a withdrawal from public affairs. In such lenient treatment it is tempting to see the intervention of Zeno, but this would again be exaggerating his closeness to Peter. It is most telling that when he became emperor, Zeno would not restore Peter to Antioch.[39] The reinstated Martyrius did not last long, with unrest forcing his resignation.[40] Not a lot is known about Martyrius' successor, Julianus, and while the lack of recorded disturbances might hint at him being 'much less controversial than his predecessors',[41] care must be taken over such an argument of silence.[42]

It is difficult to ascertain Zeno's beliefs from his dealings with Peter as it is unclear if he was acting on his own convictions or attempting to maintain the peace. Given his later proclivities to sway in whatever direction helped him get what he needed and the general orthodoxy of his religious policies, Zeno was likely only attempting to placate the rioters in Antioch. Returned to the capital by 472, sight of Zeno's religious leanings is lost until the end of 476. His initial co-rule with Leo II passes over with no hint of religious policy and there is just a single law dateable to the period of late 474 to late 476, which only concerns the failure to keep promises of giving gifts to the Church.[43]

Even if Zeno 'lacked a deeper interest in theological issues',[44] as emperor, he was faced with the continuing doctrinal fallout from Chalcedon. He therefore required input from religious individuals to deal with such problems. In the imperial capital, the foremost religious individual, aside from Daniel the Stylite, was the patriarch of Constantinople. Gennadius had been a staunch Chalcedonian, but when he died in late 471 he was succeeded by Acacius, who was regarded as a Miaphysite sympathizer. However, Acacius being a Miaphysite would be a considerable departure from the usual Chalcedonianism of the capital and raises suspicions about the depiction of the patriarch.

When Acacius succeeded Gennadius, he was a presbyter in the capital, running an orphanage.[45] If he did hold views contrary to Gennadius, it could mean that Acacius became a presbyter before Gennadius' election in 458; however, Acacius has been suggested as being an advisor to Leo and even a Chalcedonian candidate for the patriarchate opposite Gennadius.[46] It appears then that there are issues with the views of Acacius – was he always anti-Chalcedonian, did he develop such views over time or did he never hold such ideas but was successfully portrayed as such by his opponents? Ps-Zacharias has Acacius as the leader of the anti-Chalcedonian faction in Constantinople in the early 460s, with his orphanage acting as the faction's headquarters and his brother Timokletos composing hymns to propagate its anti-Chalcedonian stance.[47] The perceived unreliability of this author and the sheer oddity of a staunchly Chalcedonian city and emperor replacing 'an ardent follower of the Council of Chalcedon and Pope Leo's *Tome*'[48] with a potentially rabid anti-Chalcedonian as patriarch require investigation.

Acacius could have been a compromise candidate, but this would require polarization within Constantinople that just was not there. Some have seen the influence of Zeno in Acacius' election,[49] but this assumes, beyond the evidence, that both Acacius and Zeno held anti-Chalcedonian leanings. This raises the question of why Acacius might be portrayed as anti-Chalcedon when he was not. It could derive from attempts to depict Peter Mongus, later patriarch of Alexandria, as having never deviated from his own anti-Chalcedonianism by remaining in communion with Acacius. The creation of apocryphal letters between Mongus and Acacius bolsters the idea of a manipulated picture of Acacius.[50] To fit in with the idea of an anti-Chalcedonian Acacius, some have portrayed his support of the canon elevating Constantinople as a cynical display, supporting the one part of Chalcedon that would aid him as patriarch, while secretly opposing the rest of the council.[51] However, it would be more straightforward that Acacius was simply pro-Chalcedon rather than cherry-picking its best bits. He is not recorded calling for the reinstatement of the likes of Timothy Aeleurus or Peter the Fuller, while none of his measures demonstrate anything other than support for the council.

Rather than being so good at hiding his heterodoxy that he got elected patriarch in the most orthodox Chalcedonian see under the nose of a pro-Chalcedonian emperor, Acacius was a supporter of Chalcedon, only to be depicted as otherwise by sources with ulterior motives.[52] This further adds to the difficulty in fully uncovering the religious beliefs of Zeno due to the depictions of various individuals and their doctrines during this period being clouded by either poor or biased sources. Even if it is accepted that Peter the Fuller and Acacius reflected or influenced the beliefs of Zeno, this does not provide much clear information as it is by no means certain what either of these men believed.

The Acacian *Revanche*

While the circumstances of his restoration had exposed Zeno to all kinds of political and military pressures, the religious policies of Basiliscus caused him considerable trouble too. Therefore, four months after his return to the throne, Zeno issued a constitution on 17 December 476.[53] It annulled any religious legislation undertaken by Basiliscus and reiterated imperial support for the policies of Marcian and Leo. However, overt support for the Council of Chalcedon was not declared explicitly.[54] This could be just failing to state the obvious, but it could also have been a calculated move. An official declaration of support of Chalcedon would surely have produced provincial opposition so soon after his restoration. This leaves room to question whether Zeno should be considered the continuator of the religious policies of his predecessors or a doctrinal fence-sitter, who refused to give a clear definition of his position regarding Chalcedon.[55] Perhaps that was the point.

Zeno's constitution did demonstrate the elevation of Acacius as the key religious figure in the imperial government and praised him for his opposition to Basiliscus and Timothy Aeleurus.[56] Acacius built upon this stature with a series of synods at Constantinople which anathematized the 'Cat-weasel', Peter the Fuller, Paul of Ephesus and others. With Zeno's backing, Acacius looked to turn those anathemas into depositions. The removal of Paul of Ephesus led to the bishops of Asia Minor capitulating, declaring their support for Chalcedon and claiming that they had only accepted the *Encyclical* under duress. There may be some truth to this claim as there is no mention of the Asian bishops opposing Chalcedon during the rest of Zeno's reign.[57]

The next target for the Acacian *revanche* was the re-established patriarch of Antioch, Peter the Fuller. As a heretic and an ally of Basiliscus, he was deposed and exiled first to Pityous on the Black Sea and then to Euchaita in Pontus.[58] His immediate successor at Antioch also proved unacceptable. Installed by Trocundes, John Kodonatus served as Antiochene patriarch for just three months. His Christological views are not known for certain, but they may have been somehow anti-Chalcedonian to cause his swift deposition, although there may also have been some lingering personal issues with Acacius.[59]

Acacius and Zeno had a firm Chalcedonian called Stephen elected to replace Kodonatus, but this was not the end of affairs in the Antiochene see. Acacius felt that the conviction of Peter the Fuller for heresy was not secure, as he wrote to Pope Simplicius to pre-empt any claim from Peter that he had been poorly treated.[60] Acacius was right to worry as Stephen was soon the target of accusations of holding Nestorian beliefs. While this was a reflection of his Chalcedonianism, the new patriarch still needed to clear his name. Zeno called a synod at Laodicea in 478 to investigate the veracity of these charges and Stephen was quickly vindicated.[61] Supporters of Peter refused to accept Laodicea and took to the streets in protest. On 9 March 479, a mob murdered Stephen with sharpened reeds, his body being cast into the Orontes River like a common criminal.[62] Acacius saw to the consecration of another staunch Chalcedonian, Kalandion, as patriarch of Antioch.

While the trouble over the Antiochene patriarchate may have been somewhat unforeseen, Acacius and Zeno can have been under no illusion about the reception they would receive in Alexandria. Timothy Aeleurus had died on 31 July 477,[63] but beside his deathbed his supporters had consecrated archdeacon Peter Mongus – Peter the 'hoarse-voiced' – as his successor. The hurried nature of this consecration would be frequently held against Peter as uncanonical, with perhaps only a single bishop present.[64] Zeno responded to the elevation of Peter Mongus with hostility. Any bishop found to have taken part in Mongus' consecration was to be exiled, while Peter himself was deposed and perhaps sentenced to death. Timothy Salophakialos emerged from his Canopus exile to reclaim his see amid rioting in the streets of Alexandria.

The emperor then tried to impose his will through legislation, issuing three laws threatening the clergy, monks and laymen of Alexandria with severe penalties should they not accept the decisions of Chalcedon and the restoration of Salophakialos. These penalties also applied to anyone who gave shelter to Peter Mongus, who was now in hiding. With such imperial interference, it is not surprising that Salophakialos found that the rioting continued and support for Peter Mongus was undiminished.[65] Timothy also contacted Simplicius, declaring his support for Chalcedon and asking the pope to approve a new formula which it was hoped would appeal to opponents of Chalcedon.[66]

One supporter of the *Encyclical* to survive the Acacian *revanche* was patriarch Anastasius of Jerusalem. Despite his continued opposition to Chalcedon, Anastasius did not come under attack from Acacius and Zeno. This may be because emperor and patriarch based their reordering of the Church hierarchy more on legitimacy than removing anti-Chalcedonians. The likes of Timothy Aeleurus, Peter the Fuller and Paul of Ephesus were restored to their sees by Basiliscus, while Anastasius had been Bishop of Jerusalem for nearly twenty years. Perhaps Anastasius was willing to not be vehement in his rejection of Chalcedonians and even to be open to reconciliation.[67]

Zeno had relied heavily on Acacius and his ability to call to order the Chalcedonian clergy to give ecclesiastic legitimacy to their moves. However, the perceived dependence of several patriarchs and bishops on Constantinople and its patriarch raised concerns in Rome. The elevation of Kalandion in particular drew criticism from Simplicius, for in his haste, Acacius had overseen an uncanonical consecration. The Constantinopolitan patriarch had to go out of his way to reassure the pope that Kalandion's election would be affirmed by a synod, although the synodal letter did not reach Simplicius until 15 July 482. This might suggest that Acacius and the Antiochenes were none too keen to call a synod over Kalandion's position.[68] These interactions with the pope came as the situation in Italy was affecting the position of the papacy. The deposition of Romulus by Odoacer may have encouraged Simplicius to cement good relations between Italy, the papacy and Constantinople to prevent unrest. Conversely, the distance between Rome and Constantinople gave the pope some independence from the emperor, which was helped by the lack of interference from the new *rex Italiae* in ecclesiastical affairs.[69] This enabled popes like Simplicius more room to treat with Constantinople with 'a far-reaching, principled and uncompromising attitude'.[70]

It was not just the pope who showed concern over the growing influence of Acacius. In late 481, a delegation from Salophakialos, led by John Talaia, arrived in the capital seeking assurances that the next Alexandrian patriarch would be elected by the Egyptian church rather than imposed by Constantinople.[71] Zeno gave assurances that the Alexandrians would get to make that choice; however, this came with the proviso that their choice not be John Talaia, who was seemingly made to take an oath that he would never seek the position. When John became Bishop of Alexandria, this breach would be used as a reason for his deposition, although

THEODOSIUS II gold solidus, issued between 408–420 from Constantinople mint
OBV – DN THEODOSIVS PF AVG; diademed, helmeted and cuirassed bust, holding in right hand spear over shoulder and shield decorated with horseman
REV – CONCORDIA AVGGI, Constantinopolis enthroned, foot on prow, holding sceptre in right hand and Victory set on globe in left, CONOB in exergue

VALENTINIAN III gold solidus from Rome mint
OBV – DN PLA VALENTINIANVS PF AVG; diademed, draped and cuirassed bust
REV – VICTORIA AVGGG; emperor standing, holding long cross and Victory, foot on serpent, R V across, CONOB in exergue

MARCIAN gold solidus from Constantinople mint
OBV – DN MARCIANVS PF AVG; helmeted and cuirassed bust, holding spear and shield
REV – VICTORIA AVGGG**G*; Victory standing, holding long cross, CONOB in exergue

AELIA VERINA gold tremissis, issued between 462–466 from Constantinople mint
OBV – AEL ЧERINA AVG; diademed and draped bust
REV – cross within wreath, CONOB* in exergue

LEO I gold solidus, issued between 468–473 from Constantinople mint
OBV – DN LEO PERP ET AVG; cuirassed bust with paludamentum (cloak) and crown, holding spear and shield
REV – VICTORIA AVGGG **Q*; Victory standing, holding long cross, CONOB in exergue

LEO I gold solidus from Constantinople mint
OBV – DN LEO PERP ET AVG; cuirassed bust with paludamentum and crown, holding spear and shield
REV – VICTORIA AVGGG **Q*; Victory standing, holding long cross, CONOB in exergue

BASILISCUS gold tremissis from Constantinople mint
OBV – DN BASILISCVS P AVG diademed, draped and cuirassed bust
REV – cross in wreath, CONOB in exergue

ANASTASIUS I gold solidus, issued between 491–498 from Constantinople mint
OBV – DN ANASTASIVS PP AVG; helmeted and cuirassed bust, holding spear and shield
REV – VICTORI A AVGGG**Γ*; Victory standing, holding long cross, CONOB in exergue

ZENO gold solidus from
Constantinople mint
OBV – DN ZENO PERP AVG;
cuirassed bust with paludamentum
and crown, holding spear and shield
REV – VICTORIA AVGGG H;
Victory standing, holding long cross,
CONOB in exergue

ZENO gold solidus from
Constantinople mint
OBV – DN ZENO PERP AVG;
cuirassed bust with paludamentum
and crown, holding spear and shield
REV – VICTORI A AVGGG I;
Victory standing, holding long cross,
CONOB in exergue

ZENO gold solidus from
Constantinople mint
OBV – DN ZENO PERP AVG;
cuirassed bust with paludamentum
and crown, holding spear and shield
REV – VICTORIA AVGGG E;
Victory standing, holding long cross,
CONOB in exergue

ZENO gold tremissis from
Constantinople mint
OBV – DN ZENO PERP AVG;
diademed and draped bust
REV – VICTORIA AVGVSTORVM;
Victory advancing, holding cross on
orb, CONOB in exergue

THEODERIC I/ANASTASIUS I
gold tremissis issued by Theoderic I in the name of Anastasius I from Rome mint
OBV – DN ANASTASIVS PF AVG; diademed and cuirassed bust with paludamentum
REV – Victory to right, head to left, star in right field, around VICTORIA AVGVSTORVM, CONOB in exergue

PEROZ I silver drachm from Susa (?) mint
OBV – 'The Mazda worshipper, the fortunate Peroz' in Pahlavi; crowned and cuirassed bust
REV – 'Peroz' in Pahlavi, mint signature right, fire altar with attendants

BALASH silver drachm from Susa (?) mint
OBV – 'The good king Bala[sh]' in Pahlavi; crowned and cuirassed bust, ribbon rising from right shoulder, flame on left
REV – degraded Pahlavi legend to left, mint signature right, regal bust beside fire altar with attendants, star and crescent flanking flames

KAVADH I silver drachm issued in 521 from Dywan/Dinawar (?) mint
OBV – 'Kavadh' in Pahlavi; crowned bust
REV – fire altar with attendants; star and crescent flanking flames

Walls of Constantinople – Restored section of the walls near the Pege Gate (© *Bigdaddy1204*)

Pege Gate (*courtesy of CrniBombarder!!!*)

Missorium of Aspar – Aspar and his eldest son Ardaburius (*c*.434) (© *Sailko 2008, Museo Archeologico Nazionale in Florence*)

Right: **Leo I** – Louvre (© *Marie-Lan Nguyen 2009*)

Below: **Weight of Theoderic** – Silver inlaid bronze weight, featuring the name of Theoderic, issued by prefect Catulinus in Rome, 493–526 (*British Museum; courtesy of PHGCOM*)

Ariadne
Augusta
(*Kunsthistorisches
Museum, Vienna;
courtesy of
Andreas Praefcke,
2009*)

some felt that this 'oath' had not happened and that Zeno had promised the see to Talaia.[72] The question must be asked why the imperial court took up against John Talaia. He was an ardent Chalcedonian and seemed a good candidate to continue the Egyptian leg of the Acacian *revanche*. Perhaps Acacius was looking to increase his own influence, although the sources point to John Talaia being too close to Illus.[73]

This oath was put to the test when Salophakialos died in early 482 and the Chalcedonian bishops of Egypt quickly consecrated John Talaia as patriarch of Alexandria. Demonstrating that the reconciliation policies of the 'White Cap' had met with some success, followers of Dioscorus also took part in the election, although the supporters of Peter Mongus remained opposed, accusing the new patriarch of bribery.[74] Talaia quickly sent synodal letters regarding his consecration to Simplicius and Kalandion, but hesitated to send word to Constantinople. Perhaps he hoped that Illus in Antioch would send notifications on to the capital,[75] insulating John from any imperial backlash for breaking his oath. Instead, Zeno viewed the informing of Kalandion and Illus as further evidence of Talaia's disloyalty and determined to depose the new Alexandrian patriarch by June 482.[76] John Talaia did not wait for his formal deposition, leaving Alexandria for Rome. Zeno wrote to the pope, asking him not to recognize Talaia as patriarch, and given that Talaia would later be appointed Bishop of Nola, perhaps the pope acceded to this imperial request.[77] Zeno could not leave a patriarchal vacuum in Alexandria, but elevating another new bishop would only further split the Egyptian church. This left Zeno to seek reconciliation with the other consecrated Bishop of Alexandria, Peter Mongus.

The *Henotikon*

This attempted rapprochement with Peter may be linked to the growing divide within the anti-Chalcedonian Church, with Theodotus, Bishop of Joppe, leading a splinter group called the Aposchites.[78] Mongus may even have been the first to signal willingness for reconciliation through a delegation to the capital.[79] However, this could not happen overnight. Peter's consecration had been met with anathema from Acacius, which would have to be lifted for any reconciliation to take place, and Acacius was not going to renounce it easily. Peter would have to move away from his heretical views on Chaldecon and sign up to several conditions. He had to re-establish communion with Chalcedonian Egyptians and Pope Simplicius, and pledge not to anathematize Chalcedon at any later date. The most important part of the reconciliation was that Peter Mongus had to agree to a document of compromise – the *Henotikon*.[80]

Where had this compromise document suddenly appeared from? The originating *henosis* first emerged in a proclamation of unity made in 479/480 by the successor of Anastasius as patriarch of Jerusalem, Martyrius.[81] Originally from Cappadocia, Martyrius lived as a monk in Egypt before moving to Palestine to serve under Euthymius and then Anastasius. His views are not clear,[82] but after becoming Bishop of Jerusalem, Martyrius reportedly wrote to Zeno and Acacius denouncing the anti-Chalcedonians in Palestine, although this does not make him pro-Chalcedonian.[83] At best, Martyrius was just not a fervent advocate of the *Encyclical* while favouring anti-Chalcedonianism. This middling position may have led him to criticize the behaviour of radical anti-Chalcedonians and work to find a compromise.[84] There is no complete record of this foundation *henosis*, but the lack of theological definitions might highlight Martyrius being intentionally vague on doctrine. Acacius would follow a similar route in attempting to find a compromise with the anti-Chalcedonians of Egypt.[85]

The resultant *Henotikon* was very careful with how it dealt with contentious issues. No opinion was voiced on Second Ephesus or Chalcedon, while Leo's *Tome* was not mentioned by name. While the views of Nestorius and Eutyches were confirmed as heretical, the *Henotikon* was much more careful over Alexandrian doctrines. The formula of 'the one nature of the incarnated Word' prevalent in Alexandria was left out, but the theology of Cyril was reconciled with similar tenets of Chalcedon. Overall, the *Henotikon* marks something of a resetting of imperial Christology to its form before Second Ephesus, perhaps using the 'formula of unity' of 433.[86] The *Henotikon* was frequently portrayed as a legal document, a law laid down by the emperor – it was even called *Edictum Zenonis* by one source.[87] However, most sources do not record it as a *lex*, preferring instead to call it a 'proclamation', a 'document', a 'letter' or by name.[88] Both Zacharias and Evagrius had a legal background and did not refer to the *Henotikon* in legalistic language. There were no penalties stipulated for non-compliance, rather 'encouraging unity and promising rewards in the form of imperial commendations'.[89] This puts the *Henotikon* more in the category of imperially backed advice rather than a decree.[90]

Upon its promulgation, reaching Alexandria in late spring 482 and Rome before mid-June,[91] virtually no one was satisfied. In Egypt, the *Henotikon* was seen as a capitulation as it failed to condemn Chalcedon. Peter Mongus appeared unable to maintain balance between the factions, although he could have been appearing a willing partner of the government but 'allowing' himself to be forced into condemning Chalcedon and Leo's *Tome*. In such circumstances, Mongus might hope to prevent a schism, whilst retaining his position as patriarch from imperial interference and radical violence. It might also be that Peter genuinely tried to adhere to the *Henotikon*, only to be forced to go back on his word through pressure and threats. But whatever Mongus' thoughts and aims, the *Henotikon* had not changed anything in Egypt.[92]

The *Henotikon* received a similarly mixed reaction in Palestine. Martyrius accepted communion with Peter Mongus, while the less moderate anti-Chalcedonians, Peter the Iberian and Isaiah, refused an imperial invite to Constantinople for fear of being coerced into accepting *Henotikon*.[93] Further north in Antioch, Kalandion remained resolutely opposed to the recognition of Peter Mongus, but did not show any dislike of the *Henotikon*. There was some rejection from more fervent Chalcedonians in Constantinople due to its treatment of Chalcedon, although this may be more of a supposition than based strictly on the sources.[94] The papacy remained staunchly opposed to Peter Mongus in the absence of his full acceptance of Chalcedon. Simplicius voiced his shock at Constantinople's communion with Mongus, demanding that Zeno remove him. Some Chalcedonian monks and clergy from Alexandria travelled to Constantinople to voice their mistrust of Mongus' conversion, but they failed to persuade Acacius to take up their cause.[95]

Despite these mixed results, Zeno had achieved some politico-religious balance in Egypt and Palestine. The half-hearted complaints of the pope could be brushed off with the notion of Peter's conversion; more radical Chalcedonians could be ignored; while opposition from Kalandion could be painted as Illus sowing dissension. The *Henotikon* served its purpose, mollifying enough of the anti-Chalcedonian party without antagonizing too many Chalcedonians. However, it would not hold up to doctrinal scrutiny once the focus moved on from communion with Peter Mongus. But in the early 480s, the *Henotikon* was enough of a sticking plaster to bind Egypt and Palestine to Constantinople at a time when civil war was on the horizon.

The Acacian Schism

Zeno and Acacius may have felt capable of absorbing the complaints of the papacy over their communion with Peter Mongus, but this damaged relations between Rome and Constantinople. Pope Simplicius died on 10 March 483, but his successor, Felix III, was not slow in making his feelings known. On the day of his consecration, 13 March 483, Felix wrote to the emperor and Acacius to protest against the restoration of Peter Mongus.[96] The new pope's ire was further stoked by John Talaia, who claimed he had been deposed despite being a defender of Chalcedon and Leo's *Tome*. Accusations were also levelled at Acacius over his increasing hold over the eastern Church.[97]

The pope found eastern allies in the monks of the *Akoimetoi*[98] and a group of Chalcedonian bishops from Egypt, who arrived in Constantinople having felt harried into leaving their homeland and claiming that Mongus had already anathematized Chalcedon. Zeno's response to subsequent papal demands was to arrest his legates, confiscate their letters and then bribe/threaten them into accepting communion with Acacius and Peter. While Felix would complain that his legates were poorly treated, he did not use accusations of bribery or threatening of life in his sentence of excommunication against Acacius on 28 July 484. Perhaps the legates were never imprisoned, with tales of their poor treatment being invented in order to defend themselves before a Roman synod in July 484.[99]

But why would the legates need to explain their actions in Constantinople? In short, they had been persuaded by Acacius and Zeno that communion with Peter Mongus satisfied Chalcedonian doctrine. Acacius pointed out that the *Henotikon* had brought unity to the eastern Church, although the patriarch went out of his way to prevent the legates from meeting with the *Akoimetoi* monks.[100] Zeno also played his part in continuing to accuse John Talaia of perjury and sacrilege and explaining the Nicene basis of communion with Peter Mongus. The legates were persuaded by this 'return' to the Nicene Creed, taking part in the Eucharist and not protesting when Peter's name was read out. The emperor and the patriarch took this as papal consent to the *Henotikon*.[101]

The *Akoimetoi* monks did not accept the arguments of Acacius and Zeno, sending word to Felix of the capitulation of his legates. Upon their return to Rome, they were deposed and a synod was convened to decide their punishment, as well as to discuss the papal response to Acacius and Zeno. It was nothing if not robust. The synod declared Peter Mongus and Acacius anathematized; the former for being a heretic and the latter for communing with a heretic. Acacius was also accused of disregarding the decrees of the Council of Nicaea, elevating John Kodonatus to Bishop of Tyre, insincerity and unreliability.[102]

There were two significant things missing from Felix's anathematizing of Acacius – there was no mention of the *Henotikon* or Zeno. Felix III had picked his enemy carefully, laying 'all of the responsibility for the bad events in the Church of the East on the Bishop of Constantinople, not the Emperor'.[103] The absence of the *Henotikon* in Roman correspondence does not mean that it was accepted by the Roman Church. Felix's successor, Gelasius, would declare the *Henotikon* heretical, although this was due to Anastasius' anti-Chalcedonian slant rather than the 'crypto-Chalcedonian'[104] version of Zeno. In 484, Felix probably felt that he had an easier target in the heretical patriarch of Alexandria than delving into the doctrinal wrangling inherent in the *Henotikon*.

When word of Acacius' excommunication reached Constantinople, the Chalcedonian monks were ecstatic, nailing up a copy of the anathema in public. The patriarch's response appears mixed – it is said that he removed Felix's name from the diptychs but did not sever relations with Rome.[105] He also highlighted that in a technical sense, his papal deposition was invalid as it was a personal pronouncement of the pope rather than the proclamation of the synod. But Felix was in no mood to let any such technicality get in his way. Another synod was quickly convened for October 485, which reissued the deposition of Acacius, 'explicitly stating that it was the decision of not only the Pope himself, but also the assembled bishops of Italy'.[106]

The excommunication of Acacius would seem to be a disaster for Zeno; however, the geographical detachment of the papacy from the eastern empire and the growth of importance of Constantinople as a patriarchal see had seen a decline in papal influence in the East. Therefore, unity within the eastern provinces was more sought after than communion with the West. The extent of eastern apathy to the papal excommunication may be demonstrated in a lull in Rome-Constantinople correspondence over the next four years. When efforts at reconciliation briefly resumed in 488/489, it was not pope, patriarch or emperor who initiated it, but the king of Italy. Odoacer saw the schism over Peter Mongus and Acacius as a major hurdle to any cooperation between his regime and Constantinople, even if his relations with Felix were becoming strained. Such enmity could be put aside for the good of Italy and the *rex Italiae* asked the pope to make a conciliatory gesture. Felix refused to deal with Acacius but he did allow the Roman Senate to act as intermediaries. This senatorial intercession came to nothing as the 'gesture of conciliation' merely saw Felix reiterate his demand that Acacius accept the findings of the second Roman synod. The patriarch and emperor were in no mood to grovel for some rapprochement with the pope, and Felix's gesture went unanswered.[107]

Peter Mongus and the Aposchists

It was not just Felix III and Constantinopolitan monks who had a problem communing with Peter Mongus. Some of the Alexandrian patriarch's Aposchist allies were becoming increasingly opposed to the *Henotikon* and therefore Peter Mongus himself for accepting its compromise. This group was popular enough to 'force' Peter to condemn Chalcedon and Leo's *Tome*.[108] This declaration roused concern in Rome and Constantinople, but the record is muddled or of doubted credibility. Open condemnation of Chalcedon, while in direct contravention of his agreement with Acacius and Zeno in 482, was in line with Mongus' historic rejection of the council; however, Evagrius records a letter from Peter to Acacius in which the Alexandrian patriarch accepts the validity of Chalcedon – and in committing such thoughts to paper, they may have more credence than his verbal condemnation.[109]

Such propitious timing has seen Acacius accused of forging this letter, on the supposition that Peter Mongus, a staunch anti-Chalcedonian, would hardly affirm the council.[110] But then Peter had already accepted Chalcedon on two separate occasions. He recognized that imperial forces would get rid of him if they felt he was not toeing the party line. He may even have come to accept the *Henotikon* as not just a political necessity but also as a religious doctrine. To keep the peace and retain his position as patriarch, Peter Mongus had to wear two hats – the somewhat compliant follower of the *Henotikon* for Acacius and Zeno and the staunch anti-Chalcedonian within Egypt. While no one on either side truly believed him, it was seemingly enough to keep him in place. Acacius continued to investigate the Alexandrian patriarch. He called upon the clergy and monks of Egypt to help their patriarch retain the unity of the *Henotikon*, but in concert with Zeno, he dispatched legates to Egypt to investigate Peter's orthodoxy. At the very least, Peter put on a good show, demonstrating compliance with the agreement of 482.[111] Whether or not he believed in Peter Mongus' sincerity was largely moot as Acacius had evidence that the basis of his excommunication was incorrect, which left him with no reason to interfere in Egypt again.

However, while this outwardly professed orthodoxy was enough for Acacius and Zeno, it caused considerable trouble for the Alexandrian patriarch himself.

In trying to appear orthodox for the emperor, Peter had enflamed the Aposchists. The judgement that Peter was in line with the *Henotikon* by Zeno's legates may have helped bolster eastern Christian unity and undermine Felix III's excommunications, but it also provided the Aposchists with 'proof' that Mongus had embraced Chalcedon.[112] Tensions rose to the point where Peter Mongus had to rely on imperial forces physically removing his opponents from their monasteries. His former allies were so shocked by Mongus' apparent *volte face* that they asked Zeno for help against the violence, sending a monk called Nephalios to Constantinople to present their case.[113] Nephalios himself may represent a similar progression of beliefs over Chalcedon as Peter Mongus, starting out as a staunch opponent only to gravitate more towards moderate acceptance of the council through the *Henotikon*. That such a potential moderate could be chosen to represent the Aposchists may well demonstrate the extent of Peter Mongus' use of violence, although it may have required a moderate voice to get a hearing from Zeno.

Alarmed that his Church unity was in danger, the emperor sent his *cubicularius* Cosmas to Alexandria in March 487.[114] He found the city on the verge of armed conflict. A large number of anti-Chalcedonians – keen to exaggerate the scale of opposition to Chalcedon, Zacharias claimed 100 bishops and 30,000 monks – gathered outside the city gates. On the advice of Cosmas and the city prefect, Peter met with the protestors but found that he could not appease one side without enflaming the other. The anti-Chalcedonian demands were as to be expected: an open proclamation of anathema on Chalcedon and Leo's *Tome* and the breaking of communion with any Chalcedonian. Under pressure, Peter agreed to the anathemas but steadfastly refused to abandon communion with Chalcedonians. These anathemas not only damned Peter in the eyes of pro-Chalcedonians but provoked a split within the Aposchists. Some were willing to accept these anathemas as enough while others demanded a complete break with Chalcedonians and threatened to elect another patriarch.[115]

With the failure of negotiation, Zeno resorted to more stringent measures against the Aposchists. The new Egyptian prefect, Arsenius, was ordered to enforce unity through the *Henotikon*, with permission to forcibly remove dissidents from their monasteries. This brought the radicals back to the negotiating table but it did not change their demands and Peter Mongus refused again to break communion with Chalcedonian bishops.[116] Having reached such an impasse, Arsenius suggested to Aposchist leaders that they travel to Constantinople and present their case to Zeno.[117] However, they recognized what such an imperial audience would entail – instead of offering the Aposchists a chance to persuade Zeno, it offered Zeno a chance to 'persuade' the Aposchists to accept Chalcedon. This was exactly what happened, although those radicals who took up Arsenius' offer remained steadfast in the face of whatever pressure they faced to accept the agreement of 482. The result was continued doctrinal stalemate.

New Patriarchs and a Changing Tide?

The last years of Zeno's reign saw him become less conciliatory towards Peter Mongus in favour of healing the wounds of schism with Rome. The final defeat of Illus in 488 may have released Zeno from needing to maintain unity with an obstinate Alexandrian patriarch. Furthermore, the focus of military action had switched from Isauria to Italy, with Theoderic squaring up to Odoacer. This may have encouraged Zeno to come to a rapprochement with the pope in expectation of imperial troops arriving in Italy in the wake of Theoderic. The pope himself was likely more amenable to imperial reconciliation as his relations with Odoacer had soured so much that in 489, the city of Rome closed its gates to the *rex Italiae*.[118] It may not have just been changing political circumstances which altered Zeno's religious policies. On 26 November 489, Acacius died.[119] The Constantinopolitan patriarch had been the centre of the east/west schism over Peter Mongus, and his demise would seem to have removed a major obstacle to reconciliation.

Some have gone further, seeing the growing influence of Theoderic the Amal in the imperial court, particularly in the choice of Acacius' successor, Fravitas.[120] This is going too far. While there is no doubt that Fravitas is a Gothic name, Theoderic was in no position to influence the choice of patriarch, not only because he was in Italy at the time but also because he was an Arian Christian. It seems much more likely that Zeno knew Fravitas personally and may even have been a close friend. Before becoming patriarch, Fravitas had been presbyter at the shrine of St Thecla in Sykai, across the Golden Horn from Constantinople, and Zeno held the cult of Thecla in particularly high regard; he may even have founded the shrine at Sykai.[121]

There is another later story recorded about the accession of Fravitas. Zeno reputedly placed two pieces of paper on the altar of a church in Constantinople. On one piece was written a prayer asking God to send an angel to write the name of His chosen patriarch on the other piece. A period of forty days of fast and prayer was ordered while the church was to be safeguarded by the eunuch imperial chamberlain, possibly Urbicius, and the casket containing the papers closed with the imperial seal. Fravitas reputedly bribed the eunuch to write Fravitas' name on the blank page. At the end of the forty days, he was duly acclaimed patriarch of Constantinople. However, upon his death, the eunuch found that he had not been fully paid and badgered the executors of Fravitas' estate, who then took the tale of forgery to Zeno. The emperor entrusted the election of the new patriarch to the clergy.[122]

Communications between Rome and Constantinople in 490 saw the new patriarch and the emperor speak in glowing terms of the position taken by the pope. Zeno and Fravitas also made overtures to the monasteries of Constantinople, home to some of the most fervent support for Chalcedon and opposition to Peter Mongus. Felix put significant stock in their opinions, so winning them over would go a long way to patching up differences between patriarchate and papacy.

Pope Felix, encouraged by initial feelers sent out in the wake of Acacius' demise, wrote back to Fravitas and Zeno in friendly tones.[123]

The new patriarch also wrote to Peter Mongus. This has led some to portray Fravitas in a duplicitous light, as if the patriarch was assuring both Felix and Peter that he was still in communion with each of them whilst condemning the other. Theophanes has Fravitas' letter to Peter being intercepted and forwarded to the pope, who sent away the patriarch's delegates. This would have been a very serious setback to reconciliation; however, there are doubts about the authenticity of this development. Fravitas may have been telling different stories to Felix and Peter, but Ps-Zacharias and the letters of Felix do not mention any such incident or removal of patriarchate legates. The tone was much more convivial than confrontational. Fravitas' letter to Peter did maintain communion between Constantinople and Alexandria, but only on the basis of the 482 compromise, with the *Henotikon* conspicuously absent. With the express condemnations of Eutyches and Nestorius, these letters may show that Zeno were trying to revert to pre-*Henotikon* policy.

Fravitas may have been encouraging Peter Mongus to reach out to Felix in order to bring about church unity.[124] The Alexandrian patriarch showed that while he was willing to affirm the condemnation of Nestorius and Eutyches, he would not forget the *Henotikon*. Worse still, Mongus determined that both Chalcedon and Leo's *Tome* should be overtly condemned. Such a drastic departure from years of attempted compromise requires explanation.[125] Peter Mongus almost certainly retained an anti-Chalcedonian stance even when compromising over the *Henotikon*, but why did he now choose to reveal that stance in 490? The death of Acacius and Zeno's departure from the *Henotikon* perhaps opened the way for Peter to appropriate that compromise doctrine for himself. Mongus went as far to present himself as the successor of Acacius when it came to the *Henotikon*, with the specious claim that the deceased patriarch had followed the anti-Chalcedonian view of the compromise.[126] Peter will have been distressed by the lack of mention of *Henotikon* in Fravitas' correspondence. It had been the bedrock of the 482 compromise and if it was being sidelined by Constantinople, perhaps then so too was the compromise. In terms of his own survival then, Peter Mongus found it necessary to embrace anti-Chalcedonianism to ensure support in Egypt should Constantinople come after him.

There may be some skulduggery in the transmission of these letters between Fravitas and Peter. Other religious figures of the period, including Severus of Antioch, express no notion that Mongus had publicly stated radical anti-Chalcedonianism. The text within Peter's reply is uneven, with the section condemning Chalcedon out of character with the orthodoxy of the letter. This section may be a later addition by the Syriac compiler of Ps-Zacharias or Zacharias himself, keen to provide 'the ultimate proof for the Bishop of Alexandria's anti-Chalcedonian orthodoxy'.[127] While Peter's return to overt anti-Chalcedonianism should be treated with suspicion, the proposed reasons for such a *volte face* must be taken seriously, particularly the prevailing doctrinal wind in Constantinople. Fravitas tried to maintain a balance between Rome and Alexandria, but this alone demonstrated a change in policy away from placating just the eastern provinces and an increasing desire to repair relations with the papacy.

After at most four months as patriarch, Fravitas died in around March 490.[128] He was succeeded by Euphemius, a presbyter in charge of poor relief in Constantinople. This newest patriarch had supported a hard line on the Alexandrian patriarch and was determined to uphold the pro-Chalcedonian interpretation of the *Henotikon* and even end the compromise of 482.[129] The first interaction between Zeno and Euphemius came when a *silentarius*, Anastasius, preached anti-Chalcedonian homilies and the 'teachings of Eutyches'[130] in Constantinople. Euphemius complained, and the emperor refused to defend the *silentarius* and sent him to the patriarch to be dealt with. Zeno has been accused of allowing his personal feelings to interfere with this decision as it has been claimed that Anastasius was the lover of the empress Ariadne. However, this supposed affair between Ariadne and Anastasius during Zeno's lifetime is based on a 'casual interpretation'[131] of Ps-Zacharias and is to be rejected. Zeno may have exiled Anastasius to Egypt, although this is likely a misunderstanding of Anastasius' visit there around this time, which may have involved a shipwreck.[132] Anastasius had also been a candidate to succeed Peter the Fuller as patriarch of Antioch in 488. Therefore, it appears that it was religious issues that caused the problem between Anastasius and Euphemius and ultimately Zeno at this time, a problem which would continue and escalate after Anastasius' accession in 491.[133]

It would be unlikely that the new patriarch would have set about a more resolutely pro-Chalcedonian stance without the agreement of the emperor. However, Felix III was not going to make such a restoration a matter of course. In his reply to Fravitas' synodal letter, the pope recognized the now deceased patriarch's good intentions and orthodoxy, but remained uncompromising on Peter Mongus and Acacius. For Felix, anyone who remained in communion with either or retained their names on the diptychs could not expect recognition from Rome. Euphemius could only offer a half-solution. Peter's past radical anti-Chalcedonianism made Euphemius and Zeno willing to sacrifice communion with him in favour of alliance with the pope.

Papal demands over Acacius were trickier. The deceased patriarch remained popular at Constantinople, while Zeno was not prepared to discard the man who had provided years of good service. Euphemius too had a reason for not sacrificing Acacius as the deceased patriarch had overseen Euphemius' ordination as presbyter and he considered himself a continuer of Acacius' doctrines. By condemning Acacius, Euphemius would be undermining his own position and doctrine. Euphemius therefore attempted to compromise with Felix, declaring his adherence to Chalcedon, the removal of Peter Mongus from the diptychs but crucially an explanation of why Acacius could not be removed.[134] Felix welcomed Euphemius' orthodoxy, willingness to reconcile and the removal of Peter, but the job was only half done – for full communion to be restored, Acacius had to go. It seemed another impasse had been reached.[135]

Any such move against Peter Mongus was rendered moot on 29 October 490 when he died.[136] While a divisive character, Peter had proven useful in bringing about a compromise between two diametrically opposed viewpoints regarding Chalcedon. Finding another candidate to walk a similar tightrope would not be easy. Initially, Peter's successor, Athanasius II, seemed a placatory individual, following the *Henotikon* in an attempt to maintain communion with Constantinople.[137] However, there is a contrary portrayal of Athanasius' policies. Ps-Zacharias and Evagrius record the new Alexandrian patriarch breaking away from the compromises, condemning both Chalcedon and Leo's *Tome*. Under this Athanasius II, in the very last months of Zeno's reign, may have broken off communion with the rest of the Church.[138]

There is similar confusion over the doctrine of Sallustius, the successor of Martyrius as patriarch of Jerusalem. He sent synodal letters to all the prominent bishops, including Peter Mongus and Peter the Fuller, and may have signed up to the *Henotikon*. Sallustius is also recorded as entering into communion with Athanasius, which could portray him as having some anti-Chalcedonian leanings; however, this appears to be an error.[139] Cyril of Scythopolis is non-committal about Sallustius, but he did call him 'holy', 'which he would not, most certainly, have done if he had any doubt as to his Chalcedonian orthodoxy'.[140] Sallustius does seem to have worked with the unity movement, appointed pro-Chalcedonians and rejected the condemnations of Athanasius. At worst, Sallustius was an adherent of the compromise, if not a fully fledged pro-Chalcedonian, with Ps-Zacharias again attempting to portray Peter Mongus as having never been in communion with supporters of Chalcedon.[141] That is not to say that the entire Jerusalemite patriarchate was united in support of Chalcedon. Gaza remained a base for radical anti-Chalcedonians, including Peter the Iberian and Isaiah of Gaza.[142] Zeno again invited Peter and Isaiah to Constantinople in 487; neither took up the offer, Isaiah begging off due to poor health while Peter departed for Phoenicia. The emperor need not have worried too much about their influence, for not only would both be dead by the end of 489, but the influence of anti-Chalcedonians had been dwindling due to the rise of Chalcedonian monasticism in the region.[143]

The stance of the Antiochene patriarchate is even more muddled. As will be seen, the support of Kalandion for Illus had led to his deposition in 488, but this came at a time when the anti-Chalcedonian movement in Syria was on the rise. This division led Zeno to take a similar step as he had done in Egypt – turning to an anti-Chalcedonian who would accept the *Henotikon*. This saw Peter the Fuller reinstalled at Antioch, which brought some levels of calm, but the Fuller remained a divisive character. His deposition of various bishops could be the removal of supporters of Chalcedon or supporters of Illus.[144] He is accused by Chalcedonian sources of removing from the diptychs virtually all Antiochene patriarchs from around 430, and even anathematizing Chalcedon again.[145] Peter was not embraced by the anti-Chalcedonian party either. This was because he had agreed to support the *Henotikon*. It is likely then that Peter the Fuller remained a moderate opponent of Chalcedon but was willing to compromise. However, this is not a universal view. There are some who suggest that he remained a far more fervent opponent of Chalcedon. Perhaps then the Fuller was a religious and political opportunist, willing to lay his objections aside if it got him a third term as patriarch of Antioch.[146]

Any respite brought by the return of Peter the Fuller proved short-lived as he died in *c*.488, to be succeeded by Palladius.[147] Much like with Fravitas, Palladius' connections with the shrine of St Thecla at Isaurian Seleucia may have made him the choice of Zeno, but that is where information about Palladius ends.[148] A certain John, son of Constantine, and the future emperor Anastasius are mentioned as potential candidates for the Antiochene patriarchate upon the death of the Fuller, but this relays nothing about Palladius' views. He did refuse communion with Athanasius II, which suggests that he at least favoured compromise if not outright support of Chalcedon. If he was an appointment of Zeno, it might be expected that Palladius had signed up to the *Henotikon*, but there is no evidence for this and Zeno may have already been moving away from compromise by Palladius' elevation.[149]

It would seem that Zeno and his bishops felt that the *Henotikon* was no longer needed or that the papacy saw that compromise document as sufficiently tied up with the doctrines and personages of Acacius and Peter Mongus to taint it with schism and heresy. It could also be that Zeno's own failing health was behind the drop in support for *Henotikon*. Without his overt support for the doctrine, it may just have been seen as an unnecessary complication.

Monks, Monasteries and Churches under Zeno

It was not just doctrine and politics that saw Zeno engage with the institutions of the Christian church. Laws and sponsorship saw Zeno dealing with monasteries and churches across the empire. He was not as close to monks or Daniel the Stylite as Leo had been, but he was not a total stranger to the celebrated ascetic atop his column, and sought the advice of a Paphlagonian monk called Severus.[150] There is another account focused on Hilaria, reputedly a daughter of Zeno, which portrays the emperor giving significant gifts towards the expansion of the monasteries at Sketis in the Nile Delta. However, this account first appears in a fourteenth-century version of the narrative and not in the earlier versions of the same story, greatly undermining its credibility.[151]

Zeno was forced to look into monasteries as sections of the population were found to be becoming monks to escape their legal obligations. In a law of 28 March 484, Zeno reiterated that men tied to the land had to receive the permission of their master or landlord before they could enter a monastery. The same law also banned slaves from being ordained clergy, even with the permission of their masters. A slave would have to be freed first before they would be ordained.[152] A second law, dated 14 April 484, added the addendum that if a slave should then leave the monastic community, he would return to the status of a slave. This was to prevent slaves claiming a divine mission to join a monastic community only as a way to escape slavery. These laws were in keeping with pre-existing Roman legislation and their timing might suggest an attempt to portray normalcy in the face of the revolt of Illus.[153]

Two undated laws regarding monasteries from the *Codex Iustinianus* could belong to Zeno. The first states that those who decide to leave a monastic community could not take any movable items with them, even if they originally belonged to them at the time of their joining. It also prohibited clergy from extorting payments from laymen on the threat of excommunication, anathema or exclusion. This would be punished by removal from Church office and a fine of 10lb of gold. The second law saw an imperial interjection in the hierarchy of monasteries. The emperor ordered that no one could lead two different monasteries and that while hegumens (heads of monasteries) were to be responsible for the behaviour of those in their monastery, bishops were responsible for hegumens.[154] Zeno also built upon Canon 17 of Chalcedon regarding the sphere of authority of a bishop. The emperor ordered that every city should have its own bishop, but that no bishop should try to extend his jurisdiction to other cities on penalty of dishonour and property confiscation.[155]

Zeno's interventions had a significant effect on the Christian Church in Cyprus. Late in his third episcopate, Peter the Fuller attempted to subordinate the Cypriot church to the Antiochene see, using the argument that Cyprus was only Christian due to the Apostolic proselytising of Antioch. The discovery of the grave of the Apostle Barnabas near Salamis by Anthemius, Bishop of Cyprus, put paid to much of the Fuller's argument. The Cypriot bishop sealed the support of the emperor by travelling to Constantinople with the relics of Barnabas and then presenting him with the Gospel of Matthew which Barnabas had been buried with. Thrilled with his gift, Zeno not only backed the autocephaly of Cyprus, but he had the sanctuary of Kampanoperta built in honour of Barnabas.[156]

This building of Kampanoperta hints at Zeno's generosity to the Church. One story tells of a woman praying to the Virgin Mary, asking her to avenge a wrong committed by Zeno towards her daughter. The Blessed Virgin appeared to the woman and stated her hand had been stayed by the generosity that Zeno had shown to the Church;[157] this ties in with the portrayal of Zeno as 'one of the great builders among the Eastern emperors'.[158] If there were only literary sources to back up this portrayal, it would seem like an exaggeration played up by 'the frugal or even tight-fisted characters of his successor.[159] Only the church at Isaurian Seleucia is directly attributed to Zeno; hardly the portfolio of an 'indefatigable church-builder.'[160]

However, archaeology has provided evidence of Zenoid building in Isauria. The church at Meriamlik has been connected to the shrine of St Thecla founded by Zeno in 476, while churches at Korykos, Dag Pazari and Alatian have been linked to him.[161] The size, scope and number of these churches suggest that their benefactor was of significant means. However, this alone is far from a definitive identification of these churches as Zenoid. He was not the only Isaurian of means in the second half of the fifth century – there was Zeno the Patrician, Illus, Trocundes, Longinus and the various leaders of the Isaurian War against Anastasius. They too had the money and politico-religious reasons to build churches in their homeland. Even if it was concluded that these churches were imperial in origin, that does not mean that it was definitely Zeno who was behind the building programme. Any emperor of the period could have been attempting to reward Isaurian service or spread Christianity in the region.

There is other archaeological and anecdotal evidence to sway the identification of Zeno as the benefactor. Two types of basilica – transept and domed – have been linked with Zenoid patronage of Isaurian Seleucia, Alatian, Dag Pazari, Korykos, Kanlidivane and Okuzlu.[162] Zeno is also recorded promising to transfer the wealth of Illus to the cities of Isauria – a mass church-building could have been part of the result of that transfer.[163] 'A sudden disruption of the works in some of those locations'[164] has been linked to the outbreak of the Isaurian War in 492, placing their building before the elevation of Anastasius. After the final defeat of the Isaurians by 498, it could be argued that far from looking to build churches to unite Isauria, Anastasius would have been reluctant to pump funds into the region, especially when he had gone to such lengths of punishing Isaurian cities and deporting Isaurians to Thrace.[165]

Zeno became a devotee of St Thecla during his exile in Isauria; the saint appeared to him in a vision, predicting his return to the throne. After Zeno became emperor again, he had a huge sanctuary built to Thecla in Isaurian Seleucia, now Meriamlik in Ayatekla, to express his gratitude.[166] Zeno was also long held to be the patron behind at least part of the pilgrimage site at Alatian. This assertion has been challenged as the complex is supposedly not grand enough to require imperial patronage. It could be that Alatian was not completed to the grand specifications Zeno had planned for it by the outbreak of the Isaurian War.[167] Other churches in the region are of far less certain Zenoid attribution as they rely on architectural similarities with other Zenoid churches and a loose dating to the late fifth century. There are several other Isaurian churches which may be connected with Zeno upon further research.[168]

The cult of Thecla also became popular in Egypt, particularly in Mareotis where at Abu Mina, south-west of Alexandria, a large shrine was erected in honour of St Menas. It was not attributed to Zeno until the eighth century by the *Encomium of Saint Menas*, which is of questionable veracity. There has been some acceptance that Abu Mina is a Zenoid construction or that there is an earlier Zenoid structure below the final church.[169] Zeno may have been behind the building of Qal'at Sim'an in Syria around the column of Simeon the Stylite. It might be more likely that Leo I would have gone out of his way to celebrate Simeon the Stylite, given his closeness to Daniel, although it might be expected that the *Vita Danielis Stylitae* would mention any such building.[170] The conversion of the pagan temple of

Rhea near Cyzicus is similarly attributed to either Leo or Zeno.[171] The basilica of St Demetrius at Thessalonica could be Zenoid or of virtually any other emperor in the second half of the fifth century.[172] Other churches linked to Zeno at Gerizim and Aphrodisias are much less to do with any building programme and more to do with punishment of natives.[173]

Even if some of these churches are of dubious connection to Zeno, it does appear that he did embark on the building or rededicating of numerous religious sites. It is possible to infer some characteristics in the establishment of these churches. Quite a few are of enormous size and he showed some favour towards pilgrimage churches, while his support for Mary Theotokos could hint at a specific strand of architectural anti-Nestorianism.[174] Mosaics at Korykos and Karlik may contain messages too: the motif of the 'Peaceful Kingdom' from Isaiah 11.6-8 could be referring to the *Henotikon* and the attempts at church unification.[175] However, the pacification of Isauria after Illus' final defeat took place in a period when Zeno was moving away from the *Henotikon*. It is therefore more likely that Zeno's church-building in Isauria was connected to 'the political necessity of gaining the favour of the Isaurian clans',[176] rewarding loyalty, well-timed defection or buying future good behaviour.

It would be expected that Zeno would build heavily in the jewel of his imperial crown – Constantinople. However, while he did aid in reconstruction of the city following an earthquake, he is otherwise not recorded building any significant structures in the capital. The Church of Elias being built by soldiers with the consent of the imperial couple could be linked to Zeno and Ariadne, but these soldiers were returning from a successful Persian campaign, making it more likely that the imperial couple were Anastasius and Ariadne.[177]

Such a lack of patronage in Constantinople raises questions. Did Zeno purposefully choose to prioritize other parts of the empire out of political necessity? Or was there something more personal behind this? Could it be that for all the time he spent there, Zeno really did not like the imperial capital or its people? Constantinople had shown that it was not particularly fond of its emperor. Perhaps with his lack of building, Zeno was returning that lack of love. Zeno's somewhat muddled Christology raises another potential explanation – perhaps the emperor did lay the foundations of some buildings in Constantinople, only for later writers who considered him a doctrinal opponent to intentionally downplay his role. This might explain why Anastasius appears so prolific in religious building in the capital – twelve churches and two monasteries, plus at least twelve other churches across the empire. However, such a grudge from the sources would have to be very specific to Zeno given that Anastasius was very much an anti-Chalcedonian.[178]

Zeno and Non-Christians

As emperor, Zeno not only had to deal with the contentious issues within Christianity, but also with groups within the non-Christians of the empire. Pagans at

Aphrodisias in Caria reputedly showed support for the revolt of Illus through pagan sacrifice, but were they 'the tip of the proverbial iceberg'?[179] Or was this event blown out of proportion due to a certain Paralius travelling to Egypt and spreading word of these ceremonies? Peter Mongus complained to the metropolitan of Aphrodisias, but there is little concrete evidence of any Church or imperial reaction. Even the eventual closure and conversion of the temple of Aphrodisias by Zeno, which looks like punishment, is not clear.[180]

After spreading news of pagan rites in favour of Illus, Paralius joined the pagan community in Alexandria, intrigued by its profession of a miracle. However, after investigating this 'miracle' at the temple of Isis near Canopus, Paralius came to see the whole affair and paganism itself as a fraud. He converted to Christianity and became an increasingly vocal opponent of paganism. So vociferous were his verbal attacks that Paralius was only saved from being lynched by Isis cultists by the intervention of fellow Christian students, who included Zacharias Rhetor. Paralius and his colleagues complained to Peter Mongus about the reaction of the cultists, and the patriarch encouraged the students to take a stand against the cults. Leading pagans went into hiding, while Paralius attacked and ransacked the temple of Canopus, bringing a vast amount of pagan items back to Alexandria. In the presence of Mongus, the prefect, local commanders, officials and leading civilians, they held a mass burning.[181] Imperial delegates from Zeno had also engaged in chasing down various pagan grammarians and philosophers. There is no clear evidence that it was their paganism which made these men targets; perhaps they were instead considered allies of Illus. Whatever the charges, they must have been harsh enough to justify their arrest, torture and even death.

While individuals accepted baptism out of convenience rather than conviction,[182] care must be taken not to overplay the extent of this repression. Zeno's agents were likely acting for political reasons, hunting the allies of Illus, while the actions of Paralius were not widespread or intensive. The combination did not amount to a formalized persecution, there is no record of pagans being executed for their beliefs and many of those targeted continued in their professions. These actions 'were aiming to eliminate Zeno's adversaries in the pagan circles of Alexandria, not the pagan circles as such'.[183]

That said, some of the most prominent pagan institutions came under scrutiny. The Temple of Asclepius and the Parthenon in Athens were closed down before 485 and would be consecrated as churches. Both Proclus and Marinus, former heads of the Athenian neo-Platonic school, retired from the city due to disturbances.[184] However, linking these closures, consecrations and disturbances to Zeno's dealings with the supporters of Illus, pre- or post-revolt, and/or paganism as a whole would only be a supposition.

The spectre of pagan restoration also raised anxiety in Palestine, centred on John the Fuller, who reputedly intended to perform a human sacrifice. Informed of these plans by Zacharias, the Bishop of Berytos and an imperial *notarius* launched an investigation. John the Fuller, no doubt hearing of such official scrutiny, denounced his allies and professed his own Christianity. Such a profession was enough to see the Fuller forgiven, but the publicizing of this planned human sacrifice, real or not, saw anti-pagan discontent erupt in the city. Some pagans fled and books were burned, but there is no great attack on pagans recorded.[185] Another separate instance of book-burning is recorded in Berytos, with a jurist called Leontius being targeted for practising of divination and casting of horoscopes. Berytos Christians, endorsed by Bishop John and aided by imperial officials, chased Leontius out of the city and burned his books in front of the Church of Mary Theotokos. It is fortunate that Zacharias was present to provide a record of these Palestinian events, but it is difficult to know how much stress to put on such incidents as a snapshot of growing tension between pagans and Christians during the reign of Zeno.[186]

Damascius may also be doubted on the veracity of some of his recording of pagan-Christian relations during this period. He records Severianus of Damascus being offered the position of praetorian prefect by Zeno, but only on the condition that he converted to Christianity, a condition that Severianus rejected. Even if Damascius did invent this story, it could be used to suggest that at least some pagans felt that Zeno was opposed to paganism.[187] It must be noted that this Severianus was reputedly at the core of a plot against Zeno to restore paganism, only for it to be betrayed by the last son of Aspar, Ermanaric.[188]

Such an idea could back the identifying of two undated laws of the *Codex Iustinianus* as anti-pagan laws of Zeno. Attributing them to Zeno requires an acceptance of pro-pagan aspects of the revolt of Illus, a more concerted anti-pagan policy by Zeno and a leap of faith.[189] The first law attempted to undermine paganism's ability to self-perpetuate by prohibiting its teachers from teaching and making bequests or donations to the cult.[190] The second law demanded baptism and instruction in the Bible and canon law for all inhabitants of the empire, with the punishment of confiscations and banishments. It also forbade pagan professors from drawing public funds and made pagan sacrifice and idolatry a capital offence.[191] These laws seem like part of an extended programme of anti-pagan legislation, which puts them at odds with the rest of Zeno's reign.[192] Any action was more the reaction to decisions taken by individuals like Paralius, Peter Mongus, Zacharias or John the Fuller. Imperial interference in pagan-Christian matters under Zeno were far more a response to the supposed appeal of Pamprepius to pagan circles, whether or not this was actually true of the faction of Illus.

Christians and pagans were not the only religious groups that the regime of Zeno had to deal with. As will be seen, the Samaritans fought against imperial forces in 484, while the Jews remained a large minority across the empire. Rioting in Antioch developed an anti-Semitic tinge, with many Jews killed, the synagogue of Asabinus burnt and the bodies and tombs of their dead desecrated. It has been suggested that these Jews were targeted because they had given their support to Illus, although 'the sources do not suggest at all any Jewish sympathies for the rebellion'.[193] There could have been a Jewish element to these circus riots as the Blue faction was aligned with Jews, so rather than religiously fuelled attacks, these were attacks on allies of the Blues.[194]

Despite the seeming lack of any anti-Semitic imperial policy, Zeno's reported response to the Antiochene unrest does not reflect well on him. The emperor reputedly asked, 'Why did they only burn the corpses of Jews? They should also have burned the living Jews?'[195] There have been differing interpretations of this callous response. Some have taken it at face value – an awful proclamation by Zeno. Others have suggested that the emperor was being somewhat ironic. It could be a reply to a Jewish complaint over their treatment in Antioch, and Zeno was asking why the rioters were targeting the Jewish dead either genuinely or sarcastically. Doubts over how Malalas would have been in a position to directly quote Zeno undermines the idea that this is what the emperor actually said or meant. The desecration of graves was a serious offence in the fifth century, while Jewish synagogues received imperial protection.[196]

What might have given some basis to the suggestion of an anti-Semitic response from Zeno is that the emperor may have refused Jewish demands to punish the rival Green faction. Such a refusal to intervene could have been taken as Zeno supporting the events in Antioch. Malalas himself casts doubt on this idea that Zeno condoned the attack, as he dismissed the *comes Orientis* Theodore over the extent of the violence. Unfortunately, there are no other sources surviving regarding Zeno's policies towards the Jews; no surviving laws or suggestions that he fervently enforced any pre-existing anti-Jewish laws.[197]

There are few other extant examples of Zeno taking action against other religious groups. He does seem to have interjected in Edessa to close a theological 'School of Persians', although this was at the instigation of the Edessene bishop rather than a religious policy of Zeno. It is not clear what this 'School of Persians' really was – perhaps a heretical form of Christianity linked to the Persian Christian Church which was considered Nestorian? Or was it Manichaean or Zoroastrian?[198] A law against Manichaeans issued on 9 April during the consulship of Boethius has been linked to Zeno, with the Boethius in question being Flavius Manlius Boethius, who was western consul in 487. However, the consulship of this Boethius was not recognized by Zeno so would not be used to date a law; instead, this law should be placed in 510 during the western consulship of Ancius Manlius Severinus Boethius and therefore belongs in the reign of Anastasius.[199]

Conclusions on Zeno's Religious Policies

The fifth century as a whole was extremely important to the shaping of Christian doctrine and the Church itself; however, despite it being the time 'when the hopes of achieving unity … around the decisions of Chalcedon had ultimately fallen apart',[200] the reign of Zeno is overlooked in favour of the later reigns of Anastasius and Justinian. Such overlooking may be due to issues with the sources – their general paucity and their distortion of Zeno's doctrinal position. This leaves the student of Zeno and his religious policies having to deal with at least three different guises which the emperor takes on in the historical record:

1. Zeno the Chalcedonian, who was a committed supporter of the decisions of that council, was keen to continue the policies of Marcian and Leo, elevated a succession of Chalcedonians to patriarch of Constantinople, supported the Acacian *revanche* and hoped to restore relations with the papacy for both religious and political reasons.
2. Zeno the Pragmatic Compromiser, who was willing to do business with those of less obvious doctrinal beliefs or even suspected anti-Chalcedonianism when he felt that it would best suit his position and that of the empire, despite the protestations of popes, patriachs and imperial colleagues.
3. Zeno the Anti-Chalcedonian, who was a complete invention by Zacharias of Mitylene and other anti-Chalcedonian sources, so desperate were they to portray Peter Mongus as having never strayed from opposition to Chalcedon. The hijacking of the *Henotikon* by Anastasius also contributed to the later depiction of Zeno as an anti-Chalcedonian as the *Henotikon* itself became remembered as a stance used to undermine the council, and as the imperial sponsor of that compromise, Zeno became tarred by that anti-Chalcedonian brush.

Acacius is also presented in various lights in an attempt to make sense of his seemingly ambiguous doctrine. While there might be some truth in his ambition to increase the importance of the Constantinopolitan patriarchate, any ambition to make himself 'pope of Constantinople'[201] did not see Acacius flit back and forth over Chalcedon. Instead, he should be viewed as a committed Chalcedonian who was willing to compromise for the benefit of the Roman state, its church and his patriarchate. So successful was Zacharias in misrepresenting Acacius as an opponent of Chalcedon that Miaphysites would depict the patriarch as an anti-Chalcedonian saint.[202]

The *Henotikon* itself proved vulnerable to ambiguous, anachronistic depictions of it and its backers. The reason behind this vulnerability lies in the compromise language involved within it, allowing both pro- and anti-Chalcedonians to ascribe to it. This was its *raison d'etre* in the early 480s; however, that compromise language allowed Anastasius to manipulate the *Henotikon* for his own anti-Chalcedonian ends. The Anastasian *Henotikon* also varied from its Zenoid predecessor in terms of scope. While Zeno had intended it as a focus of communion with Alexandria and Antioch, Anastasius used his version as a doctrinal document for the entire empire.

It is not just the imperial faction which was faced with misrepresentation. Both Peter Mongus and Peter the Fuller would seem to have been far less radical than the propaganda surrounding them would have it believed. Peter Mongus proved a far more moderate critic of Chalcedon, willing to enter into negotiations with Chalcedonian authorities. He held his tongue with regards to anti-Chalcedonian pronouncements and squared up to the Aposchists over their opposition to the compromise of 482. Peter the Fuller presents a similar case; a moderate anti-Chalcedonian capable of dealing with Chalcedonian authorities, but misrepresented as a more radical opponent of the council.

While these anti-Chalcedonians represented obdurate opposition for Zeno in the religious sphere, it could be argued that he faced even more formidable opposition from within the Chalcedonian faction. While emperor and patriarch were pragmatic in achieving unity in the face of military trouble, the monasteries of Constantinople were uncompromising. They found a willing ally in Pope Felix III, who refused to countenance any communion with Peter Mongus even for the good of the Roman state. Zeno the Pragmatic Compromiser was not going to find an ally in western Christendom, so it was only after the defeat of Illus allowed Zeno the Chalcedonian to re-emerge that Felix showed any willingness to end the Acacian Schism, but even then only on his unaltered terms. With Zeno and Euphemius unwilling to condemn the now deceased Acacius, the matter had reached an impasse by Zeno's own death in early 491.

It is difficult to come to any firm conclusions about Zeno's religious policies. Politically, his compromising worked well, buying stability at a time of internal strife. This was no mean feat given the overtures of Illus and the destructive reversal of policy by Basiliscus. However, that compromise tainted Zeno and his patriarch in the eyes of many Chalcedonians and made full reconciliation impossible, opening them to scurrilous misrepresentations. In that, Zeno's religious policies should be viewed as a political success but an ecclesiastical failure. This would hardly be surprising given the strength of opposing feeling that the Council of Chalcedon incited, the mess unleashed by Basiliscus and the obduracy of the pope. Perhaps Zeno's greatest 'failure' in the realm of religion was to put the political security of his empire above what some perceived as its spiritual well-being.

Chapter 12

A Long Time Coming: The Revolt of Illus

'Who draws his sword against his prince must throw away the scabbard.'

James Howell

General, Treason and Plot

The dissolution of the Thracian Goths and the expensive reconciliation with Theoderic the Amal allowed Zeno to focus on Illus. There had long been an understandable mutual lack of trust and fear of intentions between the Isaurians.[1] The imperial family had already been responsible for two attempts on Illus' life, while the Isaurian general had held considerable influence over the emperor as his military backer. The enmity that this caused meant that 'the clash between them had seemed inevitable and they both realised it'.[2] Illus certainly appeared to be in an incredibly strong position. He had helped Zeno regain and retain his imperial position and had his own supporters promoted to high office – Pamprepius was honorary consul in 479 and *quaestor sacri palatii*, and his own brother, Trocundes, had served as *magister* in the East and at the imperial court. Together with their prominence in Isauria and in the capital, these military positions gave Trocundes and Illus influence within the Roman army. As further security against any move from Zeno, Illus still held Longinus and Verina.

While Illus had provided Zeno with the military muscle to repel Theoderic Strabo and Marcianus, the slide towards open conflict between the Isaurians was well under way by the late 470s. In 480, another conspiracy was uncovered within the walls of the capital. The perpetrators were the praetorian prefect, Dionysius, the *magister militum*, Thraustila, and that arch-schemer, Epinicus.[3] The involvement of two such highly placed officials may suggest that the Isaurian-backed regime of Zeno was unpopular, while Epinicus almost certainly retained a dislike of Illus from his imprisonment and interrogation. However, there is another way to view this conspiracy of 480; rather than an anti-Isaurian or even anti-Zeno movement, it could have been a pro-Illus movement. Perhaps politicians, generals and Epinicus were all working to remove Zeno, so Illus could replace him with someone more pliable and set himself up as the next Aspar.

Whatever its aim or backing, the conspiracy had barely gotten off the ground before being discovered and dealt with, although it again highlights that for all his seeming success in dealing with the Theoderici, Zeno was not in the most secure position.[4] The removal of Sabinianus in *c*.481, possibly for rumours of rebellion, also hints at continued anti-Zeno feeling. Indeed, there is some speculation that Sabinianus was removed by Zeno due to some collusion with Illus. Sabinianus had also been a fervent opponent of accommodation with the Amal, so his removal may have been part of the plan to facilitate negotiations with the Pannonian Goths. The replacing of Sabinianus with either Moschianus or John the Scythian suggests that the emperor was shoring up internal support in time for conflict with Illus.[5]

The growing dissension between the imperial throne and Illus was demonstrated more clearly with yet another attempt on the life of the Isaurian *magister officiorum*. The instigator this time was said to be the empress Ariadne. She was angry at the treatment of her mother and was given permission by Zeno to approach Illus with a request to release Verina. In response to Ariadne's plea, Illus reputedly asked, 'Why do you ask for her? Is it so that she can again make another emperor in place of your husband?'[6] Such a harsh rejection whipped the empress up into a murderous rage.[7] It is not certain how much Zeno had to do with the subsequent plot. He might have encouraged or even facilitated it; he might have done nothing to prevent it; he may even have known nothing about it. Malalas reports Ariadne essentially presenting an ultimatum to the emperor: 'Is it to be Illus in the palace, or I?' In replying 'Do whatever you can; as for me, I want you',[8] Zeno was giving at the very least tacit support to what Ariadne planned to do, while providing himself with some plausible deniability.

Even if her husband was not involved, Ariadne did have high-level help in orchestrating her attempt on Illus' life in the form of Urbicius. He may not be one of the recognizable names of fifth-century Constantinopolitan politics, but he was one of its constants. Such was his influence, accumulated over the course of almost sixty years of intermittent service within the imperial bedchamber to seven successive *Augusti*, it was said that he was responsible for elevating and disposing of emperors, as well as perhaps even crowning them. As imperial chamberlain, he did hand over the imperial crown to Leo I to give to Leo II, and there may be some allusion to his role in the deposing of Zeno and Basiliscus.[9] Through such a prominent position, Urbicius must have gathered innumerable contacts with which to furnish Ariadne with an assassin in 481.

For this third attempt on Illus' life sponsored by the imperial family, rather than a slave or an Alan, Urbicius employed a *scholarius* called Sporacius. He struck at the top of the staircase to the Dekimon gate into the imperial palace from the Hippodrome, perhaps as Illus answered a summons from the emperor. Swinging his sword, Sporacius succeeded in wounding Illus, cutting off his right ear, but the Isaurian's bodyguard partially blocked the blow with his hand, preventing it from being fatal. Sporacius was then set upon and was either killed by Illus' men outright or captured and executed later, after Illus had been whisked away to the safety of his palace or perhaps even to Chalcedon because his house had been burnt down.[10]

As his price for continued military backing of the current regime and not sticking a knife between Longinus' ribs, Illus extracted the position of *magister militum per Orientem* from Zeno and departed for Antioch, arriving there by at least early 482.[11] On the surface, this does not seem to be all that unusual an appointment – an emperor appointing his most prominent general to an important military command. However, when the details are examined, it becomes clear that the latest assassination attempt had 'cost Illus part of an ear, and Zeno an arm and a leg'.[12] On top of the field and border forces provided by his new magisterial position, Illus also extracted the right to appoint local commanders within the eastern provinces. He was also joined in the East by a cadre of highly placed allies – Marsus, Aelianus, Justinianus, Matronianus, Cuttules and other *comites*. This combined to give him essentially a free hand to run large parts of the East from his own capital at Antioch surrounded by his own ruling elite. No *Augustus* could allow a non-imperial individual to effectively rule significant areas of the empire for any prolonged period of time. Civil war was inevitable.[13]

The Revolt of the Samaritans 484

While relations between Zeno and Illus slid towards war, there were rumblings of discontent amongst an ethno-religious group of the eastern provinces during the mid-480s – the Samaritans. There were accusations of robbery and murder made against the Samaritans in the early 450s, which had led to an imperial enquiry. During the late 470s, the Praetorian Prefect in the East, Sebastianus, was accused of rampant corruption, which could explain some rancour amongst the Samaritans either at pre-existing conditions or at increasing imperial and religious scrutiny.[14]

The surviving sources record contradictory information about the subsequent unrest which spread through Samaria. The Samaritan account of Abu' l-Fath places a lot of the blame on Zeno himself. The emperor supposedly arrived at Nablus at the foot of Mount Gerizim, the holiest site for Samaritans, demanding that the Samaritans convert to Christianity on pain of torture or death. According to Abu' l-Fath, this was only the beginning of Zeno's repression of the Samaritans. The synagogue erected by High Priest 'Aqbun during the reign of Julian (361–363) was forcibly converted to a Christian church; many Samaritan towns were left in ruins, their people raped, brutalized and scattered. The culmination of this persecution was focused on Mount Gerizim itself. Zeno supposedly had the temple atop the holy mountain replaced with a church, complete with a tall tower and a tomb, where Zeno and one of his sons would eventually be interred.[15]

The Romano-Greek sources retell a different story, largely shifting the blame on to the Samaritans. Procopius records Samaritans attacking the Christian church at Nablus during Pentecost, killing many worshippers and cutting off the fingers of the bishop. The emperor responded by punishing those responsible for the Nablus attack, expelling the Samaritans from Mount Gerizim and building a fortified Church of Mary Theotokos atop it. He also established a garrison in Nablus to maintain the peace. The Samaritans resented this subjugation and expulsion, but they were in no position to act.[16]

Malalas presents Samaritan action as much more of a revolt to overthrow Roman control. They crowned one of their number, Iustasas, as their leader, although the title of λῃσταρχος used by the Roman historians may imply he was the 'leader of robbers'.[17] Showing his royal pretence, Iustasas established himself at Caesarea, provincial capital of Palestina Prima, and presided over a series of chariot races. Iustasas and his Samaritans then targeted the Christian community in and around Caesarea. Many were put to death and the Church of St Procopius in Caesarea was burned down. Imperial authorities in the region treated the actions of Iustasas and the Samaritans as a military revolt, with the Palestinian *dux*, Asclepiades, and the *lestodioktes*, Rheges, gathering Roman forces and taking to the field against Iustasas, defeating him utterly near Caesarea. Iustasas was captured and executed, his head and crown sent to Zeno in Constantinople. Malalas would have it that Zeno's attacks on the Samaritans and rebuilding of the Mount Gerizim synagogue as a church were reprisals for this rebellion. Samaritans were banned from public offices and property of wealthy men was confiscated.[18]

This leaves some question over which source tradition should be followed. While he drew on the Samaritan Book of Joshua and obscure chronicles, genealogies and pamphlets, Abu' l-Fath did not compose his chronicle until 1355 and his confused chronology makes it difficult to apply it to the events of the Samaritan revolt under Zeno. The *New Chronicle* has similar issues, claiming that Zeno's Samaritan intervention took place 123 years after the building of the 'Aqbun synagogue, which was 1,941 years after the Israelite arrival in Canaan. This has been correlated with the year 1639 BC, which puts the building of 'Aqbun in 302/303 and therefore Zeno's seizure of it in 425/426.[19] But just because one side of the historiographical divide must be treated with caution does not mean that the other side should be accepted out of hand. The Greek historians were much closer to events chronologically. Both Procopius and Malalas lived during the mid-sixth century, although they do not agree on certain details. Procopius, being from Palestinian Caesarea, is likely to have been more knowledgeable about Samaria and its history.[20]

Even with these chronological issues represented in the Samaritan and Greco-Roman sources, it is largely agreed that this Samaritan revolt took place in 484.[21] However, doubts have been expressed over the foundation of this 484 date in the *Chronicon Paschale*. It used Malalas as its source, who only explicitly states that the revolt took place during the reign of Zeno and lists it between the murder of Armatus in 477 and a revolt of Theoderic the Amal before moving on to the Amal's conquest of Italy. In recreating Malalas' account, the *Chronicon Paschale* puts the death of Armatus and events in Samaria in the same year, before placing Theoderic's move to Italy in 485. It may be that the *Chronicon Paschale* placing the Samaritan revolt in 484 was 'completely accidental',[22] with a reading of Malalas possibly placing events in Samaria in 477/478.[23]

The only common element in these various sources is Zeno's intervention and the building of the Mary Theotokos church on Mount Gerizim. The Samaritan tradition recording Zeno's presence in Palestine during his reign is not backed up anywhere else. Forced conversion or merely missionary work by some local Christians is possible, although not likely on Zeno's instigation. Stoking the flames of revolt in Samaria at a time when another fire was breaking out in Isauria would be foolish. Perhaps over-enthusiastic missionaries converted the 'Aqbun synagogue, causing the Samaritans to attack the church at Nablus in retaliation; however, these conversions seem more like the punishment than the provocation, with Zeno sending the garrison to Nablus and then establishing the Church of Mary Theotokos as the final reprisal.[24]

It is possible that Abu' l-Fath and Malalas have conflated the Samaritan revolt under Zeno with that against Justinian in 529–530, which contained forced conversions, acts of violence and decimation of the Samaritan population.[25] This led to many of the reported 'facts' of the Samaritan revolt against Zeno being doubted. Such is the mess of Malalas' account that the possibility of two separate Samaritan revolts in the 470s/480s has been raised, focused on Nablus and Caesarea respectively. Conversely, it has also been suggested that there was barely a Samaritan revolt at all under Zeno, merely some local riots. The archaeological record has also provided disagreement about whether or not it shows evidence of Samaritan revolt under Zeno. It is certain that a Church of Mary Theotokos was built on Gerizim, although it has yet to be verified if there was a Samaritan synagogue on that site beforehand.[26]

The study of the Samaritan revolt under Zeno is beset by problems, leading to various and vastly different versions of events. It could have been a religiously fuelled series of riots barely worthy of the name 'revolt' in the 470s, an attempt to take advantage of weak imperial government, local circus factions at each others' throats or 'a real national uprising aiming to establish Samaritan statehood'.[27] Opinion has shifted towards it being far more local in scale and religious in nature, sparked by Christian encroachment on holy Samaritan sites. Whatever the cause and timeline, limited military intervention and local policing had re-established order in Samaria before 484 was out, meaning that the Samaritan revolt could only have been of limited distraction to the outbreak of hostilities to the north.

Useful Defections and Unfulfilled Promises

Despite looking inevitable upon Illus' retiring from Constantinople in late 481, war did not break out between Zeno and his Isaurian general until 484. Having stabilised large sections of the empire through the *Henotikon* and his alliance with Theoderic the Amal, Zeno appears to have antagonized the revolt.[28] The first move came in 483 when Zeno demanded the release of Longinus. Illus refused, probably surmising that Zeno, who must have made similar demands throughout the previous seven years, was making yet another empty threat. However, this time the emperor used the refusal to follow an imperial command as justification for stripping Illus of his position as *magister militum per Orientem*, replacing him with John the Scythian. The emperor then expelled Illus' remaining relatives and supporters from Constantinople and gave their confiscated property over to the cities of Isauria. Despite these attempts to undermine his position in both the capital and in Isauria, Illus still felt comfortable. His power in the East had ascended past the need for an official position within the regime of Zeno, and he had been able to manipulate and ignore the emperor for much of the last decade.[29] But Zeno had set out his stall. Removing Illus from his command may only have been symbolic, but it was a definitive statement to the empire. By presenting himself as the wronged party who was denied the release of his brother from captivity by an imperial subject, Zeno was drawing a line – siding with Illus was treason.

Zeno knew that to remove Illus permanently was going to require military action. Therefore, when a column of troops marched east into Anatolia towards Isauria, the immediate assumption is that this was the opening gambit by Zeno to remove Illus; however, the nature of this column is disputed. Its commanders, Konon and Lilingis, were both Isaurian, raising the idea that these were defectors marching to join Illus rather than attack him. This may be further backed by the suggestion that Lilingis was Illus' half-brother. Neither Konon nor Lilingis were punished after the revolt was put down, the former returning to his position as Bishop of Apameia, while the latter served as *comes et praeses Isauriae*. This does not mean that they were allies of Zeno; he may have had to be pragmatic in dealing with former enemies. A certain Cottomenes may have been appointed *magister militum per Orientem* in 484,[30] despite being potentially an enemy of the emperor, only to be eliminated later.[31] It could be that Zeno decided not to risk provoking further revolt by punishing Illus' supporters, but it seems more likely that Konon and Lilingis were supporters of the emperor and that their advance into Isauria was the beginnings of civil war between Zeno and Illus.[32]

While he controlled most of Isauria and Syria,[33] Illus still looked around for allies. He managed to enlist parts of the Roman navy to defend the Cilician and Syrian coasts, while some leading families of Armenia offered their support.[34] But this was by no means enough; indeed, this may even have been overstating the strength of Illus' position. Major centres in Syria such as Chalcis and Edessa refused to support him.[35] Perhaps demonstrating his own worries over his lack of strength, Illus began looking outside the empire for help, with embassies being sent to Persia and Odoacer. Neither of these foreign rulers provided any tangible aid. Odoacer recognized that remaining on placatory terms with Constantinople suited him better than backing the Isaurian rebel. The response of Peroz I sounded far more promising, with the offer of an alliance, although he was distracted by ongoing trouble with Iberia, Armenia and the Hephthalites.[36]

The eastern advance of Konon and Lilingis in 484 could well be the official outbreak of civil war between Zeno and Illus, but there had been at least a few months, if not several years of cold war and preparations going on behind the scenes. However, there is one specific date which can be used to mark the definitive outbreak of revolt – 19 July 484. It was on this day that, persuaded by his lack of support and Zeno's initial move, Illus decided that he needed a focal point in order to draw in some more aid. In the process, he not only made his revolt against Zeno definitive, he elevated it to an attempted usurpation of the imperial throne. However, he did not take the imperial title for himself; he had that position bestowed upon Leontius, a *patricius*, honorary consul, *magister militum per Thracias* and 'a handsome, pock-marked, long-haired youth, pure white, with a straight nose, good eyes, and polite manners'.[37]

This choice raises a number of questions. The first would be how did the *magister militum per Thracias* come to be in Isauria where he could defect to Illus? The usual assumption is that like with Konon and Lilingis, Leontius was dispatched east with a Thracian contingent by Zeno. With the rebel controlling the eastern field army and Zeno not wanting to remove his praesental forces, the emperor will have been left with the Thracian field forces as one of his few options. His Isaurian contingent may already have been sent east, and while Theoderic the Amal had been placated, he will have been reticent to remove the Illyrian field army from the Balkans in case of trouble from the Goths or the Danube tribes. The subsequent defection of his Thracian *magister*[38] would have been a major blow to Zeno and significant boon to Illus if it included Thracian forces as well. If Leontius was in command of a large contingent on his move east to Isauria, perhaps he used that strength to bargain for his elevation to *Augustus*. It would help explain what a surprising choice it was by Illus. However, it would be expected that the sources would have made more of the defection of any significant Thracian force in 484, particularly as it could have tipped the military scales. It could be that Leontius was in Isauria to take custody of Verina and escort her back to Constantinople, perhaps even as early as 481.[39]

This then leads to another of the major questions: why did Illus not take the imperial title for himself? While Leontius held several prominent roles, he was hardly a better candidate. If it was felt that Zeno's Isaurian heritage had been holding his popularity back then it made little sense to choose Leontius, as he seems to have been from Isaurian Dalisandus.[40] Could Illus' loss of an ear have disqualified him from ascending the imperial throne? Mutilation would become part of the machinery of disqualifying imperial candidates from ruling, but it seems unlikely in the late fifth century.[41] Furthermore, if Illus was looking for someone of imperial pedigree, he had only recently had Marcianus, who had a 'better' claim than Zeno, under his control. Perhaps having a less viable *Augustus* was the point, with Illus hoping to be the power behind the throne rather than sitting on it, directly in the firing line of dissent. Leontius could be set aside far more easily than Marcianus, while if Illus had taken the purple himself, it would have been an irrevocable action, only ending in death or victory. If the political machinations of the 470s proved anything it was that virtually nothing was final except death. Zeno had accepted back into allegiance those who had raised others to the imperial throne, including members of his own family and even Illus himself. But for every tonsured Marcianus there was a beheaded/starved Basiliscus; for every rehabilitated Ricimer there was the bloody corpse of Aspar. Even without assuming the imperial title, Illus may well have burned his bridges with Zeno.

Recognizing the peril he could be in if he failed, Illus went all in with his elevation of Leontius, as the coronation at Tarsus was undertaken by another of his long-term prisoners, the empress Verina.[42] Rather than a barely explainable *volte face*, Verina was surely coerced by Illus to partake in Leontius' coronation and then to send word out to the provinces of her support of the new *Augustus* against Zeno.[43] That Verina did not join Leontius and Illus in Antioch after the coronation, but was instead sent back to the Fort of Papirius, suggests that she was still a prisoner rather than a willing participant.[44] The use of Verina not only provided an obvious link with the Leonid dynasty, but may also have helped with any potential masquerade Illus was perpetrating with Leontius. Could it be that Illus intentionally chose Leontius as emperor because his name might have seen some associate him with the Leonid dynasty? Is it even possible that due to the suggestion that he had Thracian origins, Leontius had some sort of connection to the emperor Leo I?[45] Such ideas are immensely speculative and there is no material record of Illus trying to pass off Leontius as a member of the Leonid family, but such masquerades had been shown to work in the past.[46]

Illus may not have limited himself to military and political avenues of support. Backing from Kalandion and the new patriarch of Alexandria, John Talaia, may have seen him reach out to the Church; however, there is not enough evidence to suggest that Illus was in a position to use the continuing problems over Chalcedon to garner support.[47] Even if he was, Zeno and Acacius had moved quickly to blunt any efforts through the *Henotikon*. Furthermore, religion may even have proven a detriment to Illus, particularly as much of the religious angle of his revolt came to focus on an Egyptian soothsayer called Pamprepius.

Born on 29 September 440, Pamprepius trained in grammar both in his hometown of Panopolis in Egypt and in Athens.[48] He was brought to the attention of Illus by Marsus in 476. Pamprepius quickly became a close friend of the Isaurian general, serving as a poet, thinker and court advisor in Illus' following.[49] Even with that connection, Pamprepius fell foul of imperial displeasure due to his paganism and divination. During Illus' absence from the capital in 478, Pamprepius was accused of practising magic for political purposes and banished to Pergamum or Moesia, from where Illus summoned him to Isauria.[50] As a close aide to Illus, Pamprepius played a prominent role in the establishment of Illus' quasi-independent statelet and preparations for conflict with Zeno. He is known to have travelled to Alexandria to raise pro-Illus feeling in Egypt. He met with and was rebuffed by some pagans,[51] but whether or not he met with other circles is unknown. Pamprepius either did meet with some success in drumming up support for Illus or he embellished the results.

As much as his personal religion can be deciphered along with the support of Kalandion and John Talaia, Illus appears as an orthodox Catholic;[52] however, the presence of a high-profile pagan like Pamprepius saw Illus' cause tagged with notions of pro-paganism.[53] But if Illus agreed to the dissemination of the idea that his victory would be good for paganism, it had to be handled carefully so as not to put off Christians. The proclamation letter of Leontius saw Verina refer to the usurper as a 'Christian God-loving man',[54] which could be construed as an attempt to refute rumours of paganism amongst the leaders of the revolt. Any such overt pagan support would have made little sense from a political standpoint, for by the fifth century pagans represented 'a group with limited political significance'.[55] There is also limited information as to whether or not pagans actually backed the revolt in any active way.[56] Even with such a wide range of political, religious, military and imperial appeals for aid, it appears that Illus and Leontius signally failed to draw in significant support, leaving their revolt as essentially an Isaurian rebellion against Zeno.[57]

Meanwhile, Zeno had stiffened and even expanded loyalty to him from amongst the imperial hierarchy, with John the Scythian leading a substantial force comprised of sections from four field armies. On top of that, he also had Theoderic's men, a contingent of Rugians under Ermanaric and a sizeable fleet under the otherwise unknown John and Paul. So when the emperor moved to deal with Illus, he did so from a position of strength that he probably had not yet experienced during his nine years as emperor. The force was strong enough to absorb the recall of Theoderic, who Zeno may have feared could be turned by promises from Illus.[58]

A Damp Squib: the Battle of Antioch and the 'Siege' of Papirion

After a build-up which had encompassed at least nine years of imperial rivalry, manoeuvring and brotherly imprisonment, the showdown between Zeno and Illus was finally about to happen. On top of the emotions and jealousies elicited through the struggle for power and influence at the apex of the imperial hierarchy, Illus' betrayal in 475 and his holding of Longinus as a hostage likely added a deeply personal aspect to this feud. It is recorded that Zeno and Illus had been close friends in the past.[59] After such a momentous build-up, it might be expected that this civil war between Isaurians, which had drawn in a considerable portion of the empire's resources, would live up to the hype and be of a similar extent to other imperial civil wars. Instead, the revolt of Illus was largely settled by a single engagement some time in September 484. A one-off battle by itself does not constitute a damp squib of a civil war – Theodosius' victory at Frigidus River in 394 had been a single confrontation with Arbogast but involved plenty of interesting actions and events. This is not to say that the Battle of Antioch in 484 was definitely not an epic showdown. The forces of John the Scythian may have met those of Illus in a strategically and tactically spectacular standoff on the mountainous outskirts of one of the empire's greatest cities, with both sides fighting to the death for their respective causes. Unfortunately, the source material does not go into any real detail for this battle. It is not even certain that the confrontation took place near Antioch; it may have been in Isauria.[60]

While the detail and even the basic outline of the battle are unclear, the result was anything but. John the Scythian was able to march east, seemingly through Isauria to northern Syria, and bring Illus to battle, where he decisively defeated the Isaurian general and his allies. While many of the prominent characters of the revolt – Illus, Leontius, Trocundes, Marsus and Pamprepius – survived this defeat, so many of their military forces were either killed, captured, scattered in the Isaurian highlands or caused to desert or defect that Illus had no option but to flee to the great Papirian fortress.[61] The rapid collapse of what seemed like an extremely powerful and skilled Isaurian general ensconced in the rich eastern provinces might suggest that much of the power of Illus was overplayed in the surviving sources. Or perhaps it was a damning indictment of the military weakness of the empire as a whole in the mid-480s.

The battle won, Zeno set about winning the war. John the Scythian put the Papirian fortress under blockade while the emperor went on the charm offensive amongst his countrymen. Many Isaurians had supported Illus over the emperor, and now he sought to win some of them back to his side. The valuables liberated from Illus were purposefully redistributed amongst the Isaurian people, while prominent Isaurians like Cottomenes and Longinus of Cardala were promoted to high office. The exact circumstances of these promotions are not known for certain – were these rewards for their loyalty and service in the face of revolt or the fulfilling of a bribe promised for their desertion of the rebel general?[62]

While Zeno had been victorious in battle and perhaps in diplomacy in 484, the final defeat of Illus was still a significant way off. The same holdfast from which Papirius, Indacus and even Zeno himself had resisted capture was to shelter Illus. Part of their rapid appeal to the Isaurians was due to Zeno and John recognizing that Roman forces were going to be deployed in Isaurian territory taking up Isaurian resources for a prolonged period of time. The redistribution of Illus' riches might be seen as a down-payment on future discomfort. Given the strength of the Fort of Papirius, the confrontation was more an attempted blockade than a siege as the Scythian was unlikely to waste men in futile attempts to storm the fortress. But for the rebels to hold out for another four years suggests that any blockade was incomplete. However, being secure in his mountainous hideaway with its trickle of supplies meant that the Isaurian general was isolated, solidifying the complete collapse of his position.

Illus had just two remaining cards to play: he still had Longinus and Verina. Ariadne may have been desperate to see her mother set free, but Zeno was likely not bothered. While his increased security might have seen him turn to the succession, Zeno had already looked past the threat to his brother's life in dismissing and fighting Illus. Now, with victory all but secured, the emperor was in no mood for negotiations. It was a mood which ultimately cost the empress her life. Whether through the ravages of time or the ravages of the 'siege', Verina died before the final capitulation, probably even before 484 was out. When the fortress fell, the body of the empress was recovered, allowing Ariadne to have it buried in Constantinople in the Church of the Holy Apostles.[63]

Verina *Augusta* was very much of her time. Various women of the Theodosian dynasty – Pulcheria, Galla Placidia, Eudocia – ascended to positions of considerable influence in the Roman Empire and provided a framework for Verina to aspire to a similar position. Her involvement in the reign of Leo I, plotting the deposition of Zeno, the accession of Patricius or Basiliscus, the restoration of Zeno and an assassination attempt on Illus showed that she was a formidable character and worthy successor to those Theodosian *Augustae*. The eighth/ninth-century *Parastaseis syntomoi chronikai* records two statues of her in Constantinople; the first by her husband on a pillar near St Agathonikos and the second at the Anemodourion, near St Barbara, from the reign of Basiliscus. The dedication of the second statue was welcomed by the acclamation of 'Long life to Verina, the orthodox Helena'. Such a view of her might play into Verina's abandoning of Basiliscus when he strayed from Chalcedonianism. It also records that she was responsible for the abandoning of the island of Kranos due to a curse she placed on it.[64] Another even later source, the thirteenth-century *Georgian Chronicle*, positions Verina as a dynastic ancestor of the royal house of Caucasian Iberia through a reputed third daughter called Helena, who married Vakhtang I of Iberia.[65]

The doubt over the exact year of Verina's death reflects the lack of chronological certainty about the progression of events within the Papirian fortress. Illus may have begun to lose control of the situation within the fortress through his own neglect of his duties. This was seemingly caused by the death of his daughter, Anthusa, during the blockade, although it is unknown when during the period 484-488 this took place.[66] The first signs of his growing disillusionment may have come as early as November 484 when Illus had Pamprepius executed. The lack of support from Egypt during the revolt may have been used to blacken Pamprepius' reputation. Perhaps Illus had become exasperated by the failure of Pamprepius' prophecies and his own Christian proclivities had finally won out. Or maybe he was found to be in contact with the blockading imperial forces to save himself. Whatever the reasons behind it, Pamprepius faced a fatal fall from the graces of Illus in the early stages of the 'siege'.[67]

The most obvious example of any negligence or desperation from Illus came in 485, when he inexplicably released Longinus without any guarantees of improved treatment or a slackening of the Scythian's blockade.[68] Staring defeat in the face and encouraged to take action by the increasing detachment of his older brother, Trocundes attempted a breakout from the fortress in 485. The forces of John the Scythian were well deployed, and Trocundes was quickly captured and put to death.[69] With the blockade having already taken the life of Marsus through illness,[70] the execution of Trocundes meant that the leadership of the rebels was resting more and more heavily on Illus, who may have been slumping further into depression with the death of Anthusa and now his brother.

But still the fortress held out. Only in 488 did it finally fall, and even then it required betrayal from the inside, reputedly by either Trocundes' brother-in-law or Indacus Cottunes, for John the Scythian to take the fortress. If Indacus was responsible, he was to soon regret it for as imperial forces streamed into the fortress, he was amongst those cut down. Both Illus and Leontius were captured and then executed, their heads dispatched to Constantinople as trophies for Zeno.[71] For all the trouble he had caused Zeno both as a supporter and an enemy, Illus had been a friend of the emperor and had rendered good service. This might explain why the rebel general's final requests, that his daughter be buried at Tarsus and that his wife and a faithful servant called Conon be spared, were granted. The prominence of Illus in the capital may also be demonstrated by a district in Constantinople where he owned property later becoming known as *ta Illou* and his house being consecrated as a Church of St John.[72]

Despite his overtures to various Isaurians during the revolt, Zeno did not shy away from punishing those connected to the rebellion. Several prominent individuals were executed while various strongholds were destroyed, although future events in Isauria show that not all of the region's fortresses were decommissioned.[73] Zeno also looked to punish those who had professed support for Illus. The empire was not yet in a position to challenge the Persian king over Mesopotamia and Peroz was already dead; his sons were too busy fighting each other, court officials, Zoroastrian clergy, subkingdoms and the Hephthalites to be any danger. However, the Armenians who had offered aid to Illus could be taught a lesson without risking a massive eastern war. The emperor had all but one of the Roman governors removed from their positions and altered rules governing their appointments. Only candidates chosen by the emperor would be viable, tightening Roman control over its half of Armenia.[74]

There is little in the sources to suggest that Illus attempted to undermine the unity of the *Henotikon*. The letter of Verina announcing Leontius' elevation was sent to regions such as Egypt, Libya and Palestine, but was an attempt to undermine Zeno politically rather than ecclesiastically. It could be that Illus made promises to religious opponents of the emperor, although this, while a logical supposition given the prominence of Pamprepius and Kalandion in the camp of Illus, is not recorded in the sources.[75] However, the revolt of Illus did have an impact on Zeno's Church policy. The *Henotikon* itself could be viewed as a result of such influence. There was also the Isaurian and Syrian clergy who had given strong support to Illus. The emperor had Kalandion deposed, along with a lot of his bishops.[76] But Kalandion was only one side of the doctrinal disputes in Antioch, forcing Zeno and Acacius to turn to Peter the Fuller.[77]

Christianity was not the only religion affected by the revolt of Illus. Paganism was shown some encouragement due to the more pragmatic need to cultivate support wherever he could find it.[78] It could also be speculated that Illus' scouting around for allies might have led to some contact with the Samaritans. Once he recognized that there was no hope in gaining the support of Palestine, perhaps Illus played some role in stirring up the tensions which had caused the Samaritan revolt as a way to divert some imperial attention, material and forces away from the battlefields of Isauria and Syria.

The defeat and death of Illus may have made Zeno feel safe on his imperial throne for the first time in his thirteen years as emperor. The Goths had been reconciled and settled seemingly as loyal allies, Isauria and Syria had been returned to imperial obedience and those who could be punished had been. Imperial politics seemed set to fall back into normality. However, there were still problems. Whilst not of the same stature as Aspar, the removal of Illus may raise some of the same structural problems as with the murder of the Alan *magister* – the lack of a strongman to be the focus and director of the empire's military energies, especially when the emperor did not take the field, may have encouraged military unrest. The Isaurian general had somewhat stepped into the breach left by Aspar, but now in 488, aside from perhaps John the Scythian, who harboured few political ambitions, there was no standout military leader to assume any sort of dominant position at court. As will be seen, with the positions given to him, Zeno may have meant for Longinus to assume such a role in preparation for his eventual succession. Another issue is that buoyed with his success against Illus, Zeno was unlikely to leave the Amal to enjoy the lands and political position which had been partially extorted from the empire at a time of crisis. The Pannonian Gothic question was going to require a more permanent solution.

Chapter 13

Zeno, Theoderic and the End of the Western Roman Empire

'There were, moreover, still other emperors in the west before this time, but although I know their names well, I shall make no mention of them whatsoever. For it so fell out that they lived only a short time after attaining the office, and as a result of this accomplished nothing worthy of mention.'

Procopius, *Bellum Vandalicum* VII.15-17

One Last Threat

With Illus eliminated, Zeno had narrowed his opponents down to just one, his senior *magister militum praesentalis*, Theoderic the Amal. As the Goth's present high position was largely extorted rather than rewarded and 'given Zeno's track record of tolerating political pluralism, this was not a situation that was ever likely to last'.[1] The emperor may have been initiating moves against Theoderic even before the Battle of Antioch against Illus. Theoderic was either recalled or removed himself from the battlefields of Isauria and Syria, although his Gothic contingent seems to have remained in the field until Illus was bottled up at Papirion.[2] Zeno was always likely to wonder if his barbarian general was truly loyal to the empire or if he was acting for his own and his men's benefit. Clearly 'lack of trust was already souring relations between Zeno and Theoderic, even if it did not lead to an immediate break'.[3]

Upon returning to his people, Theoderic cannot have been pleased with what he found, for the Amal was once again at war with the empire in 486. No doubt Zeno was withholding payments and resources.[4] Theoderic may have felt that such deprivations were the prelude to an all-out imperial attack, so he decided on pre-emptive action. However, such a point of view must also be attributed to the emperor himself. While it would appear that Zeno was an untrustworthy rogue of an emperor, he will have seen it that he was surrounded by traitors. Zeno may appear dishonest in the sources, but not necessarily because he himself was naturally duplicitous but because everyone around him was and if he wanted to survive, the emperor had to descend to their level.

It was Thrace that felt the wrath of Theoderic and his Goths in 486.[5] With his main armies still dealing with Illus, Zeno appears to have resorted to calling in the 'Bulgars' again, only for the Goths to defeat them, with Theoderic reputedly killing the khan in single combat.[6] The following year, Theoderic went further and advanced on Constantinople. He had no intention of besieging the enormous city, but did make things difficult for its inhabitants. Camping at Rhegium, the Goths overran the wealthy suburbs outside the Great Walls. The Amal then targeted those within the city by cutting the aqueducts that collected rain water from the Thracian hills.[7] It took a massive payment from Zeno delivered to the Gothic camp by Theoderic's sister, possibly Amalafrida, who was resident at the imperial court, to get the Goths to return to Moesia and the negotiating table.[8]

The sources do not provide much clarity over these negotiations. Those with ties to the court of Theoderic painted him in the most positive, problem-solving light,[9] while eastern sources were more likely to give Zeno more credit for breaking the impasse.[10] The crux of this deadlock was that while Theoderic could improve his negotiating position through raiding, 'this would not have solved the underlying problem … in anything but the short term, Zeno would not allow a Gothic general the kind of influence that the size of his army and understandable personal ambition dictated he should possess'.[11] The Amal also recognized that even though the emperor was reluctant to risk a full-scale campaign, Zeno's military capabilities were increasing in the wake of Illus' defeat. Repeated raids and attacks on Roman territory could provide sufficient provocation for an overwhelming Roman force arriving on Theoderic's doorstep.[12]

'Both sides recognised the impossibility of real coexistence'[13] and the need for a different, possibly permanent solution. They found it in the reputed discussions between Theoderic and Adamantius outside Dyrrhachium eight years previously. Regardless of how serious or even existent the suggestion that Theoderic would travel west to restore Julius Nepos to the western throne had been, an Italian expedition by the Goths became a reality.[14] The details of the agreement would become contentious at a later date, but for 487, Zeno and Theoderic were satisfied with the basic outline – the emperor rid himself of the last major threat to his independence and the Amal got the opportunity to establish his own realm. But why would Zeno feel that sending a barbarian nation to Italy would solve his Gothic problem? Was Italy not the seat of the western Roman emperor, who as of 472 was an eastern appointee? Clearly, there had been considerable changes.

A 'Parade of Nobodies' – The Last Western Roman Emperors

In the late 460s, Italy saw battle lines being drawn between Anthemius *Augustus* and his *magister militum*, Ricimer. Despite some promise, the early years of Anthemius' reign had been punctuated by military failure. Marcellinus had successfully removed the Vandals from Sicily and Sardinia, while Anthemiolus, the emperor's son, had made some inroads in Gaul alongside Breton allies, only for the former to come undone as part of Basiliscus' disastrous Vandal expedition of 468, while the latter was heavily defeated and killed by Euric, the Visigothic king.[15] Things were not much better in the Italian peninsula. The Senate disliked being dictated to by an emperor from the East and chosen by Constantinople, especially when Anthemius continued to look east for connections and legitimacy such as marrying his son, Marcianus, to Leontia.[16]

There were also doubts over Anthemius' Christianity due to his friends and colleagues, such as Marcellinus and Messius Phobius Severus, being pagans. In an attempt to rectify this enmity, Anthemius showered the western aristocracy with honours. The poet Sidonius Apollinaris was one such recipient, receiving the title of patrician, rank of *caput senatus* and position of *praefectus urbi*, usually reserved for members of the Italian aristocracy.[17] Watering down the exclusivity of these titles is more likely to have angered the conservative elements of the Senate, while promoting the likes of Sidonius was not going to bring much in the way of material support to Anthemius, even if the poet could provide him with some positive propaganda.

The western emperor's biggest problem was the continued presence of Ricimer as *magister militum*. The Suebo-Gothic Roman general had already done away with two western *Augusti*, and will no doubt have seen Anthemius as an obstacle rather than an ally. Anthemius' attempts at independent military action, even if they were largely failures, and the attempted promotion of Marcellinus to high military office can only have antagonized the western *magister*, while the use of an eastern practice of two *magistri* only further irritated the Senate. Even with the marriage of Anthemius' daughter, Alypia, to Ricimer early in the reign, any peace between them was not to last.

The final breach centred on Ricimer's actions when Anthemius fell ill in 470.[18] Thinking that the illness would prove to be fatal, the *magister militum* laid the groundwork for the elevation of Romanus, a senator, patrician and *magister officiorum*, as his latest puppet emperor. This in itself was not all that untoward, but when Anthemius made an unexpected recovery, it became a major problem. Romanus was now a direct threat to the emperor. This led to rumours and accusations that Romanus and other senators had brought about Anthemius' illness through sorcery. The emperor jumped on this rumour (or invented it) and accused Romanus of attempted usurpation, having him put to death. This was in opposition to Ricimer, who removed himself from the imperial court.[19] Civil war was reputedly only avoided by the intervention of Epiphanius, Bishop of Milan.[20] The truce lasted just over a year, with a fully fledged civil war breaking out between the emperor and his *magister militum* in early 472.

With the demise of Anthemiolus in 471 and the defection of Olybrius seen earlier, Anthemius was left with few military resources to oppose Ricimer; the focus of the civil war became the besieging of the emperor in Rome by the *magister*. Anthemius' last hope was the recently appointed *magister militum per Gallias*, Bilimer, who brought whatever forces he had to the very approaches of Rome.

However, Ricimer had also received reinforcement from his nephew, Gundobad, who was Bilimer's predecessor as Gallic *magister*. This may have meant that he had not lost his Gallic army, and together with the forces of Ricimer, he inflicted a decisive defeat on Bilimer in early July 472. With the city capitulating and all hope lost, Anthemius was soon captured and beheaded, either by Gundobad or Ricimer himself, on 11 July 472.[21]

It is usually thought that Olybrius was elevated to *Augustus* by Ricimer on the same day as Anthemius' execution. However, it may be that Olybrius became Ricimer's candidate for the throne from almost the very moment he arrived in Italy, whether through the discovery of a secret letter of Leo or not. Having his own candidate to play off against the besieged Anthemius would have been useful for Ricimer. The elevation of Olybrius to *Augustus* may have happened so quickly after his arrival in the West that it could have been part of Leo's plan; however, 'the facts that Anthemius was Leo's chosen candidate, his *filius*, and that Olybrius was the friend of his foe Genseric, are a strong counter-argument'.[22]

After almost two decades of attempting to ascend to an imperial throne, Olybrius did not make much of the opportunity that fell into his lap in early 472. He was referred to as a pious man, which may be reflected in his visit to Daniel the Stylite between 455 and 460 and on his coinage.[23] His *solidi* and *tremisses* minted in Rome sported a new reverse legend: SALVS MUNDI – 'Salvation of the World'.[24] It could be that this theme was chosen not just for Olybrius' own Christian piety but also in opposition to Anthemius' Neo-Platonism. The lack of any military regalia on the bust of Olybrius on his coins may also point to a lack of interest in military matters.

The most significant events of Olybrius' reign focused on his barbarian *magistri*. Within forty days of the execution of Anthemius, on 9, 18, or 19 August, the *magister militum* Ricimer died 'after vomiting much blood'.[25] But if Olybrius had any thoughts of establishing his own independence as *Augustus* he was in for double disappointment. Gundobad was in a powerful enough position to leave Olybrius no option but to promote him to patrician and *magister militum* in succession to Ricimer.[26] This was not necessarily the end for Olybrius in terms of forging his own path, as Gundobad was not the same kind of overwhelming presence Ricimer had been. And given time, Leo had proven that even the most powerful *magister* could be overcome. But time was one thing that Olybrius did not have. As little as thirteen days and no more than three months after the death of Ricimer, the emperor was struck down by dropsy.[27]

The deaths of Ricimer and Olybrius in quick succession led to an interregnum of four months. This was not unusual in the West; there had been at least a month's gap after the demise of almost every emperor since that of Petronius Maximus on 31 May 455. This interregnum was likely caused by the lack of an obvious successor and Gundobad's departure to Gaul.[28] There may have been some contact with the court at Constantinople, but not enough time had passed for any kind of real discussion. Given the response of Leo to the eventual choice made by Gundobad, it would seem that the Burgundian *magister* acted without much input from the eastern *Augustus*.

His choice fell upon the western *comes domesticorum*, Glycerius, who was elevated to the throne at Ravenna in early March 473.[29] The new emperor faired a little better than Olybrius, but not by much. He is remembered as enacting measures for the good of the people, although the one law of his which survives, dated 11 March 473, was addressed to Himilco, the Praetorian Prefect in Italy, and concerned simony.[30] Glycerius' coins appear to show that the new emperor focused a lot of his time in northern Italy, as nearly all of his issues were minted in Milan and Ravenna.[31] This fits in with the military troubles faced by Glycerius, particularly the invasion of Italy by Euric in 473. Glycerius' *comites* Alla and Sindila defeated the Visigothic general Vincentius; however, the Roman preoccupation with defending Italy saw Euric capture both Arles and Marseilles.

This Gothic danger from the West was compounded by the arrival of another group of Goths from the East. The newest arrivals were the Pannonian Goths of Videmir, who had refused to join Theodemir and Theoderic in Thessaly in 473. It is difficult to grasp just how many men Videmir brought with him. It is possible that it was only in the magnitude of hundreds rather than thousands. The threat from these Pannonian Goths was perhaps also reduced by the death of Videmir, for even though his son, also Videmir, took over the leadership of the group, the loss of an established leader may have seen some of the Pannonian Goths look elsewhere for employment. In the end, even in the crumbling West, they made little impact and Glycerius bought their removal to Gaul for 2,000 *solidi*, where they were subsumed by the realm of Euric.[32]

This was not the last threat to Glycerius' regime to come from the East. Whatever attempts the western *Augustus* had made to placate Leo had failed. To the eastern emperor, Glycerius' elevation by Gundobad was unacceptable and therefore Leo decided to choose his own candidate and empowered him to invade Italy. His choice fell upon Julius Nepos, nephew of Marcellinus, who had inherited his uncle's quasi-independent fiefdom in Dalmatia and married a relation of the imperial family.[33] The name of Nepos' wife is not recorded, but she is noted as being *neptis* of Leo and Verina, a term that can mean either 'granddaughter' or any female descendant. The lack of prevalence of both Julius and his wife in Constantinople suggests that she was a more distant relative, perhaps a niece.[34] Winter delayed Nepos' invasion, and by the time the weather was set fair for a crossing, there had been a change in regime at Constantinople with the death of Leo I in January 474. But eastern imperial policy towards Italy remained the same, with the government of Leo II and Zeno continuing to back Nepos.

The delay to Nepos' crossing should have provided Glycerius and Gundobad with time to prepare a defence. However, in the most damning indictment of the state of the western empire by 474, Gundobad, patrician and *magister militum*, chose to fight for the Burgundian crown rather than remain in Italy to defend the regime of Glycerius. Gundobad likely felt that he could grow his own position by straddling

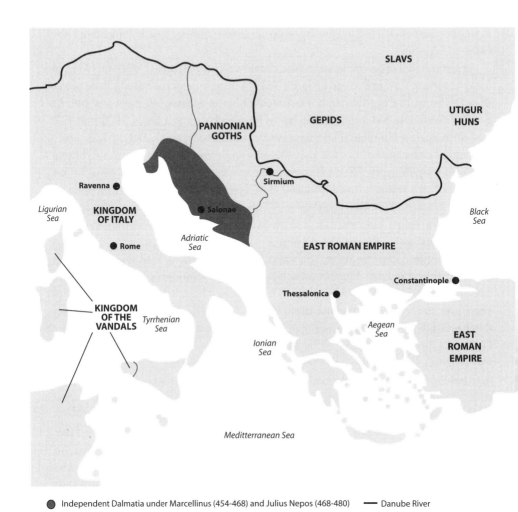

● Independent Dalmatia under Marcellinus (454-468) and Julius Nepos (468-480)   — Danube River

Dalmatia under Julius Nepos and the Balkan Provinces

the fence between Roman general and barbarian proto-king, leaving the forces which had been successful against Vincentius to defend Italy. Glycerius retreated south to Rome, where he minted a small silver coin with the legend VICTORIA AVGGG.[35] The 'AVGGG' may attest to Glycerius' continued recognition of Leo II and Zeno, along with himself, as *Augusti*. In so doing he was also demonstrating his intention to resist Nepos.

Even without his *magister* present, having served as *comes domesticorum* and commanding men capable of defeating the forces of Euric, Glycerius should have been able to lead some defence of Italy in the face of Nepos' invasion. As it was, his resistance collapsed with nary a whimper. In spring 474, Julius Nepos crossed the Adriatic, putting in at Portus, the harbour of Rome, by June. The very sight of

Nepos' army saw to the capitulation of Glycerius. The emperor was deposed and dispatched to Salona, where he was to serve as bishop until his death.[36]

The deposition of Glycerius without a fight requires inquiry. The absence of Gundobad and his forces left Glycerius to rely on the only other avenues of financial support left in western territory – the Italian and Gallic aristocracies. It is likely though that he received no useful support from these senatorial families, meaning that when it came time to face the Dalmatian invader, Glycerius' forces refused to fight as they had not been paid or there were not enough of them. Therefore, the lack of a major battle for the western empire may say less about Glycerius' leadership abilities and more about the sheer dearth of manpower and financial resources available in Italy and the ultimate lack of authority retained in the position of western *Augustus*. This did not bode well for Julius Nepos, proclaimed at Rome on 19/24 June 474.[37]

Nepos attempted to restore the stature of the western imperial position, at least in terms of numismatic output, not just in Italy but also in Gaul. He aimed for a rapprochement with the independent Roman general Syagrius and maybe some of the barbarian kingdoms. He was also active in attempting to re-establish Roman control in southern Gaul, sending embassies to Euric in an attempt to forge a peace.[38] The threat of a Roman invasion of Gothic territory brought Euric to the negotiating table, but while Nepos achieved the restoration of Provence, Arles and Marseilles, he had to give up Auvergne in return, much to the horror of Sidonius Apollinaris.[39] Such trading of Roman territory to barbarian invaders undermined the reputation of Nepos, who was already sneered at as an appointee of the eastern court. Dissent focused on the newly appointed *magister militum*, Orestes. Ordered by the emperor to march to southern Gaul, perhaps with senatorial connivance, Orestes aimed the forces under his command at a different enemy – Julius Nepos himself. The emperor suddenly found himself bereft of manpower, and when Orestes approached Ravenna, Nepos took ship for Dalmatia on 28/29 August 475.[40]

Despite Nepos not giving up the imperial title, his flight from Italy left the western throne in the hands of Orestes. It had been a meteoric rise for a Pannonian whose highest profile had been as a *notarius* to Attila the Hun and had twice served as a Hunnic envoy to Constantinople.[41] After the collapse of the Attilan empire, Orestes took service with the empire, ending up in Dalmatia, which led to him being part of Nepos' invasion force in 474 and elevation to patrician and *magister militum*. However, now in 475, with supreme Roman power within his grasp, Orestes chose to follow the example of Ricimer, Aspar, Illus and Gundobad, refusing to take the imperial title for himself. Instead, he succeeded in doing what had eluded the likes of Aetius and Aspar, two far more powerful and well-established men, and had his own teenaged son, Romulus, elevated to the purple on 31 October 475.[42]

Despite issuing new coins from Arles, Milan, Ravenna and Rome in his son's name,[43] Orestes faced a chronic resource shortage, with any promises given by the

Senate quickly proving empty. The balancing act between Italian landed interests and paying barbarian troops soon became impossible. Even with its decline in stature, the Italian field army probably 'remained the single largest military formation in western Europe – considerably larger … than the tax revenues of Italy alone could support'.[44] In lieu of cash, the barbarian soldiers demanded land, something that Orestes' senatorial allies would not accede to. With the empire unwilling to pay them, the barbarian army turned to a leader who would not depend on the cooperation of the nobility: one of their own. On 23 August 476, the various Heruli, Scirii and Torcilingi comprising the Italian field army elected Odoacer as their leader.[45] The new *rex Italiae* marched on Orestes, with the two meeting in battle near Placentia on 28 August. The rebel Italian field army overwhelmed whatever meagre forces Orestes had cobbled together. The *magister militum* was captured and executed the same day, exactly a year after he had forced Julius Nepos to Dalmatia.[46]

Within a week of Placentia, Odoacer had captured Ravenna, killed Orestes' brother, Paulus, and taken control of Romulus. With supreme power in the peninsula in his hands, and having been involved in Italian politics for a decade, Odoacer 'had enough imagination and intelligence to [understand that] trying to set up yet another short-lived regime was a waste of time'.[47] Therefore, he deposed and retired Romulus to live on a pension in Campania, and with that, the Roman Empire in Italy ceased to exist, its last emperor not even worth executing.[48]

The Emperor and the King – Zeno and Flavius Odoacer

But who was this new *rex Italiae* who had 'administered the last rites in this saga of imperial unravelling'?[49] Born in around 433, little is known about his early life and there has been considerable discussion over Odoacer's exact origins and heritage. The historical sources describe him as Rugian, Torcilingi, Heruli, Goth or Scirian, much like his mother;[50] however, his father, Edeco, is usually thought to have been a Hun, while his brother, Onoulphus, is listed as the son of a Thuringian father and a Scirian mother.[51] This could suggest either that Edceo was a Thuringian, possibly a Hunnicized one, or that Odoacer and Onoulphus were actually only half-brothers. As has already been seen, there has been some suggestion that he shared some blood with the Leonid imperial family through Verina and Armatus.

It is likely that Odoacer spent his formative years under the Attilan yolk. With the collapse of the Hunnic empire after 453, Odoacer and Onoulphus, along with their father, appear to have used their maternal connections to obtain a leading position amongst the Scirii – Odoacer is even called a Scirian 'prince'. The Scirii escaped the Huns by crossing into Roman territory, where they came into conflict with the Pannonian Goths, which resulted in the death of Valamir and then in the defeat of the Scirii by Theodemir and Videmir.[52] This defeat saw Odoacer move west, appearing at the head of a band of Saxons during the battles between the Visigothic forces of Theoderic II and Euric against the alliance of Aegidius/Syagrius, Paulus and the Frankish king Childeric I during the mid-460s. In around 463, Odoacer and his men occupied Angers in western Gaul and only surrendered the city to Childeric in 469 in return for joining Frankish service.[53]

Childeric employed Odoacer against some Alamanni/Alans in Raetia, which led to Odoacer passing through Noricum in c.470, where he met St Severinus, who encouraged Odoacer to 'Go to Italy, go, now covered with mean hides; soon you will make rich gifts to many.'[54] Arriving in the peninsula, he found a significant band of Scirii forming the core of the Italian field army, which quickly made him a prominent figure during the last years of the western empire. He supported Ricimer during the civil war against Anthemius in 472, perhaps becoming an imperial bodyguard.[55] He must have played significant roles in the inactions of the Italian field army under Olybrius, Glycerius, Julius Nepos and finally Orestes. When the opportunity came to remove the last vestiges of an exhausted imperial regime, Odoacer emerged as the first king of Italy in nearly a millennium.

While he had been responsible for the shelving of the western imperial system, Odoacer was keen to avoid conjuring up a storm from the East. It was less than two years since Constantinople had sponsored Julius Nepos. Therefore, a month after he regained the throne from Basiliscus, Zeno was visited by an embassy from the West. He might have expected ceremonial congratulations on his reclamation of his rightful position as *Augustus*; he got that and more. Seemingly as his last act as emperor, Romulus *Augustus* had been 'encouraged' by Odoacer to send a letter of resignation and his imperial vestments to Zeno. The embassy declared that 'there was no need of a divided rule and that one, shared emperor was sufficient for both territories.'[56] They proposed that Zeno confer the title of *patricius* on Odoacer and entrust him with the administration of Italy, a position that the loyalty of the army and his defeat of the usurpation of Orestes made Odoacer well qualified for.

In reaching out to Zeno in a respectful, subordinate manner, Odoacer was not only hoping to deter any eastern attempts to remove him, but also to receive legitimacy from the emperor. Given his own unstable position, Zeno could not yet challenge the situation in Italy, so it is likely that he would have accepted this proposal and appointed Odoacer as his viceroy in the West without any real caveats. However, as these negotiations progressed, another embassy arrived in Constantinople. This one was from Julius Nepos, who despite fleeing from Ravenna a year before, was still in control of Dalmatia. More importantly for Odoacer and the negotiations with Zeno, Nepos had not relinquished his imperial title and was seeking help from his Augustan colleague in restoring him to Italy. He found a willing ally in his relative Verina, who encouraged the emperor to restore Nepos to the western throne.[57]

Zeno attempted to accommodate both, granting Odoacer the title of *patricius* but demanding that he accept Julius Nepos as his imperial overlord, which did technically happen with Odoacer minting coins depicting Nepos. Ultimately though, faced with his own troubles, Zeno could offer no effective help to Nepos, beyond recognition and encouraging Odoacer to accept him back. There was no move to re-establish Nepos as effective ruler in Italy, leaving any such recognition at best a formality and at worst a meaningless gesture. Odoacer was in control of Italy and would remain so with or without Zeno's imperial consent until he was ousted militarily.

Despite that reality, Odoacer still hoped to keep that storm at bay, so he was careful not to claim titles and prerogatives which were not due to him and frequently made efforts to maintain the pretence of his subordination to Constantinople, including issuing coins of Zeno and Nepos.[58] He did appoint his own consuls, which demonstrates independence from Constantinople, although there may have been a tacit acceptance from Zeno that Odoacer needed to curry favour with the Roman aristocracy. Zeno himself had used the consulship as a political device – Illus, Trocundes, Longinus and Theoderic the Amal were all consuls after his restoration, while he also made good use of honorary consulships. Odoacer never assumed the consulship himself or gave it to his family or military allies, instead appointing what appears to be a parade of Roman senators.[59]

Perhaps dismayed by Zeno's tolerance of Odoacer, Nepos may have been planning a return to Italy to fight for his throne in early 480. If this was the case, it appears that at least some of his Dalmatian followers were none too keen. Two *comites*, Ovida and Viator, murdered Julius Nepos at his villa near Salona on 9 May 480, reputedly on the connivance of the Bishop of Salona, the former emperor Glycerius.[60] The removal of the last western Roman emperor was itself not much of an issue for either Zeno or Odoacer. He had been a distraction for both since his flight from Ravenna, with neither willing nor able to do anything about him. However, Ovida seizing control of Dalmatia allowed Odoacer to invade the province under the pretence of avenging his imperial overlord. He brushed aside whatever resistance Ovida could provide by the end of 481.[61] The *rex Italiae* continued to mint coins of Zeno, but there was no move to have Dalmatia reintegrated as a province of the Roman Empire rather than part of the realm of Odoacer.

After 481, there is a lull in recorded interaction between *Augustus* and *rex Italiae* for seven years. Internal troubles will have kept Zeno distracted throughout that period. Correspondence with Constantinople over consular appointments and lip-service over certain aspects of policy must have continued, but for the most part, Odoacer was left to consolidate his new kingdom. However, when dealing with his various internal issues, Zeno likely noticed that the *rex Italiae* was frequently mentioned as a potential ally for his enemies. While Odoacer made no promises of aid to the likes of Marcianus, Illus or the Theoderici, at least in some circles he was taken to be an adversary of the emperor. While they may have been guests of the pope, all three rebel sons of Anthemius – Marcianus, Procopius Anthemius and Romulus – were present in the territory of Odoacer by the mid-480s.[62] That alone would have been cause for Zeno to view the *rex Italiae* with suspicion.

That suspicion may have grown in 486/487 when the King of Italy attacked the Rugian kingdom of Feletheus, which sat astride the Middle Danube and took in the

Roman province of Noricum. Odoacer's Italian field army crushed the Rugians in battle, capturing and executing Feletheus and his wife, Giso. Their son, Fredericus, escaped to rally his Rugian brethren, only for Onoulphus, who had joined his brother sometime after 479, to inflict a further defeat on the Rugians.[63] Such an action against a Germanic tribe on the Middle Danube seemingly had little to do with relations between Zeno and Odoacer; however, there was much more to this episode.

If Odoacer had aimed to incorporate Noricum into his realm, his armies did a terrible job of protecting the province. It was so badly gutted that Onoulphus felt it necessary to evacuate any remaining Romans to Italy.[64] These do not seem like the actions of an expansionist. It could be that Odoacer, Onoulphus, Feletheus or Fredericus lost control of their forces, or perhaps the Rugians undertook some sort of scorched-earth policy to deprive Odoacer of conquest. However, any such policy was not all that successful, as Paul the Deacon records the Lombards establishing themselves on the former lands of the Rugii within five years of Odoacer's attack because it was better farmland than their previous home.[65] It seems then that conquest was not Odoacer's aim in attacking the Rugii. Instead, it was a pre-emptive strike to thwart a planned attack on Italy by Feletheus. This does not appear out of the ordinary; just the latest chapter of the *Völkerwanderung*. However, Zeno had been in contact with Feletheus and may have intended to use the Rugians against Odoacer. The emperor not only harboured distrust towards the *rex Italiae*, he was now actively seeking to distract, undermine or even oust him.

There is some dispute over how Zeno acted on any underlying enmity. A section of John of Antioch has been taken to mean that the emperor either 'refused' or 'feigned' accepting Odoacer's gifts. The latter has become more widely accepted, meaning that Zeno retained good outward relations with Odoacer, including recognizing his choice of consul for 488.[66] One can imagine the extent of the feigned regal smile Zeno had to employ when a delegation from Odoacer arrived in Constantinople, bringing glad tidings and the emperor's share of the loot taken from the defeated Rugians. This embassy highlights that as of 487, despite the Rugian incident and Odoacer's independent actions, there was still some want to maintain the pretence of Odoacer being Zeno's viceroy.

While Odoacer was careful to add a veneer of imperial legitimacy to his actions and cut a respectful, subordinate tone, the hollowness of his swearing of fealty to Constantinople will have been apparent to all. The embassy may also have had an underlying warning – the kingdom of Odoacer was no pushover and was fully expecting that Zeno would one day turn on his viceroy. Indeed, Zeno may have been simply biding his time, looking around for an appropriate tool to deal with the *rex Italiae*. When he felt he had found that tool, Zeno could quickly peel away the veneer of legitimacy and reveal Odoacer for what he was – a barbarian conqueror masquerading as an imperial agent. When the Rugians failed, that veneer could be stuck back in place with a few carefully chosen actions, all the while Zeno scouted around for another tool to throw at Odoacer. He found it at Novae. After applying some financial incentives and careful negotiations in 487, Theoderic the Amal would be sent west to strike against the *rex Italiae*.

Two Barbarian Birds with One Stone: The Gothic Conquest of Italy

Once the decision had been reached that Theoderic would depart for Italy, the reality must have dawned that such an imperially backed migration was not going to happen overnight. Estimating the size of such a 'nation' is notoriously difficult, particularly because the sources rarely make it clear what their figures account for – fighting strength or overall size? Numbers surmised for the Amal Goths for *c*.487 provide such issues. While they had faced periods of decline, their general trend in the 480s had been upwards. The stability provided by Theoderic's position within the imperial establishment made them an attractive proposition to wandering bands and individuals. The deaths of Strabo and Recitach perhaps doubled Amal fighting strength from *c*.10,000 to *c*.20,000. However, Theoderic's Goths remained a tribal conglomeration, so he had women and children to provide for and protect. If it is accepted that Theoderic commanded *c*.20,000 fighting men in 487, with men of fighting age representing perhaps 20-25 per cent of the total population of such a 'nation', the Amal may have been leading anything up to 100,000 souls to Italy.[67] Not all of Theoderic's followers chose to follow him to Italy and the trek across the Balkans will have included attritional losses, but such a large column will have attracted new recruits.[68]

This was a lot of mouths to feed, even before accounting for horses and pack animals. Small wonder that it was almost a year from the agreement with Zeno before Theoderic the Amal set out for Italy. When he did head west, it was autumn 488, the best time of the year to do so as the harvest will have been gathered but it was still warm enough for grass growth.[69] Some depots might have been set up along the way for the Goths to use while still in imperial territory. However, there was still a long journey from the imperial frontier through hostile lands where foraging would be difficult, so Theoderic would have to bring significant resources with him, which along with the belongings of so many thousands will have made for a vast Gothic wagon train.

Sometime in 488, either at Novae before the Goths had departed or when they were en route, Fredericus the Rugian, having been defeated by Onoulphus, joined up with Theoderic. Such forces will have provided the Goths with an extra boost in manpower for their upcoming journey to Italy (not to mention extra mouths to feed), as well as some useful intelligence about the capabilities of Odoacer and his generals.[70] Extra strike power was certainly needed, for as they approached Sirmium, Theoderic's Goths were faced by a considerable force of Gepids. It is not certain why this turned into a fight for a city that Theoderic did not want; the cynic might see Zeno's hand in such mutual barbarian slaughter, although it is more likely that the Gepids did not take kindly to the presence of such a large column sucking up the resources of their land. With the Gepids deciding to be belligerent, Theoderic had no choice but to fight them and take Sirmium.[71]

There must have been other obstacles for Theoderic's column to overcome after their Gepid escapade – Hunnic and Sarmatian raiders, unwelcoming tribes and provincials – but by the end of 488, the Goths had reached Upper Slavonia, in modern eastern Croatia, where they would spend the winter. It was still another 300 miles to the Italian frontier, but then Odoacer's kingdom ranged beyond Italy. His defeat of Ovida in 481 meant that by wintering in Slavonia, Theoderic was right on Odoacer's doorstep. As the extent of Odoacer's Dalmatia is not clear, Theoderic may have already entered the lands of the *rex Italiae*. But even if he had not, the Gothic column and its plans for the campaigning season of 489 had come to the attention of Odoacer, giving him time to gather his forces and pick his battlefield. These preparations may be on display in the suggestion by Procopius that Theoderic planned to cross the Adriatic by boat but was unable to find sufficient vessels, forcing him to march overland.[72]

Therefore, when Theoderic broke winter camp in 489 and marched through the Julian Alps into northern Italy, Odoacer and his army were waiting for him at the Isontius River, the modern Soča in Slovenia and Isonzo in Italy. Very little is recorded about the subsequent Battle of the Isontius on 28 August 489, besides that Theoderic was victorious.[73] It could be that having his entire people *in situ* worked in Theoderic's favour as he could not only call upon his full military compliment, but his men will have known the disastrous consequences of failure. Superior numbers and fighting for survival perhaps won the day for the Goths at Isontius.

Odoacer led an orderly retreat back to Verona, suggesting that Isontius had not been a calamitous defeat. However, if the *rex Italiae* felt that he would have time to regroup, he was to be disappointed. With a 1,000-mile journey from Novae behind him and encouraged by victory at Isontius, Theoderic was in no mood to slow down and advanced out of the Julian Alps, hot on Odoacer's heels. On 30 September, battle was joined again outside Verona and Theoderic was once more victorious.[74] This second Gothic victory saw a more panicked retreat by the *rex Italiae*, who fled south-east to Ravenna, while the majority of his army retreated west to Milan, where they and their *magister militum*, Tufa, and a band of Rugians surrendered to Theoderic.[75]

Two such defeats and the significant loss of manpower would usually be enough to end the rule of a tribal leader, but Odoacer's regime was made of sterner stuff. Most importantly for the *rex Italiae*, he managed to retain the loyalty of the city of Ravenna and the Roman Senate. Through the virtually impregnable defences of Ravenna and the financial support of the Italian aristocracy, Odoacer seems to have undone much of the damage caused by his defeats of Isontius and Verona even before 489 was out. Odoacer's promises lured a band of Rugians away from

Theoderic, perhaps men under the command of Tufa, despite the destruction of their kingdom by Odoacer in 487. Theoderic aided in Odoacer's recovery by being too trusting of those who had surrendered to him. The Amal had retained Tufa as *magister* and deployed him to secure the city of Faventia, modern Faenza, as part of the attempted isolation of Odoacer in Ravenna in late 489. Free from the direct oversight of Theoderic, Tufa returned to his old allegiance and handed over Theoderic's officers and elite forces to Odoacer.[76]

The defection of Tufa allowed Odoacer to emerge from Ravenna before the winter of 489/490 was out and reoccupy Cremona, put pressure on Milan and effectively besiege Theoderic at Ticinum, modern Pavia. The chances are that Theoderic and his inner circle were caught wintering at Ticinum, rather than his entire army, which was perhaps dispersed to a wider area to reduce the negative impact on the locals. The citizenry also appears to have been faced with an incursion from the Burgundians, possibly under the leadership of Gundobad, who plundered Liguria and took many Romans captive. It was not only northern Italy which was facing barbarian invasion at this time. Taking advantage of Odoacer's distraction with Theoderic, the Vandals invaded Sicily. However, in 491, demonstrating that the *rex Italiae* had not been able to bring all of his forces to bear on Theoderic, the Vandals were defeated and forced to recognize Odoacer's control of the island.[77]

Theoderic's position had seemingly declined so much since Verona that it took the timely intervention of a Visigothic army sent by Alaric II to compel Odoacer to retreat from Ticinum. Why exactly the Visigoths suddenly decided to get involved is not known for certain. Were they looking to take advantage of the turmoil caused by the invasions of Theoderic and the Burgundians? If they did, they did not stay long. Were they showing some semblance of Gothic solidarity? This would be unlikely as it was not something that happened at all often. A more likely explanation is that Theoderic had sent diplomatic feelers to Toulouse asking his Gothic brethren to send aid. A fourth, slightly different option is that rather than appealing to Alaric directly, Theoderic found his way into the Visigothic court through his cousin, Videmir.

Whatever its reasons, this Visigothic intervention proved useful for Theoderic. With Odoacer's main force now in the field and encamped near the Adda River, Theoderic collected his army and quickly marched forth to offer battle. 'Possibly near Acerrae-Pizzighettone, where the road from Lodi to Cremona crossed the river',[78] Theoderic and Odoacer met once more on 11 August 490. It proved a repeat of Isontius and Verona: a decisive Gothic victory.[79] Similarly to those previous victories though, Adda did not end the war as Odoacer escaped with enough of his men to Ravenna. Unable to capture the city or even impose an effective blockade, Theoderic 'besieged' Odoacer and tried to secure numerous pockets of resistance for the remainder of Zeno's reign.[80]

While the *rex Italiae* had been neutralized, Tufa was still at large near Tridentium, modern Trento, where he received some 'unexpected reinforcements'.[81] After being freed from Ticinum by Alaric's Visigoths, Theoderic had left Fredericus and his Rugians in control of the city. They proved unpopular enough with the locals for Theoderic to intervene and reprimand Fredericus in August 491. The Rugian princeling did not take kindly to such a dressing down, defecting with his men to Tufa.[82] For much of the next two years, these two held sway over the area, with Theoderic unable to dislodge them. A breakthrough for the Amal only came when Tufa and Fredericus fell out, perhaps over who was the overall leader. The result was the *magister* and the Rugian 'king' fighting a battle somewhere between Tridentium and Verona in 493, which saw Tufa killed. Fredericus did not get to enjoy his victory for long. Theoderic pounced on this opportunity and subdued the Rugians once more, either killing or subjugating Fredericus.[83]

This kind of piecemeal subjugation around Tridentium represented much of what the war between Theoderic and Odoacer had descended into post-Adda. Theoderic's men had managed to repel the last serious attempted breakout by Odoacer on the night of 9/10 July 491, killing the *rex Italiae*'s leading general, Livila, and a large number of his Herulian troops. However, to press any kind of adequate blockade against Ravenna, the Amal needed full control of the hinterland of northern Italy. The opportunism of various barbarian groups and local warlords made this a time-consuming endeavour. Furthermore, the position of Ravenna meant that it would also be resupplied by sea and Theoderic did not have access to sufficient ships to block those sea lanes. This changed on 29 August 492 with the capture of Arminium, modern Rimini, on the Adriatic coast. This enabled Theoderic to gather enough of a fleet to begin the blockade of Ravenna in earnest.

Things were getting desperate for Odoacer. This may be seen in his declarations of full independence from Constantinople, elevating his son, Thela, to *Caesar*, possibly as early as 490, and minting his own coinage. He also began to form an imperial administration, complete with various Roman official titles.[84] However, the only trump card Odoacer had left were the immense defences of Ravenna. The blood that would be shed in taking the city, even from a malnourished garrison, caused Theoderic to agree to negotiation. The result was that Theoderic and Odoacer would rule jointly over Italy, and on 5 March 493, the gates of Ravenna were opened to Theoderic. But within ten days it was proven that Theoderic had only 'surrendered' his winning position to gain bloodless access to Ravenna and Odoacer.[85]

At a shared banquet in the Ad Laurentum palace of Honorius,[86] the Amal plotted to have Odoacer assassinated. Reputedly, his initial plan went awry, leading Theoderic to have two of his men seize the *rex Italiae* on the pretence of supplicating before him. The Amal then drew his own sword and cleaved Odoacer from collarbone to hip. Effectively cut in half, the *rex Italiae* proclaimed 'Where is God?', to which Theoderic retorted 'This is what you did to my friends', before standing over the body of his deceased rival and proclaiming that 'there clearly was not a bone in the wretched man's body'.[87]

The recording of Odoacer's grisly demise may demonstrate Theoderic's need to dress up what was a villainous betrayal with excuses. The 'friends' who Theoderic was supposedly avenging may have been Feletheus and Giso, although 'their son was at that very moment in open rebellion against Theoderic'.[88] It was also claimed that Theoderic killed Odoacer on the spur of the moment due to the latter plotting against him.[89] However, demonstrating that this was not a spur-of-the-moment attack, the family, friends and supporters of Odoacer were rounded up and massacred, seemingly on the same day. His wife, Sunigilda, was starved to death and Onoulphus was killed by archers in a church. Thela *Caesar* sought refuge in Gaul amongst the Visigoths, but was captured and killed by Theoderic when he tried to return to Italy.[90]

Not all of Odoacer's allies were treated so violently. Showing off his prudence,[91] the Amal was clement towards the Italian aristocracy and Roman Senate. He allowed himself to be dissuaded from carrying out planned property restrictions, confiscations and purges. Theoderic's clemency also extended to the Catholic Church. Despite being an Arian, cultivating a working relationship with the pope would shut down an avenue of opposition to Theoderic. He may have been so successful in winning the acceptance of the pope that it led Zacharias to suggest that Theoderic had converted to Catholicism.[92] The aristocracy and the Church combined with Theoderic's victorious army to form the basis of a smooth transition of power to the new Amal dynasty. After thirty years spent as a hostage, trekking across Eastern Europe, negotiating with the Roman state, with betrayal, promotions, demotions, rebellions, skirmishes, sieges and battles, Theoderic the Amal had a homeland for his people; it just so happened to bring him the position of King of Italy.

Despite having been sent to Italy by Zeno and assuming the position of *rex Italiae*, Theoderic's constitutional position was extremely vague. Once again there is an East/West conflict in the sources, with the latter in the form of Cassiodorus and Ennodius stressing that Theoderic ruled in his own right from the very beginning. Eastern sources held that the Amal was only Zeno's representative, intimating that by assuming the position of *rex Italiae*, Theoderic was breaking that agreement and essentially usurping power from his imperial overlord.[93] This again raises the question of Zeno's endgame with regards to Theoderic and Italy. Was he looking to replace one viceroy with another, with the added bonus of seeing Theoderic removed from eastern territory? Or was Zeno aiming at the far loftier goal of using Theoderic to reintegrate Roman territory? The latter would have required the emperor to spell out what he demanded of Theoderic should the Goth succeed in defeating Odoacer. Any such agreement may have seen Theoderic agree to uphold the imperial framework and not to alter it through laws of his own or appointing his own men to high office. The Catholic Church would also have remained paramount, a potentially significant step for an Arian like Theoderic. Essentially, in the event of his victory, the Amal was to hold Odoacer's territories in trust until Zeno came west to claim them for himself or sent his own candidate for the western throne.[94]

It is unlikely that the agreement between Zeno and Theoderic in 487 contained such detail, aside from the need to defeat the tyrant Odoacer and that Theoderic would 'exercise vice-imperial authority until Zeno could come to Italy in person'.[95] Zeno was not necessarily thinking too far ahead, happy just to rid himself of Theoderic. This then led to the Amal sending embassies to Constantinople in an attempt to clarify his position throughout the 490s. In the autumn of 490, Theoderic dispatched a delegation to Zeno to inform the emperor of his successes at Isontius and Verona and to ask for official recognition of his rule over Italy. The negotiations led nowhere and were then cut short by the final illness and death of Zeno in April 491, with the imperial court too caught up in the fallout to impose eastern rule on Gothic Italy. Theoderic could have seen the death of Zeno as nullifying their agreement on Italy, although he continued to seek imperial recognition. A second delegation arrived in the East in late summer 492, sent by Theoderic as he tightened his grip over Ravenna with the capture of Arminium. This embassy achieved very little as well, perhaps because Anastasius was distracted by the Isaurian War; it could also be that word reached the imperial court of Theoderic's murder of Odoacer in March 493 and his appellation as *rex Italiae* by his men.

It was not until a third delegation in 497 that headway was made. The appointing of western candidates to the consulship and a slight thawing in the Acacian Schism following the death of Pope Gelasius allowed an improvement in relations between Theoderic and Anastasius. The emperor returned many of the regal vestments and ornaments sent to Constantinople by Odoacer, effectively recognizing Theoderic's rule over Italy. That said, the Amal did not receive the imperial purple and did not take the title of *Augustus*.[96] Even if Theoderic had overstepped his constitutional bounds by claiming regal authority in Italy, the imperial court had come to recognize that for all the wrangling over what Zeno and Theoderic had agreed in 487, the reality in Italy by 497 was that Theoderic the Amal was ruling his own kingdom, in his own right, and would pass it on to his descendants upon his death in 526. The empire was as yet in no position to challenge that.[97] It would be fifty years after Theoderic's first embassy to Constantinople before the Roman Empire would look to overturn Gothic control of Italy. For Zeno, upon receipt of that embassy in 490, he will have been happy knowing that Theoderic and his Goths were not returning east.

Zeno and the Vandals

Zeno's interactions with the West were not limited to Odoacer, Theoderic and the pope. The Vandals remained an important issue for Zeno and the Christian Church. Not only would the emperor want to end any Vandal raids, but he felt some obligation to protect the Catholics of Vandal Africa who were under pressure from their Arian overlords. Sometime in the mid-470s, a delegation under a patrician called either Severus or Orestes was sent to Carthage to negotiate a peace treaty. This discrepancy in the ambassadorial identification has been used to suggest that

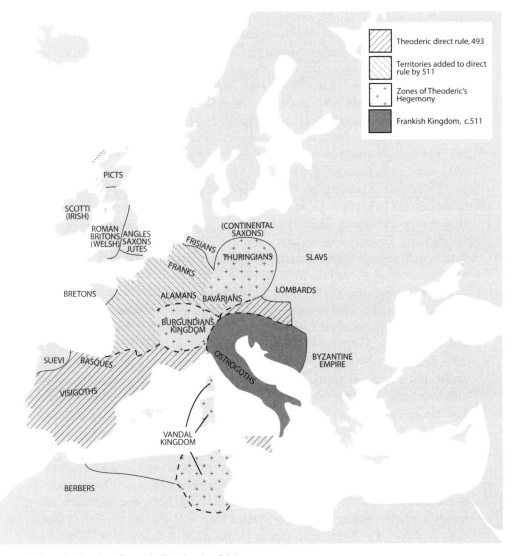

Theoderic the Great's Realm in 511

there were up to three treaties signed with Geiseric in 474–476; one negotiated by Severus for Constantinople, another by Orestes, identified as the western *magister militum* and father of Romulus, and a third by Odoacer in which the *rex Italiae* gained control of half of Sicily in return for an annual tribute.[98] The majority favour 474 as the date of the embassy of Severus or the treaty which resulted from it; however, the ταραχῆς of Malchus – 'disturbances' – affecting the empire at the time of Severus' delegation may refer to the usurpation of Basiliscus and the restoration of Zeno in 476.[99]

Regardless of the date and whether he sent the embassy or merely agreed to Severus' negotiations, Zeno will have been keen to agree some kind of peace with the Vandals in the aftermath of his restoration. The arresting of any Vandal raids and the championing of African Catholics could be presented as diplomatic victories, while the blocking of any alliance between Geiseric and the Theoderics will have brought some relief. For Geiseric and his successors, this treaty represented eastern Roman recognition of Vandal control of Africa and the islands of the western Mediterranean. The two parties also agreed not to act with hostility towards one another, while as a sign of goodwill, Geiseric released any Roman captives he still held and allowed the delegation of Severus to ransom other captives.[100]

The treaty with the Vandals in 474/476 also included implications for religion. Geiseric agreed to the return of exiled Catholic clergy and allowed them to worship openly, although the Catholic see of Carthage remained vacant.[101] Geiseric's successor Huneric was quick to send a delegation to Zeno to confirm the treaty. Perhaps sensing a weakening of the Vandal kingdom post-Geiseric, Zeno looked to bolster the position of African Catholics, including the appointment of a Catholic Bishop of Carthage, Eugenius, in 480/481.[102] Huneric demanded that in return for granting freedoms for Catholics, Zeno should give similar concessions to Arians, but given the strength of anti-Arian feeling within the empire, there was no chance of Zeno agreeing. When in 484 the Vandal king took aim at African Catholics, ordering the closure of all Catholic churches in Africa, the confiscation of all property and the banishing of all bishops, he cited the continued anti-Arianism of the Roman state.[103] Zeno was compelled to respond, but the subsequent delegation achieved little as Huneric recognized the weakened position of Zeno in the face of the revolt of Illus.[104]

Romano-Vandal relations reached an impasse with Huneric unwilling and Zeno unable to act. It took the death of Huneric on 23 December 484 and Zeno's defeat of Illus to break that deadlock. Unlike his father, Geiseric, Huneric was not popular with his people. His persecution of Catholics had seen the forcible removing of bishops from office, banishing of some to Corsica and the martyrdom of others. Such a persecution was not necessarily going to make Huneric unpopular amongst the Vandals, and neither would his persecution of Manichaeans.[105] However, Huneric did not stop there. He had many members of the Vandal dynasty murdered, and he lost territory around the Aures Mountains to Berbers. Kin-slaying and military defeat ensured the enmity of Vandals, on top of various sections of the peoples subject to him, so when Huneric died, he was neither mourned nor missed. His successor, his nephew, Gunthamund, was still dealing with that unpopularity as the revolt of Illus came to an end, allowing Zeno to pressurize Gunthamund into relaxing the anti-Catholic policies of his uncle.[106]

The interventions of Zeno in Vandal Africa saw the emperor receive a positive reception from African Catholics, with the poet Dracontius extolling his virtues of a ruler, leading to his imprisonment by Gunthamund.[107] However, this positive portrayal of Zeno should not overlook that the disastrous 468 expedition and internal distractions had seen Constantinople give official recognition to the conquest of Roman territory and treat the Vandal kingdom itself as a state rather than the tribe of Geiseric. With that, the 'perpetual' treaty between Zeno and Geiseric expected to last beyond the death of the signatories. This seems to have been the case, for 'relations remained relatively good between the eastern empire and the Vandal kingdom until the campaign of Belisarius nearly 60 years later'. [108]

Zeno's activity in the West was dominated by the weakness of his political and military position. The East retained the ability to involve itself militarily in Italy, for as much as eastern military strength had waned, that of the western empire had plummeted. Even with his manpower undermined by the Vandal disaster, Leo had launched an invasion of Italy through Julius Nepos. Had Zeno not been distracted by his reliance on various military figures, Roman and Gothic, he may well have attempted something similar without having to resort to a barbarian proxy in Theoderic the Amal. As it was, Zeno's western interactions are dominated by the fact that he was on the eastern Roman throne when the western Roman Empire was consigned to the dustbin of history and he seemingly compounded that extinction by facilitating the invasion and subjugation of Italy by the Goths.

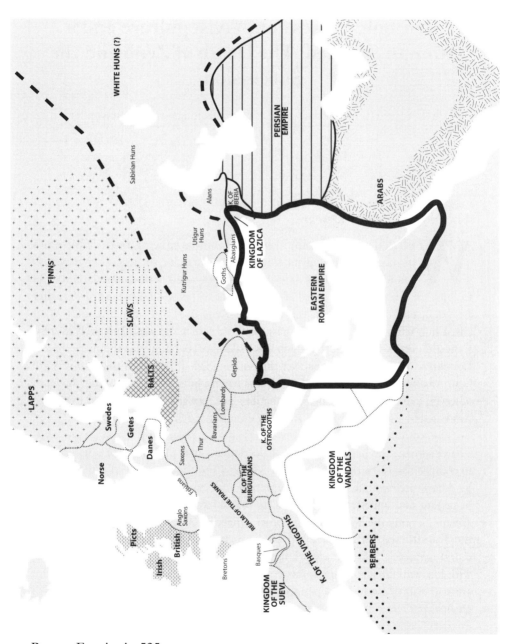

Roman Empire in 525

Chapter 14

Demonic Possession, Vivisepulture and a Woman Scorned: The Death of Zeno and the Succession

'Men regard its nature and cause as divine from ignorance and wonder.'

(Hippocrates), *On the Sacred Disease* 1

The Not So *Sacred Disease*

With all his internal political enemies removed either through defeat, death or migration and his religious policy a qualified success, Zeno may have felt by the end of the 480s that he had earned a period of peace and quiet to enjoy the fruits of his imperial labour. Fate had other ideas. On 9 April 491, after a reign of just over seventeen years, Flavius Zeno died in Constantinople.[1] What killed him is not clear. Age must have played a role as he was likely well into his sixties.[2] There is some hint that Zeno was making preparations for the succession of Longinus, suggesting that whatever illness Zeno faced, he feared that it might kill him. An attack of dysentery is recorded as having finished off the ailing *Augustus*; however, there have been other explanations put forward. It was claimed that Zeno was killed by a bout of epilepsy and may even have been buried alive.[3]

The combination of the likes of Zacharias portraying Zeno as an anti-Chalcedonian, the backlash from Chalcedonians over the emperor's willingness to compromise with the likes of Peter Mongus and the hijacking of the *Henotikon* by Anastasius contribute to the depiction of Zeno's death, his general health, behaviour and ancestry. This found its fullest expression in 1924 in a study on epilepsy among the Byzantine emperors, where Zeno was not only listed as one of those so afflicted but also as 'a depraved monster and an archetype of physical and moral ugliness'.[4] The same work lists Zeno's faults as being due to his genetics, with his brothers also being monstrous, ill-tempered individuals. Those genetics are also blamed for his epilepsy and his predisposition towards alcoholism, which encouraged such epileptic seizures.[5] That the eastern Romans were known for mixing absinthe into their wine, a drug 'known' for its potential to induce epileptic episodes, Zeno was therefore an alcoholic epileptic prone to outbursts of monstrous violence and suffering from the effects of a psychoactive hallucinogen. However, the idea that absinthe is a dangerously addictive psychoactive hallucinogen is exaggerated and the entire premise that Zeno suffered from epilepsy is based on sources out to discredit him, even if his epilepsy 'is often conceded in modern research'.[6]

The perception of epilepsy itself can shed light on the idea that Zeno was falsely accused of being a sufferer. As early as *c*.400 BC, it was opined by Hippocrates that epilepsy was a natural condition rather than 'a supernatural affliction brought on by demons or other spirit forces'.[7] Hippocrates' naturalistic approach was taken on by others, most notably Galen in the second/third century.[8] However, in the 250 years between Galen and Zeno, this naturalistic approach to epilepsy was overturned. The root of the rejection of a correct aetiology was the Gospel story of Jesus curing a boy of epilepsy by expelling the demon affecting him.[9] Given the potential dating of the Gospel's writing, it is likely that such an exorcism was reflecting popular belief at the time, both Christian and pagan, regarding the nature of the affliction. As Christianity grew in popularity, it brought the weight of God's Bible and Jesus' miracles down on the side of demonic possession rather than the naturalist approach of Hippocrates and Galen. Origen trashed the medical thinking of such doctors – for him, epilepsy was caused by 'an unclean spirit, dumb and deaf, in those suffering from it';[10] an opinion echoed by Tertullian, Athanasius and John Chrysostom.[11]

The determination of demonic influence over an epileptic required discussion over how such an afflicted should be treated by the Church, and it is here that the accusation of Zeno being epileptic starts to crumble. In believing that epilepsy was caused by actual demonic possession, the Christian Church could not differentiate between the sufferer and the demon possessing them.[12] This meant that the sufferer was condemned by their affliction and could not be in communion with the Church, as that would mean being in communion with a demon. Such thinking makes it highly unlikely that the various social, imperial, military and religious hierarchies within Constantinople would have allowed Zeno to come anywhere near the imperial title had he been epileptic. The position of *Augustus* was becoming increasingly tied up in religious ideas of being God's representative on Earth, and any physical or mental deformity would be potential grounds for disqualification from the position.

It should therefore have been impossible for someone who was epileptic to become emperor because someone possessed by a demon could not be a legitimate representative of God: 'This appears to be precisely the point of the references to Zeno's epilepsy … [he] was not and could not have been a legitimate emperor.'[13] But the polemic goes too far in its attempts to blacken Zeno's reputation. If he had epilepsy, anti-Zenoid and anti-Chalcedonian sources would have been up in arms. That Zeno managed to be *Augustus* for over seventeen years would seem to undermine this 'diagnosis' of epilepsy. But even if the accusation of epilepsy is false, tracing the origin of this smear could provide insight into the development of the reception of Zeno.

The earliest surviving source for the accusation of epilepsy is Evagrius, a sixth-century imperial bureaucrat, legal advisor and historian from Epiphaneia in northern Syria. It could be that Evagrius was reporting a rumour he had heard during his time in Constantinople; however, Evagrius owes a lot of his presentation of Zeno to another resident of Epiphaneia, Eustathius, well-regarded by contemporaries and successors as a 'most learned chronicler'.[14] Given that Evagrius used Eustathius for secular affairs, it is possible that he got the attribution of epilepsy as Zeno's cause of death from Eustathius as well. This would be a contemporary and skilled historian attesting this condition to the emperor.[15]

However, reference to Zeno's epilepsy is not made again in surviving material until the eighth/ninth-century *Chronographia* of Theophanes Confessor, where the emperor is accused of succumbing to epilepsy after a series of unwarranted executions and confiscations.[16] Theophanes does not seem to have known the work of Evagrius, but textual similarities suggest that they used the same source, which may be Eustathius. Theophanes does not need to have used Eustathius directly; perhaps an intermediary source such as the 'Greek Redactors' of Theophilius of Edessa's eighth-century Syriac chronicle.[17]

There is then another intermission in the recording of Zeno's epilepsy until the twelfth-century *Compendium Historiarum* of Cedrenus, and it is in this account where the effect of the vilification of Zeno can be best seen. The destruction of Zeno's character occurs throughout, culminating in a fitting demise. The emperor collapsed from a 'divine blow', and despite knowing of his history of epilepsy, Ariadne claimed that Zeno was dead. Eager to get rid of him due to her affair with Anastasius, she had Zeno's unconscious body taken to his tomb, with orders given not to reopen it for anyone. Despite his pleading once he regained consciousness, Zeno was left to starve to death. Zonaras records a similar demise, with Zeno buried alive by Ariadne after bringing on an epileptic seizure through overindulgence in food and drink, although he leaves room for Zeno being entombed alive by accident.[18]

Such an unfortunate death was part of the increasingly negative but largely inaccurate depiction of Zeno built up as the centuries progressed and his reputation became more and more erroneously associated with the anti-Chalcedonian version of the *Henotikon*. This demise was perhaps invented as a karmic balancing for Zeno's reported killing of Basiliscus and his family in the Cappadocian cistern. There may also be anti-female rhetoric being deployed with regard to Ariadne's role in Zeno's demise. Not only is she portrayed as an adulteress, but also potentially as a woman scorned, taking long-term, murderous revenge on her husband for his involvement in the deaths of a significant part of her family.

Anastasius may also be a target in this legend. The same ultra-Chalcedonians who were put out by Zeno's compromises with opponents of the council were outraged by Ariadne's choice of Anastasius as emperor in 491. Not only did he continue to use the *Henotikon*, which some ultra-Chalcedonians disliked, but he was using it for anti-Chalcedonian purposes. They were angry enough to riot in the capital, pulling down imperial statues.[19] It would not be surprising to find the same sources, such as the Chalcedonian Eustathius, intentionally attaching Anastasius to the legend of the epileptic Zeno's horrific demise. It enabled his story to serve a variety of purposes – it demonstrates how Zeno deserved his death due to being tainted by a demon from the very start; the divine punishment of having done to him what he had done to others; the well-established trope of the spiteful, adulterous woman becoming involved in imperial politics to the detriment of all; and it questions the legitimacy of Anastasius as an adulterer and imperial murderer.

However, the idea of Zeno meeting a horrific end is not necessarily a product of centuries of manipulation and invention. The sixth-century historian John Lydus, a financial critic of Zeno, says that the emperor met 'an ill-fated end'.[20] His failure to elucidate could suggest that while Lydus had heard rumours surrounding the fate of Zeno, he did not believe them. The same could be said for both Evagrius and Theophanes, for while they were willing to accept the dissolute portrayal of Zeno from Eustathius, his entombment is absent from both of their works. In terms of religion, they felt that Zeno should be praised for his attempts to bring unity to the Church, particularly when he did not try to force it at the point of a sword as others had done. Nicephorus Callistus may highlight that Eustathius propagated the story of Zeno's entombment as his recording of the legend comes 'in the midst of frequent citations of Eustathius'.[21]

In the end, while it can appear ubiquitous, every source to mention Zeno having epilepsy used Eustathius as a source either directly or indirectly, while the legend of his entombment 'may represent the gist of what Eustathius had to say on the matter'.[22] The Eustathian line is not the only record of how Zeno died. Much like how Evagrius, Theophanes and John Lydus rejected the live entombment tale, Malalas ignored Eustathius when it comes to the death of Zeno, despite having used him as a source. Malalas foregoes epilepsy and entombment altogether, stating that Zeno merely died of dysentery, a cause of death also listed by the *Chronicon Paschale*, Malchus and John of Nikiu.[23] There is also another collection of sources – Agathias, Agapius and the *Oracle of Baalbek* – which mention the emperor's passing but do not give any hint about how it came about or present it 'in any sort of negative context or judgemental overtones'.[24]

There is a definite split in the record of Zeno's death, and the immediate assumption is that this is the emperor being besmirched by Chalcedonians due to his connections to the *Henotikon*. That assumption is only partially correct. The polemic accusations of epilepsy and dissolute lifestyle against Zeno are the constructions of Chalcedonians, but not all Chalcedonians followed such an anti-Zenoid line. Malalas and the *Chronicon Paschale*, both Chalcedonian, are far from damning towards Zeno. The prominence of such negative views of Zeno may therefore be based in something more than solely Chalcedonian opposition. Geography may come into play, as there are two potentially identifiable anti-Zenoid groups within the more radical pro-Chalcedonian ranks – the monks of Constantinople and the patriarchate of Antioch. Both had been put out by Zeno's attempts to maintain union with Timothy Aeleurus and Peter Mongus and the *Henotikon*.[25] Zeno's reputation amongst later Chalcedonian sources may also have been coloured by his positive reception in many Monophysite sources. They take very little part in the polemic destruction of Zeno's character as a dissolute epileptic, and when they do address his death, they blame dysentery or do not mention any cause. Others who do not mention his death at all speak of the emperor in a positive manner.[26]

Epilepsy was just one of the many denigrating descriptions made of Zeno. The various historiographical accounts appear intent on throwing everything at the wall to see what stuck in attempts to portray Zeno as unfit. The list runs the full gamut of human shortcomings – repulsive physical appearance, a vicious and short temper, severe drunkenness, brutality, cruelty, cowardice, effeminacy and debauchery.[27] Ariadne is recorded commanding the Senate to select a successor to Zeno who was a Christian, Roman, regally virtuous, uninterested in money and detached from vice.[28] While such criteria is to be expected for an emperor, there is more than a hint here that Zeno is being described by his wife as a libidinous, gluttonous, brutish, barbarian heretic. While there must be some room to scale back hyperbole and perhaps suggest that these were not specifically Ariadne's thoughts, this does include the root of much of the invective aimed at Zeno. His perceived anti-Chalcedonianism is the root of the accusation of being a 'non-Christian'; his Isaurian heritage sees him painted as a barbarian, with all the incumbent uncivilized brutality and lack of virtue, which should have disqualified him from being emperor. Zeno had seemingly spent an awful lot of money on buying off the Theoderici and in his church building, although both Theoderics complained that they had rarely received their promised bribes. It would not be surprising for Zeno to have enjoyed his food and drink or be desperate to have another son in order to secure the succession. There could then be some truth to the accusations made against Zeno, particularly as 'wholesale invention was far less effective than distortion of a point already known to be associated with the other side'.[29]

However, even such a moderate approach in attempting to detect seeds of truth in invective aimed at Zeno may be going too far. The sheer fact that Eustathius required epilepsy and its religiously tainted, late antique explanation to damage Zeno's reputation might undermine everything else he said about the emperor: '[T]he effort to vilify [Zeno] on confessional grounds suggests that little – if any – of the character judgement against him can be taken at face value.'[30] Therefore, despite so much muddied water, it would seem likely that when Zeno's end came in 491, it came due to dysentery or old age. During his lifetime, he may have obtained a reputation for profligacy and excess, which opened the door for men such as Eustathius, who bore a doctrinal grudge against the emperor, to exaggerate such rumours into accusations of epilepsy, and then embellish that tale with the story of live entombment to ruin the reputations of Zeno, Ariadne and Anastasius.

The Position of Longinus and Ariadne's Choice

The death of Zeno on 9 April 491 did nothing to demote Isauria from the forefront of Roman imperial politics. While neither of Zeno's sons, Leo II and Zeno, had outlived their father and any other offspring of the deceased emperor was illegitimate, it was well expected that the imperial throne would stay in his family through Longinus. The deceased emperor had made some arrangements indicating that his brother was his preferred choice. Upon his release from incarceration at the hands of Illus, Longinus was appointed as *magister militum praesentalis* and to the consulship of 486, a position he would attain again in 490.[31] These military and political appointments could be Zeno not only positioning a loyal family member at a high rank, but also putting him in a position to inherit the throne.

Being *magister militum praesentalis* may have been more about having Longinus at the head of forces around the imperial capital to keep Zeno safe, but an opportunity to give Longinus experience of military command and connections across another section of the empire soon arose. The Tzani had been a problem for the Romans and their Caucasian allies since escaping the Lazicans in the 460s and seem to have been causing problems again in the mid-480s, likely through raiding. This would usually be a job for the *magister militum per Orientem*, but John the Scythian was preoccupied with the blockade of Papirion. Therefore, Zeno needed another loyal general to intervene in the Caucasus, and with Theoderic the Amal his other praesental *magister* and the Illyrian and Thracian *magistri* required to maintain watch over the Goths, Longinus became the only real option. Providing Longinus with some more military command experience was likely a serendipitous side effect of a military necessity. Perhaps in 486, Longinus travelled east to campaign against the Tzani. There is no record of his success or otherwise, although his camp had become a landmark for the natives – *Longini Fossatum* – by the time Sittas subdued the Tzani in 528.[32]

Longinus' consulships may also provide hints of a planned imperial future. It was somewhat customary for a newly enthroned *Caesar* or *Augustus* to hold the consulship the next available year after his elevation; however, in such situations, it was usual for the ruling *Augustus* to share the consulship with his new imperial partner. Zeno was not Longinus' colleague on either occasion. This could be more to do with maintaining good relations with the Roman Senate, perhaps recognizing one of their number as consul for the last twelve years of the reign, but it may also highlight that Longinus was not given any official recognition as Zeno's chosen heir.

When Zeno died in 491, Longinus was a prominent member of the Senate and had considerable support from that august body and the Isaurian faction which had been growing in Constantinople since Zeno's return to the capital in August 476. Longinus looked every bit a probable successor in April 491. But if he expected to be recognized as Zeno's successor,[33] Longinus was to be faced with trouble from the imperial couple, Ariadne and Zeno himself. Most importantly, if Zeno meant for Longinus to follow him as emperor, he did not make any overt recorded public declaration of that intention. Despite his prevalence and high office at court, in the Senate and at the head of the military, Longinus was not promoted to *Augustus* or *Caesar*. That does not preclude any intention for Longinus to succeed him, as there is the possibility that the emperor did make any such wish clear to the imperial court or in his will; however, the lack of public demonstration made such a desire easier to overlook, particularly if members of the court were disinclined towards having another Isaurian on the imperial throne.

However, to focus on Longinus as the natural successor to the imperial title just because he was Zeno's brother is to put too much stock in their consanguinity. Despite both Zeno and Leo II having held the imperial title, their shared bloodline – and therefore that of Longinus – was lacking in imperial pedigree. Zeno was an outlier, only inheriting the throne through his marriage and his fathering of Leo II. Longinus had no such direct link. Even if Zeno was considered to have become imperial through the ceremonies and rituals of his elevation, such status was not passed to the rest of his family, only his descendents. The weakness of Zeno's claim had already been exposed by the number of usurpers against his rule and the lack of strength in their claims: a humiliated imperial brother-in-law; the very idea of *porphyrogenitus*; and Verina's endorsement of a man with a name similar to Leo. That said, the lack of alternatives alone made Longinus a prominent candidate. The Leonid dynasty no longer contained any males; seemingly the only male of Theodosian descent was the future Vandal king, Hilderic, while Romulus, if he was still alive in Italy, was seen as a usurper in the East. Pickings were slim.[34]

Ultimately, with Zeno deceased and Longinus seemingly favoured although not openly selected, choosing who would sit on the imperial throne from this paltry selection fell to the only remaining representative of the imperial family: Zeno's widow, Ariadne. Her bloodline was not much more imperial than that of Zeno, even without questions of *porphyrogenitus*, as Ariadne's parents, Leo and Verina, had no prior imperial connections. But in times of scant authority, being the daughter of an emperor and mother of another was more than enough to see Ariadne provide legitimacy to Zeno. She may have been under pressure to provide similar marital legitimacy for Longinus, once he had set aside his wife, Valeria. However, without her father or her husband around to tell her what to do, Ariadne was now in control of who she did or did not marry. The aforementioned suggestion that she asked the Senate to choose Zeno's successor might hint at pressure coming from Constantinopolitan factions,[35] although this may have been a formality confirming her choice rather than delegating power to decide the next *Augustus*.

While Ariadne was seemingly free to make whatever choice she wished, it appeared that there was no other choice than Longinus, and given his connections and experience, he was hardly a poor choice. However, Longinus being at the centre of a powerful and successful faction at court and having the loyalty of significant Isaurian portions of the Roman army may have made him too strong an emperor for the Constantinopolitan political elite. In the century since Theodosius I departed west in May 394,[36] the Constantinopolitan court had become used to advising a weak *Augustus*. The proposed return of a well-backed, independent emperor, who was beholden to no other powerful individuals and may even have been militarily active, could have drastically reduced opportunities for influence. Any opposition to Longinus from elite Constantinopolitan circles and from the populace in general towards Isaurians may well have empowered Ariadne. Within two days of Zeno's death on 11 April 491, she snubbed Longinus and conferred the imperial title upon the *silentarius*, Anastasius.[37] Just under six weeks later, and forty days after the interment of Zeno, on 20 May, Ariadne confirmed her choice by marrying Anastasius.[38]

So why did Ariadne not choose Longinus? Had she, much like her mother, become so embedded in imperial politics that she looked to those around her for advice? Did she feel no loyalty to the family of her deceased husband? After all, the right to imperial power came through her blood, not his. She may in fact have come to hate Zeno.[39] Despite being her husband and father of her only child, Zeno had been responsible, directly or indirectly, for the deaths of a significant portion of her family. Or given that Longinus is accused of being an immoral influence on Zeno, as well as being stupid, arrogant and licentious,[40] perhaps Ariadne did not like Longinus personally; although these accusations of poor, even evil character ring like the denigration of Zeno by accusing him of all the worst personality traits.

Whatever her reasons for not picking Longinus as *Augustus*, they do not explain why she would choose Anastasius. The *silentarius* was well-known to Ariadne, fuelling rumours of a pre-existing affair,[41] but he hardly seems an inspired or even worthy choice. He was at least 60 by the time of his accession and did not come from a senatorial or military background.[42] However, his age and low rank probably worked in his favour, with Ariadne and her supporters looking for a pliable stopgap. How were they to know that Anastasius would reign for almost thirty years, outliving Ariadne herself?[43] His religious beliefs alone made him a peculiar choice. If there were any worries about Zeno's Christology, there would surely have been significant complaints over that of Anastasius, who had already presented himself as Eutychian. So worrying was this that the patriarch Euphemius only agreed to take part in Anastasius' crowning as *Augustus* after he signed a declaration of orthodoxy and promised not to refute the Council of Chalcedon.

The Isaurian War

The Isaurians refused to accept what they considered the depriving of Longinus' rightful place on the imperial throne. However, the speed with which his claim had been set aside may have seen Longinus fall into the hands of Anastasius even before what would become the Isaurian War had broken out in earnest. Longinus then found himself banished to Egypt, either the Thebaid or Alexandria, where he was ordained as a priest before he died seven or eight years later, possibly from starvation.[44] That Longinus was exiled to the Egyptian priesthood rather than executed could suggest that he held an imperial title, with Anastasius unwilling to spill the blood of an emperor. With the banishing of Longinus, the Zenoid family was reduced to three generations of women – Zeno and Longinus' mother, Lallis, and Longinus' wife and daughter, Valeria and Longina. All three were soon retired to the Brochthi convent in Bithynia.[45]

Anastasius and his allies then made something of an error. By extending the banishment to Isaurian residents in and around the imperial capital, the emperor forced Isaurian high-ranking politicians, generals, entire military units, bodyguards and their families to coalesce in their mountainous homeland. That error was compounded by an imperial failure to prevent a massacre of other Isaurians unwilling or unable to leave the capital. This will have increased the flow of Isaurians returning home and galvanized their resolve to fight the state. This banishment also provided the nascent rebellion with its leadership, which, just to confuse matters, contained several men of the same name – there were two called Athenodorus and, more problematically, two called Longinus, neither of whom were Zeno's brother. These two Longini, seemingly along with a Conon, Indes and Lilingis, became the focus of Isaurian leadership and are differentiated by geographical delimiters – Longinus of Selinus and Longinus of Cardala. That none of these named Isaurian leaders was elected as emperor to lead their fight for the crown perhaps highlights another reason why Anastasius did not execute Longinus: his continued survival made it awkward for the Isaurians to replace him as their candidate, particularly when they had no one else of similar legitimacy. Without their own candidate to rally behind, this Isaurian War became classed as a native revolt against the Roman state rather than the imperial civil war it really was.

The Isaurians quickly gathered stores, arms and money left in Isauria by Zeno, and used them and Anastasius' banishment to mobilize an army of up to 15,000 men. They then honed that army into a suitable fighting force through traditional raids on the major cities of surrounding provinces. These successes and the lack of imperial response must have emboldened the Isaurian leadership, for by 492 they had advanced out of their Isaurian strongholds and marched across Anatolia. It would appear that Constantinople was their objective, perhaps hoping to raise support along the way or from within the city. The Isaurians were within 150 miles of Constantinople before being intercepted by the imperial army of John the Scythian, John the Hunchback and Diogenianus in mid/late 492.[46] In keeping with the previous 600-year trend of results when the Isaurians faced imperial forces, the subsequent Battle of Cotyaeum saw a decisive victory for the army of the two Johns. This defeat claimed the life of Lilingis,[47] but Conon, Indes and both the Athenodori and Longini escaped east. As the cause of Longinus or the Isaurians in general had not encouraged support against the government of Anastasius from the populace or the Roman army, the rebels were left with only one option – retreat to their mountain fortresses.[48]

But if the Isaurians thought they would be free to rebuild and reconstitute their forces, they were to be mistaken. The imperial forces victorious at Cotyaeum did not let up, following their defeated adversary into the Isaurian highlands. This is understandable as the force at Cotyaeum was not just another raiding party; it had been an army looking to overthrow the imperial government. They could not be allowed to simply return home to fight or raid another day. They had to be dealt with decisively. The Isaurian army was in good enough shape to trap the forces of Diogenianus near Cilician Claudiopolis in 493; however, John the Hunchback provided relief and together these imperial forces inflicted a second heavy defeat on the Isaurians, killing Athendorus and Conon.[49]

Despite this final battlefield victory, it took six years before imperial forces finally subdued the revolt due to the impregnability of the Isaurian fortresses and their control of the coastal city of Selinus to provide supplies. Given their separation from the historic Cilician pirates, it might be somewhat strange to see Isaurians being able to rely on sea power in the late fifth century; however, it appears that their naval abilities had been growing in recent decades. In 353, they stopped sea traffic before graduating to attacking Cyprus in 404–408 and then Rhodes in 466.[50] A law of Anastasius from *c*.492 giving Cilician merchants a tax break could be compensation for Isaurian piracy.[51] Regardless of the origins of this Isaurian sea power, it was strong enough to stand up to whatever imperial navy was operating in the north-eastern Mediterranean and in combination with the holdfasts and routes to the sea, made for a difficult prospect for the imperial forces to finish the job in the 490s.

Unfortunately, such reliance on their fleet left the Isaurian rebels vulnerable to the weather, with a storm destroying their ships.[52] This loss of supply chain meant that it was only a matter of time before the tight imperial blockade of Isauria bore results, surely aided by John the Scythian's experience of blockading Illus in 484–488. Resistance finally crumbled in 497, with the Scythian defeating, capturing and beheading Longinus of Cardala and Athenodorus, sending their heads to Tarsus and then Constantinople.[53] The following year, John the Hunchback completed the subjugation of the Isaurian rebels by capturing Longinus of Selinus and Indes, sending them to Anastasius, who had them exhibited in the imperial capital and then tortured and executed at Nicaea.[54]

The end of the rebellion saw Isaurian cities and forts ravaged and considerable portions of their population deported to Thrace.[55] This process was long thought to have brought an end to the Isaurian threat not only to the imperial throne but also to the raiding of neighbouring provinces. Some *Novels* of Justinian and the increasing power of provincial governors could have been 'designed in part to curb brigandage',[56] suggesting that Isauria had not been pacified completely. However, these measures were not limited to the neighbouring provinces of Isauria – Hellespontus, Paphlagonia, Cappadocia and even Thrace were listed.[57] These laws also do not indicate that the brigands were Isaurians and the law specific to Isauria mentions nothing of brigandage, while the two Cilician governors were not provided with any extra military authority.[58] The *Novels* of Justinian also record the creation of a *dux/biocolytes* in the 540s to deal with brigandage in Asia Minor, but again neither Isauria nor Cilicia are mentioned.[59] That the likes of Lycaonia, Pisidia and Lydia are mentioned does not rule out Isaurian brigandage as they had long been targets of their raiding, but the absence of Isauria and Cilicia seems telling. These laws, far from dealing with a group of raiders like the Isaurians, may be dealing with a growing trend of localized intra-provincial raiders and private militias.[60]

That is not to say that the Isaurians suddenly lost their martial abilities post-497, only that the empire was more successful in harnessing them, with Isaurians serving prominently in Justinian's wars. They are also recorded taking part in major building projects in their homeland during the same period, including churches and the cultivation of vines and olives to provide commercial prosperity.[61] There has been some suggestion that Heraclius felt the need to garrison the Isaurian cities of Seleucia and Isaura,[62] hinting that the locals were restless. However, it may be the exact opposite: Heraclius was perhaps using Isaurian cities as his base of operations against the Persians, which hints at continuing Roman control over Isauria up to the Muslim conquests.[63] The repression by Anastasius' generals brought the Isaurian hinterland under tighter control than there had been seen since the third century. This was a far cry from the 'virtually autonomous power'[64] which fifth-century Isauria had been.

The eventual pacification of Isauria was not the only long-term consequence of Anastasius' elevation and the Isaurian War. In finding himself in direct military opposition to the Isaurians, Anastasius accentuated every stereotype there was about them. This might have been in action when the Hippodrome called specifically for a 'Roman' emperor to replace Zeno, either in the incident itself or in the retelling of it at a later date. This was already seen in the depiction of both Zeno and Longinus in a poor light, with Longinus of Cardala also described as being 'devoid of self-control'.[65] It would be easy to view this as merely the opinion of the Constantinopolitan and educated elites, but provincial sources record a similar dislike of Isaurians. The early sixth-century Syriac chronicle of Joshua the Stylite explains that Zeno and Illus were disliked because they were Isaurian.[66] Rather than indulging in a stereotype, writing in Amida in *c*.507, Joshua may have remembered or even experienced Isaurian banditry during his life and so was reflecting a local issue. But even with some room for Isaurian raiding colouring their reputation, imperial propaganda surely shifted drastically post-491, calling upon all of the negative perceptions of the Isaurians to aid Anastasius in his war against them, and while Longinus remained an imperial candidate, disparaging him and his family was of paramount importance. Therefore, on top of his hijacking of the *Henotikon* for anti-Chalcedonian ends, Anastasius saw to the tarnishing of Zeno's reputation politically, religiously and ethnically after his death.

Conclusions

The Paradoxes of Zeno *Augustus*

'How do we know what happened in the past? We cannot go back. Even historians who truly believe that in some future time historians would have assembled enough facts to understand with certainty how it was "then".'

Hoffer (2008), ix

'In this capricious world nothing is more capricious than posthumous fame. One of the most notable victims of posterity's lack of judgement is the Eleatic Zeno.'[1] This pronouncement by Bertrand Russell in his seminal 1903 work, *The Principles of Mathematics*, was referring to the fifth-century BCE philosopher, Zeno of Elea, famous for his paradoxes; however, it could also be ascribed to the man born Tarasis, son of Kodisa. His 'posthumous fame' and the lack of judgement on the Emperor Zeno stem from the various contrasting and ambiguous depictions of the sources. Rather fittingly given his Eleatic namesake, this means that the student of Zeno becomes very much caught in the 'historian's paradox' of having a wide range of different sources but being unable to trust any of them for various reasons.

So many different things, perceived or actual, have affected the record of his life, reign and actions that it is difficult to get a firm grasp on who Flavius Zeno really was. On the one hand, he was a weak leader lurching from crisis to crisis, unable to maintain the loyalty of his allies, his army and even his family; on the other, he was an emperor faced with an almost unprecedented number of threats and while unable to rely on anyone, still proved adroit in manipulating and buying the allegiance of whomever best aided him at any specific time with a mixture of cunning, ruthlessness and unscrupulousness. In religious circles, he is either a staunch Chalcedonian, keen to follow the stances of his predecessor, or a disguised anti-Chalcedonian, covertly undermining the findings of that council. He was either a well-connected man able to help plan the removal of the empire's most powerful general or a convenient ally for the emperor, merely swept along by happenstance and being in the right place at the right time. On top of that, Zeno was also an ugly, cruel, drunken, debauched, effeminate coward.

In attempting to form a clear picture of Zeno's military and political actions, it would be remiss to overlook just how much of his freedom of manoeuvre had been undermined by the damage done to the eastern army by the barbarian barrage on the Balkans and the disastrous Vandal expedition. This was even before the migration of the Pannonian Goths, the opposition of Strabo and the politicizing of the Isaurians under Illus had increased his problems and further reduced his effective military resources. Zeno therefore had to juggle two Gothic groups and an Isaurian competitor, not just because it was an age-old Roman policy to use barbarian forces against one another, but because he had no other choice due to the extent of the losses suffered at Mercurium and the damage done to his recruiting grounds. On paper, the emperor had over 40,000 men in the two praesental armies, but the poor state of the Illyrian and Thracian field forces likely saw many praesental units used to fill gaps in other field armies. Units transferred from the Constantinopolitan garrison to save other sections of the empire may never have been replaced. Even before Zeno's accession, the praesental armies were undermanned enough to see Thracian Goths make up part of Constantinople's garrison.

It is little wonder then that for large parts of his reign Zeno could be viewed as very much reactive rather than proactive. Military weakness did not allow him to plan grand campaigns, forcing him to rely on the reputation of the empire and its financial power to buy off its enemies. Such a depiction was further emphasized by the fifth/sixth-century tendency for the emperor to not lead the army and appear to stay hidden in his palace. While this reflects a growing tradition within the Roman world rather than on the emperor himself, it means that Zeno is frequently in danger of appearing as a supporting character in the story of his own reign. He had not had much opportunity to display any great leadership abilities in the field, although he had been an active commander of Roman armies and he is unlikely to have maintained a prominent position amongst the Isaurians had he not been capable of commanding loyalty amongst the highlanders. But as a stay-at-home emperor, he was overshadowed by the men active in the field – the Theoderici, Illus, Trocundes and Odoacer.

He was similarly overshadowed in ecclesiastical politics by the major players – Peter Mongus, Peter the Fuller, Timothy Aeleurus, popes and his own patriarch, Acacius. This is more understandable given that Zeno was still a layman in a world of bishops and monks. However, this did not stop his religious policies from playing a pivotal role in shaping the reception of Zeno through the ages, a role disproportionate to the actual part he played in formulating those policies. The chances are that neither of the polar-opposite depictions of a staunchly pro- or anti-Chalcedonian Zeno are true – he may even have been largely uninterested in Church doctrine or had no strongly held beliefs, only becoming involved in Church politics for the good of his reign, seeking unity in the face of revolt. This in turn sees him accused of being a religious puppet of whichever prominent churchman he was close to – Peter the Fuller in Antioch and Acacius in Constantinople. There may be some truth to this, with its seriousness for the empire mitigated or exacerbated depending on the doctrinal leanings of the Fuller, Acacius or Zeno himself.

Unlike some before him, Zeno did not resort to violence and partisan councils to get his doctrinal way. The *Henotikon* was a triumph of politically expedient compromise rather than coercion, and was relatively well-received for what could be viewed as an imperially backed 'new' orthodoxy. Unfortunately for Zeno, in creating the *Henotikon*, he and his bishops had sown the seeds of their own downfall. The looseness of language in that compromise document meant that it could be easily manipulated to fit any side of the doctrinal dispute it tried to accommodate. This was seized upon by Anastasius, who used the *Henotikon* to promote his anti-Chalcedonian stance, tarnishing the reputation of not just the *Henotikon*, but anyone associated with it. Hence the likes of Acacius and Zeno became tarred with a doctrinal brush that did not reflect their personal doctrinal stances.

From the outset of his reign, Zeno was similarly overshadowed in his political manoeuvrings: relying on Ariadne as his fountain of legitimacy, defending against the scheming Verina and Basiliscus, threatened by the forces of Theoderic the Amal and Armatus, and blackmailed by Illus and Trocundes. He showed impressive political nous and ruthlessness to emerge from the shadows of all those players by the end of his reign. His more sedate *Godfather*-like removal of so many members of his family and political opponents throughout his reign – Basiliscus, Marcus, Zenonis, Armatus, Leo Basiliscus, Marcianus, Recitach, Verina, Illus, Trocundes, Leontius – plays into his portrayal of a ruthlessly cunning individual, hidden away from the world in his palace. However, it must be noted that virtually all those on that hit list had openly rebelled against him. Zeno was hardly removing innocents from his path to uninhibited imperial power; these were past, present and future threats to his throne and his life. There was a justification of virtually all of his actions, without any real moral gymnastics coming into play.

This does not mean that Zeno was not an immoral man, perhaps only that his extrajudicial murders were on some level justified, which in turn could undermine the accusations of brutality and cruelty. Indeed, virtually all of the accusations surrounding his behaviour and private life can be undermined, appearing as transparent religiously based attempts to make Zeno appear as imperially unfit as possible through invention or exaggeration. He may well have been profligate, but that money was spent buying military support for the empire and building churches. Any personal excess may just be a reflection of life at the imperial court, although given his high-pressure existence, it would not be surprising to find that Zeno enjoyed his wine. His need for another heir and having illegitimate children may explain his 'debauchery'.

Attempts to portray Zeno as having been epileptic to discredit his reign as emperor contain the ironic paradoxical reaction of essentially proving that he did not have epilepsy because he had become emperor in the first place.

His treaty negotiations may have contained some hint of disingenuousness as he had little intention of fulfilling the terms; however, the ambitious Armatus was too dangerous to keep around and the Theoderici so frequently claimed that the

Romans had not fulfilled their treaty obligations that it was either a fact or a total fiction. Even if there is some truth in these examples, this does not prove that Zeno was disingenuous in his negotiations, only that circumstances had changed, he had trouble raising funds for a subsidy or that he had more important bills to pay. Perhaps his only action that presents Zeno in an unambiguously duplicitous light was his betrayal of Theoderic the Amal in 479; but while this might influence a negative modern reception, it is unlikely to have negatively impacted his contemporaneous reputation as he was merely playing out another episode in the Roman policy of not risking imperial forces when barbarians could be manipulated into fighting each other. To the Constantinopolitan court, it would not have been the act that was off-putting, rather its failure. Had the Theoderici knocked the stuffing out of each other near Adrianople, the emperor would have received numerous congratulatory pats on the back for reducing the empire's enemies. Similar congratulations will have come Zeno's way for his dispatching of the Amal Goths to Italy. Regardless of the outcome, it was a positive for the Roman Empire – Italy would be returned to the empire and/or barbarian enemies would be reduced in number. When it came to dealing with barbarians, any duplicity or double-dealing by Zeno would not have been seen as a negative within the empire.

While the idea of an Isauro-Gothic rivalry at the heart of Constantinople has been significantly downplayed, Zeno's origins must have played a part in his depiction. His enemies will have looked for any avenue to denigrate him, so his being an 'internal barbarian', regardless of the extent of his education and Romanization, was used against him. Not only is there some racism and elitism in the treatment of Zeno, there was some hypocrisy in play. Parts of the establishment who had been willing to find any reason to pour scorn on Zeno probably had little issue offering support to Aspar, Leo, Basiliscus or Illus. This may suggest that either Zeno was a specific personal case of mass dislike or that it was more the weakness of his position which was being preyed upon through the sneering at his 'barbarian' origins.

His Isaurian origins, fragile claim to the throne and lack of direct leadership of much of the imperial army may have put him in a weak position, but that does not mean that Zeno was a weak leader. Cutting through the source bias and misdirection, Zeno was a man faced with an incredibly difficult job of ruling and defending an empire which was under considerable political, military and religious strain. Despite the limitations of his origins and status, by the end of his reign, he was in complete control in the imperial capital, having done away with all his major political enemies; although there were some cracks, he had achieved some religious balance through the *Henotikon*; and through a Machiavellian marshalling of his meagre military resources, he had seen to the defeat, death or deporting of virtually all of his military problems. A weak leader would not have achieved such successes.

While his political, military and religious actions may have left him vulnerable to mischaracterization by indolent, unscrupulous and biased writers, he must have been a capable man, politically honed and militarily connected in the cutthroat worlds of Isauria and Constantinople to climb the imperial greasy pole. As emperor, he built on the successes of Leo I, cleared the empire of many of its opponents and put it back on a firm enough footing for Anastasius and the Justinianic dynasty to take more confident steps in securing and then expanding the imperial frontiers during the sixth century.

Ταρασικοδίσσα ʽΡουσουμβλαδεώτου was certainly much more than the man on the eastern throne when the West fell.

Zeno's Game of *Tabula*

The 'Fatal Throw' – Zeno's Game of Τάβλη

In 480, the emperor Zeno played a game of τάβλη in which he was so unlucky that he felt the need to write an epigram about it. Through this epigram or anecdotal memory, the story of his 'fatal throw'[1] survived down to the mid-sixth century when the historian Agathias, who was not born until nearly fifty years after Zeno's death in 491, reproduced the story in an epigram of his own.[2] It is through the survival of this Agathian witticism that Zeno's unfortunate throw and the nature of the game he was playing can be reconstructed.

Originally, the game being played in Agathias' anecdote was identified as *XII scripta*, although it has been demonstrated that while *XII scripta* required a board divided into three rows of twelve slots, Agathias' τάβλη required only two rows. This likely made τάβλη 'a direct descendent of *XII scripta*',[3] with both in turn being antecedents of other variations, including the modern game of backgammon. Τάβλι is still used to refer to backgammon in Greece. The likes of τάβλη and *XII scripta* were just the Roman-era developments in dice board games, which have a history dating back to the third millennium BCE with the Egyptian game Senet and the Royal Game of Ur, also known as 'The Game of Twenty Squares'.

Some of the most (in)famous events of the Roman world involved dice in some way, with Julius Caesar reputedly saying *'alea iacta est'* – 'the die is cast' – as he crossed the Rubicon in 49BCE,[4] while the dividing of Jesus of Nazareth's clothes between the soldiers by casting lots may have included the throwing of dice.[5] Even though dice gambling was illegal,[6] many of the early Roman emperors were considered to have a passion for such games, but it was Claudius who took it to the next level: 'So fervent was his devotion to dice that he published a book on the subject [now lost but referred to as *De arte aleae* – the Art of the Dice], and used to play, while out driving, on a special board fitted to his carriage which kept the dice from rolling off capriciously.'[7] Agathias' τάβλη is likely the same game that Isidore referred to as *tabula* and *alea*,[8] while the letters of Sidonius Apollinaris attest to the continued popularity of dice games like τάβλη amongst the Gallic aristocracy at the same time as Zeno's reign.[9]

The focus of Agathias' epigram is how Zeno, playing as White, rolled such numbers as to be left with no moves other than to undermine his own position by leaving eight of his pieces open for capture. As can be seen in the diagram, Zeno had a stack of seven pieces in slot 6, a stack of two pieces in slots 10, 19 and 20 and single exposed pieces in slots 9 and 23. His Black opponent had stacks of two pieces in slots 8, 11, 12, 14, 15, 18 and 21, with a single exposed piece in slot 13. Because the presence of two pieces in any one slot prevents movement to that slot by the opponent, Zeno's throwing of 2, 5 and 6 with the three dice proved disastrous. Due to Black's occupation of slots 8, 11, 12, 14 and 15, Zeno could not move any of his pieces from slots 6 or 9. Due to the rule that a player cannot move beyond the end of the board until all of his pieces are in his home table, which in Zeno's case of playing White would be slots 19-24, he could not move 5 or 6 from slots 19 or 20. His 6 could only be played by moving a single piece from slot 10 to 16; his 5 could only be used on slot 19 to 24 and his 2 on slot 20 to 22. In the process, Zeno was forced to leave eight of his pieces open to capture.

The preservation of this 'fatal throw'[10] anecdote could say something about the reception of Zeno after his death. While this story may be preserved purely because of the sheer extent of the emperor's bad luck, it may have been helped by the attempts to denigrate Zeno's name and supposed religious policies. Such poor fortune could be construed as divine displeasure, fuelled by Zeno's 'anti-Chalcedonianism'. Of course, looking for meaning in such anecdotes can work several ways. It could be said that placing Zeno in a position where he can only make his own position worse with the moves open to him also reflects the religious and political conundrums he faced during his reign – he was frequently in 'no-win' situations.

Endnotes

Introduction

1. Croke (2005a), 164; Elton, in Mitchell and Greatrex (2000), 295-98; Baldwin (1977), 91-107; Blockley (1981), I.80-85; Laniado (1991), 147-50; Shahid (1989), 100-06.
2. Jones (1964), 609; Roberto (2000), 726; cf. Feissel (1999), 11; Laniado (1991), 153-54.
3. Croke (2005a), 164.
4. Wood (2009), 134.
5. Wood (2009).
6. Laniado (1991), 170.
7. Cameron (1996); Greatrex (1994), 109-10; Grotowski (2006), 48-70.
8. Søby Christensen (2002).
9. Croke (2001).
10. Jefferys, Croke and Scott (1990); Beaucamp (2004); Treadgold (2007), 235-52; (2007b), 709-45.
11. Maskarinec in Maas (2015), 415.
12. Beaucamp, Bondoux, Lefort, Rouan-Auzepy and Sorlin (1984), 451-68; Whitby and Whitby (1989), IX-XXVIII; Treadgold (2007), 340-46.
13. Djakonov (1908), 166-360; Ashbrook Harvey (1990), 28-34; Ginkel (1995), 27-37; (2005), 35-50.
14. Assemani (1721), II.98; Nau (1896), 346-58; (1896b), 464-79; (1897), 41-68; Djakonov (1908), 202-76; Witakowski (1987), 30-36, 90-146; (1996), XIX-XXIII; Harrak (1999), 4-17; Palmer (1990), 272-84; Trombley and Watt (2000), XXI-XXXVII; Luther (1997), 1-31.
15. Kosinski (2010), 18.
16. Hansen (1971), IX-XXXIX; Lanaido (1991), 156-57; Nautin (1994), 213-43; Janiszewski (1997), 63-78; Whitby (2003), 467-72; Blaudeau (2006), 549-52, 622-48; Treadgold (2007), 168-73.
17. Allen (1980), 471-88; Lanaido (1991), 157-58; Whitby (2003), 459-66; Blaudeau (2006), 544-49; Greatrex (2009), 37-38; *PCBE* III.960-73.
18. cf. Greatrex (2009), 33-37.
19. Allen (1980), 471-88; Greatrex (2006), 40-43; (2009), 39-42; Kosinksi (2010), 16.
20. Allen (1980), 471-88; (1981); Whitby (2000), XX-LX; (2003), 480-92; Treadgold (2007), 303-07.

21. Kosinksi (2010), 17.
22. Athanassiadi (1999), 19-62; Kroll (1901), 2,039-40; Combes (1986), IX-XXVII; Szabat (1997), 194-96.
23. Dragnet (1968), 107-10; Chitty (1971), 60-65; Darling Young (1990), 312-14; Allen and Hayward (2004), 4-5; Watts (2005), 437-64; (2010), 265-68; Cameron (2007), 23-27.
24. Nau (1911), 7; Schwartz (1912); Steppa (2002), 57-80; Horn and Phoenix (2008), LVIII-LXXV.
25. Schwartz (1939), 408-15; Binns (1991), XXXVIII-LII; Baldwin and Talbot (1991), 573.
26. Kosinksi (2010), 21.
27. Delehaye (1913), 225; (1923), XXXV, LIV-LV; Baynes (1948), 6; Lanaido (1991), 166-68; Lane Fox, in Edwards and Swain (1997), 185-200; Kosinski (2006), 116-19.
28. Gunther (1894), 146-49, who dates the work to c.486; Schwartz (1934), 265-66, and Ziegler (1942), 425, to 488; and Nautin (1966-67), 139, to early 490.
29. Courtois (1954), 5-29; Moorhead (1992), IX-XX; Lancel (2002), 3-71.
30. Schwartz (1936), XVI-XVIII; Carcione (1989), 15-32; Whitby (2003), 472-77.
31. Croke (1983), 81.
32. Victor of Tunnuna sa.555.2; Placanica (1989), 327-36; (1997), XI-XXXI; Kosinski (2010), 19; Van Deun (1993), 15-21; Kollmann (2004), 58-59; (2007), 56-60.
33. Zotenburg (1883), 5-10; Charles (1916), IV-V; Carile (1981), 103-55.
34. Kosinksi (2010), 19; Mango and Scott (1997), LII-C.
35. Duffy and Parker (1979), XIII-XV.
36. http://www.stoa.org/sol/.
37. Graf (1947), 32-38; Breydy (1983); Pirone (1987), 5-14; Nasrallah (1987), 23-29; Conrad (1998), 211; Koscielniak (2004), 11.
38. Vasiliev (1904), 574-87; Graf (1947), 39-41; Nasrallah (1987), 50-51; Conrad (1998b), 63.
39. Kosinski (2010), 28 n.65; Crown (2001), 28-31; Stenhouse (1985), XXV-XXVIII; Anderson and Giles (2005), 143-46, 221-23; Di Segni (1998), 58; Sivan (2008), 108; Seligsohn (1903), VIII.
40. Chabot (1899), XXIII-XXXVII; Weltecke (2009), 112-16.
41. Agile (2005), 87-107; Takahashi (2005), 1-117; Weltecke (2009), 123-29; Teule (2003), 22-23.
42. Kedrenus-Hunger (1978), I.393-94; Zonaras-Ziegler (1972), col. 718-32; Banchich (2009), 1-10; Patzig (1896), 24-53; (1897), 322-56; DiMaio (1980), 158-85; (1981), 502-10; Nikephoros Kallistos-Beck (1959), 705-07; Gentz (1966), 154-58.
43. Jasper and Fuhrmann (2001), 61-65, 83-85.
44. Brooks (1903), V-XI; (1919), III-IX; Allen and Hayward (2004), 52-54; Van Rompay (2008), 10-11; Lebon (1909), 112-18; de Halleux (1963), 187-223.
45. Amelineau (1888), 216-20, XXXI-XLVI; Conybeare (1905), 719-40; Grumel (1932), 65; Elli (2003), 280 n.43; Revillout (1877), 103-19, and Hefele and Leclercq (1908), II.917-18; Schwartz (1934), 4-5.

46. Schwartz (1940), XI-XIII; (1934), 287-300; Grillmeier and Hainthaler (1995), 253.
47. Jones (1964), 217.
48. Robinson (1997); Honoré (1998); Harries (1999); Matthews (2000).
49. Howgego (1995).
50. Biers (1992).
51. Laniado (1991), 170.

Chapter 1: Under Pressure: The Roman Empire of the Fifth Century

1. Demandt (1984), 695.
2. Garnsey and Saller (1987), 8.
3. Lenski (2002), 127-37.
4. Alfoldi (1974); Mocsy (1974); Christie, in Christie and Loseby (1996).
5. Maenchen-Helfen (1973), 59-71; Zosimus V.22.1-3, 26.3; Sozomen VIII.25.1, IX.5.2-3; Orosius VII.37.12.
6. Maenchen-Helfen (1973), 65, 70-71; *CTh* V.6.2, 3; Orosius VII.37.3; Zosimus V.46.2, 5.
7. Olympiodorus fr.18; *CTh* VII.17.1; Thompson (1948), 30; Nikephoros Kall. XIV.1; f. *CTh* VII.8.13; XV.1.51.
8. Maenchen-Helfen (1973), 94; cf. Nestorius 366.
9. Maechen-Helfen (1973), 93, suggests that this treaty was signed with Ruga, not long before his death.
10. Maenchen-Helfen (1973), 116.
11. Priscus fr.5.
12. John of Antioch fr.199; Priscus fr.15-16; Marcellinus Comes sa.434; Jordanes, *Get.* 223-24; Theophanes, *Chron.* AM5943.
13. This battle between Aetius and Attila is known by numerous names – Catalaunian Plains, Catalaunian Fields, Châlons, Campus Mauriacus or Maurica. The battle site is also unclear.
14. Kim (2015).
15. Jordanes, *Get.* 254 on a haemorrhage; Marcellinus Comes sa.454 suggests the hand of Ildico, with a spousal murder picked up by Germanic/Norse sagas; Babcock (2005) suggests a political murder instigated by Marcian.
16. Heather (2013), 12.
17. Dagron (1974); Heather and Moncur (2001); Grig and Kelly (2012).
18. Heather (2013), 13.
19. The walls may have begun under Arcadius, in around 405/406; cf. *CTh* XV.1.51; *CIL* III.739, but credit should go to the praetorian prefect Anthemius, who oversaw their building – Socrates, *HE* VII.1.3; Bardill (2004), 122.
20. Heather (2013), 15.
21. Heather (2013), 17; Croke, in Maas (2005), 60-86; Mango (1985).
22. Jones (1964), 682-83, 1,417-50

23. Goodburn and Bartholomew (1976); Brennan, in Nicolet (1996), (1998); Kelly (1998); Kulikowski (2000).
24. Jones (1964), 1,449; Treadgold (1995), 63.
25. Treadgold (1995), 13.
26. *CTh* VII.20.4[325]; 22.8[372]; Procopius, *Anecdota* XXIV.13-14.
27. Southern and Dixon (1996), 37.
28. Procopius, *Anecdota* XXIV.21-26 records bodyguard units giving up their military pay instead of fighting.
29. Elton (1996), 151-52.
30. Procopius, *BV* III.11.3-4; IV.5.13; *BG* VII.5.13-14.
31. Whitby, in Cameron (1995), 89.
32. The works of Walter Scheidel tackle many of the problems faced with any study of late antique population.
33. Vegetius I.20; Procopius, *BV* IV.2.1-2; IV.3.4-6.
34. Heather (2009), ch.4.

Chapter 2: The Romanized 'Barbarians': Isauria and the Origins of Zeno

1. Houwink ten Cate (1965), 190-91; Mitford (1980), 1,255; Hild and Hellenkemper (1990), 98-99; Elton (2000a); Neumann (1980), 173-74, 178-80, suggests that Koine Greek had displaced Luwian, *contra Vita Sim. Sty.* 189; cf. Holl (1908), 242-43; Er (1991); Ramsay (1904), 289-92.
2. Kosinski (2010), 57; Magie (1950), 1,364-65 n.46; Jones (1971), 209-13; (1983), 195-96, 209-13, 441 n.38.; Burgess (1985), 142-50, 165-66; (1990), 121; Syme (1986), 159-64; Shaw (1990), 201-03; Lenski (1999), 415-16; Popko (1999), 95-111; Feld (2005), 37-43; Ramsay (1941), 229.
3. Lenski (1999), 431-32 n.92; Mitford (1980), 1,233; Syme (1987), 142-45.
4. Shaw (1984), 42-43; (1990), 261-70; (1993), 301-02, 312-14; (1986), 79-81; cf. Rostovzeff (1957), 258; Magie (1950), 720; Jones (1971), 214; Rouge (1966), 283-84; Stein (1959), I.64; Brooks (1893), 201.
5. Lenski (1999), 417; Shaw (1990), 261-70.
6. Wood (2009), 32; Shaw (1990), 244.
7. Isaac (2004), 363, 410.
8. Ammianus XIV.2.1; *CTh* IX.35.7; Shaw (1990), 233; Theodoret, *Ep.*40 praising a certain Neon for not following the avarice of his fellow Isaurians; cf. Lenski (1999), 448.
9. Wickham (2005), 445, 449, on such coexistence pre-existing any move away from transhumant pastoralism; Elton (2003) highlights how some Isaurian-Cilician archaeology is difficult to date due to being cut out of rock.
10. Wood (2009), 133; Lenski (1999), 417, 431-34; cf. Elton (2002a), 172-78, plays down the Roman impact.
11. MacMullen (1996), App. B; Shaw (1984), 303-07.
12. Ammianus XIV.2.5-17; XIX.13.1; Hild and Hellenkemper (1990), 143-50.

13. Lenski (1999), 418; Diodorus XVIII.22; Shaw (1990), 203-18.
14. Appian, *Mith.* 75.326; Rauh (1997).
15. Strabo XIV.5.3, 6; Cicero, *Fam.* 15.2.1; *Att.* 5.15.3, 6.1.13; cf. Syme (1987), 134-35; Appian, *BC* 75.319; Plutarch, *Ant.* 36.2.
16. Strabo XII.1.4, 6.3-5; XIV.5.6; cf. Mitchell (1993), I.72-73; Mitford (1980), 1,243.
17. Pliny, *NH* V.94; Tacitus, *Ann.* III.48, VI.41, XII.55; cf. Levick (1967), 203-14; Syme (1995), 257-69; Dio LV.28.3; cf. Velleius II.112; *AE* (1953), 251.
18. Lenski (1999), 420, 436.
19. Mitchell (1993), I.70-79; Mitford (1980); Syme (1987), 139-45.
20. Ramsay (1941), 228-32; Hopwood (1994), 376-80; Syme and Birley (1995), 217.
21. Lenski (1999), 439.
22. Lucian, *Icar.* 16.771.
23. *SHA Tyranni Triginta* 26.6; Minor (1979), 120; Shaw (1990), 238; Feld (2005), 160-63; Millar (2006), 50.
24. *SHA Prob.* 16.5-6, 16.4-17.1, 19.8; *Alex. Sev.* 58.1; *Tyr. Trig.* 26.1-7.
25. Syme (1968), 41-52; cf. Rouge (1966), 285-91.
26. Paribeni and Romanelli (1914), col.168 n.116; Bean and Mitford (1962), 207-08.
27. Zosimus I.69-70; Pashoud (1971), I.60 n.98; Mitchell (1995), 177-218; Christol (1978); Zimmerman (1996).
28. *Res Gestae Divi Saporis* II.27-31; Dodgeon and Lieu (1991), 57 nn.39-44; Kettenhofen (1982), 106-20; Wolfram (1988), 57.
29. *SHA Tyr. Trig.* 26.6; *Expositio Totius Mundi* 45; Ammianus XIV.8.2.
30. Ammianus XIV.2.14; *ND Or.* 29.7-8, 7.56.
31. Bean and Mirford (1970), n.50.
32. Lenski (1999), 422; Barnes (1996), 535-36.
33. Lenski (2002), 197; (1999b), 431-46
34. Lenski (2002), 199; (1999a); (1999b).
35. Himerius, *Or.* 25; cf. *CTh* XI.30.22; Robert (1969), 345-46; Brandt (1992), 170; Lenski (1999), 422.
36. Ammianus XIV.2.13.
37. Hopwood (1989), 191; Ramsay (1890), 366-73, 378; (1941), 232; Burgess (1985), 10-11, 20; Hild and Hellenkemper (1990), 22-29, 34-39; Mitford (1980), 1,232-234; (1990), 2,132-35; Kellener (1977), 320-22; Mutafian (1988), 14-20; Magie (1950), 260-80; Constantine Porph. *De them.* 13 on the Isaurian Decapolis.
38. Lenski (1999), 422.
39. Matthews (1989), 355-67; Santos Yanguas (1977).
40. Ammianus XIV.2.1-20; cf. Barnes (1989), 418-19, 421.
41. Ammianus XIX.13.1-2; *ILS* 740; Hellenkemper (1986), 634 n.32; Bean and Mitford (1970), n.231, with dating on p.206; Lenski (1999), 422.
42. Ammianus XXVII.9.6-7; Lenski (1999b); *CIG* 4430; Hellenkemper (1986), 628-31.

43. This episode has been doubted as it relies on Zosimus IV.20.1-2 (cf. Eunapius fr.43.4; Blockley [1983], 141 n.97); Paschoud (1971), II.2, 371-72; Santos Yanguas (1977), 366-67; Basil, *Ep.* 200, 215, 217 and milestones suggest that Valens rebuilt roads – French (1988), nn.637, 639, 648-51, 655, 660.
44. Lenski (1999), 443; *ND, Or.* 29.
45. Alfoldi-Rosenbaum (1972) = *Bull. Ep.* (1973), n.480; cf. Jones (1972); Merkelbach (1973); cf. *CTh* IX.27.3 = *CJ* IX.27.1; Malalas XIII.40; *Pan. Lat.* II(12).33.4; *ND Or.* V.66.
46. Zosimus V.14.5, 15.4-17.2, 20.1, 25; cf. Kelly (1995), 253-60; Palladius, *Dial.* XI.16; Eunapius fr.71; Sozomen VIII.25; Marcellinus Comes sa.405; *MAMA* III, n.73; John Chry. *Ep.* 108-09, 135; Jerome, *Ep.* 114.1; Philostorgius XI.8.
47. Marcellinus Comes sa.441; Priscus fr.10; Theodoret, *HR* 10.
48. Candidus fr.1; Malchus fr.22; John of Antioch fr.211.4.
49. Lenski (1999), 422-25; Shaw (1990), 244; Marcellinus Comes sa.405, 441.
50. Heather (2013), 34; Lenski (1999), 428.
51. Lenski (1999), 456.
52. Wood (2009), 133; Hill (1996), 208-34; Elton (2002b), 153.
53. Elton (2000a), 298; Wood (2009), 133, 134; Candidus fr.1.
54. Garnsey (1996), 165-66.
55. Wood (2009), 133.
56. Wood (2009), 134.
57. Stephanus of Byzantium, *Ethnika* 702.
58. *Vita Cononis* 12; *Acts of Paul and Thecla* 10-11.
59. Wood (2009), 136; cf. Amory (2003), 305-07, on Jordanes' rewriting of Gothic history.
60. Croke (2005a), 155; Elton (2000), 394.
61. Croke (2005a), 155; Elton (2000), 394; Feld (2005), 208-11; Heather (2013), 22.
62. *ACO* I.4.87; Cyril of Scythopolis, *Vita S.Sabae* I; Theophanes, *Chron.* AM5963; Elton (1996a), 133; Elton, in Mitchell and Greatrex (2000), 295.
63. John of Antioch fr.206.1, 210 and Agathias V.15.4 on Zeno having an Isaurian bodyguard; John of Antioch fr.199.1 and Priscus fr.144 on Flavius Zeno's Isaurian bodyguard; John of Antioch fr.211.4, 12 on Illus having such a bodyguard; John of Antioch fr.214.5 on Trocundes; Theophanes, *Chron.* AM5983 on Longinus.
64. Wood (2009), 131; *CJ* IX.12.10 [28 August 468]; Demandt (1970), 767; Scarcella (1997), 394-96
65. Wood (2009), 131; Lenski (1999), 448-51.
66. Wood (2009), 132; Burgess (1992); Elton (2000b).
67. Wood (2009), 133.
68. Jordanes, *Rom.* 333; Evagrius II.15; Priscus fr.14; John of Antioch fr.292; Thompson (1946), 18-31; Minor (1979), 124-25; Shaw (1990), 250-51; Feld (2005), 214-20.
69. Theodoret, *Ep.* 65, 71.
70. Priscus fr. 5, 8, 14; John of Antioch fr.199.1.

71. *CIL* V.6283; Priscus fr.8; Leo, *Ep.* 19-20; Rufius Praetextatus Postumianus was his western colleague.

72. Priscus fr.12, 13; *PLRE* II.295-97 'Chrysaphius'.

73. Lenski (1999), 426; John of Antioch, fr. 84, Priscus fr.5, 8, 12-13, 18.

74. Priscus fr.14; John of Antioch fr.199.1; cf. Thompson (1946), 23-27.

75. Dam. fr.303 = *Epit. Phot.* 290; Zeno the Patrician's growing position may be highlighted by the proposed position of his wife, Paulina, who may have been a relative of Paulinus, *magister officiorum* and friend of Theodosius II; Croke (2005a), 155 n.32; *PLRE* II.846-47 'Paulinus 8'; Feissel (1999), 9-11.

76. Jordanes, *Rom.* 333 has Flavius Zeno dying during the reign of Marcian.

77. Lenski (1999), 426.

78. Malalas XV.16, XIV.22, 27; Istrin (1914), 12; *Chron. Pasch.* sa.491; Kosinski (2010), 63 n.38.

79. *RIC* X.447; *P.Oxy* 2724.

80. Candidus = Photius, *Bibl.* 79; Agathias XIV.29.

81. Malalas XIV.46-47 – Κοδισσαῖος; *Chronicon Paschale* sa.474 – Ζήνων ὁ Κοδισσεὺς; Harrison (1981), 27-28.

82. *Exerpta de insidiis* 15; Evagrius II.15; John of Nikiu 88.80; Theophanes, *Chron.* AM5974; Istrin (1914), 10.

83. Kulakovsku (1913), 361; Henry (1959), 163.

84. Bury (1958), 318 n.1; Lippold (1972), col.151; Harrison (1981), 27; Burgess (1990), 117; Zgusta (1984), 518.

85. Burgess (1990), 109-21.

86. Malalas XIV.46-47; *Chronicon Paschale* sa.474; cf. Harrison (1981), 27-28.

87. Burgess (1990), 117-18; Zgusta (1964), 485-86; Barth (1894), 7-8, n.3; Harrison (1981), 27-28, support 'Tarasis', while Feissel (1984), 564 n.105, and Kosinski (2010), 60, support 'Tarasikodissa'; Buschhausen (1971), 190-207, on ΤΑΡΑΣΙΚΔΙΣΑ; Bean and Mitford (1970), 215-16, nn.124, 143, 240, showing the name Tarasis being a more frequent Isaurian name; cf. Gough (1955), 115-23.

88. Candidus = Photius, *Bibl.* 79; Kosinski (2010), 61 n.26.

89. Evagrius II.15.

90. Mitchell (2007), 114-15; Michael Psellus, *Historia Syntomos* 66, 68, called Leo I Zeno's natural father; Twardowska (2009), 76.

91. Croke (2005a), 169.

92. Evagrius III.3; John of Antioch fr.303, 308; Theophanes, *Chron.* AM5975; Zgusta (1964), 67.

93. Malalas XIV.12; Evagrius III.29; Marcellinus Comes sa.485; Theophanes, *Chron.* AM5975, 5983; John of Antioch fr.308; John of Nikiu 88.66-67; *Suda* Λ646; Leszka (2010), 651-66; *PLRE* II.689-90.

94. *Suda* Λ646; Zonaras XIV.2.3.

95. Candidus = Photius, *Bibl.* 79; *Parastaseis syntomoi chronikai* 32; Twardowski (2009), 76-77.

96. *Suda* A3947; *Patria KP* II.27 with Janin (1964), 312.
97. Malchus fr.9; *Suda* Z84, 885; Blockley (1983), II.350; Theophanes, *Chron.* AM5964; Wilfong (2002), 35.
98. Croke (2005a), 169; Lenski (1999b), 450-52.
99. Kosinski (2010), 61; Lippold (1972), col.150; Lainado (1991), 162-64; Konig (1997), 25-27.
100. *Excerpta Valesiana* IX.39; Brooks (1893), 212; Lippold (1972), col.152; Kulakovskij (1913), 370.
101. Thompson (1946), 18-31; Burgess (1992), 874-77; Elton (2000), 396.
102. Heather (2013), 34.
103. Haldon (1984), 130-36; *Suda* Λ267 accused Leo of employing too many officers to spy upon one another.
104. Kosinski (2010), 61, *contra* Croke (2005), 166-68.

Chapter 3: Enemies in the State: The Gothic 'Nations' of the Theoderici

1. Priscus fr.49; Procopius, *BG* VIII.49ff; *de Aed.* III.7.13; Malchus fr.18.
2. Heather (2013), 24.
3. Theophanes, *Chron.* AM5970 records Strabo as a nephew of a wife of Aspar, although Theophanes, *Chron.* AM5964, mentions Theoderic as her brother.
4. Theophanes, *Chron.* AM5931; Heather (1991), 251-63.
5. Theophanes, *Chron.* AM5931; cf. Procopius, *BV* III.2.39-40; Jordanes, *Get.* 270; Croke (1977); Marcellinus Comes sa.427 and Jordanes, *Get.* 32.166.
6. Heather (2013), 25, 24; Malchus fr.2 on their pay.
7. Heather (2009), 248.
8. Wolfram (1990), 260.
9. Malchus fr.11, 14, 15, 16; Jordanes, *Get.* 270; *Rom.* 346; Marcellinus Comes sa.481; John of Antioch fr.210.
10. Jordanes, *Get.* 270 cf. Evagrius III.25.
11. Malchus fr.11, 14, 15, 16; Jordanes, *Get.* 270; *Rom.* 346; Marcellinus Comes sa.481; John of Antioch fr.210.
12. Jordanes, *Rom.* 346; Theophanes, *Chron.* AM5970.
13. Jordanes, *Get.* 14.79-81; Cassiodorus, *Variae* 9.25.4-5; Heather (1991), 19-20; (2013), 10.
14. Heather (2013), 5; Momigliano (1955) vs Goffart (1988); cf. Heather (1991), ch.2; (1993).
15. Ammianus XXXI.3.1-2.
16. Heather (1991), 23-27.
17. Heather (1991), 27-28.
18. Priscus fr.11.2 does not mention anyone who appears to be an Amal serving Attila; Jordanes, *Get.* 48.246-52.
19. Heather (1991), 26.
20. Jordanes, *Get.* 259; Wolfram (1990), 258-59.

21. Maenchen-Helfen (1973), 144, and Burns (1984), 52, have the Pannonian Goths abstaining from the fighting, while Wolfram (1990), 258–59, considers that they fought for the Huns.
22. Jordanes, *Get.* 258-59; cf. Heather (1991), 246.
23. Jordanes, *Get.* 262.
24. Maenchen-Helfen (1973), 108-25.
25. Jordanes, *Get.* 270-71; cf. Priscus fr.37; Heather (1991), 247.
26. Jordanes, *Get.* 253, 268-69, 274-76, 283.
27. Heather (2013), 26.
28. Heather (2013), 26.
29. Heather (2013), 27.
30. Heather (2013), 28.
31. Heather (2008); (2009), 11, *contra* Gillet (2002); Halsall (2007), ch.2; Malchus fr.18.3, 20, with Heather (1991), 242ff; Blockley (1983), 430.5ff, 438.55ff, 446.199ff.
32. Jordanes, *Get.* 287; Priscus fr.37; Heather (1996), ch.3, vs Bierbrauer (1980) and Bona (1991) on the impact of the Huns on the presence of gold; Heather (2009), ch.5.
33. Jordanes, *Get.* 272-73, 274ff.
34. Jordanes, *Get.* 283.
35. Heather (1991), 250.
36. Jordanes, *Get.* 270-71; Priscus fr.28, 37; Sidonius, *Carm.* II.223-26.
37. Heather (2013), 5.
38. Heather (2013), 20; cf. Braund (1984).
39. Heather (2013), 21; cf. Cassiodorus, *Variae* I.1.

Chapter 4: Puppet on a String? The Reign of Leo I the Thracian

1. Theodore Lector, *Epit.* 367; Theophanes, *Chron.* AM 5949, gives 30 April.
2. Croke (2005a), 149.
3. His antecedents included his father, Procopius, who had risen to *magister militum per Orientem* by 422 (*CTh* VII.4.36[424]). His grandfather of the same name (*PLRE* II.93-95 'Anthemius 1') served the House of Theodosius with distinction, including as praetorian prefect of the East in 405-14, and who was himself the grandson of another eastern prefect, Philippus, who served Constantius II in 344-51 (*PLRE* I.696-97 'Flavius Philippus 7').
4. Sidonius, *Carm.* II.205-07; Marcellinus Comes sa.467; Jordanes, *Get.* 236; Demandt (1970), 771, 777.
5. Clover (1978), 174.
6. Sidonius, *Carm.* II.210-12.
7. Alan – Candidus = Photius, *Bibl.* 79; called a Goth by Jordanes, *Get.* 239 and Dam. 69 = Photius, *Bibl.* 242.
8. Claudian, *In Eutrop.* II.178, 432ff; Zosimus V.13, 17; Socrates VI.6.5; Liebeschuetz (1990a), 38, n.63.

9. Zosimus V.17.1, 18.1, 19.1; 21.9, 22.9; Socrates VI.6; Sozomen VIII.8.1

10. Whitby, in Cameron (1995), 103-10; Elton (1996a), 148 Table 4, 273 Table 7.

11. *CTh* III.13.14[370]; Eunapius fr.60; Zosimus IV.56-57; Demandt (1980), 609ff; Heather (1991), 262.

12. Marcellinus Comes sa.418; Socrates V.23; Sozomen VII.17.4, 18.20; Priscus fr.20; Evagrius II.1.

13. Croke (2005a), 153.

14. Candidus = Photius, *Bibl.* 79; Theophanes, *Chron.* AM5964, 5970; Heather (1991), 255 n.40; Demandt (1986), 114; Croke (2005a), 154 n.28, suggests the date of Ermanaric's birth being between 445 and 450 based on his consulship in 465; Croke (2005a), 153 n.25, suggests that neither daughter survived to marriageable age.

15. *PLRE* II.100 'Anthusa 1'; Demandt (1986), 113-17, links a chalice depicting Ardaburius and an Anthusa as husband and wife to Anthusa the cloud-seer in Damascius = Photius, *Bibl.* 242.69; Croke (2005a), 154 n.26.

16. Scharf (1993); *contra* Feissel (1999), 15.

17. Eustathius fr.7 = Malalas 398; Theophanes, *Chron.* AM5997; Procopius, *BP* I.8.1.

18. Socrates VII.23; Olympiodorus fr.43.

19. Cassiodorus, *Chron.* sa.425; Philostorgius, *HE* XII.4; Jordanes, *Rom.* 328; Priscus fr.14.85-90, 9.3; Aspar's consulship was commemorated in the famous silver dish now known as the Missorium of Aspar and in the Museo Nazionale del Bargello, Florence. It depicts Aspar and his family as senatorial aristocracy. Aspar himself is seated beside his son Ardaburius, flanked by the personifications of Rome and Constantinople. Above them are inserts of Romanized portraits of Ardabur and Plintha; Stewart (2014), 7 n.20; Painter, in Herring, Whitehouse and Wilkins (1991), 73-79; Zaccagnino, Bevan and Gabov (2012).

20. Procopius, *BV* I.4.7; Theophanes, *Chron.* AM5943; Malalas XIV.27; cf. *Chron. Pasch.*sa.450; Burgess (1994); Chew (2006), 207-27; Burgess (1994) rejects much of Pulcheria's role.

21. Siebigs (2010), 210.

22. Socrates VII.18, 20; Theophanes, *Chron.* AM 5918; Sidonius, *Carm.* II.89-93; cf. Cedrenus I.599, *CTh* VII.4.36, although there are some inconsistencies.

23. *Acta Syn. Hab. Rom.* 5.23-26; Arnold (2014), 159-60; cf. Moorhead (1992), 8.

24. Croke (2005a), 150 n.10.

25. Croke (2005a), 150.

26. Kaegi (1981), 26 and n.33, using Procopius, *BP* III.6.3.

27. Procopius, *BP* III.6.3; cf. Demandt (1970), 770; von Haehling, in Wissemann (1988), 97-103.

28. Croke (2005a), 150 n.12, points out that 'Bessan' does not necessarily mean an ethnic origin. Perhaps it was meant as geographical, the Bessi having been a Thracian tribe, but it is likely that Leo was from the Balkans.

29. Candidus fr.1; Constantine Porph., *de caer*. I.91; *ND Or*. VI.42; Theophanes, *Chron*. AM 5961; Zonaras XIII.25.35; Jones (1964), 221.
30. Blockley (1992), 71; Lee (2000), 46.
31. Candidus fr.1; Malalas XIV.35; Amory (1997), 277-313, on Balkan military culture.
32. Croke (2005a), 151.
33. Croke (2005a), 151.
34. Leo, *Ep*. 149.2, 150, 153.1; Marcellinus Comes sa.471 and Constantine Porph., *de caer*. I.91, also pick up on Aspar's prominence even amongst the patricians; Priscus fr.19 = *Suda* A3803; Malchus fr.3; Candidus, fr. 1 = Photius, *Bibl*. 79; Procopius, *BP* III.5.7; cf. III.6.3; Jordanes, *Rom*. 335.
35. Croke (2005a), 151.
36. Constantine Porph., *de caer*. I.91; *Paris Hebr*. 1,280.
37. Haarer (2006); Meier (2009); Kosinski (2010).
38. Siebigs (2010), 2; Stewart (2014), 4 n.7.
39. Treadgold (2007), 157; Siebigs (2010), 478-90.
40. Stewart (2014), 9.
41. *Partia KP* II.31; *PLRE* II.422-23 'Euphemia 3' voices concern about the veracity of this identification.
42. Salamon, in Mrozewicz and Ilski (1994), 187-88; Leszka, in Ceran (1998).
43. John of Antioch fr.209.1; Salamon, in Mrozewicz and Ilski (1994), 179-96; Krautschick (1986), (1995); Brandes (1993); MacGeorge (2002), 284-85, and Croke (2005a), 156 n.35, doubts this connection.
44. Croke (2005a), 158 n.41; cf. Kaster (1988), 272-73; Mathisen (1991b), 209; *PLRE* II.367-68 'Dioscorus 5'; Malalas XIV.46 lists Leontia as the elder daughter of Leo and Verina.
45. Brooks (1893), 210, using Zonaras XIV.1; Del Medico (1955), 61.
46. Croke (2005a), 157.
47. *PLRE* II.1,179-1,180 'Vivianus 2'.
48. Dagron (1982), 271-75; *V.Dan. Sty.* 38.
49. Severus of Antioch, *Ep*. 65.
50. *RIC* X.101; cf. Grierson and Mays (1992), 170-71.
51. Cumont (1921), VIII.4.224-25; cf. Pingree (1976), 147-48.
52. Holum (1982), 227-28.
53. Sidonius, *Carm*. II.224-26, 232-35.
54. Croke (2005a), 159.
55. Bury (1958), I.321-22; Marcellinus Comes sa.465; it was long held that this great fire of Constantinople took place in 465 (Snee [1998], 170), but it has been relocated to 464 (Whitby and Whitby [1989], 87 n.285, and Croke [1995], 99; [2005a], 160).
56. Janin (1964), 473-74.
57. Candidus fr.1 = Photius, *Bibl*. 79; Zonaras XIV.14-19.
58. Priscus fr.43 = *Suda* B163; Theophanes, *Chron*. AM5956; Michael the Syrian IX.1; Zonaras XIV.23; cf. Salamon, in Mrozewicz and Ilski (1994), 180 n.4; Demandt

(1970), 766f; Bersanetti (1943/1944), 335, and Ensslin (1925), 1,953, suggest that this took place in 463.

59. The identity of this Persian king is uncertain. Ardaburius was *magister militum per Orientem* from 453, which means that his tenure overlapped with Yazdegerd II (438-57), Hormizd III (457-59) and Peroz I (457-84).

60. *V. Dan. Sty.* 55.

61. *V. Dan. Sty.* 55; Croke (2005a), 160 n.48; *PLRE* II.136 'Ardaburius 3' and Lane Fox, in Edwards and Swain (1997), 190, give 466 but that is predicated on the fire of Constantinople being in 465 instead of 464; Schwartz (1934), 180 n.1, suggests that *V. Dan. Sty.* 52-54 speaking of a 'following year' could be meant as the next indiction, starting on 1 September 465, placing Ardaburius' dismissal in late 465 rather than early 465/466.

62. Croke (2005a), 160

63. *V. Dan. Sty.* 49.

64. Priscus fr.41.2 = *Exc. de leg. Rom.* 11.

65. Candidus = Photius, *Bibl.*79; cf. Ensslin (1925), 1,957.

66. Croke (2005a), 162.

67. Croke (2005a), 161 n.61, using Jones (1964), 221.

68. Bagnall, Cameron, Schwartz and Worp (1984), 466-67.

69. Lib. *Ep.* 899; *PLRE* II.1054 'Tatianus 1'.

70. Croke (2005a), 162.

71. *PLRE* II.367-68 'Dioscorus 5'; II.358 'Diapharentius'.

72. Cedrenus 607.17-18.

73. Zonaras XIV.1.

74. Pope Leo, *Ep.* 149, 151.

75. Zacharias, *HE* IV.7.

76. Croke (2005a), 163; Theodore Lector, *Epit.* 379; cf. Theophanes, *Chron.* AM5952; Evagrius *HE* II.9-11

77. Croke (2005a), 172.

78. Croke (2005a), 172.

79. Frank (1969), 65, 88-89; Palme (1998), 108ff.

80. Croke (2005a), 172; cf. Haldon (1984), 135; Kazhdan (1991), 1,600.

81. Croke (2005a), 161.

82. Brooks (1893), 211-12; Seeck (1896), 609; Bury (1923), I.317; Schwartz (1934), 180; Verdansky (1941), 60; Treadgold (1995), 13; (1997), 30; Cameron (1993), 30; Lee (2000), 46; Grierson and Mays (1992), 161.

83. Croke (2005a), 167.

84. *V. Dan. Sty.* 55.

85. Croke (2005a), 167.

86. Demandt (1989), 186; Kaegi (1981), 27; Cameron (1993), 30; Treadgold (1997), 152.

87. Lenski (1999), 426 n.60.

88. Candidus = Photius, *Bibl.* 79.
89. Procopius, *Anec.* 24.17.
90. Agathias V.15.4.
91. Procopius, *Anec.* 24.17.
92. Croke (2005a), 170; Theophanes, *Chron.* AM5969; *Anon. Val.* IX.40; Ps-Joshua the Stylite 12.
93. John of Antioch fr.206.1
94. Croke (2005a), 171.
95. John Lydus, *de mag.* I.12; Fiebiger (1909), 1,577; Grosse (1920), 270; Croke (2005b); (2005a), 170 n.75.
96. Jones (1964), 658; Mommsen (1889), 224-25; (1910), 233; Frank (1969), 204-07; Haldon (1984), 130-36.
97. John Lydus, *de mag.* I.16.3; cf. Whitby (1987), 484-88.
98. Croke (2005a), 172-73.
99. Croke (2005a), 172.
100. Croke (2005a), 172.
101. It is worth noting that dating the marriage to 466 as argued by Croke (2003), 560-63, is not universally accepted, with Kosinski (2008), 210-11, and (2010), 65, favouring 468; Theophanes, *Chron.* AM5951 has 458/459.
102. Malalas XIV.17; Michael the Syrian IX.5; cf. Croke (2003), 559-75.
103. *Cod. Par. Gr.* 1,447 fols. 257-58, in Wenger (1952), 54-55; Mango (1972), 35; Lane Fox, in Edwards and Swain (1997), 189-90, suggest that mosaic depicts Leo and Verina's dead son; cf. Croke (2005a), 173 n.83.
104. *Oratio de S. Deipara*, *PL* 115.565-66.
105. Croke (2005a), 174.
106. Croke (2005a), 175; cf. Miller (1970), 207-12.

Chapter 5: The Pressure Grows: Huns, Vandals and Assassins

1. Maenchen-Helfen (1973), 168 n.837.
2. *V. Dan. Sty.* 66, 65.
3. Croke (2005a), 166-68, 178-79.
4. Priscus fr.39.
5. Priscus fr.8.4; Maenchen-Helfen (1973), 159.
6. Sidonius, *Carm.* II.236-42, 269-80; Thompson and Heather (1996), 170.
7. Jordanes, *Get.* 276-77; *Rom.* 347.
8. Croke (2005a), 176, n.89, on the date.
9. Attila's eldest son, Ellac, was killed at Nedao; Priscus fr.38; Jordanes, *Get.* 262.
10. Priscus fr.30.
11. Sinor (1946-47), 35 suggests that Priscus' Avars are not the same Avars who founded a khaganate along the Danube in the mid-sixth century; Dobrovits (2003) on Avars, Pannonian Avars and pseudo-Avars.
12. Jordanes, *Get.* 272.

13. Croke (2005a), 176.
14. Maenchen-Helfen (1973), 166; Priscus fr.46 = *Exc. de leg.Gent*. 18.
15. Priscus fr.38, 36.
16. Croke (2005a), 177; Gordon (1960), 135; cf. Maenchen-Helfen (1973), 166.
17. Priscus fr.39; Blockley (1983), 397 n.175.
18. Jordanes, *Rom*. 338; cf. Demandt (1970), 767; (1986), 115.
19. Jordanes, *Rom*. 338; Verdansky (1941), 63-67; Croke (2005a), 177 n.93; Scharf (1993), 216-19.
20. Maenchen-Helfen (1973), 168, suggests that the Huns involved in attacks in 467 were those of Dengizich.
21. Candidus fr.1 = Photius, *Bibl*. 79; Demandt (1970), 765; Croke (2005a), 178, on the date.
22. Candidus = Photius, *Bibl*. 79; *PLRE* II.731 'Martinus 3'; Scharf (1993), 221-223.
23. Sidonius, *Carm*. II.212-15; *Fast. Vind. Prior*. sa.467; *Pasch. Camp*. sa.467; Hydatius, *Lem*. 234; Marcellinus Comes sa.467; *Chron. Pasch*. 597.16-18; Jordanes, *Get*. 236; *Rom*. 336; Procopius, *BV* I.6.5.
24. Jordanes, *Get*. 236 claims Severus only reigned three years, although this is incorrect – Severus ruled three years nine months. *Fast. Vind. Prior*. sa.465 records his death on 15 August 465 but *Novella Severi* 2 is dated 25 September 465, suggesting that either he died after that date or the law was issued in his name after his death. Cassiodorus, *Chron*. sa.465, alleges that he was poisoned by Ricimer but unless the continued presence of Severus on the western throne was seen by Leo as an obstacle to reconciliation with Ricimer, then the western *magister* really had no motive to remove an emperor who was firmly under his control (Jones [1964], 242; O'Flynn [1983], 111-14). The natural death reported by Sidonius, *Carm*. II.317-18, is more widely accepted.
25. Priscus fr.53.3, 15-20; Marcellinus Comes sa.467.1; Theophanes, *Chron*. AM5957; Sidonius, *Carm*.II.193, 224-26, 232-42, 269-80.
26. Priscus fr.64; Sidonius, *Ep*. I.5.10.
27. Procopius, *BV* III.6.5.
28. Croke (2005a), 179; Procopius, *BV* III.6.5, perhaps using Priscus as a source.
29. Merrills and Miles (2010), 120.
30. According to Malchus 366, Eudoxia wrote to Geiseric, encouraging his attack on Rome due to her forced marriage to Petronius Maximus.
31. Merrills and Miles (2010), 120.
32. Courtois (1955), 200; Merrills and Miles (2010), 120.
33. Priscus fr.41.2 = *Exc. de leg. Rom*. 11.
34. Priscus fr.40.
35. Procopius, *BV* I.5.23; Priscus fr.52.
36. Gauthier (1935), 217-71.
37. Priscus fr.42; Theophanes, *Chron*. AM5961; Cedrenus 613; Gordon (1960), 120, n.11.

38. Procopius, *BV* III.6.1; Heather (2006), 400.
39. Heather (2006), 400; Procopius, *BV* III.9.7-17.
40. Hughes (2009), 75-76; Heather (2006), 401, gives 'well over 50,000 men'.
41. Croke (2005a), 180; Courtois (1955), 202; cf. Gauthier (1935), 255.
42. Merrills and Miles (2010), 122.
43. Procopius, *BV* III.6.2; cf. Priscus fr.76; John Lydus III.43; Candidus fr.2 = *Suda* X.245; Treadgold (1995), 189-91, goes to great lengths to calculate the potential cost of the expedition.
44. *V. Dan. Sty.* 60-61; *PLRE* II.1122-23 'Titus 1'.
45. Cyril of Scythopolis, *Vita S.Sabae* I; their arrival in Constantinople is frequently placed in 469 but 'can be safely dated on internal evidence to 467/8' (Croke [2005a], 181 n.102; cf. John of Antioch fr.206.1).
46. Stewart (2014), 11.
47. Demandt (1970), 777-78.
48. Scott (1976), 65.
49. Croke (2005a), 181.
50. Damascius, *vita Isidori* = Photius, *Bibl.* 242, with Demandt (1986), 115.
51. Mango (1985), 113-14, suggests that this Heracleius of Edessa was an ancestor of the Heraclian dynasty.
52. Croke (2005a), 182.
53. Merrills and Miles (2010), 122 n.83, on this being implied by Theophanes, *Chron.* AM5961, although it could be Marcellinus' successes; Candidus fr.1 = Photius, *Bibl.* 79, has Basiliscus faced with 'successes and setbacks'.
54. Procopius, *BV* I.6.25; *Fast. Vind. Prior.* sa.468; *Pasch. Camp.* sa.468; Cassiodorus, *Chron.* sa.468; Marcellinus Comes sa.468; Damascius, *Epit. Phot.* 91 = Photius, *Bibl.* 242.
55. Damascius, *Vita Isidori* = Photius, *Bibl.* 242.
56. Procopius, *BV* I.6.10.
57. Procopius, *BV* I.6.20-21.
58. Procopius, *BV* I.6.22--24.
59. Croke (2005a), 182; Gauthier (1935), 255-57; Courtois (1955), 203.
60. Theophanes, *Chron.* AM5963
61. Procopius, *BV* I.22.16-18.
62. Merrills and Miles (2010), 123.
63. John of Antioch, fr.209.1--2.
64. Merrills (2004), 11-12, suggests that the Vandals retained respect for the imperial position as they did not replace high denomination Roman coinage out of a 'reluctance to usurp the imperial prerogative'.
65. Cedrenus 614.1-2 suggests that the war with the Vandals continued until 473-74.
66. Merrills and Miles (2010), 123.
67. Procopius, *BV* III.6.27 Nikephoros Kall. XV.27.

68. Priscus fr.53.1, 3; Theophanes, *Chron.* AM5961; Theodore Lector, *Epit.* 399; Malalas XIV.44; Nikephoros Kall. XV.27; Evagrius II.16; Jordanes, *Rom.* 337; John Lydus, *de mag.* III.43; Zonaras XIV.1.24-25.

69. Procopius, *BV* I.6.10, 11-12, 14, 22, seemingly using Priscus as a source.

70. Croke (2005a), 182.

71. Procopius, *BV* I.6.10.

72. Procopius, *BV* I.6.16.

73. Hydatius, *Chron.* 241 sa.468, with Thompson (1982), 223-26; cf Brooks (1893), 213 n.21.

74. Theophanes, *Chron.* AM5961; Zonaras XIV.1.24-25; Nikephoros Kall. XV.27; Croke (2005a), 183.

75. Procopius, *BV* III.6.3-4.

76. Procopius, *BV* I.6.4, 1-2.

77. Stewart (2014), 11.

78. Croke (2005a), 183

79. Procopius, *BV* I.6.2, 3.

80. Malchus fr.7 = *Suda* B163.

81. MacGeorge (2002), 58; Stewart (2014), 11; O'Flynn (1983), 117-18, 189.

82. John Lydus, *de mag.* III.43.4, highlights the political and financial impact of the expedition.

83. *Fasti*; *P. Oxy.* 2,724; *V. Dan. Sty.* 65; John of Antioch fr.206.2.

84. Marcellinus Comes sa.469; *Chron. Pasch.* 598.3-8.

85. Cf. Croke (1995), 54-55; (2001), 173-75; (2005a), 179 n.95.

86. John of Antioch fr.205; cf. *Suda* Y583; Zacharias, *HE* III.12.

87. Brooks (1893), 214, suggests that Anagastes revolted against the Isaurian faction, rebuffed by Croke (2005a), 184 n.115.

88. Bury (1923), 319, and Stein (1959), 360, place Anagastes' revolt in 470/71; Schwartz (1934), 183 n.3, in 471.

89. *V. Dan. Sty.* 65 and Theophanes, *Chron.* AM5962, mention no specific enemy; Brooks (1893), 215, on Pannonian Goths; Jordanes, *Get.* 278-80, on Theodemir fighting Suebi; Croke (1982), 64, on Dengizich; Heather (1991), 264-65, on Zeno being perhaps sent against Pannonian Goths in 473.

90. *V. Dan. Sty.* 65.

91. John of Antioch fr.206.2.

92. Gregory (1979), 10-11; Croke (2005a), 186.

93. Croke (2005a), 185.

94. John of Antioch fr.206.2; *V. Dan. Sty.* 65.

95. cf. Demandt (1970), 767.

96. Theophanes, *Chron.* AM5962, using Priscus (Mango and Scott [1997], 182 n.2); Brooks (1893), 213 n.17; Stein (1959), 360; Lippold (1972), col.154; Bury (1923), 318.

97. *V. Dan. Sty.* 65, with Seeck (1894), 2,022; Barth (1894), 6; Croke (2005a), 184 n.113; Kosinski (2010), 67 n.68.

98. John of Antioch fr.206.2; Downey (1961), 484
99. *V. Dan. Sty.* 65.
100. Theophanes, *Chron.* AM5962.
101. *V. Dan.Sty.* 65; Theophanes, *Chron.* AM5962.
102. Kosinski (2010), 68, on the birth of Leo II being the catalyst for Aspar's attempt on Zeno's life; *V. Dan. Sty.* 66 states that Zeno became *patricius* when Leo II was born; Bersanetti (1943-44), 346, suggests that Zeno's promotions came in the aftermath of the Vandal expedition.
103. Croke (2005a), 185.
104. Croke (2005a), 187.
105. *V. Dan. Sty.* 65; Constantine VII, *de caer.* 474, 493, on Pylai.
106. A Thracian Chersonese wall perhaps traced back to the 550s BCE (Herodotus VI.3).
107. Croke (1982), 61-63, 68-71; Whitby (1985); Crow, in Mango and Dagron (1995); Crow and Ricci (1997).
108. Whitby (1985), 563-67.
109. Croke (2005a), 188.
110. Croke (1982), 65.
111. Bury (1923), 319; Lippold (1972), 157; Demandt (1970), 767-68, suggests that Jordanes was still eastern *magister* in late 469, but this would seem to be introducing an unnecessary problem – Croke (2005a), 190 n.25.
112. Malalas XV.12.
113. Croke (2005a), 187.

Chapter 6: The Puppet Becomes the Butcher: The End of Aspar

1. Priscus fr.16; Hild and Hellekemper (1990), 374-75, and Gottwald (1936), 86-100, on the fortress of Papirius.
2. Shaw (1990), 252.
3. John of Antioch fr.206.2, 214.6.
4. Priscus fr.51; John of Antioch fr.206.2; Toumanoff (1963), 363-64.
5. Croke (2005a), 203.
6. Evagrius, *HE* II.16; cf. Theophanes, *Chron.* AM5963.
7. Croke (2005a), 191; cf. Zonaras XIV.3; Victor of Tunnuna sa.470; Arnold (2014), 159.
8. Lane Fox, in Edwards and Swain (1997), 191-92.
9. Croke (2005a), 190 n.127, Ensslin (1925), 1958, Stein (1959), 360, Demandt (1970), 772, and Lane Fox, in Edwards and Swain (1997), 192; Bury (1958), I.319, says Patricius became *Caesar* in 469/470.
10. Theophanes, *Chron.* AM5961, has it in 468/469; Stein (1959), 360, suggests 468, with the marriage of Patricius and Leontia to 470; Twardowska (2009), 98-99, puts their marriage in 469 and Patricius' elevation in 470.
11. Malalas XIV.41; *Chron. Pasch.* 597.10-12.

12. Theophanes, *Chron.* AM5952; *CJ* I.5.9; cf. Scott (1976), 68-69.

13. Croke (2005a), 193; *Vita Marcelli* 34; Theophanes, *Chron.* AM5961, 5963.

14. Seeck (1920), 489; cf. Ensslin (1925), 1,948.

15. *V. Marcelli* 32.

16. *V. Sim. Sty.* 125; cf. Lane Fox, in Edwards and Swain (1997), 193-95.

17. John Lydus, *de mag.* III.44.3.

18. Grierson and Mays (1992), 162-63.

19. Kent, Carson and Burnett (1994), 104, 109.

20. Cedrenus 613.18-21; Theophanes, *Chron.* AM5961.

21. Croke (2005a), 194.

22. Theodore Lector, *Epit.* 390-92; Cedrenus 611.20-612.10; Nikephoros Kall. XV.28; Frend (1972a), 166, 168.

23. *CJ* I.3.29; Scarella (1997), 276-82.

24. Courtois (1955), 204, followed by Croke (2005a), 194-95.

25. Courtois (1955), 204; Theophanes, *Chron.* AM5963, 5964, and Paul the Deacon, *HR* XV.2, connected Basiliscus' recall to the impending move against Aspar.

26. Procopius, *BV* III.6.27.

27. Paul the Deacon, *HR* XV.2.

28. Theophanes, *Chron.* AM5961.

29. Theophanes, *Chron.* AM5963.

30. Bersanetti (1943/1944), 344-45.

31. Croke (2005a), 192; *V. Marcelli* 34.

32. Kosinski (2010), 69 n.78, on the sources for the fall of Aspar.

33. Malalas XIV.45; cf. Bury (1886), 507-09; *V. Dan. Sty.* 55; Candidus fr.1 = Photius, *Bibl.* 79.

34. Procopius, *BV* III.6.27; Zonaras XIV.8; Malalas XIV.40; cf. Jefferys, Jefferys and Scott (1986); *Chron. Pasch.* 296.17; Damascius fr.115A on Zeno foiling a plot against Leo, with help from Ermanaric.

35. Zonaras XIV.29.

36. Jordanes, *Rom.* 338; *CJ* I.3.29; Croke (2005a), 195, suggests Basiliscus and Zeno may have been in contact.

37. *V. Dan. Sty.* 65; Baynes (1925a), 400-01.

38. Theophanes, *Chron.* AM5964; Lippold (1972), 157; cf. Seeck (1920), 370; Stein (1959), 360.

39. Theophanes, *Chron.* AM5963-5964.

40. *V. Dan. Sty.* 66; Theophanes, *Chron.* AM5964.

41. Malalas XIV.40; cf. Jones (1964), 505, on *conventus.*

42. Candidus fr. 1 = Photius, *Bibl.* 79, and Nikephoros Kall. XV.27; Croke (2005a), 197 n.147.

43. Marcellinus Comes sa.471; Jordanes, *Get.* 239; *Rom.* 338; Victor Tonn. sa.471; Evagrius, *HE* II.16; Malalas 71, fr.31; *Chron. Pasch.* sa.467; Theophanes, *Chron.* AM5963-5964.

44. Theophanes, *Chron*. AM5964; Barth (1894), 11; Verdansky (1941), 70, sticks with a more conservative 'relative of Zeno'; Damascius fr.303 = *Epit. Phot*. 290; John of Antioch fr.214.4.

45. Malalas XIV.40.

46. Malalas XIV.40; cf. Jeffreys, Jeffreys and Scott (1986), 205.

47. Malalas XIV.40; Croke (2005a), 198.

48. Scharf (2001), 51-61.

49. Malchus fr.9.4 = *Suda* A3968; Malchus fr.11.

50. Croke (2005a), 148 n.4, on Scott (1967) and Verndasky (1941).

51. Malalas XIV.40; cf. Jeffreys, Jeffreys and Scott (1986), 204-05.

52. Schwartz (1934), 184.

53. Croke (2003), 563-67.

54. *V. Dan. Sty.* 66; cf. Theophanes, *Chron*. AM5964.

55. Malchus fr.2 = *Exc. de leg. Gent.* 2.

56. Croke (2005a), 199; Kaegi (1981), 34–38.

57. Lee (2013), 98-101; Stewart (2014), 14; Priscus fr.30.

58. Stewart (2014), 13.

59. Malalas XIV.45.

60. Procopius, *BV* III.3-7; cf. Heather (2013), 49; Treadgold (1997), 149-55.

61. Evagrius II.16; Malchus fr.1.3; Baldwin (1971), 89-107.

62. Stewart (2014), 14.

63. Arnold (2014), 153; Stewart (2014), 16-20.

64. Stewart (2014), 14; Goffart (2006), 276 n.43, calls Aspar 'a courtly grand seigneur'.

65. Kaldellis (2007), 77; Börm (2013), 81, on the aristocratic threat to fifth- and sixth-century emperors.

66. Wood (2011), 310.

67. *Acta synodorum habitarum Romae* 5.

68. Procopius, *BV* III.63; Lee, in Kelly (2013), 108.

69. Arnold (2014), 159.

70. Wood (2009), 129-30; Heather (2005), 36-39, 117; Ando (2000), 23-25; Isaacs (2004).

71. Wood (2009), 130; cf. Maas (2003), 153.

72. Olympiodorus fr.33; Mathisen, in Cain and Lenski (2009), 324.

73. Stewart (2014), 16.

74. Croke (2005a), 148.

75. Brooks (1893), 212; Bury (1923), 316, 318; Vasiliev (1958), I.104; Ostrogorsky (1969), 63; Demandt (1970), 771; Treadgold (1997), 155-56.

76. Lenski (1999), 426 n.60.

77. Croke (2005a), 200, 172-73.

78. Jones (1964), 372; Guilland (1967), I.337; Palme (1998), 98-116; Croke (2005a), 172, 201; (2005b), 142-43.

79. *Patria Cons.* III.33; cf. Elton (2000), 400.

80. Croke (2005a), 201.

81. Burgess (1992), 117.
82. Croke (2005a), 200; Burgess (1990); Elton, in Mitchell and Greatrex (2000).
83. Croke (2005a), 201.
84. *Vita Dan. Sty.* 60; Stewart (2014), 17.
85. Croke (2005a), 199; Marcellinus Comes sa.471; Cedrenus 607.13
86. *Anonymus Banduri* (*PG* 122.1236C); *CJ* I.5.10.
87. Croke (2005a), 200.
88. Croke (2003), 560.
89. Croke (2005a), 147; Jones (1964), 224, provides dissent against 471 a turning point; Snee (1998), 157-86.
90. Croke (2005a), 149; Burgess (1992), 874-80; Elton (2000), 393-407.
91. Nikephoros Kall. XV.27; cf. Bury (1923), I.337.
92. Jordanes, *Get.* 276.
93. Heather (1991), 250; Jordanes, *Get.* 282.
94. Heather (2013), 22.
95. Jordanes, *Get.* 55.282ff; Heather (2013), 23.
96. Heather (2013), 23.
97. Jordanes, *Get.* 283.
98. Heather (2013), 30.
99. Heather (2013), 30.
100. Malchus fr.20; Heather (2009), 28ff., on migration habit.
101. Priscus fr.8.
102. Jordanes, *Get.* 56.
103. Heather (2013), 34.
104. Malchus fr.2.
105. Malchus fr.15.

Chapter 7: A Father Succeeding his Son: The Making of *Flavius Zeno Augustus*

1. Croke (2003), 560.
2. Malalas XIV.47; *Chron. ad 1234 pert.* 48.
3. Dawes and Baynes (1977), 81; Seeck (1919), 415.
4. Malalas XIV.22.
5. Croke (2003), 561.
6. Croke (2003), 561.
7. Lane Fox, in Edwards and Swain (1997), 191-92.
8. Ignoring Malalas XIV.47 and Victor Tonn. sa.470; Croke (2003), 562-63.
9. John of Antioch fr.206.2.
10. Croke (2003), 563.
11. Procopius, *BV* I.7.2.
12. Seeck (1919), 417-21; Brooks (1893), 20; Laszka (1999), 268; Stein (1959), 361, has Leo 6 years old in 473, born in *c*.467; Kulakoskij (1913), 397, states Leo II would have been 6 in 474, born in *c*.468.

13. Theodore Lector, *Epit.* 400.

14. Croke (2003), 564.

15. Candidus fr.1 = Photius, *Bibl.* 79; Lippold (1972), 157; Zonaras XIV.1.28; Marcellinus Comes sa.473.2.

16. Barth (1894), 19; Croke (2003), 563-64, suggests that this elevation took place in 472; Kosinski (2009a), 209-14; (2009b), 23-31, on the chronology of Leo II's reign.

17. Bury (1923), I.323; Ensslin (1961); Croke (2003), 566.

18. Croke (2003), 567.

19. Marcellinus Comes sa.472.1; Theodore Lector, *Epit.* 398; Cedrenus I.614.14-15; Hunger (1978), I.393; Jeffreys, in Jeffreys (1990), 264-65; Croke (2003), 566-67 n.42, on the issues with Victor of Tunnuna.

20. Croke (2003), 565; *Chron. Pasch.* 598.10-14; Theophanes, *Chron.* AM5966.

21. Croke (2003), 567.

22. Croke (2003), 567; *RIC* X.103.

23. Constantine Porph., *de caer.* I.94.

24. *CJ* I.23.6.

25. *CJ* XII.7.2; possibly *CJ* XII.40.11 with 'Illyriano' a corruption of 'Hilariano'.

26. Jordanes, *Get.* 286-87; Heather (1991), 264-65.

27. Croke (2003), 570; cf. Stein (1959), 361.

28. Croke (2003), 569.

29. Constantine Porph., *de caer.* I.94.

30. Malalas XIV.45-47; *Chron. Pasch.* sa.474; *PLRE* II.1202; cf. *Fasti*.

31. Malalas XIV.46; Cedrenus I.614-15; Michael the Syrian IX.4.

32. *Auct. Haun. ordo post.* 474, followed by Seeck (1919), 421, and Croke (2003), 571; Theophanes, *Chron.* AM5966; Grierson (1962), 44, on the *Necrologium*; Malalas XIV.46, followed by Bury (1923), 322; Cyril of Scythopolis, *Vita Euthymii* 43.

33. Grierson and Mays (1992), 176; cf. Victor Tonn. sa.475; *RIC* X.116; Hahn (1984).

34. The subject of such demographics is 'highly complex and encompasses a whole network of interconnected variables' (Scheidel, in Barchiesi and Scheidel [2010], 602), containing a vast amount of unknowns, including infant mortality rates, although they were high; Todman (2007).

35. Malalas XIV.47; *Chron. Pasch.* 599.8-13; *Chron. ad ann.1234 pert.* 48; Victor Tonn. sa.474.2.

36. Croke (2003), 571.

37. Kosinski (2010), 71.

38. *V. Dan.Sty.* 67; Procopius, *BV* I.7.3.

39. Malalas XIV.47; *Chron. Pasch.* sa.474; Croke (2003), 571; Kosinski (2010), 71.

40. Malalas XIV.47; Bagnall, Cameron and Worp (1987), 94; Seeck (1919), 421, 424; Kulakovskij (1913), 397; Bury (1958), I.359; Stein (1959), 362.

41. *Auct. Haun. Pros. Ordo post* sa.474.2; Theophanes, *Chron.* AM5966 records February; Schwartz (1934), 185 n.1; Kosinski (2010), 72; Croke (2003), 572.

42. *RIC* X.109.

43. *RIC* X.109; *CJ* I.14.1; II.7.16; X.15.1.
44. *CJ* X.15.1.
45. Malalas XIV.47; cf. *Chron. Pasch.* 599.13-16.
46. Theodore Lector, *Epit.* 400; Theophanes, *Chron.* AM5967.
47. Malalas XIV.47; *Vita Dan. Sty.* 67; Evagrius II.17; Theophanes, *Chron.* AM5966; Cedrenus I.615.7; Nikephoros Kall. XV.29.
48. Victor of Tunnuna sa.475.1.
49. Croke (1983), 83.
50. Candidus fr.1; Procopius, *BV* III.7.23; Malalas 382.7; Theophanes, *Chron.* AM5969.
51. Evagrius III.24; Theophanes, *Chron.* AM5969; Croke (1983), 86.
52. Ulrich-Bansa (1942).
53. Kent (1969).
54. Kent (1959), 96.
55. Candidus fr.1; Evagrius III.8; Malalas 380.16; Theophanes, *Chron.* AM5969; Zonaras XIV.2; Cedrenus I.617.3; Nikephoros Kall. XVI.8; cf. *Anon. Val.* IX.43; Victor Tonn. 476.
56. Croke (1983), 90, 89 n.28; Merchant (1851), 128; cf. Kent (1959), 95; Stein (1959), II.8-9.
57. Cedrenus I.614.23-615.2; Grierson (1962), 44 n.60; *Vita Dan. Sty.* 67.
58. Baynes (1925), 400 n.1, was suspicious but reticent to dismiss this comment; Festugiere (1961), 140 n.134.
59. Malalas XIV.47.
60. Croke (2003), 566.
61. John of Antioch fr.302; Seeck (1919), 424; Redies (1997), 213 n.23; Twardowska (2009), 109.
62. Salaman (1994), 184.

Chapter 8: A Brief Imperial Interlude: The Usurpation of Basiliscus

1. *V. Dan.Sty.* 68-69; John of Antioch fr.302; Evagrius III.24; *Synodicon Vetus* 99; Malchus fr.8.4 = *Suda* A3968; Leszka (2000), 335-43; Twardowska (2009), 39-41; Redies (1997), 214; Elton (2000), 393-407; Leszka (2005), 45-53; Theophanes, *Chron.* AM5969; Zonaras XIV.2.12-13 Lemerle (1963), 315-322; Theophanes, *Chron.* AM5970.
2. John of Antioch fr.210; Malchus fr.6.1.2.
3. John of Antioch fr.210; Salaman (1994), 191-92.
4. *Anon. Val.* IX.40; cf. *RIC* X.116; Theophanes, *Chron.* AM5967; Cedrenus I.615.
5. Jordanes, *Rom.* 341-42; Malalas XV.3; Leszka (2002), 87-93; Twardowska (2009); Theodore Lector, *Epit.* 337-38; John of Antioch fr.306; Prostko-Prostynski (2000), 259-65; Barton (2002), 60.
6. Lippold (1972), col.159-60; Leszka (1998), 132; Kosinski (2010), 80 n.16.
7. Theophanes, *Chron.* AM5967; Cedrenus I.615.

8. Malalas XV.3.
9. Brooks (1893), 217; Schwark (1950), 14; Stein (1959), 363; Bury (1958), I.390; Jarry (1968), 241; Kozlov (1985), 45; Prostko-Prostyski (2000), 259; Blaudeau (2003), 156; Feld (2005), 251.
10. Candidus fr.1.54-55; John of Antioch fr.210; Twardowska (2009), 124-26.
11. *Vita Danielis Stylitae* 55; *CJ* XII.19.9; XX.3, 4, 5.
12. John of Antioch fr.302; Schwark (1950), 14; Lippold (1972), col.161; Kozlov (1985), 46; Leszka (1998), 133; Twardowska (2009), 124, 126-27.
13. John of Antioch fr.210; *Vita Danielis Stylitae* 61.
14. Candidus fr.1 = Photius, *Bibl.* 79; John of Antioch fr.210; Jarry (1968), 241; Lippold (1972), col.160-61.
15. Theodore Lector, *Epit.* 397; Wenger (1952), 54-56; Twardowska (2009), 142-44.
16. *Alexander on Oracle of Baalbek* 150, 82; Jarry (1968), 554; Twardowska (2009), 137-40, doubted by Kosinski (2010), 82 n.26.
17. *Vita Danielis Stylitae* 68-69; Candidus fr.1.55-56; Malalas 378; *Chron. Pasch.* 600; Schwark (1950), 14; Kozlov (1985), 46; Leszka (1998), 133; Twardowska (2009), 126-27.
18. Malalas XV.2; *Chron. Pasch.* sa.477; Victor of Tunnuna sa.475.3.
19. Theophanes, *Chron.* AM5967, 5969; cf Ramsay (1890), 368; Hild and Hellenkemper (1990), 400; Elton (2004), 9; Feld (2005), 31-32; Leszka (2005), 49-50.
20. Foss (1990); Mitchell (1993); Hill (1996); Elton, in Ellis and Kidner (2004); Elton, in Elton and Reger (2007).
21. Heather (2013), 36.
22. Shaw (1990), 253, on Longinus becoming a hostage of Illus as part of Zeno's restoration in 476; Leszka (2010), 652-54, suggests Illus obtained Longinus as a prisoner during the revolt of Basiliscus.
23. Heather (2013), 37.
24. Malalas XV.3; *Chron. Pasch.* sa.478; Theophanes, *Chron.* AM5970; Bagnall, Cameron, Schwartz and Worp (1987), 486-87; Leszka (2000b), 337-38.
25. Theophanes, *Chron.* AM5970; Malchus fr.18.4.
26. Malchus fr.8 = *Suda* A3970; Malalas 378-79, 381; *Chron. Pasch.* sa.478, 484; *Fasti*; *Coll. Avell.* 60; Theophanes, *Chron.* AM5969; Zonaras XIV.2.25.
27. *Suda* A3970; Malalas 378.
28. Heather (1991), 274; Malchus fr.15.
29. *Vita Dan. Sty* 75; Heather (1991), 274 n.7.
30. Heather (1991), 255, 274; Dagron (1974), 108; John of Antioch fr.210, 211.3; Theophanes, *Chron.* AM5964.
31. Zacharias V.1, 4.
32. Kosinski (2010), 84; Ps-Zacharias V.1, 5.
33. Casson (1994), 52; (1995), 270-73, 289-90, on seasonal navigation; *CTh* 13.9.3 records the sailing season as being between 13 April and 15 October.
34. Redies (1997), 213 n.23, 215 n.46.

35. Ps-Zacharias V.1; *V. Dan.Sty.* 83; Theoctistus could also perhaps have already had a high office in Constantinople, which could then explain the appointment of Theopompus beyond coincidence.

36. Ps-Zacharias V.4; Theodore Lector, *Epit.* 402; Theophanes, *Chron.* AM5967; Blaudeau (1996), 114; (2003), 157; Frend (1972), 169-70; Redies (1997), 215 n.42; Leszka (2002), 89-90; Twardowska (2009), 145-52.

37. Dovere (1985), 169; Kozlov (1985), 6-47; (1988), 59; Kosinski (2010), 84.

38. Kozlov (1985), 47, has Acacius pleading for Timothy's recall.

39. Zacharias IV.1.4; Ps-Zacharias V.2, 5; Theodore Lector, *Epit.* 402-05; Theophanes, *Chron.* AM5967; Victor of Tunnuna sa.477.3; Liberatus XVII.122; Michael the Syrian IX.5; Malalas XV.1, 5, falsely states that it was Zeno who installed Peter at Antioch.

40. John of Nikiu 88.28 claims Timothy received a strong welcome at Constantinople *contra* Ps-Zacharias V.1.

41. Kosinski (2010), 86; Grillmeier (1987), 240, points out that Alexandrians recognizing the Council of Constantinople in the *Encyclical* is out of character as they usually ignored it; cf. Schwartz (1926), 83-85.

42. John Rufus, *Vita Petri Iberi* 106; Victor of Tunnuna sa.475 = Theodore Lector, *HE* fr.16; Dovere (1985), 153-88; Grillmeier (1987), 238-42; Brennecke (1997), 35-36; Blaudeau (2006), 161-62, 175-79.

43. Ps-Zacharias V.2; Evagrius III.4; *Vaticanus graecus* 1,431; Nikephoros Kall. XVI.3; Blaudeau (2003), 160; (2006), 173; Schwartz (1927), 49-51; Festugiere (1975), 482-84.

44. Schwartz (1927), 134; (1934), 184 n.4; Grillmeier (1987), 237 n.3; Redies (1997), 216; Blaudeau (2003), 162-64.

45. Kosinski (2010), 86; Dovere (1985), 174-76, 182-97; Grillmeier (1987), 241-42; Blaudeau (2003), 158.

46. Ps-Zacharias V.1-2; Evagrius III.4; Theodore Lector, *Epit.* 403; Michael the Syrian IX.5; Redies (1997), 213 n.23; Blaudeau (2003), 158 n.14; Szabat (2007), 256; *V. Dan. Sty.* 83 on the mob demanding Theoctistus' execution.

47. Ps-Zacharias V.1; Redies (1997), 215; Blaudeau (2006), 174-75.

48. Ps-Zacharias V.5; *V. Dan.Sty.* 70; Simplicius' letter to Acacius, 9 January 476, CA58, 132 shows knowledge of a proposed council in Jerusalem; Brennecke (1997), 36; Kosinski (2010), 89, suggests that this *Encyclical* became more anti-Chalcedonian in reaction to Acacius' opposition.

49. Ps-Zacharias V.1; Simplicius, *Ep.* CA58.131, 57.130; Blaudeau (2006), 175; Kosinski (2010), 88 n.60; Ebied and Williams (1970), 351-57.

50. Bralewski (1997), 44-45, suggests that Basiliscus called the Ephesian synod; Redies (1997) dates it to September/October; Blaudeau (2006), 180, on September; Kosinski (2010), 88 n.63, adds July/August.

51. Ps-Zacharias V.2; Evagrius III.5; Michael the Syrian IX.5; Nikephoros Kall. XVI.4; Haacke (1953), 114-16; Frend (1972), 170; Blaudeau (2006), 173; John of Nikiu 88.33; John Rufus, *Vita Petri Iberi* 106; Schwark (1950), 15-16; Perrone (1980), 125; Blaudeau (2003), 163; Gunther (1896), 127-34.

52. Ps-Zacharias V.4; *Synodicon Vetus* 99; Bar Hebraeus 69; Frend (1972), 173; Blaudeau (2003), 166.

53. Ps-Zacharias V.2; Theodore Lector, *Epit.* 410; John Rufus, *Plero.* 22; Theophanes, *Chron.* AM5967; Downey (1961), 488; Perrone (1980), 122-25; Steppa (2004), 91; (2002), 57-80; Hom (2006), 42.

54. Ps-Zacharias V.5; Evagrius III.7; Theodore Lector, *Epit.* 406; Theophanes, *Chron.* AM5968; cf. Hansen (1971), 113; Theodore Lector, *Epit.* 407; Theophanes, *Chron.* AM5967, on popular resistance; *V. Dan.Sty.* 70; Malchus fr.3; Nikephoros Kall. XVI.6; Haacke (1953), 114-15, and Blaudeau (2006), 181-82, on Acacius.

55. *V. Dan.Sty.* 70-71; Kosinski (2006), 147-54, on the conflict between Basiliscus and Daniel.

56. *V. Dan. Sty.* 71 on Basiliscus sending Danielus, a eunuch *cubicularius* to beg prayers from Daniel.

57. *V. Dan.Sty.* 72-73; Theodore Lector, *Epit.* 408; Theophanes, *Chron.* AM5968.

58. Themistius, *Or.* IV.59-61; Zosimus III.11.3; *CTh* XIV.9.2[372]; Malchus fr.11; Zonaras XIV.2.22-24; Nikephoros Kall. IV.3 on Theodosius II collecting Christian texts; Cedrenus I.618; Gamble (1995).

59. Kosinski (2010), 92; *V. Dan.Sty.* 74-84.

60. Evagrius III.7; Nikephoros Kall. XVI.7; *Vaticanus graecus* 1,431; Festugiere (175), 485; *V. Dan.Sty.* 84; Ps-Zacharias V.5; Schwartz (1927), 52, 135; (1934), 188; Dovere (1985), 180; Grillmeier (1987), 244; Brandes (1993), 419; Blaudeau (2003), 168-69; (2006), 185-87.

61. John of Nikiu 88.34.

62. John Rufus, *Plero.* 82-83; *Vita Petri Iberi* 108; Michael the Syrian IX.; Bar Hebraeus 69; Frend (1972), 173; Allen (1981), 126-27; Grillmeier (1987), 244; Redies (1997), 220; Blaudeau (2003), 168-69.

63. *V. Dan.Sty.* 85.

64. Blaudeau (2006), 185, *contra* Redies (1997), 218; Kosinski (2010), 95.

65. Theophanes, *Chron.* AM5969; Schwark (1950), 17; Jarry (1968), 250; Leszka (2005), 50-52.

66. *Suda* E2494.

67. Jordanes, *Get.* 56.288.

68. Wolfram (1988), 269-70; Ensslin (1959), 40; Heather (1991), 275.

69. *Anon. Val.* 9.42.

70. Malchus fr.18.2.

71. Heather (1991), 275; Burns (1984), 58-59.

72. Malchus fr.20; *Anon. Val.* IX.42.

73. Hoddinott (1975), 128; Poulter, in Poulter (1983), 101; Chichikova, in Poulter (1983), 11; Heather (1991), 277 n.13; Wolfram (1988), 270.

74. Wolfram (1988), 270, Schmidt (1933), 280-81, and Bury (1923), I.412, see the move as unofficial, with Heather (1991), 277; Burns (1984), 68-69, as a sign of an early alliance.

75. Malchus fr.18.2, 3, 20; Wolfram (1988), 270-71; Ensslin (1959), 44; Schmidt (1933), 279; Ensslin (1959), 44.
76. Heather (1991), 278.
77. Heather (1991), 278.
78. Theophanes, *Chron*. AM5969; Malalas XV.5; cf Stein (1959), 364; Lemerle (1963), 317.
79. Croke (1983), 84-85; Leszka (2000), 340-41; Kraus (1928), 58, 60-66, *contra* Kent (1959), 93-98.
80. Theophanes, *Chron*. AM5969; Malalas XV.5; *Chron. Pasch*. sa.478; Bar Hebraeus 69.
81. Theodore Lector, *Epit*. 413; Procopius III.7.22; Malalas XV.5 on the Great Church, followed by Stein (1959), 364; Blaudeau (2003), 170, and Twardowska (2009), 176; Croke (1983) 85 n.12, suggesting the Blachernae.
82. Procopius III.7.24-25.
83. Marcellinus Comes sa.476; Malalas XV.5; Procopius, *BV* III.7.24-25; *Chron. Pasch*. sa.477; Jordanes, *Rom*. 343; John of Nikiu 88.42; Ps-Dionysius 170; Michael the Syrian IX.5; Bar Hebraeus 69; Evagrius III.8, 24; Theophanes, *Chron*. AM5969; Victor of Tunnuna sa.477; Candidus 165; Procopius, *BV* I.7.24; Bury (1923), I.394; Heather (2013), 38; *Excerpta Valesiana* IX.43; cf Stein (1959), 364; Twardowska (2009), 176-82; Kosinski (2010), 96 n.106.
84. Brooks (1893), 218.

Chapter 9: Beholden to All: The Price of Zeno's Restoration

1. Heather (2013), 38; Malchus fr.8 = *Suda* A3968.
2. Procopius, *BV* I.7.21.
3. Malalas XV.7; *Chron. Pasch*. sa.484; Theophanes, *Chron*. AM5969; Michael the Syrian IX.6; John of Nikiu 88.45; Stein (1949), 8; Kent (1959), 93-98; Croke (1983), 81-91; Leszka (2000b), 341-42.
4. Malchus fr.9.4 = *Suda* A3968; John of Antioch fr.301; Bar Hebraeus 70; Malalas XV.7; John of Nikiu 88.46; Candidus 164; Procopius, *BV* I.7.23; *Chron. Pasch*. sa.484; Theophanes, *Chron*. AM5969; Michael the Syrian IX.6; Stein (1949), 8-9; Lippold (1972), col.165; Leszka (2006b), 342.
5. Barth (1894), 45-46; Stein (1949), 8-9; Leszka (2000b), 343; John of Antioch fr.303.
6. Candidus = Photius, *Bibl*. 79; Malalas XV.7; *Chron. Pasch*. sa.484; John of Nikiu 88.46; Theophanes, *Chron*. AM5969; Bar Hebraeus 70; Michael the Syrian IX.6; Zonaras XIV.2; Evagrius III.24; Croke (1983), 85.
7. Evagrius III.24.
8. John of Nikiu 88.65; cf Stein (1949), 8; Leszka (2000b), 342.
9. Brooks (1893), 218; Barth (1894), 77; Bury (1958), I.394; Lippold (1972), col.164.
10. John of Antioch fr.211.1, 303; Brooks (1893), 218; Stein (1949), 10; Leszka (1998), 133.

11. John of Antioch fr.303; Malchus fr.18.1; Candidus 165; Brooks (1893), 218; Barth (1894), 77-78; Stein (1949), 10; Bury (1958), I.394; Lippold (1972), col.171-72; Leszka (1998), 134.

12. Kosinski (2010), 101.

13. Malchus fr.18.4, 20 on the Amal offering to campaign with 6,000 of his best men, whilst leaving at least 2,000 to garrison Dyrrhachium (Heather [2013], 39, n.28).

14. Heather (2013), 39.

15. Malchus fr.20; Wolfram (1988), 270-71; *Excerpta Valesiana* IX.49; Theophanes, *Chron.* AM5931; Procopius, *BG* I.1.9; Jordanes, *Get.* 289; Prostko-Prostynski (1994), 113-15, has any adoption take place in 483.

16. Malchus fr.15, 18.1, 3; Stein (1949), 10-11; Heather (1991), 278-86; (1996), 159-61; Wolfram (2003), 310.

17. Malchus fr.18.2; *PLRE* II.1223 'Anonymus 21'.

18. Treadgold (1995), 48.

19. Malchus fr.20.

20. Malchus fr.18.2.

21. Heather (2013), 41.

22. Stein (1949), 12; Ensslin (1959), 45-46; Lippold (1972), col.170; Wolfram (2003), 313-14.

23. Malchus fr.18.4; Stein (1949), 12-13; Kaegi (1981), 37-39; Heather (1996), 161; Wolfram (2003), 313-14.

24. Pallas (1977); Wiseman (1984); Heather (2013), 43 n.32.

25. Heather (2013), 43.

26. Malchus fr.18.3-4, 20.

27. Malchus fr.20; Lippold (1972), col.173; Heather (1996), 161; Wolfram (2003), 314.

28. Malchus fr.18, 20; Marcellinus Comes sa.479; Ensslin (1959), 49-52; Heather (2013), 45.

29. Kosinski (2010), 101.

30. Ammianus XXVII.9.7; *Miracula S.Theclae* 19.2-6; Shaw (1990), 244-46; Allen (2006); Lee (1991), 366-74.

31. Malalas XV.12 *contra* Leszka (1998), 134; the location of Verina's imprisonment is disputed – John of Antioch fr.303 records Dalisandus; Evagrius III.27 and Theophanes, *Chron.* AM5972, suggest the fortress of Papirius, while Malalas XV.12 and John of Nikiu 88.67 just record it as an Isaurian fortress.

32. Malchus fr.11 on the senators being Anthimus, Marcellinus and Stephanus.

33. Zeno may also have been undermined by an earthquake in the late summer/early autumn of 479; Marcellinus Comes sa.480.1; Malalas XV.11; Theophanes, *Chron.* AM5970; *Chron. Pasch.* sa.487; Eutychias, *Ann.* XVI.4; Stein (1949), 12-13, 787, places the earthquake in August 479, Bury (1958), I.394, suggests 25 September 479, while Downey (1955), 597, says 25 September 477.

34. *V. Dan.Sty.* 68-69; Twardowska (2009), 188; Leszka (2007), 100.

35. John of Antioch fr.303; Bury (1958), I.395; Stein (1949), 15; Ensslin (1959), 52.

36. Theodore Lector, *Epit.* 419; Theophanes, *Chron.* AM5971; *porphyrogenitus* was mentioned during the sixth century – Ostrogorsky and Stein (1932), 199; cf. John of Ephesus, *HE* III.5.14, but may not be securely used until the mid-ninth century and not made common until the accession of Constantine VII *Porphyrogenitus* in the early tenth century; Anna Comnena, *Alexiad* 151; cf. Constantine VII, *De cer.* II.21.

37. Candidus 165-66; John of Antioch fr.303; Evagrius III.26; Theodore Lector, *Epit.* 419-20; Theophanes, *Chron.* AM5971; Malchus fr.22, 23 = *Suda* Π137; Brooks (1893), 219-20; Barth (1894), 70-73; Stein (1949), 15-16; Bury (1958), I.395; Jarry (1968), 254-58; Lippold (1972), col.175; Kozlov (1988), 63-64; Feld (2005), 260-62; Leszka (2007), 99-103.

38. Candidus 166; John of Antioch fr.303; Malchus fr.22; Ensslin (1959), 53.

39. Lenski, (2002), 75 n.41.

40. John of Antioch fr.303; Evagrius III.26 has Marcianus ordained a presbyter in Tarsus; Theodore Lector, *Epit.* 420, and Theophanes, *Chron.* AM5971, have him consecrated in the capital and then confined to Fort Papirius.

41. Malalas XIV.46; John of Antioch fr.211.4.

42. John of Antioch fr.303; Theodore Lector, *Epit.* 420; Theophanes, *Chron.* AM5971; another version of events has Procopius and Romulus being captured by Illus, only for them to escape and make their way to Rome.

43. John of Antioch fr.303; Malchus fr.22; Barth (1894), 73-74; Stein (1949), 16-17; Ensslin (1959), 53; Heather (1991), 294; Wolfram (2003), 316-17; Feld (2005), 262.

44. Heather (2013), 45-46.

45. Marcellinus Comes sa.481.1; Evagrius III.25; Theophanes, *Chron.* AM5970; John of Antioch fr.303.

46. John of Antioch fr.211.5; Marcellinus Comes sa.481.1; Evagrius III.25; Jordanes, *Rom.* 346; Stein (1949), 17; Ensslin (1959), 53; Lippold (1972), col.178; Heather (1996), 162-63; Wolfram (2003), 317.

47. John of Antioch fr.211.5.

48. It is usually accepted that Zeno had him killed for some part he played in a conspiracy, but Marcellinus Comes sa.481 mentions no such imperial role in the demise of Sabinianus or even that it was unnatural; John of Antioch fr.305; Croke (2001), 62-69; Wolfram (2003), 316-17.

49. Marcellinus Comes sa.482; John of Antioch fr.213; Michael the Syrian IX.6.

50. Heather (2013), 47.

51. Heather (2013), 47.

52. John of Antioch fr.214.3.

53. Heather (1991), 302; cf. John of Antioch fr. 214. 2.

54. Heather (2013), 47.

55. Jordanes, *Get.* 267.

56. Heather (1991), 301ff.

Chapter 10: All Quiet on the Eastern Front?

1. Dio LXXX.4
2. Crawford (2013), 25-76; Lactantius, *De Mort. Pers.* 5; Probus was planning a Persian campaign on his death in 282, perhaps leading to the opportunistic sack of Ctesiphon by Carus in 283; there was also a brief stand-off over Armenia in 286/287 (*SHA Probus* 20.1; Aurelius Victor, *de Caes.* XXXVIII.2-4; Eutropius IX.18.1).
3. Lenski (2002), 167-85.
4. Procopius, *BP* I.1.
5. Daryaee (2009), 22.
6. Cyril of Scythopolis, *Vita Euthymii* 10.
7. Holum (1977).
8. Those reinforcements included an obscure soldier who fell ill in Lycia and therefore did not take part in the war: the future emperor Marcian – Theophanes, *Chron.* AM5943.
9. Socrates VII.18 on the war of 421-22; Schrier (1992), 79-81; Greatrex (1993), 6-8; Theodoret V.37.6-10; Socrates VIII.20; Malchus fr. 1.4-7; Socrates VII.21.7-10; Greatrex and Lieu (2002), 36-45, 258 n.50.
10. Payne, in Maas (2015), 297.
11. John Lydus, *de mag.* III.52.
12. Maenchen-Helfen (1973), 51-59; Greatrex and Greatrex (1999), 65-75.
13. Blockley (1985), 66; Blockley (1985), 63-66; (1992), 50-51; Luther (1997), 104-06.
14. Payne, in Maas (2015), 298; Borm (2008), 327-46.
15. John Lydus, *de mag.* III.53.
16. Prosper Tiro sa.441; *Chron. Min.* I.478, II.80; Theophanes, *Chron.* AM5941; Moses Khorenats'i III.67; Elishe 7/61-62; Isaac of Antioch, *Hom.* 11.374-80; Theodoret, *HE* V.37.5-6.
17. Moses Khorenats'i III.57-59, 65; *NTh* 4; Marcellinus comes sa.441; cf. Procopius, *BP* I.2.12-15, 16.6; Theophanes, *Chron.* AM5921; Priscus fr.41.1.1-3.27; Greatrex and Lieu (2002), 57.
18. Moses Khorenats'i III.56-59, 64; cf. Grousset (1947), 180; Winkler (1994), 328; *Narratio de rebus Armeniae* 4-9; Blockley (1992), 60-61.
19. Certres, Donabed and Makko (2012), 258-59; Back (1978), 498; Bier (1986), 263-68.
20. Babessian (1965), 16-19.
21. Lazar 36 on Anatolius and Florentius advising Marcian not to intervene in the Armenian revolt; Grousset (1947), 194-99; Luther (1997), 141-42.
22. Lazar 66, 108; Elishe 78, 129-30.
23. *2 Maccabees*; Josephus, *AJ* XII; *BJ* I.
24. Elishe 134.185; Lazar 83, 129.
25. Elishe 127-29, 180-81.
26. Daryaee (2009), 24.

27. Involvement with the rebellion against Yazdgerd led to the Armenian Church not being represented at the Council of Chalcedon in 451, which they would later reject.

28. La Vaissiere (2003), 119-32; Zeimal (1996), 119-35; Enoki (1969), 1-26; Grenet, in Sims-Williams (2002), 203-24.

29. Priscus, *Hist.* II.348-49.

30. Pourshariati (2008), 71.

31. Procopius, *BP* I.4.

32. Tabari V.12; Howard-Johnston (2006), 172; Holland (2012), 496 n.11.

33. Agathias IV.27.3.

34. Seminal (1996), 130.

35. Originally called 'Alexander's Wall', this construction has been dated to the fifth/sixth century; Rekavandi, Sauer, Wilkinson and Nokandeh (2008).

36. Procopius, *BP* I.3.

37. Daryaee (2009), 25; Litvinsky (1996), 142

38. Daryaee (2001), 145-46.

39. Procopius, *BP* I.1-4; Ps-Joshua the Stylite 9-11; cf. Luther (1997), 116-24.

40. Ps-Joshua the Stylite 9-10.

41. Procopius, *BP* I.3.2; Holland (2012), 497 n.21, records the suggestion that Gorgo was a tent city, hence the lack of archaeology, even though Peroz razed it in 484.

42. Sebeos VIII.67.

43. Payne in Maas (2015), 288, 298.

44. *V. Dan. Sty.* 51; Priscus fr.25, 26, 33, 34; Hydatius, *Lem.* 177; Gobazes may have visited Constantinople not long after the fire of 2 September 465.

45. Priscus fr.51; Toumanoff (1963), 363-64.

46. Joshua the Stylite 8-10; Malalas XVIII.44; Braund (1994), 274; Greatrex (1998), 126 n.17.

47. Toumanoff (1963), 368-69, *contra* Greatrex (1998), 129.

48. Toumanoff (1963), 368-69; Thomson (1996), 153-251.

49. *Georgian Chronicle* 13-14.

50. Rayfield (2013), 46.

51. Grousset (1947), 217-18.

52. Adontz (1970), 173.

53. Dédéyan (2007), 193; Grousset (1947), 221.

54. Suny (1994), 23-25.

55. *Georgian Chronicle* 14; Procopius, *BP* I.12; Toumanoff (1963), 369; Suny (1994), 2; Greatrex (1998), 129.

56. Moses Kalankatuyk I.4.

57. Elishe 197-99, 242-43; Biro (1997), 53-56; Braund (1984), 274.

58. Moses Kalankatuyk I.15.

59. Daryaee (2009), 25.

60. *V. Dan. Sty.* 51; Priscus fr.25, 26, 33, 34; Hydatius, *Lem.* 177.

61. Frey in Yarshater (1983), *CHI* III.149; Hacikyan, Ouzounian, Frankchuk and Basmajian (2000), I.259; Panossian (2006), 48.

62. Procopius, *de Aed*. III.6.23.

63. Dédéyan (2007), 193-95.

64. Daryaee (2009), 25; Winter and Dignas (2001), 54-57; Ps-Joshua the Stylite 9-10.

65. Dio LXXV.3.3

66. Garnsey and Saller (1987), 8.

Chapter 11: Zeno, the Christological Crisis and Imperial Religious Policy

1. Barth (1894); Lippold (1972); Feld (2005); Polish scholars have explored Zeno's religious policies – Salamon (1996), 163-96; Leszka (1993), 71-78; (1998b), 437-53; Koczwara (2000); Kosinski (2010).

2. Greer (1961); Grillmeier (1975), 421-39; Kelly (1998), 227-31; Sullivan (1956); Gavriluk (2003), 141-43.

3. Kosinski (2010), 33; Scipioni (1956); Grillmeier (1975), 443-519; McGukin (1988), 93-129; de Halleux (1993), 163-178; Dupuy (1995), 56-64; Kosinksi (2007), 155-70; (2008a), 30-63; (2008b), 33-48.

4. Grillmeier (1975), 473-83; Kelly (1988), 237-41; Gavrilyuk (2003), 190-207; McGukin (2004).

5. McGukin (2004), 53-107; Sagi-Bunic (1965), 19-73; Grillmeier (1975), 497-501; Kelly (1988), 244-45.

6. Jalland (1941); Stockmeier (1959); Grillmeier (1975), 526-39; Kelly (1988), 249-51; Wessel (2008); Lebon (1946), 515-28, on Dioscorus, patriarch of Alexandria, supporting Eutyches.

7. The term *latrocinium* stems from the Latin term meaning 'bandit' and ultimately the Greek λατρον meaning 'hire', and was used to describe a war fought against Rome without any formal declaration.

8. Rahner (1951), 323-39.

9. *ACO* II.1.1, 27-29; 3.1, 19-22; 2.1, 1, 30; 3.1, 22-23; Schwartz (1927), 203-12; Goubert (1951), 303-21; Chew (2006), 207-27; Ilski (1992).

10. *ACO* II.1.2, 69-84; 3.2, 3-17; Galtier (1951), 354-58; Gray (1979), 9-10; Meyendorff (1989), 171-75.

11. Kosinski (2010), 37.

12. *ACO* II.1.2, 126-30, 3.2, 134-38, 1.2, 130-58, 3.2, 138-80; Galtier (1951), 358-72; de Urbina (1951), 389-418; Grillmeier (1975), 543-50; (1987b), 67-68; Gray (1979), 10-16; Meyendorff (1989), 171-78.

13. Gray (1979), 8-9; Gregory (1979), 172-81; Meyendorff (1989), 170-71; Milewski (2008), 72-76, 191-92.

14. *ACO* II.4, 55-62, 67-71; Hoffman (1953), 15-16; Grillmeier (1987), 118.

15. Ps-Zacharias III.1 on Eustathius of Berytus and Amphilochius of Side claiming that they were coerced.

16. Ps-Zacharias III.3; Evagrius II.5; Theophanes, *Chron.* AM5945; Cyril of Scythopolis, *Vita Euthymii* 27, 30.

17. John Rufus, *Vita Petri Iberi* 47, 76, 78; *Plero.* 10, 25, 52, 56; *de obitu Theodosii* 2; Ps-Zacharias III.3-5; Evagrius III.6; Cyril of Scythopolis, *Vita Euthymii* 27; Honigmann (1950), 249-50; Bacht (1953), 245-46; Steppa (2002), 1-9; Peronne (1980), 91-95; (2006), 168-69; Chitty (2008), 176; Horn (2006), 79, 83-88.

18. Ps-Zacharias III.5-9; John Rufus, *Vita Petri Iberi* 81; *de obitu Theodosii* 2; *Plerophoriae* 10; Cyril of Scythopolis, *Vita Euthymii* 30; Honigmann (1950), 256, 259; Bacht (1953), 252; Peronne (1980), 118-19; Frend (1972), 151-53; Horn (2006), 91-92; Chitty (2008), 179; Kosinksi (2010), 45 n.65.

19. Priscus fr.22; Ps-Zacharias III.2, 11; Liberatus XIV.97-98; Theodore Lector, *Epit.* 326; Evagrius II.5; *Gesta de nomine Acacii* 13, 19; John Rufus, *Vita Petri Iberi* 83; Frend (1972), 154-55; Gregory (1979), 184-88.

20. *ACOec* II.V.14; *V. Petr. Iber.* 66-67; Zacharias, *HE* IV.1.1; Evagrius, *HE* II.8.

21. Theodore Lector, *Epit.* 372.

22. Ps-Zacharias III.11, IV.1-3; John Rufus, *Vita Petri Iberi* 91-92, 95-96; *Life of Timothy Ailouros* 164-65; Victor of Tunnuna sa.457; Theodore Lector, *Epit.* 368-70; Evagrius II.8; Theophanes, *Chron.* AM5950; Grillmeier and Hainthaler (1996), 7-35; Blaudeau (2006), 149 n.246.

23. Scott (1976), 67-69; Lebon (1909), 19; Schwartz (1934), 177-78; Verdansky (1941), 55-57.

24. Frend (1972), 160-65; Schnitzler (1938), 16-20; Hofmann (1953), 25-27.

25. Ps-Zacharias IV.6; Evagrius II.10; Grillmeier (1987), 117; Blaudeau (2006), 156-57, 160-61.

26. Evagrius II.9; Ps-Zacahrias IV.5, 6; Frend (1972), 161, suggests that Leo's survey reached 1,600 church officials; Schnitzler (1938), 62; Grillmeier (1987), 116-17, 196-97; Schnitzler (1938), 63.

27. Foss (1991), 821; Janin and Stiernon (1981), col.1,091-103.

28. Ps-Zacharias IV.9-10; Theodore Lector, *Epit.* 380; John Rufus, *Vita Petri Iberi* 97; Victor of Tunnuna sa.460; Liberatus, *Brev.* 15, 16; Evagrius II.8; Frend (1972), 163; Grillmeier (1987), 201; Blaudeau (2006), 165-68.

29. Ps-Zacharias IV.10; Liberatus XVI.108; Frend (1992), 2,268-69; Grillmeier (1997), 36-37.

30. Frend (1972), 166, claims that Isauria was firmly anti-Chalcedonian despite sixteen bishops supporting Chalcedon in Leo's survey.

31. Michael Psellus, *Historia Syntomos* 66, 68; Verdansky (1941), 60; Twardowska (2009), 76

32. Theodore Lector, *Epit.* 390; Theophanes, *Chron.* AM5956; *Synodicon Vetus* 98.

33. *Gesta de nomine Acacii* 25; Liberatus XVII.122; Frite (1935), 1,933-35; Kosinski (2010c).

34. Theodore Lector, *Epit*. 390; Theophanes, *Chron*. AM5956; *Synodicon Vetus* 98; Fritz (1935), 1934; Devreese (1945), 65; Downey (1961), 485; Frend (1972), 167; Grillmeier and Hainthaler (2004), 298; Perrone (1983), 2,794; Horn (2006), 42

35. Theodore Lector, *Epit*. 390; Theophanes, *Chron*. AM5956; *Laudatio S.Barnabae* 110 on Peter attempting to curry favour with Apollinarians; Grillmeier and Hainthaler (2004), 301-02.

36. Theodore Lector, *Epit*. 390; Theophanes, *Chron*. AM5956; John Diakrin., *Epit*. 540; Downey (1961), 486; Grillmeier and Hainthaler (2004), 298; Uthemann (2006), 143; Blaudeau (2006), 169-71; Norton (2007), 93.

37. Gunther (1894), 148; Kosinski (2010), 74.

38. *Laudatio S.Barnabae* 109; Blaudeau (2006), 171 n.376.

39. *Gesta de nomine Acacii* 25; Liberatus XVII.122; *Laudatio S.Barnabae* 109-10; Theodore Lector, *Epit*. 392; Theophanes, *Chron*. AM5956; *Synodicon Vetus* 98; Kosinski (2010), 75.

40. Blaudeau (2006), 171 n.376, holds that Peter did not become bishop until Martyrius' resignation in mid-471, while Downey (1961), 486-87, suggests that Peter was patriarch on two separate occasions – during Martyrius' absence in Constantinople and then again after his resignation in mid-471.

41. Kosinski (2010), 75.

42. Theodore Lector, *Epit*. 392; Theophanes, *Chron*. AM5956; Downey (1961), 487; Grillmeier and Hainthaler (2004), 299; Schwartz (1934), 182 n.3, suggests that Julianus cannot have become patriarch later than 470.

43. *CJ* I.2.15; cf. Coleman-Norton (1966), 911 n.1.

44. Kosinski (2010), 76.

45. *Suda* A783; Theodore Lector, *Epit*. 376; Ps-Zacharias IV.11; Nikephoros Kallistos XV.16; the year 471 is broadly accepted for the election of Acacius – Leszka (1998), 437; Grumel (1958), 435, suggested 472.

46. Schwartz (1934), 198; Frend (1972), 170; Redies (1997), 212-13; Blaudeau (2006), 168.

47. Ps-Zacharias IV.11; Jugie (1912), 244; Salaville (1920), col.2,155; Frend (1972), 170; Leszka (1993), 76; Redies (1997), 212-13; Blaudeau (2006), 169.

48. Kosinski (2010), 77; Brennecke (1997), 33-34.

49. *Suda* A783; Schwark (1950), 16; *Suda* A783; Blaudeau (2006), 171.

50. Kosinski (2010), 28 n.67, 78.

51. Jugie (1912), col.244; Frend (1972), 170; Leszka (1993), 71-78.

52. Blaudeau (2006), 171-72; Kosinski (2010b), 63-97, on Acacius.

53. *CJ* I.2.16; Ps-Zacharias V.5; Evagrius III.8.

54. Kosinski (2010), 107.

55. Evagrius III.3; Martin (1953), 440-41; *contra* Blaudeau (2006), 188-89; Kosinski (2010), 107.

56. Frend (1972), 144; Brennecke (1997), 38-39; Blaudeau (2006), 189.

57. Evagrius III.9; Grumel (1932), 65; Schwartz (1934), 190-91; Brennecke (1997), 39; Blaudeau (2006), 190; Kosinski (2010), 109 n.66; Honigman (1951), 119.

58. Ps-Zacharias V.5; Theodore Lector, *Epit.* 415; Theophanes, *Chron.* AM5969; Evagrius III.8; Malalas XV.5-6; Agapius, *Kitab al-Unvan* 421; John of Nikiu 88.43; Ps-Dionysius 171; *Gesta de nomine Acacii* 25; *Synodicon Vetus* 100-01.

59. Theodore Lector, *Epit.* 392, 415; Theophanes, *Chron.* AM5969; *Gesta de nomine Acacii* 25; Liberatus XVII.122-23; Downey (1961), 489; Grillmeier and Hainthaler (2004), 299-300; Blaudeau (2006), 190-91.

60. *Gesta de nomie Acacii* 25; Frend (1972), 181.

61. Theophanes, *Chron.* AM5970; *Synodicon Vetus* 102; Blaudeau (2006), 195; Theodore Lector, *Epit.* 421; Theophanes, *Chron.* AM5973; *Synodicon Vetus* 101 and Ps-Zacharias IV.12, VI.7, seem to suggest that there were two successive Antiochene patriarchs called Stephen. However, other sources like Malalas XV.6, Evagrius III.10 and Ps-Dionysius 171 only mention one Stephen and it is more usual for modern historians to see the 'two Stephens' as an error – Downey (1961), 489-90 n.68; Whitby (2000), 144 n.3.

62. Theophanes, *Chron.* AM5973; Malalas XV.6; Evagrius III.10; John of Nikiu 88.44; Michael the Syrian IX.6; Pietri (1987), 286; Grillmeier and Hainthaler (2004), 300; Blaudeau (2001), 1,090; (2006), 195-96; although Hefele and Leclerq (1908), II.914-15; Frend (1972), 175; and Allen (1981), 130, have 481.

63. Evagrius III.11; John Rufus, *Vita Petri Iberi* 110; John of Nikiu 88.57; *Gesta de nomine Acacii* 18; Liberatus XVI.106 suggests Timothy committed suicide; Elli (2003), 278.

64. Ps-Zacharias V.5; Evagrius III.11; *Gesta de nomine Acacii* 18; Liberatus XVI.106; Theodore Lector, *Epit.* 416; Wipszycka (2006), 77-78, on the Alexandrian practice of consecrating new bishops beside the deceased.

65. Evagrius III.11; Ps-Zacharias V.5; Victor of Tunnuna sa.477; Liberatus XVI.106-07; *Gesta de nomine Acacii* 18; Theodore Lector, *Epit.* 416; Theophanes, *Chron.* AM5969; Grillmeier (1987), 249; Haas (1993), 303; (1997), 320; Blaudeau (2006), 193.

66. Liberatus XVI.107-08; Ps-Zacharias V.5; *Gesta de nomine Acacii* 19; John of Nikiu 88.58; Haas (1993), 304; (1997), 321.

67. Ps-Zacharias V.5; Stein (1949), 21; Perrone (1980), 126-27; later Miaphysite sources such as Michael the Syrian IX.5 considered Anastasius to be an opponent of Chalcedon; Leszka (1998b), 442, 444.

68. Evagrius III.10; Theodore Lector, *Epit.* 421; Theophanes, *Chron.* AM5973; Malalas XV.6; John of Nikiu 88.44; *Synodicon Vetus* 102; Michael the Syrian IX.6; Schwartz (1934), 183; Haacke (1953), 118; Downey (1961), 489; Brennecke (1997), 39; Blaudeau (2001), 1,090-91; (2006), 195-96.

69. Richards (1979), 60; Konig (1997), 117.

70. Kosinksi (2010), 118.

71. Evagrius III.12; Ps-Zacharias V.5-6; *Gesta de nomine Acacii* 21; Liberatus XVI.107; Victor of Tunnuna sa.480; Theodore Lector, *Epit.* 417; John of Nikiu 88.60; Pietri (1987), 277-95; Stiernon (2000), col.671-95.

72. Ps-Zacharias V.6; *Gesta de nomine Acacii* 21, 23; Liberatus XVI.107, XVII.110-11.

73. Liberatus XVI.107; Ps-Zacharias V.5-6; Frend (1972), 177; Blaudeau (2006), 200; Kosinski (2010), 129 n.30.

74. Liberatus XVI.108, XVII.110; Eutychius, *Ann.* XVI.4, XVII.4; Theodore Lector, *Epit.* 417; Evagrius III.12, 20; Ps-Zacharias V.7, 9; Victor of Tunnuna sa.480; Theophanes, *Chron.* AM5973; Kosinski (2010), 130.

75. Liberatus XVIII.111, 119; Frend (1972), 177; Blaudeau (2006), 201-02.

76. Ps-Zacharias V.7; Evagrius III.12; John of Nikiu 88.60-61; Sohnel (2004), 65-68; Kosinski (2010), 131 n.36.

77. Ps-Zacharias V.7; Evagrius III.13; Liberatus XVII.112, 119; Pietri (1987), 291-95; Stiernon (2000), col. 691-92; Blaudeau (2006), 206-07.

78. Ps-Zacharias V.4; Frend (1972), 176.

79. Ps-Zacharias V.7; Liberatus XVII.111-112; Theodore Lector, *Epit.* 422; Frend (1972), 177; Haas (1997), 322.

80. Ps-Zacharias V.7, 11-12, VI.2; Evagrius III.12, 13, 16; Theodore Lector, *Epit.* 422-24; Liberatus XVII.112, 119; Brennecke (1997), 42; Haas (1997), 322-25; Kosinski (2010), 132.

81. Schwartz (1939), 370; Grillmeier (1987), 251; Blaudeau (2006), 197; Kosinski (2010), 133-34 n.52.

82. Ps-Zacharias V.6; Cyril of Scythopolis, *Vita Euthymii* 32, 38-39; Allen (1981), 130.

83. Cyril of Scythopolis, *Vita Euthymii* 43; Chitty (1952), 25-26; (2008), 196-97.

84. Cyril of Scythopolis, *Vita Euthymii* 43, 45; Chitty (2008), 197; Blaudeau (2006), 197-98.

85. Ps-Zacharias V.7; Evagrius III.13; John of Nikiu 88.162; Theophanes, *Chron.* AM5976; Horn (2006), 103; Blaudeau (2006), 203.

86. Evagrius III.14; Kosinski (2010), 139.

87. *Vaticanus Graecus* 1,431; Grillmeier (1987), 251; Brennecke (1997), 40-43; Maraval (1998), 119.

88. Ps-Zacharias V.8; Evagrius III.12, 13, 14; Liberatus XVII.113; Kussmaul (1981); Dovere (1988), 179-81.

89. Kosinksi (2010), 138.

90. Devreese (1930), 256-63; Schwark (1950), 33, 61; Dovere (1988), 181-90.

91. Ps-Zacharias V.7; Evagrius III.13; Theophanes, *Chron.* AM5976; Breydy (1983), 74.

92. Ps-Zacharias V.1-2; Haas (1997), 323; Ps-Zacharias V.7 may have removed any instances of ambiguities in Mongus' application of anti-Chalcedonian doctrine; Allen (1981), 131-32; Kosinski (2010), 142.

93. John Rufus, *Vita Petr. Iberi* 103-04.

94. Ps-Zacharias V.9; Evagrius III.16; Theodore Lector, *Epit.* 426; Theophanes, *Chron.* AM5978; Haacke (1953), 120-22; Brennecke (1997), 49; Blaudeau (2006), 222.

95. Evagrius III.20; Blaudeau (2006), 209.

96. Schwark (1950), 41-42; Hofmann (1953), 44-45.

97. Liberatus XVII.120; *Gesta de nomine Acacii* 23, 27; Evagrius III.18-20; Pietri (1987), 277-95; *Gesta de nomine Acacii* 27; Blaudeau (2002), 503-28.

98. Evagrius III.19-20; Theodore Lector, *Epit.* 431; *Gesta de nomine Acacii* 28, 30.

99. Evagrius III.17, 20; Theodore Lector, *Epit.* 432-33; Nautin (1967), col.891; Blaudeau (2006), 209.

100. Blaudeau (2001), 1,097; (2002), 509-10.

101. Evagrius III.20; Schwark (1950), 45; Blaudeau (2006), 214.

102. Evagrius III.21; Theodore Lector, *Epit.* 434; Koczwara (2000), 57; Blaudeau (2002), 503-28.

103. Kosinski (2010), 183.

104. Kosinksi (2010), 144.

105. Theodore Lector, *Epit.* 434; Liberatus XVII.125; Schwark (1950), 51; Blaudeau (2001), 1,097; (2006), 223.

106. Kosinski (2010), 184.

107. Schwartz (1934), 210-11, 265-66; Schwark (1950), 55.

108. Ps-Zacharias VI.1; Evagrius III.16; Grillmeier (1987), 259; Blaudeau (2006), 225.

109. Evagrius III.17.

110. Revillout (1877), 131-33; Blaudeau (2006), 215-17; Allen (1981), 136-37, considers the letter as genuine.

111. Ps-Zacharias VI.1; Evagrius III.21.

112. Zacharias, *Vita Isaiae* 8; Dragnet (1968), 85-126.

113. Ps-Zacharias VI.1, 2; Evagrius III.22; Zacharias, *Vita Severi* 100-01; Schwartz (1934), 239; Moeller (1944-45), 84-85; Schwark (1950), 36; Bacht (1953), 267; Blaudeau (2006), 227.

114. *V. Petr. Iber.* 98; John Rufinus, *Pleroph.* 27; Zacharius, *V. Isaiae* 9; *V. Sev.* 101; Evagrius, *HE* III.22.

115. Ps-Zacharias VI.2; Evagrius III.22; Zacharias, *Vita Severi* 100-01; Moeller (1944-45), 85-86; Haas (1997), 329; Blaudeau (2006), 225-30.

116. Ps-Zacharias VI.4.

117. Evagrius III.27.

118. Ennodius, *Pan.* VIII.36-47; Caspar (1933), 53, 749; Nautin (1967), 889-95; Richards (1979), 59-62.

119. Schwartz (1934), 211 n.2, using *Le Synaxaire arabe Jacobite* II.364.

120. Blaudeau (2006), 232-33.

121. Theodore Lector, *Epit.* 440; Liberatus XVIII.127; Schwartz (1934), 212 n.1; Nautin (1977), col.1,128; Blaudeau (2006), 231-33; Janin (1969), 143, on the shrine of Thecla and its location.

122. Nikephoros Kall. XVI.18-19.

123. Barth (1894), 114; Schwartz (1934), 212-13; Schwark (1950), 56-58; Bacht (1953), 274; Blaudeau (2001), 1,098-99, 1,106; (2006), 233.

124. Ps-Zacharias VI.5; Theophanes, *Chron.* AM5981.

125. Ps-Zacharias VI.6, VII.1; Blaudeau (2006), 234-35.

126. Ps-Zacharias VI.6.

127. Kosinski (2010), 191; Ps-Zacharias VI.4; Grillmeier (1987), 264; Haas (1997), 330; Blaudeau (2006), 234.

128. Theodore Lector, *Epit.* 440; Evagrius III.23; Schwartz (1934), 213 n.2; Schwark (1950); Blaudeau (2006), 234.

129. Kosinski (2010), 191; Ps-Zacharias VI.4; Theodore Lector, *Epit.* 440.

130. Theodore Lector, *Epit.* 441; Theophanes, *Chron.* AM5982; *Suda* Φ136.

131. Kosinski (2010), 192 n.93; Ps-Zacharias VII.1; Blaudeau (2006), 239 n.810; Capizzi (1969), 74 n.16; Twardowska (2009), 95-96.

132. John of Nikiu 89.2-17; Theophanes, *Chron.* AM5984; Victor of Tonn. sa.494.

133. Theodore Lector, *Epit.* 445; Theophanes, *Chron.* AM5984; Charanis (1939), 12; Capizzi (1969), 69-70; Grillmeier (1987), 264; Haarer (2006), 2.

134. Theodore Lector, *Epit.* 440; Ps-Zacharias VI.4; Evagrius III.23; Barth (1894), 115; Kosinski (2010), 193 n.97

135. Theophanes, *Chron.* AM5983; *Synodicon Vetus* 108; Grillmeier (1987), 265.

136. *Le Synxaire Arabe Jacobite* II.246; Schwartz (1934), 213; *contra* Elli (2003), 285, who suggests 29 October 489.

137. Liberatus XVIII.127.

138. Ps-Zacharias VI.4, 6, VII.1; Evagrius III.31; cf. Allen (1981), 147-49; Perrone (1980), 142-43 n.2.

139. Ps-Zacharias VII.1; Frend (1972), 189; Blaudeau (2006), 231.

140. Kosinski (2010), 195.

141. Cyril of Scythopolis, *Vita Sabae* 30, 65; Evagrius III.31; cf. Perrone (1980), 142-44.

142. Grillmeier (1987), 259; Ps-Zacharias VI.3; Zacharias, *Vita Isaiae* 9-10; John Rufus, *Plero.* 27; *Vita Petri Iberi* 140; Chabot (1895), 383 n.4.

143. Zacharius VI.2, 3; *V. Petr. Iber.* 98; *V. Isaiae* 9-10; John Rufus, *Plero.* 27; Cyril of Scythopolis, *Vita Sabae* 15-21; Grillmeier (1987), 261-62; Horn (2006), 107-08; Chitty (2008), 205-08; Kosinski (2010), 196 n.115.

144. Theophanes, *Chron.* AM5982; Gray (1979), 33, and Blaudeau (2006), 220; Downey (1961), 496.

145. Victor of Tunnuna sa.485, 487; *Laud. S. Barnabae* 110.

146. De Halleux (1963), 34; Grillmeier and Hainthaler (2004), 302; Blaudeau (2006), 231, follow the moderate view of Peter the Fuller; Gray (1979), 23, sees him as a fervent anti-Chalcedonian, while van Esbroeck (1996), 469, highlights his political opportunism.

147. Victor of Tunnuna sa.488.3.

148. Theophanes, *Chron.* AM5983; Bar Hebraeus, *Chron. Ecc.* 40; Devreese (1945), 118; Downey (1961), 507-08 n.19; Blaudeau (2006), 231.

149. Evagrius III.23, 31; Ps-Zacharias VI.6; Theophanes, *Chron.* AM5983.
150. Theodore Lector fr.37; Kosinski (2006), 142-47.
151. Amelineau (1888), 181-85; Lichtheim (2006), 90-94; Evelyn-White (1932), 224-27.
152. *CJ* I.3.36; cf. Valentinian III, *Nov.* 35.6; Jones (1964), 802, 920-21, 931; Lippold (1972), col.203-04.
153. *CJ* I.3.37; Lippold (1972), col.204; Coleman-Norton (1966), 936; *ACO* II.1.355; Jones (1964), 802.
154. *CJ* I.3.38, 39; *ACO* II.1.355; Coleman-Norton (1966), 937, 939, places these two laws between 484 and 524.
155. *CJ* I.3.35; Leszka (1998b), 442-44; Browning and Kazhdan (1991), 2,092, on Tomis; Popescu (1994), 154, 212; Belke (1984), 180-81; Stiernon (1997), col.131-36; Lippold (1972), 203; Jones (1964), 877, 1,364 n.8.
156. *Laudatio S. Barnabae* 112-8; Victor of Tunnuna sa.488.1; cf. Theodore Lector, *Epit.* 436; Mitsides (1976), 3-18; Downey (1961), 496-97; Grillmeier and Hainthaler (2004), 301; Roux (1998), 35; Kollman (2004), 58.
157. John Moschos, *Pratum Spirituale* 175.
158. Krauthmeier (1986), 112; cf. Megaw (2006), 400.
159. Kosinski (2010), 203.
160. Megaw (2006), 400.
161. Herzfeld and Guyer (1930), 32; Forsyth (1957), 225; Mango (1966), 364; Gough (1972), 199-212, although Forsyth (1957), 233, has some reservations, dating the majority of Isaurian churches to the sixth century.
162. Hill (1996), 51-54; Nauerth (1987), 55.
163. John of Antioch fr.306; Gough (1972), 210.
164. Kosinski (2010), 204.
165. Theophanes, *Chron.* AM5988; Jordanes, *Rom.* 355; Priscian, *Pan.* 130-32; Procopius, *Pan.* 10; Stein (1949); Capizzi (1969), 95-100; Hill (1996), 6-9, 51-54; Lenski (1999), 428-29; Feld (2005), 332-38; Meier (2009), 75-84; Haarer (2006), 21-28, urges caution over the extent of the repression of Isauria by Anastasius.
166. Evagrius III.8; cf. Dagron (198), 59; Herzfeld and Guyer (1930), 73-74, and Hellenkemper (1980), 81-88, see the domed basilica as a foundation of Zeno, while Forsyth (1957), 224-25, and Dagron (1978), 60-61, thought that the main basilica on the site belongs to Zeno. Hill (1996), 51, 213-14, suggests that both these basilicas and the North Church are all Zenoid foundations. Elton (2000), 153, agrees that all three were Zenoid in date but suggests that only the main basilica was a foundation of Zeno, while the other two were by local patrons.
167. Hill (1996), 51, 68-72; Harrison (1993), 40; Gough (1972), 201; Feld (2005), 301, although Forsyth (1957), 233, dated it mid-sixth century; Gough (1972) vs Elton (2002b) over Alatian being Zenoid or Justinianic.
168. Forsyth (1957), 234-36; Feld (1965), 131-43 – Dag Pazari, Korykos, Alaklise, Anemourion and Karlik; Kosinski (2010), 210 n.31 – Anavarza, Batisandal,

Bodrum, Cennet, Cehennem, Kardirli, the Tomb church at Dag Pazari and the monastery at Mahras Dagi.

169. *Encomium of Saint Menas* 146-47; Grossman (2001), 8; Krautheimer (1986), 110-12; Feld (2005), 298-99; Kosciulk (2009), 37-38; Severin and Severin (1987), 9; Hahn (1997), 1,090 n.84.

170. Tchalenko (1953), I.223-33; Maraval (2004), 342-44; Peeters (1950), 126; Doran (1992), 36.

171. Malalas IV.12; John of Nikiu 88.1-9; Downey (1935), 56; Buresch (1889), 111-12, on *The Oracle of the Hellenic Gods*; Mango (1995), 202-03; Hasluk (1910), 24; Janin (1975), 203-05; Deichmann (1982), 81.

172. Sotiriou and Sotiriou (1952), 246; Cormack (1969), 17-18; Kleinbauer (1970), 36-37; Janin (1975), 365; Krautheimer (1986), 128; Sotiriou and Sotiriou (1952); Lemerle (1953), 660-94; Cormack (1985).

173. Procopius, *de Aed.* V.7.5-8; Magen (1990), 333-41; (1993), 129-33; Sivan (2008), 123-24; Cormack (1990), 75-88; Smith and Ratte (1995), 44-46; Ward-Perkins (1999), 234; Liebeschuetz (2001), 36; Trombley (1994), II.52-53; Bayliss (2004), 53.

174. Mango (1978), 44-51; Kosinski (2010), 215, 216.

175. Gough (1972), 210-22; Hill (1996), 53.

176. Kosinski (2010), 217.

177. Malalas XV.11; *Patr. Cons.* III.66; Janin (1969); Twardowska (2009), 155; Berger (1988), 88-89.

178. Kosinski (2010), 218; Capizzi (1969), 196-99, 206-32; Haarer (2006), 238-42.

179. Trombley (1994), I.62; Zacharias, *Vita Severi* 39-41; Szabat (2007), 187-89; Fowden (1982), 46-48.

180. Zacharias, *Vita Severi* 36-47; Trombley (1994), I.94, II.14-25, 52-53, 68-72; *contra* Bayliss (2004), 53; Kosinksi (2010), 57, 213-14.

181. Zacharias, *Vita Severi* 14-35; Rodziewicz (1991), 119-30, records a discovery in 1982 of the burnt remains of pagan artefacts near the Via Canopea, which Haas (1997) links to Mongus and Paralius.

182. Damascius fr.117b, 120b, 126c, 131a, b; Kosinski (2010), 160-62; Fowden (1982), 46-47, 54; Athanassiadi (1993), 20; Dzelska (1998), 57; Szabat (2007), 177-78, 213-14, 225.

183. Kosinski (2010), 163; Damascius fr.107, 148c; Szabat (2007), 234; van Haeling (1980), 94.

184. Damascius fr.101c; Marinus, *Vita Procli* 15.

185. Zacharias, *Vita Isaiae* 7; *Vita Severi* 57-66; Zacharias was in Berytus between 487/488 and 491; Kugener (1900), 206; Allen and Hayward (2004), 6.

186. Zacharias, *Vita Severi* 66-70, 73; Trombley (1994), II.39-40; Chuvin (2008), 131-34.

187. Damascius fr.108; van Haeling (1980), 90; Kosinski (2010), 165.

188. Damascius fr.303 = *Epit. Phot.* 290.

189. Trombley (1994), I.81-94.
190. *CJ* I.11.9.
191. *CJ* I.11.10.
192. Kosinski (2010), 166.
193. Kosinski (2010), 175; Malalas XV.
194. Starr (1939), 43-44; Cameron (1976), 149-152; Roueche (1993), 130-31; Horst (2006), 53-58.
195. Malalas XV.15.
196. *CTh* IX.38.3, 7; XVI.8.22.
197. Malalas XV.5, 15; Michael the Syrian IX.6; Jarry (1968), 241, 265.
198. Jacob of Sarug, *Ep.* XIV; *Chronicle of Edessa* 73; Symeon of Bet Arsham 34; John Diakrinomenos, *Epit.* 548; Voobius (1965), 32; Pigulewska (1989), 68; Becker (2006), 41-76; (2008), 2.
199. *CJ* I.5.11; Bagnall, Cameron, Schwartz and Worp (1987), 509, 555; Kosinski (2010), 123.
200. Kosinski (2010), 12.
201. Schwark (1950), 61-62.
202. Frend (1972), 190.

Chapter 12: A Long Time Coming: The Revolt of Illus

1. Damascius fr.113e; Ps-Joshua the Stylite 14.
2. Kosinski (2010), 125.
3. Thraustila may not have been an actual *magister militum* but held only a titular/honorary post – *PLRE* II.1118.
4. John of Antioch fr.303; Stein (1949), 16-17, 781; Lippold (1972), col.178.
5. John of Antioch fr.305; Stein (1949), 18.
6. Malalas XV.13.
7. Jordanes, *Rom.* 349ff suggests that Illus also began plotting the death of Ariadne.
8. Malalas XV.13.
9. Theodosius, *De Situ Terrae Sanctae* 28; the seven emperors were Theodosius II, Marcian, Leo I, Leo II, Zeno, Basiliscus and Anastasius; Callinicus, *V. Hypatii* 12.4 has Urbicius as a *cubicularius* from 434-449; he retired in *c*.450, perhaps on the death of Theodosius II, but was back in office by 470 if not earlier – Malalas fr.35; Theophanes, *Chron.* AM5972; John of Antioch fr.211.1.
10. Malalas XV.13; Jordanes, *Rom.* 351; Theophanes, *Chron.* AM5972; Ps-Joshua the Stylite 13; John of Nikiu 88.68-73; John of Antioch fr.211.3; despite the failure of his plot, Urbicius remained imperial chamberlain until the end of Zeno's reign and took part in Anastasius' elevation ceremony – Zonaras XIV.3.1; Cedrenus I.626; Constantine VII, *de caer.* I.92.
11. Liberatus, *Brev.* 17 records Illus in Antioch to receive a letter from the new Alexandrian patriarch, John Talaia.
12. Heather (2013), 48.

13. Jordanes, *Rom.* 349ff; Joshua the Stylite 12-13; Marcellinus Comes sa.484; Malalas 388; Theophanes, *Chron.* AM5972; Evagrius, *HE* III.27; Zacharias, *HE* V.6; John of Nikiu 88.74-75.

14. *ACOec* II.1.3.127, 129; Malchus fr.9 = *Suda* Z283.

15. Abu' l-Fath, *Kitab al-Tarikh* 53, 239-242; *New Chronicle* 75; Pummer (1987), 13; (1989), 145-47; (1999), 123, 133; Crown (1993b), 217-19; Magen (1993), 220-21; Negev and Gibson (2005), 175-76.

16. Procopius, *de Aed.* V.7.1-9.

17. Michael the Syrian IX.6 called him 'Iustus'.

18. Malalas XV.8; Michael the Syrian IX.6; a *lestodioktes* likely was a leader of local police forces; cf. Rabello (1987), I.378 n.9; Di Segni (1996), 579.

19. *New Chronicle* 75; Crown (1993b), 46-49; (2001), 28-29; Anderson and Giles (2005), 143-46; Di Segni (1998), 58; Sivan (2008), 108; Kosinksi (2010), 169.

20. Cameron (1996), 5-6; Sivan (2008), 123; Crown (1986-87), 112-13; (1989), 59-60; Levine (1975), 107; Atwater (1927) went as far as to suggest that Procopius was a Samaritan; backed by Adshead (1996), 35-41, but rejected by Pummer (2002), 291-94.

21. Montgomery (1907), 110; Avi-Yonah (1976), 242; Crown (1986-87), 128; Kohen (2007), 26; Pummer (2002), 256; Sivan (2008), 117.

22. Kosinski (2010), 171.

23. Stein (1949), 32 n.1; Whitby and Whitby (1989), 96 n.308; cf. Kosinski (2010d); (2010), 170-71.

24. Crown (1989), 73.

25. Malalas XVIII.35; Cyril of Scythopolis, *Vita Sabae* 70; Procopius, *de Aed.* V.7.16-17; *Chronicon Paschlae* 530; Theophanes, *Chron.* AM6021; Ps-Zacharias IX.8; John of Nikiu 93.4-9; Michael the Syrian IX.21.

26. Rabello (1987), I.375-79; Whitby and Whitby (1989), 96 n.308; Pummer (2002), 256-57; Di Segni (1993), 140; (1996), 586-87 n.64; (1998), 62 n.21, 64; Holum (1982), 69-70, suggests that Malalas demonstrates the Romanization of Samaria; Dar (1995), 157-68, vs Di Segni (1998), 57-58, on Samaritan archaeology; Crown (1986-87), 109-18; (1989), 57-58; Pummer (2002), 257-58, 289; (1999), 132-33.

27. Kosinski (2010), 174, using Schur (1989), 84-85.

28. Dam. *Epit. Phot.* 169.

29. John of Antioch fr.306; Evagrius III.35; Theophanes, *Chron.* AM5985.

30. John of Antioch fr.214.6.

31. Theophanes, *Chron.* AM5983; there is some issue with this proposed shared name of Cottomenes and Cottais, for the former is also linked to a Cato, who is attested alive in 490.

32. Malalas XVI.3; John of Antioch fr.306; Evagrius III.35; Theophanes, *Chron.* AM5985; Barth (1894), 83; Kosinski (2010), 147.

33. Downey (1961), 491, suggests that Illus attempted to shore up support in Antioch with a building programme.

34. Procopius, *De Aef.* III.1.25.
35. Theophanes, *Chron.* AM5976; John of Nikiu 88.85-86; Ps-Joshua the Stylite 16; Brooks (1893), 227.
36. John of Antioch fr.306; Ps-Joshua the Stylite 15.
37. Malalas XV.13; Theophanes, *Chron.* AM5972-5973, 5985; Theodore Lector, *Epit.* 437; Joshua the Stylite 14 calls him *stratelates* in 484.
38. Joshua the Stylite 14; Jordanes, *Rom.* 252.
39. Malalas, *de insid* XV.13; Evagrius III.27; Ps-Joshua the Stylite13; John of Nikiu 88.74-78; Theophanes, *Chron.* AM 5972; Damascius fr.115a; Marcellinus Comes sa.484.1.
40. John of Antioch fr.306; Theophanes, *Chron.* AM5972 suggests that he was of well-educated Syrian descent, while Malalas XV.13 has him as a Thracian; Downey (1961), 494 n.5; Twardowska (2009), 165-66.
41. Justinian II had a false nose made to 'reverse' his disqualification through mutilation.
42. Jordanes, *Rom.* 349ff; John of Antioch fr.214.2; Joshua the Stylite 14-15; Marcellinus Comes sa.484.
43. Malalas XV.13; John of Antioch fr.306; Theodore Lector, *Epit.* 437; Theophanes, *Chron.* AM5973; Marcellinus Comes sa.484.1.
44. Theodore Lector, *Epit.* 437.
45. Malalas *slav* XV.13.
46. The use of deceased emperor's names and claims to their personage had happened in the past – three men claiming to be Nero – while in the early seventh century a pseudo-Theodosius claimed to be the son of Mauricius.
47. Stein (1949), 19-20; Elton (2000), 402-04.
48. Asimus (1913), 320-47; Gregoire (1929), 22-38; Salamon (1996), 163-95; Feld (2002), 261-80; Kaster (1997), 329-32; Szabat (2007), 253-54.
49. Dam. *Epit. Phot.* 109 = Photius, *Bibl.* 242; Dam. fr.178 = *Suda* PI137; Malchus fr.20 = *Suda* PI137.
50. Malchus fr.23; Rhetorius 221, 2-4, 224, 4-9; Dam. fr.77d; *Suda* Π137.
51. Rhetorius 224, 13-15; Damascius fr.112a.
52. Theodore Lector, *Epit.* 435; Zacharias, *HE* V.9; Liberatus, *Brev,* 16; cf. Evagrius, *HE* III.6.
53. Damascius fr.77b, 113c; Zacharias, *Vita Isaiae* 7; *Vita Severi* 39-41.
54. John of Nikiu 88.80-82; Malalas XV.13; Theophanes, *Chron.* AM5974.
55. Kosinski (2010), 156.
56. Salamon (1996), 187-89.
57. John of Antioch fr.306; Kosinksi (2010), 149.
58. John of Antioch fr.306; Malalas XV.14; Ps-Joshua the Stylite 15; Evagrius III.27; John of Nikiu 88.86; Theophanes, *Chron.* AM5976-5977 suggests that Theoderic only returned west after the siege.
59. Jordanes, *Rom.* 349; Malalas XV.12; Joshua the Stylite 12.
60. Downey (1961), 495-96 n.105.

61. Ps-Joshua the Stylite 17; John of Antioch fr.306; Malalas XV.14; John of Nikiu 88.87-88; McCail (1976), 54.
62. John of Antioch fr.306; Brooks (1893), 228; Stein (1949), 30; Bury (1958), I.400; Lippold (1972), 187.
63. John of Antioch fr.214.6, 12; Theophanes, *Chron*. AM5975, 5976.
64. *Parastaseis syntomoi chronikai* 29, 89.
65. *Georgian Chronicle* 13-14.
66. John of Antioch fr.214.6, 9.
67. Malalas XV.14; Theophanes, *Chron*. AM5975 states that Pamprepius was not killed until 488; John of Nikiu 88.89; Dam. *Epit. Phot*. 242; Rhetorius 221.6-7, 223.10-19; Ps-Joshua the Stylite 15; Asmius (1913), 338-40; Cameron (1965), 499; Salamon (1996), 191-92 nn.137-39.
68. Marcellinus Comes sa.485; Theophanes, *Chron*. AM5975; cf. *Patr. Const*. II.227.
69. John of Antioch fr.306; Malalas XV.14; Theophanes, *Chron*. AM5975, 5976; Damascius fr.115a.
70. Damascius fr.303; John of Antioch fr.214.6.
71. Jordanes, *Rom*. 349ff; John of Antioch fr.214.10-11; Joshua the Stylite 17; Marcellinus Comes sa.488; Theodore Lector, *Epit*. 438; Dam. fr.303 = Photius, *Bibl*. 242; Victor Tonn. sa.488; Malalas 389; John of Nikiu 88.88-91; Theophanes, *Chron*. AM5976, 5980.
72. John of Antioch fr.214.10-11; *Patr. Const*. II.227, 281 cf. Theophanes, *Chron*. AM6020.
73. John of Antioch fr.306.
74. Procopius, *de Aed*. III.1.26; Stein (1949), 31.
75. Elton (2000), 402; Feld (2005); Twardowska (2006), 140; (2009), 165.
76. Evagrius III.6; Liberatus XVII.125; Michael the Syrian IX.6; Bar Hebraeus, *Chron. Ecc*. 39; Frend (1972), 181, 188; Blaudeau (2006), 219-20.
77. Ps-Zacharias V.9-10; Evagrius III.16; Malalas XV.6; Theodore Lector, *Epit*. 444; Theophanes, *Chron*. AM5982; *Synodicon Vetus* 105; *Laudatio S. Barnabae* 112; Cyril of Scythopolis, *V. Sabae* 32; John of Nikiu 8.63; *Chron. Iacobi. Edesseni* 235; Michael the Syrian IX.6; Agapius, *Kitab* 421; Schwark (1950), 53; Blaudeau (2006), 220-22; de Halleux (1963), 31-39.
78. Trombley (1994), I.81; Chuvin (2008), 118; Salamon (1996), 189-90.

Chapter 13: Zeno, Theoderic and the End of the Western Roman Empire

1. Heather (2013), 49.
2. John of Antioch fr.306; Malalas XV.14; Ps-Joshua the Stylite 15; Evagrius III.27; John of Nikiu 88.86; Theophanes, *Chron*. AM5976-5977.
3. Heather (1991), 304.
4. Jordanes, *Get*. 290; Heather (1991), 304.
5. John of Antioch fr.214.7; Zacharias, *HE* III.27.
6. Ennodius, *Pan*. 19.

7.   John of Antioch fr.214.4.

8.   John of Antioch fr.214.8-9; Marcellinus Comes sa.487; Procopius, *BG* I.1.9; Malalas XV.8; Theophanes, *Chron.* AM5977; Michael the Syrian IX.6; cf. Stein (1949), 39; Bury (1958), I.422 n.1.

9.   Ennodius, *Pan.* 14, 25; cf. *Vita Epiph.* 109; Jordanes, *Get.* 57.

10. Procopius, *BG* V.1.9-12; Evagrius III.27; Theophanes, *Chron.* AM5977; Jordanes, *Rom.* 348.

11. Heather (1991), 306.

12. Procopius, *BG* V.1.12; cf. Wolfram (1984), 279; Heather (1991), 306.

13. Heather (2013), 50.

14. *Anon. Val.* XI.49; Jordanes, *Get.* 290ff; Procopius, *BG* I.1.10-11; Theophanes, *Chron.* AM5977.

15. *Chronicon Gall. 511* n.649 sa.470, 471; Sidonius, *Ep.* III.9.

16. *CJ* I.11.8 is the last eastern law to record the western emperor, Anthemius.

17. Sidonius, *Ep.* I.9.1-7.

18. John of Antioch fr.207.

19. John of Antioch fr.207; Cassiodorus, *Chron.* 1289 sa.470; Paul the Deacon, *HR* XV.2.

20. Ennodius, *Vita Epiphanii*, 51-53, 60-68; Paul the Deacon, *HR* XV.203.

21. John of Antioch, fr.209.1-2; *Fast. Vind. Prior.* sa.472; *Pasch. Camp.* sa.472; Marcellinus Comes sa.472; Jordanes, *Get.* 236; *Rom.* 336; Procopius, *BV* I.7.1; Malalas XIV.45; *Chron. Gall. 511* no.650; Cassiodorus, *Chron.* sa.472; Victor Tonn. sa.473; Theophanes, *Chron.* AM5964; Evagrius, *HE* II.16.

22. Bury (1886), 508.

23. Ennodius, *Vita Epiphanius* 79; cf. *Vita Dan. Sty.* 35.

24. *RIC* X.422 nn.3,001-03; Olybrius' Milanese issues also featured a cross (*RIC* X.423 n.3,004).

25. John of Antioch fr.209.2; Cassiodorus, *Chron.* 1,293, sa.472; *Fast. Vind. Prior.* 607.

26. *Fast. Vind. Prior.* 608; Paul the Deacon, *HR* XV.5.

27. John of Antioch *fr.* 209.2; *Fast. Vind. Prior.* 609 has 22 October; *Pasch. camp.* has 2 November; cf. Cassiodorus, *Chron.* 1293; Ennodius, *Vita Epiphanii* 350.

28. Malalas XIV.45.

29. John of Antioch fr.209.2; Jordanes, *Get.* 239; Ennodius, *Vita Epiphanii* 79; Evagrius II.16; *Fast. Vind. Prior.* sa.473; *Pasch. camp.* sa.473; Marcellinus Comes sa.473.

30. Ennodius, *Vita Epiph.* 79; Haenel (1857), n.1,226 = *PL* 56, 896-98.

31. *RIC* X.424-26.

32. Jordanes, *Get.* 283-84; *Rom.* 347; Videmir the Younger may be the recipient of two letters from Bishop Ruricius of Limoges (*Ep.* II.61, 63); Mathisen (1990).

33. Malchus fr.10; Marcellinus Comes sa.474; Jordanes, *Get.* 239; *Rom.* 338 on Nepotianus being his father; *CJ* VI.61.5 shows Nepos in power in Dalmatia at least by 1 June 473; *Anon. Val.* 7.36; *Auct. Haun. ordo. post* sa.474; Marcellinus Comes sa.474; Evagrius II.16; John of Antioch fr.209.

34. This might fit in with Julius becoming known as 'Nepos' as that can be translated as 'nephew'. He also owed his position in Dalmatia due to being Marcellinus' nephew, although his father was called Nepotianus.

35. *RIC* X.426 n.3,111.

36. *Anon. Val.* 7.36; *Auct. Haun. ordo. post* sa.474; Marcellinus Comes sa.474; Evagrius II.16; John of Antioch fr.209; Glycerius being promoted to Bishop of Milan is a corruption of Ennodius, *Carm.* 82; cf. *CIL* V.11.67.5.

37. *Anon. Val.* 7.36; John f Antioch fr.209; *Fast. Vind. Prior.* sa.474; *Pasch.Camp.* sa.474; *Auct. Haun. ordo post* sa.474; Marcellinus Comes sa.475; Ennodius, *V. Epiph.* 80; Theophanes, *Chron.* AM5965

38. *RIC* X.461 nn.3,76668; Sidonius, *Ep.* V.16.1-2.

39. *Ennodius, Vita Epiph* 91; Sidonius, *Ep.* V.7.4.

40. *Anon. Val.* 7.36; *Fast. Vind. Prior.* sa.475; *Pasch. Camp.* sa.475; *Auct. Haun. ordo prior* sa.475; *Auct. Haun. ordo post* sa.475; Marcellinus Comes sa.475; Jordanes, *Get.* 241; *Rom.* 344; Evagrius, *HE* II.16.

41. *Anon. Val.* 8.38; Priscus fr.7-8, 12

42. Jordanes, *Get.* 241; *Rom.* 344; *Fast. Vind. Prior.* sa.475; *Pasch. Camp.* sa.475; *Auct. Haun. ordo prior* sa.475; *Auct. Haun. ordo post* sa.475; *Auct. Haun. ordo post marg.* sa.475; Marcellinus Comes sa.475; *Anon. Val.* 7.36, 8.37; Cassiodorus, *Chron.* sa.475; Evagrius II.16; Theophanes, *Chron.* AM5965; Procopius, *BG* I.1.2.

43. *RIC* X.438-41.

44. Heather (2006), 428.

45. Procopius, *BG* I.1.6; Malchus fr.14; Jordanes, *Get.* 242, *Rom.* 344; Ennodius, *V. Epiph.* 95ff; *Fast. Vind. Prior.* sa.476; *Pasch. Camp.* sa.476; *Auct. Haun. ordo prior* sa.476; *Auct. Haun. ordo post* sa.476.

46. Ennodius, *V. Epiph.* 95-100; *Anon. Val.* 8.37; Eugippius, *Ep. ad Pasc.* 8; Jordanes, *Get.* 242; Procopius, *BG* I.1.5; *Fast. Vind. Prior.* sa.476; *Auct. Haun. ordo prior* sa.476; *Auct. Haun. ordo post* sa.476; *Auct. Haun. ordo post marg.* sa.476; Cassiodorus, *Chron.* sa.476; Marcellinus Comes sa.476.

47. Heather (2006), 428.

48. Jordanes, *Get.* 241-42; *Rom.* 344; Procopius, *BG* I.1.7; Theophanes, *Chron.* AM5965; *Anon. Val.* 8.38; Marcellinus Comes sa.476; Cassiodorus, *Variae* III.35 suggests Romulus was still there in 511.

49. Heather (2013), xvi.

50. Jordanes, *Rom.* 344; *Get.* 242; Marcellinus Comes sa.476; John of Antioch fr.209.1.

51. *Anon. Val.* 10.45; John of Antioch fr.209.1; *Suda* K393; Eugippius, *V. Sev.* 44.4; Reynolds and Lopez (1946); MacBain (1983); Maenchen-Helfen (1973), 388 n.104, doubts the connection between Odoacer and Edeco.

52. Edeco disappears after his Scirians suffered a second Gothic defeat – Jordanes, *Get.* 277.

53. Gregory of Tours, *HF* II.18-19.

54. Eugippius, *V. Sev.* 6.6, 7.1; *Anon. Val.* 10.45-46.

55. John of Antioch fr.209.1; Procopius, *BG* I.1.6.
56. Malchus fr.14.
57. Malchus fr.14.
58. Stein (1949), 46-49; Thompson (1982), 66-68; O'Flynn (1983), 139-40; Henning (1999), 206-07; Kent (1966), 146-50; (1994), 207, 215-19.
59. Chastagnol (1966), 55 n.123, thought none were recognized, while Stein (1949), 47 n.1, Jones (1962), 126, and Cameron and Schauer (1982), 131-33, thought some were; O'Flynn (1983), 141-42.
60. Marcellinus Comes sa.480; *Auct. Haun. ordo prior* sa.480; *Anon. Val.* VII.36; Malchus = Photius, *Bibl.* 78.
61. Cassiodorus, *Chron.* sa.481; *Fast. Vind. Prior.* sa.482; *Auct. Haun. ordo prior* sa.482.
62. Theodore Lector, *Epit.* 420 = Theophanes, *Chron.* AM5971; John of Antioch fr.214.2.
63. Eugippus, *V. Sev.* 44.4.
64. Eugippus, *V. Sev.* 44.4.
65. Paul the Deacon, *Hist. Lang.* I.19.
66. John of Antioch fr.306; Eugippius, *V. Sev.* 44.4-5; Cassiodorus, *Chron.* 1,316; *Excerpta Valesiana* X.48; Procopius, *BG* III.2.1-2; McCormick (1977), 216-22; Heather (1991), 307; Wolfram (2003), 319.
67. Burns (1973); Heather (1991), 298, 302; Schmidt (1904), I.152; Bury (1923), I.422.
68. O'Flynn (1983), 14445; Wolfram (2003), 320-22.
69. Heather (2013), 418 n.38.
70. Eugippius, *V. Sev.* 44.4
71. Jordanes, *Get.* 292; *Rom.* 349; *Anon. Val.* XI.49; Ennodius, *Pan.* 26ff; *V. Epiph.* 109; Marcellinus Comes sa.488; *Chron. Gall. 511* no.670; Paul the Deacon, *HR* XV.15; Procopius, *BG* I.1.12.
72. Procopius *BG* I.1.13
73. *Fast. Vind. Prior.* sa.490.
74. *Anon. Val.* XI.50; Cassiodorus, *Chron.*sa.489; Ennodius, *Pan.* 39ff.
75. *Anon. Val.* XI.50-51.
76. *Anon. Val.* XI.51-52; Ennodius, *V. Epiph.* 111; Wolfram (1990), 281.
77. Wolfram (1990), 281.
78. Wolfram (1990), 282.
79. *Anon. Val.* XI.53; *Auct. Prosp. haun.* sa.491; Cassiodorus, *Chron.* sa.490; Jordanes, *Get.* 292ff; Ennodius, *V. Epiph.* 109-11, 127; *Pan.* 36-47.
80. Procopius, *BG* I.1.15-24; Cassiodorus, *Chron.* sa.490.
81. Wolfram (1990), 282.
82. Ennodius, *V. Epiph.*118-19.
83. *Fast. Vind. Prior.* sa.493; *Auct. Prosp. Haun.* sa.493; Ennodius, *Pan.* 55.
84. John of Antioch fr.214a; Wolfram (1990), 282; (2003), 322-25; Kent (1994), 213-14, and Grierson and Blackburn (2007), 28, on Odoacer's late coins.

85. *Anon. Val.* 11.55; *Fast. Vind. Prior.* sa.493; *Auct. Haun.* sa.493; *Chron. Gall. 511* no.670 sa.493; Marcellinus Comes sa.489; Cassiodorus, *Chron.* sa.493; Jordanes, *Get.* 295; *Rom.* 349; Procopius, *BG* I.1.2-25; John of Antioch fr.214a; Theophanes, *Chron.* AM5977.

86. *Anon. Val.* XI.55; *Liber pontificalis ecclesiae Ravennatis* 39.

87. John of Antioch fr.214a.

88. Wolfram (1990), 283.

89. John of Antioch fr. 214a; Ennodius, *Pan.* 25, 50-52; Cassiodorus, *Chron.* sa.493.

90. John of Antioch fr.214a; *Anon. Val.* II.54.

91. Theophanes, *Chron.* AM5977; cf. Zacharias, *HE* IX.18; *Anon. Val.* XII.61.

92. Zacharias, *HE* VII.12; *Anon. Val.* XI.60; Theophanes, *Chron.* AM5991, 5993; Ennodius, *Pan.* 80; *Ep.* IX.30.

93. Jones (1962); Moorhead (1984), 263-64; Wolfram (1990), 284-90; Heather (1991), 308.

94. Prostko-Prostynski (1994), 103-29; cf. Moorhead (1984), 263-64; Heather (1991), 307-08.

95. Wolfram (1990), 285.

96. *Anon. Val.* XI.53, XII.64; Gelasius, *Ep.*12; Procopius, *BG* I.1.26; Evagrius, *HE* III.27; Theodore Lector, *Epit.* 461; Theophanes, *Chron.* AM5992; Chastagnol (1966), 80; O'Flynn (1983), 146; Prostko-Prostynski (1994), 131-49, on relations between Theoderic and Anastasius.

97. *Anon. Val.* XII.59, 16.94-95; Procopius, *BG* I.1.31, 39.

98. The date and identity of this delegation is not agreed. While Malchus fr.3 and Victor of Vita I.51 record Severus as the Roman ambassador, Paul the Deacon XV.7 records Orestes the patrician negotiating with Geiseric; Feld (2005), 328; Merrils and Miles (2010), 131.

99. Barth (1894), 23 n.3; Courtois (1955), 54 n.231; Moorhead (1992), 23 n.51; Wolfram (1997), 173, *contra* Errington (1983), 88 n.12, usng Malchus fr.5 and followed by Merrils and Miles (2010), 123, and Kosinski (2010), 118-19; Procopius, *BV* I.7.18-25; Victor of Vita I.51 links the treaty to Geiseric's death.

100. Merrils and Miles (2010), 123.

101. Victor of Vita I.51; Lancel (2002), 121 n.111; Feld (2005), 326; Strzelczyk (2005), 144.

102. Malchus fr.17; Victor of Vita II.1-2; Courtois (1954), 21-22, 58 n.285; Lancel (2002), 295 n.119, 296 n.124, although this is doubted by Kosinski (2010), 120; Strzelczyk (2005), 147, on the dates of Eugenius.

103. Victor of Vita II.3-5, III.3-14; Courtois (1955), 293-94; Lancel (2002), 296 n.123; Strzelczyk (2005), 147; Merrils and Miles (2010), 189.

104. Victor of Vita III.2, III.32; Paul the Deacon XV.19; Schwartz (1934), 204 n.1; Lancel (2002), 324 nn.430-31; Strzelcyzk (2005), 149.

105. Victor of Vita II.1-2.

106. *Laterculus regnum Vandalorum* 8; Courtois (1955), 300; Strzelczyk (2005), 157.

107. Dracontius, *Satisfactio* 93-94; Brozek (1980), 553-62; Feld (2005), 330; Strzelczyk (2005), 274; Clover (1989), 62-66, suggests that it could be Zeno or Anastasius; Merrills and Miles (2010), 220, suggest Huneric.

108. Merrills and Miles (2010), 123.

Chapter 14: Demonic Possession, Vivisepulture and a Woman Scorned

1. Marcellinus Comes sa.491; Victor Tonn. sa.491; *Chron. Pasch.* sa.491; Malalas 391; Zacharius VI.6; VII.1; Stein (1949), II.76 n.3, on the date.

2. Malalas XV.16 on 60 years 9 months; Malalas *slav.* 113 on 65 years 9 months; Michael the Syrian IX.6 on 60 years.

3. Malalas XV.16; Evagrius III.29; Theophanes, *Chron.* AM5983; Haarer (2006), 21 n.52; Leszka (2010), 657, is sceptical; Conrad (2000).

4. Conrad (2000), 61, on Jeanselme (1924).

5. Jeanselme (1924), 226-28.

6. Conrad (2000), 62; Padosch, Lachenmeier and Kroner (2006).

7. Conrad (2000), 62; [Hippocrates], *De morbo sacro* I.1-4; Temkin (1971), 3-27, on pre-Hippocratic beliefs on epilepsy; Stol (1993), 16-19, on how in ancient Babylonia epilepsy was attributed to a specific demon.

8. Galen, *de locis affectis* III.9-11.

9. Matthew 17:14-10; Mark 9:14-29; Luke 9:37-43.

10. Origen, *Comm. Matt.* XIII.3-7.

11. Athanasius, *Vita sancti Antonii* XXXVI.1-2.

12. Smith (1965), 403-26.

13. Conrad (2000), 66-67.

14. Malalas XVI.9; Evagrius I.19, II.15, III.26, 27, 29, 37; Allen (1988); Laniado (1991), 152; Conrad (2000), 68.

15. Evagrius III.29; Brooks (1893), 216; Allen (1981), 7-8, 120, 121, 140; Conrad (2000), 69.

16. Theophanes, *Chron.* AM5938.

17. Allen (1981), 9, 106, 139; Conrad, in Cameron and Conrad (1991), 334-36; Conrad (1996), 170-72; Conrad (2000), 69-70.

18. Cedrenus I.622.7-23; Zonaras XIV.2.

19. Theodore Lector, *Epit.* 441; Theophanes, *Chron.* AM5982; Suda Φ136; Marcellinus Comes sa.491.

20. John Lydus, *de Mag.* III.45.

21. Conrad (2000), 73; Nikephoros Kall. XVI.22-24.

22. Conrad (2000), 74.

23. Malalas 398.11-399.6, 391.1-4; *Chron. Pasch.* I.607.3-4; Malchus fr.85.9; John of Nikiu 89.97.

24. Conrad (2000), 75; Agathias IV.29.2; Agapius, *Kitab* 317.7-8; *Oracle of Baalbek* 19:159-62.

25. Evagrius III.14; Liberatus XVII; Frend (1972), 143-83.

26. Zacharias VI.6; Ps-Dionysius I.248.22-24; Michael the Syrian II.149; *Chron. Min.* II.138: 27-28, II.218: 9-15.

27. Malchus fr.83, 85; John Lydus, *de mag.* III.45; Evagrius III.1.29; Theophanes, *Chron.* AM5983; Cedrenus, I.615, 11-17; Zonaras XIV.2; Nikephoros Kall. XVI.1.24; cf. Laniado (1991).

28. Constantine VII, *de cer.* I.92; Conrad (2000), 77.

29. Conrad (2000), 77.

30. Conrad (2000), 81.

31. Malalas XV.12; Procopius, *de Aed.* III.6.23; *AE* (1911), 90; (1928), 83; John of Antioch fr.214.7; *Anon. Val.* XI.53; Theophanes, *Chron.* AM5983; *CIL* V.7531, XII.2058; *P. Flor.* I.94.

32. Procopius, *de Aed.* III.6.23; *PLRE* III.1,060-1,063 'Sittas'.

33. Theophanes, *Chron.* AM5983; cf. Evagrius III.29.

34. Zeno reputedly asked an astrologer, Maurianus, about the future of the imperial throne. The astrologer replied that his successor would be a *silentarius*. Zeno may also have been looking to get rid of another *silentarius*, Pelagius, an outspoken critic of Zeno. He was executed for plotting to accede to the throne and for being a pagan – Marcellinus Comes sa.490; John of Nikiu 88.93-94; *Chron. Pasch.* sa.490; Theophanes, *Chron.* AM5982-5983; Michael the Syrian IX.6; Zonaras XIV.2; Cedrenus I.621.

35. Constantine VII, *de cer.* I.92; Conrad (2000), 77.

36. Zosimus IV.57.4.

37. Constantine VII, *de caer.* I.92; Theodore Lector, *Epit.* 446; *Anon. Val.* XII.56; Zacharius, *HE* VII.1; Marcellinus Comes sa.491; Jordanes, *Rom.* 354; *Chron. Pasch.* sa.491; Evagrius, III.29, 32; Victor Tonn. sa.491; Theophanes, *Chron.* AM5983; Zonaras XIV.3.1.

38. Zacharius, *HE* VII.13; Malalas 392; Evagrius, *HE* III.29; Zonaras XIV.3.10; Theophanes, *Chron.* AM5983.

39. Constantine VII, *de cer.* I.92; Conrad (2000), 77.

40. *Suda* Λ646; Theophanes, *Chron.* AM5983.

41. Zacharias VII.1.

42. Evagrius III.29.

43. Marcellinus Comes sa.515; Victor Tonn. sa.515; Theophanes, *Chron.* AM6008; Malalas XIV.22 lists Anastasius dying at 90 years and 5 months.

44. John of Antioch fr.214b; Theophanes, *Chron.* AM5984; Zonaras XIV.3.20.

45. John of Antioch fr.214b; cf. Procopius, *de Aed.* I.8.2-3.

46. Malalas XVI.3 suggests that there were Scythians and Bessians, as well as Goths, in this imperial army, perhaps reflecting its leadership – John the Hunchback was a Thracian and Diogenianus was a relative of Ariadne, with all the Thraco-Bessian connotations. It could have involved the field army of Thrace.

47. Malalas XVI.3; Theophanes, *Chron.* AM5985; John of Antioch fr.214b; Jordanes, *Rom.* 355; Marcellinus Comes sa.492; Michael the Syrian IX.11.

48. Theophanes, *Chron*. AM5986; John of Antioch fr.214b.5; Marcellinus Comes sa.492; Stein (1959), II.83 n.1.

49. Theophanes, *Chron*. AM5986; the presence of a Claudiopolis in both Phyrgia near Cotyaeum and in Cilicia raises the potential for chronological and geographical issues with this second battle.

50. Ammianus XIV.2.2-3; Philostorgius XI.8; John of Antioch fr.214.2-4.

51. Durliat and Guillou (1984).

52. Priscian, *Pan*. II.103-17; Theophanes, *Chron*. AM5987, on Selinus as an important Isaurian supply centre.

53. Evagrius, *HE* III.35; Marcellinus Comes sa.497; Cedrenus I.627; John of Antioch fr.214b; Theophanes, *Chron*. AM5987, 5988; Victor Tonn. sa.495; Theodore Lector, *Epit*. 449.

54. Marcellinus Comes sa.498; Evagrius, *HE* III.35; Theophanes, *Chron*. AM5987-5988; for their Isaurian victories, John the Scythian and John the Hunchback were awarded consulships in 498 and 499 respectively.

55. Theophanes, *Chron*. AM5988; Jordanes, *Rom*. 355; Priscian, *Pan*. II.83; cf. Stein (1959), II.84 n.2.

56. Lenski (1999), 429; Shaw (1990), 255-59.

57. Justinian, *Nov.* 24-30; cf. Jones (1964), 280-83.

58. Hild and Hellenkemper (1990), 42.

59. Justinian, *Nov.* 145 *praef.*, 1; cf. Jones (1964), 294.

60. cf. Justinian, *Nov.* 8.12-13, 128.21, 134.2; cf. Whittaker (1983).

61. Teall (1965); Elton (2000a); Mango (1966).

62. *Suda* H465, B579; Minor (1979), 127; Shaw (1990), 259.

63. Lenski (1999), 430 n.87; Foss (1975), 729-30.

64. Lenski (1999), 430.

65. Malchus fr.8; Malalas XIV.3.

66. Joshua the Stylite 12-14; cf. Evagrius III.29.

Conclusions: The Paradoxes of Zeno *Augustus*

1. Russell (1903), 347.

Appendix: The 'Fatal Throw' – Zeno's Game of Τάβλη

1. Austin (1934a), 205.

2. *AP* IX.482; Austin (1934a), 202; Becq de Fouquieres (1863), 371-83.

3. Austin (1934a), 202; Austin (1934b); (1935).

4. Plutarch, *Pompey* 20; Suetonius, *Divi Iulii* 33.

5. Matthew 27:35.

6. Faris (2012).

7. Suetonius, *Claudius* V.33.

8. Isidore, *Orig*. XVIII.60; Austin (1934a), 202.

9. cf. Sidonius, *Ep*. I.2; II.9.4; V.17.6.

10. Austin (1934a), 205.

Bibliography

Abbreviations

ACO	*Acta Conciliorum Oecumenicorum*
AE	*L'Année épigraphique*
Anon. Val	*Anonymous Valesianus*
CIG	*Corpus Inscriptionum Graecarum*
CIL	*Corpus Inscriptionum Latinarum*
CJ	*Codex Iustinianus*
CTh	*Codex Theodosianus*
ILS	*Inscriptiones Latinae Selectae*
ND	*Notitia Dignitatum*
NJ	*Novels of Justinian*
P. Amh.	*The Amherst Papyri*
P. Flor.	*Papiri Fiorentini*
P.Oxy	*The Oxyrhynchus Papyri*
Pan. Lat.	*Panegyrici Latini*
PLRE	*Prosopography of the Late Roman Empire*
RIC	*Roman Imperial Coinage*
SHA	*Scriptores Historiae Augustae*

Primary

Abu' l-Fath, *Kitab al-Tarikh* (Stenhouse, P., trans., 1985)

Acta Pauli et Theclae (Eliott, J.K., trans., 1993)

Acta synodorum habitarum Romae (MGH edition, Mommsen, T., 1894)

Agapius, *Kitab al-Unvan* (Vasiliev, A.A., trans., 1910-12)

Agathias, *De imperio et rebus gestis Iustiniani* (Frendo, J.D., trans., 1975)

Ammianus Marcellinus (Rolfe, J.C., trans., Loeb Classical Library, 1939-50; Hamilton, W., trans., Penguin Classics, 1986)

Anna Comnena, *Alexiad* (Sewter, E.R.A., trans., Penguin, 2009)

Anonymus Banduri, see *Patria of Constantinople*

Anonymus Valesianus (Gardthausen, V., trans., Teubner, 1874)

Appian, *Roman History* (White, H., trans., Loeb Classical Library, 1913; Gabba, E., trans., 1958-70)

Appian, *The Civil Wars* (Carter, J., trans., Penguin Classics, 1996)

Athanasius, *Against the Pagans* (Thomson, R.W., trans., 1971)

Athanasius, *Festal Index* (Payne-Smith, J., trans., 1892)

Athanasius, *Festal Letters* (Payne-Smith, R., and Robertson, A., trans., *NPNF*, 1891)

Athanasius, *Life of Antony* (White, C., trans., 1998)

Auctarii Hauniensis, see *Consularia Italica*

Aurelius Victor, *de Caesaribus* (Bird, H.W., trans., Translated Texts for Historians, 1994)

Bar Hebraeus (Wallis Budge, E.A., trans., 1932)

Basil of Caesarea, *Letters* (Deferrari, R.J., trans., Loeb Classical Library, 1930)

Callinicus, *Vita S. Hypatii* (Bartelink, G.J.M., trans., 1971)

Candidus (Blockley, R.C., trans., *The Fragmentary Classicising Historians of the Later Roman Empire*, 1981)

Cassiodorus, *Chronica* (Mommsen, T., edition, 1894)

Cassiodorus, *Variae* (Barnish, S.J.B, trans., Translated Texts for Historians, 1992)

Cassius Dio, *Historia Romana* (Cary, E., trans., Loeb Classical Library, 1914-27)

Cedrenus, *Historiarium Compendium* (Bekker, I., edition, 1838)

Chronica Gallica 452 (Burgess, R.W., trans., 2001)

Chronica Gallica 511 (Burgess, R.W., trans., 2001)

Chronica Minora (Mommsen, T., edition, Teubner, 1892)

Chronicle of Arbela (Kroll, T., trans., 1985)

Chronicle of Jacob of Edessa (Brooks, E.W., and Chabot, J-B., trans., 1903)

Chronicle of Zuqnin/Pseudo-Dionysius of Tel-Mahre, *Chronicle* (Witakowski, W., trans., 1997)

Chronicon ad annum Christi 1234 pertinens (Chabot, J-B., trans., 1920)

Chronicon Edessenum (Brooks, E.W., and Chabot, J-B., trans., 1903)

Chronicon Paschale (Whitby, M., and Whitby, M., trans., Translated Texts for Historians, 1989)

Cicero, *Letters to Atticus* (Winstedt, B.O., trans., Loeb Classical Library, 1912)

Cicero, *Letters to Friends* (Shackleton Bailey, D.R., trans., Loeb Classical Library, 2001)

Claudian, *In Eutropium* (Platnauer, M., trans., Loeb Classical Library, 1922)

Collectio Avellana (Guenther, O., edition, *CSEL*, 1895; Coleman-Norton, P.R., trans., 1966)

Constantine VII Porphyrogenitus, *De Administrando Imperio* (Jenkins, R.J.H., trans., 1967)

Constantine VII Porphyrogenitus, *De Caerimoniis* (Reiske, J.J., trans., 1828)

Consularia Constantinopolitana (Burgess, R.W., trans., 1993)

Consularia Italica (Mommsen, T., edition, 1892)

Continuatio Prosperi Hauniensis (Mommsen, T., edition, 1892)

Cyril of Scythopolis, *Vita S. Euthymii* (Price, R.M., trans., 1991)

Cyril of Scythopolis, *Vita S. Sabae* (Price, R.M., trans., 1991)

Damascius (Sambursky, S., trans., 1971)

Diodorus Siculus (Geer, R.M., trans., Loeb Classical Library, 1947)

Diogenes Laërtius, *Lives and Opinions of Eminent Philosophers* (Hicks, R.D., trans., Loeb Classical Library, 1925)

Dracontius, *Satisfactio* (Vollmer, F., edition, 1905)

Elishe, *History of Vardan and the Armenian War* (Thomson, R.W., trans., 1982)

Encomium of Saint Menas (Drescher, J., trans., 1942)

Ennodius, *Carmina* (Vogel, F., edition, 1885)

Ennodius, *Panegyricus dictus Theoderico regi* (Vogel, F., edition, 1885)

Ennodius, *Vita Epiphanii* (Cook, G.M., trans., 1942)

Eugippius, *Letter to Paschasius* (Robinson, G.W., trans., 1914)

Eugippius, *Vita S. Severini* (Butler, L., trans., 1965)

Eulogius of Alexandria (= Photius, Bibl. 230) (Henry, R., trans., 1967)

Eunapius, *Historiarum Fragmenta* (Blockley, R.C., trans., *The Fragmentary Classicising Historians of the Later Roman Empire*, 1981)

Eutropius, *Breviarium ab urbe condita* (Bird, H.W., trans., Translated Texts for Historians, 1993)

Eutychius, *Annals* (Breydy, M., trans., 1985)

Evagrius Scholasticus, *Historia Ecclesiastica* (Whitby, M., trans., Translated Texts for Historians, 2000)

Excerpta Valesiana (Rolfe, R.C., trans., Loeb Classical Library, 1939)

Expositio totius mundi et gentium (Rouge, J., trans., 1966)

Fasti Vindobonenses priores (Mommsen, T., edition, 1892

Festus, *Breviarium* (Eadie, J.W., trans., 1967)

Frontinus, *Strategems* (Bennett, C.E., trans., Loeb Classical Library, 1925)

Galen, *de locis affectis* (Siegel, R.E., trans., 1976)

Gelasius, *Letters* (Migne, J.P., edition, 1862)

Georgian Chronicle (Bedrosian, R., trans., 1991)

Gesta de nomine Acacii (Geunther, O., edition, 1895)

Gregory of Tours, *Historia Francorum* (Thorpe, L., trans., Penguin Classics, 1974)

Herodotus, *Histories* (de Selincourt, A., and Marincola, J., trans., 2003)

Himerius, *Orationes* (Colonna, A., trans., 1951)

[Hippocrates], On the Sacred Disease (DeBevoise, M.B. trans., 1999)

Hydatius, *Chronicle* (Burgess, R.W., trans., 1993)

Jacob of Sarug, *Letters* (Olinder, G., trans., 1939)

Jerome, *Epistulae* (Mierow, C.C., trans., 1963)

John Chrysostom, *On the Priesthood, Ascetic Treatises, Select Homilies and Letters* (Stephens, W.R.W., Brandram, T.P., and Blackburn, R., trans., 1889)

John Diakrinomenus (Hansen, G.C., edition, 1971

John Lydus, *De Magistratibus reipublicae Romanae* (Carney, J.F., trans., 1971)

John Malalas, *Chronographia* (Jeffreys, E., Jeffreys, M., and Scott, R., trans., 1986)

John Malalas, *Excerpta de Insidiis* (de Boor, C., trans., 1905)

John Moschus, *Pratum Spirituale* (Wortley, J., trans., 2001)

John Moschus, *Pratum Spirtuale* (*PG* LXXXVII, III.2851-3112)

John of Antioch (Mariev, S., trans., 2008)

John of Ephesus, *Historia Ecclesiastica* (Payne-Smith, R., trans., 1860)

John of Nikiu, *Chronicle* (Charles, R.H., trans., 1916)

John Rufus, *de obitu Theodosii* (Horn, C.B., and Phenix, R.R., trans., 2008)

John Rufus, *Plerophoriae* (Nau, F., trans., 1912)

John Rufus, *Vita Petri Iberi* (Horn, C.B., and Phenix, R.R., trans., 2008)

Jordanes, *Getica* (Mierow, C.C., trans., 1915)

Jordanes, *Romana* (Mommsen, T., edition, Teubner, 1882)

Josephus, *Antiquitates Judaicae* (Whiston, W., trans., 1987)

Josephus, *Bellum Judaicum* (Whiston, W., trans., 1987)

Joshua the Stylite, *Chronicle* (Trombley, F.R., and Watt, J.W., trans., 2000)

Lactantius, *De Mortibus Persecutorum* (Creed, J.L., trans., 1984)

Laterculus Regum Vandalorum et Alanorum (Mommsen, T., edition, 1898)

Laudatio S. Barnabae (Kollmann, B., trans., 2007)

Lazar P'arpets'i, *The History of Lazar P'arpets'i* (Thomson, R.W., trans., 1991)

Leo, *Letters* (da Silva-Tarouca, C., trans., 1932)

Libanius, *Epistulae* (Norman, A.F., trans., Loeb Classical Library, 1992)

Liber Pontificalis (Davis, R., trans., 1989)

Life of Hilaria (Wensinck, A.J., edition, 1913)

Life of Timothy Ailouros (Evelyn-White, H.G., trans., 1926)

Livy, *Ab Urbe Condita* (de Selincourt, A., trans., Penguin Classics, 1965)

Lucian, *Icaromenippus* (Harmon, A.M., trans., Loeb Classical Library, 1915)

Malchus, *Historia* (Blockley, R.C., trans., *The Fragmentary Classicising Historians of the Later Roman Empire*, 1981)

Marcellinus Comes, *Chronicon* (Croke, B., trans., 1995)

Marinus, *Vita Procli* (Rita Masullo, R., trans., 1985)

Michael Psellus, *Historia Syntomos* (Aerts, W.J., trans., 1990)

Michael the Syrian, *Chronicle* (Palmer, A., trans., Translated Texts for Historians, 1993)

Miracles of Thecla (Dagron, G., trans., 1978)

Moses Kalankatuyk, *History of the Caucasian Albanians* (Dowsett, C.J.F., trans., 1967)

Movses Khorenatsi, *History of Armenia* (Thomson, R.W., trans., 2006)

Narratio de rebus Armeniae (Garitte, G., trans., 1952)

New Chronicle (Adler, E-A., and Séligsohn, E., trans., 1903)

Nikephoros, *Short History* (Mango, C., trans., 1990)

Notitia Dignitatum (Jones, A.H.M., trans., 1964)

Olympiodorus (Blockley, R.C., trans., *The Fragmentary Classicising Historians of the Later Roman Empire*, 1981)

Optatus Milevitanus, *Against Parmenian* (Edwards, M., trans., Translated Texts for Historians, 1998)

Oracle of Baalbek (Alexander, P.J., trans., 1967)

Orientus, *Commonitorium* (Tobin, M.D., trans., 1945)

Orosius, *Historiae adversum paganos* (Deferrari, R.J., trans., 1964)

Palladius, *Dialogus de vita S. Joannis Chrysostomi* (Meyer, R.T., trans., 1985)

Panegyrici Latini (Mynors, R.A.B., Nixon, C.E.V., and Rodgers, B.S., trans., 1994)

Parastaseis syntomoi chronikai (Cameron, A., and Herrin, J., trans., 1984)

Paschale Campanum (Mommsen, T., edition, 1892)

Patria of Constantinople (Preger, T., edition, 1907)

Paul the Deacon, *Historia Langobardorum* (Foulke, W.D., trans., 1906)

Paul the Deacon, *Historia Romana* (Crivellucci, A., trans., 1914)

Philostorgius, *Historia Ecclesiastica* (Amidon, P.R., trans., 2007)

Pliny the Elder, *Natural History* (Bostock, J., and Riley, H.T., trans., 1855)

Plutarch, *Lives* (Perrin, B., trans., Loeb Classical Library, 1923)

Priscian of Caesarea, *Panegyricus* (Coyne, P., trans., 1991)

Priscus (Blockley, R.C., trans., *The Fragmentary Classicising Historians of the Later Roman Empire*, 1981; Given, J., trans., 2014)

Procopius, *Anecdota* (Williamson, G.A., trans., Penguin Classics, 1967)

Procopius, *De Aedificiis* (Dewing, H.B., trans., Loeb Classical Library, 1940)

Procopius, *De Bello Gothico* (Dewing, H.B., trans., Loeb Classical Library, 1919)

Procopius, *De Bello Persico* (Dewing, H.B., trans., Loeb Classical Library, 1914)

Procopius, *De Bello Vandalico* (Dewing, H.B., trans., Loeb Classical Library, 1916)

Prosper Tiro, *Epitoma Chronicon* (Mommsen, T. edition, Teubner, 1892)

Ps-Joshua the Stylite (William, W., trans., 1882; Brooks, E.W., trans., 1924)

Res Gestae Divi Saporis (Frye, R.N., trans., 1984)

Rhetorius, *Astrological Compendium* (Holden, J.H., trans., 2009)

Sallust, *Historiae* (Rolfe, R.C., trans., Loeb Classical Library, 1931)

Scriptores Historiae Augustae (Magie, D., trans., Loeb Classical Library, 1921-32)

Sebeos, *History* (Thomson, R.W., trans., 1999)

Sidonius Apollinaris, *Carmina* (Anderson, W.B., trans., Loeb Classical Library, 1936)

Sidonius Apollinaris, *Epistulae* (Anderson, W.B., trans., Loeb Classical Library, 1936-65)

Socrates Scholasticus, *Historia Ecclesiastica* (Zenos, A.C., trans., 1890)

Sophronius, *Anacreontica* (Gigante, M., trans., 1957)

Sozomen, *Historia Ecclesiastica* (Hartranft, C.D., trans., 1890)

Stephanus of Byzantium, *Ethnika* (Billerbeck, M., trans., 2008-17)

Strabo, *Geography* (Jones, H.L., trans., Loeb Classical Library, 1917-32)

Suda, *Lexicon* (Adler, A., trans., 1928-38)

Symeon of Bet Arsham (Becker, A.H., trans., 2008)

Synaxaire arabe Jacobite (Basset, R., edition, 1909)

Synodicon Vetus (Duffy, J., and Parker, J., trans., 1979)

Tabari (Yar-Shater, E., trans., 1985-99)

Tacitus, *Annales* (Grant, M., trans., Penguin Classics, 1957)

Tacitus, *Histories* (Wellesley, K., trans., Penguin Classics, 1964)

Themistius, *Orationes* (Heather, P., and Moncur, D., trans., 2001, *Politics, Philosophy, and Empire in the Fourth Century: selected orations of Themistius*, 2001)

Theodore Lector, *Historia Ecclesiastica* (Hansen, G.C., trans., 1971)

Theodoret, *Epistulae* (Jackson, B., trans., 1892)

Theodoret, *Historia Ecclesiastica* (Jackson, B., trans., 1892)

Theodoret, *Historia Religiosa* (Canivet, P., and Leroy-Molinghen, A., trans., 1977-79)

Theodosius, *De Situ Terrae Sanctae* (Gildemeister, J., edition, 1882)

Theophanes, *Chronographia* (Mango, C., and Scott, R., trans., 1997)

Vegetius, *De rei militari* (Milner, N.P., trans., 1993; Reeve, M.D., trans., 2004)

Velleius Paterculus, *Roman History* (Shipley, F.W., trans., Loeb Classical Library, 1924)

Victor of Tunnuna, *Chroncion* (Martyn, J.R.C., trans., 2008)

Victor Vitensis, *Historia persecutionis Africanae* (Moorhead, J., trans., 1992)

Vita Cononis (Halkin, F., trans., 1985)

Vita Marcelli (Dagron, G., trans., 1968)

Vita S. Danielis Stylitae (Dawes, E., and Baynes, N.H., trans., 1948)

Vita Simeon Stylitae (Doran, R., trans., 1992)

William of Malmesbury, *Gesta Regnum Angolorum* (Mynors, R.A.B., Thomson, R.M., and Winterbottom, M., trans., 1998)

Xenophon, *Hellenica* (Cawkwell, G., trans., Penguin Classics, 1979)

Zacharias of Mytilene, *Chronographia* (Phenix, R.R., and Horn, C.B., trans., 2011)

Zacharias of Mytilene, *Historia ecclesiastica* (Brooks, E.W., trans., 1899)

Zacharias of Mytilene, *Vita Isaiae* (Brooks, E.W., trans., 1907)

Zacharias of Mytilene, *Vita Petri Iberi* (Lang, D.M., trans., 1956)

Zacharias of Mytilene, *Vita Severi* (Kugener, M-A., trans., 1903)

Zonaras, *Epitome* (Banchich, T.M., and Lane, E.N., trans., 2009)

Zosimus, *New History* (Ridley, R.T., trans., 1982)

Secondary

Adontz, N., *Armenia in the Period of Justinian: The Political Conditions Based on the Naxarar System* (Leuven, 1970)

Adshead, K., 'Procopius and the Samaritans', in Allen, P., and Jefferys, E. (eds), *The Sixth Century: End of Beginning?* (Brisbane, 1996), 35-41

Agile, D., 'Bar Hebraeus et son public a travers ses chroniques en syriaque et en arbe', *Le Museon* 118 (2005), 87-107

Alexander, P.J., *The Patriarch Nicephorus of Constantinople: Ecclesiastical Policy and Image Worship in the Byzantine State* (Oxford, 1958)

Alfoldi, G., *Noricum* (London, 1974)

Alfoldi-Rosenbaum, M., 'Matronianus, comes Isauriae: an inscription from the sea wall of Anemurium', *Phoenix* 26 (1972), 183-86

Allen, J., *Hostages and Hostage-Taking in the Roman Empire* (Cambridge, 2006)

Allen, P., 'Zachariah Scholasticus and the Historia Ecclesiastica of Evagrius Scholasticus', *JTS* 31 (1980), 471-88

Allen, P., *Evagrius Scholasticus the Church Historian* (Louvain, 1981)

Allen, P., 'An Early Epitomator of Josephus: Eustathius of Epiphaneia', *Byzantinische Zeitschrift* 81 (1988), 1-11

Allen, P., and Hayward, C.T.R., *Severus of Antioch* (London, 2004)

Allen, P., and Jefferys, E. (eds), *The Sixth Century: End of Beginning?* (Brisbane, 1996)

Alston, R., 'Managing the Frontiers: Supplying the Frontier Troops in the Sixth and Seventh Centuries', in Erdkamp, P. (ed.), *The Roman Army and the Economy* (Amsterdam, 2002), 398-419

Amelineau, E., 'Histoire des deux filles de l'empereur Zénon', *Proceedings of the Society of Biblical Archaeology* 10 (1888), 181-206

Amory, P., *People and Identity in Ostrogothic Italy, 489-554* (Cambridge, 1997)

Anderson, R.T., and Giles, T., *Tradition Kept: the Literature of the Samaritans* (Peabody, 2005)

Ando, C., *Imperial Ideology and Provincial Loyalty in the Roman Empire* (Berkeley, 2000)

Arnheim, M.T.W., *The Senatorial Aristocracy in the Later Roman Empire* (Oxford, 1972)

Arnold, J., *Theoderic and the Roman Imperial Restoration* (Cambridge, 2014)

Arslan, M., Bahce, N., and Bulut, E., 'Revolts in Isauria during the Hellenistic and Roman Periods in the Light of Ancient Sources', Uluslararasi Sempozyum: Gecmisten Gunumuze Bozkir (2016), 49-64

Ashbrook Harvey, S., *Asceticism and Society in Crisis: John of Ephesus and the Lives of the Eastern Saints* (Berkeley, 1990)

Asmus, R. 'Pamprepios, ein byzantinischer Gelehrter und Staatsmann des 5 Jahrhunderts', *Byzantinische Zeitschrift* 22 (1913), 320-347

Assemani, J.S., *Bibliotheca Orientalis Clementino-Vaticana* (Rome, 1721)

Athanassiadi, P., 'Persecution and Response in Late Paganism: The Evidence of Damascius', *JHS* 113 (1993), 1-29

Athanassiadi, P., *Damascius: The Philosophical History* (Athens, 1999)

Atiya, A.S., 'Peter III Mongus', in Atiya, A.S. (ed.), *The Coptic Encyclopaedia* (New York, 1991), 1,947-48

Atiya, A.S., (ed.), *The Coptic Encyclopaedia* (New York, 1991)

Atwater, R., 'Introduction', in Procopius, *Secret History* (New York, 1927), 1-20

Ausbüttel, F.M., 'Die Vertrage zwischen den Vandalen und Romern', *RomanoBarbarica* 11 (1991), 1-20

Austin, R.G., 'Zeno's Game of Τάβλη', *JHS* 54 (1934a), 202-05

Austin, R.G., 'Roman Board Games I', *G+R* 4 (1934b), 24-34

Austin, R.G., "Roman Board Games II', *G+R* 4 (1935), 76-82

Avi-Yonah, M., *The Jews of Palestine: A Political History from the Bar Kokhba War to the Arab Conquest* (Oxford, 1976)

Babcock, M.A., *The Night Attila Died: Solving the Murder of Attila the Hun* (New York, 2005)

Babessian, H., 'The Vartanantz Wars', *The Armenian Review* 18 (1965), 16-19

Bacht, H., 'Die Rolle des orientalischen Monchtums in den kirchenpolitischen Auseinandersetzungen um Chalkedon (431-519)', in Grillmeier, A., and Bacht, H. (eds), *Das Konzil von Chalkedon* (Wurzburg, 1953), 193-314

Back, M., 'Die sassanidischen Staatsinschriften : Studien zur Orthographie und Phonologie des Mittelpersischen der Inschriften, zusammen mit einem etymologischen Index des mittelpersischen Wortgutes und einem Textcorpus der behandelten Inschriften', *Acta Iranica* 18 (Leiden, 1978)

Bagnall, R.S., 'Landholding in Late Roman Egypt: the Distribution of Wealth', *JRS* 82 (1992), 128-49

Bagnall, R.S., *Reading Papyri*: *Writing History* (Ann Arbor, 1995)

Bagnall, R.S. (ed.), *Egypt in the Byzantine World 300-700* (Cambridge, 2007)

Bagnall, R.S., Cameron, A., Schwartz, S.R., and Worp, K.A., *Consuls of the Late Empire* (Atlanta, 1987)

Baldwin, B., 'Malchus of Philadelphia', *DOP* 31 (1971), 89-107

Baldwin, B., and Talbot, A-M., 'Cyril of Skythopolis', in Kazhdan, A.P. (ed.), *The Oxford Dictionary of Byzantium* (Oxford, 1991), 573

Banaji, J., *Agrarian Change in Late Antiquity: Gold, Labour and Aristocratic Dominance* (Oxford, 2001)

Banchich, T.M., and Lane, E.N., *The History of Zonaras: from Alexander Severus to the Death of Theodosius the Great* (London, 2009)

Barchiesi, A., and Scheidel, W. (eds), *The Oxford Handbook of Roman Studies* (Oxford, 2010)

Bardill, J., *Brickstamps of Constantinople* (Oxford, 2004)

Barnes, T.D., 'Patricii under Valentinian III', *Phoenix* 29 (1975), 155-70

Barnes, T.D., 'Structure and Chronology in Ammianus Book 14', *HSCP* 92 (1989), 413-22

Barnes, T.D., 'Statistics and the Conversion of the Roman Aristocracy', *JRS* 85 (1995), 188-212

Barnes, T.D., 'Emperors, Panegyrics, Prefects, Provinces and Palaces (284-317)', *JRA* 9 (1996), 534-52

Barnes, T.D., 'Foregrounding the Theodosian Code', *JRA* 14 (2001), 671-85

Barnish, S.J.B., 'Taxation, Land and Barbarian Settlement', *Papers of the British School at Rome* 54 (1986), 170-95

Barnwell, P.S., *Emperor, Prefects and Kings: The Roman West 395-565* (London, 1992)

Barnwell, P.S., 'Emperors, jurists and kings: law and custom in the late Roman and early medieval west', *Past and Present* 168 (2000), 6-29

Barth, W., *Kaiser Zeno* (Basle, 1894)

Barton, T., *Power and Knowledge: Astrology, Physiognomics, and Medicine under the Roman Empire* (Madison, 2002)

Batty, R., *Rome and the Nomads: The Pontic and Danubian Realm in Antiquity* (Oxford, 2007)

Bauml, F.H., and Birnbaum, M.D. (eds), *Attila: The Man and His Image* (Budapest, 1993)

Bayliss, R., *Provincial Cilicia and the Archaeology of Temple Conversion* (Oxford, 2004)

Baynes, N.H., 'The Vita S. Danielis Stylitae', *EHR* 40 (1925a), 397-402

Baynes, N.H., *The Byzantine Empire* (London, 1925b)

Baynes, N., *Three Byzantine Saints: Contemporary Bibliographies of St Daniel the Stylite, St Theodore of Sykeon and St John the Almsgiver* (London, 1948)

Baynes, N.H., *Byzantine Studies and Other Essays* (Westport, 1955)

Bean, G.E., and Mitford, T.B., 'Sites Old and New in Rough Cilicia', *Anatolian Studies* 12 (1962), 185-217.

Bean, G.E., and Mitford, T.B., 'Journeys in Rough Cilicia in 1962 and 1963', *Denkschriften der 6sterreichischen Akademie* 85 (Vienna, 1965)

Bean, G.E., and Mitford, T.B., 'Journeys in Rough Cilica 1964-1968, *Denkschriften der osterreichischen Akademie* 102 (Vienna, 1970)

Beaucamp, J., *Recherches Sur La Chronique de Jean Malalas I* (Paris, 2004)

Beaucamp, J., Bondoux, R-C., Lefort, J., Rouan-Auzépy, M-F., and Sorlin, I., 'La Chronique Pascale: Le temps approprié', in *Le temps chrétien de la fin de l'Antiquité au Moyen Age, IIIe-XIIIe siècles* (Paris, 1984), 451-68

Beck, H-G., *Kirche und theologische Literatur in byzantinischen Reich* (Munich, 1959)

Becker, A.H., *Fear of God and the Beginning of Wisdom: The School of Nisibis and Christian Scholastic Culture in Late Antique Mesopotamia* (Philadelphia, 2006)

Becker, A.H., *Sources for the History of the School of Nisibis* (Liverpool, 2008)

Becker, A.H., and Reed, A.Y., *The Ways That Never Parted: Jews and Christians in Late Antiquity and the Early Middle Ages* (Tübingen, 2003)

Becq de Fouquieres, L., *Les Jeux des Anciens* (Paris, 1863)

Belke, K., *Tabula Imperii Byzantini* (Vienna, 1984)

Bell, R.C., *Board and Table Games from Many Civilizations* (New York, 1979)

Berger, A., *Untersuchungen zu den Patria Konstantinupoleos* (Bonn, 1988)

Bersanetti, G.M., 'Basilisco e l'imperatore Leone I', *RPAA* 20 (1943/1944), 331-46

Bier, L., 'Notes on Mihr Narseh's Bridge near Firuzabad', *Archaologische Mitteilungen aus Iran* 19 (1986), 263-68.

Bierbrauer, V., 'Zur chronologischen, soziologischen und regionalen Gliederung des ostgermanischen Fundstoffs des 5. Jahrhunderts in Südosteuropa', in Wolfram, H., and Daim, F. (eds), *Die Vöiker an der mittleren und unteren Donauim fünften und sechsten Jahrhundert, Denkschriften der Östereichischen Akademie der Wissenschaften, phil.-hist. Kl. 145* (Vienna, 1980), 131-42.

Biers, W.R., *Art, Artefacts and Chronology in Classical Archaeology* (London, 1992)

Binns, J., *Cyril of Scytholpolis: The Lives of the Monks of Palestine* (Kalamazoo, 1991)

Biro, M., 'On the presence of the Huns in the Caucasus: To the chronology of the 'Ovs' raid mentioned in Ĵuanšer's Chronicle', *Acta Orientalia Academiae Scientiarum Hungaricae* 50 (1997), 53-60

Bivar, A.D.H., 'Cavalry Equipment and Tactics on the Euphrates Frontier', *DOP* 26 (1972), 271-91

Blaudeau, P., 'Le *cas Pierre Monge* au regard des sources monophysites d'origine palestinienne (fin Ve-début VIe s.)', *StPat* 37 (2001), 353-60

Blaudeau, P., '*Antagonismes* et convergences : regard sur les interprétations confessantes du gouvernement d'un usurpateur, Basilisque (475-476)', *Mediterraneo Antico* 6 (2003), 155-93

Blaudeau, P., *Alexandrie et Constantinople (451-491): De l'histoire a la geo-ecclesiologie* (Rome, 2006)

Blockley, R.C., *The Fragmentary Classicising Historians of the Later Roman Empire: Eunapius, Olympiodorus, Priscus and Malchus* (Liverpool, 1981)

Blockley, R.C., *The Fragmentary Classicising Historians of the Later Roman Empire: Eunapius, Olympiodorus, Priscus and Malchus; Text, Translation and Historiographical Notes* (Liverpool, 1983)

Blockley, R.C., *The History of Menander the Guardsman* (Liverpool, 1985a)

Blockley, R.C., Subsidies and Diplomacy: Rome and Persia in Late Antiquity', *Phoenix* 39 (1985b), 62-74

Blockley, R.C., 'The Division of Armenia Between the Romans and the Persians at the end of the Fourth Century AD', *Historia* 36 (1987), 222-34

Blockley, R.C., *Eastern Roman Foreign Policy: Formation and Conduct from Diocletian to Anastasius* (Leeds, 1992)

Blockley, R.C., 'The Development of Greek Historiography: Priscus, Malchus, Candidus', in Marasco, G. (ed.), *Greek and Roman Historiography in Late Antiquity: Fourth to Sixth Century AD* (Brill, 2003), 289-316

Boak, A.E.R., 'Imperial Coronation ceremonies of the Fifth and Sixth Centuries', *HSCP* 30 (1919), 37-47

Bodel, J., *Epigrahic Evidence: Ancient History from Inscriptions* (London, 2001)

Bona, I., *Das Hunnenreich* (Stuttgart, 1991)

Börm, H., '"Es war allerdings nicht so, dass sie es im Sinne eines Tributes erhielten, wie viele meinten...": Anlässe und Funktion der persischen Geldforderungen an die Römer (3. bis 6. Jh.)', *Historia* 57 (2008), 327-46

Börm, H., 'Justinians Triumph und Belisars Erniedrigung. Überlegungen zum Verhältnis zwischen Kaiser und Militär im späten Römischen Reich', *Chiron* 43 (2013), 63-91

Bowersock, G., Brown, P., and Grabar, O. (eds), *Late Antiquity: A Guide to the Postclassical World* (Cambridge, 1999)

Bowman, A.K., and Woolf, G. (eds), *Literacy and Power in the Ancient World* (Cambridge, 1994)

Braaten, C.E., 'Modern Interpretations of Nestorius', *Church History* 32 (1963), 251-67

Bradbury, S.A., 'Constantine and Anti-pagan Legislation in the Fourth Century', *CP* 89 (1994), 120-39

Bralewski, S., *Imperatorzy poznego cesarstwa rzymskiego wobec zgromadzen biskupow* (Lodz, 1997)

Brandes, W., 'Familienbände? Odoaker, Basiliskos und Harmatios', *Klio* 75 (1993), 407-437

Brandt H., *Gesellschaft und Wirtschaft Pamphyliens und Pisidiens im Altertum* (Bonn, 1992)

Braund, D., *Rome and the Friendly King: The Character of the Client Kingship* (London, 1984)

Brennan, P., 'The Last of the Romans: Roman Identity and the Roman Army in the Late Roman Near East', *MedArch* 11 (1998), 191-203

Brennecke, H.C., 'Chalkedonense und Henotikon Bemerkungen zum Prozeß der östlichen Rezeption der christologischen Formel von Chalkedon', in van Oort, J., and Roldanus, J. (eds), *Chalkedon: Geschichte und Aktualität : Studien zur Rezeption der christologischen Formel von Chalkedon* (Leuvain, 1997), 24-53

Breydy, M., *Etudes sur Sa'id ibn Batriq et ses sources* (Louvain, 1983)

Brodka, D., and Stachura, M. (eds), 'Continuity and Change. Studies in Late Antique Historiography', *Electrum* 13 (Kraków, 2007)

Brooks, E.W., 'The Emperor Zenon and the Isaurians', *EHR* 30 (1893), 209-38

Brooks, E.W., *The Sixth Book of the Select Letters of Severus Patriarch of Antioch in the Syriac Version of Athanasius of Nisibis* (Oxford, 1903)

Brooks, E.W., *A Collection of Letters of Severus of Antioch from Numerous Syriac Manuscripts* (Paris, 1919)

Brown, P.R.L., *Authority and the Sacred: Aspects of the Christianisation of the Roman World* (Cambridge, 1995)

Browning, R., 'Where was Attila's camp?', *JHS* 73 (1953), 143-45

Browning, R., and Kazhdan, A.P., 'Tomis', in Kazhdan, A.P. (ed.), *The Oxford Dictionary of Byzantium* (Oxford, 1991), 2,092

Brozek, M., 'Drakoncjusz – poeta w wiezieniu', *Meander* 35 (1980), 553-62

Bullogh, V.L., 'The Roman Empire vs Persia, 363-502: A Study of Successful Deterrence', *Journal of Conflict Resolution* 7 (1963), 55-68

Buresch, K., *Klaros. Untersuchungen zum Orakelwesen des spaten Altertums* (Leipzig, 1889)

Burgess, R.W., 'The accession of Marcian in the light of Chalcedonian Apologetic and Monophysite Polemic', *BZ* 86-87 (1993-94), 47-68

Burgess, W.D., 'The Isaurians in the Fifth Century AD', Unpublished Diss. (Madison, 1985)

Burgess, W.D., 'Isaurian Names and the Ethnic Identity of the Isaurians in Late Antiquity', *AncW* 21 (1990), 109-21

Burgess, W.D., 'Isaurian Factions in the Reign of Zeno the Isaurian', *Latomus* 51 (1992), 874-80

Burgess, W.D., 'Isauria and the Notitia Dignitatum', *Ancient World* 26 (1996), 79-88

Burns, T.S., 'The Battle of Adrianople: A Reconsideration', *Historia* 22 (1973), 336-45

Burns, T.S., 'Calculating Ostrogothic Population', *Acta Antiqua* 26 (1978), 457-63

Burns, T.S., *The History of the Ostrogoths* (Bloomington, 1984)

Bury, J.B., 'A Note on the Emperor Olybrius', *EHR* I (1886), 507-09

Bury, J.B., *History of the Later Roman Empire from the Death of Theodosius I to the Death of Justinian* (London, 1923/1958)

Buschhausen, H., *Die spätrömischen Metallscrinia und frühchristlichen Reliquiare* (Vienna, 1971)

Butcher, K., *Roman Syria and the Near East* (Los Angeles, 2003)

Cain, A., and Lenski, N. (eds), *The Power of Religion in Late Antiquity* (Aldershot, 2009)

Cameron, Alan, 'Wandering Poets: A Literary Movement in Byzantine Egypt', *Historia* 14 (1965), 470-509

Cameron, Alan, *Circus Factions: Blues and Greens at Rome and Byzantium* (Oxford, 1976)

Cameron, Alan, 'The Empress and the Poet: Paganism and Politics at the Court of Theodosius II', YCS 27 (1982), 217-89

Cameron, Alan, *The Last Pagans of Rome* (New York, 2001)

Cameron, Alan, 'Vergil illustrated between Pagans and Christians', *JRA* 17 (2004), 501-25

Cameron, Alan, 'Poets and Pagans in Byzantine Egypt', in Bagnall, R.S. (ed.), *Egypt in the Byzantine World 300-700* (Cambridge, 2007), 21-46

Cameron, A., Bagnall, R.S., Schwartz, S.R., and Worp, K.A., *Consuls of the Late Empire* (Atlanta, 1987)

Cameron, Alan, and Long, J., *Barbarians and Politics at the Court of Arcadius* (Oxford, 1993)

Cameron, Alan, and Schauer, D., 'The Last Consul; Basilius and his Diptych', *JRS* 72 (1982), 126-44

Cameron, Averil, *The Mediterranean World in Late Antiquity AD395-600* (London, 1993)

Cameron, Averil (ed.), *The Byzantine and Early Islamic Near East III: States, Resources and Armies* (Princeton, 1995)

Cameron, Averil, *Procopius and the Sixth Century* (London, 1996)

Cameron, Averil, *Fifty Years of Prosopography: The Later Roman Empire, Byzantium and Beyond* (Oxford, 2003)

Cameron, Averil, *The Mediterranean World in Late Antiquity AD395-700* (London, 2012)

Cameron, A., and Herrin, J., *Constantinople in the Early Eighth Century: The Parastaseis Syntomoi Chronikai: Introduction, Translation, and Commentary* (Leiden, 1984)

Cameron, Averil, and Garnsey, P. (eds), *The Cambridge Ancient History XIII: The Late Empire AD337-425* (Cambridge, 1998)

Cameron, A., Ward-Perkins, B., and Whitby, M. (eds), *The Cambridge Ancient History XIV: Late Antiquity: Empire and Successors AD425-600* (Cambridge, 2001)

Campbell, J.B., and Trittle, L.A., *The Oxford Handbook of Warfare in the Classical World* (Oxford, 2013)

Caner, D., *Wandering, Begging Monks: Spiritual Authority and the Promotion of Monasticism in Late Antiquity* (Berkeley, 2002)

Capizzi, C. *L'imperatore Anastasio I (491-518). Studio sulla sua vita, la sua opera e la sua personalita* (Rome, 1969)

Carcione, F., *Liberato di Cartagine, Breve storia della contraversia nestoriana ed eutichiana* (Anagni, 1989)

Carile, A. (ed.), *Teoderico e I Gota tra Oriente e Occidente* (Ravenna, 1995)

Caspar, E., *Geschichte des Papsttums. Von den Anfangen bis zur Hohe der Weltherrschaft* (Tubingen, 1933)

Casson, L., *Travel in the Ancient World* (Baltimore, 1994)

Casson, L., *Ships and Seamanship in the Ancient World* (Princeton, 1995)

Cataudella, M.R., 'Historiography in the East', in Marasco, G. (ed.), *Greek and Roman Historiography in Late Antiquity: Fourth to Sixth Century AD* (Brill, 2003), 391-448

Ceran, W. (ed.), *Mélanges D'histoire Byzantine Offerts à Oktawiusz Jurewicz à L'occasion de Son Soixante-Dixième Anniversaire* (Lodz, 1998)

Certrez, O., Donabed, S., and Makko, A. (eds), *The Assyrian Heritage: Threads of Continuity and Influence* (Uppsala, 2012)

Chabot, J-B., 'Pierre l'Iberien, eveque monophysite de Mayouma (Gaza) a la fin du V siècle d'apres une recente publication', *Reveu de l'Orient Latin* 3 (1895), 367-93

Chabot, J-B., *Chronique de Michel le Syrien: Patrarche Jacobite d'Antioche (1166-1198)*, (Paris, 1899)

Chadwick, H., *East and West: The Making of a Rift in the Church from Apostolic Times until the Council of Florence* (Oxford, 2003)

Charanis, P., *The Religious Policy of Anastasius I: Emperor of the Later Roman Empire 491-518* (Madison, 1935)

Charanis, P., *Church and State in the Later Roman Empire: The Religious Policy of Anastasius the First 491-518* (Madison, 1939)

Charanis, P., 'Ethnic Changes in the Byzantine Empire in the Seventh Century', *DOP* 13 (1959), 25-44

Charanis, P., *Studies in the Demography of the Byzantine Empire* (London, 1972)

Charanis, P., 'Cultural diversity and the breakdown of Byzantine power in Asia Minor', *DOP* 29 (1975), 1-20

Charles, R.H., *The Chronicle of John, Bishop of Nikiu* (Oxford, 1916)

Chastagnol, A., *Le Senat romain sous le regne d'Odoacre. Recherches sur l'Epigraphie du Colisee au V Siecle* (Bonn, 1966)

Cheesman, G.L., *The Auxilia of the Roman Imperial Army* (Oxford, 1914)

Chew, K., 'Virgins and Eunuchs: Pulcheria, Politics and the Death of Emperor Theodosius II', *Historia* 55 (2006), 207-27

Chichikova, M., 'Fouilles du camp romain et de la ville paléobyzantine de Novae (Mésie Inférieure)', in Poulter, A.G. (ed.), *Ancient Bulgaria* (Nottingham, 1983), 11-18

Chitty, D.J., 'Jerusalem after Chalcedon AD451-518', *The Christian East* II (1952), 22-32

Chitty, D.J., 'Abba Isaiah', *JTS* 22 (1971), 47-72

Chitty, D.J., *A pustynia stała się miastem...: wprowadzenie do dziejów monastycyzmu w Egipcie i Palestynie pod panowaniem chrześcijańskim* (Krakow, 2008)

Christie, N., 'Urban defence in later Roman Italy', in Herring, E., Whitehouse, R., and Wilkins, J. (eds), *Papers of the Fourth Conference of Italian Archaeology* 2 (London, 1991), 185-99

Christie, N., 'Barren fields? Landscapes and settlements in late Roman and post-Roman Italy', in Shipley, G., and Salmon, J. (eds), *Human Landscapes in Classical Antiquity* (London, 1996), 255-83

Christie, N., 'Towns and people on the Middle Danube in late antiquity and the early Middle Ages', in Christie, N., and Loseby, S.T. (eds), *Towns in Transition: Urban Evolution in Late Antiquity and the Early Middle Ages* (Aldershot, 1996), 71-98

Christie, N., *From Constantine to Charlemagne: An Archaeology of Italy AD300-800* (Aldershot, 2006)

Christie, N., and Loseby, S.T. (eds), *Towns in Transition: Urban Evolution in Late Antiquity and the Early Middle Ages* (Aldershot, 1996)

Christol, M., 'Un duc dans une inscription de Termessos (Pisidie)', *Chiron* 8 (1978), 529-40

Chrysos, E,. and Schwarcz, A. (eds), *Das Reich und die Barbaren* (Vienna, 1989)

Chuvin, P., *Ostatni poganie: zanik wierzeń pogańskich w cesarstwie rzymskim od panowania Konstantyna do Justyniana* (Warsaw, 2008)

Clover, F.M., 'Geiseric and Attila', *Historia* 22 (1972), 104-11

Clover, F.M., 'The Family and Early Career of Ancius Olybrius', *Historia* 27 (1978), 169-96

Clover, F.M., 'The Symbiosis of Romans and Vandals in Africa', in Chrysos, E., and Schwarcz, A. (eds), *Das Reich und die Barbaren* (Vienna, 1989), 57-73

Clover, F.M., *The Late Roman West and the Vandals* (Aldershot, 1993)

Coakley, J.F., and Parry, K. (eds), *The Church of the East: Life and Thought*, Bull. John.Ryl.Lib 78 (1996)

Coleman-Norton, P.R., *Roman State and Christian Church: A Collection of Legal Documents to AD535* (London, 1966)

Collatz, C-F, Dummer, J., Kollesek, J., and Werlitz, M-L. (eds). *Dissertiunculae criticae. Festschrift für G.Chr. Hansen* (Würzburg, 1998)

Collins, R., 'Law and Ethnic Identity in the Western Kingdoms in the Fifth and Sixth centuries', in Smyth, P.A. (ed.), *Medieval Europeans: Studies in Ethnic Identity and National Perspectives in Medieval Europe* (London, 1998), 1-23

Combes, J., *Damascius, Traite des premiers principes* (Paris, 1986)

Conant, J., *Staying Roman: Conquest and Identity in Africa and the Mediterranean, 439-700* (Cambridge, 2012)

Conrad, L.I., 'The Conquest of Arwad: a Source-Critical Study in the Historiography of the Early Medieval Near East', in Cameron, Averil, and Conrad L.I. (eds), *The Byzantine and Early Islamic Near East I: Problems in the Literary Source Material* (Princeton, 1992), 334-336

Conrad, L.I., 'The Arabs and the Colossus', *JRAS* 6 (1996), 170-72

Conrad, L.I., 'Eutychius', in Meisami, J.S., and Starkey, P. (eds), *Encyclopedia of Arabic Literature* (London, 1998a), 63

Conrad, L.I., 'Agapius' in Meisami, J.S., and Starkey, P. (eds), *Encyclopedia of Arabic Literature* (London, 1998b), 211

Conrad, L.I., 'Zeno, the epileptic emperor: historiography and polemics as realia', *BMGS* 24 (2000), 61-81

Conybeare, F.C., 'Anecdota Monophysitarum', *AJTh* 9 (1905), 719-40

Cormack, R., 'The Mosaic Decoration of St Demetrios, Thessalonica: a Re-examination in the Light of the Drawings of W.S. George', *The Annual of the British School of Athens* 64 (1969), 17-52

Cormack, R., *The Church of Saint Demetrios: The Watercolours of W.S. George* (Thessaloniki, 1985)

Cormack, R., 'The Temple as the Cathedral', in Rouche, C., and Erim, K.T. (eds), *Aphrodisias Papers* (Ann Arbor, 1990), 75-88

Courtois, C., *Victor de Vita et son oeuvre* (Alger, 1954)

Courtois, C., *Les Vandales et l'Afrique* (Paris, 1955)

Crawford, J.S., 'Jews, Christians, and Polytheists in Late-Antique Sardis', in Fine, S. (ed.), *Jews, Christians and Polytheists in the Ancient Synagogue Cultural Interaction during the Greco-Roman Period* (London, 1999), 174-89

Crawford, P.T., *The War of Three Gods: Romans, Persians and the Rise of Islam* (Barnsley, 2013)

Croke, B., 'Evidence for the Hun Invasion of Thrace', *GRBS* 18 (1977), 347–67

Croke, B., 'Anatolius and Nomus: Envoys to Attila', *ByzSlav* 42 (1981a), 159-170

Croke, B., 'Two Early Byzantine Earthquakes and their Liturgical Commemoration', *Byzantion* 51 (1981b), 131-44

Croke, B., 'The Date of the "Anastasian Long Walls" in Thrace', *GRBS* 23 (1982), 59-78

Croke, B., '476: The Manufacture of a Turning Point', *Chiron* 13 (1983), 81-119

Croke, B., *Christian Chronicles and Byzantine History, 5th-6th Centuries* (Aldershot, 1992)

Croke, B., *The Chronicle of Marcellinus: Translation and Commentary* (Sydney, 1995)

Croke, B., *Count Marcellinus and His Chronicle* (Oxford, 2001)

Croke, B., 'Latin Historiography and the Barbarian Kingdoms', in Marasco, G. (ed.), *Greek and Roman Historiography in Late Antiquity: Fourth to Sixth Century AD* (Brill, 2003), 349-90

Croke, B., 'The Imperial Reigns of Leo II', *ByzZ* 96 (2003), 559-75

Croke, B., 'Dynasty and Ethnicity: Emperor Leo I and the Eclipse of Aspar', *Chiron* 34 (2005a), 147-203

Croke B., 'Leo I and the palace guard', *Byzantion* 75 (2005b), 117-51

Croke, B., 'Justianian's Constantinople', in Maas, M. (ed.), *The Cambridge Companion to the Age of Justinian* (Cambridge, 2005), 60-86

Croke, B., 'Ariadne Augusta: Shaping the Identity of the Early Byzantine Empress', in Dunn, G.D., and Mayer, W. (eds), *Christians Shaping Identity from the Roman Empire to Byzantium: Studies inspired by Pauline Allen* (Leiden, 2015), 291-320

Crow, J.G., 'The Long Walls of Thrace', in Mango, C., and Dagron, G. (eds), *Constantinople and its Hinterlands* (Aldershot, 1995), 100-24

Crow, J.G., and Ricci, A., 'The Anastasian Long Wall', *JRA* 10 (1997), 253-88

Crown, A.D., 'The Samaritans in the Byzantine Orbit', *Bulletin of the John Rylands University Library* 69 (1986-87), 96-138

Crown, A.D., 'The Byzantine and Moslem Period', in Crown, A.D. (ed.), *The Samaritans* (Tubingen, 1989), 55-81

Crown, A.D. (ed.), *The Samaritans* (Tubingen, 1989)

Crown, A.D., 'Shechem', in Crown, A.D., Pummer, R., and Tal, A. (eds), *A Companion to Samaritan Studies* (1993), 217-19

Crown, A.D., *Samaritan Scribes and Manuscripts* (Tubingen, 2001)

Crown, A.D., Pummer, R., and Tal, A. (eds), *A Companion to Samaritan Studies* (Tubingen, 1993)

Crown, A.D., and Davey, L. (eds), *Essays in Honour of G.D. Sixdenier. New Samaritan Studies of the Société d'Etudes Samaritaines III and IV* (Sydney, 1995)

Cumont, F., *Catalogus Codicum Astrologorum Graecorum VIII.4: Codices Parisini* (Brussels, 1921)

Curta, F. (ed.), *Borders, Barriers and Ethnogensis: Frontiers in Late Antiquity and the Middle Ages* (Turnhout, 2005)

Curta, F. (ed.), *Neglected Barbarians* (Turnhout, 2011)

Dąbrowa, E., Dzielska, M., Salamon, M., and Sprawski, S. (eds), *Hortus Historiae: Studies in Honour of Professor Jozef Wolski on the 100th Anniversary of His Birthday* (Krakow, 2010)

Dagron. G., *Naissance d'une capitale: Constantinople et ses institutions de 330 à 451* (Paris, 1974)

Dagron, G., 'Le fils de Léon Ier (463) Témoignages concordants de l'hagiographie et de l'astrologie', *Analecta Bollandiana* 100 (1982), 271-75

Dagron, G., *Emperor and Priest: The Imperial Office in Byzantium* (Cambridge, 2007)

Dar, S., 'Additional Archaeological Evidence of the Samaritan Rebellions in the Byzantine Period', in Crown, A.D., and Davey, L. (eds), *Essays in Honour of G.D. Sixdenier. New Samaritan Studies ofthe Société d'Etudes Samaritaines III and IV* (Sydney, 1995), 157-68

Darling Young, R.A., "Zacharias, *The Life of Severus*', in Wimbusch, V.L. (ed.), *Ascetic Behaviour in Greco-Roman Antiquity: A Sourcebook* (Minneapolis, 1990), 312-28

Daryaee, T., *Sasanian Persia: The Rise and Fall of an Empire* (New York, 2009)

De Blois, L., and Rich, J. (eds), *Transformation of Economic Life Under the Roman Empire* (Amsterdam, 2002)

de Halleux, A., *Philoxene de Mabbog. Sa vie, ses ecrits, sa theologie* (Louvain, 1963)

de Halleux, A., 'Nestorius, Histoire et Doctrine', *Irenikon* 66 (1993), 38-51, 163-78

de Souza, P., Arnaud, P., and Buchet, C. (eds), *The Sea in History. Vol I: The Ancient World* (Rochester, 2017)

de Urbina, I.O., 'Das Glaubenssymbol von Chalkedon – sein Text, sein Werden, seine dogmatische Bedeutung', in Grillmeier, A., and Bacht, H. (eds), *Das Konzil von Chalkedon* (Wurzburg, 1951), 389-418

Debie, M. (ed.), *L'historiographie syriaque* (Paris, 2009)

Dédéyan, G., *History of the Armenian People* (Paris, 2007)

Deichmann, F.W., 'Fruhchristliche Kirchen in antiken Heiligtumern', in Deichmann, F.W. (ed.), *Rom, Ravenna, Konstantinopel, Naher Osten: Gesammelte Studien zur spätantiken Architektur, Kunst und Geschichte* (Wiesbaden, 1982), 56-94

Deichmann, F.W. (ed.), *Rom, Ravenna, Konstantinopel, Naher Osten: Gesammelte Studien zur spätantiken Architektur, Kunst und Geschichte* (Wiesbaden, 1982)

Del Medico, H.E., 'Le couronnemeni d'un empereur byzantin vu par un juif de Constantinople', *ByzSlav* 16 (1955), 43-75

Delehaye, H., 'Vita S. Danielis Stylitae', *Analecta Bollandiana* XXXII (1913), 121-214

Delehaye, H., 'Les Saints Stylites', *Subsidia Hagiographica* XIV (1923)

Demandt, A., 'Magister Militum', *RE Suppl.* 12 (1970), 553-790

Demandt, A., 'Der spatromische Militaradel', *Chiron* 10 (1980), 609-36

Demandt, A., *Der Fall Roms: Die Auflösung des römischen Reiches im Urteil der Nachwelt* (Munich, 1984)

Demandt, A., 'Der Kelch von Ardabur und Anthusa', *DOP* 40 (1986), 113-17

Demandt, A., *Die Spätantike: römische Geschichte von Diocletian bis Justinian 284-565 n. Chr.* (Munich, 1989)

Derdy, T., and Wipszyckiej, E. (eds), *Chrześcijaństwo u schyłku starożytności. Studia źródłoznawcze, praca zbiorowa pod redakcją* (Warsaw, 1997)

Devreese, R., 'Les premieres annees du monophysisme. Une collection antichalcedonienne', *Revue des Sciences Philosophiques et Theologiques* 19 (1930), 256-63

Devreese, R., *Le Patriarcat d'Antioche depuis la paix de l'Eglise jusqu' a la conquete arabe* (Paris, 1945)

Di Segni, L., 'Justasas', in Crown, A.D., Pummer, R., and Tal, A. (eds), *A Companion to Samaritan Studies* (Tubingen, 1993), 140

Di Segni, L., 'Metropolis and Provincia in Byzantine Palestine', in Raban, A., and Holum, K.G. (eds), *Caesarea Maritima: A Retrospective after Two Millennia* (Leiden, 1996), 575-89

Di Segni, L., 'The Samaritans in Roman-Byzantine Palestine: Some Misapprehensions', in Lapin, H. (ed.), *Religious and Ethnic Communities in Later Roman Palestine* (Potomac, 1998), 51-66

Diesner, H.-J., 'Das Buccellariertum von Stilicho und Sarus bis auf Aetius', *Klio* 54 (1972), 321-50

Dignas, B., and Winter, E., *Rome and Persia in Late Antiquity* (Cambridge, 2007)

DiMaio, M., 'The Antiochene Connection: Zonaras, Ammianus Marcellinus, and John of Antioch on the Reigns of the Emperors Constantius II and Julian', *Byzantion* 50 (1980), 158-85

DiMaio, M., 'Infaustis Ductoribus Praeviis: The Antiochene Connection Part II', *Byzantion* 51 (1981), 502-10

Dmitriev, S., 'John Lydus and His Contemporaries on Identities and Cultures of Sixth-Century Byzantium', *DOP* 64 (2010), 27-42

Dobrovits, M., '"They called themselves Avar" – Considering the pseudo-Avar question in the work of Theophylaktos', *Transoxiana Webfestschrift Series I Webfestschrift Marshak* (2003)

Dodds, E.R., *Pagan and Christian in an Age of Anxiety* (Cambridge, 1965)

Dodgeon, M.H., and Lieu, S.N.C., *The Roman Eastern Frontier and the Persian Wars (AD 226-363)* (London, 1991)

Doran, R., *The Lives of Symeon Stylites* (Kalamazoo, 1992)

Dovere, E., 'L'EGKUKLION BASILISKOU. Un caso di normativa imperiale in Oriente su temi di dogmatica teologica', *Studia et Documenta Historiae et Iuris* 51 (1985), 153-88

Dovere, E., 'L'Enotico di *Zenone Isaurico*. Preteso intervento normativo tra politica religiosa e pacificazione sociale', *Studia et Documenta Historiae et Iuris* 54 (1988), 170-90

Dovere, E., 'Constitutiones divae memoriae Marciani in Synodo Calchedonensi', *Annuarium Historiae Conciliorum* 24 (1992), 1-34

Downey, G., 'References to Inscriptions in the Chronicle of Malalas', *TPAPA* 66 (1935), 55-73

Downey, G., 'Earthquakes at Constantinople and Vicinity AD342-1454', *Speculum* 30 (1955), 596-600

Downey, G., *A History of Antioch in Syria* (Princeton, 1961)

Draguet, R., *Les cinq recensions de l'Ascéticon syriaque d'Abba Isaie* (Louvain, 1968)

Drake, H.A. (ed.), *Violence in Late Antiquity: Perceptions and Practices* (Aldershot, 2006)

Drijvers, J.W., and Hunt, D. (eds), *The Late Roman World and its Historian: Interpreting Ammianus Marcellinus* (London, 1999)

Drinkwater, J., and Salway, B. (eds), *Reflections in Wolf Liebeschuetz* (London, 2007)

Duffy, J., and Parker, J., *The Synodicon Vetus* (Washington, 1979)

Duncan-Jones, R.P., 'Economic Change and the Transition to Late Antiquity', in Swain, S., and Edwards, M. (eds), *Approaching Late Antiquity: The Transformation from Early to Late Empire* (Oxford, 2004), 20-52

Dunlap, J.E., *The Office of Grand Chamberlain in the Later Roman and Byzantine Empires* (New York, 1924)

Dunn, G.D., and Mayer, W. (eds), *Christians Shaping Identity from the Roman Empire to Byzantium: Studies inspired by Pauline Allen* (Leiden, 2015)

Dupuy, B., 'La christologie de Nestorius', *Istina* 40 (1995), 56-64

Durliat, J., and Guillou, A., 'Le Tarif d'Abydos (vers 492)', *Bulletin de Correspondance Hellenique* 108 (1984), 581-98

Dvornik, F., 'Emperors, Popes and General Councils', *DOP* 6 (1951), 1-23

Dvornik, H., *Early Christian and Byzantine Political Philosophy: Origins and Background* (Washington DC, 1966)

Dzelska, M., 'Boscy mezowie', *Znak* 4 (1998), 41-54

Ebied, R.Y., and Wickham, L.R., 'A Collection of unpublished Syriac letters of Timothy Aelurus', *JTS* 21 (1970), 351-57

Elli, A., *Storia della Chiesa copta vol.1; L'Egitto romano-bizantino e cristiano* (Cairo, 2003)

Ellis, L., and Kidner, F. (eds), *Travel, Communication and Geography in Late Antiquity: Sacred and Profane* (Aldershot, 2004)

Elton, H., *Warfare in Roman Europe AD350-425* (Oxford, 1996a)

Elton, H., *Frontiers of the Roman Empire* (London, 1996b)

Elton, H., 'Defining Romans, Barbarians and the Roman Frontier', in Mathisen, R.W., and Sivan, H.S. (eds), *Shifting Frontiers in Late Antiquity* (Aldershot, 1996), 126-35

Elton, H., 'Illus and the Late Roman Aristocracy under Zeno', *Byzantion* 70 (2000), 393-407

Elton, H., 'The Nature of the Sixth-century Isaurians', in Mitchell, S., and Greatrex, G., (eds), *Ethnicity and Culture in Late Antiquity* (Swansea, 2000), 293-307

Elton, H., 'Economic fringe – the reach of the Roman Empire in Rough Cilicia', in De Blois, L. and Rich, J. (eds), *Transformation of Economic Life Under the Roman Empire* (Amsterdam, 2002), 172-78

Elton, H., 'Zeno and Alatian', *Anatolian Studies* 52 (2002), 153-57

Elton, H., 'The economy of Cilicia in late antiquity', *Olba* 8 (2003), 173-79

Elton, H., 'Romanization and some Cilician Cults', in de Ligt, L., Hemelrijk, E.A., and Singor, H.W. (eds), *Roman Rule and Civic Life: Local and Regional Perspectives* (Amsterdam, 2004), 231-41

Elton, H. 'Cilicia, Geography and the Late Roman Empire', in Ellis, L., and Kidner, F. (eds), *Travel, Communication and Geography in Late Antiquity: Sacred and Profane* (Aldershot, 2004), 5-10

Elton, H., 'Ecclesiastical politics in fifth- and sixth-century Isauria', in Drinkwater, J., and Salway, B. (eds), *Reflections in Wolf Liebeschuetz* (London, 2007), 77-85

Elton, H., 'Geography, Labels, Romans and Cilicia', in Elton, H., and Reger, G. (eds), *Regionalism in Hellenistic and Roman Asia Minor* (Bordeaux, 2007), 25-31

Elton, H., 'Imperial Politics at the Court of Theodosius II', in Cain, A., and Lenski, N., *The Power of Religion in Late Antiquity* (Aldershot, 2009) ,133-42

Elton, H., Jackson, M., Mietke, G., Newhard, J., Özgenel, L., and Twigger, E., 'A New Late-Roman urban centre in Isauria', *JRA* 19 (2006), 300-11

Elton, H. and Reger, G. (eds), *Regionalism in Hellenistic and Roman Asia Minor* (Bordeaux, 2007)

Enoki, K., 'On the Date of the Kidarites', *Memoirs of the Research Department of the Toyo Bunko* 27 (1969), 1-26

Ensslin, W., 'Leo I', *RE* 12.2 (1925), 1,947-62

Ensslin, W., 'Zur Frage nach der ersten Kaiserkrönung durch den Patriarchen und zur Bedeutung dieses Aktes im Wahlzeremoniell', *ByzZ* 42, 43 (1943-49, 1951), 101-15, 369-72

Ensslin, W., *Theoerich der Grosse* (Munich, 1959)

Ensslin, W., 'Witigis', *RE* II (1961), 395

Er, Y., 'Diversith e interazione culturale in Cilicia Tracheia. I monumenti funerary', *Quaderni Storici* 76 (1991), 105-40

Erdkamp, P. (ed.), *The Roman Army and the Economy* (Amsterdam, 2002)

Erdkamp, P. (ed.), *A Companion to the Roman Army* (Oxford, 2007)

Errington, M., 'Malchus von Philadelphia, Kaiser Zenon und dei zwei Theoderiche', *Museum Helveticum* 40 (1983), 82-110

Evelyn-White, H.G., *The Monasteries of the Wadi'n Natrun* (New York, 1932)

Faris, S.B., 'Changing Public Policy and the Evolution of Roman Civil and Criminal Law on Gambling', *GLJ* 3 (2012), 199-219

Feissel, D., 'Notes d'Épigraphie chrétienne (VIII)', *BCH* 108 (1984), 564-66

Feissel, D., 'Deux grandes familles isauriennes du Ve siècle d'après des inscriptions de Cilicie Trachée', *Mitteilungen zur christlichen Archäologie* 5 (1999), 9-17

Feissel, D., and Gascou, J., *La pétition à Byzance*. Centre de Recherche d'Histoire et Civilisation de Byzance, *Monographies* 14 (Paris, 2004)

Feld, K., 'Pamprepius – Philosoph und Politiker oder Magier und Aufrührer?', in Goltz, A., Luther, A., and Schlange-Schöningen, H. (eds), *Gelehrte in der Antike. Alexander Demandt zum 65. Geburtstag* (Cologne, 2002), 261-80

Feld, K., *Barbarische Burger. Die Isaurier und das Romische Reich* (Berlin, 2005)

Feld, O., 'Beobachtungen an spatantiken und fruhchristlichen Bauten in Kilikien', *Romische Quartalschrift* 60 (1965), 131-43

Ferrill, A., *The Fall of the Roman Empire: The Military Explanation* (London, 1986)

Ferris, I.M., *Enemies of Rome: Barbarians through Roman Eyes* (Stroud, 2000)

Festugiere, A-J., 'Evagre, *Histoire ecclesiastique*', *Byzantion* 45 (1975)

Fiebiger, H.O., 'Excubitores', *RE* 6.2 (1909), 1,577

Fine, S. (ed.), *Jews, Christians and Polytheists in the Ancient Synagogue Cultural Interaction during the Greco-Roman Period* (London, 1999)

Fisher, G., *Between Empire: Arabs, Romans and Sasanians in Late Antiquity* (Oxford, 2011)

Forsyth, G.M., 'Architectural notes on a Trip through Cilicia', *DOP* 11 (1957), 223-36

Foss, C., 'The Persians in Asia Minor and the End of Antiquity', *EHR* 90 (1975), 721-43

Foss, C., *History and Archaeology of Byzantine Asia Minor* (Aldershot, 1990)

Foss, C., 'Gangra', in Kazhdan, A.P. (ed.), *The Oxford Dictionary of Byzantium* (Oxford, 1991), 821

Foss, C., *Cities, Fortresses, Villages of Byzantine Asia Minor* (Aldershot, 1996)

Fowden, G., 'The Pagan Holy Man in Late Antique Society', *JHS* 102 (1982), 33-59

Fowden, G., *Empire to Commonwealth: Consequences of Monotheism in Late Antiquity* (Princeton, 1993)

Frakes, F.M., 'Late Roman Social Justice and Origin of the Defensor Civitatis', *CJ* 89 (1994), 337-48

Frank, R.I., *Scholae Palatinae* (Rome, 1969)

Frazee, C.A., 'Late Roman and Byzantine Legislation on the Monastic Life from the Fourth to the Eighth Centuries', *CH* 51 (1982), 263-79

Freeman, P., and Kennedy, D. (eds), *The Defence of the Roman and Byzantine East* (Oxford, 1986)

French, D.H., *Roman Roads and Milestones of Asia Minor, Fasciule 2: An Interrim Catalogue of Milestones*, BAR Intl Series 392 (1988)

French, D.H., and Lightfoot, C.S. (eds), *The Eastern Frontier of the Roman Empire: Proceedings of a Colloquium held at Ankara in September 1988* (Oxford, 1989)

Frend, W.H.C., *The Rise of the Monophysite Movement* (Cambridge, 1972a)

Frend, W.H.C., 'The Monks and the Survival of the East Roman Empire in the Fifth Century', *Past and Present* 54 (1972b), 3-25

Frend, W.H.C., 'Timothy Salofacilus', in Atiya, A.S. (ed.), *The Coptic Encyclopaedia* (New York, 1991), 2,268-69

Frézouls, E. (ed.), *Sociétés urbainses, sociétés rurales dans l'Asie Mineure et la Syrie* (Strasbourg, 1987)

Fries, P.R., and Nersoyan, T. (eds), *Christ in East and West* (Macon, 1987)

Fritz, G., 'Pierre le Foulon', in *Dictionnaire de theologie catholique* (Paris, 1935), col.1,933-35

Frye, R.N., 'The Political History of Iran under the Sasanians', in Yarshater, E. (ed.), *The Cambridge History of Iran Vol.III: The Seleucid, Parthian and Sasanid Periods* (Cambridge, 1983), 116-80

Galtier, P., 'Saint Cyrille d'Alexandrie et saint Leon le Grand a Chalcedoine', in Grillmeier, A., and Bacht, H. (eds), *Das Konzil von Chalkedon* (Wurzburg, 1951), 345-87

Gamble, H.Y., *Books and Readers in the Early Church: A History of Early Christian Texts* (London, 1995)

Gamq'relidze, D., 'Juansher Juansheriani, The Life of Vakht'ang Gorgasali', in Jones, S. (ed.), *Kartlis Tskhovreba. A History of Georgia* (Tbilisi, 2014), 78-82

Garipzanov, I., Geary, P., and Urbanczyk, P. (eds), *Franks, Northmen, and Slavs: Identities and State Formation in Early Medieval Europe* (Turnhout, 2008)

Garnsey, P., *Ideas of Slavery from Aristotle to Augustine* (Cambridge, 1996)

Garnsey, P., and Saller, R., *The Roman Empire: Economy, Society and Culture* (Berkley, 1987)

Gauthier, E-F., *Genseric, Roi des Vandales* (Paris, 1935)

Gavrilyuk, P.L., *The Suffering of the Impassible God: The Dialectics of Patristic Thought* (Oxford, 2003)

Geanakoplos, D.J., 'Church and State in the Byzantine Empire: A Reconsideration of the problem of Caesaropapism', *CH* 34 (1965), 381-403

Gentz, G., *Die Kirchengeschichte des Nicephorus Cillistus Xanthopulos* (Berlin, 1966)

Giardina, A. (ed.), *The Romans* (Chicago, 1993)

Gillett, A., 'The Date and Circumstances of Olympiodorus of Thebes', *Traditio* 48 (1993), 1-29

Gillett, A., 'Rome, Ravenna and the last western emperors', *PBSR* 69 (2001), 131-67

Gillett, A. (ed.), *On Barbarian Identity: Critical Approaches to Ethnicity in the Early Middle Ages* (Turnhout, 2002)

Gillett, A., *Envoys and political communiction in the Late Antique West 411-533* (Cambridge, 2003)

Goffart, W., *Barbarians and Romans AD418-584* (Princeton, 1980)

Goffart, W., 'Rome, Constantinople and the Barbarians in Late Antiquity', *AHR* 76 (1981), 275-306

Goffart, W., *The Narrators of Barbarian history (AD550-800): Jordanes, Gregory of Tours, Bede, and Paul the Deacon* (Princeton, 1988)

Goffart, W., *Rome's Fall and After* (London, 1989)

Goffart, W., *Barbarian Tribes: The Migration Age and the Later Roman Empire* (Philadelphia, 2006)

Goldsworthy, A., *The Roman Army at War 100BC-AD200* (Oxford, 1996)

Goltz, A., Luther, A., and Schlange-Schöningen, H. (eds), *Gelehrte in der Antike. Alexander Demandt zum 65. Geburtstag* (Cologne, 2002)

Goodburn, R., and Bartholomew, P. (eds), *Aspects of the Notitia Dignitatum* (Oxford, 1976)

Gordon, C.D., *The Age of Attila* (Ann Arbor, 1960)

Gottwald, J., 'Die Kirche und das Schloss Paperon in Kilikisch-Armenien', *ByzZ* 36 (1936), 86-100

Goubert, P., 'Le role de Sainte Pulcherie et de l'eunuque Chrysaphios', in Grillmeier, A., and Bacht, H. (eds), *Das Konzil von Chalkedon* (Wurzburg, 1951), 303-21

Gough, M., 'Early Churches in Cilicia', *Byzantinoslavica* 16 (1955), 201-11

Gough, M., 'The Emperor Zeno and Some Cilician Churches', *Anatolian Studies* 22 (1972), 199-212

Gough, M., 'Alatian: An Early Christian Monastery in Southern Turkey', *AJA* 91 (1987), 638-39

Gracanin, H., 'The Huns and South Pannonia', *ByzSlav* 64 (2006), 29-76

Graf, G., *Geschichte der christlichen arabischen Literatur* (Vatican City, 1947)

Grafton, A., and Mills, K. (eds), *Conversion in Late Antiquity and the Early Middle Ages* (Rochester, 2003)

Graindor, P., 'Pamprepios (?) et Theagenes', *Byzantion* 4 (1929), 469-75

Gray, P.T.R., *The Defense of Chalcedon in the East (451-553)* (Leiden, 1979)

Gray, P.T.R., 'The Legacy of Chalcedon: Christological Problems and their Significance', in Maas, M. (ed.), *The Cambridge Companion to the Age of Justinian* (Cambridge, 2005) 215-38

Greatrex, G., 'The Two Fifth-Century Wars between Rome and Persia', *Florilegium* 12 (1993), 1-14

Greatrex, G., 'The Dates of Procopius' works', *BMGS* 18 (1994), 101-14

Greatrex, G., *Rome and Persia at War 502-532* (Leeds, 1998)

Greatrex, G., 'The Background and Aftermath of the Partition of Armenia in AD 387', *Ancient History Bulletin* 14 (2000), 35-48

Greatrex, G., 'Roman Identity in the Sixth Century', in Mitchell, S., and Greatrex, G. (eds), *Ethnicity and Culture in Late Antiquity* (London, 2000), 267-92

Greatrex, G., 'Justin I and the Arians', *SP* 34 (2001), 72-81

Greatrex, G., 'Byzantium and the East in the Sixth Century', in Maas, M. (ed.), *The Cambridge Companion to the Age of Justinian* (Cambridge, 2005), 477-509

Greatrex, G., 'Pseudo-Zachariah of Mytilene: The Context and Nature of his Work', *Journal of the Canadian Society for Syriac Studies* 6 (2006), 39-52

Greatrex, G., 'Le Peudo-Zacharie de Mytilene et l'historiographie syriaque au sixieme siele', in Debie, M. (ed.), *L'historiographie syriaque* (Paris, 2009), 33-55

Greatrex, G., and Bardill, J., 'Antiochus the Praepositus: A Persian Eunuch at the Court of Theodosius II', *DOP* 50 (1996), 171-97

Greatrex, G., and Greatrex, M., 'The Hunnic invasion of the East of 395 and the fortress of Ziatha', *Byzantion* 69 (1999), 65-75

Greatrex, G., and Lieu, S.N.C. (eds), *The Roman Eastern Frontier and the Persian Wars Part II AD 363-630: A Narrative Sourcebook* (London, 2002)

Greer, R., *Theodore of Mopsuestia: Exegete and Theologian* (Westminster, 1961)

Gregoire, H., 'Au camp d'un Wallenstein byzantine. La vie et less vers de Pamprepios aventurier paien', *Bulletin de l'Association Guillaume Bude* 24 (1929), 22-38

Gregory, S., *Roman Military Architecture on the Eastern Frontier from AD200-600* (Amsterdam, 1995)

Gregory, T.E., *Vox Populi: Popular Opinion and Violence in the Religious Controversies of the Fifth Century AD* (Columbus, 1979)

Grenet, F., 'Regional Interaction in Central Asia and North-West India in the Kidarite and Hephthalite Period', in Sims-Williams, N. (ed.), *Indo-Iranian Languages and Peoples: Proceedings of the British Academy* (London, 2002), 203-24

Grierson, P., 'Three Unpublished coins of Zeno (474-491)', *NC* 8 (1948), 223-26

Grierson, P., 'The tombs and Obits of the Byzantine emperors (337-1042)', *DOP* 16 (1962), 3-60

Grierson, P., and Blackburn, M., *Medieval European Coinage I: The Early Middle Ages (5th-10th centuries* (Cambridge, 2007)

Grierson, P., and Mays, M., *Catalogue of Late Roman Coins in the Dumbarton Oaks Collection and in the Whittemore Collection. From Arcadius and Honorius to the Accession of Anastasius* (Washington DC, 1992)

Grig, L., and Kelly, G. (eds), *Two Romes: Rome and Constantinople in Late Antiquity* (Oxford, 2012)

Grillmeier, A., *Christ in Christian Tradition I: From the Apostolic Age to Chalcedon (451)* (Atlanta, 1975)

Grillmeier, A., *Christ in Christian Tradition II.1: From Chalcedon to Justinian I* (Atlanta, 1987a)

Grillmeier, A., 'The Understanding of the Christological Definitions of Both (Oriental Orthodox and Roman Catholic) Traditions in the Light of the Post-Chalcedonian Theology (Analysis of Terminologies in a Conceptual Framework)', in Fries, P.R., and Nersoyan, T. (eds), *Christ in East and West* (Macon, 1987b), 65-82

Grillmeier, A., and Bacht, H. (eds), *Das Konzil von Chalkedon* (Wurzburg, 1951/1953/1954)

Grillmeier, A., and Hainthaler, T., *Christ in Christian Tradition II.2: From the Council of Chalcedon (451) to Gregory the Great (590-604); the Church of Constantinple in the Sixth Century* (London, 1995)

Grillmeier, A., and Hainthaler, T., *Jesus der Christus m Glauben der Kirche: Die Kirchen von Jerusalem und Antiochien nach 451-600* (Freiburg, 2004)

Grosse, R., *Römische Militärgeschichte von Gallienus bis zum Beginn der Byzantinschen Themenverfassung* (Berlin, 1920)

Grossman, P., *Christliche Architektur in Aegypten* (Leiden, 2001)

Gruen, E. (ed.), *Cultural Borrowings and Ethnic Appropriations in Antiquity* (Stuttgart, 2005)

Grumel, V., 'Les regestes des actes du patriarcat de Constantinople', in *Les actes des patriarches: Les regestes de 381 a 715* (Istanbul, 1932)

Grumel, V., *La Chronique* (Paris, 1958)

Guilland, R., *Recherches sur les Institutions Byzantines* (Berlin, 1967)

Guilloi, A., *La civilta bizantina aggetti e messagio* (Rome, 1993)

Gunther, O., 'Zu den *Gesta de nomine Acacii*', *ByzZ* 3 (1894), 146-49

Gunther, O., *Avellana-Studien* (Vienna, 1896)

Haacke, R., 'Die kaiserliche Politik in den Auseinandersetzungen un Chalcedon (451-553)', in Grillmeier, A., and Bacht, H. (eds), *Das Konzil von Chalkedon* (Wurzburg, 1951), 95-177

Haarer, F., *Anastasius I: Politics and Empire in the Late Roman World* (Cambridge, 2006)

Haas, C., 'Patriarch and People: Peter Mongus of Alexandria and Episcopal Leadership in the Late Fifth Century', *JECS* 1 (1993), 297-316

Haas, C., *Alexandria in Late Antiquity* (Baltimore, 1997)

Hacikyan, A.J., Ouzounian, N., Franchuk, E.S., and Basmajian, G. (eds), *The Heritage of Armenian Literature: From the Oral Tradition to the Golden Age I* (Detroit, 2000)

Haehling von, R., '"Timeo, ne per me consuetudo in regno nascatur." Die Germanen und der romische Kaiserthron', in Wissemann, M. (ed.), *Roma Renascens. Beitra'ge zur Spa'tantike und Rezeptionsgeschichte* (Frankfurt, 1988), 88-113

Haenel, G., *Corpus Legum* (Leipzig, 1857)

Hahn, C., 'Seeing and Believing: The Construction of Sanctity in Early Medieval Saints' Shrines', *Speculum* 72 (1997), 1.079-106

Haldon, J.F., *Byzantine Praetorians: An Administrative, Institutional and Social Survey of the Opsikion and Tagmata c.580-900* (Bonn, 1984)

Haldon, J.F., *Byzantine Warfare* (Aldershot, 2007)

Haldon, J.F., *The Byzantine Wars* (Stroud, 2008)

Halsall, G., 'Movers and Shakers: the barbarians and the fall of Rome', *EME* 8 (1999), 131-45

Halsall, G., *Barbarian Migrations and the Roman West 376-568* (Cambridge, 2007)

Hansen, G.C., *Theodoros Anagnostes, Kirchengeschichte* (Berlin, 1971)

Harl, K.W., 'Sacrifice and Pagan Belief in Fifth- and Sixth-Century Byzantium', *P+P* 128 (1990), 7-27

Harrak, A., *The Chronicle of Zuqnin, Parts III and IV: AD 488-775* (Toronto, 1999)

Harries, J., 'The Roman Imperial Quaestor from Constantine to Theodosius II', *JRS* 71 (1988), 148-72

Harries, J., *Sidonius Apollinaris and the Fall of Rome AD 407-485* (Oxford, 1994)

Harries, J., 'Pius princeps: Theodosius II and Fifth Century Constantinople', in Magdalino, P. (ed.), *New Constantines. The Rhythm of Imperial Renewal in Byzantium, 4th-13th Centuries. Papers from the Twenty-Sixth Spring Symposium of Byzantine Studies, St Andrews, March 1992* (Aldershot, 1994), 35-44

Harries, J., *Law and Empire in Late Antiquity* (Cambridge, 1999)

Harries, J., 'Law', in Barchiesi, A., and Scheidel, W. (eds), *The Oxford Handbook of Roman Studies* (Oxford, 2010), 637-50

Harries, J., *Imperial Rome AD284 to 363: A New Empire* (Edinburgh, 2012)

Harries, J., and Wood, I. (eds), *The Theodosian Code* (Ithaca, 1993)

Harrison, M., 'The Emperor Zeno's Real Name', *BZ* 74 (1981), 27-28

Harrison, M., 'Monumenti e urbanistica nella cita', in Guilloi, A., *La civilta bizantina aggetti e messagio* (Rome, 1993)

Hasluk, F.W., *Cyzicus* (Cambridge, 1910)

Heather, P., 'Cassiodorus and the Rise of the Amals: Genealogy and the Goths under Hun Domination', *JRS* 79 (1989), 103-28

Heather, P., *Goths and Romans 332-489* (Oxford, 1991)

Heather, P., 'The Historical Culture of Ostrogothic Italy', *Teoderico il Grande e i Goti d'Italia. Atti del XIII Congresso internazionale di studi sull'Alto Medioevo, Milano 2-6 novembre 1992* Vol. 1-2 Spoleto (1993), 317-54

Heather, P., 'New men for new Constantines? Creating an imperial elite in the eastern Mediterranean', in Magdalino, P. (ed.), *New Constantines. The Rhythm of Imperial Renewal in Byzantium, 4th-13th Centuries. Papers from the Twenty-Sixth Spring Symposium of Byzantine Studies, St Andrews, March 1992* (Aldershot, 1994), 11-33

Heather, P., 'The Huns and the End of the Roman Empire in the West', *EHR* 110 (1995a), 4-41

Heather, P., 'Theoderic as war-leader', *EME* 4 (1995b), 145-73

Heather, P., *The Goths* (Oxford, 1996)

Heather, P., 'The late Roman art of client management: Imperial defence in the fourth century west', in Pohl, W., Wood, I., and Reimitz, H. (eds), *The Transformation of Frontiers* (Leiden, 2001), 15-68

Heather, P., *The Fall of the Roman Empire: A New History* (London, 2006)

Heather, P., 'Ethnicity, Group Identity and Social Staus in the Migration Period', in Garipzanov, I., Geary, P., and Urbanczyk, P. (eds), *Franks, Northmen, and Slavs: Identities and State Formation in Early Medieval Europe* (Turnhout, 2008), 17-50

Heather, P., *Empire and Barbarians: Migration, Development and the Birth of Europe* (London, 2009)

Heather, P., *The Restoration of Rome: Barbarian Popes and Imperial Pretenders* (Oxford, 2013)

Heather, P., and Moncur, D., *Politics, Philosophy, and Empire in the Fourth Century: selected orations of Themistius* (Liverpool, 2001)

Hefele, C.J., and Leclercq, H., *Histoire des Conciles* (Paris, 1908)

Hellenkemper, H., 'Zur Entwicklung des Stadtbildes in Kilikien', *ANEW* II.7.1 (1980), 1,262-83

Hellenkemper, H., 'Die Kirchenstiftung des Kaisers Zenon im Wallfahrtsheiligtum der Heiligen Thekla bei Seleukeia', *Wallraf-Richartz-Jahrbuch* 47 (1986), 63-90

Henning, D., *Periclitans Res Publica. Kaiserteum und Elite in der Krise des westromischen Reiches 454/5-493 n. Chr.* (Stuttgart, 1999)

Henry, R. Photius, *Bibliothque* (Paris, 1959)

Herring, E., Whitehouse, R., and Wilkins, J. (eds), *Papers of the Fourth Conference of Italian Archaeology* (London, 1991)

Herzfeld, E., and Guyer, S., *Meriamlik und Korykos. Zwei christliche Ruinenstatten des Rauhen Kilikiens* (Manchester, 1930)

Hild, F., and Hellenkemper, H., *Tabula Imperii Byzantini* (Vienna, 1990)

Hill, G., *A History of Cyprus I: To the Conquest of Richard Lion Heart* (Cambridge, 1949)

Hill, S., 'Matronianus "Comes Isauriae": An inscription from an Early Byzantine Basilica at Yanikhan, Rough Cilicia', *Anatolian Studies* 35 (1985), 93-97

Hill, S., *The Early Byzantine Churches of Cilicia and Isauria* (Aldershot, 1996)

Hoddinott, R.F., *Bulgaria in Antiquity: An Archaeological Introduction* (London, 1975)

Hoffer, P.C., *The Historian's Paradox: A Study of History in Our Time* (London, 2008)

Hofmann, F., 'Der Kampf der Papste um Konzil und Dogma von Chalkedon von Leo dem Grossen bis Hormisdas (451-519)', in Grillmeier, A., and Bacht, H. (eds), *Das Konzil von Chalkedon* (Wurzburg, 1951), 13-94

Holl, K., *Amphilochius von Iconium in seinem Verhaltnis zu den grossen Kappadoziern* (Tubingen, 1904)

Holland, T., *In The Shadow Of The Sword: The Battle for Global Empire and the End of the Ancient World* (London, 2012)

Holum, K.G., 'Pulcheria's Crusade AD421-422', *GRBS* 18 (1977), 153-72

Holum, K.G., *Theodosian Empresses: Women and Imperial Dominion in Late Antiquity* (Berkeley, 1982)

Honigmann, E., 'Juvenal of Jerusalem', *DOP* 5 (1950), 209-79

Honigmann, E., *Eveques et Eveches Monophysite d'Asie Anterieure au VI siècle* (Louvain, 1951)

Honoré, T., *Law and the Crisis of Empire 379-455AD: The Theodosian Dynasty and its Quaestors with a Palingenesia of Laws of the Dynasty* (Oxford, 1998)

Hopkins, K., 'Eunuchs and Politics in the Later Roman Empire', *CPS* 9 (1963), 62-80

Hopkins, K., 'Taxes and Trade in the Roman Empire (200BC–AD400)', *JRS* 70 (1980), 101–25

Hopwood, K., 'Policing the Hinterland Rough Cilicia and Isauria', *BAR Intl. Ser.* 156 (Oxford, 1983), 173–78

Hopwood, K., 'Consent and Control: How Peace was Kept in Rough Cilicia', in French, D.H., and Lightfoot, C.S. (eds), *The Eastern Frontier of the Roman Empire: Proceedings of a Colloquium held at Ankara in September 1988* (Oxford, 1989), 191-201

Hopwood, K., 'Who were the Isaurians?' XI. Türk Tarih Kongresi, Ankara, 5-9 Eylül 1990, Kongreye Sunulan Bildiriler, 1. Cilt (Ankara, 1994), 375-386

Hopwood, K., 'Ammianus Marcellinus on Isauria', in Drijvers, J.W., and Hunt, D. (eds), *The Late Roman World and its Historian: Interpreting Ammianus Marcellinus* (London, 1999), 224-35

Horn, C., *Asceticism and Christological Controversy in Fifth-Century Palestine. The Career of Peter the Iberian* (Oxford, 2006)

Horn, C., and Phoenix, R.R., *John Rufus, the Lives of Peter the Iberian, Theodosius of Jerusalem and the Monk Romanus* (Atlanta, 2008)

Houwink ten Cate, P.H.J., *The Luwian Population Group of Lycia and Cilicia Aspera during the Hellenistic Period* (Leiden, 1965)

Howard-Johnston, J., 'The Two Great Powers in Late Antiquity: a Comparison', in Cameron, Averil (ed.), *The Byzantine and Early Islamic Near East III: States, Resources and Armies* (Princeton, 1995), 157-226

Howard-Johnston, J., *East Rome, Sasanian Persia and the End of Antiquity: Historiographical and Historical Sources* (Aldershot, 2006)

Howgego, C., *Ancient History from Coins* (London, 2001)

Huffman, J.P., 'The Donation of Zeno: St Barnabas and the Modern History of the Cypriot Archbishop's Regalia Privileges', *Church History* 84 (2015), 713-45

Hughes, I., *Belisarius: The Last Roman General* (Barnsley, 2009)

Humphries, M., 'Valentinian III and the City of Rome (AD425-455): Patronage, Politics and Power', in Grig, L., and Kelly, G. (eds), *Two Romes: Rome and Constantinople in Late Antiquity* (Oxford, 2012), 161-82

Ilski, K., *Sobory w polityce religijnej Teodozjusza II* (Poznan, 1992)

Iricinschi, E., and Zellentin, H.M. (eds), *Heresy and Identity in Late Antiquity* (Tubingen, 2008)

Isaac, B., *The Limits of Empire* (Oxford, 1992)

Isaac, B., 'The Army in the Late Roman East: the Persian Wars and the Defence of the Byzantine Provinces', in Cameron, Averil (ed.), *The Byzantine and Early Islamic Near East III: States, Resources and Armies* (Princeton, 1995), 125-55

Jacobsen, T.C., *A History of the Vandals* (Yardley, 2012)

Jalland, T., *The Life and Times of St Leo the Great* (London, 1941)

James, L., *Empresses and Power in Early Byzantium* (Leicester, 2001)

Janin, R., *La Géographie ecclésiastique de l'Empire byzantin. 1. Part: Le Siège de Constantinople et le Patriarcat Oecuménique. 3rd Vol.: Les Églises et les Monastères* (Paris, 1953)

Janin, R., *Constantinople byzantine: developpement urbain et repertoire topographique* (Paris, 1964)

Janin, R., *La Géographie ecclésiastique de l'Empire byzantin. 1. Part: Le Siège de Constantinople et le Patriarcat Oecuménique. 3rd Vol.: Les Églises et les Monastères* (Paris, 1969)

Janin, R., *La Géographie ecclésiastique de l'Empire byzantin. 1. Part: Le Siège de Constantinople et le Patriarcat Oecuménique. 2nd Vol.: Les Églises et les Monastères des grands centres byzantins (Bithynie, Hellespoint, Latros, Galesios, Trebizonde, Athenes, Thessalonique)* (Paris, 1975)

Janin, R., and Stiernon, D., 'Gangres', in *Dictonnaire d'Histoire et de Geographie Ecclesiastiques* (Paris, 1981), col.1,091-103.

Janiszewski, P., 'Jan Diakrinomenos i jego Historia kościelna', in Derdy, T., and Wipszyckiej, E. (eds), *Chrześcijaństwo u schyłku starożytności. Studia źródłoznawcze, praca zbiorowa pod redakcją* (Warsaw, 1997), 63-78

Jankowiak, M., 'Bizancjum a kryzysy sukcesyjne w Cesarstwie Zachodniorzymskim w ostatnich latach jego istnienia (465-747)', in Derdy, T., and Wipszyckiej, E. (eds), *Chrześcijaństwo u schyłku starożytności. Studia źródłoznawcze, praca zbiorowa pod redakcją III* (Warsaw, 2000), 193-244

Jarry, J., *Hérésies et factions dans l'empire byzantin du IVe au VIIe siècle* (Cairo, 1968)

Jasper, D., and Fuhrmann, H., *Papal letters in the Early Middle Ages* (Washington, 2001)

Jean, E., Ali, M., Dinçol, A.M., and Durugönül, S. (eds), *La Cilicie: Espaces et Pouvoirs Locaux. Table Ronde Internationale, Istanbul 2-5 Novembre 1999* (Istanbul, 2001)

Jeanselme, E., 'L'epilepsie sur e trone de Byzance', *Bulletin de la societe francaise d'histoire de la medecine* 18 (1924), 225-74

Jeffreys, E.,. '*Malalas in Greek*', in Jeffreys, E., Croke, B., and Scott, R. (eds), *Studies in John Malalas* (Sydney, 1990), 245-68

Jeffreys, E., 'The Beginning of Byzantine Chronography: John Malalas', in Marasco, G. (ed.), *Greek and Roman Historiography in Late Antiquity: Fourth to Sixth Century AD* (Brill, 2003), 497-528

Jeffreys, E. (ed.), *Byzantine Style, Religion and Civilization. In Honour of Sir Steven Runciman* (Cambridge, 2006)

Jeffreys, E., Croke, B., and Scott, R. (eds), *Studies in John Malalas* (Sydney, 1990)

Jeffreys, E., Jeffreys, M., and Scott, R., *The Chronicle of John Malalas* (Melbourne, 1986)

Johnson, D.W., 'Anti-Chalcedonian Polemicin Coptic Texts', in Pearson, B.A., and Goehring, J.E. (eds), *The Roots of Egyptian Christianity* (Philadelphia, 1986), 216-34

Jones, A.H.M., 'The Constitutional Position of Odoacer and Theoderic', *JRS* 52 (1962), 126-30

Jones, A.H.M., *Later Roman Empire 284-602* (Oxford, 1964)

Jones, A.H.M., 'Review of Frank (1969)', *JRS* 60 (1970), 227-29

Jones, A.H.M., *The Cities of the Eastern Roman Provinces* (Amsterdam, 1983)

Jones, C.P., 'The Inscription from the Sea Wall of Anemurium', *Phoenix* 26 (1972), 396-99

Jones, S. (ed.), *Kartlis Tskhovreba. A History of Georgia* (Tbilisi, 2014)

Jugie, M., 'Acace', in *Dictionnaire d'Histoire et de Géographie Ecclésiastiques* (Paris, 1912), 244-48

Kaegi, W.E., *Byzantium and the Decline of Rome* (Princeton, 1968)

Kaegi, W.E., *Byzantine Military Unrest 471-843: an interpretation* (Amsterdam, 1981)

Kaegi, W.E., *Some Thoughts on Byzantine Military Strategy* (Brookline, 1983)

Kaegi, W.E., 'The capability of the Byzantine army for operations in Italy', in Carile, A. (ed.), *Teoderico e I Gota tra Oriente e Occidente* (Ravenna, 1995), 79-99

Kaldellis, A., *Hellenism in Byzantium: the Transformation of Greek Identity and the Reception of the Classical Tradition* (Cambridge, 2007)

Kaster, R., *Guardians of Language: The Grammarian and Society in Late Antiquity* (Berkeley, 1988)

Kazhdan, A.P. (ed.), *The Oxford Dictionary of Byzantium* (Oxford, 1991)

Kellner, H-J., 'Zwei neue Flottendiplome zur Grenze von Pamphylien und Kilikien', *Chiron* 7 (1977), 315-22

Kelly, C., 'Emperors, Government and Bureauracy', in Cameron, Averil, and Garnsey, P. (eds), *The Cambridge Ancient History XIII: The Late Empire AD337-425* Cambridge (1998), 138-83

Kelly, C., *Ruling the Later Roman Empire* (Cambridge, 2004)

Kelly, C., *Attila the Hun: Barbarian Terror and the Fall of the Roman Empire* (London, 2008)

Kelly, C. (ed.), *Theodosius II: Rethinking the Roman Empire in Late Antiquity* (Cambridge, 2013)

Kelly, J.N.D., *Golden Mouth. The Story of John Chrysostom-Ascetic, Preacher, Bishop* (Ithaca, 1995)

Kent, J.P.C., 'Zeno and Leo, the Most Noble Caesars', *NC* 19 (1959), 93-98

Kent, J.P.C., 'Julius Nepos and the Fall of the Western Empire', in *Corolla Memoriae Erich Swoboda Dedicata* (Cologne, 1966), 146-50

Kent, J.P.C., Carson, R.A.G., and Burnett, A.M. (eds), *Roman Imperial Coinage X: The Divided Empire and the Fall of the Western Parts AD395-491* (London, 1994)

Kettenhofen, E., *Die römisch-persischen Kriege des 3. Jahrhunderts n. Chr. nach der Inscrift puhrs I. an der Ka'be-ye Zartost (SKZ)* (Wiesbaden, 1982)

Kiel-Freytag, A., 'Betrachtungen zur Usurpation des Illus und des Leontius (484-488 n.Chr.)', *ZPE* 174 (2010), 291-301

Kim, H.J., *The Huns, Rome and the Birth of Europe* (Cambridge, 2013)

Kim, H.J., 'Herodotean Illusions in Late Antiquity: Priscus, Jordanes, and the Huns', *Byzantion* 85 (2015), 127-42

King, C.E. (ed.), *Imperial Revenue, Expenditure and Monetary Policy in the Fourth Century AD*, Bar Intl Series 76 (Oxford, 1980)

Kislinger, E., 'Zwischen Vandalen, Goten und Byzantinern: Sizilien im 5. und frühen 6. Jahrhundert', in Różycka-Bryzek, A., and Salamon, M. (eds), *Byzantina et Slavica Cracoviensia* (Krakow, 1994), 31-51

Kitchen, T.E., 'Contemporary Perceptions of the Roman Empire in the Later Fifth and Sixth Centuries', PhD diss (Cambridge, 2008)

Kleinbauer, W.E., 'Some Observations on the Dating of S. Demetrius in Thessaloniki', *Byzantion* 40 (1970), 36-44

Koczwara, S., *Wokół sprawy Akacjusza* (Lublin, 2000)

Kofsky, A., and Strousma, G.G. (eds), *Sharing the Sacred: Religious Contacts and Conflicts in the Holy Land, First-Fifteenth Centuries CE* (Jerusalem, 1998)

Kohen, E., *History of the Byzantine Jews. A Microcosmos in the Thousand Year Empire* (Lanham, 2007)

Kollmann, B., *Joseph Barnabas. His Life and Legacy* (Collegeville, 2004)

Kollmann, B., *Alexander Monachus, Laudatio Barnabae. Lobrede auf Barnabas* (Turnhout, 2007)

König, I., *Aus der Zeit Theoderichs des Großen. Einleitung, Text, Übersetzung und Kommentar einer anonymen Quelle* (Darmstadt, 1997)

Kopecek, T.A., *A History of Neo-Arianism* (Philadelphia, 1979)

Kościuk, J., *Wczesnośredniowieczna osada w Abû Mînâ* (Wrocław, 2009)

Kosiński, R., ΑΓΙΩΣΥΝΗ ΚΑΙ ΕΞΟΥΣΙΑ. *Konstantynopolitańscy święci mężowie i władza w V wieku po Chr* (Warsaw, 2006)

Kosiński, R., 'The Life of Nestorius as seen in Greek and Oriental sources', in Brodka, D., and Stachura, M. (eds), *Continuity and Change. Studies in Late Antique Historiography. Electrum* 13 (Kraków, 2007), 155-70

Kosiński, R., 'Dzieje Nestoriusza, biskupa Konstantynopola w latach 428-431', in Janiszewski, P., and Wiśniewski, R. (eds), *U schyłku starożytności. Studia Źródłoznawcze VII* (Warsaw, 2008a), 30-63

Kosiński, R., 'The Fate of Nestorius after the Council of Ephesus in 431', *Fen Edebiyat Dergisi* 10 (2008b), 33-48

Kosiński, R., 'Leo II – some chronological questions', *Palamedes* 3 (2009a), 209-14

Kosiński, R., 'Dziecko na tronie. Leon II', in Patka, A. (ed.), *Zeszyty Naukowe Uniwersytetu Jagiellońskiego MCCCIV*, Prace Historyczne 136 (Kraków, 2009b), 23-31

Kosiński, R., *The Emperor Zeno: Religion and Politics* (Kraków, 2010)

Kosiński, R., 'Kilka uwag o Henotikonie i domniemanym zwrocie w polityce religijnej cesarza Zenona', in Olszańca, S., and Wojciechowskiego, P. (eds),

Społeczeństwo i religia w świecie antycznym. Materiały z ogólnopolskiej konferencji naukowej (Toruń, 2010a), 433-51

Kosiński, R., 'Dzieje Akacjusza, patriarchy Konstantynopola w latach 472-489, U schyłku starożytności', *Studia Źródłoznawcze* 9 (2010b), 63-97

Kosiński, R., 'Peter the Fuller, patriarch of Antioch (471-488)', *Byzantinoslavica* 68 (2010c), 49-73

Kosiński, R., 'The 316th Olympiad as presented in the *Chronicon Paschale*', in Musiał, D. (ed.), *Society and religions: studies in Greek and Roman history III* (Toruń, 2010d), 79-88

Kosiński, R., 'The Emperor Zeno's Church Donations', in Dąbrowa, E., Dzielska, M., Salamon, M., and Sprawski, S. (eds), *Hortus Historiae: Studies in Honour of Professor Jozef Wolski on the 100th Anniversary of His Birthday* (Kraków, 2010e), 635-49

Kraus, F.F., *Die Münzen Odovacars und des Ostgotenreiches in Italien* (Halle, 1928)

Krautschick, S., 'Zwei Aspekte des Jahres 476', *Historia* 35 (1986), 344-71

Krautschick, S., 'Die unmögliche Tatsache: Argumente gegen Johannes Antiochenus', *Klio* 77 (1995), 332-38

Krautheimer, R., *Early Christian and Byzantine Architecture* (London, 1986)

Kroll, W., 'Damaskios', in *Paulys Realencyclopädie der classischen Altertumswissenschaft* (Stuttgart, 1901), col.2,039-42

Kugener, M-A., 'La compilation historique de Pseudo-Zacharie le Rhéteur', *Revue de l'Orient Chrétien* 5 (1900), 201-14, 461-80

Kulakovskij, J., Историа Византіи, Томъ I *(395-518)* (Kiev, 1913)

Kulikowski, M., 'The Notitia Dignitatum as an historical source', *Historia* 49 (2000), 358-77

Kulikowski, M., 'Marcellinus of Dalmatia and the dissolution of the fifth-century Empire', *Byzantion* 72 (2002), 177-91

Kussmaul, P., *Pragmaticum und Lex. Formen spätrömischen Gesetzgebung 408-457* (Göttingen, 1981)

La Vaissiere, E., 'Is there a Nationality of the Hephthalites?', *BAI* 17 (2003), 119-32

Ladner, G., 'On Roman Attitudes towards Barbarians in Late Antiquity', *Viator* 7 (1976), 1-26

Lafferty, S.D.W., *Law and Society in the Age of Theoderic the Great: A Study of the Edictum Theoderici* (Cambridge, 2013)

Laidlaw, R., *Theoderic: Imitation of an Emperor* (Edinburgh, 2008)

Lancel, S., *Victor de Vita, Histoire de la persécution Vandale en Afrique suivie de La Passion des Sept Martyrs, registre des provinces et des cités d'Afrique* (Paris, 2002)

Lane Fox, R., 'The Life of Daniel', in Edwards, M.J., and Swain, S. (eds), *Portraits: Biographical Representation in the Greek and Latin Literature of the Roman Empire* (Oxford, 1997), 175-225

Laniado, A., 'Some Problems in the Sources of the Reign of the Emperor Zeno', *BMGS* 15 (1991), 147-73

Lapin, H. (ed.), *Religious and Ethnic Communities in Later Roman Palestine* (Potomac, 1998)

Lebon, J., 'La christologie de Timothée Aelure, archevêque monophysite d'Alexandrie d'après les sources syriaques inédites', *Revue d'histoire ecclésiastique* 9 (1908), 677-702

Lebon, J., *Le monophysisme sévérien. Étude historique, littéraire et théologique sur la résistance monophysite au concile de Chalcédoine jusqu'à la constitution de l'église jacobite* (Louvain, 1909)

Lebon, J., 'Autour du cas de Dioscore d'Alexandrie', *Le Muséon* 59 (1946), 515-28

Lee, A.D., 'The Role of Hostages in Roman Diplomacy with Sasanian Persia', *Historia* 40 (1991), 366-74

Lee, A.D., *Information and Frontiers* (Cambridge, 1993)

Lee, A.D., 'The Army', in Cameron, A., and Garnsey, P. (eds), *The Cambridge Ancient History Vol. XIII* (Cambridge, 1998), 211-37

Lee, A.D., 'The Eastern Empire: Theodosius to Anastasius', in Cameron, A., Ward-Perkins, B., and Whitby, M. (eds), *The Cambridge Ancient History Vol. XIV* (Cambridge, 2000), 45-49

Lee, A.D., 'Decoding Late Roman Law', *JRS* 92 (2002), 185-94

Lee, A.D., *War in Late Antiquity* (Oxford, 2007)

Lee, A.D., *From Rome to Byzantium AD363 to 565: The Transformation of the Ancient Roman World* (Edinburgh, 2013)

Lee, A.D., 'Theodosius and his Generals', in Kelly, C. (ed.), *Theodosius II: Rethinking the Roman Empire in Late Antiquity* (Cambridge, 2013), 90-108

Lee, A.D., 'Roman Warfare with Sasanian Persia', in Campbell, J.B., and Trittle, L.A., *The Oxford Handbook of Warfare in the Classical World* (Oxford, 2013), 708-25

Lemerle, P., 'St-Démétrius de Thessalonique et les problèmes du martyrion et du transept', *Bulletin de Correspondance Hellénique* 77 (1953), 660-94

Lemerle, P., 'Fl. Appalius Illus Trocundes', *Syria* 40 (1963), 315-22

Lemerle, P., *The Agrarian History of Byzantium from the Origins to the Twelfth Century* (Galway, 1979)

Lenski, N., 'Basil and the Isaurian Uprising of AD375', *Phoenix* 59 (1999a), 308-29

Lenski, N., 'Assimilation and Revolt in the Territory of Isauria, from the 1st Century BC to the 6th Century AD', *JESHO* 42 (1999b), 413-65

Lenski, N., 'Relations between Coast and Hinterland in Rough Cilicia', in Jean, E., Ali, M., Dinçol, A.M., and Durugönül, S. (eds), *La Cilicie: Espaces et Pouvoirs Locaux. Table Ronde Internationale, Istanbul 2-5 Novembre 1999* (Istanbul, 2001), 417-24

Lenski, N., *Failure of Empire: Valens and the Roman State in the Fourth Century AD* (London, 2002)

Lenski, N., 'Valens and the Monks: cudgelling and conscription as a means of social control', *DOP* 58 (2004), 93-117

Leppin, H., 'The Church Historians (I): Socrates, Sozomenus, and Theodoretus', in Marasco, G. (ed.), *Greek and Roman Historiography in Late Antiquity: Fourth to Sixth Century AD* (Brill, 2003), 219-56

Leszka, M.B., 'Patriarcha Akacjusz wobec uzurpacji Bazyliskosa 475-476 roku', *Acta Universitatis Lodziensis, Folia historica* 48 (1993), 71-78

Leszka, M.B., 'Między ortodoksją a monofizytyzmem. Obsada tronów patriarszych Konstantynopola, Aleksandrii, Antiochii i Jerozolimy w polityce cesarza Zenona', *Vox Patrum* 18 (1998), 437-53

Leszka, M.B., *Rola duchowieństwa na dworze cesarzy wczesnobizantyńskich* (Łódź, 2000)

Leszka, M.J., '*Empress-Widow Verina's Political Activity during the Reign of Emperor Zeno*', in Ceran, W. (ed.), *Mélanges D'histoire Byzantine Offerts à Oktawiusz Jurewicz à L'occasion de Son Soixante-Dixième Anniversaire* (Łódź, 1998), 128-36

Leszka, M.J., 'Armatus: A Story of a Byzantine General from the 5th Century', *Eos* 87 (2000), 335-43

Leszka, M.J., 'Aelia Zenonis, żona Bazyliskosa', *Meander* 57 (2002), 87-93

Leszka, M.J., 'Illus Izauryjczyk wobec uzurpacji Bazyliskosa', *Acta Universitatis Lodziensis, Folia historica* 80 (2005), 45-53

Leszka, M.J., 'Kilka uwag na temat losów Illusa Izauryjczyka w latach 479-484', *Meander* 62 (2007), 99-107

Leszka, M.J., 'Dzieje Longina, brata cesarza Zenona', in Dąbrowy, E., Dzielskiej, M., Salamona, M., and Sprawskiego, S. (eds), *Hortus historiae. Księga pamiątkowa ku czci profesora Józefa Wolskiego w setną rocznicę urodzin* (Kraków, 2010), 651-66

Levick, B., *Roman Colonies in Southern Asia Minor* (Oxford, 1967)

Levine, L.I., *Caesarea under Roman Rule* (Leiden, 1975)

Lichtheim, M., *Ancient Egyptian Literature. A Book of Readings, vol. III, The Late Period* (London, 2006)

Liebeschuetz, J.H.W.G., *Barbarians and Bishops: army, church and state in the reign of Arcadius and Chrysostom* (London, 1990a)

Liebeschuetz, J.H.W.G., *From Diocletian to the Arab Conquest: change in the late Roman Empire* (Northampton, 1990b)

Liebeschuetz, J.H.W.G., *The Decline and Fall of the Roman City* (Oxford, 2001)

Liebeschuetz, J.H.W.G., 'Pagan Historiography and the Decline of the Empire', in Marasco, G. (ed.), *Greek and Roman Historiography in Late Antiquity: Fourth to Sixth Century AD* (Brill, 2003), 177-218

Lilie, R-J., 'Die Krönungsprotokolle des Zeremonienbuchs und die Krönung Kaiser Leos I', in Collatz, C-F., Dummer, J., Kollesek, J., and Werlitz, M-L. (eds), *Dissertiunculae criticae. Festschrift für G.Chr. Hansen* (Würzburg, 1998), 395-408

Limor, O., and Stroumsa, G.G. (eds), *Christians and Christianity in the Holy Land. From the Origins to the Latin Kingdoms* (Turnhout, 2006)

Lippold, A., 'Zenon 17', *RE* 2 (1972), 149-213

Luibheid, C., 'Theodosius II and Heresy', *JEH* 16 (1995), 13-38

Luther, A., *Die syrische Chronik des Joshua Stylites* (New York, 1997)

Luttwak, E.N., *Grand Strategy of the Byzantine Empire* (Cambridge, 2009)

Maas, M., 'Delivered from their ancient customs: Christianity and the question of cultural change in early Byzantine ethnography', in Grafton, A., and Mills, K. (eds), *Conversion in Late Antiquity and the Early Middle Ages* (Rochester, 2003), 152-88

Maas, M. (ed.), *The Cambridge Companion to the Age of Justinian* (Cambridge, 2005)

Maas, M. (ed.), *The Cambridge Companion to the Age of Attila* (New York, 2015)

MacBain, B., 'Odovacer the Hun?', *CP* 78 (1983), 323-27

MacCormack, S., *Art and Ceremony in Late Antiquity* (Berkeley, 1981)

MacGeorge, P., *Late Roman Warlords* (Oxford, 2002)

MacMullen, R., *Soldier and Civilian in the Later Roman Empire* (Cambridge, 1963a)

MacMullen, R., 'Barbarian enclaves in the northern Roman Empire', *Antiquité Classique* 32 (1963b), 552-61

MacMullen, R., *Enemies of the Roman Order* (New Haven, 1966)

MacMullen, R., 'How big was the Roman Imperial Army?', *Klio* 62 (1980a), 451-60

MacMullen, R., 'The Roman Emperors' Army Costs', *Latomus* 43 (1980b), 451-60

MacMullen, R., *Corruption and the Decline of Rome* (New Haven, 1988)

Maenchen-Helfen, O.J., *The World of the Huns: Studies in Their History and Culture* (London, 1973)

Magdalino, P. (ed.), *New Constantines. The Rhythm of Imperial Renewal in Byzantium, 4th-13th Centuries. Papers from the Twenty-Sixth Spring Symposium of Byzantine Studies, St Andrews, March 1992* (Aldershot, 1994)

Magen, Y., 'The Church of Mary Theotokos on Mount Gerizim', in Bottini, G.C., di Segni, L., and Alliata, E. (eds), *Christian Archaeology in the Holy Land. New Discoveries, Essays in Honour of Virgilio C. Corbo* (Jerusalem, 1990), 333-41

Magen, Y., 'Samaritan Synagogues', in Manns, F., Alliata, E., and Testa, E. (eds), *Early Christianity in Context. Monuments and Documents* (Jerusalem, 1993), 193-230

Magie, D., *Roman Rule in Asia Minor to the End of the Third Century After Christ* (Princeton, 1950)

Man, J., *Attila: the Barbarian King Who Challenged Rome* (New York, 2006)

Mango, C., 'Isaurian builders', in Wirth, P. (ed.), *Polychronion: Festschrift for P. Dolger* (Heidelberg, 1966), 358-65

Mango, C., *The Art of the Byzantine Empire, 312-1453:Sources & Documents in History of Art* (Englewood Cliffs, 1972)

Mango, C., *Byzantine Architecture* (Milan, 1978)

Mango, C., *Byzantium: the Empire of New Rome* (London, 1980)

Mango, C., 'Deux études sur Byzance et la Perse sassanide', *Travaux et mémoires* 9 (1985), 91-118

Mango, C., 'The Conversion of the Parthenion into a Church: The Tübingen Theosophy', *DCAH* 18 (1995), 201-03

Mango, C., and Dagron, G. (eds), *Constantinople and its Hinterlands* (Aldershot, 1995)

Mango, C., and Scott R., *The Chronicle of Theophanes Confessor. Byzantine and Near Eastern History AD 284-813* (Oxford, 1997)

Manns, F., Alliata, E., and Testa, E. (eds), *Early Christianity in Context. Monuments and Documents* (Jerusalem, 1993)

Marasco, G. (ed.), *Greek and Roman Historiography in Late Antiquity: Fourth to Sixth Century AD* (Brill, 2003)

Marasco, G., 'The Church Historians (II): Philostorgius and Gelasius of Cyzicus', in Marasco, G. (ed.), *Greek and Roman Historiography in Late Antiquity: Fourth to Sixth Century AD* (Brill, 2003), 257-88

Maraval, P., 'La réception de Chalcédoine dans l'empire d'Orient', in Mayeur, J-M., Charles et Luce Pietri, C., Pietri, L., Vauchez, A., and Venard, M. (eds), *Les Églises d'Orient et d'Occident (432-610): Histoire du christianisme des origines à nos jours* (Paris, 1998), 107-45

Maraval, P., 'The Earliest Phase of Christian Pilgrimage in the Near East (before the 7th century)', *DOP* 56 (2002), 63-74

Maraval, P., *Lieux saints et pèlerinages d'Orient. Histoire et géographie. Des origines à la conquête arabe* (Paris, 2004)

Marinis, V., *Architecture and Ritual in the Churches of Constantinople: Ninth to Fifteenth Centuries* (New York, 2014)

Martin, G.R.R., *A Song of Ice and Fire: A Game of Thrones* (London, 1996)

Martin, G.R.R., *A Song of Ice and Fire: A Dance with Dragons* (London, 2011)

Martin, T.O., 'The Twenty-Eight Canon of Chalcedon: A Background Note', in Grillmeier, A., and Bacht, H. (eds), *Das Konzil von Chalkedon* (Wurzburg, 1953), 433-58

Maskarinec, M., 'Selected Ancient Sources', in Maas, M. (ed.), *The Cambridge Companion to the Age of Attila* (New York, 2015), 414-23

Mathisen, R.W., 'Resistance and reconciliation: Majorian and the Gallic aristocracy after the fall of Avitus', *Francia* 7 (1979a), 597-627

Mathisen, R.W., 'Sidonius on the reign of Avitus: a study in political prudence', *TAPA* 109 (1979b), 165-71

Mathisen, R.W., 'Emperors, Consuls and Patricians: Some Problems of Personal Preference, Precedence and Protocol', *Byzantinische Forschungen* 17 (1991a), 173-90

Mathisen, R.W., 'Leo, Anthemius, Zeno, and Extraordinary Senatorial Status in the Late Fifth Century', *Byzantinische Forschungen* 17 (1991b), 191-222

Mathisen, R.W., 'Adnotatio and Petitio: The Emperor's Favour and Special Exceptions in the Early Byzantine Empire', in Feissel, D., and Gascou, J., *La pétition à Byzance*, Centre de Recherche d'Histoire et Civilisation de Byzance, Monographies 14 (Paris, 2004), 23-32

Mathisen, R.W., 'Ricimer's Church in Rome: How an Arian Barbarian Prospered in a Nicene World', in Cain, A., and Lenski, N. (eds), *The Power of Religion in Late Antiquity* (Aldershot, 2009), 307-26

Mathisen, R.W., and Shanzer, D. (eds), *Romans, Barbarians and the Transformation of the Roman World* (Farnham, 2011)

Mathisen, R.W., and Sivan, H.S. (eds), *Shifting Frontiers in Late Antiquity* (Aldershot, 1996)

Matthews, J.F., 'Olympiodorus of Thebes and the History of the West (AD407-425)', *JRS* 60 (1970), 79-97

Matthews, J.F., *Western Aristocracies and Imperial Court AD364-425* (Oxford, 1975)

Matthews, J.F., *The Roman Empire of Ammianus* (London, 1989)

Matthews, J.F., *Laying Down the Law: A Study of the Theodosian Code* (New Haven, 2000)

Mattingly, D.J., 'Vulgar and weak "Romanisation" or Time for a Paradigm Shift?', *JRA* 15 (2002), 163-67

McCail, R.C., 'P. Gr. Vindob. 29788C: Hexameter Encomium on an Un-named Emperor', *JHS* 98 (1978), 38-63

McCormick, M., 'Odoacer, emperor Zeno and the Rugian Victory Legation', *Byzantion* 47 (1977), 212-22

McCormick, M., *Eternal Victory: Triumphal Rulership in Late Antiquity: Byzantium and the Early Medieval West* (Cambridge, 1990)

McCotter, S.E.J., 'The Strategy and Tactics of Siege Warfare in the Early Byzantine Period', Ph.D Thesis Queen's University, Belfast (1996)

McDonough, S.J., 'A Question of Faith? Persecution and Political Centralization in the Sasanian Empire of Yazdgerd II (438-457 CE)', in Drake, H.A. (ed.), *Violence in Late Antiquity: Perceptions and Practices* (Aldershot, 2006), 69-85

McEvoy, M., 'Becoming Roman?: The Not-So-Curious Case of Aspar and the Ardaburii', *JLA* 9 (2016), 483-511

McGill, S., Sogno, C., and Watts, E. (eds), *From the Tetrarchs to the Theodosians* (New York, 2010)

McGuckin, J., 'The Christology of Nestorius of Constantinople', *Patristic and Byzantine Review* 7 (1988), 93-129

McGuckin, J.A., 'Nestorius and the Political Factions of Fifth-Century Byzantium: Factors in his Personal Downfall', in Coakley, J.F., and Parry, K. (ed.), *The Church of the East: Life and Thought*, Bull.John.Ryl.Lib 78 (1996), 7-21

McGuckin, J.A., *St. Cyril of Alexandria and the Christological Controversy* (New York, 2004)

McLynn, N.B., 'From Palladius to Maximinus: Passing the Arian Torch', *JECS* 4 (1994), 477-93

McMahon, L., 'The foederati, the phoideratoi, and the symmachoi of the late antique east (ca. A.D. 400-650)', unpublished MA thesis, University of Ottawa (2014)

Megaw A.H.S., 'The Campanopetra reconsidered: the pilgrimage church of the Apostle Barnabas?', in Jeffreys, E. (ed.), *Byzantine Style, Religion and Civilization. In Honour of Sir Steven Runciman* (Cambridge, 2006), 394-404

Meier, M., *Anastasios I. Die Entstehung des Byzantinischen Reiches* (Stuttgart, 2009)

Meisami, J.S., and Starkey, P. (eds), *Encyclopedia of Arabic Literature* (London, 1998)

Merkelbach, R., 'Maurbaueepigramm aus Anemurion', *ZPE* 10 (1973), 174

Merrills, A., 'Vandals, Romans and Berbers: Understanding Late Antique North Africa', in Merrills, A. (ed.), *Vandals, Romans and Berbers: New Perspectives on Late Antique North Africa* (Farnham, 2004), 3-28

Merrills, A. (ed.), *Vandals, Romans and Berbers: New Perspectives on Late Antique North Africa* (Farnham, 2004)

Merrills, A., 'Rome and the Vandals', in de Souza, P., Arnaud, P., and Buchet, C. (eds), *The Sea in History. Vol. I: The Ancient World* (Rochester, 2017), 496-507

Merrills, A., and Miles, R., *The Vandals* (Chichester, 2010)

Meyendorff, J., *Imperial Unity and Christian Division. The Church 450-680 AD* (New York, 1989)

Milewski, I., *Depozycje i zsyłki biskupów w Cesarstwie Wschodniorzymskim (lata 325-451)* (Gdańsk, 2008)

Millar, F., 'Ethnic Identity in the Roman Near East 325-450: Language, Religion and Culture', *MedArch* 11 (1998), 159-76

Millar, F., 'The Greek East and Roman Law: The Dossier of M. Cn. Licinius Rufinus', *JRS* 89 (1999), 90-108

Millar, F., 'Repentant Heretics in Fifth-century Lydia: Identity and Literacy', *SCI* 23 (2004a), 111-30

Millar, F., 'Christian Emperors, Christian church and the Jews of the Diaspora in the Greek East, CE379-450', *JJS* 55 (2004b), 1-25

Millar, F., 'The Theodosian Empire CE408-450 and the Arabs: Saracens or Ishmaelites?', in Gruen, E. (ed.), *Cultural Borrowings and Ethnic Appropriations in Antiquity* (Stuttgart, 2005), 297-314

Millar, F., *A Greek Roman Empire: Power and Belief Under Theodosius II 408-450* (London, 2006)

Miller, D., 'The Emperor and the Stylite: a Note on the Imperial Office', *GOTR* 15 (1970), 207-12

Minor, C.E., 'The Robber Tribes of Isauria', *Ancient World* 2 (1979), 117-27

Mitchell, S., *Armies and Frontiers in Roman and Byzantine Anatolia*, BAR 156 (Oxford, 1993)

Mitchell, S., *Cremna in Pisidia: An Ancient City in Peace and in War* (London, 1995)

Mitchell, S., *A History of the Later Roman Empire AD 284-641: The Transformation of the Ancient World* (Oxford, 2007)

Mitchell, S., and Greatrex, G. (eds.), *Ethnicity and Culture in Late Antiquity* (Swansea, 2000)

Mitford, T.B., 'Roman Rough Cilicia', *ANRW* II 7.2. (Berlin, 1980), 1,230-61

Mitford, T.B., 'The Cults of Roman Rough Cilicia', *ANRW* II.18.3 (1990), 2,131-60

Mócsy, A., *Pannonia and Upper Moesia: a history of the middle Danube provinces of the Roman Empire* (London, 1974)

Moeller, C., 'Un représentant de la christologie néochalcédonienne au début du sixième siècle en Orient: Nephalius d'Alexandrie', *Revue d'Histoire Ecclésiastique* 40 (1944-45), 73-140

Momigliano, A., 'Cassiodorus and the Italian Culutre of His Time', *ProBAcad* 41 (1955), 215-48

Mommsen, T., 'Ostgothische Studien', *Neues Archiv* 14 (1889), 224-25

Mommsen, T., 'Das römische Militärwesen seit Diocletian', *Hermes* 24 (1889); Gesammelte Schriften VI (Berlin, 1910), 206-83

Montgomery, J.A., *The Samaritans. The Earliest Jewish Sect, Their History, Theology and Literature* (Philadelphia, 1907)

Moorhead, J., 'Boethius and Romans in Ostrogothic Service', *Historia* 27 (1978a), 604-12

Moorhead, J., 'The Laurentian Schism: East and West in the Roman Church', *CH* 47 (1978b), 125-36

Moorhead, J., 'The Last Years of Theoderic', *Historia* 32 (1983), 106-20

Moorhead, J., 'Theoderic, Zeno and Odovaker', *Byzantinische Zeitschrift* 77 (1984), 261-66

Moorhead, J., *Theoderic in Italy* (Oxford, 1992)

Moravcsik, G., *Principles and Methods of Byzantine Diplomacy* (Belgrade, 1963)

Mrozewicz, L., and Ilski, K. (eds), *Studia Moesiaca I* (Poznan, 1994)

Muhlberger, S., *The Fifth-Century Chroniclers. Prosper, Hydatius, and the Gallic Chronicler of 452* (Leeds, 1990)

Musiał, D. (ed.), *Society and religions: studies in Greek and Roman history III* (Toruń, 2010)

Mutafian, C., *La Cilicie au Carrefour des empires* (Paris, 1988)

Nasrallah, J., *Histoire du mouvement littéraire dans l'Église Melchite du Ve au XXe siècle. Contribution à l'étude de la littérature arabe chrétienne, vol. II.2* (Louvain, 1987)

Nau, F., 'Note sur la chronique attribuée par Assémani à Denys de Tell-Mahré, patriarche d'Antioche', *Journal Asiatique* 8 (1896a), 346-58

Nau, F., 'Nouvelle étude sur la chronique attribuée à Denys de TellMahré', *Bulletin Critique* 17 (1896b), 464-79

Nau, F., 'L'histoire ecclésiastique de Jean d'Asie, patriarche jacobite de Constantinople (+ 585)', *Revue de l'Orient Chrétien* 2 (1897), 455-93

Nau, F., 'Sur la christologie de Timothée Aelure', *Revue de l'Orient Chrétien* 14 (1909), 99-103

Nau, F., *Jean Rufus, Plérophories. Témoignages et révélations contre le Concile de Chalcédoine* (Paris, 1911)

Nauerth, C., 'Kaiser Zenon und Dalisandos – ein Theklakloster in Alahan Monastir?', *Dielheimer Blätter zum Alten Testament und seiner Rezeption in der Alten Kirche* 23/24 (1987), 46-65

Nautin, P., 'L'ecclésiologie romaine à l'époque du schisme d'Acace', *Annuaire de l'École Pratique des Hautes Études, Section des Sciences Religieuses* 74 (1966-67), 138-41

Nautin, P., 'Felix III (II)', in *Dictionnaire d'Histoire et de Géographie Ecclésiastiques* (Paris, 1977), col. 889-95.

Nautin, P., 'Fravita', in *Dictionnaire d'Histoire et de Géographie Ecclésiastiques* (Paris, 1977), col. 1,128-29

Nautin, P., 'Théodore Lecteur et sa "Réunion de différentes histoire" de l'Église', *Revue des Études Byzantines* 52 (1994), 213-43

Nechaeva, E., 'The Runaway Avars and Late Antique Diplomacy', in Mathisen, R.W., and Schanzer, D. (eds), *Romans, Barbarians, and the Transformation of the Roman World* (Burlington, 2011), 175-84

Negev, A., and Shimon, G., *Archaeological Encyclopedia of the Holy Land* (London, 2005)

Neumann, G., and Untermann, J. (eds), *Die Sprachen im romischen Reich der Kaiserzeit. Beihefte der Bonner Jahrbücher 40* (Cologne, 1980)

Neumann, G., 'Kleinasien', in Neumann, G., and Untermann, J. (eds), *Die Sprachen im romischen Reich der Kaiserzeit. Beihefte der Bonner Jahrbücher 40* (Cologne, 1980), 167-85

Neusner, J., and Frerichs, E.S. (eds), *To See Ourselves as Others See Us: Christians, Jews and 'Others' in Late Antiquity* (Chico, 1985)

Nicolet, C. (ed.), *Les Litteratures techniques dans l'antiquité romaine* (Geneva, 1996)

Noethlichs, K.L., 'Kaisertum und Heidentum im 5. Jahrhundert', in van Oort, J., and Wyrwa, D. (eds), *Heiden und Christen im 5. Jahrhundert* (Leuven, 1998), 1-31

Norris, R.A., *Manhood in Christ. A Study in the Christology of Theodore of Mopsuestia* (Oxford, 1963)

Norton, P., *Episcopal Elections 250-600. Hierarchy and Popular Will in Late Antiquity* (Oxford, 2007)

O'Donnell, J.J., *Cassiodorus* (London, 1979)

O'Donnell, J.J., 'The Aims of Jordanes', *Historia* 31 (1982), 223-40

O'Flynn, J.M., *Generalissimos of the Western Roman Empire* (Edmonton, 1983)

O'Flynn, J.M., 'A Greek on the Roman Throne: A Fate of Anthemius', *Historia* 41 (1991), 122-28

Olszańca, S., and Wojciechowskiego, P. (eds), *Społeczeństwo i religia w świecie antycznym. Materiały z ogólnopolskiej konferencji naukowej* (Toruń, 2010)

Onur, F., 'The Roman Army in Pamphylia: From the Third to Sixth Centuries AD', *ADALYA* XII (2009), 299-316

Oost, S.I., 'Aetius and Majorian', *CPh* 59 (1964), 23-29

Oost, S.I., *Galla Placidia Augusta* (Chicago, 1968)

Ostrogorsky, G., *The History of the Byzantine State* (Oxford, 1969)

Padosch, S.A., Lachenmeier, D.W., and Kroner, L.U., 'Absinthism: a ficticious 19th century syndrome with present impact', *Substance Abuse Treatment, Prevention and Policy* 1.14 (2006), 1-14

Painter, K., 'The silver dish of Ardabur Aspar', in Herring, E., Whitehouse, R., and Wilkins, J. (eds), *Papers of the Fourth Conference of Italian Archaeology* (London, 1991), II.73-80

Pallas, D., *Les Monuments paleochretiens de Grece decouverts de 1959 a 1973* (Vatican City, 1977)

Palme, B., 'Flavius Epiphanius, *comes domesticorum*', *Eirene* 34 (1998), 98-116

Palme, B., 'The Imperial Presence: Government and Army', in Bagnall, R.S. (ed.), *Egypt in the Byzantine World 300-700* (Cambridge, 2007), 244-70, 491-555

Palmer, A.N., 'Who wrote the Chronicle of Joshua the Stylite?', in Schulz, R., and Görg, M. (eds), *Lingua Restituta Orientalis. Festgabe für Julius Assfalg* (Wiesbaden, 1990), 272-84

Papadogiannakis, Y., *Christianity and Hellenism in the Fifth-Century Greek East* (Washington DC, 2012)

Paribeni, R., and Romanelli, P., 'Studi e ricerche archeologiche nell'Anatolia Meridonale', *Monumenti Antichi* 23 (1914), 5-274

Paschoud, F., *Zosime: Histoire nouvelle* (Paris, 1971-1989)

Patka, A. (ed.), *Zeszyty Naukowe Uniwersytetu Jagiellońskiego MCCCIV*, Prace Historyczne 136 (Kraków, 2009)

Patzig E., 'Über einige Quellen des Zonaras', *ByzZ* 5 (1896), 24-53

Patzig E., 'Über einige Quellen des Zonaras II', *ByzZ* 6 (1897), 322-56

Payne, R., 'The Reinvention of Iran: The Sasanian Empire and the Huns', in Maas, M. (ed.), *The Cambridge Companion to the Age of Attila* (New York, 2015), 282-302

Pearson, B.A., and Goehring, J.E. (eds), *The Roots of Egyptian Christianity* (Philadelphia, 1986)

Peeters, P., *Orient et Byzance. Le trefonds oriental de l'hagiographie byzantine* (Brussels, 1950)

Perrone, L., *La chiesa di Palestina e le controversie cristologiche. Dal concilio di Efeso (431) al secondo concilio di Constantinopoli (553)* (Brescia, 1980)

Perrone, L., 'Rejoice Sion, Mother of all Churches; Christianity in the Holy Land during the Byzantine Era', in Limor, O., and Stroumsa, G.G. (eds), *Christians and Christianity in the Holy Land. From the Origins to the Latin Kingdoms* (Turnhout, 2006), 141-73

Pietri, C., 'D'Alexandrie à Rome: Jean Talaïa, émule d'Athanase au Ve siècle', in ΑΛΕΞΑΝΔΡΙΝΑ, *Hellénisme, judaïsme et christianisme à Alexandrie, Mélanges offerts au P. Claude Mondésert* (Paris, 1987), 277-95

Pigulewska, N.W., *Kultura Syryjska we wczesnym średniowieczu* (Warsaw, 1989)

Pingree, D., 'Political Horoscopes from the Reign of Zeno', *DOP* 30 (1976), 133-50

Pirone, B., *Eutichio, Gli Annali* (Cairo, 1987)

Placanica, A., 'Da Cartagine a Bisanzio: per la biografia di Vittore Tunnunense', *Vetera Christianorum* 26 (1989), 327-36

Placanica, A., *Vittore da Tunnuna, Chronica. Chiesa e impero nell'età di Giustiniano* (Florence, 1997)

Pohl, W. (ed.), *Kingdoms of the Empire: The Integration of Barbarians in Late Antiquity* (Leiden, 1997)

Pohl, W., and Diesenberger, M. (eds), *Integration and Authority in the Early Middle Ages* (Vienna, 2002)

Pohl, W., Ganter, C., and Payne, R. (eds), *Visions of Community in the Post-Roman World: The West, Byzantium and the Islamic World 300-1100* (Farnham, 2012)

Pohl, W., Wood, I., and Reimitz, H. (eds), *The Transformation of Frontiers* (Leiden, 2001)

Popescu, E., *Christianitas Daco-Romana* (Bucharest, 1994)

Popko, M., *Ludy i języki starożytnej Anatolii* (Warsaw, 1999)

Popovic, V. (ed.) *Villes et Peuplement dans l'Illyricum protobyzantin.* Rome (1984)

Potter, D.S., 'The Unity of the Roman Empire', in McGill, S., Sogno, C., and Watts, E. (eds), *From the Tetrarchs to the Theodosians* (New York, 2010), 13-32

Poulter, A.G. (ed.), *Ancient Bulgaria* (Nottingham, 1983)

Poulter, A.G., 'Town and Country in Moesia Inferior', in Poulter, A.G. (ed.), *Ancient Bulgaria* (Nottingham, 1983), 74-118

Pourshariati, P., *Decline and Fall of the Sasanian Empire: The Sasanian-Parthian Confederacy and the Arab Conquest of Iran* (London, 2008)

Price, R., and Gaddis, M., *The Acts of the Council of Chalcedon* (Liverpool, 2005)

Prostko-Prostyński, J., *Utraeque res publicae. The Emperor Anastasius I's Gothic Policy (491-518)* (Poznań, 1994)

Prostko-Prostyński, J., 'Basiliskos: Ein in Rom anerkannter Usurpator', *Zeitschrift für Papyrologie und Epigraphik* 133 (2000), 259-65

Pummer, R., *The Samaritans* (Leiden, 1987)

Pummer, R., 'Samaritan Material Remains and Archaeology', in Crown, A.D. (ed.), *The Samaritans* (Tubingen, 1989), 135-77

Pummer, R., 'Feasts and Festivals', in Crown, A.D., Pummer, R., and Tal, A. (eds), *A Companion to Samaritan Studies* (Tubingen, 1993), 91-94

Pummer, R., 'Samaritan synagogues and Jewish synagogues. Similarities and differences', in Fine, S. (ed.), *Jews, Christians and Polytheists in the Ancient Synagogue Cultural Interaction during the Greco-Roman Period* (London, 1999), 118-60

Pummer, R., *Early Christian Authors on Samaritans and Samaritanism: Texts, Translations and Commentary* (Tübingen, 2002)

Pyatnitsky, Y., 'New Evidence for Byzantine Activity in the Caucasus During the Reign of the Emperor Anastasius I', *American Journal of Numismatics* 18 (2006), 113-22

Raban, A., and Holum, K.G. (eds), *Caesarea Maritima: A Retrospective after Two Millennia* (Leiden, 1996)

Rabello, A.M., *Giustiniano, Ebrei e Samaritani alla luce delle fonti storico-letterarie, ecclesiastiche e giuridiche* (Milan, 1987)

Rahner, H., 'Leo der Große, der Papst des Konzils', in Grillmeier, A., and Bacht, H. (eds), *Das Konzil von Chalkedon* (Wurzburg, 1951), 323-39

Ramsay, A.M., 'The Early Christian Art of Isaura Nova', *JHS* 24 (1904), 260-92

Ramsay, W.M., *The Historical Geography of Asia Minor* (London, 1890)

Ramsay, W.M., *The Social Basis of Roman Power in Asia Minor* (Aberdeen, 1941)

Rance, P., 'The Fulcum, the late Roman and Byzantine Testudo: The Germanisation of Late Roman Tactics?', *GRBS* 44 (2004), 265-326

Rapp, C., 'Hagiography and Monastic Literature between Greek East and Latin West in Late Antiquity', *Settimane di studio LI Centro Italiano di Studi sull'Alto Medioevo* (2003), 1,221-82

Rapp, C., 'Hellenic Identity, Romanitas, and Christianity in Byzantium', in Zacharia, K. (ed), *Hellenisms. Culture, Identity and Ethnicity from Antiquity to Modernity* (2008), 127-47

Rapp, S.H., *The Sasanian World through Georgian Eyes: Caucasia and the Iranian Commonwealth in Late Antique Georgian Literature* (Farnham, 2014)

Rauh, N., 'Who were the Cilician Pirates?', Swiny, S., Hohlfelder, R.L., and Swiny, H.N. (eds), *Res Maritimae. Cyprus and the Eastern Mediterranean from Prehistory to Late Antiquity* (Atlanta, 1997), 263-83

Raven, C.E., *Apollinarianism. An Essay on the Christology of the Early Church* (Cambridge, 1923)

Rayfield, D., *Edge of Empires: A History of Georgia* (London, 2013)

Redies, M., 'Die Usurpation des Basiliskos (475-476) im Kontext der aufsteigenden monophystischen Kirche', *Antiquité Tardive* 5 (1997), 211-21

Rekavandi, H.O., 'Sasanian Walls, Hinterland Fortresses, and Abandoned Ancient Irrigated Landscapes: the 2007 Season on the Great Wall of Gurgan and the Wall of Tammishe', *Iran 46* (2008), 151-78

Rekavandi, H.O., Sauer, E.W., Wilkinson, T., and Nokandeh, J., 'An Imperial Frontier of the Sasanian Empire: Further Fieldwork at the Great Wall of Gurgan', *Iran 45* (2007), 95-136

Revillout, E., 'Le premier schisme de Constantinople', *Revue des Questions Historiques* 22 (1877), 83-134

Reynolds, L.D., and Wilson, N.G., *Scribes and Scholars: A Guide to the Transmission of Greek and Latin Literature* (Oxford, 1991)

Reynolds, R.L., and Lopez, R.S., 'Odoacer: German or Hun?', *AHR* 52 (1946), 36-53

Richards, J., *The Popes and the Papacy in the Early Middle Ages, 476-752* (London, 1979)

Robert, L., 'Les Inscriptions', in DesGagniers, J., Devambez, P., Kahil, L., and Ginouves, R. (eds), *Laodicle du Lycos. Le Nymphie* (Quebec, 1969), 345-46

Roberto, U., 'Sulla tradizione storiografica di Candido Isaurico', *Mediterraneo Antico* 3 (2000), 685-727

Robinson, O.F., *The Sources of Roman Law: Problems and Methods for Ancient Historians* (London, 1997)

Rodziewicz, E., 'Remains of a Chryselephantine Statue in Alexandria', *Bulletin de la Société Archéologique d'Alexandrie* 44 (1991), 119-30

Rohrbacher, D., *The Historians of Late Antiquity* (London, 2002)

Rostovtzeff, M., *Social and Economic History of the Roman Empire* (Oxford, 1957)

Roueché, C., *Performers and Partisans at Aphrodisias in the Roman and Late Roman Periods* (London, 1993)

Roueché, C., and Erim, K.T. (eds), *Aphrodisias Papers* (Ann Arbor, 1990)

Rouge, J., 'L'Histoire Auguste et l'Isaurie au IV siecle', *REA* 68 (1966), 282-315

Roux, G., *La basilique de la Campanopétra* (Paris, 1998)

Różycka-Bryzek, A., and Salamon, M. (eds), *Byzantina et Slavica Cracoviensia* (Krakow, 1994)

Rubin, Z., 'Diplomacy and War in the Relations between Byzantium and the Sassanids in the Fifth Century AD', in Freemann, P., and Kennedy, H. (eds), *The Defence of the Roman and Byzantine East* (Oxford, 1986), 677-95

Rubin, Z., 'The Mediterranean and the Dilemma of the Roman Empire in Late Antiquity', *MHR* 1 (1986), 13-62

Russell, B., *The Principles of Mathematics* (Cambridge, 1903)

Šagi-Bunić, T., *'Deus perfectus et homo perfectus' a Concilio Ephesino (a. 431) ad Chalcedonense (a. 451)* (Rome, 1965)

Sahin, S., 'Inschriften aus Seleukeia am Kalykadnos', *Epigraphica Anatolica* 17 (1991), 155-63

Salamon, M., 'Basiliscus cum Romanis suis', in Mrozewicz, L., and Ilski, K. (eds), *Studia Moesiaca I* (Poznan, 1994), 179-96

Salaville, S., 'Hénotique', in *Dictionnaire de Théologie Catholique* (Paris, 1920), col. 2,153-78

Santos Yanguas, N., 'Algunos problemas sociales en Asia Menor en la segunda mitad del siglo IV d.C: Isaurios y Maratocuprenos', *HispAnt* 7 (1977), 351-78

Sarantis, A., 'The Justinianic Herules: from allied barbarians to Roman provincials', in Curta, F. (ed.), *Neglected Barbarians* (Turnhout, 2011), 361-402

Sarkissian, K., *The Council of Chalcedon and the Armenian Church* (London, 1965)

Sarris, P., *Empires of Faith: The Fall of Rome to the Rise of Islam 500-700* (Oxford, 2011a)

Sarris, P., 'The Early Byzantine Economy in Context: Aristocratic Property and Economic Growth Reconsidered', *EMedE* 19.3 (2011b), 255-84

Sarris, P., Dal Santo, M., and Booth, P. (eds), *An Age of Saints? Power, Conflict, and Dissent in Early Medieval Christianity* (Leiden, 2011)

Scarcella, A.S., *La legislazione di Leone I* (Milan, 1997)

Scharf, R., 'Der Kelch des Ardabur und der Anthusa', *Byzantion* 63 (1993), 213-23

Scharf, R., *Foederati: Von der volkerrechtliihen hategprie zur byzantinischen Truppengattung. Tyche*, Supplementband 4 (Vienna, 2001)

Scheidel, W., *Measuring Sex, Age and Death in the Roman Empire* (Ann Arbor, 1996)

Scheidel, W. (ed.), *Debating Roman Demography* (Leiden, 2001)

Scheidel, W., 'Progress and Problems in Roman Demography', in Scheidel, W. (ed.), *Debating Roman Demography* (Leiden, 2001), 1-81

Scheidel, W., 'Demography', in Scheidel, W., Morris, I., and Saller, R. (eds), *The Cambridge Economic History of the Greco-Roman World* (Cambridge, 2007), 38-86

Scheidel, W., 'Marriage, Families and Survival: Demographic Aspects', in Erdkamp, P. (ed.), *A Companion to the Roman Army* (Oxford, 2007), 417-34

Scheidel, W., 'Economy and Quality of Life', in Barchiesi, A., and Scheidel, W. (eds), *The Oxford Handbook of Roman Studies* (Oxford, 2010), 593-609

Scheidel, W., Morris, I., and Saller, R. (eds), *The Cambridge Economic History of the Greco-Roman World* (Cambridge, 2007)

Schindel, N., *Sylloge Nummorum Sasanidarum Paris-Berlin-Wien III: Shapur II-Kawad I* (Vienna, 2009)

Schmidt, L., *Geschichte der deutschen Stämme bis zum Ausgang der Völkerwanderung: Die Ostgermanen* (Munich, 1933)

Schmidt, L., *Geschichte der Wandalen* (Munich, 1942)

Schnitzler, T., *Im Kampfe um Chalcedon. Geschichte und Inhalt des Codex Encyclius von 458* (Rome, 1938)

Schulz, R., and Görg, M. (eds), *Lingua Restituta Orientalis. Festgabe für Julius Assfalg* (Wiesbaden, 1990)

Schur, N., *History of the Samaritans* (New York, 1989)

Schwarcz, A., 'Relations between Ostrogoths and Visigoths in the Fifth and Sixth Centuries and the Question of Visigothic Settlement in Aquitaine and Spain', in Pohl, W., and Diesenberger, M. (eds), *Integration and Authority in the Early Middle Ages* (Vienna, 2002), 217-26

Schwark, B., 'Die Kirchenpolitik Kaiser Zenos', unpublished diss. (Würzburg, 1950)

Schwartz, E., *Johannes Rufus, ein monophysitischer Schriftsteller* (Heidelberg, 1912)

Schwartz, E., 'Das Nicaenum und das Constantinopolitanum auf der Synode von Chalkedon', *Zeitschrift für neutestamentliche Wissenschaft und die Kunde der älteren Kirche* 25 (1926), 38-88.

Schwartz, E., *Codex Vaticanus gr. 1431, eine antichalkedonische Sammlung aus der Zeit Kaiser Zenos* (Munich, 1927)

Schwartz, E., 'Publizistische Sammlungen zum acacianischen Schisma', Abhandlungen der Bayerischen Akademie der Wissenschaften. Philosophisch-historische Abteilung. Neue Folge. Heft 10 (Munich, 1934)

Schwartz, E., 'Praefatio', in Schwartz, E. (ed.), *ACO, tomus alter, Concilium Universale Chalcedonense, volumen quintum, Collectio sangermanensis* (Berlin, 1936), V-XXII

Schwartz, E., 'Bemerkungen', in Schwartz, E. (ed.), *Kyrillos von Skythopolis* (Leipzig, 1939), 317-415

Schwartz, E. (ed.), *ACO, tomus tertius, Collectio Sabbaitica contra Acephalos et Origeniastas destinata. Insunt Acta Synodorum Constantinopolitanae et Hierosolymitanae* (Berlin, 1940)

Schwartz, E., 'Praefatio', in Schwartz, E. (ed.), *ACO, tomus tertius, Collectio Sabbaitica contra Acephalos et Origeniastas destinata. Insunt Acta Synodorum Constantinopolitanae et Hierosolymitanae* (Berlin, 1940), V-XIIII

Scipioni, L.I., *Ricerche sulla cristologia del 'Libro di Eraclide' di Nestorio* (Freiburg, 1956)

Scott, L.R., 'Aspar and the Burden of the Barbarian Heritage', *Byzantine Studies* 3 (1976), 59-69

Seeck, O., 'Anagastes', *RE* 2 (1894), 2022

Seeck, O., 'Ardabur 1', *RE* 2 (1896), 606-07

Seeck, O., 'Ardabur 2', *RE* 2 (1896), 607-10

Seeck, O., 'Geisericus', in *Paulys Realencyclopädie der classischen Altertumswissenschaft* (Stuttgart, 1910), col. 935-45

Seeck, O., *Regesten der Kaiser und Päpste für die Jahre 311 bis 476 n. Chr.: Vorarbeit zu einer Prosopographie der chrislichen Kaiserzeit* (Stuttgart, 1919)

Seeck, O., *Geschichte des Untergangs der antiken Welt VI* (Stuttgart, 1920)

Sellers, R.V., *The Council of Chalcedon* (London, 1953)

Sessa, K., 'Ursa's Return: Captivity, Remarriage, and the Domestic Authority of Roman Bishops in Fifth-Century Italy', *JECS* 19 (2011), 401-32

Sessa, K., *The Formation of Papal Authority in Late Antique Italy* (Cambridge, 2012)

Severin, G., and Severin, H-G., *Marmor vom heiligen Menas* (Frankfurt, 1987)

Shahid, I., *Byzantium and the Arabs in the Fifth Century* (Washington DC, 1989)

Shaw, B.D., 'Autonomy and Tribute: Mountain and Plain in Mauretania Tingitana', *Revue des mondes musulmans et de la Méditerranée Année* 41-42 (1986), 66-89

Shaw, B.D., 'Bandits in the Roman Empire', *Past and Present* 105 (1984), 3-52

Shaw, B.D., 'Bandit Highlands and Lowland Peace: The Mountains of Isauria-Cilicia', *JESHO* 33 (1990), 199-233, 237-70

Shaw, B.D., 'The Bandit', in Giardina, A. (ed.), *The Romans* (Chicago, 1993), 300-41

Shepherd, J., and Franklin, S. (eds), *Byzantine Diplomacy* (London, 1992)

Shipley, G., and Salmon, J. (eds), *Human Landscapes in Classical Antiquity* (London, 1996)

Siebigs, G., *Kaiser Leo I: Das oströmische Reich in den ersten drei Jahren seiner Regierung (457-460 n. Chr.)* (Berlin, 2010)

Sims-Williams, N. (ed.), *Indo-Iranian Languages and Peoples: Proceedings of the British Academy* (London, 2002)

Sinor, D., 'Autour d'une migration des peuples au Ve siècle', *Journal Asiatique* (1946-47), 1-78

Sirks, A.J.B., *Food for Rome: The Legal Structure of the Transportation and Processing of Supplies for the Imperial Distributions in Rome and Constantinople* (Amsterdam, 1991)

Sirks, A.J.B., *The Theodosian Code: A Study* (Norderstedt, 2007)

Sivan, H., *Palestine in Late Antiquity* (Oxford, 2008)

Sizgorich, T., *Violence and Belief in Late Antiquity: Militant Devotion in Christianity and Islam* (Philadelphia, 2009)

Smith, R.R., and Ratté, C., 'Archaeological research at Aphrodisias in Caria, 1993', *AJA* 99 (1995), 33-58

Smith, W.D., 'So-called Possession in Pre-Christian Greece', *TAPA* (1965), 403-26

Smyth, P.A. (ed.), *Medieval Europeans: Studies in Ethnic Identity and National Perspectives in Medieval Europe* (London, 1998)

Snee, R., 'Gregory of Nazianzen's Anastasia Church: Arianism, Goths and hagiography', *DOP* 52 (1998), 157-86

Søby Christensen, A., *Cassiodorus, Jordanes, and the History of the Goths. Studies in a Migration Myth* (Copenhagen, 2002)

Sode, C., and Takács, S. (eds), *Novum Millennium: Studies on Byzantine History and Culture dedicated to Paul Speck* (Aldershot, 2001)

Sontag, S., *Regarding the Pain of Others* (London, 2003)

Sotinel, C., 'How Were Bishops Informed? Information Transmission across the Adriatic Sea in Late Antiquity', in Ellis, L., and Kidner, F. (eds), *Travel, Communication and Geography in Late Antiquity: Sacred and Profane* (Aldershot, 2004), 63-71

Sotiriou, G., and Sotiriou, M,. Η βασιλική του Αγίου Δημητρίου Θεσσαλονίκης (Athens, 1952)

Southern, P., and Dixon, K.R., *The Late Roman Army* (London, 1996)

Spoerl, K.M., 'Apollinarian Christology and the Anti-Marcellan Tradition', *JTS* 45 (1994), 545-68

Starr, J., *The Jews in the Byzantine Empire* (New York, 1939)

Stein, E., *Geschichte des spätrömischen Reiches. Band I. Vom römischen zum byzantinischen Staate (284–476 n. Chr.)* (Vienna, 1928); (Palanque, J.R., French trans., Paris, 1959)

Stein, E., *Histoire du Bas-Empire II: De la disparition de l'Empire d'Occident à la mort de Justinien (476-565)* (Paris, 1949)

Stenhouse, P., *The Kitāb al-Tarīkh of Abu'l-Fath* (Sydney, 1985)

Steppa, J-E., *John Rufus and the World Vision of Anti-Chalcedonian Culture* (Piscataway, 2002)

Steppa, J-E., 'Heresy and Orthodoxy: the Anti-Chalcedonian Hagiography of John Rufus', in Bitton-Ashkelony, B., and Kofsky, A. (eds), *Christian Gaza in Late Antiquity* (Boston, 2004), 89-106

Stevens, C.E., *Sidonius Apollinaris and His Age* (Oxford, 1933)

Stewart, M.E., 'The First Byzantine Emperor? Leo I, Aspar and Challenges of Power and Romanitas in Fifth-century Byzantium', *Porphyra* XXII (2014), 4-17

Stiernon, D., 'Jean le Tabennèsiote', in *Dictionnaire d'Histoire et de Géographie Ecclésiastiques* (Paris, 2000), col. 671-95.

Stockmeier, P., *Leo I. des Grossen. Beurteilung der kaiserlichen Religionspolitik* (Munich, 1959)

Stojanovic, D., *Circling* (1993)

Stol, M., *Epilepsy in Babylonia* (Gronigen, 1993)

Strzelczyk, J., *Wandalowie i ich afrykańskie państwo* (Warsaw, (2005)Sullivan, F.A., *The Christology of Theodore of Mopsuestia* (Rome, 1956)

Suny, R.G., *The Making of the Georgian Nation* (Bloomington, 1994)

Swain, S., and Edwards, M. (eds), *Approaching Late Antiquity: The Transformation from Early to Late Empire* (Oxford, 2004)

Swiny, S., Hohlfelder, R.L., and Swiny, H.N. (eds), *Res Maritimae. Cyprus and the Eastern Mediterranean from Prehistory to Late Antiquity* (Atlanta, 1997)

Syme, R., *Ammianus and the Historia Augusta* (Oxford, 1968)

Syme, R., *Isauria in Pliny*, Anatolian Studies 36, (1986), 159-64.

Syme, R., *The Augustan Aristocracy* (New York, 1986)

Syme, R., 'Isaura and Isauria. Some Problems', in Frézouls, E. (ed.), *Sociétés urbainses, sociétés rurales dans l'Asie Mineure et la Syrie* (Strasbourg, 1987), 131-47

Syme, R., and Birley, A., *Anatolica. Studies in Strabo* (Oxford, 1995)

Szabat, E., 'Prozopografia środowisk twórczych', in *Chrześcijaństwo u schyłku starożytności. Studia źródłoznawcze VI* (Warsaw, 2007), 172-319

Takahashi, H., *Barhebraeus. A Bio-Bibliography* (Piscataway, 2005)

Tchalenko, G., *Villages antiques de la Syrie du Nord. Le Massif du Bélus a l'époque romaine* (Paris, 1953)

Teall, J.L., 'The Barbarians in Justinian's Armies', *Speculum* 40 (1965), 294-322

Temkin, O., *The Falling Sickness: a History of Epilepsy from the Greeks to the Beginnings of Modern Neurology* (London, 1971)

Teule, H.,'Gregory Barhebraeus and his Time. The Syrian Renaissance', *Journal of the Canadian Society for Syriac Studies* 3 (2003), 21-42

Thompson, E.A., 'The Isaurians under Theodosius II', *Hermathena* 68 (1946), 18-31

Thompson, E.A., 'The Foreign Policies of Theodosius II and Marcian', *Hermathena* 76 (1950), 58-75

Thompson, E.A., *Romans and Barbarians: the Decline of the Western Empire* (London, 1982)

Thompson, E.A., and Heather, P., *The Huns* (Oxford, 1996)

Thomson, R.W., *Rewriting Caucasian History: The Medieval Armenian Adaptation of the Georgian Chronicles* (Oxford, 1996)

Todman, D., 'Childbirth in ancient Rome: from traditional folklore to obstetrics', *ANZJOG* 47 (2007), 82-85

Townsend, W.T., 'The Henotikon Schism and the Roman Church', *JRel* 16 (1936), 78-86

Traina, G., and Cameron, A., *428AD: An Ordinary Year at the End of the Roman Empire* (Woodstock, 2009)

Treadgold, W., *Byzantium and its Army 284-1081* (Stanford, 1995)

Treadgold, W., *A History of the Byzantine State and Society* (Stanford, 1997)

Treadgold W., *The Early Byzantine Historians* (New York, 2007a)

Treadgold W., 'The Byzantine World Histories of John Malalas and Eustathius of Epiphania', *IHR* 29 (2007b), 709-45

Trombley, F.R., *Hellenic Religion and Christianisation c.370-529* (Leiden, 1994)

Trombley, F.R., 'War and Society in Rural Syria *ca*.502-613AD: Observations on the Epigraphy', *BMGS* 21 (1997), 154-209

Trombley, F.R., and Watt, J.W., *The Chronicle of Pseudo-Joshua the Stylite* (Liverpool, 2000)

Trout, D.E., *Paulinus of Nola: Life, Letters and Poems* (Berkeley, 1999)

Tsangadas, B.C.P., *The Fortifications and Defence of Constantinople*, East European Monographs 71 (New York, 1980)

Twardowska, K., *Cesarzowe bizantyjskie 2 poł. V w. Kobiety a władza* (Kraków, 2009)

Ulrich-Bansa, O., *Moneta Mediolanensis* (Venice, 1949)

Uthemann, K-H., 'Petros der Walker', in *Lexikon für Theologie und Kirche* (Freiburg, 2006), col. 143

Van Dam, R., *Becoming Christian: The Conversion of Roman Cappadocia* (Philadelphia, 2003)

Van Dam, R., *Rome and Constantinople: Rewriting Roman History During Late Antiquity* (Waco, 2010)

Van Deun, P., *Hagiographica Cypria. Sancti Barnabae Laudatio auctore Alexandro Monacho et Sanctorum Bartholomaei et Barnabae Vita e Menologio imperiali deprompta* (Leuven, 1993)

van Esbroeck, M., 'The Memra on the Parrot by Isaac of Antioch', *Journal of Theological Studies* 47 (1996), 465-76

Van Ginkel, J.J., *John of Ephesus: A Monophysite Historian in Sixth-Century Byzantium* (Groningen, 1995)

Van Ginkel, J.J., 'Monk, Missionary and Martyr: John of Ephesus, a Syriac Orthodox Historian in Sixth Century Byzantium', *Journal of the Canadian Society for Syriac Studies* 5 (2005), 35-50

Van Milligan, A., *Byzantine Constantinople: The Walls of the City and Adjoining Historical Sites* (London, 1899)

van Oort, J., and Roldanus, J. (eds), *Chalkedon: Geschichte und Aktualität: Studien zur Rezeption der christologischen Formel von Chalkedon* (Leuvain, 1997)

van Oort, J., and Wyrwa, D. (eds), *Heiden und Christen im 5. Jahrhundert* (Leuven, 1998)

Van Rompay, L., 'A Letter of the Jews to the Emperor Marcian concerning the Council of Chalcedon', *Orientalia Lovaniensia Periodica* 12 (1981), 215-24

Van Rompay, L., 'Severus, Patriarch of Antioch (512-538), in the Greek, Syriac, and Coptic Traditions', *Journal of the Canadian Society for Syriac Studies* 8 (2008), 3-22

Vasiliev, A.A., 'Агапій Манбиджскій, христіанскій историкъ X века', Византийский Временник 11 (1904), 574-87

Vasiliev, A.A., *The Goths in the Crimea* (Cambridge, 1936)

Vasiliev, A.A., *History of the Byzantine Empire* (Madison, 1952)

Velkov, V., *Cities in Thrace and Dacia in Late Antiquity* (Amsterdam, 1977)

Velkov, V., *Roman Cities in Bulgaria: Collected Studies* (Amsterdam, 1980)

Vernadsky, G., 'Flavius Ardabur Aspar', *Sudostforschungen* 6 (1941), 38-73

Voicu, S.J., 'Martiri di Antiochia', *Dizionario patristico e di antichita cristiana* 2 (1983), col. 2,154

von Haehling, R., 'Damascius und die heidnische Opposition im 5. Jahrhundert nach Christus', *Jahrbuch für Antike und Christentum* 23 (1980), 82-95

Vööbus, A. *History of the School of Nisibis* (Louvain, 1965)

Walbank, F.W., *The Awful Revolution: The Decline of the Roman Empire in the West* (Liverpool, 1969)

Ward-Perkins, B., *The Fall of Rome and the End of Civilisation* (New York, 2005)

Watts, E.J., 'Winning the Intracommunal Dialogues. Zacharias Scholasticus' *Life of Severus*', *JECS* 13 (2005), 437-64

Watts, E.J., *City and School in Late Antique Athens and Alexandria* (Los Angeles, 2006)

Watts, E.J., *Riot in Alexandria. Tradition and Group Dynamics in Late Antique Pagan and Christian Communities* (Los Angeles, 2010)

Webster, L., and Brown, M (eds), *The Transformation of the Roman World AD400-900* (London, 1997)

Weltecke, D., 'Les trois grandes chroniques syro-orthodoxes des XIIe et XIIIe siècles', in Debie, M. (ed.), *L'historiographie syriaque* (Paris, 2009), 107-35

Wenger, A., 'Notes inédites sur les empereurs Théodose I, Arcadius, Théodose II, Léon I', *REByz* 10 (1952), 47-59

Wensinck, A.J., *Legends of Eastern Saints chiefly from Syriac sources* (Leiden, 1913)

Wessel, S., 'The Ecclesiastical Policy of Theodosius II', *Annuarium Historiae Conciliorum* 33 (2001), 285-308

Wessel, S., *Cyril of Alexander and Nestorian Controversy: The Making of a Saint and of a Heretic* (Oxford, 2004)

Wessel, S., *Leo the Great and the Spiritual Rebuilding of a Universal Rome* (Leiden, 2008)

Whitby, L.M., 'The Long Walls of Constantinople', *Byzantion* 55 (1985), 560-83

Whitby, L.M., *Rome at War AD229-696* (Oxford, 2002)

Whitby, M., 'Recruitment in Roman armies from Justinian to Heraclius (*ca.* 565-615)', in Cameron, A. (ed.), *The Byzantine and Early Islamic Near East III: States, Resources and Armies* (Princeton, 1995), 61-124

Whitby, M., *The Ecclesiastical History of Evagrius Scholasticus* (Liverpool, 2000)

Whitby, M., 'The Church Historians and Chalcedon', in Marasco, G. (ed.), *Greek and Roman Historiography in Late Antiquity: Fourth to Sixth Century AD* (Brill, 2003), 449-98

Whitby, M., and Whitby, Mary, *Chronicon Paschale 284-628AD* (Liverpool, 1989)

Whitby, Mary, 'On the Omission of a Ceremony in Mid-Sixth Century Constantinople: Candidati, Curopalatus, Silentiarii, Excubitores and Others', *Historia* 36 (1987), 462-88

Whittaker, C.R., *Frontiers of the Roman Empire: A Social and Economic Study* (London, 1994)

Whittow, M., 'Ruling the Late Roman and Early Byzantine City: A Continuous History', *Past and Present* 129 (1990), 3-29

Whittow, M., *The Making of Orthodox Byzantium 600-1025* (Houndmills, 1996)

Wickham, C., *Early Medieval Italy: Central Power and Local Society 400-1000* (London, 1981)

Wickham, C., *Framing the Early Middle Ages: Europe and the Mediterranean, 400-800* (Oxford, 2005)

Wickham, C., *The Inheritance of Rome: Illuminating the Dark Ages 400-1000* (London, 2009)

Wiewiorowski, J., 'The Defence of the Long Walls of Thrace (Μακρά Τείχη τῆς Θράκης) under Justinian the Great (527-565AD)', *Studia Ceranea* 2 (2012), 181-94

Wilfong, T.G., *Women of Jeme: Lives in a Coptic Town in Late Antique Egypt* (Madison, 2002)

Wimbusch, V.L. (ed.), *Ascetic Behaviour in Greco-Roman Antiquity: A Sourcebook* (Minneapolis, 1990)

Winter, E., and Dignas, B., *Rom und das Perserreich, Zwei Weltmachte zwischen Konfrontation und Koexistenz* (Berlin, 2001)

Wipszycka, E., 'The Origins of Monarchic Episcopate in Egypt', *Adamantius* 12 (2006), 71-90

Wirth, P. (ed.), *Polychronion: Festschrift for P. Dolger* (Heidelberg, 1966)

Wiseman, J., 'The City in Macedonia Secunda', in Popovic, V. (ed.), *Villes et Peuplement dans l'Illyricum protobyzantin* (Rome, 1984), 289-313

Wissemann, M. (ed.), *Roma Renascens. Beitra'ge zur Spa'tantike und Rezeptionsgeschichte* (Frankfurt, 1988)

Witakowski, W., *Syriac Chronicle of Pseudo-Dionysius of Tel-Mahre: A Study in the History of Historiography* (Uppsala, 1987)

Witakowski W., *Pseudo-Dionysius of Tel-Mahre, Chronicle (known also as the Chronicle of Zuqnin). Part III* (Liverpool, 1996)

Wolfram, H., *History of the Goths* (Berkeley, 1988)

Wolfram, H., *Das Reich und die Germanen. Zwischen Antike und Mittelalter* (Berlin, 1990)

Wolfram, H., *The Roman Empire and its Germanic Peoples* (London, 1997)

Wolfram, H., and Daim, F. (eds), *Die Völker an der mittleren und unteren Donauim fünften und sechsten Jahrhundert, Denkschriften der Östereichischen Akademie der Wissenschaften, phil.-hist. Kl. 145* (Vienna, 1980)

Wood, P., 'Foundation myths in late antique Syria and Mesopotamia: the emergence of Miaphysite political thought, 400-600AD', unpublished PhD thesis (Oxford, 2007)

Wood, P., 'The Invention of History in the Later Roman World; the Conversion of Isauria in "The Life of Conon"', *Anatolian Studies* 59 (2009), 129-38

Wood, P., 'Multiple Voices in Chronicle Sources: The Reign of Leo I (457-474) in Book Fourteen of Malalas', *JLA* 4 (2011a), 298-314

Wood, P., 'Being Roman in Procopius' Vandal Wars', *Byzantion* 81 (2011b), 424-47

Wood, P., 'Excluded from power? The Boundaries of Orthodoxy in the Works of Athanasius and John of Ephesus', in Sarris, P., Dal Santo, M., and Booth, P. (eds), *An Age of Saints? Power, Conflict, and Dissent in Early Medieval Christianity* (Leiden, 2011), 62-76

Wozniak, F.E., 'East Rome, Ravenna and Western Illyricum 454-536AD', *Historia* 30 (1981), 351-82

Yarshater, E. (ed.), *The Cambridge History of Iran Vol.III: The Seleucid, Parthian and Sasanid Periods* (Cambridge, 1983)

Young, F., *From Nicaea to Chalcedon: A Guide to the Literature and Its Background* (London, 2010)

Zaccagnino, C., Bevan, G., and Gabov, A., 'The Missorium of Ardabur Aspar: new considerations on its archaeological and historical contexts', *ArchCl* LXIII (2012), 419-54

Zecchini, G., 'Latin Historiography: Jerome, Orosius and the Western Chronicles', in Marasco, G. (ed.), *Greek and Roman Historiography in Late Antiquity: Fourth to Sixth Century AD* (Brill, 2003), 317-48

Zeimal, E.V., 'The Kidarite kingdom in Central Asia', *History of Civilizations of Central Asia, Volume III: The Crossroads of Civilizations: AD 250 to 750* (Paris, 1996), 119-35

Zgusta L., *Kleinasiatische Personennamen* (Prague, 1964)

Zgusta L., *Kleinasiatische Ortsnamen* (Heidelberg, 1984)

Ziegler, A.K., 'Pope Gelasius I and His Teaching on the Relation of Church and State', *CHR* 27 (1942), 412-37

Ziegler, K., 'Zonaras', in *Paulys Realencyclopädie der classischen Altertumswissenschaft* (Munich, 1972), col. 718-32

Zimmerman, M., 'Probus, Varus und die Rauber im Gebiet des pisidischen Termessos', *ZPE* 110 (1996), 265-77

Zotenberg, H., *Chronique de Jean, évêque de Nikiou, texte éthiopien* (Paris, 1883)

Zuckerman, C., 'L'Empire d'Orient et les Huns. Notes sur Priscus', *Travaux et Mémoires* 12, (1994), 159-82

Index